WAGONS WEST

France and the Jacobite Rising of 1745
The Jacobite Army in England
The Jacobites
Invasion: From the Armada to Hitler
Charles Edward Stuart
Crime and Punishment in Eighteenth-Century England
Stanley: The Making of an African Explorer
Snow Upon the Desert: The Life of Sir Richard Burton
From the Sierras to the Pampas: Richard Burton's Travels in the Americas, 1860–69
Stanley: Sorcerer's Apprentice
Hearts of Darkness: The European Exploration of Africa
Fitzroy Maclean
Robert Louis Stevenson
C.G. Jung
Napoleon
1066: The Year of the Three Battles
Villa and Zapata

WAGONS WEST

THE EPIC STORY OF
AMERICA'S OVERLAND TRAILS

Frank McLynn

GROVE PRESS
New York

First published in Great Britain in 2002 by Jonathan Cape, a division of Random House, London, England

Published simultaneously in Canada
Printed in the United States of America

FIRST AMERICAN EDITION

Library of Congress Cataloging-in-Publication Data
McLynn, Frank.
Wagons west : the epic story of America's overland trails / Frank McLynn.
p. cm.
Includes bibliographical references (p.) and index.
ISBN 0-8021-1731-7
1. Overland journeys to the Pacific. 2. Trails—West (U.S.)—History—19th century. 3. Frontier and pioneer life—West (U.S.) 4. Pioneers—West (U.S.)—History—19th century. 5. West (U.S.)—History—To 1848. 6. West (U.S.)—History—1848–1860. I. Title.

F593 .M475 2003
978'.02—dc21   2002033859

Grove Press
841 Broadway
New York, NY 10003

03 04 05 06 07 10 9 8 7 6 5 4 3 2 1

For Pauline, my partner on the trails
and Lucy who was there in spirit.

CONTENTS

ILLUSTRATIONS

A woman collecting buffalo chips: Culver Pictures
A pioneer family on a log bridge: Denver Public Library (Z–223)
Appleton Milo Harmon's journal: © by Intellectual Reserve, Inc. Courtesy
of Museum of Church History and Art. Used by Permission
A Chief forbidding passage: Collection of the New-York Historical Society
Oglala Sioux on horseback: © Corbis
A pioneer hunting buffalo: Culver Pictures
John Grey being attacked by 5 grizzly bears: Washington State University
Library
Donner Party going through Donner Pass: Brown Brothers
James Reed: Peter Newark's Western Americana
The Donner party struggling up the Sierra Nevada: Peter Newark's
Western Americana
The rescue party reaching the Donner camp: © Bettmann/Corbis
Patty's doll: © James L. Amos/Corbis
Brigham Young: Peter Newark's American Pictures
Winter Quarters by C.C.A. Christensen: courtesy of Brigham Young
University Museum of Art. All Rights Reserved.
Mormons crossing the Platte River on rafts: courtesy Daughters of Utah
Pioneers, Salt Lake City
A Mormon family with their wagons, 1870: Denver Public Library (X-
11929)
Mormon pioneers in South Pass by Charles R. Savage, 1866: courtesy LDS
Family and Church History Archives
Clark Kelly Price, 'Shall We Not Go On In So Great A Cause?': courtesy of
Museum of Church History and Art
Salt Lake City in c. 1860: Peter Newark's Western Americana

MAPS

PREFACE

Having covered every inch of the 3,000 miles of the California and Oregon Trails, sometimes, it seemed, almost on my hands and knees, I must first of all acknowledge the help and kindness of dozens of nameless individuals in the United States: officials of the U.S. National Parks and National Monuments Service, park rangers, librarians, archivists, local historians and even specialist bookshop owners. If they asked me, I could write a book about this part of the research alone. Back in England, I must particularly pay tribute to the superb visual talents of Paul Taylor, the mapmaker, and John Lindsay, the illustrator. Their wonderfully efficient organisation, Data Reprographics, in Ashford, has made straight the paths in more ways than one.

Others whose talent, competence and assistance have been invaluable include Lila Mauro in California and Sophie Hartley, Tony Whittome and James Nightingale, all at Random House in London. But above all I must single out my editor Will Sulkin for praise. Many editors commission books grudgingly, without enthusiasm or through gritted teeth. Will, however, was one hundred per cent committed to this project from Day One, and his support and encouragement have been a priceless gift. My wife Pauline has been indispensable to this book. It could not have been written without her, and her skills as researcher, critic and lateral thinker make her in all but a formal sense the true co-author of this volume. I thank all my collaborators for their various contributions, but warn that, as 'director' of this venture into early U.S. history, I alone must be held responsible for any shortcomings.

FRANK MCLYNN, Twickenham, 2002

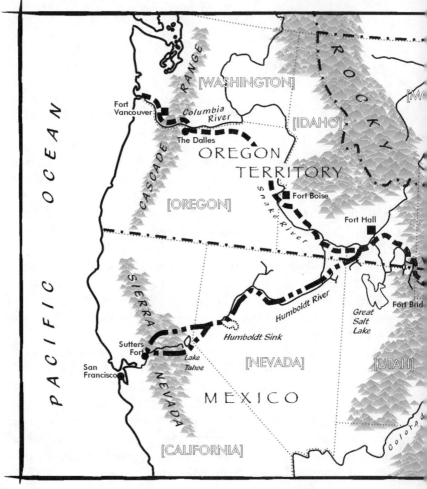

ails 1841-46

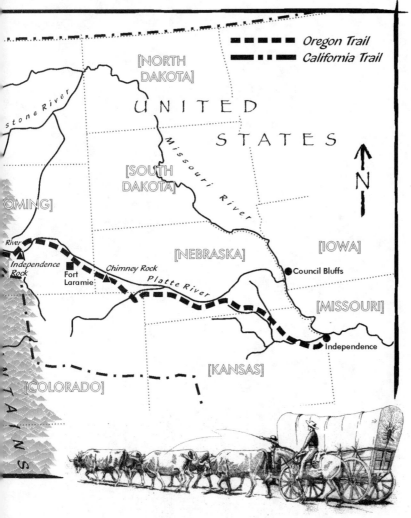

- ▪▪▪▪▪ Oregon Trail
- ▪═▪═▪═ California Trail

[NORTH DAKOTA]

UNITED

STATES

↑ N

stone River

Missouri River

[SOUTH DAKOTA]

[OMING]

River

Independence Rock

Fort Laramie

Chimney Rock

Platte River

[NEBRASKA]

[IOWA]

● Council Bluffs

[MISSOURI]

● Independence

[KANSAS]

[COLORADO]

⋮ T A I N S

INTRODUCTION

The days of the pioneers of the American West are long gone now, lost in the limitless past. It is more than 150 years since wagon trains first headed westwards from Missouri, bound either for California or Oregon. How can we recapture that era, where events seem almost to have happened on another planet? We live in a world of television, e-mail, mobile phones, computers, jet airliners, movies, rock music, antibiotics, psychoanalysis and billionnaire sports players. In the 1840s, by contrast, when wagons first headed west, the transatlantic cable had not been laid and even steamships were essentially a phenomenon of the future. Railways were in their infancy, and the great technological breakthrough of the age was the building of the Erie Canal. Repeating rifles had not been invented and firearms were still muzzle-loading. Not even the Pony Express operated yet in the West. Oregon was essentially a British province, and California, settled from 'New Spain' in 1769, a territory the new state of Mexico had inherited from the old Spanish Empire in 1821. Between Missouri and the Pacific coast lay uncharted wilderness.

The decision to emigrate was itself a bizarre one. Take the case of a family living in reasonable comfort in Missouri. Nearby there are friends and neighbours; in times of trouble there is help, advice and expertise close at hand. But then the father of the family makes a decision that changes everything, leading them into supreme peril and maybe costing all the family their lives. That decision is to buy a wagon and head west in search of a better life. This means his wife must dispose of her domestic treasures and join her man in an enormous gamble. For to go west means to leave civilisation and the rule of law, to leave behind towns, stores, schools, churches, doctors. It means going where there are no proper maps, where savage Indians lurk who are said to prey on whites and where the only food is what you take yourself. Wagon, stock, oxen, money and pure grit are the only resources on the trail.

The trail. But of course the truth is that there is no trail in a recognisable sense. All pioneers must be literally that, they will travel in ignorance of the terrain unless they can find a mountain man who knows the country to guide them through the labyrinth. Soon, the trail *will* be clear, for it will be marked by the bleaching bones of oxen, horses and mules and the crude graves of humans. For many, the route will be a trail of tears: for the old and sick who should never have gone along; for the infants who were too young to endure the rigours of the trek; for the stupid and careless who will fall victim to drowning, accidentally discharged firearms or death by wagon wheel; for the unlucky who succumb to disease or straggle and fall victim to Indian arrows. It is the survivors who will forge the myth of the golden age under canvas, when everyone allegedly collaborated and made common cause, free from envy, malice, lust, sloth or greed.

Five years earlier, in 1836, the Boers of South Africa had set out on their own Great Trek, out of Cape Province and into what would later become Natal, Transvaal and the Orange Free State. Their course was bloodier and harder fought, for they had first to subdue the mighty military nations of the Zulu and Ndebele. Sanguinary battles like Vegkop, Weenen, Marico River and Blood River do not feature in the chronicles of those who left Missouri in wagons in the 1840s. But the western pioneers had twice as much ground to cover, just a few kilometres short of 2,000 miles. And the westward movement would eventually become a mass phenomenon that would take 250,000 people to the West before the American Civil War. The early pioneers had one golden rule: follow the rivers. The crucial water artery in Nebraska was the Platte, after which the route followed the Sweetwater and the Bear. Travellers to California then followed the Humboldt until it disappeared in the deserts of Nevada; many of the notorious problems of the latter stage of the California-bound journey derived from one simple fact: there were no clear rivers to follow, only the ice wall of the Sierra Nevada blocking the way. From a riverine point of view the Oregon-bound settlers had it easier, as they could follow the Snake until it suddenly swerved away sharply north through impenetrable canyons, eventually to join the mighty Columbia. The pioneers, meanwhile, made their way north-west through what is today eastern Oregon to debouch on the Columbia further west.

From Independence, Missouri, the first 'jump-off' point, the covered wagons made their way painfully across the Kansas River watershed, angling north-west. This was a region striated with large rivers and extremely vulnerable to flooding. Flash floods and hailstorms usually accompanied the overlanders all the way to the broad Platte River, 320 miles from Independence, where at last there was something like a trail, blazed on both sides of the stream by the mountain men and fur traders. After negotiating the difficult fords at the fork in the river, the travellers held on along the North Platte, still heading north-west. After passing the notable landmarks of Courthouse Rock, Scotts Bluffs and Chimney Rock, they came to the first resting place, the military fort at Fort Laramie, nestling at the foot of the Rockies. Fort Laramie was 535 miles from the start of the so-called 'Platte River Road'.

The next stage, 180 miles to Independence Rock, was difficult for wagons, for this was the broken terrain of the Rockies' foothills, where grass gave way to sage and greasewood. The trail left the Platte for the valley of the Sweetwater, which took the wagons to the halfway point at South Pass, a hundred miles beyond Independence Rock, sometimes thought of as the gateway to the real West. Here there was a choice of routes, either due west to the Bear River or (after 1843) south-west to Fort Bridger, where there was another chance to restock and revictual. Those who went due west had to endure a difficult 130 miles to the Bear, fording the Big Sandy and the Green rivers and sometimes travelling forty miles over waterless tracts of desert. Oregon travellers now adjusted their compasses for the 125 miles north-west from the Bear to Fort Hall via Soda Springs. California-bound emigrants had a number of choices. They could either go all the way to Fort Hall and hope to pick up a guide there for the long south-western trek to California; or they could branch off on what became known as Hudspeth's Cutoff, five miles west of Soda Springs; or they could essay one of the more perilous routes south-west from Fort Bridger to the Great Salt Lake, hoping to pick up the Humboldt River at Cathedral Rock; or on the even more southerly route that eventually bore the infamous title of Hastings' Cutoff.

At Fort Hall, the parting of the ways became definitive. Oregon-bound emigrants would now follow the Snake until it left them. They would then travel north-north-west through Fort Boise and the Grande Ronde area of eastern Oregon until they hit the Columbia River. Unfortunately for them, their problems were just beginning, for the turbulent Columbia was a harsh, unforgiving, rapid-filled cauldron. Prudence indicated a slow slog along the southern shore to The Dalles, but usually at this stage time was against them. Assuming a departure date of mid-May from Independence, by the time the overlanders reached the Columbia River, winter was coming on, and land-based travellers faced the prospect of being cut off and starving to death in Oregon's mountains; the foamy perils of the Columbia usually seemed a better option.

The California-bound pioneers, meanwhile, faced nearly six hundred

3

miles just to get from Fort Hall to the Humboldt Sink, the point where the Humboldt River vanished into the sands of the Nevada Desert. Then came the Forty-Mile Desert, fifty-five miles of utter desolation, to the Truckee River. The advantages of sufficient grass and water were now offset by the gruelling uphill pull, one hundred miles twisting and turning through the anfractuous Californian Sierras before emerging at the pass and down into the Bear Valley. From Bear Valley, there was hard work along forested ridges and canyons, but at least the route now lay downhill to Sutter's Fort in the Sacramento valley. Like the Oregonians on the Columbia River, the California emigrants had probably only just beaten the snows. It was mid-October and both at Sutter's Fort and far away to the north in the newly founded Oregon City, the overlanders could chew the fat and discuss which itinerary was the more gruelling. So much for the physical obstacles. But of course the story of the overland treks was always much more than Man pitted against Nature. It was also a complex story involving international statesmen, geopolitics, imperialism and the quest for riches, to say nothing of its implications for individual psychology.

ONE

MANIFEST DESTINY

It has been said that Anglo-Americans were the last people to arrive in the West. Even if we except the three million or so Native Americans who occupied most of the two million square miles between the Mississippi River and the Pacific, the British had penetrated the Oregon Territory from Canada in the north, the Spanish had occupied Arizona, New Mexico, Texas and California as part of colonial New Spain, and the Russians and even the Chinese had made the journey from the east to the Pacific seaboard. Until the 1840s, the West was a backwater in the life of the United States. Even in 1845, when emigration to California and Oregon had already begun, fewer than 20,000 whites lived west of the Mississippi, if we exclude the (then) still independent state of Texas.

The Spanish had been in Texas and Arizona intermittently since the days of Juan Coronado and the conquistadores in the sixteenth century, but found the territories difficult to settle because of the hostility of Indian tribes, especially the formidable Comanche. This was the origin of the fateful decision to admit Anglo colonists to Texas after 1821, when Mexico gained its independence from Spain. Stephen Austin completed his father Moses's groundwork by founding the first colony of three hundred American families, each of whom received one square league of free land in return for taking an oath of allegiance to the Mexican government. The colony of San Felipe de Austin numbered 2,021 souls by 1824. Further land grants meant that by 1835 there were nearly 30,000 Americans living in Texas as against just 3,500 Mexicans. The seeds of future trouble were obviously present.

The Spanish had more success in New Mexico. By 1827, with 44,000 inhabitants, the territory had ten times the population of California or Texas. New Mexico, a land riven by grotesque social inequalities, drew its wealth from sheep-rearing and mining: millions of sheep grazed the upper valley of the Rio Grande between El Paso and Taos while the mines of south-western New Mexico churned out a thousand tons of copper a year; south of Santa Fe there were also rich-yielding gold mines. The territory's chief drawbacks, apart from its corrupt and archaic administration, were the old-fashioned mercantilist economic policy carried out there, and the lack of a seaport: the nearest maritime outlet was faraway Vera Cruz, 2,000 miles distant on mountain tracks. But, in contrast to Arizona, New Mexico was a prize worth saving, which was why, in the 1820s, the Mexican authorities opened up this previously closed economy to trade with the USA.

California, colonised by the Spanish as late as 1769, and only then in response to feared Russian encroachment from the north, was another sleepy backwater, whose main feature was the string of twenty Franciscan missions established from San Diego in the south to Sonoma in the north. But in the early nineteenth century a new power had interposed itself between Spanish California and Russian Alaska. Through the Hudson's Bay Company, Britain controlled the territory from 54° N40' (roughly where the present state of Alaska sweeps down to meet British Columbia near Queen Charlotte Islands) to the present Oregon–California border. From the company's north-western headquarters at Fort Vancouver on the Columbia River, the British dominated the lucrative fur trade. The company's position was a strong one, for Fort Vancouver could be supplied and reinforced from Vancouver and most of the local Indian tribes were friendly.

US interest in the Far West really began with the Lewis and Clark expedition and the architect of this was the much maligned US president Thomas Jefferson. When Napoleon's dreams of an American empire faded with the defeat of his forces in Haiti in 1803, he sold the massive French holdings in North America – the so-called Louisiana Territory – to the United States. For $15 million, Jefferson bought 800,000 square miles between the Mississippi and the Rockies, and doubled the size of his country. At the same time, he asked Congress for the funds to send an expedition to explore his new acquisition and to continue on to the Pacific. Meriwether Lewis, an army captain, was appointed as expedition leader, but he shared the leadership with his friend Lieutenant William Clark. Leaving Missouri in May 1804, Lewis and Clark reached the Mandan territory of North Dakota in late October and spent the winter there. In April 1805, they resumed their journey and followed the headwaters of the Missouri to, successively, the Clearwater, Snake and Columbia rivers. Rafting down the Columbia, they reached the Pacific in early November. They wintered at Fort Catslop (which they built) and began the homeward journey in late March 1806. They returned via the

6

Yellowstone and upper Missouri, reaching St Louis late in September 1806, after an absence of two years and four months.

The United States did not immediately follow up on the Lewis and Clark expedition. Exploration of the vast area between the Mississippi and the Pacific was largely the work of the 'mountain men' who, between 1820 and 1840, reconnoitred the routes that would later be recognised as the Santa Fe, California and Oregon trails. Living beyond the pale of civilisation, often with Indian wives and thus linked by kinship to the potentially hostile tribes, the mountain men had their own way of life and even their own canting argot. Among them were some of the most famous names of the old West – Kit Carson, Jim Bridger, Joseph Walker, Jedediah Smith, Thomas 'Pegleg' Smith, Caleb Greenwood, Thomas Fitzpatrick and the Sublette brothers.

The mountain men made their living trapping beaver, for the fur trade was *the* salient fact of economic life in the West c. 1820–40. At first, the fur trade was a three-way commercial contest between the British-chartered Hudson's Bay Company, operating in the Oregon territory, the Rocky Mountain Fur Company, whose operatives used Taos in New Mexico as its jump-off point, and the American Fur Company based in St Louis. In the early days, the Hudson's Bay Company trapped along the Pacific Rim while the other two disputed the interior, but after 1830 the Hudson's Bay Company expanded inland, complicating the situation. The American Fur Company won its long battle with the Rocky Mountain Fur Company, but was about to succumb to the greater resources of the Hudson's Bay Company when the fur trade itself came to an abrupt end: in their competition mania, the mountain men had all but exterminated the beaver. But the indirect consequences of the fur trade era were incalculable. The mountain men, seeking new employment, were able to guide the first wagon trains of emigrants along trails they themselves had pioneered. And throughout the 1830s they brought back letters and travellers' tales from California and Oregon, thus acting as transmission belts in the spreading of knowledge about the West.

Mountain men apart, until the late 1830s the only other significant white American presence west of the Mississippi (always excepting the special case of Texas) was that of missionaries. In 1833, the Methodists established their first mission in the Oregon territory under the Reverend Jason Lee. Dr John McLoughlin, chief of the Hudson's Bay Company in Oregon, did not want Americans north of the Columbia River, so steered them towards the fertile Willamette valley; the Methodists accepted the suggestion, but set up a branch office at the Dalles on the Columbia. Stung by the success of the Methodists, the Presbyterians sent out their

7

own missionaries in 1835. Accompanied by Dr Marcus Whitman, the Reverend Samuel Parker reconnoitred the Oregon territory and decided that his denomination's missions would be in eastern Oregon, at Waiilatpu, among the Cayuse Indians, and at Lapwai, among the Nez Percé. Warnings from McLoughlin about the danger of working with such warlike tribes went unheeded.

Parker and Whitman returned east by ship. In the spring of 1836, Whitman set out for Oregon again. But his situation was difficult. Because the American Board of Commissioners for Foreign Missions, fearing the miscegenation and 'immorality' of the mountain men, would send only married couples to work among 'savages', Whitman had to find a wife. He found one in the twenty-eight-year-old Narcissa Prentiss, a dedicated New York Presbyterian. Whitman married her in February 1836 after returning from his first trip to Oregon with Samuel Parker. But there was a complication. Accompanying Whitman to Oregon was another missionary, Henry Spalding, who had earlier been rejected by Narcissa when he proposed marriage. By now Spalding had made a marriage of convenience, so he and his wife joined the Whitmans for an embarrassing and uncomfortable journey into the unknown. Some historians have speculated that many of the later difficulties between Spalding and Whitman can be traced to Narcissa's initial rejection. There were other problems on the journey, as Thomas Fitzpatrick, leading a party of fur traders into the interior, did not want to take the missionaries along, fearing that their wives would be targeted by the Indians. He tried to slip away unnoticed, but the intrepid Whitman caught up with his party in a series of forced marches.

By becoming the first white women to cross the Rockies, Narcissa Whitman and Mrs Henry Spalding proved that the way west was feasible for women and children. The Whitmans set up their mission station at Waiilatpu, near modern-day Walla Walla, Washington, while the Spaldings settled at Lapwai, near present-day Lewiston, Idaho. Narcissa became one of the great characters of the early West, 'vivacious, attractive, gregarious, idealistic and sentimentally religious', as she has been called. But the Presbyterians made few converts. The Cayuse and Nez Percé were interested only in what benefits they could winkle out of the white men and accordingly merely feigned interest in Christianity. Spalding wrote in despair: 'I fear that they will all prove to be a selfish, deceptive race of beings.' But the missionaries sowed seeds that would germinate later. President Andrew Jackson sent an agent out to investigate missionary endeavour in Oregon. William Slocum's report, enthusiastically stressing the potential of the Oregon territory, interested

8

Senator Lewis Linn of Missouri, who soon began to lobby for US annexation of the territory. And the existence of the missions encouraged a trickle of early settlers: fifty-one to Jason Lee's Methodist foundation in the Willamette valley in 1839, many more in 1840. By the end of that year, there were already five hundred whites in the Willamette valley.

Such was the context for the first wagon train emigration of 1841. The 1840s was, in economic terms, an odd decade, wedged between the fur trade bonanza years of 1820–40 and the gold rush of 1849 and the subsequent inland mining boom era. Almost by pre-established harmony, the last great annual market or rendezvous of the fur trappers took place the year before the first wagon train set out. The other peculiarity of the 1840s was that the United States suddenly became an aggressive, expansionist nation. *Pace* the historian Bernard de Voto, some say that America's real 'year of decision' was 1844 not 1846. The election of James Polk that year as US president gave the green light for a process that would, four years later, see all of Mexico north of the Rio Grande and all the Oregon territory south of the forty-ninth parallel of latitude in US hands. The watchword was sounded by the editor of the New York *Morning News*, John L. O'Sullivan, who wrote in December 1845 that it was the 'manifest destiny' of the United States 'to overspread and to possess the whole of the continent which Providence has given us for the development of the great experiment of liberty and federated self-government entrusted to us'.

Manifest Destiny was a peculiar mixture of assertiveness and fear, of ideology and crude political calculation. Economic motives such as the export of surplus capital or the acquisition of new markets do not seem to have played a primary role. Ideologically, the notion of Manifest Destiny can be seen as a weird mixture of evangelical Protestantism, ultramontane republicanism and Hegelian philosophy. History, as in Hegel's system, had a purpose or destiny, and Providence had obviously chosen the United States as its vessel. Since the white race was self-evidently superior to the black, the red or the Hispanic, only the lily-livered or the cretinous would draw back from fulfilling the obvious design of the transcendent order, whether this was called God, Spirit or Providence. There has always been a strand in US republican thought that has emphasised continual expansion as the only way to preserve the peculiar virtue of republicanism, just as there has always been a countervailing strand that stresses that expansion or foreign adventures pervert the sanctity both of republican virtue and of Providence's mandate itself.

But Manifest Destiny was not a product of pure ideology. Alongside these 'positive' aspects, at least two negative facets should be noted. Some historians see fear of foreign nations, and especially Britain, as the real impulse towards expansion. British meddling in California and Texas was particularly resented, and the fear was that, if the United States did not move quickly to annex the territories north of the Rio Grande held in Mexico's grasp, some other nation, probably Britain, would acquire them. Even if former Spanish territories were not added to the British Empire, London could maintain them as independent states, as a curb on American economic ambitions; both Britain and France looked on Texas as a profitable target for markets and investment. Alongside this was a desire for expansion by southern slave-owning states, fearful that the balance of power in the United States was swinging away from them. The incorporation of slave-owning Texas would be a powerful brake on the ambitions of the abolitionists. Even those who wavered were won round by scare stories about British desire to abolish slavery worldwide.

So, for their own reasons, Southerners who might otherwise have been disposed to oppose Polk supported him. But whatever the explanation of Manifest Destiny (and it continues to be disputed), the spectacular results could scarcely be doubted. Alongside the earlier settlement of the Oregon Question, the 1848 Treaty of Guadalupe Hidalgo, which sealed the US victory in the Mexican War, added 1.2 million square miles to the United States, out of which would arise the states of California, Oregon, New Mexico and Arizona, as well as much of Nevada, Utah and Colorado. Polk's aggression had secured an increase of 66 per cent in the nation's size.

In subtle ways, Manifest Destiny was important as an ideological support for the pioneers who struck west in their wagons in the 1840s. Just as the Boers and Mormons trekked into the wilderness with a conviction that God was on their side, so the emigrants could feel they were caught up in a movement of inevitability, that they were history's 'winners'. Racial prejudice and a feeling of cultural superiority were important aspects to this. The traveller Walter Colton is eloquent on the sentiments of cultural and ethnic superiority, when he describes the California pioneers: 'They seem to look upon this beautiful land as their own Canaan, and the motley race around them as the Hittites, the Hivites, and the Jebusites, whom they are to drive out.' Everything they heard and read convinced the wagon train emigrants that right, justice and the main historical currents were on their side. John O'Sullivan reassured them: 'There is in fact no such thing as title to the wild lands of the new world, except that which actual possession gives. They belong to whoever will redeem them from the Indian and the desert, and subjugate them to the use of man.'

Thereafter, the would-be emigrant had just two main decisions to make: which route should he follow; and was the 'pull' of the Pacific sufficient to draw him out of the farmlands of the Midwest?

Wagons first went west on the Santa Fe Trail from Missouri to Santa Fe, and the trail itself was born in the very year of Mexico's independence from Spain, in 1821. But it took twenty years for the first emigrants to reach California from Missouri via the Santa Fe Trail. There is an interesting historical 'synchronicity' here. It took twenty years from the time the British acquired the Cape Colony to the moment (in 1836) the first Boers trekked west and north out of the colony in search of the promised land. The great migrations in South Africa and North America were virtually simultaneous events. But overland migration in the south-west proved a false dawn. The Santa Fe Trail is important in the story of the wagon trains mainly as (literally) the road not taken. Why it was not taken is important to establish, for in this case the flag most certainly did not follow trade.

By the late 1820s the route from Independence, Missouri, to Santa Fe was well trodden. The trail ran to the Arkansas River, then traversed the arid Cimarron Desert before debouching on the Cimarron River; thereafter there were crossings of the Canadian and Pecos rivers before the settlers could ascend the Glorieta Pass and then make their way down to the town of Santa Fe, eight hundred miles from Independence. On this itinerary, the intricacies of travel by wagon were first mastered and valuable lessons learned which the pioneers on the later Oregon and California trails would take to heart. But the journey was dangerous, for it crossed the hunting grounds of the Arapaho and the Comanche, the 'Spartans of the plains'. So serious did Comanche depredations on the wagon trains become that in 1829 the US Army found itself fighting a long and difficult campaign against these Indians. It was their mixed fortune that was the genesis of the famed US Cavalry, for Washington soon decided that using infantry against mounted warriors on the great plains was consummate idiocy. That same year, the Mexicans pioneered a trading route between Santa Fe and Los Angeles in California. There already existed an Old Spanish Trail, which ran north-west from Santa Fe, across the continental divide in northern New Mexico, into the Rockies at Colorado, then, after fording the Green and Colorado rivers above their junction, looped round the northern rim of the Grand Canyon into Utah, creeping south-west through the deserts of Nevada and California to Los Angeles. But the Old Spanish Trail was an impossibly roundabout route. Traffic in trade goods between New

Mexico and California began only when Antonio Armijo blazed a new trail in 1829–30. Starting from Santa Fe on 6 November 1829, Armijo, with thirty companions, followed the Old Spanish Trail north-west only as far as Abiquiu, then cut almost due west to the Four Corners region near Mesa Verde and proceeded via the Goose Neck gorge of the San Juan River to the so-called 'Crossing of the Fathers' – the series of man-made stone steps at the Colorado River north of the Grand Canyon where the Franciscan fathers Dominguez and Escalante had made the crossing in 1777.

After fording the Colorado with great difficulty on 6 December, Armijo's band reached the Virgin River on New Year's Day 1830 about a hundred miles north of present-day Las Vegas, Nevada, then survived the Mojave Desert by eating mule and horse flesh and arrived at the San Gabriel mission about fifty miles east of Los Angeles on 31 January; they had thus completed the journey in less than three months. Even though they had killed some of the pack animals, they arrived in California with most of their mules still loaded with serapes, blankets, quilts and other woollen goods, which they traded for mules and horses from the Californian ranches. The expedition did even better on the return journey: Armijo's flying column got back to Santa Fe in forty days and Armijo himself on 25 April, after a two-month trip that saw him robbed by the Navajo Indians.

Every year thereafter, a mule train picked its way across the continent from Santa Fe to Los Angeles, thus in effect extending the Santa Fe Trail so that it ran from Missouri to California. Apart from the occasional raid by the Navajo, these trains fared better in terms of Indian attacks than the wagon trains on the Santa Fe Trail proper, to the point where Mexican traders took their wives and children along with them. Silver, woollen goods and blankets went to California, whence the intrepid merchants brought back horses and mules and even luxury items that had arrived in Californian ports from China and New England. Americans entered the horse-trading business in California and emulated the Mexicans by driving livestock back to Santa Fe; soon they were taking mules and horses all the way from California to Missouri. The new trails had become genuine extensions of the Santa Fe Trail and thus, potentially, an emigrant route lay open from the Midwest to the Pacific.

The 1830s was a troubled decade in the south-west. Massive Anglo-Saxon immigration into Texas led to calls for the state's independence and for an immediate military solution from men like William Barret Travis, who soon eclipsed the gradualists led by William Austin. Events played into Travis's hands. The hardliner Antonio de Santa Anna became dictator of Mexico and tried to bring his recalcitrant northern province to heel. The result was war: the heroism of the Alamo, the grim massacre of Goliad and finally Sam Houston's victory over Santa Anna at San Jacinto in 1836 which secured Texan independence. The hero of the hour became the president of independent Texas, but was succeeded by Howard L. Lamar, who pursued a 'forward' policy aimed at the annexation of New Mexico and the acquisition of the Santa Fe trade. There were numerous skirmishes and minor battles between Texans and Mexicans in New Mexico and by 1841 the two infant republics were once again on the brink of all-out war. This was the tangled context in which the first American emigrants came to California. In September 1841, William Workman and John Rowland led a party of twenty-five along the Old Spanish Trail, from Santa Fe to California. Workman and Rowland were secret supporters of the Anglo-American faction in New Mexico that wanted the territory annexed by Texas and had been in correspondence with the plotters in Austin; there is even a suspicion that it was their intercepted letters that alerted the Mexicans to the conspiracy at an early stage. When Workman and Rowland's 'treachery' became known, there was a move among Mexican patriots to lynch them, narrowly prevented by Armijo's personal intervention. Nonetheless, the writing was on the wall: it was no longer safe for Workman, Rowland and their American associates to remain in New Mexico. They laid plans for an overland trek to California.

Workman was a forty-one-year-old native of Cumberland, England, who after coming to America spent some time as a trapper before settling down with a Mexican wife, as a storekeeper and naturalised Mexican citizen in Taos. Rowland, a Pennsylvanian, had a similar background except that he had a more extensive history of Indian fighting and was a more successful businessman, having diversified into the flour and distillery business. The two gathered together a small party of emigrants, mainly Americans who had been living for some time in New Mexico, together with a few new arrivals from the Santa Fe Trail. All twenty-five men were either professionals or skilled craftsmen, except for a French Creole gambler named Tibeau (or Tiboux). The emigrant party could boast two physicians, a naturalist, a mineralogist, an engineer, a musician, a tailor, a gunsmith, three carpenters, two coopers and a blacksmith; there were also two native New Mexicans, the only ones in the party to take families.

Some historians of the Old Spanish Trail claim that the crisis of 1841 was the occasion rather than the cause of Rowland and Workman's departure from New Mexico, that they had been planning to leave the territory long before the crisis with Texas, but that the tension of that year gave them the final nudge. This interpretation would explain how the men were able to liquidate their assets in real estate so rapidly and turn them into cash and livestock. Certainly, there was no sign of money shortage at the beginning of the journey. At Santa Fe, they took on supplies of flour, hard tack, dried and jerked beef and buffalo meat. Following Armijo's 1829–30 route they travelled north-west to Abiquiu, where they bought 150 sheep and employed local drovers for the journey. The prosperity of the emigrants is casually indicated by the number of Mexican servants they employed in the village. Some of the travellers were amazed to find the Mexicans prepared to follow them into the unknown with just an hour's notice; standard pay for the trip was two dollars, issued together with a set of Californian clothes on arrival.

The emigrants had a stroke of luck just before heading out into the wilderness. The Mexican Secretary of State was at first inclined to make a clear distinction between loyal and treacherous Anglo-Americans in Mexican territory, but in September 1841 he finally concluded that the first loyalty of gringos would always be to Texas or the United States. He therefore issued an order prohibiting foreigners from leaving their places of residence. The decree reached Abiuquiu only days after the Workman party had left; they quit the village in the first week of September. After Abiuquiu, they took the classic northerly route of the Old Spanish Trail – a more roundabout journey than Armijo's. Travelling north-west, they hit the Colorado River just below the mouth of the Dolores (near present-day Moab), then crossed the 'Great American Basin' to the Sevier River. At first the going was easy, with plenty of ice-cold water trickling down from the mountains and rich pasturage for the animals. But then the landscape gradually became more arid and sterile, and the going difficult, across treeless wastes striated by ravines.

At the Sevier they swung sharply south-west to the Virgin River (passing close to present-day St George), and followed this down to the Colorado. The next obstacle was the Mojave Desert, where there was no water, the sands drifted frighteningly and the route was littered with the carcasses of horses that had perished on previous attempts to cross this Sahara of the West. Because of the lack of moisture in the atmosphere, the flesh of the dead horses had not rotted but rather mummified as if embalmed. Finally, they completed the crossing of the Mojave and proceeded through the Cajon Pass to San Bernadino, and thence to Los Angeles, which was reached in early November, eight weeks out from Santa Fe. The Mexican authorities, alerted to the coming of the

Americans by the regular annual Spanish Trail caravan, rode out to inspect the new arrivals but found them of good character. Evidently, Armijo in New Mexico had not complained to his counterpart in California or, if he had, his words were disregarded. Workman's explanation for their emigration, that they had grown tired of Comanche depredations in New Mexico, was found totally satisfactory.

The successful Workman–Rowland emigration should on paper have opened up an obvious conduit for emigrants from Missouri, for by now both the Santa Fe Trail and the Old Spanish Trail were well-trodden pathways. Yet until the California Gold Rush of 1849, the route to the Pacific through the south-west remained a dead letter. Why was this? Why were wagon trains destined to settle Oregon and California only by the more northerly Oregon and California trails? This question seems at first sight difficult to answer, both because the route along the Old Spanish Trail was not, in theory, as strenuous as the Oregon and California trails and because the Workman–Rowland party did spectacularly well in California and should presumably have spawned imitators. Within three months of arriving at Los Angeles, Workman and Rowland owned a 48,000-acre ranch. Workman's eventual failure as a banker did not occur until 1876. Rowland became a cattle tycoon and pioneer of the California wine industry, while another of the 1841 emigrants, Benjamin D. Wilson, also became a millionaire rancher and businessman.

Three principal factors explain the failure of the Santa Fe Trail to develop in the early 1840s as a continental migration route to rival the Oregon and California trails. First, there was the unsuitability of the route for wagons, which meant that the San Juan area and the 'Crossing of the Fathers' were never to see the building of first-class roads. On the Old Spanish Trail, the distances between rivers was vast, as it never was on the Oregon Trail; since wagons moved so much more slowly than mule trains, the problem of water supply was acute, and those who had faced the rigours of the Cimarron Cutoff on the Santa Fe Trail proper did not relish further jousts with waterless deserts. The consequence was, as the historian John Hawgood remarked: 'No covered wagons followed "in the steps of the Fathers", no railroad was to be built along Armijo's route.' When the building of a wagon road became a necessity in 1846, with the outbreak of war between Mexico and the US, General Kearny ordered St George Cooke and the Mormon Battalion to make one. Significantly, they built it on a much more southerly route, along the Gila River to Yuma and San Diego, and this was the route later taken by the stagecoach lines.

Second, the south-western trails were plagued by Indian attacks as the

Oregon and California trails never were. Whereas the US government had from the very earliest days of migrant travel attempted to constrain or co-opt the Sioux, Cheyenne and other potentially hostile northern tribes, no such policy emerged in the south-west in the 1840s. The political context was simply too difficult. Not only was there an independent state of Texas until late 1845, but the problem of the south-western tribes inevitably impinged on the larger issue of relations with Mexico. There was, in some quarters, the feeling that the Comanche and the Apache were primarily Mexican problems or that, even if they were pressing issues for the US, the fact that the tribes could always seek sanctuary across the Mexican border made punitive action by US forces impracticable.

Any traveller proceeding along the Santa Fe and Old Spanish trails from Missouri to California had to reckon on possible encounters with a plethora of hostile or unpredictable Indian tribes: Pawnee, Kiowa, Gros Ventres, Arapaho, Southern Cheyenne, Comanche, Apache, Navajo, Ute. The eastern end of the trail was vulnerable to the Pawnee who, though decimated by smallpox, were by no means out of the reckoning, as a serious assault on the Santa Fe wagon train in February 1840 showed. Anyone taking the Canadian River route was likely to fall foul of the Kiowas, while the southern end of the trail was within striking distance of the Apache. One traveller taking a southerly route from Santa Fe was attacked by Navajo 150 miles from Santa Fe and then, one hundred miles further on, by Apaches. Even the Californian end of the Old Spanish Trail was not immune to the Indian menace, which became acute in the early 1840s with increasingly daring Ute raids, which even took them into the sleepy town of Los Angeles itself.

Worst of all the menaces were the Comanche. Contemporary accounts do not permit a modern-day 'noble savage' reading of this tribe. Bernard de Voto comments:

No one has ever exaggerated the Comanche tortures. The authenticated accounts fill thousands of pages, and some are altogether unreadable for men with normal nerves. They had great skill in pain, and cruelty was their catharsis. In short, the Comanche killed and tortured more whites than any other Indians in the West, stole more horses and cattle, were a greater danger. With their allies, the Kiowa, they were for many years what the title of a recent book calls them, a barrier to the advancement of the plains.

Some contemporaries were struck by the apparent immunity of much of New Mexico to Comanche attack even as they waged ferocious war on

Texas, and speculated that the Mexicans and Comanches had a secret understanding. More likely, it was simply that the pickings were richer in Texas, and that if they raided in both Texas *and* New Mexico, the US and Mexican governments might then combine for joint punitive action.

Anyone proposing to take an emigrant wagon train from Missouri to California along the south-western route would certainly have been given pause by the tales of Comanche massacre, atrocity and depredation, which reached a height in the years 1837–40. So audacious were the Comanche that not even Texan settlements on the shores of the Gulf of Mexico were safe. In a daring raid on Linnville, Matagorda Bay, on 8 August 1840, the Comanche gutted and razed the town, forcing the townspeople to take refuge on a ship in the bay. Although Texas Rangers caught up with the raiders, defeated them and recovered the white captives, this was just one successful battle in a grinding war of attrition. As Josiah Gregg reported:

> War parties have frequently penetrated to the very heart of the settlements, perpetrating murderous outrages, and bearing away into captivity numerous women and children. They have entered the city of Austin, then the seat of government, in open day; and, at other times, have been known to descend to the very sea coast, committing many frightful depredations.

Third, and by far the greatest deterrent to overland emigration by the south-western trails, was the sheer unpredictability of the political three-way imbroglio involving Texas, Mexico and the United States. The years 1842–43 saw Texas and Mexico in a state of open war. Santa Anna followed up his earlier raid on San Antonio with a further swoop under General Adrian Woll and 1,200 men in September, which again captured the town; meanwhile, Corpus Christi had been attacked by a large Mexican force. Even though Sam Houston had been re-elected on a programme of retrenchment and economy, he could not ignore this provocation, nor indeed the panic in Texas and the clamour for firm action. The Texans prepared three separate expeditions, each of which ended in fiasco or worse.

Santa Anna's response to the events of 1843 was to issue a decree in August, prohibiting all overland commerce with the United States via the Santa Fe Trail. Missouri, whose economy depended so heavily on this trade, faced immediate ruin. But Santa Anna was also under pressure from the merchants of New Mexico. Unable to back down unless he could find a face-saving formula, Santa Anna 'allowed' himself to be convinced that Sam Houston's recent actions were an earnest of American good faith; he therefore rescinded his decree of interdict in March 1844. But New Mexico was anyway by now slipping out of Santa Anna's orbit. The Spanish-speaking inhabitants of the state, who detested the centralism emanating from Mexico City but had no enthusiasm for annexation by the United States, faced the coming Mexico–United States conflict, all but inevitable by 1845, with a 'plague on both your houses' attitude.

The story of how US imperialism, aka 'Manifest Destiny', triumphed in the war of 1846–48 against Mexico is well known. These were dramatic years, since in the 1,078 days between the annexation of Texas on 1 March 1845 and the signing of the Treaty of Guadalupe Hidalgo on 2 February 1848, which brought the Mexican War to an end, the US added 1.2 million square miles to its national domain. Once the issue of Mexico was solved, the Santa Fe and the Old Spanish trails became what they would otherwise always have been – national arteries used by emigrants as well as traders. In some ways, the late 1840s were the great days of the Santa Fe Trail, and this was to be a favourite route to the gold fields for the gold-fevered overlanders of 1849. But by that time the classic era of covered-wagon emigration was already over. Pioneers had found other routes to their Pacific Utopias.

TWO

THE REASONS WHY

Why did so many men and women risk the unknown to travel 2,000 miles to the Pacific when there was perfectly good and fertile land closer at hand? Why did this diaspora take place in the 1840s? The question is all the more intriguing since majority opinion until the 1840s held that to travel overland to California or Oregon was virtually to commit suicide. Savage Indians barred the way, it was said, as did ferocious wild beasts, death-dealing rivers and impassable deserts. Moreover, the journey could not be made in one season, so that emigrants would have to winter in the Rockies in ice and snow. Death was certain, either from drowning, starvation, scalping or being eaten alive. A particularly potent argument was that the 'Great American Desert' barred the way to the West to all but fanatics and lunatics. Until the Civil War, maps of the West routinely showed a blank space labelled 'Great American Desert', which stretched from the hundredth meridian to the Rockies.

In short, then, the overland journey was impossible and it was too cruel on women and children for heads of families even to contemplate it. Dr John McLoughlin, the Hudson's Bay Company chief at Fort Vancouver, said that would-be overland emigrants to Oregon might just as well plan to travel to the moon. Of course, the British interest in dissuading American westward expansion and American colonists was obvious, so his opinion (though sincerely held) could be set aside. But many prominent Americans shared McLoughlin's view. Horace Greeley, editor of the influential New York *Daily Tribune* regularly inveighed in the 1840s against the very idea of travel to the West by wagon train: 'It is palpable homicide to tempt or send women and children over this thousand miles of precipice and volcanic sterility to Oregon.' Particularly hostile to the great emigration to Oregon in 1843, Greeley poured scorn on the intelligence of the pioneers:

For what, then, do they brave the desert, the wilderness, the savage,

19

the snowy precipices of the Rocky Mountains, the weary summer march, the storm-drenched bivouac, and the gnawings of famine? Only to fulfil their destiny! There is probably not one among them whose outward circumstances will be improved by this perilous journey.

Since California in the early 1840s was a Spanish domain, most anti-emigration propaganda was directed at Oregon. An article in the *Daily Missouri Republican* was typical:

[Oregon] is mountainous and rugged; its plains are dry and barren, nothing but sun in summer; very few fertile valleys, and those of very limited extent, and no navigable rivers to compare with the great watercourses of the Mississippi valley. This is Oregon. In truth, no man of information . . . in his right mind would think of leaving such a country as this [Missouri] to wander over a thousand miles of desert and five hundred [miles] of mountain to reach such as that.

In a nutshell, then, the anti-Oregon case peddled so assiduously by some sections of the press was threefold: the journey was too dangerous for women and children; there was much better land available in the east; and in any case the US Army could not march overland to defend it against the British.

So why was such anti-emigration propaganda so contemptuously dismissed and why did the wagon trains insist on trekking west? Some writers insist that this is a non-problem, that in the late 1830s and early 1840s, for particular reasons, the world was in a migratory ferment: Boers in South Africa trekked out of Cape Colony to find the promised land because of British policies on slavery; the Irish emigrated to the eastern United States en masse because of the potato famine, and so on. It just so happened that the early 1840s saw a conjunction of different, discrete migrations related in some obscure way to the imperatives of a global economy, but there is really no general explanation. A variant of this 'empirical' particularist approach is to suggest that the entire problem of motivation is so complex that only an exhaustive enumeration of the motives of every single patriarch would suffice, and that the mosaic thus revealed would not show any single overarching pattern. While not committing himself to such 'impossibilism', a distinguished scholar of the frontier has written: 'It is impossible, of course, to generalize with confidence about the motives of a variety of individuals.'

Another approach is to subsume the overland emigrations under the rubric of exploration and to relate them to the Victorian thirst for charting new lands and new rivers under the banner of science. An article in the *Washington National Intelligencer* for 1855 makes the point clearly.

> The present is emphatically the age of discovery. At no period since the days of Columbus and Cortez has the thirst for exploration been more active and universal than now. One by one the outposts of barbarism are stormed and carried, advanced parallels are thrown up, and the besieging lines of knowledge, which when once established can never be retaken, are gradually closing around the yet unconquered mysteries of the globe. Modern exploration is intelligent, and its results are therefore positive and permanent. The traveller no longer wanders bewildered in a cloud of fables prepared to see marvels, and too ready to create them. He tests every step of his way by the sure light of science and his pioneer trail becomes a plain and easy path to those who follow. The pencil, the compass, the barometer, and the sextant are his aids; and by these helps and appliances his single brain achieves results now which it would once have required an armed force to win.

The problem is that the motivations of explorers and pioneers are very different; reason is a good guide to the latter but not to the former, whose psychological wellsprings tend to be sexual or pathological.

Yet others allege that the instinct to go west is a constant of human nature, deeply embedded in human psychology and biology, and that to seek structural reasons for western emigration is otiose. The most famous statement is Thoreau's 'eastward I go only by force; but westward I go free . . . we go westward as into the future, with a spirit of enterprise and adventure'. Less cautious writers have married Thoreau to the spirit of Mark Twain's 'lighting out for the territory' and produced formulations such as the following: 'The westward urge was a human instinct, like the need to love or to taste spring air and believe again that life is not a dead end after all.' It has even been stated that the urge to go west 'was as natural as swimming upstream is to a salmon'. The burden of all such statements is clear: although there may be theoretical explanations for western emigration, they are unnecessary, for we are dealing with human impulses, urges and instincts. The 'cause' of the wagon trains is a non-issue, except to esoteric specialists, just as the reason for falling in love is.

Another interpretation is that the wagon train is an aspect of a unique American culture; it may stand in need of explanation from outside the USA but not from within. American culture is characterised by permanent restlessness, marked by spatial mobility, relocation and the belief in the Fresh Start. The dream of escape to the open frontier, where you can change occupation, lifestyle or even identity, is part of the process of reinvention that Americans understand by liberty. The covered wagon thus functions as a pilot version of the automobile in the twentieth century, and trekking west is a pre-echo of being 'on the road' in the manner of Jack London, Jack Kerouac or the Easy Riders. The theme of restlessness receives powerful endorsement from the French historian Alexis de Tocqueville who toured the United States in the 1830s, just before the wagons set out. He wrote: 'An American will build a house in which to pass his old age and sell it before the roof is on; he will plant a garden and rent it just as the trees are coming into bearing; he will clear a field and leave others to reap the harvest.'

This notion of restlessness receives ample support from the diaries, memoirs and recollections of the pioneers of the 1840s. The plainsman James Clyman noted that it was a peculiarly American thing for people with comfortable homes in Missouri and elsewhere to set out for the unknown. The Sager family, whose story will be told later, set out for Oregon in 1844 largely because of the restlessness of the head of the household. The emigrant Sarah J. Cummins gives a clear example of itchy-footedness which comes close to the neurotic. She relates how she returned to her Illinois home on a Friday evening and found her mother with a long face. 'What do you think father has done?' her mother asked. 'I do not know,' she replied. 'He has sold the farm and as soon as school closes we are to move to Missouri.' Needless to say, Missouri did not suit either, and the family was soon on its way to Oregon. Medorem Crawford, pioneer of the journey to Oregon in 1842, told of one family who had spent twenty years in a wagon, staying in one place just long enough to raise a crop, which they had done in every state and territory in the Mississippi valley; again, it hardly needs to be added that, once they reached Oregon, they were dissatisfied with what they found and the following year pressed on to California.

Part of the explanation for restlessness may be that the American farmer was a completely different kind of animal from the European peasant. The European peasant looked on land as a lifetime investment; he was prepared to defer gratification, had a mystical relationship with it, waged vendettas and feuds over it, as Zola's *La Terre* shows. The American farmer looked on it as a source of get-rich-quick wealth, wanted instant gratification and was prepared to move on if his present situation dissatisfied him. Some of the tension between men and women on the overland trail arose from the simple fact that the men were wandering stars, perennial movers, while the women wanted a settled hearth and home. It may be, too, that this was why honeymoon emigrations were such a tradition, as it was the one time when a man could disguise his restlessness with a romantic pretext. Certainly in the West the fabled restlessness was carried to extremes: only 25 per cent of those present in San Francisco in 1850 were still there in 1860.

The notion of restlessness and its role in American culture is seminal and fruitful, and its truth cannot be denied. But it does not, on its own, explain why emigration on such a large scale should have taken place in the 1840s. Mass migrations take place when 'push' and 'pull' factors both operate at the same time, and by the end of the 1830s a combination of factors produced such a unique conjuncture. National financial panic led to depression in 1837; as a result of the speculation mania in the railways, land prices plummeted, farm produce was unsaleable and most settlers in the Mississippi valley were already heavily mortgaged. By 1842, wheat was selling for twenty-five cents a bushel when the profit margin did not begin until fifty cents, while hogs had dropped in price from $4.20 per hundredweight in 1839 to under a dollar – always assuming you could find a buyer. Thirty-two-year-old Jesse Applegate, once a prosperous farmer in St Clair County, Missouri, sold a steamboat full of bacon and lard for $100 when the curing salt alone cost $150. As one historian has written of the years after 1839, 'the United States entered upon an era of declining prices and a succession of lean years for the farmer, so long continued that men became 'restless, visionary, even revolutionary'. In other words, the restlessness in the American psyche needed to be triggered by events.

But even as severe financial crisis wracked the land, the United States changed its attitude on land policy. The Preemption Act of 1841 nudged the government away from the idea of public lands as a source of revenue and towards free homesteads – a principle not accepted fully until the great Homestead Act of 1862. The 'pre-emption' principle was accepted: any squatter on unclaimed land could exercise the right, once the land was surveyed and auctioned, to buy at a minimum price, usually $2 an acre, with the squatter getting first refusal. Missouri senator Lewis Linn tried to push matters a stage further by introducing a bill into the Senate, granting free land as a reward for those prepared to travel across the Rockies to claim it. Linn's bill was expressly aimed at wresting control of the Oregon territory from Britain by deluging it with American settlers. He and his fellow Missouri senators were rabid Anglophobes, who mendaciously asserted that the Hudson's Bay Company had murdered five hundred Americans since 1829 (it had not killed one).

Dr Linn introduced his bill in December 1841 and laboured manfully to secure its passage through the Senate. He faced tough opposition from South Carolina senators Calhoun and McDuffie, who argued that the bill would upset the status quo in Washington, alienate Britain and lead to war; by the 1818 treaty (renewed in 1827), Britain and the United States had agreed to 'joint occupation' of Oregon. The South was bound to Britain by economic and political ties which lasted until the Civil War, but beyond this Calhoun and Linn were both involved in a wider struggle over the 'peculiar institution' of slavery, with pro-slavers and abolitionists trying to steal a march on each other. McDuffie alleged that Oregon was useless for agricultural and farming purposes and that he for one would not give a pinch of snuff for the entire territory.

Linn hit back with some vintage irony:

The Senator from South Carolina somewhat inconsistently urges that the country is bleak, barren, volcanic, rocky, a waste always flooded when it is not parched; and insists that, worthless as it is, Great Britain will go at once to war for it. Strange that she should in 1818 have held so tenaciously to what is so worthless! Stranger still, that she should have stuck yet closer to it in 1827, when she had still ampler time to learn the bootlessness of the possession! And strangest of all that she should still cling to it with the grasp of death! Sir, I cannot for my life help thinking that she and the senator have formed a very different estimate of the territory, and that she is (as she ought to be) a good deal better informed.

The upshot was that the bill passed the Senate on 3 February 1843 by a vote of twenty-four to twenty-two. But it fell in the House of Representatives. It was not until the Oregon Donation Act of 1850 that Linn's aim was achieved. This gave 320 acres to single men and 640 to married men, with claims to be lodged by 1855.

The talk of free land in the Senate helped to free the logjam in the Midwest. The problem for so many farmers in the upper Mississippi valley and Missouri was that 'moving on' did not seem to be an option, since the frontier had already reached the edge of the plains and the 'Great American Desert', all of which were Indian territory. Such men tried at first to solve their problems by pressurising Washington to annex the Indian lands in Iowa and Minnesota. But for those in the lower Mississippi valley the only viable option seemed to be to move into precariously independent Texas. True, there were 'wild men' who spoke of settling beyond the Great Divide, but how could anyone equip himself and his family properly for a trek west until he could get a decent price for his farm? One of the reasons the overland route to Oregon took off so dramatically in early 1843 was that for the first time in five years economic conditions were returning to something like normal. But once bitten, the men of the Midwest did not intend to wait for the next downturn in the boom-and-bust economic cycle. They had had enough and they wanted to get out, to a land where their futures were not determined by the vagaries of the New York stock market.

The same applied to all those on the frontier who depended on the farmers for their living. Peter Burnett, a storekeeper in Weston, Missouri, could not meet the interest on his debts. When he heard of Linn's bill before Congress that proposed to offer land to anyone emigrating to the Far West, he seized his opportunity. He called his creditors together, explained the situation, and asked their permission to emigrate to Oregon. He pointed out that, since he would receive 640 acres of land for himself and 160 acres for each child, he would at once be able to pay off his debts from the value of the real estate alone – always assuming the bill passed Congress. The creditors were convinced. 'Take what may be necessary for the trip,' they said, 'leave us what you can spare, and pay the balance when you can do so.'

That economic depression and land hunger were the principal 'push' factors in the decision to migrate to the Far West can scarcely be doubted. John Minto, emigrant in 1844, was an obvious victim of recession: an ex-coal miner from Pittsburgh, he went west when his fellow miners struck in a futile bid for living wages – futile, because the market for coal was already glutted. Minto's case is an interesting one, illustrating as it does that motives were usually 'overdetermined'. Having established that he was a classic economic refugee, Minto confessed that he had always had a hankering to see the Rocky Mountains and, when young, once announced: 'If I live, I will go across the Rocky Mountains.' Another man who later made his mark on the frontier was Solomon Sublette, who had begun as a storekeeper in the Mississippi valley but given up once the 1837 panic and subsequent recession bit deep.

As for the prospect of free land, its impact can hardly be overestimated. Two very different witnesses are worth citing, first a pioneer, and second an expert on agriculture.

The motive that induced us to part with the pleasant associations and dear friends of our childhood days, was to obtain from the government of the United States a grant of land that 'Uncle Sam' had promised to give to the head of each family who settled in this new country.

And:

The impulse towards removal to the West did not arise from a desire to

25

recreate the pattern of eastern farms left behind but came from a vision of a rich soil producing an abundant surplus of products, readily salable for cash upon markets which, if not immediately available, would certainly develop and could somehow be reached.

The other great 'push' factor was the desire to avoid the fever-infested swamps of the Missouri and Mississippi and to migrate to a land where the climate was more salubrious and disease less frequent. Malaria and the ague were endemic in the Midwest and settlers there had to reconcile themselves to sweating and shivering throughout the summer months. Over and over again in their own accounts of their motivation, overlanders mentioned the fevers of Illinois, Iowa and Missouri, and their desire to live a healthy life in the West. In 1846, Francis Parkman found this the most frequently mentioned topic: 'The bad climate seems to have been the motive that has induced many of them to set out.' George McKinstry, travelling in the same year with the Russell party, included a significant throwaway detail in his diary: 'Mr Ames is travelling for his health and cares not whether he goes to California or Oregon.' Jesse Quinn Thornton, again in the same year, mentioned avoidance of disease in his list of actuating factors, before concluding with bathos: 'The motives which thus brought this multitude together were, in fact, almost as various as their features. They agreed in one general object – that of bettering their condition.'

Part of the success of the 'pull' propaganda, inducing people to travel to Oregon and California, was the myth of a disease-free paradise. A favourite 'rural myth' related to a 250-year-old Californian who finally decided he wanted to die. Since California was a kind of Shangri-La in more ways than one, he had to leave the state to achieve mortality. But when his body was brought back to California for burial, the miraculous climate at once restored him to health. John Bidwell, leader of the first party of emigrants from Missouri to California via the Platte River, recalled writing to Antoine Robidoux to ask him whether they had fever or ague in California. 'I remember his answer distinctly. He said there was but one man in California that ever had a chill there, and it was a matter of so much wonderment to the people of Monterey that they went eighteen miles into the country to see him shake.'

As a 'pull' factor, it is difficult to overrate the impact of propaganda portraying California and Oregon as Utopias. This process may be said to have begun in sincerity and quickly developed into hyperbole. Richard Henry Dana's *Two Years Before the Mast*, describing his experiences as a seaman on the California coast in 1835–36, was published to great acclaim in 1840. Dana shared the usual Yankee contempt for the indolence and lethargy of Spanish Californians and wrote: 'In the hands of an enterprising people, what a country this might be! Yet how long would a people remain so in this country? If the "California fever," laziness, spares the first generation, it is likely to attack the second.' Dana was one of the more moderate California 'boosters', but more intemperate advocates alleged that ranches the size of principalities could be had there for the asking. Typical of the hype was this from the adventurer Lansford Hastings (on whom more later) who wrote in his *Emigrants' Guide* that, compared with California, 'the deep, rich, alluvial soil of the Nile, in Egypt, does not afford a parallel'.

Successful American settlers in California sent back glowing reports to the States about the riches there, the balmy climate, the fertility of the soil. Prominent among these was John Marsh, an adventurer in both senses, who was evading a warrant for his arrest for running guns to the Sioux when he arrived in Los Angeles in 1836. On the basis of a BA diploma written in Latin from Harvard – scarcely more than a certificate of attendance – he professed himself a physician, set up practice and even performed operations successfully, accepting hides and tallow as payment. With his profits, he bought a ranch (Rancho Los Meganos) at the foot of Mount Diablo in the San Joaquin Valley and soon made a second fortune, with a spread of 50,000 acres and thousands of cattle and horses. Marsh was one of those men who grew more avaricious the richer he became, and soon he developed an obsession that the Mexican authorities might expropriate his holdings. He therefore began to lobby unceasingly for US annexation of California. His letters to friends and newspapers in the East became ever more lyrical and rhapsodic in their praise of the wealth and beauty of California, and they found a ready audience.

Perhaps even more influential was John Sutter, who fled his native Switzerland to escape a bankruptcy warrant in 1834, abandoning a hated wife and five children in the process. Where Marsh employed brazen cheek and effrontery as his main weapons, Sutter preferred guile, bluff and outright deceit. Unable to place him in the European pecking order, the people of New York, his first port of call in North America, accepted his story that he was a travelling nobleman and made straight the ways with letters of introduction to wealthy merchants and investment banks. Sutter's speciality was to persuade investors to advance venture capital on which he returned a healthy profit. Step by step he advanced to riches, first with a caravan on the Sante Fe Trail, next with the American Fur Company. Having reached Fort Vancouver in 1838 he sailed to Hawaii, where he made his first big 'killing' by persuading local merchants to advance him the money to buy a schooner. He reached California on this in January 1839, carrying a cargo which he sold at huge profit.

Sutter then asked Governor Juan Bautista Alvarado for a land grant so that he could settle Swiss families in California. Alvarado advised him to buy a private ranch instead, and Sutter chose, whether by luck or inspiration, the best possible site. His eleven-league land grant, formally notarised in 1841 after he became a citizen of California, lay between the Sacramento and Feather rivers and dominated three important routes: the inland waterways from San Francisco Bay, the future emigrant trail to California across the Sierra Nevada, and the Oregon–California road. With eight Kanakas, who had come with him from Hawaii, three white assistants and one Indian, he began building an empire. First, he showed the local Indian tribes he was not to be trifled with by massive retaliation for theft. Then he gulled the California authorities into making him loans for seeds and livestock, again turning a handsome profit on the ultimate outcome. Finally, he hired an army of workers to construct a massive adobe fort, with walls eighteen feet high and two feet thick, surrounded by a courtyard where an army of one thousand men could be mustered. In the summer of 1843, the fort was completed. It was an entire world unto itself, complete with a village full of shops, houses, mills and warehouses, where blacksmiths, flour millers, bakers, carpenters, gunsmiths and blanket-makers carried out their trades. Sutter ruled like a feudal lord. 'I was everything –' he wrote, 'patriarch, priest, father and judge.'

The importance of Sutter and Marsh was threefold. They showed what could be achieved in the Arcadia of the Pacific coast by men of acumen and determination. As he surveyed the cannon and gun emplacements on the walls of the fort in 1842, the British traveller George Simpson noted that if Sutter really was as talented as he seemed, he could become California's Sam Houston. And Sutter and Marsh provided the prospect of safe refuge for the emigrants at the end of the 2,000-mile journey. They knew that if they could reach Sutter's Fort, there would be food and shelter and even jobs, for it was Sutter's proud boast that he always employed those with no money even if there was no real work for them. 'All of them,' he wrote in his diary, 'was allways hospitably received under my roof and all those who could or would not be employed could stay with me as long as they liked, and when leaving, I gave them passports which was everywhere respected.' Most of all, Sutter and Marsh underwrote the golden legend of California as the Promised Land; Sutter plugged away at this theme and liked to tell the story of how a French-Canadian trapper had first opened his eyes to California when he spoke to him at Taos about the 'perpetual summers' at Los Angeles. The 'pull' impact of men like Marsh and Sutter was enhanced by verifiable facts about Spanish California that trickled back to the United States. Many observers pointed out that California's population was so small that incremental influxes of American migrants could easily convert it into a second Texas. Excluding Indians, California's population at the time of Mexican independence in 1821 was 3,320, but at least two-thirds of these Mexicans were women and children, which meant that even a few hundred male immigrants would alter the population balance significantly. In the 1820s and 30s though, few 'Anglos' settled in California; their land hunger could be satisfied far more easily in Texas and, besides, the Mexican government, mindful of the possibility of the repetition of the revolt in Texas, forbade foreigners to own land without ratification by both chambers of Congress in Mexico City. Finally, and clinchingly, all the best land in California was held by the missions, whose position was historically inviolable, to the point where, under Spanish rule, no more than thirty land grants had been made to individual ranchers.

This is to say nothing of the fact that in the 1820s and 30s Mexican authorities actively discouraged foreigners from settling in California. This was one reason, as we have seen, why the Santa Fe Trail was never properly extended to southern California. The situation was, nonetheless, a difficult one for Mexico since the territory needed immigrants to function effectively, and Russian settlements in northern California were a source of anxiety. Americans evaded the regulations in a number of ways, such as by buying directly from Mexicans in private sales that bypassed officialdom, by squatting and by intermarriage. They did not attract the attention of the authorities by forming separate enclaves, as the 'Anglos' had in Texas, but assimilated and operated, as it were, in disguise. When John Bidwell arrived in California with the first party of overland emigrants from the United States in 1841, he was amazed to find a number of his countrymen who had married Spanish women and 'gone native'.

The turning point in California's economic history came in 1834–36, when the twenty-two Franciscan missions, extending north from San Diego to Sonoma, were 'secularised'. This meant, technically, that Franciscan regular clergy were replaced by secular priests, but in a deeper sense it meant the end of the paternal communalism by the Fathers and the triumph of private property. Just as chieftains in the Scottish Highlands after 1745 ceased to be the 'Fathers' of their clan and kinsfolk and became capitalists instead, turning the clansmen into mere units of labour, so the secularisation of the missions meant that California's Indian labourers on the communal lands were turned loose, either to return to 'savagery' or seek other employment. This was exactly the development that Mexico City had feared and why it had long opposed secularisation: above all, the fear was of widespread Indian rebellion. But pressure from the aristocratic Spaniards of California, the so-called *gente de razón*, overrode such considerations. Although such was not the original intention, the effect of secularisation of the missions was to release vast tracts of land on to the market.

The officials, or mayordomos, appointed by the governor to oversee and administer the former Franciscan missions largely looted and pillaged them for their own advantage and sold off huge swathes of land. Meanwhile, secularisation had created a dearth of workers. As private ranches grew up on the former mission lands and the Indians decamped to their tribes, entered domestic service or became beggars, the question arose: who was to work the lands or even, come to that, serve in the army if the worst happened and there was a general Indian uprising? At the same time, the Russians had built Fort Ross on Bodega Bay, refused to budge and began casting covetous eyes on San Francisco Bay. An attempt to colonise northern California from Mexico foundered over a dispute between Mexico City and the local authorities in California. Mexico wanted to distribute mission land to new emigrants, but the old Spanish elite wanted the land for itself. Attempts to colonise California from Mexico were anyway foredoomed. There was no 'push' from Mexico, since there was no pressure of population on resources and no real land hunger, as there was plenty of vacant land south of the Rio Grande. The northern regions of Mexico, including Arizona, New Mexico and California, had a poor reputation in terms of opportunities offered, and were known to be the cockpit of continual Indian warfare. Emigration was also expensive, and Mexico lacked sufficient numbers of the 'middle sectors' with the money to migrate. In desperation, Mexico City tried to turn California into its own Botany Bay and sent convicts north, but this scheme also faltered. The only possible long-term answer was a government-assisted migration scheme, which the government in Mexico City could not afford to underwrite, especially given the paradox that her far richer northern neighbour was able to send migrants to California and Oregon without spending a penny. As always, the costs of migration kept the very poor at home.

The result of all this was that in the early 1840s the Mexican authorities virtually conceded defeat and began to sell vast tracts of public land to private bidders. Despite the widespread fears of the 'Texas game' – that incoming 'Anglos' would soon overwhelm Spanish-speakers – a third of all lands alienated were sold to Anglo-Americans. Some cynical entrepreneurs even acquired such lands in the expectation that the United States would soon annex Mexico and property values would then rise. Apart from the obvious lure of land speculation, the objective 'pull' of California to immigrants from the United States was threefold: the secularisation of the missions had created a large pool of cheap Indian labour; it had freed most of the choice coastal lands for development; and improved transport had created a market for the products of Californian ranches, especially hides and tallow. Anglo-Americans were keen to get their snouts in the trough. The Pilate-like stance of California's governors in the late 1830s and early 1840s meant that between 1834 and 1846 no fewer than seven hundred grants for private ranches were made, which represented more than 90 per cent of all such grants made during the entire history of Spanish-speaking California.

This land boom reached its height in the mid-1840s. Successive governors, Juan Bautista Alvarado (1836–42), Manuel Micheltorena (1842–45) and Pio Pico (1845–46), together made 370 rancho grants, with Micheltorena especially generous to Americans as he needed their support against Mexican pretenders to the governor's chair – one-third of his grants went to foreigners. Most of the land grants to 'Anglos' were in the Central valley, and the newcomers were a different breed from their countrymen in the 1820s and 30s; they held themselves aloof and did not mix, blend or intermarry with Spanish Californians. Alvarado was heard to remark sadly: 'Would that the foreigners that came to settle in California after 1841 had been of the same quality as those who preceded them.' The difference between the early Anglo-American settlers and those arriving by wagon train after 1840 was so great that one historian has proposed the idea that the early ones were the 'maritime interests' and the overlanders the pioneering interests; the former were prepared to use Fabian tactics to play the 'Texas game' but the latter group, in the Sacramento valley, were the zealots who wanted to settle the issue of American annexation by staging an armed revolt, as indeed they did in the 'Bear Flag Revolt' of June 1846.

By the mid-1840s, what far-sighted Mexicans had feared had largely come to pass. In 1830, about 120 foreigners lived in California, by 1835 the number had doubled and by 1840 it was still only 380. But by 1845, at 680, 'Anglos' already made up 9 per cent of the population. Spanish Californians, meanwhile, had increased from 3,320 in 1821 to 6,500 in 1846 when the USA acquired California as part of the spoils of war with

Mexico. The combination of a change in land policy after 1836 with the exhortations of men like Marsh and Sutter had proved a decisive magnet for American immigrants. Unquestionably, 'pull' factors were more powerful than 'push' in inducing Midwestern farmers to emigrate. There was little the Mexican authorities could do about it, for their own efforts to 'countercolonise' Mexico had failed, and the only other option was brutal physical repression of Anglo-Americans. Not only would this have been unwise – even if it had not provoked Washington into open intervention, how could Mexico's frontier armies combat hostile Indians and Americans simultaneously? – but it would have set the military against California's financial interests. To oppose the workings of the market with armies seems like issuing a papal bull against a comet.

It is worth re-emphasising the key role of Sutter in this process. Since more unworthy individuals, such as John Fremont, have been sometimes wrongly singled out as key players actuating the emigrants to turn their wagons west, one should underline the psychological fillip and self-confidence provided to the overlanders by this bizarre Swiss adventurer. Sutter's town of New Helvetia provided a 'home from home' for the emigrants, who might otherwise have felt alienated and disoriented in a Spanish culture and milieu. Pioneers could deal directly with him and bypass the troublesome Mexican authorities, especially as Sutter's growing confidence led him to issue passports, sell land and draw up deeds in flagrant violation of Mexican law. General Mariano Vallejo was particularly incensed by Sutter's activities and rightly concluded that Sutter's Fort was 'the gateway of communication between the United States and this country which they covet so much'. But Vallejo drew back from military confrontation. He feared that an attack on Sutter's Fort would be perceived in the USA as a second Alamo, and he probably lacked the troops to do the job anyway.

Sutter certainly thought so. As early as 1841 he remarked smugly: 'It is too late now to drive me out of the country . . . I am strong now,' adding that if Mexican forces moved against him, 'I will make a declaration of Independence and proclaim California for a Republique.' In any case, during the years 1842–45, the hard-pressed governor Micheltorena needed Sutter more than Sutter needed him, and in return the irrepressible Switzer received twenty-two more square leagues of land to add to his domain. After the overthrow of Micheltorena in 1845, Pio Pico, the new governor, finally seems to have realised the size of the cuckoo that had been invited into the nest but, anxious not to alienate Washington, attempted to get rid of him by peaceful means. He tried to buy him out, but Sutter wanted an astronomical sum to give up his empire. To Vallejo's disgust, Pico would not pay the asking price. As he himself bitterly remarked: 'It is the security of the country that is to be bought, and that is priceless.'

In the Oregon territory, the issue of land did not loom so large. It was not a question of whether emigrants could acquire it, since the United States had joint occupation rights, but about the terms on which it could be had. Yet, if anything, the Oregon 'boosters' were even more vociferous in their paeans to the beauty of the land and their urgent demands that the flower of American manhood and womanhood should make its way there. Perhaps there was a feeling that in Oregon there was a tougher nut to crack in the shape of the British; many Americans hated 'John Bull' but they did not despise Britain as they despised Mexico. Another obvious difference was that in Oregon the role of forerunner and anchor was played by missionaries rather than adventurers like Marsh and Sutter. The missionaries' attitude was rather like that of St Augustine to sin: not so much 'make me good, Lord, but not yet', but 'let emigrants come, but not until we have converted the heathen'. As one observer put it, they wanted the Indians to 'hear the Gospel before they are prejudiced against it by the fraud, injustice, and dissolute lives' of immigrants. In other words, do as the white man says, not as he does.

The missionaries had a clear ten years, from their first appearance in the Oregon country in 1831, to gather in the spiritual harvest before their more uncouth secular brethren put in an appearance. Methodists, Presbyterians and eventually Catholics made a greater or lesser attempt at saving souls, and some of the most famous names in the history of the West – Jason Lee, Marcus and Narcissa Whitman – were prime movers in this evangelical endeavour. Nez Percé, Flathead, Snake and Cayuse Indians were particular targets of the proselytisers. Although an important episode in the history of the West, the missionary travels and endeavours in the Pacific north-west form no part of the story of the wagon trains, except in one respect. Their enthusiastic reports and speeches, reprinted in the East, limned yet another picture of a land flowing with milk and honey. So hyperbolic were their accounts of Oregon that it almost seemed that the laws of God's universe had been breached and that the missionaries had found themselves back in the Garden of Eden. Edwin Bryant, the journalist and emigrant of 1846, remarked sardonically that reports of the Pacific coast contained 'such fascinations as almost to call the angels and saints from their blissful gardens and diamond temples in the sky'.

But the missionaries were not the only Oregon 'boosters'. As early as 1818, full of fury with Washington for its 'pusillanimous' agreement with the British over Oregon, opinion-formers like Hall Jackson Kelley and John Floyd, together with their powerful supporters in Congress like the Missouri Senators Lewis F. Linn and Thomas Hart Benton, began a sustained campaign for the US annexation of Oregon and to that end lauded both Oregon and the putative Oregon Trail, of which they knew nothing. An amusing exercise could be undertaken, juxtaposing the writings of Horace Greeley with the speeches of Lewis Linn. For Greeley, Oregon was a rocky wilderness not worth the American equivalent of the bones of a single Pomeranian grenadier, to use Bismarck's phrase; for Linn, it was the ultimate test of American grit and republican virtú. For Greeley, the Rockies were an impassable barrier, where men and horses would die in their hundreds from starvation; for Linn, the passage of the Rockies was little more than a stroll in a New England meadow, since it was full of 'easy passes'. Greeley emphasised the snow and ice of Oregon's mountains; Linn spoke of the 'almost tropical' climate of the Willamette valley. In Greeley's imagination, hostile Indians lurked behind every rock; in the Linn scenario, they were gentle, peaceful, noble savages. Greeley thought that only a sociopath would take his women on the way west; Linn said the trip was a walkover even for 'delicate females'. From California, John Marsh weighed in on Linn's side. Speaking of the 1841 Bidwell party, he said: 'A young woman with a child in her arms came in the company . . . after this the men ought to be ashamed to think of the difficulties.'

The propaganda of the Oregon boosters was shrewd and subtle, aimed as it was at the archetypes of the Golden Age, Arcadia and the lost Eden. Not only were the valleys in Oregon beautiful and well watered, but the soil was so fertile that anything could be grown there, both the temperate produce of the East and the exotic crops of the Tropics. The climate was perfect, for the lack of rain was balanced by heavy dews, and there were no frosts. Since wheat could be planted in January and corn and beans in April, a newcomer could be assured of a first-year's crop and thereafter he could enjoy two or three crops a year. Wheat was said to grow as tall as a man, with each stalk sprouting seven kernels; clover also attained a height of five feet and grew so densely that the farmer could barely get into the field to harvest it. Oats reached heights of eight feet or more, with stalks half an inch thick; beets could be dug out of the ground fully three feet in circumference and turnips were five feet tall. While such abundant crops fed the body, the soul was nourished by the rapture of gazing on a verdant wilderness and contemplating its conquest. Lewis Linn suggested that every man could be his own Daniel Boone, and that pioneers could acquire an almost godlike status, venturing out from civilisation 'to the wilderness like our first parents, when God sent them forth from the Garden of Eden to subdue the earth'. In his enthusiastic rhetoric, Linn forgot that he had earlier described Oregon as Paradise; now it seemed it had declined to the status of the Land of Nod, east of Eden.

Aware that the California boosters had already grabbed some of the best 'soundbites' with their tall stories about the ease of acquiring land for a song and the miraculous health-giving qualities of Mexico's neglected northern territory, the pro-Oregon publicists endeavoured to 'niche-market' the Pacific north-west in four distinctive ways. First, where the rural myths about California had spoken of Lazarus-like miracles and an Erewhonian absence of illness, those to do with Oregon stressed the joys of table and board and the good eating to be had there. Edward Lenox, an emigrant of 1843, remembered that his parents had been influenced by a soapbox orator in Missouri, who appealed directly to their gulosity: 'pigs are running about under the great acorn trees, round and fat, and already cooked, with knives and forks sticking in them so that you can cut off a slice whenever you are hungry.'

The second approach was to stress that Oregon had an English-speaking milieu and culture, unlike California where one had to deal with the swarthy, tricky, untrustworthy 'dons'. In Oregon there was, additionally, a pre-existing internal migration, caused by a population 'implosion' of former mountain men leaving the Rockies as the fur trade declined and died. Already, by 1840, there was a thriving settlement of 120 farms in the Willamette valley, with a population of five hundred whites and a thousand Indian servants, together with 3,000 cattle, 2,500 horses and teeming numbers of hogs (some of them doubtless with knives and forks attached). This was a more settled and welcoming environment than Sutter's Fort. Sutter, after all, was Swiss and there was no guarantee that California-bound emigrants would not have to fight a bitter war against the Mexicans, either if they decided to dispossess Sutter by main force or if war broke out between Mexico and the United States.

The third angle was to stress the ease of running a pastoral economy in Oregon. The trick was to insinuate that the climate was marginally preferable to California's so that one did not fall into the 'laziness' trap of the Mexicans, while still assuring oneself vast amounts of leisure time. That this idea was taken very seriously indeed can be seen from the simple fact that a clergyman propagandist addressed himself on this theme to the notable pioneer and plainsman Joel Palmer, who knew the West intimately and would not be taken in by flimflam. Spalding wrote:

I cannot but contrast the time, labor and expense requisite to look after lands in this country with that required in the States, especially in the Northern and Middle States, where two-thirds of every man's time, labor and money is expended on his animals, in preparing and fencing pasture grounds and meadows, building barns, sheds, stables and granaries, and feeding and looking to animals through the winter. In this country, all is superceded [sic] by Nature's own beautiful hand. In this country a single shepherd with his horse and dogs can protect and look after 5,000 sheep. A man with his horse and perhaps a dog can easily attend to 2,000 head of cattle and horses, without spending a dollar for barns, grain or hay. Consider the vast amount of labor and expense such a number of animals would require in the States. Were I to select for my friends a location for a healthy, happy and speedy wealth, this would be the country.

In short, mild and wet weather eliminated the need to shelter and feed stock through long, cold winters, thereby cutting down on arduous labour and saving money. But the fourth advantage of Oregon was potentially the most momentous of all. This was the potentially unlimited market for goods produced there. The Hudson's Bay Company was ready to buy supplies in vast quantities and, even if that market dried up, still greater opportunities lay across the sea in the Orient where the teeming millions of China and India were desperate for American exports 'with nothing intervening but the blue and stormless Pacific' (evidently written by someone who had never sailed on the inaptly named ocean). Palmer's correspondent, the Reverend Mr Spalding, suggested that the Oregon settlers begin by supplying Pacific whalers and then graduate to satisfying the material wants of 360 million people in China, to say nothing of the many millions more in Australasia and the East Indies. Spalding neglected to mention that California was even better positioned than Oregon to carry out this lucrative trade. But his words struck a chord and were evidently in the mind of Hudson's Bay factor Dr John McLoughlin when he made his famous recantation in 1847. Having previously stated that emigrants might as well try to go to the moon by covered wagon as Oregon, he told a friend 'he was ready to aver that the Yankees could go right over to China with their ox wagons if they desired to do it'.

That all this propaganda affected the perceptions and motivations of emigrants can scarcely be doubted, and indeed we know from unimpeachable first-hand evidence that people were actuated accordingly. 'Why, man alive, money grows there!' – the answer given to John Minto in 1844 when he asked a fellow emigrant why he was going to Oregon – reveals a man who had taken the roast hog story perhaps too seriously.

Another Missouri farmer, after hearing all the pro-Oregon propaganda from the 'boosters', called his family together and exhorted them thus: 'Out in Oregon I can get me a square mile of land. And a quarter section for each of you all. Dad burn me, I am done with this country. Winter it's frost and snow to freeze a body; summers that overflow from Old Muddy drowns half my acres; taxes take the yield of them that's left. What say, Maw, it's God's country.' 'Oregon fever' was spurred on by the chance of evading actual fever, since the endemic diseases in Missouri included smallpox, flu, cholera and malaria. The boosters even said the journey out was good for your health and had medical pundits to back them.

The Oregon boosters definitely won the battle for hearts and minds over the pro-California faction. In the years before the 1849 California Gold Rush, 11,512 overlanders migrated to Oregon and just 2,735 to California. In only one year (1846) did emigration to California exceed that to Oregon, but then the California bubble burst, largely because of the Donner tragedy and the controversy over Lansford Hastings and his cutoff. Surprisingly, most emigrants found that the Canaans they reached fitted the lands of their imagination, for the rate of 'turn-around' or 'go-back' was very low. One study finds no more than fifty emigrants turning back in the years 1841–46, and then only for reasons that had nothing to do with the promised land as such: some were scared off by Indians, some impoverished by theft, some lost heart after illness or simple homesickness. But there were not many who felt as an 1847 'turn-back' felt: 'In Oregon there are no bees, and you can't raise corn, and if you can't raise corn, you can't raise hogs, you can't have bacon, so I'm going back to Missouri where I can have cornbread, bacon and honey.'

'Oregon Fever' is a story of a publicity campaign almost faultlessly carried out, with propaganda streams from missionaries, senators, boosters and travellers coalescing into a mighty river. It caught popular imagination with its clever use of archetypes, myths, collective images and frontier ideologies. It appealed to the 'why not?' mentality engendered by an economic depression in the Mississippi valley where wheat sold for ten cents a bushel, corn had to be given away and bacon was so worthless on the market that river steamboats used it for fuel. And, although the propaganda and travellers' tales contained palpable and absurd exaggeration, the truth was not impossibly far from the image created. California *did* need the injection of new immigrant blood and was a political prize ripe for the taking; the soil of the Pacific states *was* fertile, and California would soon become the agricultural phenomenon of the USA; the landscape in the American West *was* the most sublime and beautiful in the entire country. Oregon *was* a country where it was possible to generate a healthy economic surplus without expending toilsome and prematurely ageing labour.

Undoubtedly, there were key tracts that had a huge influence, but the 'books that won the West', such as Edwin Bryant's *What I Saw in California*, mainly made their biggest impact after the 1849 gold rush. It has sometimes been claimed that Lieutenant John 'Pathfinder' Frémont was a powerful influence in motivating pioneers to trek west, and this is a claim that merits consideration, since opinion is divided on this point. It was a view first advanced by the expansionist pro-emigration senator Thomas Hart Benton, who conveniently forgot to mention that Frémont was an army lieutenant in the Topographical Corps, and his son-in-law. Aware, unlike some incautious later writers, that the great 1843 emigration to Oregon took place before Frémont completed the great transcontinental odyssey of 1843–44 that won him international fame, Benton tried to locate the influence further back in time, to Frémont's first surveying expedition of 1842. Unfortunately for Benton, there was still a twofold objection to be overcome: Frémont in 1842 got no further than South Pass, whence he diverted to explore the Wind River Mountains; meanwhile, pioneers in wagon trains had already crossed the Sierra Nevada.

Frémont wrote up his expeditions in the style later perfected by African explorers like Livingstone and Stanley: that is to say, he larded his text with scientific observations while making the basic drive in the narrative rest on a romantic sensibility. He also played down the huge contribution made, in men, money and matériel, to his journeys by the US Topographical Corps, in which he was a mere Lieutenant of Engineers, not a trailblazing colossus. Typical of Frémont's romanticism (and romancing in another sense) is the famous passage in his account of the 1842 expedition when he describes his ascent of the highest peak in the Wind River range. When he set up a specially designed US flag on the summit, showing a triumphant eagle grasping a bundle of arrows and a peace pipe, it was the most famous raising of the American flag before the Marine Corps hoisted the Stars and Stripes on Iwo Jima in 1945. The other famous passage dealing with the summit of 'Frémont's Peak' was the description of a bumblebee, meant to juxtapose the sublime with the mundane workings of nature, but really artfully devised to strike directly at the American unconscious. Yet, what Frémont did not admit in all his myth-making was that 'Frémont's Peak' was not the highest peak in the Rockies, as he claimed, nor was he the first to climb it; Major B.L.E. Bonneville and his men had been there in the 1830s.

Without question, Frémont's 1843–44 expedition was a major achievement, probably the greatest pure epic of adventure in the history of the West since the Lewis and Clark expedition. He began by following the Oregon Trail along the Platte for a while, then turned south to explore the Kansas River. He proceeded on the Upper Arkansas to Pueblo, then followed the Cache de la Poudre River into the Laramie Mountains. Next he turned north to the Sweetwater, and crossed the Rockies via South Pass to Green River and Bear River, which he followed to the Great Salt Lake. After exploring the Weber River, which flows into the Great Salt Lake from the east, he proceeded to Fort Hall, then continued up the Snake River past Fort Boise, and on to the Columbia River, thus going in the footsteps of the 1843 pioneers.

After stopovers at the Walla Walla mission, The Dalles and Fort Vancouver (where he met Dr McLoughlin), he turned south in December 1843, explored Klamath Lake and, after a foolish search for a legendary river named the Buenaventura (said to flow from the Rockies to the Pacific), which Frémont ought to have known did not exist, he descended into the Great Basin in parallel with the Sierra Nevada before turning west for California. The passage through the Sierras in the depths of winter, in massive snowdrifts, was a touch-and-go affair in which several men lost their minds because of the hardship. Finally, they struggled down to Sutter's Fort, then struck due south along the San Joaquin valley to modern-day Bakersfield, where he turned and entered the Tehachapi Pass. He next struck the Old Spanish Trail, found the Colorado River, then followed the Sevier River to Utah Lake. From Utah Lake, he headed due east across present-day Utah into Colorado, surveyed the Rockies near the headwaters of the Arkansas and Colorado rivers, proceeded east to Pueblo and Bent's Fort and eventually arrived in St Louis to a hero's welcome on 6 August 1844.

This near-legendary odyssey made Frémont a household name. He used it as a springboard to launch an unauthorised adventure to California in 1846 during the war with Mexico and later to present himself as a candidate for the presidency of the USA. But in many respects, Frémont's second expedition was no more impressive than his first. He met the wagon trains on their way west, but did not lead them or blaze trail for them, he located no new pass or new route into Oregon or California, and made contact with Jesse Applegate's 'cow column' (see p. 168) only when it was already floating down the Columbia River in flatboats. He achieved no 'firsts' at all. The expert on the early fur trade, Hiram Chittenden, flatly refused to concede the title 'Pathfinder' to him. As the historian William Goetzmann remarks: 'Analysed in detail, his scientific findings seem either inconclusive or anticipated by others . . . Everywhere he went, it seems, someone had been there before, sometimes even official explorers.'

Frémont was a populariser and self-publicist of very high talent and a myth-maker extraordinary; he it was who propelled his friend the mountain man Kit Carson into such national prominence that a few years later he was mentioned in Melville's *Moby Dick*. Frémont's influence is best considered under three categories. Of his general impact there can be no doubt. He drew Brigham Young's attention to the potential of the Great Salt Lake valley and helped in a general sense to win the propaganda battle for the 'boosters'. But whether in any significant sense he motivated people to emigrate in the 1840s seems much less likely. He did inspire young men to go travelling and exploring in the West and thrilled many a romantic soul with his purple passages, but that is not the same thing as convincing someone to emigrate. There is no evidence for the historian Unruh's remark that 'thanks to Frémont's enthusiastic reports, many emigrants launched out for Oregon'.

There is not even general agreement on whether Frémont's books were useful as an emigrants' guide. Some students of the overland trail are adamant that the pioneers found Frémont's writings useless; for example, he had crossed the Rockies over mountain paths that were unusable by wagons and had followed desert trails across Utah rather than the emigrants' Humboldt River route. But at this level there is certainly some evidence in Frémont's favour. Some emigrant parties, for better or ill, did use Frémont's maps and data to guide them, and among them was Sarah Royce, mother of the Californian philosopher Josiah Royce, who recalled that her westward journey to California had been 'guided only by the light of Frémont's *Travels*'.

Since Frémont's account of his great 1843–44 odyssey was not available to emigrants before 1846 at the earliest, we can safely discount him as a *motivating factor* for overlanders making the journey before that date. Of course, after that no one can say with certainty what residue might have been left in the unconscious of a reader of Frémont's stirring narratives. But who can say for sure what went on in the minds of the 14,000-plus emigrants to Oregon and California in the years 1841–48 and what mixture of 'push' and 'pull' operated in each case? Clearly in some cases, neither push nor pull had much to do with it. Some men went west to forget a romance gone sour; in this sense the wagon train operated as an early version of the French Foreign Legion. Some were on the run from justice, and criminals were noticeable among those who trekked out in 1846. 'Gone to Texas' was the early euphemism for those who left the territorial jurisdiction of the United States to avoid punishment; 'in the wagon train to Oregon and California' could have been a suitable substitute after 1841.

There were overlanders actuated by missionary zeal, Utopianism, the desire to get away from the United States for whatever motive or simply to move beyond civilisation. Some of the stated motives seem extreme or highly eccentric. Samuel Barlow, a native of Massachusetts of Scots descent, was a fanatical partisan of Henry Clay in the 1844 presidential election. When Polk was elected instead, Barlow declared he wanted nothing more to do with such an accursed country: 'the nation failed to elect Clay so Mr Barlow declared his determination to go where he would not feel the force of failure.' And Benjamin Bonney, an emigrant of 1845, mentioned the horrors of shivering each summer with malaria and ague and being wracked each winter with 'congestive fever' in Missouri, adding: 'Father was a great fisherman, and while he caught pike and red horse there [Missouri], he wanted to move to a country where he could catch trout and salmon.'

Another good example of the mixture of hard-headed common sense and sentimentality can be seen in the stated motivation of William Case. Like many emigrants, he saw that there were potentially rich pickings in the West – Peter Burnett, an 1843 emigrant, reckoned that you could buy heifers for $300 in Missouri and sell them for $4,000 in Oregon – and could see no future in a dead-end job in Indiana where wage rates were twenty-five cents a day, six dollars a month or, if you were really lucky, $100 a year. He saw clearly that there was big money to be made by buying land cheaply now and waiting for the real-estate boom that would come later when California and Oregon were incorporated in the United States. But non-material factors played a part in his decision also. As a child, he had read the journals of Lewis and Clark and vowed to go to Oregon when he was an adult. His father advised him that, if such was his intention, he should get married first. His wife proved the ideal mate for a would-be pioneer. She told him: 'My father used to dip me in the surf of the Atlantic on the New Jersey shore, and I would like to go and dip in the surf of the Pacific Ocean.'

Undoubtedly, a few emigrants hoped to carry the struggle over slavery, destined to bring the country to civil war in twenty years, to the Far West. There were Southerners who hoped to perpetuate slavery in the territories of Arizona, New Mexico and California once they had been wrested from Mexico by Washington, and to spread the 'peculiar institution' into the empty lands to redress the growing power of the North. Similarly, there were abolitionists who wanted to pre-empt this and tip the balance against slave states by creating new 'free' states in the West. John Minto reported in 1844 that many of his fellow overlanders would have gone to Texas, other things being equal, but they could not abide slavery. He also mentioned the case of a mulatto who had left Missouri because of slavery and was anxious to see how his colour would be viewed in Oregon; if he encountered prejudice there, he intended to re-emigrate to Mexican California. History does not relate what happened to this man when he reached Oregon, for laws there banned settlement by free blacks until 1861. Emigration to California would scarcely have helped, for after US annexation in 1846 the pattern was the same. Three thousand blacks reached California in 1850 but failed to achieve rights as US citizens; anti-black legislation placed them firmly as second-class citizens, so most chose to settle in Canada instead.

One group whose motives were seldom discussed or even considered was pioneer women. With rare exceptions, such as Mrs Case, women entered into the westward trek reluctantly. Women's need for a home, their 'separate spheres' domestic role and their distaste for gypsying and wandering stars would have militated against the idea of emigration even if their opinion had been asked, which in most cases it was not. One historian of women on the trail was unable to find a single instance where the idea of trekking west was the woman's idea rather than the man's. Men wanting to persuade their wives had to choose their moments carefully. This explains why families on the trail tended to be young; in 22 per cent of all cases the wife was pregnant at some stage during the journey. Families were most likely to move at marriage or soon after the birth of children; if they missed that moment of opportunity, men often had to wait until their children were approaching adulthood.

Less than one-quarter of women who kept journals on the trail agreed with the decision to emigrate, but simply acquiesced, with fully one-third obeying their husbands only reluctantly or sullenly. Even women who bore themselves bravely on the trail had usually not wanted to go in the first place. Because they did not want to go on the overland trail, women tended to blame their men for anything that went wrong, even if only in the privacy of their own diaries. But, though reluctant to go, women tended to be even more reluctant to let their husbands go west alone; there was a deep fear of casual infidelity, abandonment and, possibly at a deeper level, anxiety lest the Mormon paradigm of polygamy take hold as the norm at the frontier. Knowing of these fears and anxieties, men often threatened recalcitrant wives with 'going it alone' to bring them to heel.

One of the most intriguing issues concerning motivation is this: did the overlanders in any sense see themselves as the agents of Manifest

Destiny? They were certainly often exhorted to do so. Senator Linn often praised the overlanders as the crème de la crème, because they went west to found an American empire. Those who went to Oregon would drive out the detested Hudson's Bay Company; those who went to Mexico would rout the lazy and indolent Mexicans. By contrast, Lansford Hastings spoke in semi-oracular terms of a divine mission to establish republicanism throughout North America: he had Machiavelli's hatred for kingdoms, principalities, empires, and spoke of the emigrants' destiny to establish a 'land of genuine Republicanism and unsophisticated democracy' which would 'stand forth as an enduring monument to the increasing wisdom of Man, and the infinite kindness and protection of an all-wise, ever-ruling Providence'.

It was certainly tempting for emigrants motivated by common-sense desire for land or even the yearning for speculative riches to wrap their mundane considerations in an ideological coating and to rationalise their essentially selfish aims as patriotism; as has been well said, ideology is to the mass what rationalisation is to the individual. But there is no need to make such 'camouflage' evidence of utter insincerity. Bernal Diaz said that the aims of the conquistadores were at once to serve God and become rich. In the case of the emigrants, not only was there no conflict between material and political aims, but the two were in a functional relationship: all the looked-for economic benefits, whether from internal markets, trade across the Pacific or land speculation, would only accrue when Manifest Destiny had gathered Oregon and California to its bosom. The intended victims were well aware of their peril, and there was an air of desperation about the various schemes floated in Mexican California to prevent the inevitable: selling California to a Prussian entrepreneur or paying off British bondholders with vacant lands north of San Francisco. However, all these quixotic schemes came to nothing.

It is safest to assume that nearly all the alleged motivation to roll back frontiers and found empires was routine jingoism or gallery-touch fustian. The fact that newly arrived emigrants served with American troops against Mexicans in California need mean no more than that they were 'spring-cleaning' prior to settling down to enjoying wealth and prosperity; it need not imply a thoroughgoing commitment to Manifest Destiny. It is peculiarly difficult to know how to take the more gung-ho utterances of some emigrants: were they caught up in mindless excitement; were they role-playing for posterity; or had the boosters genuinely convinced them that they were important historical actors in a drama that found them at the crossroads of history? One emigrant proclaimed himself to be among 'the benefactors of their race – the founders of a new, enlightened and powerful state'. Cornelius Gilliam, one of the wagon train captains in 1844, told his daughter that his prime motive was patriotism: 'Father had come to Oregon not only to make a home but to help hold Oregon for the United States.'

Motive is often bracketed with means and opportunity, making the obvious point that, as Thomas Hobbes put it, 'covenants without swords are but words'. In short, the very poor could not be motivated to become emigrants, as they lacked the means to be so. Wagon-train emigration required one to be on an equilibrium point in terms of social stratification: too rich and there was no reason why one should want to move; too poor, and there was no way one could. Every single sociological study done of wagon-train emigration before the Californian Gold Rush of 1849 reinforces the point that, by and large, the overlanders came from the 'middling sort' – previously prosperous farmers, traders, artisans and craftsmen, who had fallen on hard times because of the depression but who still had sufficent savings to get to the West before being sucked into terminal financial quicksands in the Mississippi valley or points north.

Considerable financial resources were needed to uproot from the Midwest, trek for six months across 2,000 miles of country hostile in many senses and then relocate successfully in the Pacific coast territories, for on top of the journey one had to wait for the first harvest to come in at the other end. The absolute minimum required to make the journey and start up at the other end was $500, but more realistically for a man with a family it was nearer to $1,000. This assumed that one already owned wagons and draft animals; former city residents who had to buy these might need an extra $400 for a farm wagon made of hardwood that could carry up to 2,500 pounds of goods; to pull such a load one would need six mules or four yoke of oxen. To cut down on the impedimenta taken, some writers of guidebooks recommended sending tools and farm implements separately, by sea round Cape Horn; not until the late 1850s could tools be bought on the west coast.

Such sums of money were a tall order, but there were several ways round the problem of financing the trip. Many emigrants sold their farms and all their household goods to raise the money. It was also possible to purchase shares in a joint-stock emigrating company, and the shares could be bought 'on margin'. Even if an individual could thus shave down the initial outlay for the entire journey to $100, there were still the incidentals en route – tolls for ferries and bridges, supplies at trading posts, goods bought from other travellers – which might consume another $50 to $100. The problem of money at the other end was partially solved by the generosity of John Sutter in California or Dr McLoughlin of the Hudson's Bay Company in Oregon.

Luck and entrepreneurship also determined the overall cost of the trip. John Smith, an 1853 overlander, spent more than $342 getting from Indiana to Council Bluffs on the Missouri, then $233.50 outfitting at Council Bluffs, and a further $650 on the plains, replacing oxen, paying bridge and ferry tolls, buying more food and equipment. He sold the oxen and surplus food at the end of the journey for $389, but even so the total cost for himself and his family came to more than $846. In addition, he sent baggage by sea, so that the total cost was not far short of $1,500. On the other hand, a six-man outfit in 1849 spent $954 for the whole trip, including the fare to Independence, provisions, wagon, six mules and a horse, and a further $48 en route for tolls, food and alcohol. On arrival in Sacramento, they still had $100 worth of supplies left and were able to sell the wagon and team for $250. The total cost of crossing the continent to the five surviving men was just over $100 a head.

Poor single men had a chance to work their passage. An 1846 poster in Missouri laid out the terms. 'Who wants to go to California without costing them anything? As many as eight young men, of good character, who can drive an ox team, will be accommodated by gentlemen who will leave this vicinity about the first of April. Come, boys!' F.X. Matthieu in 1842 noticed destitute Irishmen panhandling round the camp; one of these Irish beggars re-emigrated from Oregon to California and struck it rich, becoming one of the Golden State's prominent citizens. In 1844, John Minto persuaded the Morrison family to give him bed and board in exchange for his labour and soon found himself adopted as an honorary son. Of course, it was much easier for poor single males to work their way across the continent than it was for single females; unless planning to work as schoolteachers, prostitutes or domestic servants, migration was almost impossible for impoverished single women.

Finally, something can be discerned about overlanders' motivation from the very pattern of migration. The classic wagon train-emigrant parties were kinship-based; indeed the reluctant women agreed to go because, unable to hold together the extended family, they were determined to make the nuclear one endure. They were basically satisfied with their way of life, be it farming, storekeeping or blacksmithing, but discontented with the opportunities for practising it successfully in the Midwest. Obviously, very different motivations were at play from the case of the Mormons, who migrated en masse for religious reasons, to find an almost literally biblical Promised Land instead of a material paradise, and even more so from the case of the gold rush migrants, whose intention was to make money quickly in the Far West and then return home. Statistics make this clear. Fifty per cent of those migrating in the mid-1840s went as members of a family, with adult females forming 15–20 per cent of the total; the California Gold Rush reduced the percentage of family travellers to 20–30.

Native-born migrants tended to move along the same lines of latitude: those from Ohio, Indiana, Illinois and Missouri, the principal source of emigrants, went to California and Oregon; those from Mississippi went to Texas. The reason was obvious: they were farmers and their animals and seeds were adapted to specific latitudes. So northern farmers tended to use horses and oxen, which thrived better in cool climates; southerners used mules, better able to stand the heat. Large numbers of migrants were born outside the USA – in 1850, 32 per cent of California's population was foreign-born as against 10 per cent in the United States as a whole – but as these were largely Canadians and northern Europeans with a penchant for temperate climates, the preference for Oregon and California was obvious. Patterns of migration also heavily underscore the thesis of national restlessness. The 1850 census showed that three-quarters of adult males arriving in Oregon in 1840–50 were from the Atlantic states but that 80 per cent of their children had been born in the Midwest.

The California Gold Rush changed everything utterly, but before 1849 the intriguing question was why some emigrants chose California over Oregon or vice versa. While in most years the bulk of settlers headed for Oregon, in 1846 1,500 emigrated to California and only 1,200 to Oregon. The most plausible explanation is that the conservative 'steady as she goes' people chose Oregon and the risk-takers opted for California. This hypothesis is not just consistent with common sense – Oregon had a farming pattern more familiar to pastoralists with small herds, and was more obviously Anglo-Saxon – but receives a lot of support from contemporary sources. Even Lansford Hastings, most barefaced of the California boosters, admitted that Oregon attracted a better class of emigrant:

> The Oregon emigrants are, as a general thing, of a superior order to those of our own people, who usually emigrate to our frontier countries. They are not the indolent, dissolute, ignorant and vicious, but they are, generally, the enterprising, orderly, intelligent and virtuous.

Oregonians perceived themselves to be superior and liked to tell the

46

following story. At Pacific Springs, on the crossroads of the Oregon and California trails, there was a pile of gold-bearing quartz marking the road to California for the illiterate; on the other road there was a sign saying 'To Oregon' for the benefit of those who could read. Jesse Applegate, the pioneer of 1843, was adamant that all respectable folk went to Oregon. Reading the subtext, later historians have concluded that 'respectable' meant Protestant, imbued with Puritan morality, content with modest gains, as opposed to the Catholic, hedonistic gamblers who wanted big, quick returns; in this respect, the Irish-Catholic majority on the Murphy–Stephens trailblazing party to California in 1844 is thought to be significant. One historian suggests that the paradigm of conservative Oregon and experimental, novelty-seeking California can be extended to give a complete social explanation for differential emigration, thus aristocrats go to Oregon, Jeffersonian radicals to California, deists to Oregon, Methodist revivalists to California, and so on.

The historian Dorothy Johansen has pointed out that Oregon boosters used certain key epithets in their propaganda: 'pious', 'well-educated', 'of good character', 'religious', 'industrious', etc., and that, when asking the US Congress for American sovereignty, they referred indirectly to California when they spoke of a region settled by 'the reckless and unprincipled adventurer . . . the Botany Bay refugee . . . the renegade of civilization from the Rocky Mountains . . . the profligate deserter seaman from Polynesia, and the unprincipled sharpers from Latin America'. Oregon had the advantage, too, that slavery was excluded, thus acting as a barrier to migration from the South. Most of all, what the conservative emigrants to Oregon wanted was a life of ease and quiet contentment, well summed up in this statement from the Virginia-born cabinet-maker William Rector:

The health of pine forests and limpid streams took my fancy . . . I had lost much of my ambitions for welth [sic] or society. And often I indulged in visions of a happy retreat from the agua and fevour [sc. ague and fever] and from the toils and vexations of a business life.

And so we come full circle. We are back with Thoreau again and the dream of withdrawal from the world to a Walden Pond Utopia. For the emigrants to the Pacific, the dream was especially unreal, for they were going to the precise area where Manifest Destiny required conflict. Thoreau wrote that his compass needle pointed him inexorably westward.

It is hard for me to believe that I shall find fair landscapes or sufficient wildness and freedom behind the eastern horizon. I am not excited by the prospect of a walk thither; but I believe that the forest which I see in the western horizon stretches uninterruptedly towards the setting sun, and there are no towns nor cities in it of enough consequence to disturb me.

Yet Manifest Destiny produced the war with Mexico, which Thoreau so opposed that he recommended civil disobedience. He could never solve the paradox: that the impulse that pointed him ever westward would take him into harm's way. Perhaps in their simple acceptance of the war of all against all, the 'irreligious' California-bound emigrants displayed greater practical sense than their 'respectable' Utopian Oregon-bound cousins.

THREE

TO BOLDLY GO

Chance, fate and contingency play a greater role in history than strait-laced scholars like to admit. Nowhere is this more evident than in the story of John Bidwell, the name indelibly associated with the first proper emigrant crossing to California. His exploit has always inspired historians to superlatives. Here are Charles and Mary Beard on the Bidwell expedition:

> Compared to the trials and sufferings endured by this party on its tedious journey of six months, the hardships of the voyagers in the *Mayflower* seem positively slight. The colonial pilgrims were in the hands of good sailors who knew the seas and the stars and were at home on the wide ocean paths. The Bidwell adventurers, on the contrary, crossed an almost uncharted continent, their wisest guides knowing little about the route save that it lay in a westerly direction.

Who was this alleged Columbus of the wagon trains? Aged twenty-two at the time of his great adventure, John Bidwell was a restless spirit whose short life had already taken him from New York to Pennsylvania, then on to Ohio. Finally attempting to settle in Westport, Missouri, he taught in a school there, but made the mistake of travelling to St Louis for his summer vacation in 1840. When he got back, he found that his farm had been stolen from him by a gun-toting claim-jumper whose reputation was so fearsome that the authorities of Platte County baulked at enforcing Bidwell's rights; moreover, the gunman hired a corrupt lawyer, who found a legal technicality in Bidwell's being under twenty-one when he came into possession of his land, and this gave the law enforcement officers the excuse they needed to do nothing.

That winter, Bidwell continued to teach, determined to seek a fortune away from the corrupt folkways of Missouri. The opportunity came when he heard wondrous stories from an eyewitness about the Utopia in the

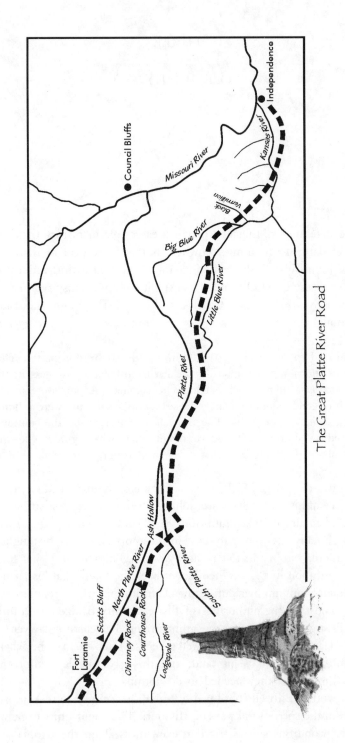

The Great Platte River Road

West called California, then still under Mexican rule. The teller of tales, Antoine Robidoux, painted such a rosy picture of the promised land that Bidwell decided there and then to make California his Mecca: 'his [Robidoux's] description of the country made it seem like a paradise.' He began to seek out like-minded souls. Others were inspired by Robidoux and by Americans who had already settled near the mouth of the Sacramento River at New Helvetia (Sutter's Fort), principally Thomas Larkin, John Augustus Sutter and John Marsh, the self-styled Dr Marsh.

Bidwell eagerly embraced the idea of emigration to California in a huge wagon train. He and his associates appointed a secretary and a committee and set up what they called the Western Emigration Society. All correspondents pledged to purchase a suitable outfit for pioneering and to rendezvous at Sapling Grove, in the present-day state of Kansas, on 9 May 1841. The enquiries flooded in, from Illinois, from Kentucky, from Arkansas. Soon the society had over five hundred names on its books, all pledged to the rendezvous. But then came the backlash. Missouri shopkeepers mounted a sustained propaganda campaign aimed at dissuading emigrants to the Far West. The manifold dangers of the routes, from Indians to wild animals, were stressed, and the rigours of the 'Mexican yoke' in California. Just when many would-be emigrants were stopped in their tracks by newspaper scare stories or began dithering, uncertain whether to believe the press or Robidoux and Marsh, the Jeremiahs received a propaganda gift. Thomas J. Farnham, leader of a party from Peoria, Illinois, made his way with thirteen followers to the Willamette valley in Oregon with a train of pack horses, but was so disillusioned by the gruelling trek that he wrote a notably dyspeptic book. Farnham's *Travels in the Great Western Prairies* came out early in 1841 and was widely read and discussed. The travails of the 'Peoria Group' lost nothing in Farnham's telling. He flatly counselled all would-be emigrants to the West to stay at home, and painted a particularly lurid picture of the hardships women would face on the trail.

The result of all this was that when the emigrants assembled at Sapling Grove early in May 1841, only about one-tenth of those expected showed up. When Bidwell arrived, there was just one wagon ahead of him. Gradually, a few more travellers trickled in, but on the date Bidwell had earmarked for the beginning of the trek his companions numbered no more than forty-five. Most were young men with a straightforward and simple-minded love of adventure. Nicholas Dawson, like Bidwell aged twenty-two, had set out from his native Pennsylvania three years earlier in the spirit of 'lighting out for the territory'; after he had paid for mules and provisions, he was left with just seventy-five cents in his pocket.

Josiah Belden set out for Sapling Grove, as he put it, 'being rather fond of that kind of adventure'. All told, this penurious band of emigrants could not raise more than one hundred dollars between them.

Even more alarming than their poverty was the group's total ignorance of the way west, the trails and routes that would take them to the promised land. Although they must have gleaned something from Marsh, Sutter, Farnham and others, Bidwell was probably not exaggerating by much when he said: 'Our ignorance of the route was complete. We knew that California lay west, and that was the extent of our knowledge.' In such circumstances, the participation of women in the enterprise seemed particularly foolhardy, but five of them set out with Bidwell, most of them attached by kinship to the numerous Kelsey clan. The Kelseys who came to Sapling Grove included Andrew, Benjamin and his eighteen-year-old wife Nancy and their one-year-old daughter, Isaac and Samuel (together with wife and five children). Richard Williams and his wife and daughter (who would shortly marry Isaac Kelsey) made up the rest of the sept, while the quintet of women was completed by a young widow named Mrs Gray, who had a young child.

In retrospect, two things strike one about the initial Bidwell party. One is the high calibre of the would-be emigrants. The Kelseys, it is true, were roughnecks who had been in trouble with the law, though Benjamin, the strongest of the brood, proved to have natural leadership qualities. His wife Nancy, married at fifteen, was herself a tough character. When asked why she braved the dangers of the trail, she replied matter-of-factly: 'Where my husband goes I go. I can better endure the hardships of the trail than the anxieties for an absent husband.' By contrast, Grove Cook was a Kentuckian related to the renowned fur-trading Sublette brothers, so pioneering was in his genes. He had decided that the rigours of the trail were too much for a woman and had left his wife at home.

Yet there were many more impressive personalities in this party than Cook or the Kelseys. Apart from Bidwell himself, Robert Thomes, Josiah Belden and Charles Weber would all eventually become millionaires, while Joseph B. Chiles and Talbot Green would both, in different ways, make their mark on Californian history. The other salient aspect of the party was that factionalism was present within the party from the earliest days. Nicholas Dawson, an important diarist of the trek, found himself 'messed' with the fifty-four-year-old John Bartleson and his coterie, which included the hunter Charles Hopper, his relative Gwyn Patton, Grove Cook and the enigmatic character Talbot Green, who had some medical supplies with him and acted as doctor to the wagon train.

Dawson described Green as 'a young man of evident culture and very pleasing address' who intrigued Dawson by carrying around with him a heavy parcel, which he claimed was a quantity of lead for trading in California.

The first decision Bidwell and his comrades had had to make, even before the rendezvous, was the type of wagon to take on the trek and the kind of transport animal. Fortunately, despite their ignorance of the country ahead of them, most of the travellers knew a great deal about the mechanics of the covered wagon, by this date overwhelmingly the favourite choice of vehicle for long-range travel. Wagons scored over pack mules in that they did not have to be unloaded at night and then reloaded next morning; they provided shelter and refuge for pregnant women and children and an improvised hospital for the sick or wounded. These factors more than compensated for the obvious drawbacks: wagons were slower than mule trains and less adapted to fording swift and deep rivers or scaling precipitous mountains. Moreover, in an emergency, the covered wagons could be formed into a defensive circle – the method of 'forming laager' the South African Voortrekkers had used in 1836–38 when under attack from Zulu or Matabele.

There were three types of covered wagon in regular use in the early 1840s. The classic model was the huge Conestoga wagon, developed in Pennsylvania around the time of the Seven Years War in the eighteenth century. In the West, the Conestoga wagon, the hardy conveyance for lugging freight, was mainly seen on the Santa Fe Trail, where the road was wide and straight. Emigrants to California or Oregon used either a medium-sized wagon with sloping sides and ends or, even better, a light wagon that in theory was pulled by one or two horses depending on the load; in fact, the pulling power in the early years on the trail was nearly always supplied by mules and oxen. The optimum aim was to have a light load in a light wagon, drawn by as many animals as possible.

Since the wagons had to be as tough as human labour could make them, only the best woods were used in their construction. The favoured types of lumber were oak, hickory, maple and other hardwood such as poplar, ash, beech, elm and Osage orange. The cover, invariably of double thickness, was a heavy rainproof canvas, caulked, oiled and painted, usually linen, sailcloth or oilcloth. The bed was a wooden box nine or ten feet long, about two feet wide, with ends and sides about two feet high, rising perpendicularly. From the straight bed of the wagon, the wagon bows (usually five or six per vehicle) were hooped to a height of about five feet, though sometimes the bows were made square, providing extra headroom. On the wagon bed were placed wooden boxes containing provisions, and the lids of the boxes provided the support for the mattresses on which the pioneers could sleep at night. Sometimes a false floor was built, about a foot from the bottom of the box, and this space was used for storage. A refinement was to caulk the bed or cover it with hides or canvases, to make the wagon more buoyant when crossing rivers. One or two wealthier travellers on the later emigrations had a double-deck arrangement, with supplies on the floor and bedding above, but none of the Bidwell party could rise to such luxury.

Flaps at the front of the wagon and 'puckering strings' at the back for opening and closing completed the upper ensemble of the wagon. Few problems occurred in the top half of a wagon, even though bows did sometimes break and snap and canvas tear, especially in heavily wooded terrain where overhanging branches caught and ripped the cloth. And in high winds, the emigrants sometimes carried out a manoeuvre equivalent to reefing the sails on a ship by heading into the storm 'bareheaded' to reduce pressure. Such 'prairie schooners' could carry loads up to 2,500 pounds, but the recommended maximum was 1,600 pounds. Some travellers well versed in primitive ergonomics suggested building a wagon capable of carrying 6,000 pounds, then loading with just one-third of that weight. Assuming the pulling power of four yoke of oxen or six mules, such a rig would provide the smoothest and fastest ride over the prairies. Most of the Bidwell party made do with half the recommended animals and loads. There were no Conestoga freight leviathans pulled by twenty-four oxen on this trip.

Most of the problems on the journey concerned the lower half of the wagon – what we might call the running gear. Although the tyres were made of iron, and iron was used also to reinforce the wagon at crucial points, the metal had to be used sparingly in construction since it was heavy, and an over-heavy wagon would simply exhaust the teams. A top-class wainwright had the enviable knack of making a wagon that was at once light and sturdy. An indestructible wagon would be too heavy to be pulled, but if it was too light, it would soon disintegrate under the jolting on the plains. Yet, inevitably, tyres buckled, wagon tongues snapped on sharp bends and front axles failed when the wagon lurched into a sudden 'hole in the prairie'. The snag about carrying extra axles was the extra weight in the wagon, but a snapped axle could be replaced, even by a skilled wheelwright, only if there was timber nearby; on the high plains the nearest trees could sometimes be a day's ride away. And even on a daily basis the wheels had to be greased to prevent friction building up in the wheel bearings in the form of a 'hotbox'. So, along with the tongues, spokes, ropes, chains, whips and goads slung under the wagon bed, the emigrants had to carry grease buckets and water (either in barrels or India rubber bags). When the store-bought grease was used up, the men improvised with fat from buffaloes or wolves.

To aid in manhandling or double-teaming wagons through mud, across creeks and ravines, and in braking downhill, it became the practice to take along a minimum of one hundred feet of rope, though such niceties were unknown to the Bidwell party. And since front wheels were slightly smaller than rear ones, the manoeuvrability of the wagons was cut down and the vehicle could not turn at an angle sharper than thirty degrees. If one attempted to combat this by constructing wheels so low that they could swing under the wagon bed and allow the wagon to turn at right angles, it was found that the smaller front wheels made the task of the team animals much more onerous. But even on flat, level ground tyres were a headache. Many wheels began to fail because they shrank in the dry air of prairie and desert. When wagon rims became dislodged because of dryness or jolting, there were three main stages in the repair process. First, wedges would be driven under the tyre to tighten it. Second, if that did not work, the wheel would be soaked in water and wedged with buffalo hide. But finally the tyre might have to be taken off, heated in an improvised fire pit until red-hot and then reset on the wheel.

Amazingly, to modern ears, the wagons had no brakes or springs, but since they rarely travelled at more than two miles an hour, the bouncing effect was not what people in stagecoaches would have experienced. But, with no shock-absorbers, the stresses on the wagon would have been severe and cumulative. As for the absence of brakes, this meant that on steep downhill slopes chain locks, log-dragging and improvised wind-lasses were the gravity-defying weapons. At the top of a slope, it was customary to lock at least one wheel, and on very steep descents, wheels were 'rough locked' by using a length of chain on which the tyre rested, allowing the wagon to grip. In wooded country, trees were especially useful for braking power. A tree could be felled and hauled behind the wagon to supply drag, or a wagon could be lowered over a cliff using a rope wrapped round a tree trunk as a windlass.

Since Bidwell's emigrants came from the four corners of the United States, the shared wagon lore must have been impressive. But all the eyewitness accounts suggest that the party had not yet definitively solved the conundrum of whether to place more reliance on oxen or mules. Some arrived with wagons drawn by oxen; others had horse-drawn vehicles; a few went on horseback and a handful did not even have an animal to their name. In the later years, emigrants debated fiercely the relative merits of mules and oxen. The case for mules, as on the Santa Fe

Trail, was that they were tough and durable, moved faster, did not get sore feet as oxen did and could subsist on cottonwood bark and alkaline water. By contrast, oxen 'spooked' easily and would become headstrong and reckless when hot and thirsty, causing stampedes in a mad rush for waterholes. The pro-oxen camp argued that oxen were less likely to be stolen than mules, were more valuable on arrival on the Pacific coast (especially in Oregon), were better able to withstand fatigue, could exist on a wider variety of sparse vegetation, were less likely to stray from camp, were safer, more reliable and almost as fast. Much play was made of the mule's notorious stubbornness and recalcitrance, the way they threw riders and could be constrained only by 'nose sticks' – a rope placed in a loop around the upper lip of the animal and twisted tight with a stick. There was also disagreement on the Indian threat. The usual opinion was that the tribes coveted the oxen more as a desirable source of food, but some countered that the Sioux, to name just one tribe, always stole mules rather than oxen.

During the whole period of the overland emigrations from 1840 to 1860, well over half of emigrants' wagons were pulled by oxen. In fact, in the later period, mules were pipped for second place by horses, possibly, it has been suggested, because the emigrants in the late 1840s who used St Joseph, Missouri, as their jumping-off point came from the northern states of Michigan, Iowa, Wisconsin, Illinois and Indiana, where mules were scarce. One set of statistics establishes the ratio of oxen, mules and horses on the overland trails as respectively, 60:20:20, but some experts would amend that to more like 60:15:25. The clinching argument in favour of oxen was surely that they were so much cheaper than mules; one estimate finds a mule, at $75, three times as expensive in the early 1840s as an ox at $25.

The Bidwell party was just about to move off into the wilderness when a late arrival mentioned that a party of Jesuits was a day behind them on the trail, headed for Fort Hall and thence on a mission into the country of the Flathead Indians. Some of the party thought it would be a good idea to join forces with them, but majority opinion was at first against this; the argument was that an unwieldy missionary party would slow them down. Then second thoughts prevailed. It was known that the Jesuits were being guided by one of the most famous names in frontier lore, the mountain man Thomas Fitzpatrick. Since none of the Bidwell party knew anything about the route to California, it seemed the merest common sense to wait and take advantage of his expertise. As Bidwell wrote later: 'it was well we did, for otherwise probably not one of us would ever have reached California, because of our inexperience.'

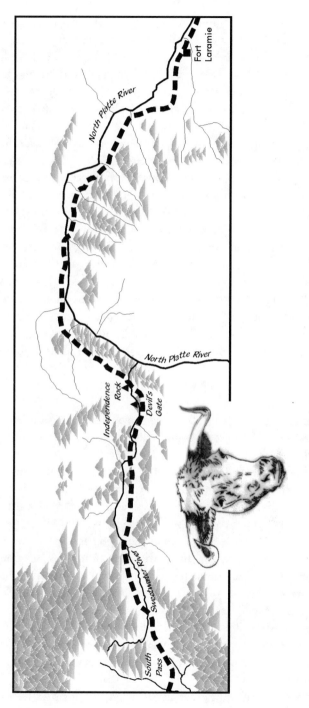

Into the Rockies: Fort Laramie to South Pass

The leader of the Jesuit mission was a remarkable man, hailed by some as the greatest missionary in the entire nineteenth century. Pierre-Jean de Smet was born at Termonde, Belgium, in 1801, educated in Flanders and came to the United States in 1821. In 1838, he achieved his lifetime's ambition of going as a missionary among the Indians when he was sent to the Powatomi, near present-day Council Bluffs, Iowa. After making contact with the Flathead tribe of western Montana, who, he claimed, were seeking Christian instruction, he was sent by his superior on a mission to the tribe in their fastnesses in the Rocky Mountains.

De Smet was given two Jesuit fathers and three lay brothers as his assistants and, after a winter of careful preparation, he and his party boarded the riverboat at St Louis on 24 April 1841, reaching Westport, Missouri, on 30 April. There followed nine frantic days of preparation. When de Smet's wagon train set off in single file, four carts and the missionaries' small wagon took the van, followed by eight wagons drawn by mules and horses and finally five wagons drawn by seventeen yoke of oxen. De Smet had hired the famous mountain man Thomas Fitzpatrick as guide to the Flathead country, and Fitzpatrick had signed up other members to the party. Alongside the Jesuits, the three brothers and their two teamsters, he had recruited the trappers Jim Baker, John Gray, George Simpson and William Mast, plus a trio of pleasure-seeking 'sportsmen', including an English milord named Romaine, and five extra teamsters.

It is fascinating to observe the interpersonal dynamic as recorded in diaries, journals and letters as soon as the Bidwell and de Smet parties merged. The three lay brothers – William Clessens, a twenty-nine-year-old Belgian blacksmith, Charles Huet, a Belgian carpenter, and Joseph Specht, a German tanner and factotum – merged seamlessly with the Kelseys and others. The three Jesuits were at first regarded warily by the Americans. The forty-two-year-old Father Nicolas Point had the reputation of being an irascible Frenchman who had already been kicked out of two countries (Spain and Switzerland) for his religious zeal. Actually, he was a tough character who had been in America since 1835 and had served on Jesuit missions in Kentucky, Louisiana and St Louis. A talented amateur painter, Point soon struck up an unlikely rapport with the cross-grained Bartleson, whom he described as the most remarkable of the Americans, 'already somewhat advanced in years, calm in temperament but enterprising in character, he was kind to us during the whole trip'.

The thirty-one-year-old Father Gregorio Mengarini was the scion of a rich Neapolitan family, who had volunteered in Rome for a mission in the

American West and arrived in the USA in 1840. A talented musician, he seemed at first bemused by the rough folkways of the trappers and mountain men and noted that the trapper John Gray was an Iroquois. There were signs, too, that he was missing the Tiber, for his journal contained the following entry: 'Plains on all sides! Plains at the morning; plains at noon, plains at night. And this day after day.' The Americans took longer to warm to Mengarini than to Point or de Smet but at least there was not the contempt evinced, for example, by Nicholas Dawson when the drawling English aristocrat Romaine went buffalo-hunting and got lost.

But easily the most impressive of the Jesuits was de Smet himself. Impetuous and energetic, a wandering star who could never settle anywhere, and a born optimist who hated desk jobs and paper work, the short and portly priest of Flemish peasant stock bowled everyone over with his enthusiasm and good spirits. Bearded, with heavy-lidded eyes and bushy eyebrows, de Smet was proud of his very strong teeth, which he liked to show off by bending coins with them. He could often be seen chewing jerky on the trail like a mountain man. His easy rapport with Thomas Fitzpatrick was much remarked on, and each man later paid tribute to the other's quality. In private, de Smet was much less sanguine than his public image suggested. On 16 May, just after joining up with Bidwell's party, he confided gloomily to his journal: 'I hope that the journey will end well; it has begun badly. One of our wagons was burned on the steamboat; a horse ran away and was never found; a second fell ill, which I was obliged to exchange for another at a loss. Some of the mules took fright and ran off, leaving their wagons; others, with wagons, have been stalled in the mud. We have faced perilous situations in crossing steep declivities, deep ravines, marshes and rivers.'

If de Smet was the heart and soul of the expedition as far as Fort Hall, Fitzpatrick was its mind and guiding spirit. It is hard to overrate the serendipity involved in the spontaneously organised Bidwell's party lighting on him. Born in County Cavan in Ireland, Fitzpatrick reached America in 1816, started in the Midwest trading with Indians and made his first ascent of the Missouri River in 1823. He, Jedediah Smith and the fur trader William Henry Ashley trapped and explored on the Green River, moved into the Flathead country of Montana in 1829, made contact with the Blackfeet on the upper Missouri the following year, and thoroughly reconnoitred the Three Forks Country. The early 1830s saw him in St Louis and on the Santa Fe Trail. The veteran of a dozen major Indian fights – with the Blackfeet, Crows and Gros Ventres – he had endured so much razor-edged stress that his hair went prematurely white. Strangely enough, his nickname 'Broken Hand' derived not from one of these engagements but from an accident when his left hand was crippled by a misfiring pistol. An entrepreneur, he had purchased the Rocky Mountain Fur Company in 1830, but sold it to the American Fur Company in 1836, hiring himself out to them on an annual basis and guiding several parties into the Rockies. His engagement as a guide by de Smet was in itself the surest possible sign that the fur-trading days of the Far West were over. With an extensive knowledge of every Indian tribe from the Sioux to the Comanche, Fitzpatrick was one of the greatest mountain men of the age, perhaps second only in fame and achievement to the legendary Kit Carson.

Fitzpatrick ran the wagon train in a tight and disciplined way. He placed the Jesuits in the van and insisted that everyone except himself and de Smet take turns at sentry duty. Every day he sounded reveille and got the column on the march; thereafter, he would ride up and down with many a cry of 'Close up!', reserving for himself the prerogative of where to halt for meals or bivouac for the night. Whenever possible, he liked to pitch camp on the wooded bank of a river so that there was plenty of firewood and drinking water. On arrival at the overnight sites, Fitzpatrick would mark the spot for the Jesuits' tent, then draw up the vehicles one beside another in a circle or square, depending on the nature of the terrain, but always in such a way as to keep the pack animals securely penned. At night, both priests and traders stood guard against possible attack.

On 12 May, the combined party got under way. The missionaries' four carts formed the vanguard, each drawn by two mules hitched in tandem. The main party consisted of eight wagons drawn either by mules or horses. In the rear were the slowest-moving vehicles – six wagons drawn by oxen. They followed the Santa Fe Trail for two days, then branched off on a faint path, previously beaten by the handful of missionaries and fur traders who had already made the journey to Fort Laramie. On 17 May, they crossed the Kansas River with help from the Kansa Indians. Nancy Kelsey, who would live another fifty-five years, always remembered vividly how the Indians towed them across the river in rawhide boats made from buffalo skins. There were two Kansa Indians who were particularly skilled at using a hollowed tree trunk as a kind of pirogue for transporting the wagons and baggage; de Smet reflected that the pirogue looked like a Venetian gondola. On 18 May, the three Jesuits made a two-day visit to the Kansa chieftain Fool Chief's twenty-lodge village at Soldier Creek. The visit provided de Smet and Point with a mass of anthropological and ethnological data.

While they were away, the Bidwell party conducted their own business, principally the organisation of the so-called Western Emigration Society. Although Dawson and others claimed (inaccurately) that there were a hundred people on the 1841 trek, an accurate headcount established clearly that there were only sixty-nine; though de Smet, with an eye to practicalities, said the significant figure was only fifty people – that being the number who could shoot a rifle. Talbot Green presided at the meeting and Bidwell acted as secretary. Bidwell urged on the company the need for each person to have a barrel of flour. He himself took an extra hundred pounds, fearing that they would run out of carbohydrates in the mountains and have to live on meat alone.

Despite strong opposition, mainly from the Kelseys, who pressed the considerable claims of Benjamin Kelsey, and another faction who favoured the forty-one-year-old Charles Hopper on the grounds of his experience and hunting prowess, Bartleson, the fifty-four-year-old martinet from Jackson County, Missouri, was elected captain, which meant that he would be the chief decision-maker once Fitzpatrick got them to Fort Hall. Bidwell and others were dismayed at this appointment, but Bartleson 'bounced' them: in Bidwell's word, 'he was not the best man for the position but we were given to understand that if he was not elected he would not go; and he had seven or eight men with him and we did not want the party to be diminished, so he was chosen'. Bidwell would doubtless have been even more alarmed had he known then that Bartleson and his coterie had a stash of alcohol in their wagons which they were hoping to trade with the mountain men of the Rockies.

The combined party finally started making serious inroads into the wilderness on 19 May. After the crossing of the Kansas River and the two-day halt for business, the wagons turned north towards the Blue River, the first of eighteen streams they had to cross between the Kansas and the Platte. This part of the journey was difficult, for much of it was tall grass interspersed with trees; anyone who had been foolish enough to bring heavy furniture jettisoned it here. A disgruntled Father Point noted: 'The terrain between Westport and the Platte is one of those endless undulations which bear a perfect resemblance to those of the sea when it is agitated by a storm.'

They got their first taste of the travails of the trek on 20 May (and again on the 22nd) when valuable time was spent rounding up straying oxen. Four days from the Kansas (on 23 May), they were overtaken by yet another group – six men and a wagon, led by Joseph B. Chiles of Jackson County, Missouri. Chiles was a thirty-one-year-old red-headed Missourian, fully six feet four, awkward and gangling, who liked to play practical jokes and prided himself on his sense of humour. He was a widower, the father of four children (whom he had not brought with him) and a veteran of the Seminole wars, in which he had fought at the battle of Lake Okeechobee. Repaying his pawky humour in kind, the Bidwell party nicknamed him 'the colonel'. His five comrades were Charles Weber, James John, James Shotwell, Robert Rickman and Henry Peyton. Chiles explained that they had all been swayed by the eloquence of John Marsh in faraway California.

The newcomers were given a hearty welcome but less enthusiasm was evinced for the next apparition that overtook them. Three days after the arrival of the Chiles party, an eccentric sixty-three-year-old Methodist preacher rode into camp, babbling about his burning desire to bring the gospel to the heathen Indian. Born in Pennsylvania in 1778, like most of the others Joseph Williams had led an itinerant existence. Hearing of the wagon train west, he set out from Indiana to St Louis, only to learn that all the emigrants were far ahead of him. When he arrived at Westport and found all the wagons gone, he rode alone through Indian country and arrived penniless and weaponless. An ingrate and a hothead, Williams did not reflect on the dangerous folly of his solitary odyssey, when he could have been easy prey for a Kansa, Pawnee or Cheyenne hunting party, but acted as though he were doing the Bidwell party a favour.

Williams, who was so naive and inexperienced in wilderness life that he had never seen an antelope before he joined the overlanders, nevertheless tried to preach a sermon to his new messmates on Sunday 30 May but was rebuffed. In his journal, he wrote: 'There were some as wicked people among them as I ever saw in all my life' – doubtless a reference to the Kelseys. He nourished an obscure grudge against Bartleson for being a renegade Methodist, but the man who really stuck in his craw was Fitzpatrick, who, predictably, would have none of his nonsense. Williams sought revenge in the secrecy of his journal: 'Our leader, Fitzpatrick, is a wicked worldly man, and is much opposed to missionaries going among the Indians. He has some intelligence, but is deistical in his principles.' That this was palpable nonsense would have been clear to Williams if he had just reflected for a moment that, of all potential assignments in Missouri, Fitzpatrick had expressly chosen to guide de Smet to the Flathead country.

The country between the Kansas and the Platte teemed with game and Father Point, the wildlife artist, was in his element. Wolves howled at night and skulked by day just out of rifle range; there were white wolves, grey wolves and coyotes among the lupine hordes. Inquisitive antelopes also approached closely, again usually out of range of the hunters, their budlike horns and white throats just visible above the grasstops, peering eagerly with their round, black eyes at the interlopers. Sometimes their curiosity was literally the death of them, as on 28 May when the hunters made their first antelope kill, and then capped it with the 'bag' of an elk. Five years later, the historian Francis Parkman, travelling this route, saw in a single morning a pack of coyotes, a flock of curlews, an antelope, a herd of some two hundred elk and a rattlesnake.

The numbers of snakes always amazed the overlanders, and it is surprising that there are no authenticated cases of death from snakebite in the 1840s. Serpents could be seen slithering away from the horses' feet by day or trying to glide into tents at night. Point noted that on a single day the wagoners killed a dozen rattlesnakes with their whips without ever once leaving the trail. More to his taste was the profusion of bird life: crows, ravens, turkey buzzards, grey owls and vultures, preying on snakes, beetles and lizards. By day, the birds' raucous calls mingled with the hum of bees, grasshoppers, locusts, butterflies, while the characteristic sound of night was the whining of mosquitoes and, from marsh and puddle, the bellowing, croaking and trilling of cohorts of frogs, multitudinous in colour, shape and dimension.

As the travellers approached the Platte on the last day of May, they were overwhelmed by a torrential downpour of a kind for which this valley was notorious. To reach the Pacific coast before the winter snows, it was essential to set out from Missouri early in May, but this meant debouching on the Platte at the very time the spring rainfall was at its height. To make matters worse, the heaviest deluges always seemed to occur at night. Alonzo Delano, a later traveller on the Platte, described the fury of Nebraska thunderstorms thus: 'King Lear in the height of his madness would have been troubled to have got his mouth open to vent his spleen on such a night . . . a worse night than [that] on which Tam O'Shanter outran the witches.' The combination of Jovian thunder, permanently coruscating forked lightning and hailstones as large as lemons or small apples persuaded many travellers on the Platte that they had entered the infernal regions. Even worse, oxen could be killed by lightning or they stampeded in terror. By no means untypical was Amelia Knight's experience in 1852 when twelve inches of rain fell in an hour, everything in her wagon was soaked and there was no possibility of lighting a fire, so the company went to bed supperless. Since most of the Bidwell party were greenhorns and had not brought special clothing, they were more than once exposed to the dreadful hailstorms and flash floods of the Great Plains.

Next morning, on the first of June, as they reached the banks of the

Platte, the sodden and demoralised company tried to lift their spirits by attending the wedding of Miss Williams and Isaac Kelsey. They gathered at the river bank, lined with a thin fringe of timber – the only trees on the horizon now that they had left the dense groves of tall green hardwood. The Revd. Joseph Williams finally earned his keep by officiating at the ceremony though, typically, he grumbled at the task, confiding in his diary that the marriage was 'without law or license, for we were a long way from the United States'. And his lamentations over the 'ungodly' continued: 'That night dreadful oaths were heard all over the camp ground. O, the wickedness of the wicked . . . I am still weary of hearing so much swearing by the wicked white men.'

Three days later (4 June), they were just about to make camp on the banks of the Platte, making steady progress of at least fifteen miles a day, when they experienced the most dramatic moment of the entire continental crossing. Contrary to Fitzpatrick's advice about solo forays, Nicholas Dawson went out hunting alone and ran into a war party of some sixty Cheyenne braves, operating rather far from their normal haunts. Dawson seems to have panicked and either pointed his gun at them or actually got off a shot. The Cheyenne, who could easily have killed him on the spot, relieved him of his clothes, mule, rifle and handgun, and slapped his horse contemptuously to get it to bear the white man away. The naked Dawson galloped off in the direction of the wagons, whooping and hollering that massacre was imminent. Infected by Dawson's panic the Cheyenne gave chase and came charging up to the Platte.

Fitzpatrick quickly ordered the wagons to draw up along the river bank and form square, at sight of which the Indians drew away and positioned themselves out of rifle range. When they made moves as if to bivouac, the worst fears subsided, though the Americans still wondered why they wore war paint. Fitzpatrick, who spoke their language, said that Cheyenne on the warpath did not act thus and pointed out the single female, a medicine woman, with the warriors. He then rode forward with John Gray for a parley with the war chief. The Cheyenne proved affable and readily returned Dawson's mule and rifle but kept the pistol. These terms were deemed acceptable, the peace pipe was produced, and the Cheyenne invited Fitzpatrick and the others to smoke with them.

That afternoon, they traded for tobacco and beads, while Fitzpatrick calmed the quaking Nicholas Dawson. The unruffled Father Point noted in his journal that the Cheyenne were better-looking than the Kansa and was impressed by their geniality. Even so, with the Cheyenne camped nearby, Fitzpatrick was taking no chances, posting double sentries and a strong guard over the animals. Next morning, they gave the Cheyenne time to move well ahead of them before they inspanned the oxen. For the next two days, the Cheyenne rode a couple of miles ahead of them. Curiously, other Indians, presumably Pawnee on whom the Cheyenne would normally have preyed, accompanied the overlanders, begging and panhandling. As for the terrified Dawson, ever afterwards he bore the nickname 'Cheyenne' and even referred to himself as 'Cheyenne Dawson' to distinguish him from his namesake, 'Bear' Dawson, also in the party.

The afternoon following the Cheyenne incident the pioneers were assailed by the most ferocious hailstorm yet: Bidwell spoke of hailstones larger than a turkey's egg, while Williams, using similar imagery, recorded that one of the panhandling Indians was knocked down by a hailstone as big as a goose's egg. That was not the only alarming natural phenomenon, for the Bidwell party shared with Joseph Berrien (travelling the same route eight years later) the dubious privilege of witnessing a tornado, its long funnel small end downwards as black as ink. Bidwell noted: 'Dark clouds rushed in wild confusion around and above us, soon with amazement we saw a lofty water spout, towering like a huge Column to support the arch of the sky.'

On either side of the Platte River, a broad, well-defined trappers' trail now led westwards across the plains, following the wide yet shallow Platte into dusty, arid territory but promising at last the prospect of easy going. The barren wastes of the great river valley stretched before them: level plains measureless to the eye, soft green undulations like the gentle motionless swell of the becalmed ocean, winding streams followed along their course by thin wisps of groves and inchoate woods, where at dusk the whispering of the whippoorwills succeeded the diurnal whistle of the quails. Viewed from the summit of a sandhill, this was how the Platte struck Francis Parkman in 1846: 'For league after league a plain as level as a lake was outspread beneath us; here and there the Platte, divided into a dozen thread-like sluices, was traversing it, and an occasional clump of wood, rising in the midst like a shadowy island, relieved the monotony of the waste.'

On 7 June, they came in sight of the junction of the North and South Platte. This was a good day for the larder, for the hunters killed not just an elk but three bison, the first of the myriad 'buffalo' they encountered in the next week. The Bidwell party began a trend that would be repeated on thousands of occasions, ultimately with catastrophic ecological consequences; at first they killed the bison for fresh meat but soon, intoxicated with the sheer profusion of the beasts, they followed the cynical advice of the hunter John Gray and began slaughtering them just to remove the tongues and marrow bones, the most prized delicacies. As they trod in the steps of the Cheyenne who had so recently given them such a fright, they noticed that the Indians did not believe in such prodigal squandering of the gifts of the Great Spirit; when they killed buffaloes, they used all the meat, leaving only the bones.

To those accustomed to the 'turkey-shoots' of the deep South, killing bison was child's play. All the hunters had to do was stay out of sight and to leeward of the beasts, and the massacre could begin. This part of the Platte valley seemed to be the buffaloes' happy grazing grounds, for they swarmed in continually from the southern plains to lap water and swim in the turbid waters of the great river. Bidwell remembered seeing the horizon black with the beasts for three days' journey ahead, as far as the eye could see; as the animals bulldozed into the Platte in their thousands, they changed not only the colour of the water but its taste, making it unfit for human consumption; but as Bidwell said, the emigrants were forced to drink it anyway. On 9 June, when the party was encamped on the south fork of the Platte, the whole party had to sit up all night and fire guns at the herds to prevent them trampling over them; in fact, the danger was so acute that Fitzpatrick made the sentries form a *cordon sanitaire* some distance ahead of the camp; Fitzpatrick advised them that otherwise the leading bulls would not be able to swerve in time because of the pressure from those behind.

Having passed the junction of the North and South Platte on 8 June, they crossed the South Platte on the 9th and next day travelled fourteen miles up the north bank of the Platte's southern arm. Whether it was the continuing availability of easy hunting in the form of bison (the hunters shot three this day) or euphoria at the impressive daily mileage they were clocking up, they grew careless and neglected to post sentries that night. The consequences of this error could have been disastrous, but the real fear hit them only the next day when there was an Indian scare – a war party of Sioux was seen in the distance. On the 11th, the mileage was even more impressive, fully twenty miles, and so good was their progress that on the 12th they left the South Platte (near the present-day town of Paxton) to march the twelve miles to the North Platte. Joseph Williams continued to grumble about the ungodly: 'I am still weary of hearing so much swearing by the ungodly white men.'

The 13th renewed its reputation as an unlucky ordinal number, for as they neared Ash Hollow on the morning of this date, the party sustained its first fatality. Bidwell wrote: 'A young man by the name of Shotwell, while in the act of taking a gun out of the wagon, drew up the muzzle towards him in such a manner that it went off and shot him in the heart.

He lived about an hour and died in full possession of his senses.' The party gave him a makeshift burial after a funeral service preached by Joseph Williams but, grief-stricken or not, pressed on another five miles that afternoon, being forced by hills that came down to the banks of the North Platte to leave the river at Cedar Grove and loop round the hills before descending to the river again by the dry channel of Ash Creek.

After five uneventful days they came to one of the most famous sights in the Platte valley: Chimney Rock, marking the five-hundred-mile point from their starting place in Missouri. The landscape changed after Ash Hollow, and more and more bizarrely shaped rock formations, the product of erosion by wind and rain, began to be seen. First there was Court House Rock, and then the cynosure of western Nebraska, a slender column on a broad conical base, standing apart from the principal ridge bounding the North Platte valley. Composed of indurated clay with alternating layers of red and white sandstone, Chimney Rock resembled an inverted funnel, with the top of the 'chimney' towering 325 feet above the base of the cone. The 120-foot vertical spire may even have been a hundred feet higher in 1841 than it is today, and some geological scholars posit a still higher chimney at the end of the eighteenth century, whose height was allegedly reduced by a lightning strike.

Visible up to forty miles away, and thus on the horizon for at least two days before travellers reached it, Chimney Rock, essentially a Brûlé clay phenomenon from the Oligocene age, with interspersed layers of volcanic ash, was *the* great sight on the Oregon and California trails, if we judge solely by travellers' tales; more than 90 per cent of extant emigrants' diaries and writings mention it. Looking at first sight like an old tree with all its limbs truncated, it appeared, as one got closer, like the crater or chimney of a volcano and, finally, like a shot tower. Although some observers compared it to Cleopatra's Needle or other obelisks and many easterners mentioned the Bunker Hill monument, the word almost everyone reached for was 'chimney', variously located depending on the imagination of the observer: that of a glass-house furnace, a steam mill, a sugar refinery, a chemical works and iron foundry. The great British explorer and adventurer Sir Richard Burton, who passed this way in 1860, wrote: 'the name is not, as is that of the Court-House, a misnomer; one might almost expect to see smoke or steam jetting from the summit . . . Nothing could be more picturesque than this lone pillar of pale rock lying against a huge black cloud with forked lightning playing over its great head.'

A great natural wonder, then, by common consent one of the most striking sights on the Great Plains; according to one writer, it is to the

Oregon–California Trail what Old Faithful is to Yellowstone National Park. The clarity of the atmosphere on the high plains produced a magnifying effect when one looked towards the horizon, and the mirage produced by Chimney Rock was such that it seemed to stay in the same relative position to travellers even while they trekked to and past it over four to five days. Bidwell was certainly impressed: 'The Chimney was seen towering like a huge column at a distance of thirty miles.' De Smet, one of those who used the inverted funnel imagery, had been at the rock in 1840 so was renewing his acquaintance. Father Point got out his paints and sketching materials, but sadly produced only a pedestrian and uninspired picture. Point, though, did his sketch from the bluffs looking north towards the Platte; this was unusual, since most nineteenth-century views were painted from the south, showing the high bluff background.

After pausing to allow the rite of climbing the base sections of Chimney Rock (not the chimney itself), Fitzpatrick urged his party on over this hinterland between the Great Plains and the foothills of the Rockies. The party experienced many mirages as the heat haze hid the folds of the highest hills and the trail shimmered in a dun and ochre flickering of dusty hallucination. Next day, after passing a series of curious mounds and bluffs, they came to another famous trail landmark, Scotts Bluff, which an informed minority of travellers thought more impressive than Chimney Rock. The bluff, yellow clay and soft sand rock, washed and broken into fantastic shapes by wind, rain and storm, presented the appearance of an immense city of towers and crenellations. Once again, a host of dubious analogies was cited over the years by hyperbolic emigrants: the Hanging Gardens of Babylon, Nineveh, Thebes, Petra, Baghdad, Rome, Athens, Gibraltar, the Alhambra at Granada, the castle at Heidelberg, Chinese temples, *Arabian Nights* palaces, Rhine castles and the Capitol at Washington, DC. More prosaically, these high beetling cliffs of indurated clay and sandstone were the haunt of mountain or bighorn sheep, a species so agile it was often taken for goats. While more poetic souls rhapsodised over the bluffs, Fitzpatrick's hunters killed two of the bighorns for the pot.

Three days later (22 June), the travellers reached Fort Laramie in eastern Wyoming, situated on a tongue of land formed by the junction of the Laramie and North Platte rivers. This was not yet the thriving military post it would become after 1849; in 1841 it was a curious amalgam of three different trading posts, named Fort John, Fort Platte and Fort William. It was well known both to de Smet, who had smoked the calumet the year before with Cheyenne chiefs, camped there in forty lodges, and more particularly to Thomas Fitzpatrick. Fort William was founded by William Sublette and Robert Campbell in 1834, but the following year they sold it to Fitzpatrick and James Bridger, who in turn sold it on in 1838 to the American Fur Company, trading in the West as Pierre Chouteau, Jr & Co. In the winter of 1840–41 a rival establishment was set up on the nearby banks of the North Platte, known as Fort Platte. Since Fort William was rotting, and to spite the newcomer, the Chouteau interests constructed a new adobe fort named Fort John or, as it was already more commonly termed, Fort Laramie. The building work was still going on when the Bidwell party rolled in, as Joseph Williams casually observed; he was far more interested in the number of Indians camped around the fort and the 'scandal' that whites lived openly with Indian 'wives'.

While Fitzpatrick decreed a day of rest, allowing the emigrants to take advantage of the fort's abundant wood, grass and water, to trade, bathe and wash clothes, de Smet took the opportunity to record his own impressions of the egregious Joseph Williams. The Jesuits had held some theological disputations with him and found him to be a mixture of naivety, ignorance and credulity. De Smet wrote:

He wished some religion, it being well understood that his was the best. I say this, because he was neither a Methodist, a Protestant nor a Catholic – not even a Christian; he maintained that a Jew, a Turk or an Idolater may be as agreeable as any other in the sight of God. For the proof of his doctrine he relied (strange to say) on the authority of St Paul, and particularly on his text: *Unus dominus una fides*. In fact, these were the very words with which he greeted us, the first time we saw him, and which formed the subject of a long valedictory discourse that he delivered in one of the meeting houses of Westport. previous to his departure for his western mission. By whom was he sent? We have never ascertained. His zeal frequently induced him to dispute with us; it was not difficult to show him that his ideas, with the exception of one, were vague and fluctuating. He acknowledged it himself; but after having wandered from point to point, he always returned to his favourite tenet, which, according to him, was the fundamental belief, 'that the love of God is the first of duties, and that to inculcate it we must be tolerant.' This was his strongest point of support, the foundation of all his reasoning, and the stimulus of his zeal. The term Catholic, according to him, was but another word for 'love and philanthropy.' He carried his absurdities so far that he excited the hilarity of the whole camp. His ingenuous simplicity was even greater than his tolerance.

While the object of these observations fretted about the numbers of

Sioux in and around Fort Laramie and pondered their fearsome reputation as warriors, the barrack-room lawyers in the Bidwell party viewed the future with trepidation arising from another quarter. In short, they had increased misgivings about Fitzpatrick's hard-driving style on the trail. On paper theirs was a spectacular achievement. They had fetched Fort Laramie on their forty-second day of trekking, having covered 635 miles at an average of fifteen miles a day. Fitzpatrick believed in going at the rapid speed of his carts in the van, but many of the party complained that this was *too* fast. Oxen covered two miles an hour, which meant that the hard-pressed beasts were in the yokes up to ten hours a day. Already Bartleson had held a meeting to discuss whether those in the wagons should not slow down, but the majority opinion had been that it was better to go at Fitzpatrick's pace than risk losing his expert leadership. But with the Laramie mountains clearly in sight, from which the Laramie River itself plunged in waterfalls to the broad lazy waters of the Platte, there seemed no choice but to go on with Fitzpatrick or return to Missouri. Anything else was out of the question: to the north was the Bozeman or Montana Trail, jealously guarded by the Sioux, while to the south was the inhospitable Cherokee Trail.

It was an unhappy and demoralised party that got under way on 24 June. After Fort Laramie the going was particularly difficult for wagons, few of which had ever come this far west. In the broken terrain of the foothills, the brown grass gave way to sage and greasewood, the streams were bitter with alkali and only a few creeks provided sufficient water, wood and grass for the animals to make their banks feasible camping grounds. There was no longer a distinct trail: they had to clear passage through bushes, on the slope of rocks and even in the middle of a ravine; they made their own crude road as they went, levelling stream banks, removing rocks, infilling gulches. So indistinct was the trail that on 26 June even the great Broken Hand himself took the wrong turning and then had to retrace steps. The Jesuits fared no better: Mengarini took six tumbles from his horse, Point many more, and even de Smet, who prided himself on his horsemanship, suffered the indignity of sailing through the air when his horse fell and he was pitched over its head.

The overlanders trekked grimly on, over a succession of creeks – Horseshoe, La Bonté, La Perle, Box Elder, Deer – still trying to hug the south bank of the North Platte. But the terrain did not always permit this, so there was much toil working up and down hills. These were the Black Hills, a poor relation of their greater namesake in South Dakota, mainly sombre pines and cedars. Although this was Sioux country, the Indians mostly seen were the Lakotas' traditional enemies – the Crow and the Blackfeet. Bear were plentiful too, both black and grizzly. But more formidable than Indians or wildlife was the Platte itself. The South Fork had been crossed with ease, since the water was no more than two feet deep and there was no sign of either quicksands or water mocassins – the two traditionally dreaded scourges at river crossings.

Now, a week out from Fort Laramie, came the dreaded North Fork crossing, close to present-day Casper, Wyoming. Suddenly, just after Deer Creek, the North Platte swung sharply away to the south, while the California–Oregon Trail lay due west, on to the Sweetwater River. The North Platte was in spate, much too deep for fording, so the emigrants had to improvise a crossing. De Smet candidly admitted that he was afraid of the swollen waters, but the hunter Gray showed a spirited example with his own form of troika: ahead of him he lashed a horse on which his wife was mounted, then he urged his own mount into the foaming waters, while finally pulling a colt that bore Nancy Kelsey's one-year-old daughter strapped to its back. Seeing such signal courage and aware of being watched by Indians, whose whispers would precede him to the Flathead, de Smet took the plunge and got to the other side with difficulty. The pioneers got across with the loss of just one drowned mule – a small price to pay, for the North Fork often claimed human lives.

There was no respite on the other side. A severe canyon forced the trail away from the river, and the water they encountered was brackish and alkaline – bad enough to kill cattle who drank the poisonous liquid. In this area were dry beds of shining white; in the rainy season they were shallow salt lakes. On 3 July, the party gained the banks of the Sweetwater and next day came to Independence Rock, another of the great landmarks on the trail. Mountain men started the custom of scratching their names on the rock and in years to come this monument would be graffiti-covered. Bidwell's comrades did not neglect to add their names to the roster, carving and painting their signatures or marking primitive doodles with axle grease. It was an easy climb to the top, and from the summit could be seen the meandering Sweetwater and, more ominously, the first sight of snowcapped peaks to the west.

It was now one hundred miles to the continental watershed at South Pass. After Independence Rock, for the eight days or so spent negotiating the Sweetwater, the going was easy – remarkably so, considering that the travellers were now in the Rockies, with high peaks and precipitous ridges all around them. The Sweetwater boasted a valley that was huge in relation to the size of the river itself, and here were plentiful water and grass, herds of bison and antelope and gentle gradients. The one worry was that flour and provisions were running out rapidly. Yet it was in good spirits that they came to Devil's Gate on Sunday 5 July. Here, the river cut through perpendicular cliffs on either side, but there was no need to take the wagons through the gorge, since nature had provided an easy pass just half a mile to the south. Small wonder that de Smet wrote: 'In my opinion they should rather have called it Heaven's Avenue.'

The overlanders celebrated their good fortune that night with a rousing campfire hoedown, which predictably drew the fire of the curmudgeonly Sabbath-observing Joseph Williams, who wrote: 'This night we have the sound of the violin, but not much dancing. "Woe unto the wicked, for they shall have their reward." Our company is mostly composed of universalists and deists.' One of Williams's unfavourite deists, Thomas Fitzpatrick, was now seriously worried about the food supply and ordered that the party 'make meat' – that is, hunt buffalo and dry the meat. But the hunters' tallies could not keep pace with consumption. Even though twenty bison were killed on 8 July, none of the meat was saved, and it was the same story next day when the bag was ten.

They passed close to the Granite Range and saw the snowcaps of the even loftier Wind River Range to the north of their destination at South Pass. Whether it was snowblindness or a real perception, Joseph Williams claimed to have seen both white bears and white wolves. More interesting to the travellers was Ice Slough, a boggy location where one could dig down through a foot of mud and touch layers of ice, even in summer. But tempers were beginning to fray again, for bison were scarce along the Sweetwater during this season, and the hunters' kills were dwindling to vanishing point. On 11 July the tally was two, on the 12th four, and only one on the 13th. Like ravenous sharks, the overlanders started attacking each other. There were several altercations, one of which was gleefully reported by Williams as follows: 'Today Col. Bartleson gave some of our deists a down-setting, which pleased me very well.'

The 13th was living up to its unsavoury reputation. On this date in June, Shotwell had accidentally killed himself and on 13 July the single buffalo that was slaughtered, raised the spectre of short commons and even starvation. Fortunately, next day the hunters bagged no less than nine of the lumbering bison. Spirits rose once more and positively soared on the 18th when they reached South Pass and at last found waters that flowed towards the Pacific. Against the expectations of an alpine defile, the travellers found they could see for many miles to the west across a sweeping, sage-covered plateau. Here, at 8,000 feet, even though this was the high point of the Rockies, the pass was easy, like a broad plain, though there was frost at night and ice formed on the water buckets.

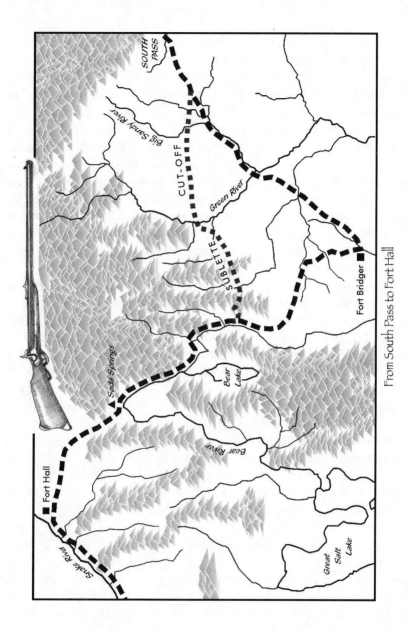

From South Pass to Fort Hall

Until they reached the Bear River there was no longer a river valley, like those of the Platte and Sweetwater, to follow, but a gruelling trek across north–south rivers and mountain ranges. A long day's journey downhill brought them to Little Sandy Creek, then, a day later, there was Big Sandy Creek. Beyond that, all the way to Green River, they were in a wilderness more hostile than any yet encountered. This was simply desert land, with no waterholes and no forage. The effective buffalo range ended at South Pass, and deer and antelope on the desert stretches were as rare as the water that sustained them. This was the worst stretch so far, and it was with feelings of more than just relief that after a five-day slog they descended the bluffs above Green River and made a euphoric descent to the grass and water in the valley. This area seemed to teem with grizzly bears, but more welcome were the mountain sheep, a few of which the hunters managed to shoot for the larder.

The peaks and troughs of the grim trek from South Pass left the travellers in a volatile, manic mood, with some exhibiting signs of hypermania. One of Bidwell's *bêtes noires* was an illiterate loudmouth named Bill Overton. At the campfire on Green River, he boasted that he had never been surprised by anything in his life. Bidwell tried to get a rise out of him by leading him into further extravagant claims, but Overton simply said he would not be surprised if he saw a steamboat suddenly appear on the wild Green River. Overton's words seemed borne out on 23 July when John Gray, who had been sent ahead to scout, returned with a large party of trappers. This epiphany was not as miraculous as it seemed, for Fitzpatrick, who knew the probable movements of the trappers, had actually conjectured their likely presence and sent Gray out with this in mind.

This was the moment when Bartleson and his cronies produced the kegs of alcohol they had secreted and began a brisk trade, bartering it mainly for buffalo meat, by now no longer on the Bidwell party's menu. The leader of the newcomers was Henry Fraeb, an old comrade of Fitzpatrick's, and the Green River was one of his favourite trapping grounds. Fraeb, who was returning from a successful trading trip to the sleepy little town of Los Angeles on the southern Californian coast, where he had sold hundreds of beaver skins, counselled the travellers that they would not reach their destination in wagons. He proved such a Job's comforter that six men (Gray, Peyton, Frye, Romaine, Rogers and Jones) left the party immediately, while Jim Baker said farewell to de Smet, having elected to join Fraeb. This was a fairly typical drop-out rate; scholars have estimated that the total 'turn-round' figure on the emigrant trail was around 10 per cent. In Baker's case, the decision was perhaps not a wise one. A month later, Fraeb and several of his companions were killed in a fight with Sioux and Cheyenne braves on a branch of the Yampa River near the Colorado–Wyoming border; Baker, however, survived and made old bones, dying at eighty in 1898.

Easily fording the low-running Green River, the travellers followed its banks for a few miles and then struck into very rough mountain country. The hills were so challenging that Cheyenne Dawson recorded that the wagons were kept upright 'only by having fastened to the top of our loads ropes to which men clung'. But after the desert between the Big Sandy and the Green, even the high country was a relief, especially as it boasted clear streams and springs among the verdant pine. Prairie dogs and sage hens were the only wildlife noted as they crossed the creek known as Ham's Fork and headed for the Bear. Seven days' travel took them close to the Bear, where de Smet conducted the second wedding ceremony of the journey. A man named Fillan, or Phelan (whom Bidwell, unaccountably, insisted on calling Cochrum), had joined the party at Fort Laramie and in the intervening month he and the widow Gray had formed an attachment. Doubtless feeling that de Smet had performed the rites with an aplomb that he, in his earlier doubting mode, had lacked in the previous trail marriage, Williams decided to try his hand at preaching once more. Two days after the Fillan wedding, he tried a sermon but simply elicited anger and derision from the 'deists and swearers'.

The Bear River valley promised another easy stretch, but getting there did not prove easy. On 2 August, the great Broken Hand again lost the way, got trapped in a defile and had to backtrack two miles. Next day, though, he found the way through a high divide and brought the party down to the Bear River. Here, the trail swung sharply northwards and, for the first time, the overlanders found Rocky Mountain scenery to match the Rockies of their imagination: rushing streams, luxuriant grassy meadows, geese, ducks, trout in clear waters, wild berries, even the unaccustomed sound of songbirds. Bathing and washing of clothes were again possible. Six days of easy travel brought them to another highlight of the California–Oregon Trail: Soda Springs, on the northernmost bend of the Bear, set among beautiful fir and cedar, full of bubbling soda fountains and sulphurous mud pools, later to be given individual names such as Beer Spring and Steamboat Spring. For once, Joseph Williams was enraptured by natural phenomena and forgot about his fellow sinners.

The travellers had taken forty-eight days to cover the 560 miles from Fort Laramie; the nature of the terrain had slowed their progress to an average of twelve miles a day. There was a short pause at Soda Springs for hunting, and among the exotic beasts brought back to the communal table was a six-foot-tall pelican, whose flesh, however, was found to be coarse and unpleasant to eat. The joint party proceeded six miles beyond Soda Springs where the trail definitively divided, with one branch leading north to Fort Hall and Oregon and the other to California. Fitzpatrick and the Jesuits would continue to the Snake, another party would head for the Willamette valley in Oregon, while only the most intrepid or foolhardy would continue for California. The Bidwell–Bartleson party, properly so-called, had hitherto sheltered behind Fitzpatrick and his hunters, but from now on they would be on their own.

The parting of the ways came on 11 August. Only thirty-two people elected to go to California with Bartleson and Bidwell. Of those who have featured so far in the narrative there were the two Dawsons, Belden, Chiles, Cook, Hopper, John, Patton and Talbot Green. Only one woman continued on the California trail – the dauntless Nancy Kelsey with her one-year-old daughter. The Kelsey clan fractured, with Andrew and Benjamin heading south-west for the Mexican territory and Samuel and Isaac (with wives and children) heading north-west towards the land of Oregon over which the Union Jack still fluttered. The names of the other California pioneers deserve to be recorded: Elias Barnett, William Belty, Henry Brolaski, David Chandler, John Schwartz, George Kenshaw, Henry Huber, Thomas Jones, John McDowell, Green McMahon, Nelson McMahon, Michael Nye, Robert Rickman, John Roland, James Springer, Robert Thomes, Ambrose Walton and Major Walton.

The overland party had already shrunk with the tragic death of Shotwell and the defection or departure of eight other males, including Gray and Romaine. And at Fort Hall there would be further splintering, when Isaac and Samuel Kelsey and their families, plus Joseph Williams, Richard Fillan and his new bride (together with her child from a previous marriage), the loudmouth Overton and nine other persons headed for the Willamette valley while the de Smet party pushed on up the Snake River towards their mission. In an ideal world one would like to have had journals or memoirs from *all* the adult travellers, but this was scarcely possible in an era of low literacy. One would particularly like to know the impressions of de Smet's French-Canadian teamsters, descendants of the old *coureurs de bois*, of the one-eyed trapper Fillan who had married Mrs Gray, or indeed of Overton, the Thersites of the piece, or the turbulent Kelseys.

What is abundantly clear is that the California-bound emigrants parted from Fitzpatrick and the Jesuits with genuine regret. De Smet had undoubtedly raised the moral and spiritual tone of the party, to say nothing of its morale. Bidwell paid him this handsome compliment:

> He was genial, of fine presence, and one of the saintliest men I have ever known, and I cannot wonder that the Indians were made to believe him divinely protected. He was a man of great kindness and great affability under all circumstances; nothing seemed to disturb his temper . . . Sometimes a cart would go over, breaking everything in it to pieces; and at such times Father de Smet would be just the same – beaming with good humor.

De Smet repaid the compliment and said of the California-bound emigrants: 'They started purely with the design of seeking their fortune in California . . . and pursued their enterprise with the constancy which is characteristic of Americans.'

Thomas Fitzpatrick spoke seriously and earnestly to Bartleson and Bidwell, and asked them to abandon their quixotic quest and proceed instead to Oregon. When the Missourians remained adamant, he gave them such information as he possessed – which was not much, as he himself had not travelled the route and he was relying on ill-remembered fragments of anecdotage from Jedediah Smith and Joseph Walker, who had traversed the terrain in the 1820s. Bidwell and Bartleson were hopeful that Walker might be at Fort Hall and be willing to guide them – they had often comforted themselves around the campfire with the thought that they could simply exchange Fitzpatrick for Walker – and sent four of their party on with Fitzpatrick. Alas for their hopes, Walker was not there, and they were on their own.

The Jesuits and the Oregon-bound party arrived at Fort Hall on 15 August, where they found an advance deputation of Flathead Indians waiting to guide them to their ancestral homelands. De Smet paused for three days to rest and recuperate, but obtained precious little in the way of provisions, for Fort Hall was a minor fur-trading post of the Hudson's Bay Company and in 1841 could provide travellers with even fewer supplies than Fort Laramie. The post commander Francis Ermatinger's spirit was willing but his commissariat was weak. This is one of the rare instances where one can detect de Smet playing to posterity's gallery. In his journal, he noted that Ermatinger, though a Protestant, went out of his way to pledge help to the new Catholic mission among the Flatheads and promised to lobby his superiors in the Hudson's Bay Company on the Jesuits' behalf: 'Not only did he repeatedly invite us to his table and sell us, at first cost, or one-third the value, in a country so remote, whatever we required; but he also added, as pure gifts, many articles which he believed to be particularly acceptable.' This hardly squares with Mengarini's account. According to the third-ranking Jesuit, all Ermatinger had to sell was two bags of pemmican of which Mengarini reported: 'Though this was our first experience of it, it was far from unpleasant.'

The Jesuits left Fort Hall on 18 August and followed the course of the dangerous and swift-flowing Snake River, sustaining greater losses of horses and baggage than on all the trail hitherto; the only compensation was the abundant salmon the Flatheads caught with ease in the limpid waters. They also had to negotiate the gorge at Hell's Gate, on which Mengarini commented: 'If the road to the infernal regions were as uninviting as that of its namesake, few, I think, would care to travel it.' Finally, they became the first wagon train to cross western Montana and at the end of September they founded a mission on the right bank of the Bitter Root River, thirty miles north of present-day Missoula, Montana.

Despite his many disputations with the Jesuits, Joseph Williams was genuinely sorry to part from them and admitted to Father Point that he owed them a lot. To be impressed with de Smet was not unusual, and his later career was even more remarkable. Having survived a narrow brush with death on the rapids of the Columbia River in 1842 (five of his boatmen were drowned), he returned to Europe, went back to the United States (he would eventually cross the Atlantic nineteen times), founded a convent in the Willamette valley, charted the Columbia, made peace between the Blackfeet and the Flathead (hitherto irreconcilable enemies), met Brigham Young, and in 1851 attended the great meeting at Fort Laramie to solve the 'Indian problem'. In the last years of his life, he negotiated with the Lakota chiefs Sitting Bull and Gall during the Sioux wars. Williams, by contrast, returned to honest obscurity. The Oregon-bound party took advice about the way west, abandoned their wagons at Fort Hall and followed the Snake River down to American Falls, eventually reaching Fort Boise after the Snake had swung away northwards to Montana. The emigrants reached the Willamette valley safely, having first detoured to the Walla Walla mission and rafted down the perilous Columbia River.

Meanwhile, the four men from Bidwell's party who had gone to Fort Hall for guides and information returned to the main group with none of the former and very little of the latter. It took them ten days to catch up with their comrades who had been travelling in a south-westerly direction towards the great Salt Lake, armed only with primitive maps. The best intelligence available from Fort Hall was that the California-bound emigrants should go north of the Salt Lake before swinging due west, but should not proceed too far north for fear of running into a maze of rugged canyons, precipices and gulches; on the other hand, if they went too far south, they were likely to end by dying of thirst in the trackless desert. Armed with this anodyne information, dire warnings about deserts and the useless exhortation that they should look for the 'Mary River', said to flow all the way to California, the Fort Hall party were reunited with their comrades a day's trek west of the Bear River. So far the Bidwell party had made good progress: the expected dearth of water and pasture had not materialised, though there had been some false trails through mud flats which had bamboozled them.

Bidwell regaled the returnees with an amusing tale. Suffering from excessively hot days (which alternated with chillingly cold nights), on 13 August he and James John had set out down the Bear River on a fishing trip but, seeing snowcapped peaks in the distance, had suddenly conceived a mad desire to wallow in the snow, thinking they could get there and back by sundown. They proceeded at the double but their goal seemed to recede before them. When nightfall came, they found themselves marooned on a snowless peak that stood between them and their objective, and which they had been unable to make out because of the distance magnification common in the Rockies. Bidwell suggested camping overnight but John proposed they go at a brisk trot through the darkness. Passing Indian encampments in their wild helter-skelter, they descended the valley and began puffing up the ridge on the far side. Sharp rocks cut through their mocassins and made them bleed. Up and up they went, past midnight, above the treeline until, exhausted, they crawled under a solitary stunted fir tree and waited until dawn.

Two hours after dawn, they finally reached the snow. They then started on the return journey, but were too tired and maimed in the feet to retrace their steps, so opted for a short cut. This turned into a labyrinth of chasms, dark thickets and gorges full of rapid, raging streams. All around them were copious signs of grizzly bears, with whom any encounter would probably have been fatal, for in their crazy initial impulse they had not returned to camp for firearms but started for their snowy Shangri-La armed only with butcher's knives. Once in the valley, they quickened their pace, noticing as they went that last night's Indians had moved on. Gaining the summit of the next hill they saw below them the diminished wagon train hugging the Bear valley. It was about 2 p.m. and the party had been on the march for about three miles, having given up on John and Bidwell, whom they assumed to have fallen victim to a Blackfoot hunting party. They clambered down the hillside and ran whooping and shouting towards their astonished comrades. They heard a sad story of a sleepless night spent on maximum alert, expecting an Indian attack, followed by a wasted morning fruitlessly searching for their lost orphans. It is doubtful if anyone was placated by Bidwell's insouciant and cavalier explanation: 'We have been up to the snow!' The most exciting twenty-four hours in Bidwell's life (during which he probably travelled fifty miles on a whim) was, objectively considered, a piece of dangerous folly.

The ignorant overlanders began working round the western and northern end of the Salt Lake. On 22 August, they were camped by a large spring of brackish water, surrounded by grass barely edible by the animals. In search of decent water and pasture, the unyoked oxen began wandering off, so the party had to remain camped the rest of that day while scouts went out to round up the strays. Once they were away from rivers, the oxen had a yen to roam in search of water, which meant that most days there was a delay while they were found and coralled. All travellers reported the same thing: thirsty oxen were nervous and unpredictable, likely to stray, panic, get bogged down in the mud, collapse from overexertion or even stampede.

Out in quest of his errant oxen one day, this time partnered by Cheyenne Dawson, Bidwell had another of his amazing adventures. The two men set out with a double ration of water as it was a furnace-like day, but Dawson soon tired of the heat and told Bidwell there were enough cattle in California for them not to be on this wild-goose chase. Bidwell went on alone and tracked the animals till sundown, but was alarmed to find parallel tracks of an Indian hunting party, evidently on the trail of the oxen. Eventually, he found the oxen but had the nagging feeling the Indians were now tailing him. After a near-disastrous episode when his horse sank in quicksand and Bidwell dragged him out by a rope only with supreme difficulty, he was alarmed to find that his gun had become clogged with mud and was in no condition to shoot. Just at that moment he saw two riders approach and feared they were Indians. Without a serviceable firearm he was helpless. Fortunately, the riders proved to be two of his comrades, who had come to find him, bringing much needed provisions and water.

The new problems with oxen, coupled with shortages of food, absence of game and a new, inhospitable desert terrain, took its toll on the party. There was a sense of foreboding and palpable anxiety that they would now have to trek across country away from river valleys. Many recalled the halcyon days along the Platte, Sweetwater, Green and Bear when they were under the protection of Fitzpatrick and his hunters. Yet there was nothing for it but to plod on. On 23 August, they headed westwards, having taken rough-and-ready bearings from some barren hills when they looked towards the northern arm of the lake. After a long haul, they camped near the lake at a spring, but once again the water was brackish and had a bad smell of sulphur. The only way the liquid was palatable was when it was brewed into strong coffee, when even the horses, which had refused the crude water, would consent to take a drink.

On 24 August, the oxen strayed again, so that the party did not get under way until noon. They made ten miles in a north-westerly direction, then camped near the northern tip of the lake, again near brackish springs. After a rest on the 25th, they made an early start next day and continued until full dusk, but without finding water. Having completed twenty-five miles in a single day, leaving the Salt Lake far behind, Bartleson was proving as hard a driver as Fitzpatrick had been, but this time the mules and oxen were suffering from thirst. The travellers were too exhausted even to loose the animals, and spent a dismal night with no fresh water, little food and no forage for the animals. Next morning, though – relief. A five-mile trek brought them to good water and abundant grass at the foot of a mountain range. They decided to rest for some days and send out scouts.

Again the anxiety in camp was palpable. At the end of August, days were getting shorter and the good weather likely to hold for no more than another month, but what choice did they have? The exhausted animals were almost at the point of death, and needed to be fed and watered before moving on. Besides, there was no clear route to follow. On 29 August, Bartleson decided to scout ahead for the fabled Mary's River, taking Hopper with him. Meanwhile, his comrades traded with some Shoshone Indians – traditionally friendly to whites – exchanging precious powder and bullets for edible berries. It was expected that Bartleson and Hopper would soon be back. In fact, by 5 September, after more than a week at the 'oasis', and the grass now nearly exhausted after ten days' munching by the animals, the two had still not returned. It was decided to proceed west in easy stages. One of the wagons was found to be unserviceable and abandoned, reducing the total number of vehicles to eight.

In three days they covered twenty-two miles, along the southern base of the mountains. They had already realised that their best chance of water and grass was close to hill country, and the hunch paid off. They found both pasture and water and even a handful of junipers and desert birch. They slaughtered the ox released from the abandoned wagon and, when the hunters bagged some rabbits and antelope, the immediate food crisis passed. Even so, the way ahead was long and hard: the smoke from hundreds of Indian fires reduced visibility, so that they sometimes stumbled into obstacles unawares; steep banks and gulches barred their way; and they were driven to new heights of frustration by the prevalence of artemisia or sagebrush, difficult for the wagons to penetrate. The only saving grace about the sagebrush was that it made excellent fuel for the campfires and harboured dozens of hares (the prairie 'jackrabbit') and sage hens.

On 7 September, there was an acrimonious split in the party. Even with the controversial Bartleson absent, feelings ran very high. It was observed that the mountain range they had been following curved sharply to the south, suggesting that westward progress with the wagons was not feasible. Unless they were to sit idly by, waiting in vain for the return of Bartleson and Hopper (whom all now assumed to have been killed by Indians), the only practicable solution seemed to be to swing south with the range. Using sign language, the dissident minority negotiated with a nearby band of Indians (Native Americans never seemed very far away after Fort Hall) and got them to agree to act as guides. There is some controversy about the ability of the 1841 California overlanders to communicate effectively with Indians; whether the travellers got their intentions across, whether the Indians understood, told them what they wanted to hear or just wanted to decoy them out of their territory is unclear. What is remarkable is that on this and subsequent occasions, the emigrants trusted the Indians to guide them and to find food and water even though they consistently suspected them of hostile intentions.

Those who opted to move south rather than 'wait and see' were few. Even so, they detached two wagons and got under way, guided by the Indians. Bidwell and the majority with the other six wagons stayed in camp, increasingly anxious, especially when an icy night, with the water buckets frozen solid, reminded them that the season was advanced and time was running out on them. But next day, to general astonishment, Bartleson and Hopper returned, having been away eleven days. They had found a small stream, which they thought was a feeder of the fabled Mary's River, but thought the way unsuitable for wagons. A decision was therefore taken to trek south. That evening they caught up with the two dissident wagons, and the party was physically reunited if still full of simmering discontents and rivalries. The itinerary cannot be followed with exactitude: all one can say is that it lay along a line taking in Rabbit Spring and Pilot Peak (so named by 'Pathfinder' Frémont in 1845).

Having dismissed the Indian guides with pay on 10 September, they set out across a desert 'glimmering with heat and salt', through arid stretches where wagons sank so deeply in drifting sand that the men could scarcely pull them. They camped the first night without water after a long trek, then the next day continued south-westwards for fifteen miles to Rabbit Spring. Had they turned west at this point, they would have come in a single day to the headwaters of Thousand Spring Creek and thence, after perhaps another five days, to the head of Mary's River. Still following Indian trails, they arrived at Mountain Spring (Pilot Peak) and made camp. Here the Kelseys threw in the sponge and abandoned their two wagons, which by now contained little food or anything else of value; it is not clear if Nancy, with her baby, proceeded on horseback or found space in one of the other wagons.

For three days, the six remaining wagons moved south, across Silver Zone Pass and Gosiute valley, picking out their route between the mountains to the west and the salt flats to the east. On the evening of 13 September, they made camp at a good spring – almost a lake in size – but then blundered for two days, south-west, then north-west, finding springs of fresh water, but hopelessly lost. Finally, on the 15th, at the foot of the Pequops, the decision was taken to abandon the wagons. The reasoning was clear: they could get on faster, could negotiate rough and hilly country more easily, and would have meat on the hoof in the form of the oxen, now surplus to pulling requirements. Naturally, they would no longer be able to claim that they were the first wagon train to reach California, but by now survival was the issue. Equipment and supplies were unloaded and packed on to the backs of mules and oxen. Unused to loads, the oxen became skittish and bucked the packs off. A smug Cheyenne Dawson noted: 'Bidwell and Kelsey were to miss the wagons most, for their teams were oxen, and an ox is not easy to pack or to stay packed.'

Making better progress, the travellers passed some hot springs at the foot of Ruby Mountains on 21 September, crossed the mountains by Harrison Pass and came at last to Mary's River (later called the Humboldt) and followed its south fork northwards to the so-called Humboldt Sink. By now at least half the party was on foot, and the mounted portion seemed likely to diminish further, as some of the emigrants, craving tobacco, were prepared to trade their horses for the weed with the Shoshone. One by one they killed the oxen for food, and sometimes the hunters got an antelope, jackrabbits, wild duck and even coyotes, though all wildlife was hard to kill; on the south fork of the Humboldt, James John, an expert fisherman, caught a few trout. Occasionally they encountered Indians, smoked the peace pipe with them and bartered for food. The Shoshone liked to collect tule rushes from the banks of the Humboldt, extract the honey that covered the tule, and then wrap locusts, crickets and grasshoppers inside the honey, making a kind of primitive toffee apple. At first the emigrants relished this 'delicacy', but lost their appetites once they discovered the core component.

It was the Indian issue that first divided Bartleson and Bidwell, and caused notable bad blood between them. Earlier in the trip, they had encountered a war band of unidentified Indians (probably Ute or Paiute), ninety strong, who suddenly came upon their bivouac in the morning just as the emigrants were striking camp ready for the day's march. Bidwell wanted to send an armed guard out to keep the warriors at a distance until the wagon train was properly equipped and prepared, and the confusion of the morning's packing was over. Bartleson demurred, on the ground that the sight of armed defenders might provoke the braves. Bidwell and his faction ignored his advice and rode out, half a dozen strong, to confront the intruders. According to Bidwell, once the Indians saw the fully armed defenders, they ceased all thought of marauding; whereas if Bartleson's advice had been followed, the warriors would have realised that they had caught the overlanders on the hop and that there were easy pickings to be made. All that day the war party followed the wagon train at a respectful distance, making it clear they wanted to trade for guns and ammunition. Bartleson was inclined to humour them, but once again Bidwell berated him for naivety, speaking his mind freely on the subject of the captain's incompetence with Indians. Josiah Belden bore out Bidwell's account: he said that on the Humboldt they were often dogged by war parties and were in constant fear of attack.

Bartleson neither forgot nor forgave the insult. A little later, when Bidwell was out on one of the frequent round-ups of stray oxen, Bartleson ordered the wagon train to trek on, even though he had given his word that they would all wait for Bidwell's return. When two of the party turned aside to find Bidwell and bring him fresh water and food, Bartleson remarked sardonically that if they had such surplus energy they would be better employed scouting the trail ahead. When they reached the end of the South Fork of the Humboldt and turned abruptly west on the main river, Bartleson's men suggested abandoning the oxen, on the ground that they would soon be in California and among plentiful beef. Bidwell refused, pointing out that they were now doing well even with the oxen, covering eighteen to twenty miles a day, and that the beasts were the only assured source of fresh meat.

Bartleson responded by setting such a cracking pace for the caravan that Bidwell, lumbered with the oxen, could not keep up. Left behind in the wilds, Bidwell was forced to sleep out in the wilderness, without

84

supper or breakfast. A tough nine-mile march brought him up with the wagon train next day and, predictably, he was not in the best of humours. He found the party with their tongues hanging out, waiting for him to arrive with the oxen, for there was nothing else to eat. Bidwell gave Bartleson another verbal lashing, but the wily Bartleson took it on the chin and said nothing. An ox was slaughtered and the whole party dined well. Then Bartleson sent one of his cronies to ask if he could have the loan of another whole ox carcass until the hunters obtained more meat. Foolishly, generously, or both – Cheyenne Dawson recorded that Bidwell never charged hungry emigrants for the oxen they ate – Bidwell acquiesced. Having secured his food supply, Bartleson and his eight closest associates mounted up. Bartleson then revealed his true feelings: 'Now we have been found fault with long enough and are going to California. If you can keep up with us, all right; if you cannot, you may go to the devil.'

It was about two o'clock in the afternoon when Bartleson and his comrades swept out of the camp. Those who were left were understandably cast down, and some began to despair of seeing the promised land. Urgent voices were raised for a return to Fort Hall or Soda Springs; a vote was called for, and the decision to go on taken by just one vote. Bidwell followed gamely in the tracks of the deserters for a couple of days, then lost them in the sandy wastes of the Humboldt. This river, whether masquerading as the Swampy, Ogden's, St Mary's, or the name it finally adopted when in 1848 Frémont named it in honour of the explorer Baron Alexander von Humboldt, was universally detested by western travellers. Some called it the 'Humbug River' and commented bitterly on it as the meanest, muddiest, filthiest, stream imaginable, 'nothing but horse broth seasoned with alkali and salt', as one of them put it.

Feculent and forbidding as it was, the Humboldt provided a good western artery to Nevada and California. Unfortunately, it petered out in the Humboldt Sink, a marshy area where the Humboldt finally gave up the ghost in the middle of the desert. Had Bidwell known, there were no less than three passes through the Californian Sierra Nevada, about three days' march due west of the Sink: the Carson, Truckee and Lassen. He himself later blamed Bartleson for the error; he had, he said, been so intent on following the treacherous captain's tracks that he branched off south after the Humboldt Sink and rode south through the desert to the fast-flowing Walker River as it spumed out of the mountains. Mid-October found them on the west fork of the Walker, at the extreme eastern foot of the Sierras.

Bidwell sent two men ahead to see if the Sierras were passable, and meanwhile killed two more oxen in preparation for the ascent. On the evening of the 16th, the men returned, with news that the mountains, though steep, could be scaled. They were just eating their supper, with dusk coming on, when sentries brought word that a party of horsemen was approaching. Fearing Indian attack, they sprang to arms but were dumbfounded some half-hour later when Bartleson and his eight renegades rode dejectedly into camp. The nine-strong party had gone even further south and arrived at Carson Lake, where Indians fed them with fish and pine nuts. But the fish turned out to be contaminated, and the men were violently ill, suffering from what Bidwell called *cholera morbus*. Never a man to gloat over an enemy's misfortunes, Bidwell forgave the treacherous Bartleson and shared his meat. There was a quarter of a side of beef left, which was set before the ravenous returnees. Bartleson, previously a portly man, had by now lost half his body weight since May and declared vociferously: 'Boys, if ever I get back to Missouri, I will never leave that country. I would gladly eat out of the trough with my hogs.' Sadly, it was a case of 'the devil a monk', for as Bidwell noted sardonically: 'He seemed to be heartily sick of his late experiences, but that did not prevent him from leaving us twice after that.'

Daunted by the prospect of crossing the Sierra Nevada, the reunited party knew, however, they would die of starvation if they tried to retrace their steps. On 18 October, they started up the north bank of the Walker River among 'mountains whose summits still retained the snows perhaps of a thousand years'. They met an Indian who agreed to be their guide, but he led them along anfractuous mountain tracks, from which unsteady animals plunged over precipices, and finally abandoned them in a walled canyon. Grove Cook caught up with him on 27 October and shot him dead, thus notching up the first fatality in the enduring white–Indian duel on the overland trail. They lost four animals in the mountain passes and to save the rest had to hoist the mules up the sheer sides of the canyon, with four men pushing and another four pulling. But this was not the only aspect of the via dolorosa among the Sierras. On 22 October, they killed the last ox, and thenceforth existed on the flesh of horses and mules. The last two weeks of October saw them all close to starvation, so impatient to fill their bellies that they could not take the time to roast carcasses adequately, often tearing and ravening at blood-red meat.

Exhausted, they reached the summit somewhere near modern-day Sonora Pass and, descending on the far side, finally stumbled on a fast-flowing westward stream, the Stanislaus River, which they followed along twisting canyons, increasingly nervous now that the snows would soon be on them and death by starvation rather than merely rumbling stomachs would be their lot. Progress was slow, for they often had to leave the river bank and climb ridges to avoid getting into deep canyons that were blocked with immense boulders. Some of the men began hallucinating to the point where their genuine ordeal augmented in imagination and retrospect. Josiah Belden later claimed that he was famished with hunger for twenty-two days and lived on nothing but acorns for two weeks. The actual length of the ordeal by hunger was ten days, but the suffering was real enough. When all the mules and horses were eaten, they killed crows and even a wildcat.

On 29 October, their morale took another jolt when they saw looming ahead of them fold on fold of yet another mountain range; they assumed California lay beyond the peaks and that there was still another five hundred miles to go. The dauntless duo of Bidwell and John set out to scout ahead and learn the worst. After no more than three-quarters of a mile, Bidwell concluded that they had got into a box canyon and declared it was pointless to continue; John shrugged and said he was going on anyway, at which point he fired his gun as a signal for the rest of the party to come on. Bartleson and the others rode up, and spent the rest of the day in another nightmare of dead ends and beetling cliff walls, from which they were lucky to extract themselves. John, meanwhile, seemed to have disappeared, to general bafflement, for no one could work out how a solitary man could have got out of the canyon unaided.

Next morning, another two men set out to reconnoitre the way ahead. Andrew Kelsey and Thomas Jones were the men chosen. Bidwell, feeling humiliated that he had turned back when John, the bravest of the brave, had gone on, went off on another of his solitary reconnoitres. He was gone for more than twenty-four hours, once again spending a night in the wilderness. He followed an ancient trail and met many Indians who, though they did not molest him, seemed hostile in attitude. At dusk, he became the first white man to report seeing the giant sierra redwood, *Sequoia giganteum* (the broadest tree in the world, its cousin *Sequoia sempervirens*, the coastal redwood, being the tallest); some have thought he found the Calaveras Grove, but the best scholarship rules this out. Finding sleep impossible – for he either froze if he was too far from his fire or scorched if he tried to get closer – Bidwell endured a sleepless night. Next morning, he claimed to have come upon Indians at the camp which Bartleson had by now abandoned, eating horses which the dastardly captain had abandoned. Here, Bidwell undoubtedly enters the realm of fiction, for he elsewhere clearly states that all the horses were eaten before they reached the summit of the Sierra Nevada, and the Big

Trees, as is well known, are on the Californian side of the Sierra, not in Nevada. More soundly based is the story that when Bidwell caught up with the others, they had just finished eating a coyote and that he frenziedly devoured the lights and windpipe – all that was left of the butchered animal.

Trekking on, full of foreboding, the party finally came to a flat plain on 31 October. Without knowing it, they had reached the San Joaquin valley and safety. It seems they struck the plains not far from the later Knight's Ferry but at first found no grass or good drinking water. They reached the open plains about 10 p.m. and spent a night without fresh water, still uncertain where they were. Next morning, they made for a belt of timber and found themselves back on a loop of the Stanislaus. Suddenly, their luck turned. They found water and a spoor of deer, and soon the hunters had solved immediate food problems by killing thirteen deer and antelope. A passing Indian told them that Marsh's Fort was nearby, and on 4 November Jones and Kelsey returned from Marsh's, loaded with supplies, pack animals and Indian guides. The great Bidwell–Bartleson odyssey was over.

A little later, the thirty-three weary travellers traipsed into Marsh's ranch at the foot of Mount Diablo. What they found was a depressing anticlimax. Instead of the paradisical settlement portrayed by Marsh in his letters, they saw drought-stricken fields and a collection of rude adobe buildings. As Cheyenne Dawson wrote: 'We had expected to find civilization, with big fields, fine houses, churches, schools, etc. Instead, we found houses resembling unburnt brick kilns, with no floors, no chimneys, and with the openings for doors and windows closed by shutters instead of glass.' The travellers also found Marsh much meaner than the commanders of Fort Laramie and Fort Hall. He entertained them liberally the first night with pork, beef tortillas and a keg of mature *aguardiente*, but then presented them with a bill for five dollars each next morning. Grumbling over Marsh's 'nearness', the emigrants decided they could not afford another night of Marsh's 'hospitality' and dispersed at once in search of work and contacts.

For Bidwell, Marsh was but the first of a series of disillusionments. He found Mexican rule in California oppressive, but the authorities, mindful of the earlier 'stealth colonisation' of Texas by the gringos, were suspicious of 'Yankee' emigrants. There were only about one hundred white natives of the United States in California in 1841 and, as Bidwell put it, 'they were not generally a class calculated to gain much favour with the people'. Some were sailors who had deserted from US ships, while others were ex-trappers, trying to diversify now that the fur trade was dying. There was also a gang of American desperadoes who hovered around the frontier areas of the Mojave Desert, specialising in stealing horses from Mexican rancheros. But Bidwell, as he had proved already, was an enterprising character. He went to work for Sutter in 1844 and soon demonstrated a talent for land speculation. A premature rebel against the Mexican government in 1844, he was imprisoned but came to prominence after the revolt in 1846 and the Mexico–US war brought California under American hegemony. He struck it rich in the gold rush of 1849 and became the owner of the 22,000-acre Rancho Chico, spread north of Sacramento. Famous for his agricultural techniques, he entered politics, made another fortune through speculating in the transcontinental railroad, was a delegate to the convention that nominated Abraham Lincoln in 1860, served in the US Congress and even ran for president in 1892 on a prohibition ticket. He died at eighty in 1900.

As a source for the first major emigrant party to reach the Far West, Bidwell is invaluable but his animus towards Bartleson sometimes made him bend the facts, so that for the period after Soda Springs his version of events should always be checked against the other eyewitness accounts. As well as the story about Bartleson and the horses, even more absurdly, he claims that he uttered grave warnings about the thievery of California Indians in the San Joaquin valley, but that his warnings were twice ignored. On the first occasion, the Indians stole and roasted two horses belonging to an unnamed emigrant, and on the second, at the foot of Mount Diablo, Bartleson and his cronies flounced out, but were then attacked and had all their animals stolen. But since all the animals had allegedly been killed for meat in the dark last week of October when scaling the Sierra, how were such things possible?

Though they had failed to take wagons all the way to the Pacific from Missouri, the Bartleson–Bidwell party was the first company of emigrants to enter California overland. In the opinion of many scholars of the American West, it was the most talented bunch of individuals ever found in one wagon train. Of the thirty-four who arrived (for James John found his way to Sutter's Fort and met up with Bidwell early in the new year), about a dozen returned to the east, and a dozen others faded into historical obscurity. Chiles and Hopper had further adventures on the California Trail and died in the Golden State after long and conventionally successful lives. But others made serious money. Robert Thomes became the proprietor of the huge Tehama Ranch in Tehama County. Charles Weber made a fortune and founded the city of Stockton, and Josiah Belden, the first mayor of San Jose, was another who became extremely wealthy.

As the first woman to cross from Missouri to California, Nancy Kelsey has naturally attracted a lot of attention. Cheyenne Dawson paints a memorable picture of a stoical barefooted woman grimly ascending the mountains, with her one-year-old in her arms. She had all the legendary toughness of the pioneer woman and died at seventy-two in 1895, after a roving life with her husband on the frontier that took them from California to Oregon and thence to Texas. Her husband Benjamin was an Indian-hater, so there is perhaps an element of hubris and nemesis in the story that one of the later Kelsey children was scalped by the Comanches in Texas in 1861. This was not Anne, who, after being the first American child to cross the Sierra Nevada, presumably died young (infant mortality was a habitual fact of life in the nineteenth century), since we hear of her no more. The black reputation of the Kelseys was enhanced by Andrew, who reduced the Indians working for him on his ranch near Clear Lake to virtual peonage, and was then murdered by them in 1849.

Cheyenne Dawson, who died in 1903, aged eighty-three, is the last known survivor of the Bartleson–Bidwell party of 1841. But the palm for most amazing story must go to a man he observed minutely on the trail: Talbot Green. Dawson, obsessed (after his experience with the Cheyenne) with the danger from Indian attack, noted that in the latter stages of the journey his fellow emigrants began caching their possessions in hiding places along the trail, but they stopped when they saw an Indian watching them and realised that he would simply unearth their possessions once they had moved on. It was therefore not until they had got into the San Joaquin valley that Green, aided by Cook, finally cached his mysterious chunk of lead.

Soon after the parting of the ways at Marsh's, Green and Cook returned to the secret stash and removed the 'lead'. Immediately, Cook and Green began to cut a dash in the streets of San Francisco, and Green soon became one of the city's most respected businessmen. By 1851, married and a solid citizen of the growing city by the Golden Gate, Green put himself forward as candidate for mayor and seemed likely to sweep the board. Suddenly, he was denounced as an impostor and embezzler. His real name, it was alleged, was Paul Geddes, who had been a humble bank clerk back East before decamping with the bank's money, abandoning a wife and children. Green pulled out of the election and took ship for the East, vowing to clear his name and return. Large numbers of his supporters accompanied him to the dockside to show their contempt for the 'lies' told about their man. Green/Geddes was never seen again. The 'lead' which had so intrigued Dawson was obviously the bullion with which Green had absconded for the West.

Possibly even more villainous than Kelsey and Green was the latter's one-time partner, Grove C. Cook. He already had the murder of one Indian to his score and added to it in 1844 when he murdered Elijah Hedding, an educated Oregon Indian who had come to Sutter's Fort to trade horses and mules for cattle to be driven north. With a black reputation already, in December 1845 Cook married Rebecca Kelsey who, as one memorialist put it, 'presently had some reason to regret it'. In 1846, Cook settled at San Jose, took a minor part in the US military operations that year against Mexican California, then struck it rich in the gold rush of 1849. Within two years he had lost the lot and died in 1852 a broken man. If Bidwell was the angel of light on the 1841 overland journey, Cook was the imp of darkness. Hubert Howe Bancroft's classic description of Cook is a masterpiece of understatement: 'a man whose wit and generosity went far to counterbalance some less desirable qualities.'

The year 1841 marked a breakthrough in Western history. True, no one had yet managed to take wagons from Missouri clear to the Pacific, but the Bidwell–Bartleson adventure was a genuine milestone. Some scholars would even rate it as *the* most significant event in the history of the world that year. Elsewhere, processes were set in train which would have their dénouement the following year or in the long-term, and there were incidents that formed a coda to dramas enacted in previous years. The British in Afghanistan, the Treaty of Waitangui in New Zealand, the Straits Convention on Turkish sovereignty in the Bosphorus and Dardanelles are examples of the former; the formal ending of the Opium War in China illustrates the latter. But nowhere else is there discernible the beginning of a causal chain that would change national destinies almost overnight. On calm reflection, the Beards' description of Bidwell as a new Columbus does not seem so far-fetched, after all.

FOUR

THE WOMAN IN THE SUNBONNET

The year 1842 was a blank one for wagon-train emigration to California. But the restless Joseph Chiles was determined that others would follow where he had blazed trail. While Bidwell and most of the other veterans of '41 dispersed to new careers in California, Chiles and a dozen men rendezvoused at Sutter's Fort in April 1842 for a return trip to Missouri. Among those who foregathered were Bartleson, Hopper and Springer. Departure was delayed when Hopper went down with typhoid, but the dauntless Chiles simply rigged up a litter strung between two mules, one ahead, one behind. Joltingly, the more dead than alive Hopper followed his comrades thus to Tejon Pass, seventy miles from the sleepy Spanish town of Los Angeles. From there, they struck into the desert with inadequate water. Hopper claimed to have seen the exact whereabouts of a spring in a dream, guided the party to the location, and there, miraculously, was the waterhole as promised.

Having survived the desert, they swung north along the eastern side of the Sierra Nevada, picked up familiar landmarks to the Humboldt Sink, then followed the Humboldt River to Fort Hall. Having suffered for 1,500 gruelling miles, four men left the party here, but the other nine pressed on east to the Green River. Here, learning that the Sioux were on the warpath, they swung sharply south by south-east to Santa Fe, picking up the Old Spanish Trail in the latter stages. Hopper again saved the party near Santa Fe when they ran into a band of marauding Mescalero Apaches, but the details of this encounter are obscure. From Santa Fe, they followed the regular Santa Fe Trail to Missouri, reached on 9 September. Chiles and his comrades had completed a little-known odyssey of 4,000 miles, following two sides of a triangle from Los Angeles to Fort Hall and Santa Fe instead of the direct route along the Old Spanish Trail. They had travelled through California, Nevada, Utah, Idaho, Wyoming, Colorado, New Mexico, Kansas and Missouri. It was a

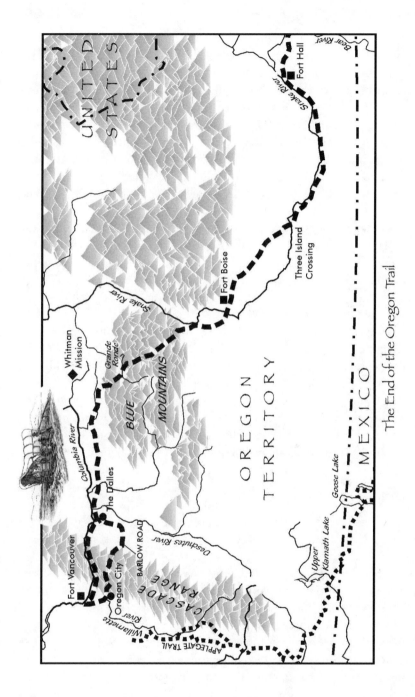

The End of the Oregon Trail

great journey, and it taught Chiles a lot, but strictly speaking it did not immediately advance emigration to California one jot.

In 1842, the emigrant interest shifted from California to Oregon, and the man largely responsible for the change was a Methodist missionary named Elijah White, described as being of light complexion, blue eyes, dark hair and an 'elastic frame'. A native of New York State, the thirty-seven-year-old White had trained as a physician and in 1837 sailed from Boston around Cape Horn to reinforce the Methodist mission in the Willamette valley headed by Jason Lee, a legendarily energetic convert. Six-foot-three, the black-bearded, powerfully built former backwoods farmer Lee was in many respects the David Livingstone of the West, in that his initial missionary impulse was gradually abandoned in the search for fame and fortune. In 1840, Elijah White quarrelled with Lee and returned east on board ship. It should not be assumed that White's quarrel with Lee was ideological or religious, for the good Dr White has been described as 'fussy . . . self-important . . . quarrelsome . . . a pompous little busybody'.

In Washington, White insinuated his way into the circles led by Senator Lewis Linn of Missouri, who was campaigning vigorously for the extension of US sovereignty over the Oregon territory, even if this meant war with Great Britain. Since few people in Washington possessed first-hand knowledge of Oregon, White was offered the post of subagent for the Oregon Indians at half salary, with the promise of a full agency and a full salary if Congress passed a bill for the occupation of Oregon. He was also authorised to promote 'Oregon fever' by using the government's secret service fund to subsidise and finance the western movement of emigrants: the slush funds were supposed to cover the costs of newspaper advertisements puffing Oregon and the cost of any guides or pilots needed to take the emigrants to the promised land. White saw the chance to turn himself into a kind of American viceroy in Oregon and jumped at it.

White made his way from the east coast to Independence in a leisurely fashion, all the time speechifying and making grandiose promises of what lay ahead in the promised land of Oregon for those brave enough to accompany him into the wilderness. He stressed the equable climate, the plentiful land, the market forces that meant any worthwhile entrepreneur could make a fortune. At the end of each of his talks, men would come to him and promise to emigrate, though many stressed that it would be 1843 before they were ready to leave, as they needed time to sell their farms. Even so, he extracted five hundred firm promises to meet him at the rendezvous point near Independence. From St Louis onwards, White began to gather around him the nucleus of what he imagined would be 'his' team. His first 'signing', using the secret service money, was the noted mountain man and guide Andrew Sublette. But Sublette soon discerned the dark side of the 1842 emigration: nobody was prepared to take orders and everyone wanted to command. Even the experience of trying to maintain discipline among the two dozen or so emigrants who accompanied White from St Louis to the rendezvous point at Elm Grove was too much for Sublette; he quit in disgust once the caravan reached Independence.

Once at the inaptly named Elm Grove (only a handful of elms were still standing), twenty-five miles south-west of Independence, White surveyed his fellow-travellers. By 15 May, more than a hundred had assembled, though exact statistics are hard to come by: each eyewitness account gives a different figure, largely because each diarist counted the party at a different time, taking no account of how many had already turned back and how many had joined en route. White claimed that 112 persons in eighteen wagons were in the party at the start, but that later recruits swelled the numbers to 125. Frémont, who crossed the tracks of the pioneers on a number of occasions, said there were sixteen to seventeen families, sixty-four males and a wealth of cattle and household furniture. Later, more careful estimates fined down the numbers to sixteen wagons, 105 persons all told, with fifty-one males aged over eighteen – the effective fighting strength of the wagon train.

The first business of the caravan was the election of officers. The 1842 wagon train started the way it meant to go on by evincing a high degree of turbulence and rancour during the voting on 15 May. Elijah White had confidently expected to be elected captain of the expedition but, to his great irritation, he found himself opposed by a self-publicist even more talented and unscrupulous than himself: the twenty-four-year-old Lansford Hastings, an ambitious control freak from Ohio, whose glib tongue would later make him notorious. Hastings was what Disraeli would have called 'spendaciously mendacious'; his cavalier way with the truth is evident on the very first page of his self-serving *Emigrants' Guide to Oregon and California*, where he confidently asserts that the wagon train on 15 May consisted of 160 persons, eighty of them armed men. White had always considered that he had a winning personality: it was said of him that he had manners 'of that obliging and flattering kind which made him popular, especially among women, but which men often called sycophantic or insincere'. Yet even so, the plausible rogue Hastings outpointed him in the personal popularity stakes; it was only his knowledge of Oregon and the prestige of his role as government subagent that enabled him to win the ballot against Hastings. Nevertheless, the crafty voters decided they would give no man a blank cheque for the whole journey but would hold fresh elections each month, when incumbents would have to reapply to the electors for their position.

The other appointments shed some light on the personnel of this expedition. One James Coates, of whom little is known, was chosen as guide on the strength of having once travelled as far west as the Green River. Hastings and two other men, Columbia Lancaster and Asa L. Lovejoy, constituted the so-called 'scientific corps'; Nathaniel Crocker served as secretary, Hugh Burns as official blacksmith and John Hoffstutter as master wagon-maker. Travelling with White and in his charge were two half-Chinook youths, John Alexander McKay and Alexander McKay, sons of the former Hudson Bay Company's employee Thomas McKay, himself a quarter-Cree and formerly an employee of the Astoria Fur Company. Though McKay himself never rose very high in the Hudson's Bay Company and became an independent trader in Oregon in 1834, his sons had apparently been targeted by Jason Lee as 'ones to note'. These boys had travelled the Oregon Trail in 1838 with missionaries, on their way to mission school in the east, and were now returning. Also with White was the most reliable diarist of the 1842 emigration, Medorem Crawford, whom White had recruited in New York City.

There are many on the 1842 wagon train, of whom we know the names but little else. In this category come three people named Smith, one of whom had a bevy of shapely daughters whose beauty featured in the story of the caravan. Another attractive woman was the widow Hannah Abel, travelling with her baby girl in a wagon owned by one W.T. Perry. Also along on the journey was Sidney Walter Moss, later a hotelier in Oregon City, who claimed to be the author of the first Oregon novel, *The Prairie Flower*. Two of the better known recruits, and valuable for their backwoods experience, were the twenty-seven-year-old Eldridge Trask and his great friend Osbourne Russell. They were expert trappers and knew the beaver lodges along the Snake River as intimately as Elijah White knew the smoke-filled rooms of Washington.

Potentially White's most valuable recruit was the mountain man Stephen Meek, who joined the expedition on 17 May. Now thirty-seven, Meek had experience with William Sublette and Joseph Walker as well as his more famous younger brother Joseph Meek. Meek would not have been eligible to succeed James Coates as pilot until the elections due on 15 June, but in any case it is unlikely that he would have suited a man of Elijah White's temperament. Stephen Meek had a dark reputation at this time, as a result of having spent two years as assistant to the notorious Belfast-born scalp-hunter James Kirker. Operating from a ranch in Chihuahua, Arizona, Kirker and Meek had hunted Apaches for their scalps and, not surprisingly, had been involved in several dangerous skirmishes with the Chiricahuahua and other Apache clans. Nevertheless, Meek's importance did apparently increase as the wagon train of 1842 went further west.

The martinet Elijah White got backs up immediately when he produced a code of caravan laws almost as complex as the Constitution itself, though admittedly the code was drawn up with the agreement of the 'elders' in the wagon train. Every male over eighteen was to have a horse, mule or ox, a gun, three pounds of powder, twelve pounds of lead, one thousand caps or suitable flints, fifty pounds of flour or meal, and thirty pounds of bacon, with suitable proportions of the same for women and children. The 'scientific corps' was to keep a record of everything concerning the road and the journey that might be useful to the government or future emigrants. A further code of laws would be drafted and submitted to the company, which would be enforced by reprimand, fines or, at the limit, banishment. Grounds for expulsion from the wagon train would be committing anything defined by the party as a crime, indulging in lewd or immoral conduct and even obscene conversation or profane swearing. The names of every man, woman and child on the expedition would be recorded by the secretary. The code ended with a formal adjournment and the wish expressed that the committee would not need to meet again until 'Fort Vancouver, on the Columbia River, on the first day of October next, the powers of Heaven willing'.

White was well pleased with himself and in upbeat mood as the wagon train moved out. As he reported it to his biographer later:

A noble sight. The eighteen wagons with their snow white coverings, winding down the long hill, followed by the immense train of horses, mules and cattle of all kind, their drivers walking by their sides, merrily singing or whistling, to beguile their way. As Dr White stood on an elevation, he cast his eyes forward towards the wastes and wilds of the savage world they were to traverse, and back to his own loved, pleasant land, and it need not be enquired whether his reflections were of a very joyous nature.

Lansford Hastings, who knew the mood of the emigrants rather better, still allowed himself an effusion of bogus Panglossianism:

Now all was high glee, jocular hilarity, and happy anticipation, as we

97

thus darted forward into the wild expanse, of the untrodden regions of the 'western world.' The harmony of feeling, the sameness of purpose, and the identity of interest, which here existed, seemed to indicate nothing but continued order, harmony, and peace, amid all the trying scenes incident to our long and toilsome journey.

Hastings shifted gear towards the truth when he later admitted to the presence of a serpent in this paradise, namely, as he put it: 'The American character was fully exhibited. All appeared to be determined to govern but not to be governed.' On the first day out, the meddlesome White convened a jury to try a man on the charge of having stolen a horse from the Kansa Indians. His henchmen bitterly denounced the culprit, for putting at risk relations with the Kansa, on whose goodwill they depended during the initial stages of the trek. But a hardline 'libertarian' faction at once made strenuous representations for the defence, alleging that stealing horses from Indians was neither a crime nor any kind of evil action and, further, that as this action was not expressly forbidden in White's code – the only set of laws governing them, situated as they were in the 'state of nature' – all charges should be dismissed. The matter was referred to the jurymen, who had no hesitation in finding the horse-stealer not guilty, by unanimous vote.

A wise man would have read the runes and opted for minimalist government thereafter. But White, smarting from the rebuff, wasted no time in returning to the fray. On 18 May, just three days after departure from Elm Grove, he produced a draconian decree that had the caravan in uproar and which further hardened the division between factions. It is said that it is the English who spell God backwards, but the overlanders too seemed to cherish their dogs just this side of idolatry. Household pets were one thing: they were valuable for hunting and herding and as watchdogs. But most wagon trains were followed by packs of scavenging curs, who fought, snarled and snapped the livelong day, annoying the cattle and horses, while by night they disturbed sleep and frayed tempers with their incessant yapping and howling. Even worse, their barking encouraged coyotes to join in the midnight cacophony, and it was said that one coyote could make as much noise as five domestic dogs.

In an evil hour, White took it into his head that the problem of dogs could be cured by extermination. He exhorted the company to take drastic action, after highlighting a threefold problem. In the first place, they would soon be worn out from lack of sleep, since the barking dogs encouraged their wild cousins, the coyotes, to come out in sympathy and five hundred howling prairie wolves would create an ear-splitting bedlam.

Second, the barking of the dogs would alert any Indian war party within earshot that here was a defenceless wagon train ready for the plundering. Third, as they approached the arid plains and the pariah dogs among the caravan's canines got hungrier, they were likely to turn savage, go mad and infect the emigrants with the dreaded and incurable rabies. In vain did the libertarian faction protest that the Indian argument was two-edged: dogs could just as well warn the overlanders of the approach of otherwise undetectable hostile Indian bands. After vociferous and acrimonious discussion, when feelings ran high, especially among the women, who regarded White as no better than a murderer, White obtained a majority vote to implement the slaughter of all dogs.

White describes the sequel:

> While the destruction was going on, the poor creatures would run to their mistresses for protection, crying most piteously. Even the men, while engaged in their task, found their hearts were not sufficiently steeled to permit its performance without feelings of sorrow and regret. However, the recollection of a freshly related account of the mad wolf which had bitten eleven men in two encampments, strengthened their fortitude. The death of the dogs was preferred to those of their herds, and perhaps members of their families, and they went resolutely about the work, amid the cries and screams of the women and children, as well as of the victims.

It is just possible, however, that White did not have matters entirely his own way. Hastings, always an unreliable source, claims that violence escalated once the dog-killing commenced. Faced with threats that the dog owners would resist seizure of their animals, the execution squad went about fully armed. According to Hastings, the hardline owners threatened that they would shoot dead anyone who tried to kill their dogs; faced with the likelihood of civil war in the caravan, White backed down, called another meeting and annulled the anti-dog decree. We know for certain that White's executioners made serious inroads on the canine population, for Medorem Crawford, the best source for the 1842 emigration, noted in his laconic and throwaway fashion: 'May 18. A violent rain this morning. much excitement in camp about Dogs: 22 dogs shot. stopped raining at one o'c.' It may be, then, that the mendacious Hastings reported what he would like to have happened rather than what actually did; alternatively, it may be that the number of dogs in the camp was greater than twenty-two, and that threats of armed opposition made White call off his killers after they had attained that tally.

In sombre mood, the travellers trekked on to the Kansas River, slogging through heavy rains, which increased the discomfort, gloom, uncertainty and apprehension of the emigrants. Three days after the dog-killing, death of a more depressing kind struck when the Lancasters' sixteen-month-old daughter died; she had the dubious distinction of being the first white child to perish on the overland trail. White pronounced the unhelpful diagnosis of 'symptomatick fever accompanied with worms'. Having buried the little girl, they forded the engorged Kansas River with the help of the Kansa Indian ferrymen, all the time battling with continued heavy rains. They made good progress on the far side, where they shifted the direction of the march from west to north-west. On 22 May, they clocked up twenty-five miles, on the 24th another ten and by the 26th they were at Vermillion Creek, close to where the Black Vermillion flows into the Big Blue.

Here the grief-stricken Mrs Lancaster decided she could stand it no longer; she kept thinking of her daughter's lonely grave and insisted that her husband take her back. Playing for time and hoping his distraught wife might come to her senses. Columbia Lancaster announced to the wagon train that his wife was sick and begged them to wait until she was better again. Some refused forthwith and pressed on, but most agreed to wait until Mrs Lancaster was better. But her grief did not slacken nor her mood improve. Finally, on 30 May, Lancaster realised he could stall no longer and agreed to return with his wife to Missouri. Dr White accompanied them back to the Kansas, then rode hard to catch up with the company, who set a blistering pace to reach the Big Blue on the evening of 31 May.

Thereafter, they made steady progress towards the Platte, first to the junction of the Little Blue and Big Sandy Creek. They had many streams still to cross, swollen with the spring rains, but apart from that the journey tended towards monotony, with the beauties of emerald-green grass and abundant wild flowers a partial palliative. Usually this was not a good area for wildlife, with the occasional white-bobbed antelope the only creature making an appearance, but the travellers in 1842 found it a cornucopia of living things: deer, elk, rabbit, hare and wildfowl. This was Pawnee country, but smallpox had decimated them and few Indians were seen. The main enemy was the rain, still monsoon-like in its insistence. White continued to post sentinels to guard against Pawnee depredation – this was likely to take the form of petty theft rather than armed attack – but sentry-go was extremely unpopular on the march to the Platte, for it meant being drenched by heavy rains and buffeted by strong winds.

By now, life on the trail had settled into a routine. At first light, the shouts of the sentries drew bleary-eyed men and women from tents and wagons to start the day's chores: rounding up the cows that had been left to graze on the nearby prairie and bringing them in ready for the march; collecting buffalo chips (dung) and starting fires; cooking breakfasts, stowing away blankets, striking camp, yoking oxen. At 7 a.m., the bugle sounded the advance. The wagoners walked beside their teams, giving an occasional flick of the whip, while the women and children broke off from the column to pick wild flowers. Ahead of them, the pilot planted a flag at each stream, indicating the best places for fording. There would be a break, preferably by a stream, at noon when a light meal was taken – very quickly, so that it was not worth unyoking the oxen. Already the travellers were tired, and perhaps most of all the drovers at the rear, herding the cattle and driving the spare horses before them.

The afternoon was a sleepy time. Women and children would usually take the opportunity for a nap in the wagons, drivers seemed to nod off as they walked like automata, and some said the oxen seemed to doze as they plodded. As night came on, they would reach the campsite – wherever the pilot had marked a large circle on the ground. A circular barricade or laager was now formed, against possible Indian attacks. Outside the wagons they pitched their tents, and then in the outer perimeter beyond this they made fires. Within the inner corral of wagons the precious horses and mules were placed. Since there was no room for the cattle inside the corral, and as Indians were reputed not to be interested in stealing cattle, they were turned loose on the plains; the drovers always hoped that, come morning, they would not have been stampeded by lightning storms or 'spooked' by a buffalo herd. Meanwhile, children gathered buffalo chips while the women prepared the evening meal – typically salt meat, fresh-baked bread and black coffee. The period after dinner was the best part of the day. This was the time when men spun yarns with gusto around the campfires, the young men and women carried on furtive courtship, and decisions were made at full meeting.

Inevitably, the greatest concern of the emigrants centred on food, and the heaviest loads on the wagons consisted of water and provisions. Lansford Hastings recommended that each emigrant take two hundred pounds of flour, 150 pounds of bacon, ten pounds of coffee, twenty pounds of sugar and ten pounds of salt. T.H. Jefferson, who published a trail guide called *Brief Practical Advice*, stressed the importance of bread as a staple and recommended two hundred pounds of flour per adult: 'Take plenty of bread stuff; this is the staff of life when everything else runs short.' The staff of life was often carried as crackers or hard tack, with Southerners tending to opt for corn meal or pinole rather than wheat flour. Because of the difficulties of boiling water, rice and beans were little used, except at the forts where the caravans made stopovers and fuel was abundant. The other main staple of the overlanders was bacon, which covered cuts of meat we would nowadays construe as pork, was cheap and readily available, but suffered the disadvantage that it became rancid in extreme heat. Salt, coffee, sugar and dried fruit were also considered essentials of life on the trail.

Most families tended to carry a small store of luxury goods – tea, maple sugar, vinegar, pickles, smoked beef – but only aristocratic or upper-class travellers in the West used the canned goods that were rapidly coming into use, though still at the experimental stage in the years before the Civil War; nonetheless, there are occasional mentions in the sources of tins of oysters, sardines, meat, cheese and fruit. A few pioneers seem to have carried eggs and butter packed in barrels of flour and some brought dairy cows along. The overlanders also supplemented their diet by hunting, most notably buffalo, but also antelope, deer, mountain sheep, wildfowl, trout, freshwater lobster, catfish and wild berries. In desperate times and when faced with starvation, travellers would slaughter their oxen, mules and horses, and when they ran out, would eat anything: coyote, fox, the usually unpopular jackrabbit, prairie dogs, marmots and even rattlesnakes, which later emigrants called 'bush fish'.

Kegs of water were an important item, but alcohol was rarely used on the trail; drunkenness was a feature only of the stopovers at the forts and trading posts. Whisky was carried for medicinal purposes – it was thought useful in cases of snakebite – and especially as a pick-me-up after being drenched by violent thunderstorms or turbulent river crossings, for special celebrations such as the Fourth of July, and to trade with Indians and trappers at the forts. If there was something sad about the overlanders' touching belief that whisky could ward off cholera or purify brackish water, their abstemiousness on the trail was commendable, for there are almost no cases of inebriation 'on the road'. The fact that large numbers of emigrants were teetotal or members of temperance societies is significant; some of these would not allow a drop of alcohol to pass their lips even if dying.

Food, though, was another matter, for to set a good table was a value highly prized in emigrant and farming culture; it must be remembered too that most overlanders were 'middling' people, far from destitute. It was a matter of pride for pioneer women to bake good bread, even though it was difficult to operate Dutch ovens or even knead dough in prairie conditions. Some of the more skilled even managed to produce succulent pies, using raisins, peaches and dried apples. A later California emigrant described his daily menu: 'For breakfast, coffee, bacon, dry or pilot bread: for dinner, coffee, cold beans, bacon or buffalo meat; for supper, tea, boiled rice and dried beef or codfish . . . our appetites are good, our digestive organs strong, our sleep sweet.' Another overlander, invited to supper in a friend's tent near Fort Laramie, noted a menu of hot biscuit, fresh butter, honey, rich milk, cream, venison steak with green peas gathered that day from wild vines along the trail, tea and coffee. It is not surprising, especially given the numbers of gooseberries, chokeberries and serviceberries collected, especially along the Platte, that scurvy was not (except for the 1847 Mormons) a plague that normally assailed the emigrants.

The skill of the pioneer women in preparing meals was even more remarkable given the difficulty of heating food on the prairie and the shortage of fuel. Sometimes wood from cedar, willow or cottonwood would be available, and occasionally dry prairie grass, but for the most part emigrant fires were fuelled by the dried buffalo dung euphemistically called 'buffalo chips'. When dry, it resembled rotten wood and would make a clear, hot fire, but its drawback was that it burned very rapidly, so that it took up to three bushels of chips to heat a meal and left a great pile of ash behind. In the early days, the women, especially, found the chips repulsive, but they soon came to appreciate their value. Collecting chips for the fire was one chore to which children could usefully be set; memoirs written by those who were very young when they made the journey west invariably refer to this aspect of life on the trail.

Enjoying mainly good weather, the 1842 wagon train pushed on steadily towards the Platte, always heading north-west, to Big Sandy Creek and then along the northern bank of the Little Blue; on 9 June they completed in one day the twenty-five-mile stretch between the Little Blue and the Platte. Once on to the Platte, the women demanded a day's rest to catch up with laundry, arguing that there was no guarantee they would find the present combination of good water and dry weather further ahead. It was agreed that the halt would be made on 15 June, the day Elijah White's one-month stewardship expired, so that new elections for principal officers could be held. Hastings was jubilant, confident that this time his challenge would succeed; White had lost caste enormously after the dog incident and by his general autocratic demeanour. Sure enough, in the elections of 15 June White was decisively rebuffed. Hastings was elected as the new captain, with Lovejoy as his deputy.

White did not accept his demotion meekly, but instead headed a breakaway faction; thereafter, until Fort Laramie, two sections of the wagon train travelled apart, separated by a few miles of trail, with White's smaller party going ahead. In the wilds of Nebraska, he allowed himself a typical self-pitying aside: 'I am now in Indian country with foes on every hand, subtle as the devil himself.' The divided wagon train was now moving at great speed, since it was a point of honour for White to keep ahead of Hastings, while Hastings for his part strained every muscle to try to overtake the smaller party in the van. Hastings set such a cracking pace that Medorem Crawford complained his haste was counter-productive, since the animals began to suffer: 'cattle's feet very sore. travelled slow' was a typically laconic diary entry.

Since the Platte valley was *the* place for buffalo along the Oregon Trail, not surprisingly both the White and the Hastings parties sent out their hunters to get fresh meat for the travelling larders. But the caravans were notably deficient in men with real experience in this difficult art of mounted slaughter, with possibly only Meek, Trask and Russell as assured veterans. Predictably, then, the greenhorn nimrods generated more noise than kills. The other problem about emigrant buffalo-hunting was that usually the men had to ride long distances from the wagon train to find their prey. Inevitably, then, even if they managed to kill one of the furry leviathans, they could not haul the entire carcass back to the caravan, but were reduced to cutting off the choice portions – tongue, ribs and hump – leaving the rest to rot or for wolves to find and devour. And great appreciation was not necessarily shown for the hunters' labours, for opinions differed on the worth of buffalo meat. The mountain man Charles Larpenteur, who claimed to have lived exclusively on bison steaks in the 1830s, said that it was tougher than whalebone. Other travellers found it unchewable. The usual opinion was that it was palatable only if jerked, dried, cut into small strips and roasted over a fire.

White's party experienced a further problem when buffalo-hunting along the Platte. While eighteen-year-old Phil Bennett was out hunting, his mother suddenly took it into her head that her son was in mortal danger and became hysterical. A giant of a woman, she alarmed the company by running through the camp, ululating, tearing her hair and wringing her hands. 'Oh, my Philly is dead! My Philly is dead!' she shrieked. 'Turn out, men, turn out!' In vain did they try to calm her, and there is no knowing how matters would have ended had not her boy suddenly come into camp with a hunk of meat on his shoulder. White commented: 'It affected all her hearers rather comically though they sympathised with the distracted woman; for her agony, though drolly acted, was terrible.'

Since 1842 was a drought year, the wagon train did not experience the usual problems with swollen streams and flooded fords and so made good progress along the Platte towards Fort Laramie. The only serious obstacle was at the always formidable South Fork, where the emigrants had to endure a three-quarter-mile crossing through boisterous, boiling waters. They chained the horses and wagons together, six or eight teams at a time, and forced them through the seething foam, having to shout and bellow at their charges through the din of the roaring waters. Once on to the North Platte, it was smooth progress again. White ticked off the landmarks in easy progression: Court House Rock, Chimney Rock, Scotts Bluff. They arrived at Fort Laramie on 23 June. Nothing so far on this trip justified the hyperbole with which one historian sought to characterise the usual condition of emigrants on arrival at the fort: 'The emigrants commonly arrived at their destination destitute, naked, starving and dispirited, with their nerves frayed to breaking point.'

In 1842, trading competition was stiff between Fort Laramie, at the junction of the North Platte and Laramie rivers, and Fort Platte, just two miles away on the banks of the North Platte. Both were adobe-walled, Laramie Fort being the property of the American Fur Company, aka Pierre Chouteau, Jr & Co., which had extensive interests in the Far West, and Fort Platte being part of the commercial empire of Sybille Adams & Co. In charge at Fort Laramie was the mountain man James Bordeaux, while almost within a stone's throw, in command at Platte, was the perhaps even more renowned frontiersman Joseph Bissonette. Both men had reputations 'as none too scrupulous' fur traders: Bissonette had taken a Sioux wife, spoke the language fluently, and traded with the Lakota for buffalo robes, sometimes using alcohol for the purpose; Bordeaux, a veteran fur trader, had married a Sioux, his first (Arikara) wife having left him. Throughout the 1840s the men were bitter trade rivals, but in the 1850s, after the two forts were sold to the US government, the two men joined forces and set up a trading post, Fort Bernard, eight miles away. Medorem Crawford noted in his diary that about twenty-five to thirty men were employed by Bordeaux and about fifteen to twenty by Bissonette.

The natural tendency was for the White faction to gravitate to one of the forts, while the Hastings party bivouacked at the other. But Bissonette told White that the Sioux were in an ugly mood after the bruising encounter with Henry Fraeb the previous August (see page 75) and were contemplating revenge against the next sizeable party of whites. Bordeaux and other trappers at the fort confirmed the rumour to Hastings when he and his footsore party came in a couple of days later. Dr White therefore thought it best to make soothing overtures to Hastings and the main party when they arrived. Hastings and his men played hard to get and consented only reluctantly to a reunion of the factions. In typically self-serving style, not mentioning the obvious prudential factor, Hastings wrote that he had acted magnanimously in burying the hatchet with White for 'in view of the fact, that they must either travel with us, remain at these forts, or return to the States, they were permitted to join us again'.

The combined wagon train spent a week at the two forts, making careful preparation for the rigours ahead. They rested, bought food and supplies and traded exhausted animals, always at exorbitant prices. The mountain men at the forts were adamant that wagons could not get through to Oregon, so many dejected emigrants exchanged oxen and wagons for horses or cut down the worst of the wagons into carts. Others, seeing the raw and bleeding feet of their cattle, concluded that they could go on no farther and traded them in. The more hard-hearted, cynical or optimistic held on to their beasts and were rewarded for their blind faith by discovering that the cows' hooves hardened and grew another layer of skin, allowing even previously exhausted cattle to make a full recovery. Although the leaders of the expedition praised Bissonette and Bordeaux for the warm welcome they had given the caravan, the rank-and-file emigrants complained vociferously about the high prices charged at the forts: a dollar a pint for flour at Fort Platte and a dollar a pound for coffee and sugar at Fort Laramie were the going rates.

Two of the most famous names in Western history endorsed the emigrants' complaints about profiteering at the forts. Frémont, who arrived in July 1842 in the wake of the White–Hastings expedition, reported of the overlanders: 'They disposed of their wagons and cattle at the fort, selling them at the prices they had paid in the States, and taking in exchange coffee and sugar at one dollar a pound and miserable, worn-out horses which died before they reached the mountains. Mr Boudeau [sic] informed me that he had purchased 30 and the lower fort 80 head of fine cattle, some of them of the Durham breed.' By 1846, Francis Parkman reported that inflation and money-grubbing at the forts were seriously out of hand and said of the emigrants: 'They were plundered and cheated without mercy. In one bargain, concluded in my presence, I calculated the profits that accrued to the fort, and found that at the lowest estimate they exceeded *eighteen hundred per cent.*'

Among the handful of unemployed trappers who joined the caravan at Fort Laramie was the twenty-four-year-old French Canadian, François Xavier Matthieu, who left a valuable memoir of the journey. Born in Terrebonne near Montreal, Matthieu had been in service with the American Fur Company, where he developed a reputation as a tough bargainer: on one occasion he bought ten buffalo robes worth ten dollars each for a single-gallon jar of diluted whisky. Already a veteran of the American North-West, who could count Kit Carson, George Bent and Joseph Meek among his friends and acquaintances, Matthieu was a shrewd observer of his fellow man (and woman). He tells us, as none of the other diarists do, that among the party was an elderly woman and her daughter, both of whom had at one time been captives among the Comanche. And his pen portraits are incisive: White was 'a sleek-looking gentleman . . . a quick talker'; Amos Lovejoy, a cross-grained individual, 'more quick-tempered than any man I ever knew'; while he described Hastings as a man of heavy build and swarthy complexion.

Matthieu and his trapper friends went supperless the first night out from Fort Laramie. Furthermore, they were condemned to the torture of having their senses assailed by savoury cooking smells. As Matthieu wrote: 'They could not but look on with a little envy and self-commiseration at the various campfires where the emigrants were despatching fried bacon and mountain biscuit and drinking coffee.' But next day Matthieu's descriptive powers found a new focus, for the wagon train had barely got out of sight of Fort Laramie, slowly ascending the juniper scrub and steep ravines of the Laramie foothills, than they met Thomas Fitzpatrick and Jim Bridger returning to the forts with a quantity of furs. Matthieu described Fitzpatrick as taciturn, tall and spare with grey hair, but withal an Irishman of gentlemanly bearing, at home anywhere in the mountains or the prairies.

Since Fitzpatrick's service with Bridger was due to expire at Fort Laramie, he was more than pleased when White at once offered him an appointment as guide as far as Fort Hall. Hastings and Lovejoy were annoyed at this, Lovejoy noting that Fitzpatrick and his party were deeply sceptical about the project of taking wagons to Oregon and that they poured cold water on the emigrants' idea of the Pacific north-west as a promised land. 'There was not land enough in Oregon for our party' were the words Lovejoy put into Fitzpatrick's mouth. We may take leave to doubt that this was actually said. Lovejoy and Hastings were at pains to play down Fitzpatrick's contribution to the 1842 wagon train, even alleging, absurdly, that the Indians disliked the Irishman. They were particularly incensed at the 'astronomical' sum Fitzpatrick demanded from White and which the doctor, flush with secret service funds, readily agreed to. Hastings's references to Fitzpatrick are invariably hostile: he consistently writes him out of his narrative and implies, confusingly, both that Fitzpatrick was greedy in asking and receiving five hundred dollars for the relatively short leg of the journey to Fort Hall, and that he was not paid. Five hundred dollars was certainly a lot of money, but Fitzpatrick was soon to prove he was worth every cent.

The emigrants made steady progress through the hundred miles of the Black Hills (effectively the foothills of the Laramie mountains), crossing off the succession of creeks that lay athwart their path – the Horseshoe, the La Bonté, the La Perle, the Box Elder and the Deer – and even managing the usually difficult crossing of the North Platte at the confluence with Cooper Creek, where the water was low because of the drought. Leaving the North Platte, they swung across country, crossing Poison Spider Creek and debouching on to the Sweetwater just before Independence Rock. In his usual gung-ho way, Hastings described the mood in the party thus: 'Perfect unanimity of feeling and purpose now having been fully restored, we passed on very agreeably.' In reality, the two factions continued to dislike each other intensely but were held together by fear of the Sioux. That organic solidarity was the very last thing characterising the caravan is clear from Elijah White's shocked and fastidious description of a violent altercation between two of the emigrants over a plug of tobacco.

The mutual antipathy and seething feuding was, however, put into some sort of perspective by a genuine tragedy which occurred on 13 July, within sight of Independence Rock. A young man named Bailey, a native of Massachusetts who had been blacksmithing in Iowa before joing the wagon train, was accidentally shot by an emigrant carelessly wielding his rifle. The name of the accidental killer was Adam Horn. Since the bullet entered the groin, the mountain men warned Hastings that the wound was bound to be fatal. There followed two hours of excruciating agony before Bailey expired. His death occurred in the evening and cast a shadow over the entire wagon train. Next morning, the funeral was held at the foot of the mountains some way from the main trail. Gloom and depression was everywhere evident, and the black pall that descended on the caravan was enhanced by the lurking fear of the Sioux. Even as the obsequies took place, heavily armed guards stood watch, fearful that at any moment the last rites might be interrupted by whooping savages.

The very different temperaments of the 1842 diarists emerge clearly from their treatment of this episode. The somewhat bogus religiosity of Elijah White contrasts starkly with the laconic, matter-of-fact entry in the Medorem Crawford journal. This is White:

> He [Bailey] was a useful man, and it gave a dreadful shock to us all. The next day at eight o'clock, as there was no clergyman, I was called upon to deliver a funeral discourse, near Independence Rock, in the

midst of the mountains. While I talked to all the company, who went on foot a mile to the grave, a general weeping prevailed among us. When in the course of my brief, solemn lecture, I said, 'Let us pray,' to my astonishment nearly every man, woman and child dropped upon their knees to implore the divine blessing and protection. It was the most solemn funeral by far that any of us ever attended or probably ever will.

And this is Crawford:

July 14. Buried Baily [sic] near Independence Rock, *half a mile* [my italics] from camp. My feelings on this occasion can hardly be described. A young man . . . wrapped in a buffalo robe and buried in this dismal prairie.

Gloomy and morbid, the overlanders decided to stage a period of mourning, at least ostensibly, since they rested for two days, drying buffalo meat and holding fresh elections. On 15 July, Hastings and Lovejoy were re-elected as captain and deputy; the intense antipathy towards Elijah White still lingered. But, if there was any doubt about Hastings's incapacity to be captain of a wagon train, he clinched the case for his unsuitability by his next action. Having tarried for two days by Independence Rock, he waited until the wagons had drawn well clear and were heading up the Sweetwater towards Devil's Gate before he belatedly decided he wanted to inscribe his legend on the famous rock, where so many previous travellers had carved names and initials. Even more foolishly, he persuaded Lovejoy to accompany him. If he and Lovejoy really were as indispensable to the 1842 wagon train as he later claimed, was it not consummate folly for the two senior officers in the caravan to absent themselves at the same time, when the threat from the Sioux still loomed? Still more absurdly, the two men started climbing the rock, having left their guns at the bottom with the horses.

They had no sooner gained the summit than seven Lakota warriors galloped up to the base, yelling and whooping. Lovejoy and Hastings quickly scrambled down from the rock in a high state of panic and just managed to get to their horses and seize their weapons before the Sioux arrived. The two sides then squared off, the Americans with their guns primed, the Indians with drawn bows. After a few minutes' tense stand-off, the Sioux appeared to blink first and lowered their weapons. But as soon as Lovejoy and Hastings mounted up, the warriors closed in on them and made it plain they intended to stop them leaving. While they were in two minds about what to do, the Americans saw dozens more

Lakota arriving. The boastful and lying Hastings falsely claimed that he and Lovejoy killed five of the initial seven braves; had that really been the case, they would have been massacred on the spot. Nonetheless, their situation was parlous, for they could neither outrun nor outfight such a large number of warriors.

Concluding that a meek submission to the overwhelmingly superior force was the best policy, the two men made no demur when the Indians seized their bridles and motioned to them to dismount. Once on the ground, they were subjected to jeering, poking and prodding from the excited braves. Forced to sit, they endured blows and buffets until the leader of the new arrivals, evidently a war chief of some standing, made it plain by sitting down alongside them that he would not tolerate any more such behaviour by his young hotheads. Lovejoy, indeed, seemed to excite particular rancour in one warrior, who smote him a heavy blow, then tried to shoot him; fortunately, his primitive flintlock misfired. Why Lovejoy was made such a target is uncertain; maybe the cross-grained character that Matthieu had detected came to the fore and he acted unwisely for a captive by a show of temper. At any rate, faced by this insensate behaviour from one of his 'bucks', the chief ordered his men to form a protective cordon around the two whites.

There followed a furious altercation between doves and hawks, which ended with the Sioux chieftain ordering his men to fire at the enraged warrior who had tried to kill Lovejoy. This man and his supporters galloped off at speed before the order could be carried out but, once out of range, turned round and taunted the chief. His reproaches and imprecations evidently had an effect, for the entire argument broke out anew, with more warriors asking the chief for permission to execute the whites. The clamorous dialectic was suddenly broken off when the irate hawks turned their attention to a dog, which had unhappily followed Lovejoy and Hastings to Independence Rock. The Sioux quickly shot the dog, then seemed to delight in spearing the dead animal with their lances, as if it was some kind of substitute for the two humans they were forbidden to kill.

Having taken horses, saddles, bridles and anything of value they could find on the whites, the Sioux settled down to await the coming of superior officers, whose advent was communicated to them by Lakota heralds. Early in the afternoon, some half-dozen Sioux elders, who clearly outranked the original chieftain, arrived. Hastings discovered that one of them, a man of mixed Indian and French-Canadian blood, spoke some English. Using the few primitive words the man possessed, Hastings explained the purpose of the emigrants' trip to the Pacific, including the

John Bidwell,
the Columbus of the overland trail

John Sutter,
entrepreneur and 'California booster'

John McLoughlin, secular saint
of the Hudson's Bay Company

Marcus Whitman, controversial missionary
and 'Oregon booster'

Narcissa Whitman,
'vivacious, attractive, gregarious, idealistic
sentimentally religious'

Jim Bridger,
legendary mountain man and trail guide

Pierre-Jean de Smet,
Jesuit, explorer and visionary

Independence, Missouri, principal 'jump-off' point in the early years of the overland trails

Fort Laramie, the stopover oasis of the Great Platte River Road

At Fort Laramie white man and Indian lived in harmonious coexistence

Independence Rock. This was always a happy stopover for the emigrants

Three Island Crossing. Here the pioneers could avoid the worst dangers of the Snake

Oregon City. Journey's end for the overlanders on the Oregon Trail

A close-up of the pioneer wagon

Hearth and home on wheels: the wagon's interior

Greasing the wagon wheels

Ghosts of the past:
wagon ruts mark the epic journey

Wagons on a difficult river crossing

Wagons descending a mountain

Wagons ascending a mountain

usual bromides about the 'great father' in Washington. The English-speaking Sioux 'senator' then explained that his warriors were irate because a rumour had been spread at Fort Laramie that the whites in the wagon train intended to join the Sioux's traditional enemy, the Blackfeet. Hastings scouted the absurd rumour by pointing out to the chief that the white emigrants had women and children with them; it was well known that no war party, white or red, ever travelled thus encumbered. The Anglophone Sioux communicated these remarks to his venerable colleagues; from the body language of the speakers, Hastings inferred that they seemed more relaxed after receiving this information. At any rate, the white men were invited to mount up, whereupon the entire party turned in the direction the wagon train had taken.

Initially, their Sioux escort seemed friendly, but, after two hours' riding, a scout returned; after that, the Sioux seemed to be making preparations for battle and their demeanour was much less affable. Finally, they came in sight of the wagon train, now camped for the evening. Hastings tried to speak to the chief elder to explain that the emigrants might fire if the Sioux evinced any hostility. The chief seemed to take this to heart, but meanwhile his young headstrong warriors had commenced a charge on the wagon train. For a while chaos took over, with the chief trying to halt the charge and recall his riders. The emigrants formed their wagons into a circle and stood ready to receive the attack. Fitzpatrick rode out to meet the warriors to remonstrate with them, but they seemed not to be in a mood to listen. White recalled: 'His [Fitzpatrick's] repeated signs were disregarded and they rode steadily forward till nearly within gunshot, when they suddenly halted, apparently intimidated by our array.'

Fitzpatrick now took charge, though the mendacious Hastings later tried to take the credit for himself. Meek, Fitzpatrick and Matthieu were able to speak to the Sioux leaders in their own tongue. They asked the Lakota to return the stolen property, and the chiefs replied they would be willing to do so in exchange for ammunition, which was the one thing they needed for their coming campaign against the Blackfeet. Protracted negotiations then took place, with the Sioux chiefs having to save face in the eyes of their warriors by extracting major concessions from the white man while at the same time reining them in so that general fighting did not break out. When Fitzpatrick asked for a guarantee that the Sioux would camp at a respectable distance from the wagon train, the chiefs protested at this attempt to 'give them laws' in their own territory. Nevertheless, according to Matthieu, the Indians were in general good-natured and seemed only to want to drive a hard bargain before letting their prisoners go. Peace terms were agreed. The pipe of peace was then smoked, with the calumet being passed alternately from a red hand to a white.

After receiving ammunition and gifts of tobacco, the Sioux released Lovejoy and Hastings and returned all the stolen property. Hastings later vaingloriously claimed that he made his escape from the Sioux ranks while the charge on the wagon train went on. The myth-making Hastings hated having to admit that he had been handed over like a parcel of goods, so pretended that he had made a daring escape *and* that he then took charge of the subsequent negotiations. Matthieu, though, revealed the truth: 'A great band of Sioux developed out of the prairie, galloping in wild fashion upon their ponies or in large part running on foot . . . in full war dress and paint. Lovejoy and Hastings were among them, being held as captives and looking very crestfallen.' The truth is that Hastings had botched every aspect of relations with the Sioux, and had placed the wagon train in jeopardy by his stupidity, and that only the experience and statesmanship of Fitzpatrick prevented a major confrontation between red man and white.

Although Matthieu and Medorem Crawford played down the threat from the Indians, the truth is that there was more danger than they realised. After the trade and for most of the way to South Pass, the Sioux hung on the flanks of the wagon train. On 22 July, Crawford estimated that 4–5,000 Lakota were camped within sight. Such a formidable host would have made even a regiment of US regulars more than a little nervous; its effect on a caravan boasting no more than fifty or so fighting men can be imagined. The fact that another gun went off accidentally in the emigrants' camp, this time doing no harm, was thought to be a particularly bad omen while the 'savages' dogged their footsteps. And whenever the caravan sent out hunting parties to shoot buffalo, the Sioux would relieve the hunters either of their meat, if successful, or their horses, if they were not. Increasing signs of hostility built up to a crisis. There was another armed demonstration in front of the emigrants' encampment, so the overlanders had to stand to, ready to repel imminent assault. Yet curiously, even while all these hostile manifestations went on, throngs of Indian women and children came to sightsee and gawk at the travellers. And the martial ethos did not entirely overcome the commercial spirit. Some of the emigrants continued to barter with the Sioux; some later boasted they had traded good horses out of them.

Nevertheless, an anxious Fitzpatrick thought it necessary to bring matters to a head. Just before South Pass, where the Sweetwater swung off to the north, he asked for a parley with the Indian chiefs. They told him that they had vetoed an attack on the emigrant train only with great difficulty, that majority opinion (and almost unanimous opinion among the young braves) favoured an all-out campaign against the whites. The chiefs solemnly assured him that only the great reputation of 'Broken Hand' and his known wisdom had finally enabled them to carry the day, but they 'assured him that his path was no longer open and that any party of whites which should hereafter be found upon it should meet with certain destruction'. Even then the danger was not over. Fitzpatrick invited the chiefs into his camp to smoke the peace pipe but grew alarmed when hundreds of braves seemed disposed to follow their elders. Naturally, this presented a risk too dangerous to contemplate. Using a nice blend of tact and firmness. Fitzpatrick informed the chiefs that the invitation to smoke the calumet was not a general one, but reserved for them only. They accepted his rebuke affably, but Fitzpatrick was glad to see the back of them finally at South Pass. As Frémont rightly remarked: 'I have no doubt the emigrants owe their lives to Mr Fitzpatric [sic].'

One of the principal concerns that preyed on Fitzpatrick's mind was the perceived threat to the emigrant women. In the Victorian era, white men of all nations really did think that rape was the 'fate worse than death', and viewed with particular horror any manifestation of lust by 'savages' towards white women. This is a proposition as true of David Livingstone in Central Africa as of Frémont in the Far West. During the latter days along the Sweetwater, Matthieu recorded one less than welcome Sioux incursion: 'About five or six thousand of the Blackfoot Sioux, under a great war chief, appeared. By this immense multitude the train was compelled to halt and be inspected by band after band of the curious savages. They were especially curious to look at the women of the train.'

It was the beautiful Smith women who particularly attracted attention. The Sioux came cautiously to Smith's tent, pulled the flaps apart, and gazed in silent admiration upon his wife and daughters. The patriarch Smith appealed to Matthieu to help him get rid of the intruders. At Matthieu's insistence, all withdrew except one young warrior. He told Matthieu, who was interpreting, that he wanted to talk with Mr Smith and seemed impatient for Matthieu to translate Smith's words. It soon became clear that the brave was offering twenty good horses for one of Smith's daughters. Smith was angry, and Matthieu had to explain to the bemused Lakota that it was not the practice among white men to sell their wives and daughters. But the young Sioux had a ready answer. Since it was well known that white men bought Indian girls as wives, why not have the system work both ways? Eventually he was persuaded that his quest was hopeless, but went away reluctantly, casting longing looks on the Smith girls.

As a parting shot, the Blackfoot Sioux asked for alcohol; they were about to attack the Shoshone, it was explained, and needed Dutch courage. Since the emigrants possessed only the medicinal supplies of whisky and anyway made it a policy not to sell liquor to Indians, this request too was refused. All Indians regularly approached wagon trains for whisky, with the Sioux, by universal consent, being the most persistent importuners; the later emigrant Alonzo Delano declared that the Sioux would sell their own children for whisky. As for Matthieu, his success in turning away the Blackfoot Sioux from Smith's tent produced an attack of boasting. He claimed it was he, not Fitzpatrick, who had been the mastermind in conciliating the Sioux. Truly, failure is an orphan and success has a thousand fathers!

But in dealing with the proposed trade for the Smith girls, Matthieu's account is undoubtedly authentic. This was far from the only such proposal by Indian to emigrant. The 'going rate' was anything from six to twenty horses, but old-timers soon invented stories involving the offer of entire herds, containing up to four hundred horses, for some legendary beauty. There are even accounts of Indian women offering horses for handsome young emigrant men.

Those sceptical of the potentiality of human nature would have taken cynical satisfaction at the way the solidarity temporarily engendered by the Sioux threat immediately disintegrated once the emigrants were clear of Lakota territory. As soon as the Indians turned back at the Continental Divide, White and a dozen others who were well mounted pressed on ahead, taking Fitzpatrick with them. Hastings was left in charge of the main train, without a guide. Even among those left, there was a disinclination for duty. One man declined to stand guard, was found guilty by a jury of his peers, but refused to abide by their decision. When told he would be expelled from the caravan if he failed to submit to his sentence, the malefactor continued obstinate and defiant. When ten armed men arrived at his tent, with orders to remove him forcibly, 'dead or alive' to a distance one mile behind the wagon train, the man turned into a snivelling wreck, who pleaded and implored for a retrial. This was granted and, amazingly, this time the scrimshanker was found not guilty. But he had learned his lesson, and henceforth took his watch and obeyed every order issued by the caravan's officers.

From South Pass the emigrants proceeded down the Big Sandy River to the junction with the Green. At the Green River the caravan reunited only to break apart once again into factions. White and his acolytes proposed abandoning the troublesome wagons, cutting them up, making packsaddles and completing the journey with horses. They won some support, but Hastings and Lovejoy were adamant that they wanted to roll on wheels all the way to Oregon. The consequence was that about half the wagons were retained, and the others broken up. With eight reconstructed wagons, one of which soon collapsed, the Hastings party pressed sullenly ahead, leaving the White group behind to chop up the abandoned wagons and use the wood for making packsaddles. White insisted that as he had hired Fitzpatrick at an exorbitant rate, the mountain man had to stay with him, even though Hastings was now acting as pathfinder. In desperation, and despite his misgivings, Hastings finally took on Stephen Meek as his guide.

Once the White party was properly outfitted, they travelled fast and soon overtook Hastings and the wagons along the Bear River. Bears were frequently seen along the aptly named river, not just browns and blacks but also the more formidable grizzlies. One morning a grizzly bear walked into White's camp and caused pandemonium. White's hunters chased the animal off, pursued him into a copse and then tried to smoke him out, but the grizzly escaped. Encounters with bears were one of the hazards of the emigrant trail but, it must be said, mainly because the overlanders went looking for trouble. In 1854, the mountain man Isaac Glover died after hand-to-hand combat with a grizzly. In 1843, Overton Johnson's party went out of their way to hunt three bears. They shot one, it fell, they thought it dead, but it rose again, charged, took a second volley, and still kept coming on. Then the bears' two comrades joined in the charge but became confused as the men were downwind of them. Even so, the bears got so close to them that the hunters were beginning to panic; finally, amid much whooping, the humans scrambled on to their horses. Seeing the rearing, bucking and skittish horses, the bears ran off. Seeing the wounded one streaming with blood, the hunters dismounted and finished him off.

Both parties were severely hampered by heavy rainstorms along the Bear River. One lasted for seventy-two hours non-stop and was described by Fitzpatrick as the worst downpour he had ever been in. Yet, despite the torrents and the general sterility of the landscape, with only sagebrush and prickly pear growing in any abundance, Hastings claimed to have found along this valley the best camping ground on the entire route between the Atlantic and the Pacific. Needless to say, both sets of travellers went into raptures over the half-dozen hot springs producing boiling soda-flavoured water and ever afterwards known as Soda Springs. Set in a beautiful grove of small cedars, fifty miles east of Fort Hall, surrounded by rich valleys and plains and high rolling hills, the springs impressed as much by their spa waters as by the anthill-like conical springs – not strictly speaking the *soi-disant* Soda Springs – which were nearby.

White's horsemen reached Fort Hall a day before Hastings's wagons, though naturally this was too much for Hastings's pride; he rewrote the events so that the rivals reached the fort at the same time. (Fort Hall was a trading post of the British Hudson's Bay Company which the British had purchased as recently as 1837 from the enterpreneur Nathaniel Wyeth, whose extravagant plans for trade on the Green River led him to build it in 1834.) In charge at the Fort was a new commandant, Richard Grant, described by Matthieu as a large, good-looking man, a forty-eight-year-old with twenty-one years' service in the Hudson's Bay Company behind him. Although Grant, like John McLoughlin at Fort Vancouver, was under strict orders from the company to give no assistance that might encourage emigrants from the United States to flock into the Oregon territory, Grant, again like McLoughlin, welcomed the overlanders warmly. He warned them, though, that it was impossible to take wagons over the Blue Mountains, and he knew whereof he spoke, having come from Fort Vancouver and Fort Walla Walla by a horse-only trail. In later years, Grant had a reputation for encouraging all emigrants arriving at the fort to proceed to California rather than Oregon, and he was suspected of machiavellianism; the plain truth is that he genuinely did think travel by wagon to Oregon was impracticable.

Grant anyway proved his good faith by selling provisions to the travellers at below market price and encouraging them to take their wagons as far as Walla Walla, if that was their choice. Even though he had no use for wagons at Fort Hall, he was prepared to accept them and worn-out oxen in exchange for food and supplies. By a majority vote, it was decided to abandon the wagons and proceed by horseback. Some sold worn-out wagons to Grant for a pittance; others, convinced they could get a higher price by private trading, missed the once-only opportunity and ended up receiving nothing for their conveyances. But the men of 1842 were unanimous in speaking highly of Grant's efforts on their behalf. He alone, of all the forts' commandants, retained the reputation of being always kind and helpful to the traveller. The fact that the travellers spent eight days in rest and recuperation at the fort speaks volumes.

Since Fitzpatrick's contract expired at Fort Hall, and Grant was able to draw detailed maps and supply local guides, White and his party pressed on two days ahead of the Hastings caravan; this had to travel more slowly as it was still leading weary and worn-out cattle. The trail to Oregon now lay along the powerful and treacherous Snake River, which almost immediately claimed a victim. At the crossing of the Snake below Salmon Falls, Adam Horn, the man whose gun had killed Bailey near Independence Rock, was drowned. If approached carefully, this island ford was not particularly dangerous, but every year brought some foolish or 'intrepid' young man who liked to find his own way across and was swept away by the torrent. Horn slipped from his horse and for a moment seemed to be standing in the river as if caught in quicksand. Then, in an instant, he was swept away by the swift current. As White remembered it, 'His implorings for help were most touching, but it was impossible to reach him.' Neither he nor his horse was ever seen again. The superstitious pioneers thought it significant that God or the Fates had 'punished him' for causing the death of Bailey at Independence Rock.

Drownings were second only to accidental shootings as a cause of fatalities on the overland trails. More than three hundred drownings were recorded in the twenty years 1840–60, more than ninety in 1850 alone, when highly inexperienced travellers went west in the California Gold Rush. At the start of the trek the great dangers were the Kansas, the Blue and, especially, the Platte. Nineteen emigrants drowned at the Fort Laramie crossing of the Platte in 1850, and forty-nine at the North Fork in 1849–50. Further west, the principal perils were the Green (which claimed thirty-seven lives in 1850), the Snake and the Columbia. Overwhelmingly, the victims were male – men who through impatience, drink, recklessness, meanness or simple poverty would not, or could not, cross by ferry or use the tried and tested fords.

Hastings's party, meanwhile, avoided the crossing of the Snake and proceeded along the south side of the river as far as the lower crossing at Fort Boise, where they crossed the track of the advance party. It was a dreary journey: Hastings described the landscape as 'extremely hilly, mountainous and sterile, generally producing neither timber nor vegetation . . . one continued succession of high mountains, stupendous cliffs, and deep, frightful caverns, with an occasional limited valley'. But White's vanguard had already suffered its own splintering. Since the pack animals could not keep up with the furious pace White tried to set, the good doctor rode ahead at his own speed with Angus McDonald of the Hudson's Bay Company and a handful of friends; the rest of the pack-animal cavalcade was left to shift for itself.

Both parties found the 270-mile journey along the Snake from Fort Hall to Fort Boise an ordeal. The lava boulders, with sharp obsidian rock, cut into the flesh of the horses and mules as they bumped against them; the sagebrush, sometimes as tall as the mules, was a constant irritant;

clouds of mosquitoes plagued them; the stench of exhausted sweating animals and bruised artemisia assailed them; and then there were the choking whorls of dust, thrown up from the arid, crumbly soil that disintegrated into light powder under hooves, and stung eyes with noxious alkali. To be sure, they could obtain plentiful supplies of salmon from the Shoshone fishermen along the banks of the Snake, and there was also the example of mountain man Newell to hearten them; he had travelled this trail in 1840 even more loaded and encumbered than they. But Hastings at least negated the effect of this by his obsessive anxiety that he might meet a war party of Blackfeet; for some reason he feared and dreaded these Indians even more than the Sioux and Cheyenne.

The rear of the vanguard, with the pack animals, reached Fort Boise on 3 September. There was so little to buy or trade there that the overlanders did not tarry more than a couple of hours, just time to buy and consume some indifferent melons. They bade goodbye to the Snake and commenced the long, hard pull up Burnt Canyon, out of the valley where the Snake met the River Boise. Medorem Crawford's diary gives the flavour of the next ordeal: 'Left camp at 11 o'clock and travelled briskly over a sandy country, suffered considerable for water as the day was exceedingly hot. Came to a creek about six o'clock and never was water to me more acceptable though of a very indifferent quality. Passed down the creek a short distance at the foot of a mountain and found boiling water running out of the ground.' He could not believe that horses could negotiate the gradient and spoke of 'frightful precipices and in many places if our animals make one mis-step it would be certain death'.

Once at the top of Burnt Canyon, the overlanders were able to gaze at a vast valley, pullulating with luxurious vegetation. Right in the middle of the vale was a single pine tree, which was already famous in the annals of the West. French-Canadian mountain men called it *l'arbre seul*, the lone tree, and subsequent travellers dubbed the valley 'Lone Tree Valley'. They made camp at the Powder River, close to the solitary tree, and Crawford noted in his diary: 'The tree is a large pine standing in the midst of an immense plain, entirely alone. It presented a truly singular appearance and I believe is respected by every traveller through this almost treeless country.'

The next obstacle was the Blue Mountains and the emigrants' initial impressions were gloomy. The first glimpse of the snowcaps, said Crawford, 'struck us with terror . . . their lofty peaks seemed a resting place for the clouds'. Struggling upwards along a rocky canyon, the overlanders needed every ounce of moral fibre to keep going on the morale-crushing winding track. But about forty miles north-west of Lone Tree Valley, they came to a second oasis, nestling in the middle of the Blue Mountains: the valley of La Grande Ronde, not just extensive like Lone Pine, but well timbered and full of fresh-water springs and with fertile soil that marked it out as a future spot for colonisation. The shape of the valley was nearly circular, hence its name – literally 'The Big Round'. Massive pines, firs and cedar made La Grande Ronde a lumberman's paradise, and it can well be imagined that many a tired horseman marked the valley down as 'one to note'.

On the far side of La Grande Ronde the travellers commenced another steep ascent, finally breasting the western ridges of the Blue Mountains to descend to the western base near the Umatilla River. Fort Walla Walla and the nearby Presbyterian mission run by Dr Marcus Whitman were the next staging posts. Crawford's diary gives the essential information: 'Sept 14. We arrived at 3 o'clock and camped near his house . . . He has a very considerable house and is farming to a considerable extent. He has a threshing machine and a grinding mill all under one roof drived [sic] by water power. Many Indians around him. I was never more pleased to see a house or white people in my life.' By this time the gap between the two sections of the 1842 caravan had widened alarmingly. Before Crawford and Hastings reached Walla Walla, Elijah White had already called on Whitman, delivered a letter of rebuke from his missionary superiors and departed down the Columbia River by boat. Hastings's straggling rearguard was received with great kindness by Whitman, described by Matthieu as a dark-haired Yankee, slender in build but impressive in manner. The latecomers stayed several days, attended Sunday service when Whitman preached, admired his evangelical progress among the Cayuse, and traded horses with the Indians to acquire the supplies and equipment that would enable them to complete the difficult final stage of the journey.

After leaving the Whitman mission on 16 September, the horsemen now rode along the south bank of the Columbia, 'heads bent against a sand-laden wind that whipped through the upper gorge full into their faces'. At the Methodist mission at The Dalles they rested a few days and found Indian guides for the coming trek through the Cascades. Evidently Hastings was satisfied with his welcome here, even though the mission became notorious later for its curmudgeonly attitude towards emigrants in distress. Beyond The Dalles the horsemen found their way blocked by the deepening gorge of the Columbia and diverted into the Cascades. These mountains proved as formidable as had been feared. The emigrants encountered 'horrid road, logs and mud holes', to say nothing of rocks, precipices, yawning chasms, boiling streams, damp, dripping conifers and little grass; the animals grew 'hollow and weak'. In addition, they ran into heavy snowstorms. Matthieu remembered the journey over the Cascades, following an old Indian trail at the base of Mount Hood, as the worst part of the entire trip.

Eventually, the main body of emigrants made it through to the falls of Willamette River, just as Dr John McLoughlin of the Hudson's Bay Company founded a new settlement called Oregon City. Because of the heavy snowfall in the Cascades, the cattle drovers took their herds along the north bank of the Columbia and swam them over to the south side much further down – a risky business which this time paid off. The horsemen on the south bank reached the end of the trail on 5 October, two weeks after White, who had arrived at Fort Vancouver on 20 September with news of his commission as Indian agent. Unfortunately for him, the settlers of Oregon City paid little attention to him or his authority. He was obliged to take a back seat in Oregon affairs and continue as a humble Indian agent. The restless Hastings soon found Oregon not to his liking and emigrated to California. The most cheering story at trail's end was that of Elbridge Trask, who won the heart of Hannah Abel. They arrived in Oregon City on 22 September and were married a month later.

Lovejoy and White also played a minor role, albeit indirectly, in the great Oregon-bound migration of 1843. When White delivered his letter of reprimand during his stay at Waiilatpu from 9 to 13 September, the effect of the bombshell was to make Marcus Whitman head for Boston at full speed. Whitman left for the east on 3 October, accompanied by Lovejoy, and it is a fair inference that it must have been pressing business that made him leave Narcissa alone at the mission throughout the winter of 1842–43. Whitman's biographer uncovered a threefold motivation. First, he was concerned at Roman Catholic influence in the Pacific northwest: it is possible that he had met de Smet some time in 1842 and that de Smet had told him he was going to Europe to recruit more missionaries. Second, and most immediately pressing, Whitman went east to rescind the orders White had brought him, particularly the directive to dismiss H.H. Spalding and close the missions at Waiilatpu and Lapwai.

But Whitman's third motive is the one that has caused most controversy among historians of Oregon, for Whitman was a fervent supporter of US annexation of Oregon and to this end wanted to see large-scale settlement in the territory. Learning that a major pioneering exodus was planned for the spring of 1843, he intended to reach Boston by Christmas and then return to Missouri in time for the wagon train season in early May. Whitman's importance as an Oregon 'booster' was that he actually lived there and knew the country. He spoke convincingly of opportunities there, he explained how trappers and traders had already mapped the important routes and argued that Captain Bonneville had proved that one could take wagons through the Rockies to Oregon. He argued, plausibly, that the path to the Willamette valley was easier than the arduous trek across the intermontane plateau to California followed by a crossing of the formidable Sierras. In fact, Whitman did play an important part in the 1843 emigration, to the point where some have credited him single-handedly with being the man who 'saved' Oregon from the British and the Hudson's Bay Company. This is of course a risible exaggeration; the most careful studies show that the 1843 emigration was not a significant factor in the solution of the Oregon boundary dispute.

But the steady drip-drip of emigrants to Oregon in the early 1840s did create a situation where the position of the Hudson's Bay Company ('Here Before Christ', as one wag put it) was untenable. The 1827 Treaty of Joint Occupation between Britain and the United States worked only so long as the area was the domain of a handful of trappers. Although the Oregon territory extended from the forty-second parallel to 54°40' in the north, the British had no interest in the lands below the Columbia River. The real area of contention was between the Columbia River and the forty-ninth parallel (the present-day state of Washington). The British turned down a four-times repeated offer by Washington to partition the territory along the forty-ninth parallel, fearing they would be cut off from the southern half of Vancouver, denied access to the straits of Juan de Fuca and prohibited from navigation on the Columbia River. They thus played into the hands of hardliners in the USA who wanted American occupation of all lands to 54°40'.

The pressure for an American Oregon began in 1842 and reached a high point in 1844. In 1842, a number of 'Oregon Conventions', demanding US annexation, were held throughout the West and there was a national convention on the subject at Cincinnati in 1843. There was surprising unanimity on the subject. Abolitionists wanted to create a new free state; slavers saw that this would be an acceptable quid pro quo, removing northern opposition to the annexation of Texas. Those who were worried about British influence in Texas and California saw the Oregon issue as a way to strike back. In the 1844 presidential election, James Polk campaigned on a jingoistic slogan of 'Fifty-Four Forty or Bust'. When he was elected, he faced a dangerous situation, committed to wresting the Oregon territory from Britain even if it meant war. As he was at the same time committed to annexing Texas, which would mean war with Mexico, he faced the peril of a two-front war and it was by no means certain he could win. Nevertheless, his inaugural message in March 1845 was uncompromising. War over Oregon seemed certain.

Behind the scenes, Polk made Richard Pakenham, the British Minister in Washington, the old offer of the forty-ninth parallel, but by this time passions were running high in London. The Gordian knot was cut by the Hudson's Bay Company. Concluding that human population in the Willamette valley was anyway throttling the fur trade in the Puget Sound area, in January 1845 the company shifted its base of operations from Fort Vancouver to Fort Victoria on Vancouver Island. Dr John McLoughlin had already warned his superiors in London that the presence of so many American frontiersmen around the Columbia meant that Fort Vancouver could not be defended militarily; £100,000 worth of goods would go up in flames if the Americans stormed the fort, as they had often threatened to. This action was a de facto acceptance of the forty-ninth parallel, and it remained only to see if London could swallow the loss of face involved. Sir Robert Peel, the Prime Minister, and Lord Aberdeen, the Foreign Secretary, privately concluded that the lands between Vancouver Island and the Columbia River could not be defended. The trick was to find a formula which would allow them to sell the acceptance of the forty-ninth parallel to a truculent British public opinion.

Peel and Aberdeen had other motives, as well as military incapacity, for seeking to avoid war with the United States. They both agreed that Oregon – 'a pine swamp' as Aberdeen called it – was not worth fighting for, and that a tariff agreement with Washington was more in the British national interest. Besides, they had hefty problems in Ireland, in China and Afghanistan, and with France, to say nothing about their plans for the repeal of the Corn Laws, which could not be solved if they indulged in a costly and unwinnable war on the other side of the globe. Selling the idea of a 'climbdown' over Oregon to the Whig opposition, especially the fire-eating Lord Palmerston, was supremely difficult, but when the Tories fell from power in December 1845, the incoming Whig leader Lord Russell found his position impossible; many of his own party refused to serve with the warmongering Palmerston and share prices plummeted on the Stock Exchange. Unable to make headway, Russell resigned and Peel returned as Prime Minister. Peel then 'squared' the hostile London press and signified his acceptance of the forty-ninth parallel to Washington. On 10 June 1846, the Senate, by thirty-eight votes to twelve, authorised Polk to accept the British offer and on 15 June the treaty was ratified. The Oregon territory was now American. The overlanders may not have been the sufficient condition for winning Oregon, but they were certainly a necessary one.

The year 1842 saw women on the overland trail in significant numbers, and their presence as emigrants would increase exponentially right through to the American Civil War. It is impossible to overstate the importance of women in the story of the covered wagon, as indicated in the classic statement from Emerson Hough: 'The chief figure of the American West . . . is not the long-haired, fringed-legged man riding a raw-boned pony, but the gaunt and sad-faced woman sitting on the front seat of the wagon, following her lord where he might lead . . . That was the great romance of all America – the woman in the sunbonnet.' But the Sister in a Sunbonnet was only one collective image of the wagon trains, and there were many other archetypes of women on the trail which have since been worked over by historians: Earth Mothers, Petticoat Pioneers, Loose Ladies, Calamity Janes, Feisty Pioneers and Fighting Feminists.

Doubtless because family responsibilities precluded the leisure needed to write a journal, most female diarists on the overland trail were young women, either unmarried or newly married. For most male diarists, however, women featured as bit players or 'noises off'. Some of them could be dismissive or patronising, like J.M. Shiveley in his well-known *Guide to Oregon and California*, published in 1846:

> However much help your wives and daughters have been to you at home, they can do but little for you here – herding stock through either dew, dust or rain, breaking brush, swimming rivers, attacking grizzly bears or savage Indians, is all out of their line of business. All they can do, is to cook for camps, etc.

Of the hundreds of male diarists, only James Clyman and Randall Hewitt reveal great powers of empathy for women. At first sight, Clyman's empathy reads like a susceptibility for a pretty face, but further reading reveals it as far more than that. While crossing the plains in 1844, Clyman often had occasion to notice women at work. What begins as a perception of women from an egotistical standpoint – '20 May. Two fine looking young ladies in camp'; '23 May. Several fine intelligent young ladies. Engaged one of them to make me a pair of pantaloons' – soon blossoms into a genuine appreciation of the feminine principle: '29 July. Beautiful covey [*sic*] of young ladies and misses while they gathered wild currants and chokeberries which grow in great profusion in this region and of the finest kind.'

Soon Clyman's admiration becomes more and more abstract in its general appreciation of women. When spirits drooped under the constant downpours and monsoon-like precipitation of May 1844, Clyman noted: 'I thought I never saw more determined resolution even amongst the men than most of the female part of our company exhibited.' He particularly liked the stoical way women continued with their chores while the elements loosed their fury around them. 'Here let me say there was one young lady which showed herself worthy of the bravest undaunted pioneer of the West, for after having kneaded her dough, she watched and nursed the fire and held an umbrella over the fire and her skillet with the greatest composure for near two hours and baked bread enough to give us a very plentiful supper.'

Without question, men had an easier time on the overland trail than women. Their heavy labour was balanced by easy male cameraderie, the freedom of the wide open spaces, the excitement of the buffalo hunt, the general sense of 'becoming' and evolving from Midwestern farmer to founding father of a new society. When their chores were over in the evening, they could eat their dinner, then relax, smoke and yarn around the campfire. They were content if they had wife and children along with them. Women, by contrast, had been uprooted from home and hearth to face the perils of the unknown, with fear of being scalped, raped or murdered by Indians uppermost in their minds. They had had to give up friends and kin in the extended family to travel with the nuclear family, on a quest whose outcome and utility they often doubted deep down. Worst of all, on the trail their work was literally never done. There was no post-dinner relaxation for them, for there was always cooking, washing, mending, childcare and other chores to perform; any talking they did had to be done while working. Since the rapport of woman with woman tends to be deeper than that of man with man, it took longer to establish, but time was what the non-stop skivvies of the plains did not have. Both because there was so little time absolutely for socialising and because women had *relatively* less time to make friends, their contacts with other women tended to be fleeting.

Some historians claim that women enjoyed greater freedom on the overland trails, for they were able to cast off the conventional shackles of hidebound society and reinvent themselves existentially; in a word, they were very far from being the traditional feminist victims. The evidence from emigrant diaries, on the other hand, tends to show women mainly enduring passively and stoically, but all generalisations have to be expressed with care. Much depended on the individual social and economic circumstances of the woman, and her own qualities of independence and assertiveness. For the prosperous, the inconvenience of life on the plains could be kept to a minimum. Mrs Francis Sawyer, who went overland to California in 1852 in a conveyance that was more carriage than wagon, wrote somewhat complacently:

'I have been in bed in my carriage all day, for it is very disagreeable out. The wind commenced blowing at a high rate last night and it has continued to blow a perfect gale . . . Mr Sawyer got up in the night and pulled the carriage, with me in it, out into the prairie, for fear that timber would fall on us. The men do all the cooking in bad weather, though I never have to do anything but make up the bread.'

Other frontier women found ways to break out of traditional sex roles. The most extreme cases involved women masquerading as men. Elizabeth Smith of Missouri, dressed as a man, called herself Bill Newcom and fought in the Mexican War of 1846–48 for ten months before her true sexual identity was discovered. Naturally, such actions were not really possible on the emigrant trail, but a woman calling herself Mountain Charlie worked for thirteen years in heavy disguise as a frontier scout and wagonmaster before being revealed. More usually, rebellion took the form of acidulous and ironical comments in the privacy of one's diary about the singular misfortune of being 'only a woman'. But the very circumstances of trail life made some departure from the old values and norms imperative. The first time a woman rode a horse like a man, instead of side saddle, it was considered 'daring' and even shocking but the practice soon ceased to raise eyebrows.

For most pioneer women, though, their lot was everywhere and at all times the same: managing the family, looking after children, doing household chores, acting as the family historian. A recent study of their trail diaries notes three predominant and recurring themes: discussions of practical matters; concern for health and safety; and expressions of appreciation for the natural beauty encountered on the way west. Their anxieties tended to centre on the (much exaggerated) threat from Indians, fear of disease, the dust and heat of the trail, wild animals (especially rattlesnakes) and the general sense of being at sea, not just on the grassy oceans of the prairies but in the sense of having left civilisation behind. As one historian has written sardonically: 'Disquiet, anxiety, melancholy and anger were repressed and hidden from husbands, brothers and fathers, those most responsible for such feelings.' Undoubtedly, most women frequently broke down and wept when no one could observe them.

It is worth reviewing in turn the various chores women had to perform on the trail. Cooking obviously loomed large, and was one reason why women got less rest and sleep than men. They had to get up at 4 a.m. – an hour before the men – to cook breakfast, and had to work longer into the night clearing up after supper. Then there were the manifold difficulties on the plains with inadequate ovens and fragile and fissile cooking pots, contending all the time with rain and high winds that put out the fires. Women also hated the burden of having to collect buffalo chips as fuel. Even when they got used to the smell – a sterner trial to them than to their menfolk because of their keener sense of smell and greater general fastidiousness – they never really got used to gathering the dung, especially since for some reason the chips seemed to attract rattlesnakes, which often clattered menacingly alongside the 'fuel'.

Under these testing conditions, pioneer women produced a wide variety of foods: bacon, beans, coffee, milk, butter, cheese, boiled potatoes, mashed potatoes, gravies, stewed dried fruit, bread, biscuits, pies, cakes, puddings and rice, as well as making preserves, jams and jellies from the many wild berries collected en route. Some of the women were even sophisticated enough to know that the vitamin C obtained from the gooseberries, chokeberries and serviceberries they collected along the trail could ward off scurvy. They were also alive to the dangers from contaminated water. Alkaline water was corrosive and made people sick, more severely polluted liquid could bring on typhoid, while the sparse waterholes in the desert were often crawling with infusoria and noisome with bison urine, which could cause dysentery and cholera. Naturally, the chore of having to boil water to extract weevils, microbes and other pests simply increased the mechanical and psychological toll on women, as guardians of the family's health.

By far the most unwelcome task on the trail was the family wash, which was back-breaking toil, done with no modern aids or detergents, simply with pumice stones and running water. Yet even to achieve a stopover to perform this dreaded chore, emigrant women often had to battle with their male leaders, who liked to press on without stopping, either through impatience, competitiveness with other wagon trains or (real or alleged) fear of Indians. Since men and women differed strongly on their view of Sabbath observance – with women worried about the 'impiety' of working and travelling on a Sunday and the men taking the gung-ho view that God's rules applied only within the pale of civilisation – cynical males rationalised the problem of laundry breaks by, in effect, dumping the problem back with the women: they could either travel on Sundays and have a day's stopover for the wash in the week, or they could spend their precious Sabbath washing clothes; the Lord would surely understand. As James Longmire, in the first emigrant train to Puget Sound in northern Washington State, archly put it: 'our washing . . . was not done always on Monday, to the annoyance of our excellent housekeepers.' Naturally, the clergymen on the trail did not like this 'compromise' solution at all, but were powerless to prevent its implementation.

Childcare and childbirth could not stop just because wagon trains were crossing the continent. The latter was more dangerous on the overland trail than at home, the former more onerous and tiresome. The battle against infant mortality and disease was further hampered by the poor hygiene on the overland trek, which also oppressed women in such 'delicate' areas as menstruation. At times it seemed to the hard-pressed female emigrants that the very forces of nature conspired against them; this was especially the case when their voluminous dresses became filled with mosquitoes. On top of this, they had to put up with male behaviour which back home they would have regarded as unacceptable. They had to turn a blind eye to crudeness, spitting and hawking, swearing and even obscene oaths routinely rasped out by exasperated patriarchs.

Perhaps the worst cross women had to bear was the lack of privacy in which to bathe, do ablutions, or even answer the call of nature. The nineteenth century was a prudish age in the Western world, so the sources are by and large silent about the arrangements for urination and defecation on the trail. One historian disposes of this issue as follows: 'Did they rig up a canvas screen at the campground, or were there slop jars in the wagons? . . . This is, however, scarcely a matter of concern for an epic tale; Homer does not tell us of the arrangements in the Greek camp along the Hellespont.' Oral testimony suggests that on many caravans the captains separated the sexes on a simple left/right basis. Men would make off to the right to relieve themselves while women would go to the left, often in convoys, so that each one could achieve a measure of privacy behind the spread skirts of her 'sisters', which acted as a modesty screen.

Nevertheless, some details do seep out from the diaries, and it is clear from this testimony that some encampments made use of hastily dug and improvised latrines, where considerations of convenience easily won out over hygiene. As John Faragher puts it: 'the animal and human excrement that littered the trail was a constant injury to women's habits.' This is reinforced by contemporary testimony from Charlotte Pengra, another intrepid lady diarist: 'The stench is sometimes almost unendurable, it arises from a ravene [sic] that is resorted to for special purposes by all the Emigration.' Sometimes, the foetor was just too much. When the captain on her caravan chose a campsite filthy from earlier travellers, Lavinia Porter threatened to take her blankets and go out on the prairie if her husband did not find her a clean place to sleep. She then engineered a revolt among the other women, and the captain had to find a new place to camp.

The sources are likewise generally silent about the role of sexuality on the emigrant trail. Rape, certainly before the 1849 gold rush, must have been almost non-existent, as also children born out of wedlock, for otherwise there would surely be more in the diaries about these aspects of relations between the sexes. One historian has gone so far as to suggest that men and women acted in a more hot-blooded way on the overland trail because of the danger and uncertainty of living on the edge, and that even sexual intercourse was heightened by the emigrant experience. Certainly, there were many wagon-train romances, but these hardly seemed extraordinary enough to merit more than passing mention, unless they impacted on some other aspect of the journey. When Joel Palmer was travelling back east in 1846, he had barely got started before one of his young companions abandoned the journey. At The Dalles, the young man caught sight of a beautiful young woman who had spent the winter with her parents there after being delayed in the Blue Mountains by the early snows – perhaps she was even one of the fair unknowns who had earlier elicited James Clyman's admiration. The besotted suitor promptly followed her back to the Willamette valley, whence he had just started.

Women's attitudes to Native Americans encountered en route deserve a separate study. Certainly, generalisations are risky. Women force-fed a diet of rape fantasies, atrocities and horror stories before they left home usually found that the reality of the Indians of the high plains belied their terrible reputation, to the point where many endorsed the judgement made by Elizabeth Gilliam Collins, an emigrant of 1844: 'I have always liked Indians.' What upset some female observers was that Indians had no sense of the nuances of polite society, had no chivalric feelings towards the 'weaker sex', and behaved casually, for instance by entering dwelling places before knocking. Gertrude Burlingame, an emigrant of 1858, experienced this aspect of the Kansa Indians even before she set out on the overland journey. She was combing her hair in her own house when she saw two large Indians in the mirror. To the great amusement of the braves, she ran out of the house screaming, convinced she was about to be scalped. The Kansa men laughed heartily and mimicked the actions of scalping. But Gertrude could not be prevailed upon to enter her house again while the intruders were still there, even though her husband made light of the incident and told her that the Kansa had simply been entranced by her beautiful hair.

Although rape of white women by Indians was uncommon (but certainly not unknown), even when the women had been made captive by ferocious tribes like the Comanche, Cheyenne or Sioux, what attracted most attention in white woman–Indian relations was the real or imagined lust of the Native American male. Emigrants scarcely knew whether to be amused or shocked by the many attempts made by Indians to buy white women. Struck by the beauty of some fair-skinned girls, wealthy chieftains would offer up to a good number of horses for them. And it was a great mistake for emigrant males to use levity on such occasions or regard the whole matter as a joke. In 1853, an emigrant so coveted a Pawnee's horse that he told the man he had a good mind to trade his own wife for the animal. The Pawnee took him literally, agreed, and tried to 'possess' her on the spot, to the consternation of all present. The Pawnee became very angry when the emigrant failed to honour the 'bargain', expressed incomprehension when the 'joke' was explained to him and was finally placated only when given a blue coat with shiny brass buttons.

The year 1842 decisively changed the motivational picture of the emigrants. In 1841, with few women present, it was still possible to take the line sometimes peddled even today, that the western impulse was a purely romantic phenomenon. Here is one view of 1841: 'We may suspect that many of them were driven on by mere boredom. To exist for a few years on a backwoods farm with almost no means of amusement or stimulation meant the build-up of an overwhelming desire to see new places and people.' And it is true that the unmarried men of the Bidwell–Bartleson party had variously explained their motives as living out fantasies inspired by the reading of Fenimore Cooper and Washington Irving and as a desire to see Indians, to hunt and to experience the great outdoors. But once wagon-train emigration became primarily a family affair, reason rather than romance had to take over. The inevitable effect of the 'feminisation' of the wagon trains was to enthrone home, hearth, roots and family as the supreme values, over the male camaraderie of free-spirited, open-ended, devil-may-care adventure. The penates and lares won out over Mars.

FIVE

THE GREAT MIGRATION

The great exodus to Oregon in 1843 was more meticulously planned than any caravan so far. Already, primitive guidebooks were starting to appear, based on the experiences of the Bidwell–Bartleson party, the Rufus Sage expedition, the 1842 Hastings trip and even on Fremont's first journey. All the books were at one in warning that loads of more than a ton could not be taken over the mountains by wagon, but somewhat spoiled their case by adding ominously that each family should take double the quantity of provisions they would need at home in Missouri for the relevant months. The old idea that one could fill the larder by shooting game on the march was firmly knocked on the head: it might be possible, but only a reckless fool would regard the possibility as a certainty. Moreover, the traders of the West were widely regarded as exploiters, who would think nothing of charging twenty-five cents a pint for flour or fifty cents for a pint of sugar or coffee. As a result, the emigrants were hard at their preparations in the early months of 1843, buying oxen and cows that could be sold in Oregon, packing bacon in strong bags, storing flour and sugar in double sacks to keep out water.

Accordingly, the 1843 pioneers were urged to bring no less than two hundred pounds of flour and one hundred pounds of bacon for every family member, as well as other provisions – beans, rice, ship's biscuits and dried fruit being particularly recommended. A typical family of four was found to be carting along eight hundred pounds of flour, two hundred pounds of lard, seven hundred pounds of bacon, two hundred pounds of beans, one hundred pounds of fruit, seventy-five pounds of coffee and twenty-five pounds of salt and pepper. If in doubt, it was best to cut down on the coffee and sugar rather than the staples proper. Emigrants were warned not to take furniture, as this would simply have to be jettisoned, and to leave behind all heavy articles except cooking utensils, a shovel and a pair of pot hooks. They were enjoined to bring clothes enough to last for a year and several pairs of stout walking shoes each. Other recommended items were butcher's knives, a water keg, tin plates, tin saucers and a grindstone for honing tools.

Those setting out for Oregon and worth less than $1,000 were hopelessly unrealistic, unless they were prepared to work their passage as teamsters, cooks, nannies or governesses. A single wagon and team would cost between $300 and $600 (and some emigrants had two or three wagons), with the same amount spent on provisions, and a nest egg with which to set up home in the promised land; all this in an era when a dollar a day was considered a good wage. As said before, the emigration west by wagon was almost by definition a middle-class movement, since the poor could not afford to go and the rich had no reason to. But the penniless employees gave the 1843 caravan the same ambiguous character that the Bidwell–Bartleson expedition had possessed. As Narcissa Whitman said: 'There are many intelligent and excellent people, and also many who are lawless and ignorant.' To which added Hubert Bancroft, the nineteenth-century historian who knew many of the emigrants, 'The immigration of 1843 was composed of people of pronounced character, rudely arrogant and aggressive rather than tame and submissive.'

The emigrants came straggling into Independence during April and early May. More than one thousand people and 1,800 oxen and cattle arrived and then moved on the thirty-three miles to the final rendezvous point at Elm Grove. It was clearly necessary to have talks about talks. On 20 May, the Oregon Emigrating Company came into existence and set a firm departure date of Monday 22 May. Committees were formed to formulate rules and procedures for the elections for officers, and it was agreed that all adult males over sixteen were deemed by the mere act of participation to have agreed to military service if required. Decision-making would be by adult male suffrage, with a one-third vote needed to recall the officials who would be elected before they crossed the Kansas River. A council of nine would function as judge and jury to try crimes and adjudicate disputes.

The long haul from Independence to Elm Grove saw many of the emigrants pensive, sad or wistful. The twenty-two-year-old Jim Nesmith noted: 'This day was fine and clear. Took a farewell look at the State of Missouri.' Another young bachelor, Pierson Reading, was in more facetious mood: 'We have now bid farewell to the Palefaces.' Another of the emigrants, Peter Burnett, used to the heavily wooded Mississippi valley, got a shock when he reached the inaptly named Elm Grove and found just a couple of elms. 'I have learned for the first time,' he wrote, 'that two trees could compose a grove.' Once at the rendezvous, the travellers spent the 21st dancing and singing to the joyous strains of the fiddle, making friends or simply chewing the fat around the campfires. Burnett noted: 'No scene appeared to our enthusiastic vision more exquisite than the sight of so many wagons, tents, fires, cattle and people, as were here collected. At night the sound of joyous music was heard in the tents. Our long journey thus began in sunshine and song, in anecdote and laughter.'

On 22 May 1843, the first wagons started on the trail, at first over lush prairie with no danger from Indians. Eight miles from Elm Grove a solitary signpost on the barren plain bore the legend 'Road to Oregon'; they followed the route to the next rendezvous point at Big Springs on the fertile bottom land of the Wakarusa River, where the trail divided to lead to two fords over the Kansas River. The first part of the elections was held here. Fifty-three-year-old John Gantt was chosen as guide. We may be sure that Gantt did not tell his emigrant employers that in 1829 he had been cashiered from the army for falsifying accounts, but his money-grubbing instincts were on display in the form of the fee – one dollar per head – that he levied for his services. Canny, too, was his decision not to join the caravan until it was ready to trek on for the Kansas River in earnest. He let the emigrants work out the crossing of the Wakarusa for themselves. Predictably, they made heavy weather of it. Baffled by the steep forty-five-degree banks, they eased the wagons down at the end of a tether, tying ropes to the wagons' rear axles, then allowing them to roll gently down the bank as several muscular teamsters paid out the line. The teamsters then transferred to the opposite shore and used teams of oxen to haul the wagons up the equally steep opposite slopes. This was the standard procedure at difficult stream crossings.

Gantt also made sure he missed the speech-making and fustian rhetoric of the office-seekers. Realising that the enforced togetherness, deferred gratification and general hardships of the trail would be bound to bring out the worst in human nature, and aware that the concourse of more than a thousand people made crime a statistical certainty, the overlanders had no choice but to create their own machinery of self-government and law enforcement. A temporary chairman presided as speakers at first exhorted the assembled pioneers to adopt the constitutions of either Tennessee or Missouri. When it was objected that this was using a sledgehammer to crack a nut, they drew up a simpler code of laws, suited to the primitive travelling society. The original nine 'guardians' were expanded to a Council of Ten who would act as judge and jury in cases 'subversive of good order and military discipline'; the original recall provision for officers was retained; and in addition a captain and orderly sergeant were to be elected by ballot of all males over sixteen. A short period of electioneering would be allowed.

The next task was to cross the swollen Kansas River. Since fording was out of the question, the choice was simple: pay the exorbitant charges on the existing Papins' ferry or build a new one. The Papin brothers, Louis and Joseph, were notorious for their high prices and general surliness: they would not even rent out a platform to allow the emigrants to build their own ferry except at prohibitive rates. As the overlanders slowly and painfully began to construct their own rafts and barges, the more impatient among them broke rank and agreed to pay the Papins' charges. The hoped-for organic solidarity among the trekkers was thus shattered before they even reached the wilderness proper. This manifestation of 'rugged individualism' was only the first of such antisocial outbursts on the 1843 exodus.

Peter Burnett was already disgusted with the behaviour of some of his fellow-travellers. He noted with distaste that even on the way to the Kansas, the pushier members of the party raced the others to get to the river bank first and thought, reasonably enough, that this boded ill for a journey with 2,000 miles still to go. But this time the so-called donkeys had the last laugh on the so-called lions, for the impatient faction that had hired the Papins' platform suffered the indignity of seeing their ferry sink beneath them. This was largely because the foolish wagoners had overloaded the barge. When it capsized in the middle of the stream, Kansa Indians jumped in and rescued the women; this they did without payment, but to retrieve the equipment and provisions they demanded a hefty fee.

Those who had built their own ferry demonstrated genuine pioneering ingenuity. They laid round poles between two dugout canoes, rolled their wagons on to the improvised platform one by one, then pulled them across by tugging at the long ropes attached to each end of the raft, unloaded the wagon, and motioned to the men on the other side, who would then pull the raft back to their bank and begin again; they then repeated the process for more than one hundred wagons, which, not surprisingly, the emigrants regarded as a very tedious process. Once again, despite the contempt evinced for them by many emigrants, the Kansa Indians proved their worth, pulling ropes and swimming alongside the ferries in return for minimal wages. Their usefulness was offset, in the minds of most emigrants, by their bizarre appearance, all shaven heads, feathered scalp locks, and heads and bodies daubed with vermilion in 'rings, streaks and stripes'.

To the young men in the wagon train the sight of Indians swimming in the river was just too much of a temptation. In they plunged, splashing, turning turtle and generally indulging in horseplay. But this was another example of dangerous folly: the Kansas had treacherous currents and was not to be trifled with. It could not compare in danger with the Snake, the Columbia, the Green, and still less with the North Fork of the Platte, the scene of innumerable emigrant drownings, but Jim Nesmith got personal experience of the peril on the Kansas on this very day. A man named William Vaughan was leading his stock across the stream when he was suddenly attacked by cramp and disappeared under the waters. Seeing what was happening, Nesmith swam to his aid but found himself in desperate straits when the panic-stricken Vaughan clung to his saviour like a limpet and bade fair to take him down to a watery grave also. Fortunately, a third man named Stewart lent a hand, enabling the shaken rescuer to scramble disconsolately up the bank. By this time Vaughan had lost consciousness. While Nesmith and Stewart attempted artificial respiration, a teenager named Edward Lenox rushed to his wagon to get help. His father returned with hot coffee. Nesmith and Stewart had by now despaired of reviving the comatose Vaughan by physical manipulation and pumping. Seeing signs of life, the elder Lenox forced coffee down the victim's throat. Vaughan gradually came round and, after two days, made a complete recovery.

Once on the far side of the Kansas, there was another pause while fresh officials were elected. The pause was in any case necessary, to allow the unwieldy wagon train finally to uncoil itself to its full length. It took six days for the entire grandly named Oregon Emigrating Company to cross the Kansas; in nine days the travellers had covered just fifty-five miles from Elm Grove, and already were heard the Jeremiahs who said that at this rate of progress the caravan would never get to Oregon before the winter snows. Cynics called the campsite on the far side of the Kansas Camp Delay, and it is noteworthy that the last days of May saw a spate of letter writing and more voluminous diary entries than usual.

Despite the growing contempt expressed for the Kansa Indians because of their petty pilfering, the method chosen for the election of officials suggests an Indian chautauqua rather than the normal practice of democracy. Each candidate was called out and, with his back to the electorate, began walking out into the prairie; those voting for him would fall in behind, forming a 'tail' like that behind a Highland chieftain of old. As the more popular candidates acquired longer and longer lines, they were required to speed up the electoral process by breaking into a run, forcing their supporters to canter with them. The man with the longest tail was declared the winner, and in this way Peter Burnett became captain of the company and Jim Nesmith orderly sergeant. The newspaper reporter Matthew Field happened to be in Camp Delay that day and he wrote up the bizarre event thus:

> These men were running about the prairie in long strings; the leaders – in sport and for the purpose of puzzling the judges – doubling and winding in the drollest fashion; so that the all-important business of forming a government seemed very much like the merry schoolboy game of 'snapping the whip' . . . 'Running for office' is certainly performed in more literal fashion on the prairie than we see the same sort of business performed in town.

The same process was adopted for the selection of the Council of Ten. Since these were the men who were to rule over the 'travelling commonwealth', enacting laws, amending those that turned out unsatisfactory, trying offenders, settling disputes and enforcing laws, the gap between image and reality was even more unsettling. To use Bagehot's terminology, if the Council of Ten was efficient, it was certainly not dignified. One emigrant could hardly wait to reach Oregon before writing to a newspaper in New Orleans about this serio-comic interlude: 'It was really very funny to see the candidates for the solemn council . . . run several hundred yards away to show off the length of their tails, and then cut a half circle, so as to turn and admire their longitudinal popularity *in extenso* themselves.'

The new officers clearly seem to have been elected by a 'cattleman's ramp' and represented the interests of those, like Jesse Applegate, who had brought huge herds of cattle to the rendezvous in defiance of the tenets of the founding fathers of the Oregon Emigration Society.

The extended Applegate family was one of the wealthiest and most influential on the trek. The original patriarch of the clan, Daniel, had fought in the American War of Independence, and then moved west to Kentucky, where his three sons – Charles, Lindsay and Jesse – were born. The restless Daniel then moved further west, to St Louis, Missouri, where he bought extensive acreage for his sons in the 'Platte Purchase' of 1832. The Applegate males seemed to get more impressive through the generations, for Lindsay made more of a showing than Charles and was in turn eclipsed by Jesse. In 1843, Charles was thirty-seven and Lindsay, a veteran of the Black Hawk War, thirty-five, but it was thirty-two-year-old Jesse who made the biggest historical impact. After attending Rock Creek Seminary in Shiloh, Illinois, he had a brief spell as a schoolteacher before developing a consuming interest in surveying. He became deputy to the surveyor-general in St Louis and was, by the standards of the Midwest, an educated man: he knew some law, was well versed in history, literature and science, and was passionate about mathematics. His brothers seemed to be in awe of him, and Lindsay named his third son after him. This boy, Jesse A. Applegate, aged seven in 1843, left a most valuable memoir of the 1843 emigration.

Burnett and Nesmith were controversial from the start. They began inauspiciously by abandoning one of the principles agreed at Independence, which limited each emigrant to three head of cattle for each adult male in the party. This new measure was immediately seen as divisive, for since guard duties and rosters were apportioned equally, it would mean that the onus of looking after the stock of wealthy emigrants would fall on the poor and dispossessed. Not only did the measure breed discontent and disharmony at the bottom end of the social scale, but it encouraged the greedy and irresponsible among the wealthier sectors. It was impossible to guard vast herds of cattle at night: Indians stole and killed them; the owners then complained to the officers and the Council of Ten; they in turn rebuked the propertyless and reluctant guards, whose resentment was thus ratched up another notch.

The poorer emigrants also complained that the big cattle owners, like Jesse Applegate, whose herd numbered upwards of two hundred head, were slowing down the rate of march; if they got caught in the winter snows, Applegate, with his glut of beef on the hoof, would doubtless survive, while they starved. The council, aware how high feelings were running, therefore implemented two measures. They got the cattle owners to agree to make their herds available as an emergency food supply at a fixed price to be decided by the council. The other decision was more dramatic: henceforth the caravan would split in two, with a faster vanguard proceeding unencumbered and a slower 'cow column' under Jesse Applegate following behind.

The rougher elements in the wagon train were barely placated by this. There was always a hard core of troublemakers who believed in communalism when it suited their book on Monday and rugged individualism when it worked to their advantage on Tuesday. There were standing orders for the wagons to be corralled in a circle at camp, not out of fear of Indian attack so much as to pen the oxen and mules in the centre and stop them from straying. But no sooner had the elected officers promulgated their first decrees than hotheads in the party tested their authority by a deliberate act of defiance. Having ostentatiously camped their two wagons by themselves, a party of roughnecks drove down to the creek next morning in blatant defiance of the council and made ready to cross. 'The commander' (it is uncertain from the context whether this was Nesmith or Gantt) sent two men after them with orders to stop them or shoot them if they refused. But the recalcitrant wagons boasted a formidable party. When they drew their guns and made as though to shoot it out, the 'policemen' decided not to press their luck.

At night, the overlanders made their camp outside the corralled wagons and freight animals, taking turns to guard the vast herds of loose cattle. Contrary to the myth of 'organic solidarity' among pioneers, standing together to face a common threat, with all hearts beating as one, the nightly coexistence was fraught with petty irritation, bickering and worse. Especially for those who had been used to a lonely life on an isolated Midwestern farm, the enforced togetherness of the trail and the almost total lack of privacy badly affected the nerves. When to this was added the resentment of scrimshankers, freeloaders, professional hypo-chondriacs, card-sharps or simply the different manners and morals of people from the next state or county, it was not surprising that tempers often flared, particularly in the early weeks of the journey. To begin with, the fist fight was a regular occurrence, but the overlanders soon learned that this was counter-productive. As one of them put it: 'The man with a black eye and battered face could not well hunt up his cattle or drive his team.'

With morale low, the elements took a hand and gave the emigrants a different kind of buffeting. Now three weeks out on the trail, the travellers were assailed by a storm of rare fury, blowing up suddenly and unexpectedly as if from nowhere, as so often on the prairie. All night the noise of thunder rolled, seeming to one overlander, Overton Johnson, like the cannonade of heavy artillery. Tents and even wagons were blown down by violent winds. The lightning flashed and coruscated as if a demented Zeus were throwing thunderbolts by the second. All vertical surfaces seemed like pillars of flame or corposant, and even the animals' ears seemed to be on fire. The biggest danger from lightning was not to humans, though emigrants were sometimes killed by the bolts, but to panic-stricken animals; the greatest risk of stampede always came during fierce lightning. This time the travellers were lucky: there were no runaways and only one horse was killed by the thunderbolts.

The violence of a prairie storm was a novel experience for most of the overlanders, who, in their journals, reckoned it one of their most memorable, if terrifying, experiences. William Newby declared that it passed belief that such a deluge of rain could beat unceasingly from 10 p.m. till well after dawn the next day and remarked on the special terror entertained by the women and children in the party. Pierson Reading concurred, and suggested that the dangers might have been more acute even than was realised: 'The whole atmosphere seemed charged with the electric fluid, and during some five hours seemed a continuous blaze. I felt much uneasiness, sleeping in the back part of a tent, at the foot of which were six guns with the horns full of powder near them.'

It was bad luck for the emigrants that the storm hit them just as they had crossed the west fork of the Blue River. The banks of the engorged river were now flooded for a quarter of a mile on either side, and there was eight inches of water even in the 'safe' encampment; where they had crossed at twilight the night before there was, next morning, a massive lake forty feet deep. All were soaked, chilled and damp, with children miserable and crying, women in despair and sleepless men cursing their ill fate. But there was no respite from the elements. Nineteen-year-old John Boardman left a diary which summed up the experiences of early June: 'Tuesday 6th . . . Rained hard all night; all wet.' 'Wednesday 7th . . . Rain all night . . . no sleep.' 'Thursday 8th . . . Laying by for high water. Rain all night; wet as usual; little sleep.'

The heavy rains caused havoc in the caravan. Bedding and clothes were saturated, large quantities of corn and meal ruined, soaked and rotten provisions abandoned on the trail. Worst of all, many overlanders began to panic when they discovered their wagons hub-deep in a quagmire, immovable even with the most frantic exertions of the oxen. Dozens of men had to push and heave at a single wagon to make any impression, the oxen meanwhile slipping and floundering in the deep mud. The stalled teams and furious, frustrated drivers and teamsters all the time contended with a continuing deluge of rain, the noise of the precipitation magnified in the great echo chamber that was the empty, treeless prairie.

The mood of the travellers, which had been dark even before the Little Blue, now turned positively ugly. They were victims of the whims of nature and the waywardness of wind and weather, but this did not satisfy the jaundiced travellers. They felt betrayed by human agency, they needed to fasten responsibility on a leader who had led them into this mess, they wanted scapegoats. The obvious candidate as recipient of mass vitriol was the captain, Peter Burnett, especially as he had chosen a campsite on the evening of the 7th which he guaranteed would be dry but turned out to be very far from it. Having endured one verbal lashing too many, he finally resigned on 8 June, ostensibly on grounds of 'ill health'. He was anyway tired of the indiscipline of the caravan and the inability of American 'freedom-loving democrats' to take orders. As he put it understatedly later: 'I adopted rules and endeavoured to enforce them, but found much practical difficulty and opposition.'

The net result of the debacle at the Blue River was that the gap in attitudes between the vanguard and the rearguard, or 'cow column', under Jesse Applegate widened still further. William Martin succeeded Burnett as captain, and the advance party was divided into four divisions, with a captain and an orderly sergeant assigned to each; the rule that each wagon in the vanguard could take no more than ten cattle with it was strictly enforced. Jesse Applegate followed and extended the 'small is beautiful' principle, dividing his sixty wagons and the bulk of the cattle into fifteen platoons. His task was easier, for all the malcontents, barrack-room lawyers and troublemakers naturally went with the faster column. Applegate was glad to see the back of them: 'They were probably brave enough but would never submit to discipline as soldiers. If the president himself had started across the plains to command a company, the first time he would choose a bad camp or in any way offend them, they would turn him out and elect someone among themselves who would suit them better.'

Applegate proved a born leader. He rotated his platoons, so that the four wagons in the vanguard one day would be in the extreme rear the next and would then work their way up the column for the next fortnight until they once again headed the cow column; if any of the teamsters or owners disobeyed rules or proved indolent, negligent or incompetent, they would be given an extraordinary 'punishment' – being a rearguard to the rearguard. Applegate's leadership qualities, though, were such that punitive acts were rarely necessary, and his platoons operated with such efficiency that the ostensibly much slower cow column kept pace with the so-called rapid runners at the front, and often camped within hailing distance of the vanguard at night.

Applegate has left us a clear account of the daily routine of the rear column. Reveille, signalled by the firing of rifles, was at 4 a.m. Sixty herders then made sure that none of the more than 2,000 cattle had strayed during the night or been stolen by Indians. At 5 a.m., they started rounding up the animals, contracting the huge grazing circle, herding them into a narrow circle ready for the morning trek. From 6 to 7 a.m., the smoke from a hundred fires announced breakfast time, after which the tents were struck, the wagons loaded, the teams yoked and hitched to them, and all made ready for the seven o'clock signal that marked the beginning of the day's march. The bullwhackers cracked their whips, harsh and guttural voices rasped the words of command to the oxen, and finally the clear notes of a trumpet sounded the advance. Onlookers often marvelled that a scene of confusion at, say, a quarter to seven could transform itself fifteen minutes later into a military manoeuvre of clockwork precision, with each wagon in its preordained place.

Both columns were tailed for a stretch by a group of Kansa and Osage Indians, eighty to ninety strong, described by some of the emigrant diarists as a war party and by others as a ragtag tatterdemalion gang of beggars. Gantt advised the overlanders to buy them off with food, to avoid the otherwise predictable thefts. Opinions were divided on the wisdom of such 'appeasement'; the vanguard gave the Indians some bread and a calf after the 'warriors' begged and cajoled, whimpering that they had not eaten for three days. The cow column proved a tougher nut for the Indians to crack; it was, after all, concern for their cattle that had led them to break with their comrades in the first place. When the Kansa braves asked for beef, Applegate refused; instead, he offered them shirts and tobacco. The general feeling of the 1843 overlanders for the Kansa was deeply contemptuous: Peter Burnett described them as 'the most miserable, cowardly and dirty Indians we saw east of the Rocky Mountains'.

On 10 June, the emigrants came across the body of a Pawnee who had earlier fallen foul of the Kansa–Osage party. The travellers were revolted by the atrocities that been committed on his corpse; every extremity had been hacked off, not just the scalp. A frisson of apprehension ran through the caravan, and all the wild rumours of Indian massacres once more surfaced to terrify the Oregon-bound hopefuls. The general nervousness made the sentries more jittery than ever, and there was a legendary incident when a young man named Nathan Sutton, standing guard in the inky blackness of a prairie night, blazed away at a 'prowling Indian', only to discover at daybreak that the savage he had shot was a mule, valued at $300. 'Nate the Indian-killer' was ribbed more mercilessly for this exploit on the 1843 journey than Cheyenne Dawson ever was for his experience two years earlier.

As the caravan slowly snaked its way north-west along the Little Blue River, the monsoon-like rains struck again. Later records showed that most of 1843's precipitation on the plains pelted down during these two weeks. This was bad luck for the travellers, for otherwise the rolling treeless plains abutting the Little Blue would have been easy country for wagons. The lack of trees was advantageous for the Indian tribes, at least in the short term, for it meant that the pioneers were not tempted to divert and settle in this vast tract of Indian territory. According to the ethos and culture of 1840s pioneers, treeless lands were valueless lands, for they lacked the timber necessary for log cabins, outhouses, fence posts and furniture, to say nothing of wood for heating and cooking. Peter Burnett expressed the common prejudice: the country, he said, was 'generally fertile but destitute of timber except upon the streams . . . I saw only a few places where good farms could be made, for want of timber'.

When the rain stopped, soft breezes caressed the glistening grass, making it seem 'to spread a stream of light along the surface of the wave-like expanse'. It was on the trek up the Little Blue valley to the junction with the Platte that the 1843 party had their first encounter with the wild animals of the plains. A party of six hunters, including Gantt and Nesmith, pursued a rogue male buffalo, detached from his herd. After a running battle, they managed to bring the elderly bison down, but only after pumping seven shots into him. Buffalo did not succumb easily to the firepower available in the 1840s; in 1841, Joseph Williams noted that it took between fifteen and twenty bullets to kill a single buffalo bull. Nor were the hunters' exertions rewarded with a feast of venison-like meat; Nesmith found the flesh of the old bull tough and stringy.

Like all their predecessors, the men of '43 took careful note of the prairie fauna. Overton Johnson noted the peculiarity that east of the Rockies there was plenty of big game but very little smaller fry or wildfowl; also that bees were not found west of the Kansas River. Pronghorn antelope were abundant in this area, but they proved too good for the guns of the 1843 hunters. Second only to the buffalo in numbers, distinctive with sloe eyes and a white spot on the hips and appearing to some observers like a cross between a deer and a sheep, the antelope typically grazed in small herds up to thirty in number and attracted all who saw them by their beauty, speed and grace and their loping run. They seemed to have an instinctive sense of the exact range of the hunters' guns and would commonly halt just outside this perimeter, examine the emigrants curiously, then vanish, only to reappear inquisitively on the other flank of the caravan.

In the 1840s, antelope were still common in Wyoming and western Nebraska but positively teemed along the Little Blue and the Platte. Though much prized for their flesh, which tasted like the finest mutton, they were more than a match for the weapons technology of the day and could be 'bagged' only by subterfuge. Typically, a hunter would construct a hide, conceal himself inside and wait, meanwhile attracting the animal by planting a red handkerchief or bandanna on a stick. If an antelope then approached, giving the hunter a perfect shot, it was indeed likely to be dead meat. Largely, though, this 'American gazelle' was untouchable except by expert marksmen. Some foolish hunters thought they could use dogs to overhaul them. Jesse Applegate's son Lindsay had a pet dog called Fleet which he loosed to pursue an antelope. At first, Fleet seemed to be gaining on his prey, but the antelope was merely toying with the black cur. When the dog was within a few yards of him, the antelope lengthened his stride. There was a flurry and a whorling cloud of dust, but when it cleared the antelope was seen to have gained a full fifty yards on the inaptly named Fleet.

In mid-June, the emigrants passed an invisible frontier into the territory of the Pawnee. These Indians always drew mixed opinions from travellers. They had a reputation as thieves, and Gantt immediately doubled the guard at night. Some who met them positively loathed the Pawnee, and the great historian Francis Parkman was one of these. Pondering his experiences on the plains in 1846 when he met them migrating from their winter villages on the lower Platte southwards to their summer hunting grounds, he described them as 'a treacherous, cowardly banditti, who by a thousand acts of pillage and murder, have deserved chastisement at the hands of government'. Overton Johnson concurred: they were 'the most notorious rascals anywhere east of the Rocky Mountains'.

On 17 June, the wagon train met a small party of Pawnee, enabling the diarists to form further opinions. Pierson Reading, appreciating the fact that, unlike the Kansa, they were too haughty to beg and were much better looking than those mendicant Indians, described them as worthy representatives of 'a proud and honourable nation'. Peter Burnett liked the fact that their hairstyles were similar to those of white men, unlike the shaven-headed Kansa. No one gave a thought to the real plight of the Pawnee, who were being hit by a triad of adverse circumstances. The buffalo range was narrowing because of overhunting; the Teton Sioux, who had arrived in the Platte hinterlands around 1830, were literally hounding them to destruction, aided by their eight-to-one superiority in population; and in 1838 the Pawnee were devastated by smallpox. Gradually, this proud people, who once controlled the country from the forks of the Platte south to the Republican, Kansas and Arkansas rivers, were being driven out of their traditional hunting grounds. In the middle of the eighteenth century they had boasted a population of 20,000 but already by 1843 their numbers were down to 6,000.

On 18 June, the wagon train left the Little Blue and began a strenuous thirty-mile trek across picturesque prairie country and low sand dunes to the banks of the Platte; the sentries were on maximum alert, for this was the territory where the destitute Pawnee liked to do most of their thieving. Additionally, for this arduous overland section of the journey the travellers were out of sight of water for a full two days, so for the first time the pioneering experience was truly dangerous. Water shortages were a much more severe threat to a wagon train than Indians or prairie storms as, although men and women could just about survive for a few days without the life-giving liquid, cattle, oxen and draught animals could not. Rivers, and especially the Platte itself, were vital arteries; even experienced guides could locate no more than two freshwater springs between the headwaters of the Blue and the Sweetwater.

The wagons hit the Platte River at Grand Island, later to be the site of Fort Kearny, 316 miles from Independence. Grand Island in the middle of the stream was heavily timbered, but the south bank of the Platte, where the wagon train debouched, was treeless. The Platte River always annoyed overlanders, since it seemed neither fish nor fowl in riverine terms. It was, they remarked ruefully, a mile wide and six inches deep and useless to man on every count. On the one hand, the water was too thick to drink and 'too thin to plow'. On the other, it was too shallow for floating boats and too perilous to ford because of quicksands; fur trappers had long since given up on it as they spent more time running aground on sandbars and shallows than floating their loaded canoes. To Peter Burnett, the Platte seemed like the Nile of his imagination, flowing hundreds of miles through sandy deserts, while Pierson Reading was more impressed by the rapid current in a shallow river, the sandy soil impregnated with sulphate and the barren sandhills running parallel with the south bank.

As they trekked in a gradual north-westerly direction along the great river road, the teamsters and bullwhackers, beguiled by the barren landscape, the warm genial sunshine of languorous early summer along the placid Platte and the mirage-like miasmata from the broad stream, increasingly succumbed to waking dreams or found themselves nodding off at the reins. Monotony and sunshine induced drowsiness, it was difficult to keep awake, and many drivers fell asleep when they should have been urging their charges forward; grateful for the respite, the oxen, somnolent also, came to a halt and dozed fitfully until the drivers, recovering from their slumbers, snapped the animals out of sleep with cracking whips. Jesse Applegate remembered the dreamy summer days in the same way and recalled how 'a drowsiness has fallen apparently on man and beast; teamsters drop asleep in their perches and even when walking by their teams, and the words of command are now addressed to the slowly creeping oxen in the soft tenor of women or the piping treble of children, while the snores of the teamsters make a droning accompaniment.'

There were two obvious aspects of the great Platte River trail: the multitudes of bison and the scarcity of timber for fuel. The overlanders solved the latter problem, as had previous travellers, by using a by-product of the former, in the shape of dried buffalo dung. Sometimes the concentration of dung chips determined the location of an overnight camp but more often the gatherers, usually children, had to range far and wide to bring in a sufficient quantity. Each company vied with the others to see which could accumulate the biggest pile of chips. Inevitably, jealousy and resentment built up, there were attempts at theft by 'trespassers' and fisticuffs resulted, one of which violent encounters involved Lindsay Applegate's seven-year-old son Jesse.

Even when sufficient buffalo chips had been collected, a high wind could be an implacable enemy of a pioneer wife trying to cook a meal. Matches, carried in sealed containers, were highly valued by the pioneers. Lacking a camp stove, their usual procedure on the high plains was to dig a shallow slit trench two or three feet long, in line with prevailing winds, or to create a kind of natural oven by choosing a spot a short distance from a steep river bank, digging a hole about twelve inches deep for a fire, and then providing an air tunnel; this was done by forcing a ramrod horizontally from the river bank to provide the necessary draft. As Peter Burnett noted: 'It is necessary to dig a narrow ditch, about eight inches wide, one foot deep, and two or three feet long. This confines the heat and prevents the wind from scattering the fire.'

Once on to the Platte, the buffalo herds appeared in their tens of thousands. Here was a chance for fresh meat, and the captains of the 1843 party took it. The evidence suggests that their hunting parties were better organised than most such emigrant expeditions, which usually took after the bison with wild cries and little thought to the considerable problems of downing the prey. Lacking any understanding of the physiology of giant bulls weighing between 1,500 and 2,000 pounds, emigrants often needed fifty shots to finish off a single animal. Many blasted away face-to-face with the prairie leviathans, not realising that the front of a bison's thick skull was given extra armour-plating by accretions of sand and dirt several inches thick matted into the animal's woolly forehead. The best opinion was that bison were most vulnerable when shot between the forelegs and the lower body.

Largely ignorant of such considerations, on 20 June Colonel Martin commissioned twenty men to go buffalo-hunting with him and bring in fresh meat for the wagon train. Their orders were to swing in an outer arc and make contact with the main party again further ahead on the trail when their kill-quotas were filled. Among those who drew the straw (whether short or long was uncertain at the time) for the hunt were Overton Johnson, Jim Nesmith and Pierson Reading. All three recorded the dismal experience of being caught in the open by the pelting of a pitiless storm. Johnson wrote that the rain 'poured down upon us as if all the windows of heaven had been at once unbarred. The lightning and the thunder were dimming to the eye and deafening to the ear; and, withal, it was certainly just as cold as it could be without the water congealing . . . [the men] were as far as wet and cold were concerned, about in the same condition that they would have been had they been soaked an age in the Atlantic Ocean, and just hung out on the North Cape to dry.'

Such was the monsoon-like ferocity of the storm that they lay all night in sodden blankets, unable to sleep, but glad to be sheltered from the biting wind. Reading wrote of the irony of going supperless when they had already killed enough bison to feed an army: 'It is to me rather hard, but there is no remedy. Misery loves company. There are twenty of us in the same situation. It is provoking to have plenty of meat in camp and suffer hunger.' Still, after a four-day hunt, the twenty dauntless buffalo-killers were able to rejoin the main column with horses laden with fresh meat. The emigrants devoured the steaks and, especially, the tongues; Peter Burnett testified that it was not just the hunger on the prairies that made him regard bison meat as the sweetest-tasting of all viands.

By 26 June, the universal complaint was not of rain but the sweltering heat and the plagues of mosquitoes. Whether through paranoia or objective observation, successive parties of overlanders became convinced that the plains variety of mosquito was especially noisome; one theory was that the insects were particularly bloodthirsty as they lived principally on the blood of bison and savage Indians. The mosquitoes particularly irritated the men of '43 as they seemed to make their most maddening attacks at the precise moment Martin and his men were searching unsuccessfully for a place shallow enough to cross the South Platte. On 29 June, they abandoned the quest and settled down to build a flotilla of primitive ferry boats. The hammers of carpenters and wheelwrights echoed through the cottonwood grove where the wagon train had come to an uncertain and perplexed halt.

To construct the boats, the pioneers used two fresh buffalo hides sewn together, tightly stretched out over the wagon beds with the fleshy side facing the sun; when the hides were thoroughly dry and blanched, they covered them with tallow and ashes to provide waterproofing. The snag was that to obtain the number of hides required a further buffalo safari was needed. The cliché about more haste came into its own: in their haste to obtain the skins, the hunters grew negligent. Two men were injured in firearm accidents and a mule was killed in the same way, all through sheer carelessness on the part of those bearing the firearms.

These accidents illustrated a perennial truth about the overland migrations. As has been said, the safety record of the wagon trains was appalling. Armed to the teeth as most of the emigrants were, much like Mexican bandoleros with entire arsenals of rifles, shotguns and revolvers, they wounded, maimed and killed themselves in alarming numbers. Partly this was because of fundamental ignorance about firearms – many bought so-called sophisticated Indian-killing weapons with which they were totally unfamiliar – and partly because of the absence of safety catches on the firearms. But also, it must be acknowledged, shooting accidents happened because of the sheer pigheaded stupidity and laziness of many emigrants, who neglected to take their caps out before stowing weapons in the wagon. 'Shot himself accidentally' was seen on dozens of trailside grave markers and was undoubtedly *the* major cause of accidental death. Then there the other injuries: men with bloody noses from recoils, with amputated thumbs after they had been caught in the hammer of a revolver, crippled after literally shooting themselves in the foot, with dislocated shoulders from bullets or even blinded by a burst gun.

Once the shell of the wagons had been covered with skins and waterproofed, the emigrants reloaded their effects and ferried the improvised barges across the Platte. For the one-mile crossing through deep water, each 'boat' was assigned six men, who waded or swam alongside or tugged at a long rope attached to the front. The men with the tow ropes usually had to swim like gundogs, with the rope in their mouths, until they found water shallow enough for secure footing; in so doing, they often swallowed foul or foetid water and consequently were ill with fever. Further upstream, where the river was wider but shallower, teams of animals were chained together in a long row, harnessed to empty wagons (with horses in the front and oxen in the rear) and pulled across by a rope attached to the lead team by groups of thirty to forty men tugging from the opposite bank. Between twenty and fifty wagons might be chained together during this manoeuvre.

The crossing of the South Platte took six days, long enough for Jesse Applegate and the cow column to catch up once more. There was no slackening of the pace on 4 July, and the national holiday was largely subsumed in the effort to get the wagons across the dangerous waters. All the diarists spoke of the 'Glorious Fourth' in a formulaic way, but then went on to record that they had spent the holiday swimming the Platte, hauling on a tow rope, pushing a 'skinboat' or shepherding the cattle, horses and oxen across the river. Many emigrants appeared indifferent to

Independence Day and they were probably the wise ones, for Jim Nesmith noted in his diary that some of the overlanders had tortured themselves by imagining the riotous celebrations going on 'back East' and salivating at the mere idea of ice cream, soda, mint juleps, cognac, sherry, porter and ale.

The base for the six-day crossing was a wooded campsite on the south of the river dubbed Sleepy Grove by the emigrants. At Sleepy Grove, the first childbirth on the '43 emigration was recorded in the form of a baby daughter born to a Mr and Mrs Stewart. Here, too, the Oregon veteran Dr Marcus Whitman caught up with the overlanders. Whitman had made a late start from Missouri but, travelling fast on horseback, he threaded his way from wagon train to wagon train, handed from one to another like a baton in a relay race, until he caught up with the main body of the emigrants. Coming in with no supplies and equipment, Whitman was assigned to Daniel Waldo's company, where Captain Waldo moaned about the expense of having to feed the newcomer who, the captain jeered, had arrived with just one boiled ham to see him clear across the continent. Most of the company, though, thought it was cheap at the price to have a qualified physician in their ranks. Certainly, morale was high on the last night at Sleepy Grove when, with all wagons and impedimenta safely across the Platte, the rearguard held a boisterous sand-kicking dance, with country fiddlers bowing and trilling with accelerated rhythms and the women excluded because of the unseemly whooping and hoofing.

Whitman's role in the 1843 emigration has been overstated and overrated, but it is clear that he made an impact on the emigrants. A notably sloppy dresser – described by one observer as looking like Robinson Crusoe in the first illustrations to Defoe's book – with the languid body language of a *flâneur*, Whitman was surprisingly energetic, optimistic and upbeat, always ready to urge on despairing or recalcitrant emigrants. Jim Nesmith testified that Whitman 'possessed a great and good heart, full of charity and courage, and utterly destitute of cant, hypocrisy, shams and effeminacy, and always terribly in earnest'. Jesse Applegate went further:

From the time he joined us on the Platte until he left us at Fort Hall, his great experience and indomitable energy were of priceless value to the emigrating column. His constant advice, which we knew was based upon a knowledge of the road before us was 'travel, travel, TRAVEL – nothing else will take you to the end of your journey; nothing is wise that does not help you along, nothing is good for you that causes a moment's delay.' His great authority as a physician . . . saved us many prolonged and perhaps ruinous delays . . . it is no disparagement to others to say, that to no other individual are the emigrants of 1843 so much indebted for the successful conclusion of their journey as to Dr Marcus Whitman.

Once over the south fork, the emigrants made rapid progress to the North Platte and camped on its south bank on 9 July. The fissiparous nature of the 1843 wagon train was never so clearly on display, with more and more parties of emigrants seeming to make a point of splitting off from the main body. Daniel Waldo, friend and former Missouri neighbour of Jesse Applegate, had left Independence a week later than the bulk of the emigrants, caught up with the wagon train at the south fork of the Platte, then immediately struck off again, in company with the California-bound party led by Joseph Chiles. Overton Johnson's party, too, largely travelled on its own, rejoining the main party entirely at whim. A certain amount of bitterness was caused by this eclectic approach: those who persevered with the main column felt that the 'occasionals' were cherry-picking the aspects of emigrant solidarity that appealed to them, bunching together for security when the going got tough, but lurching into selfishness and egotism when travel was easy. The word 'deserter' rose to many lips. Had they been on the Bartleson–Bidwell expedition in 1841, they would have known that this 'pick 'n' mix' attitude was par for the westward course.

Along the south bank of the North Platte the emigrants had the predictable encounter with the famous sights: Court House Rock, Jail Rock, Chimney Rock and Scotts Bluff. They rhapsodised over the imaginary castles, towers, cities, temples and palaces, as so many had before them and so many would in the future. But, in contrast with later travellers, it might be said that the reactions of the men of '43 were somewhat subdued and formulaic. Where other travellers, trying to describe Chimney Rock, spoke of towering clouds, necks of ostriches, mosque minarets or even 'some vast giant leaning against the distant clouds, standing sentinel at the entrance to an enchanted fairyland', the best Jim Nesmith could muster was the banal observation that the famous landmark looked like 'a funnel reversed'. And where Scotts Bluff drew comparisons with the Alhambra, the castle at Heidelberg, Gibraltar, Tadmor, Nineveh, Thebes and Babylon, all Overton Johnson could muster was the jaundiced remark that the bluff was 'a range of high Sand Hills'.

Soon after leaving Scotts Bluff, the wagon train came to the foothills of the Laramie mountains, the boundary of the present-day states of Nebraska and Wyoming. They were in the territory of the Sioux who, with their allies the Cheyenne, had the reputation of being the most warlike Indians of the northern plains. Having come through a brush or two with Osage, Kansa and Pawnee, the emigrants braced themselves for a possible trial of arms with these much more formidable Spartans of the prairie. On paper this was unlikely, for the white intruders were numerous and well-armed and would give a good account of themselves; not even the Sioux would risk heavy casualties to engage travellers who destroyed few buffalo and would anyway soon move out of their territory. What the older and wiser heads in the overland party most feared was not a premeditated attack by the Sioux but some contretemps caused by the idiocy of the younger members of their party. One young man had already nearly ignited armed conflict by offering gratuitous insult to a Cheyenne chief; trouble was averted only when Peter Burnett gave the chief to understand by sign language that the emigrants regarded the errant young man as feeble-minded. The chief, well versed in the many ways his own tribe incorporated madness into their culture, expressed himself satisfied.

After leaving the sights of the North Platte behind, the wagon train made good progress to Fort Laramie, situated on the north bank of the Laramie River near its junction with the North Platte. The Laramie River proved almost as difficult an obstacle as the south fork of the Platte itself and so deep that a brave volunteer had to swim the boiling waters with a rope in his teeth before they could commence the now familiar process of hauling the wagons across as improvised ferry boats. Shortly afterwards, the fifteen-foot adobe walls of Fort Laramie loomed before them. The weary travellers took in the wooden palisade, the entrance with its square earthern tower with embrasures and loopholes, and the picturesque setting, with the Black Hills in the near foreground and Laramie Peak soaring in the background. Jesse Applegate's young son remembered just two things about the 1843 migration: one was Independence Rock, and the other was the 'white' appearance of Fort Laramie.

Inside the fort, the housing was primitive, with small apartments, each with a door and window opening internally, giving on to the main courtyard. But after the trail, anything resembling a house was welcome, and here was a chance to buy provisions, wash clothes, use the smithy to shoe horses and repair wagon wheels, and generally rest and recuperate. It was with gusto and euphoria that the overlanders set up camp next to the fort. But they were grievously disappointed at the meagre range of goods available and the astronomical prices. Many items were unobtainable and those that could be bought – coffee, brown sugar, flour, powder, lead, percussion caps and calico – were at a premium, much to the disgust of would-be purchasers.

Nonetheless, the emigrants were glad to make an extended stopover of several days. They counted themselves lucky to have lost no one in the Laramie River, for this was one of the most dangerous streams on the entire overland trail, notorious for the victims of drowning it claimed. Some enthused about the Laramie Peak, especially majestic at sunset when, still snowcapped, it provided a wondrous backdrop for the isolated fort. The overlanders did not even seem to mind the curious custom, later taken over by the army, when it converted Fort Laramie into a military establishment, of taking a census of all who passed through its portals. After all, the fort, for all its limitations, represented the first glimpse of anything like civilisation since leaving Kansas. And, when it did not affect their pocketbooks, the fort's traders were affable and accommodating: 'the boys at Fort Platte gave us a ball in the evening, where we received hospitable treatment', noted Jim Nesmith. This may have been the same dance recorded in sibylline fashion by John Boardman, who wrote that 'some of the company got gay' – presumably a reference to the alcohol available at the fort.

The inference is strengthened by reports from two other travellers. In 1844, John Minto reported: 'We had a beautiful camp on the bank of the Laramie, and both weather and scene were delightful. The moon I think, must have been near the full . . . at all events we levelled off a space and one man played the fiddle and we danced into the night.' And here is Rufus Sage in 1841 with an even blunter account:

> The night of our arrival at Fort Platte was the signal for a grand jollification to all hands . . . who soon got most gloriously drunk . . . Yelling, screeching, firing, shouting, fighting, swearing, drinking and such like interesting performances, were kept up without intermission . . . The scene was prolonged till near sundown the next, and several made their egress from this beastly carousal minus shirts and coats – with swollen eyes, bloody noses and empty pockets . . . liquor, in this country, is sold for four dollars per pint.

Fort Laramie was also the awaited opportunity for the 'turn-arounds' – those emigrants who had had enough of the hardships on the trail and wanted to return to the Midwest. Up to eight overlanders are thought to have turned back. Since this action brought them the stigma of cowards or 'quitters', the returnees had to rationalise their actions. 'Turn-arounds' liked to claim, on arrival at forts, that they had received news of the death of a loved one back in Missouri or Kansas and that they were so overwhelmed with grief that they had to turn back. The more common tactic was to pretend that hostile Indians barred the way or that frequent attacks by the tribes had worn them down. Naturally, to justify their own pusillanimous actions, the returnees spread the wildest rumours of massacre, atrocity, starvation or disease, to such an extent that frontier newspapers warned their readers never to trust the word of a 'turn-around'.

Naturally, there *were* cases – though none on the 1843 emigration – where overlanders had lost so much equipment, provisions or cattle that they had no realistic chance of a new life on the Pacific coast, so that turning back really was the most intelligent option. And the 'turn-around' phenomenon was not all negative, since returnees often had valuable intelligence to relay to the next wave of would-be emigrants. But the usual familiar excuses failed to convince. The motive of grief would have been more convincing had not emigrants overwhelmingly simply buried their dead and pressed on when they suffered family tragedy. On 18 July, shortly after leaving Fort Laramie, the 1843 party sustained its first fatality. Six-year-old Joel Hembree was riding the wagon tongue in 'boys will be boys' mode, when a sudden jolt threw him off; moments later, the entire wagon rolled over him. The mangled boy lingered for a day in agony before dying. His parents buried him, placed a headstone over the grave and proceeded to clock up seventeen miles on the day's march.

As for the threat from Indians, although tall stories to this effect might come to have a superficial plausibility in the 1850s, they had none in 1843. The emigrant Jesse Looney stated categorically in a letter to his brother on arrival in Oregon that they had experienced no 'interruptions' from Indians. The much-feared Sioux proved their hardiness not by exploits in battle against the whites but in swimming stock across the Platte and Laramie rivers. Overton Johnson reported that Fort Laramie had no fear of the Sioux, since most of the French-speaking occupants had taken Sioux women as wives and were regarded as 'part of the family'. Although William Newby must have seen Indians at Fort Laramie, they were evidently so docile as to make no impression on him, for he noted in his diary that he had not seen an Indian between 17 June and 23 August. But this did not stop one 'turn-around' family claiming they had returned to Missouri because of 'some Indian depredations'.

Tearing themselves away with some reluctance from the easier life at Fort Laramie, the overlanders recommenced their journey in the middle days of July and began heading through the Red Buttes towards the north fork of the Platte. Many of them were in sullen, wilful, wayward and mutinous mood, unwilling to take orders, nitpicking and arguing about every single issue: where to cross, who should go first, whether it was fair to ask the column to look after its weakest members. Rugged individualism joined hands with social Darwinism to produce a nasty, cynical, selfish mood, evidently so acute at this point in the journey that Nesmith despaired of his fellow-travellers. He noted in his diary the wish that all emigrant caravans should be run by the military, with martial law the rule and firing squads for the recalcitrant.

Perhaps the absence of timber and kindling contributed to the generally sour mood in the caravan, for west of Fort Laramie they could no longer rely on buffalo chips for fuel but had to forage for scarce scrub lumber. On the other hand, the absence of Indians should have encouraged them, for this was sparsely populated terrain and many travellers later foolishly concluded that, once past Fort Laramie, they need no longer even think about Indians. At all events, the journey to the farewell point of the Platte was uneventful. The travellers reached the north fork on 22 July and began to cross in the way that by now was second nature – hauling wagons across with ropes. The notionally slow-moving cow column, actually in better shape than the main body, beset as it was by an epidemic of 'camp fever', crossed first, ahead of the 'flying column'. The north fork was notoriously treacherous, with insidiously swift currents at play even when it was shallow enough to ford. William Newby nearly drowned through overconfidence, and ended up losing gun, powder, axe and other implements.

The last week in July saw the emigrants finally clear of the prairie and climbing upwards towards the foothills of the Rockies. The landscape changed, becoming more barren and forbidding, the hills blue-grey and the vegetation mainly sagebrush, with here and there the odd dwarf cedar. This was desolate country where the few waterholes were so adulterated with salt that even the animals refused to drink. Although the pioneers had encountered alkali-infested pools along the Platte valley, there had always been clean, fresh water nearby. But now, as they cut further across country to the Sweetwater, there were only the poisonous streams. Blinded and choked by dust, the suffering oxen and mules eventually slaked their thirst at any handy pool, and soon began collapsing. The humans meanwhile, scorched under a pitiless late July sun, suffered grievously from sunburn and dehydration even while they tried to prevent maddened animals from drinking at the poisoned pools. Many a man who had cursed the inundations of the Platte a month before now wished they could travel back in time. For the women, their own misery was compounded by the ululations of crying children.

After two days of the utmost misery and privation, they found relief at the oasis of Willow Springs, ever afterwards a landmark for westbound emigrants, a place where, as Overton Johnson put it, there was 'a beautiful spring, of very clear cold water, rising in a green valley, through which its water flows about one mile'. They spent a day at this waterhole, sending out hunting parties to track bison. They found few enough of the great beasts, largely because they had already been shot out in this area. Overton Johnson, however, blamed the 'pleasure party' led by the Scots adventurer Sir William Stewart. This group of sixty 'sportsmen' and their guides had left Independence at about the same time as the emigrants but was now travelling about two days' march ahead, killing whatever game was available. Just as Nesmith had yearned for military discipline, so Johnson now yearned for laws that would compel any such party of sightseers, especially of British milords, to travel in the rear of an emigrant train instead of ahead of it. He conveniently overlooked the ways his own party was posing even more of a threat to the viability of 'Pathfinder' Frémont's expedition that year.

The trail climbed steeply to the rushing waters of the Sweetwater and along its banks to Independence Rock, 838 miles from Independence, Missouri. Jim Nesmith wrote drily of 'an unshapen pile, about half a mile long, and half that breadth, and 100 feet high. The composition of the rock is a flinty, gray substance, mixed with limestone and very hard. Sweetwater River runs by the foot of it about fifty yards distant, and a great many high mountains and peaks are in the neighbourhood.' Here, the pioneers clambered to the top of one of the most famous landmarks on the trail and wrote their names in the soft stone, alongside those of the fur traders, missionaries and tourists who had already passed that way. Most of the travellers inscribed their names within six or eight feet of the ground, but some were daring enough to carve with knives or daub with tar at a height of sixty to eighty feet. Nesmith escorted 'five or six young ladies' to the rock and boasted of having inscribed on the south-east point, near the trail, the names of Miss Mary Zachary and Miss Jane Mills, using gunpowder, tar and buffalo grease.

But the euphoria of reaching the famous landmark did not last long, and indeed it almost seemed to lash the emigrants into fresh rages of factionalism. Colonel Martin had words with members of his group, as a result of which it splintered, and he went on ahead with his own coterie. On the trail he fell in with some men who had quarrelled with Jesse Applegate, leading the cow column. The two lots of malcontents made common cause and formed a new grouping of nineteen wagons. Then Nesmith's group split: he found himself demoted as orderly sergeant by the new leader and wrote forlornly that he must now get used to mounting guard as a private. The council, though described as a high court and a senate, seemed completely powerless to prevent these manifestations of anarchy and permanent revolution. Jesse Applegate proudly mentions the 'most respected fathers' sitting in judgement on trivial cases, such as that involving an owner and a young man who was working his passage in his employment, but is ominously silent about the 'Senate's' impotence at Independence Rock.

After the rock, the pioneers had an even more serious issue to deal with: the outbreak of disease. Pierson Reading, suffering from a malady he inaccurately describes as 'vertigo', was ministered to and bled by no less an expert than Marcus Whitman, though Reading raised an eyebrow at Whitman's idea of surgery, describing the incision he made as 'large enough for a beaver to make his ingress'. Reading was actually suffering from what the pioneers called 'mountain fever', identified by modern medical science as being either Rocky Mountain spotted fever or Colorado tick fever, but in either event a potential killer, and second only to cholera as a fatal disease for overlanders.

The second death among their number appears to have been a case of cholera, for Clayborne Payne of Arkansas went down with what was described as 'an inflammation of the bowels'. They buried him after a service preached by a Methodist minister. Cholera was essentially a product of impure water, a disease that was imperfectly understood at the time. Pioneers knew that it was unpleasant to drink from stagnant pools, but did not realise that it was also dangerous. Killing bacteria by boiling was something they did by chance, not design; only the American mania for hot coffee warded off greater fatalities. One of the women with the party recalled what they were often up against: they had to take a bucket and hit the water to get the bugs away before they could dip a bucket into the water, then had to strain it before making coffee.

The inroads of disease were fortunately curtailed as the overlanders progressed to higher and higher altitudes, where nights were cold, with severe frosts and water freezing in the kettles; many of the travellers began huddling over stoves with their overcoats on once darkness fell. For the few who had leisure enough to appreciate the picturesque, the Wind River range made an impressive snow-covered backdrop. One such was Peter Burnett, who had never before seen in summer the kind of eternal snows the Rockies boast. Overton Johnson, while no expert on the cause of disease, instinctively felt that the mountain air was doing them good. He noted a new spring in the stride of his companions, and declared that altitude was more of a panacea than all the folk nostrums, fairground snake oil, patent medicines and bogus elixirs put together.

After Independence Rock, the next significant landmark along the Sweetwater was Devil's Gate, a massive granite formation of almost perpendicular rock where the river runs through a narrow chasm, forcing the rock to tower three hundred feet above the water. This was a sight to admire from the trail a few hundred yards away, where many observers wondered why the river had not simply followed the obvious line of the valley. Contemplating the 'wondrous ways of the deity', as one of Frémont's party put it as he pondered Devil's Rock, was very much on the emigrants' minds a few days later when, on the afternoon of Friday 4 August, out of a cloudless sky they heard what sounded like a clap of thunder, followed by the sight of a ball of fire in the sky pursuing a zigzag course and a vapour trail two hundred yards long. The artillery-like banging sound continued for a while. The best estimate is that the pioneers probably saw and heard a meteor.

On 8 August, they came to the Continental Divide at South Pass, such an easy defile through the Rockies that everyone concurred in the judgement that it felt just like being on the high plains. This was a watershed event in more ways than one, and should have given the travellers a psychological boost, but the prevailing atmosphere was downbeat and querulous. The mood was not improved by the third death among the party when a young man named Edward Stevenson finally succumbed to the 'mountain fever' that had been plaguing him since Fort Laramie. They buried him on the bank of a creek, where, as Pierson Reading noted, none of his Kentucky relatives would ever find his final resting place. *Memento mori* was very much on Reading's mind, for he had only just come through a severe tussle with mountain fever himself and therefore regarded Stevenson's death as the road not taken. Some of the more eupeptic pioneers, balancing life with death, took comfort from the birth of a daughter to Mrs John Pennington on 6 August.

By early August, the travellers had reached Pacific Springs, the first water flowing towards the Pacific (actually south-west, into the Big Sandy). Although most of the terrain was sage and alkaline, the women in the party were delighted to find blue gooseberries growing in profusion, and used them to vary the monotonous fare they cooked for their menfolk. From Pacific Creek they proceeded south-west across rough, arid country, fording the Little Sandy and the other streams of Sandy Creek, until they reached the rapid-flowing Green River, broad and beautiful, pursuing its long course through Wyoming, Flaming Gorge and Colorado before finally debouching into the Colorado River and south-east Utah. Throughout June and July the swift and deep Green could be crossed only by ferry; by arriving so late, the pioneers forded without difficulty, since the snow at the headwaters had long since melted and the aridity of high summer had taken over.

After the halt at the Green River, they continued in a south-westerly direction, over Ham's Fork (a major tributary of the Green), then running south of and parallel to Black's Fork, making for the newly opened Fort Bridger. They soon found themselves in a wasteland as grim, arid and barren as any they had encountered, tormented by mirages, which the animals apparently also saw and were maddened by. Trekking in nil visibility through whorls of dust, the overlanders suffered grievously from billowing sand, intense heat and wagons that creaked from cracking hubs and loosened tyres. They were caught between the perils of the desert, pressing down on the parched and plodding oxen with pulverised particles of sand, and those of the mountain, whose arid atmosphere caused all iron tyres on wood that was not properly seasoned to work loose. Some of the travellers tried driving wedges between the tyre and the wheel but there was neither time nor opportunity to try the usual expedient of removing the wheel and soaking it in a stream overnight. There was nothing for it but to hold on grimly and await the blacksmith's shop at Fort Bridger.

They reached the fort on 14 August, but the post was in its infancy and not able to supply more than the most basic requirements. Begun in late 1841 as a joint venture between the trader Louis Vasquez and the legendary mountain man Jim Bridger, the fort had not long had the finishing touches put to it by the time the 1843 overlanders arrived. Bridger explained his scheme in a famous letter to his supplier:

> I have established a small store with a Blacksmith Shop, and a supply of iron in the road of the Emigrants, on Black's Fork, Green River, which promises fairly. They, in coming out, are generally well supplied with money, but by the time they get there, are in want of all kinds of supplies. Horses, Provisions, Smith work etc brings ready cash from them; and should I receive the goods hereby ordered, will do a considerable business in that way with them!

The location was certainly well chosen, for Bridger had selected a riparian oasis amid fields of grass and tree-lined streams. Black's Fork of the Green River was situated at the head of a long valley and split into several forks that flowed independently before rejoining, thus forming several islands, and it was on the most westerly of these islets that Bridger had placed his fort. The emigrants, however, were more concerned about the dearth of provisions at the fort than the beauty of its location. To their consternation, they learned that the Sioux and Cheyenne had not only stolen most of Bridger's horses in a recent raid but had hunted the local buffalo out. Instead of staying at the fort and making leisurely expeditions to replenish the supply of fresh meat, they had to send out an emergency group of hunters on a long trawl just to have sufficient in the larder for the onward trek. To dampen spirits even further, three-year-old Catherine Cary died at the fort, so to the shortage of food was added the gloom of a funeral service.

In sombre and disgruntled mood, the travellers set off again, travelling due west along the Muddy, again through barren country. In crossing the Muddy to head for the Bear River, Jim Nesmith capsized his wagon; although all clothing and blankets were soaked, the water did not reach his food and flour and no one was drowned. Once across the Muddy, they ascended a steep divide to the Bear, which then headed due north. By trekking south-west from South Pass, then west, then due north, they had in effect gone up and down two sides of the triangle formed by South Pass–Fort Bridger–Soda Springs; not until Sublette engineered his famous cutoff would this absurdly circuitous route be altered. The crossing of the Bear, too, proved difficult, but the valley they entered thereafter was more promising, teeming as it did with geese, ducks, trout and other fish.

Like previous travellers, the men and women of 1843 found the beautiful Bear valley – about six miles wide – a land flowing with good things, if not milk and honey, then certainly wildfowl, salmon, trout, which they had never tasted before, and other delicious fish, plus a profusion of wild berries, wild goat, elk and deer; and even the meat of bears proved surprisingly rich and toothsome. After the short commons of Fort Bridger, they were overjoyed to find themselves so soon surfeited with good things. The only disappointment was that the ducks and geese had learned to be wary of humans and kept their distance, so that only crack shots could bring them down. The animals did well too, for the soil was fertile, the grass good and flax grew in great quantities. The sensuous paradise was topped off with rushing streams, luxuriant grassy meadows, songbirds and cottonwood trees.

In the Bear valley the emigrants had two sets of visitors. The first were the Shoshone (or Snake) Indians, traditionally as mild and friendly to the white man as the Sioux were warlike and hostile. Normally, the Shoshone habit of begging irritated overlanders, but the 1843 party seem to have got on well with them and bought horses in exchange for blankets and knives – the trappers and fur traders had spread the word that Shoshone horses were the best in the world. Possibly acting as a social lubricant on this occasion, and preventing the petty pilfering that so often soured relations between Indians and emigrants, was an old mountain man who had married into the Snake tribe, Peg-Leg Smith; he got his name, allegedly, from having amputated a gangrenous leg with his own Bowie knife after an accident in the wilderness. The portly, round-headed Smith, aged around fifty, with a twenty-five-year career in the mountains behind him, was an important person in the valley, who kept pigs and horses as well as very young squaws but earned his place in the Shoshone community by sharing his wealth with them and, on occasion, saving them from starvation.

The other visitors were less welcome, for now at last 'Pathfinder' Frémont and his men had caught up with the overlanders and, as always, the two parties were in competition for food and resources. But where the emigrants thought of Frémont mainly as a threat, he viewed them as a nostalgic reminder of home comforts and described their encampment as:

> a picture of home beauty that went directly to our hearts. The edge of the wood, for several miles along the river, was dotted with the white covers of emigrant wagons, collected in groups at various camps, where the smokes were rising lazily from the fires, around which the women were occupied in preparing the evening meal, and the children playing in the grass; and herds of cattle grazing about in the bottom, had an air of quiet security, and civilized comfort, that made a rare sight for the traveller in such a remote wilderness.

The overlanders continued to swing north-west along the Bear River valley until the Bear made its sudden hairpin bend due south, almost doubling back on itself before emptying into the Great Salt Lake. Just at the turn-off point, along the valley of a clear mountain stream running south-west and entering into the Bear, the travellers encountered the series of springs and geysers that earned the generic title Soda Springs. Producing the appearance of the kind of effervescence obtained from a combination of alkali and acid, the springs issued from the earth in channels of various sizes and popped and blubbered like porridge as they came into contact with air. Often the sediment formed cones, from which the springs issued forth. The travellers vied with each other to taste the waters, which they invariably described as tasting like soda without the syrup. According to Frémont, the misnomer Beer Springs, sometimes given to the first set of fountains, arose from wishful thinking by the early mountain men, who fantasised about the foaming head of a glass of beer. One mile further on, on the banks of the Bear River, was the so-called Steamboat Spring, usually considered the most curious of the plopping vats of boiling water. Issuing from a hole six to eight inches in diameter, at intervals of half a second, this seethed and foamed at a height of anything from six inches to three feet (though Theodore Talbot reported a maximum height of ten feet), combining the look and noise of the foam behind a steamboat wheel; one foot away, gas hissed out at regular intervals from a crack in the rock. Around the spring, too, were several holes to which the emigrants bent their ears and claimed to hear the sound of a steam engine at full throttle. The water here was not so palatable: Talbot said it was warm but with a rusty, reddish colour, while Newby said it tasted like warm dishwater.

After leaving the Bear, the emigrants travelled twenty miles to the Portneuf River, a tributary of the mighty Snake. A few miles north of the point where the Portneuf flowed into the Snake stood the palisaded Fort Hall where the agent in charge was still Richard Grant, whose kindness and generosity to overlanders was remarked on by all who passed that way. Unfortunately for the 1843 party, provisions were as short here as they had been at Fort Bridger; part of the fault lay with Frémont who, foreseeing that he would be in competition for supplies with the overlanders, sent Kit Carson on ahead to buy up everything he needed. The emigrants of '43, arriving in euphoria at a 'regular' fort, found the cupboard largely bare.

This was the beginning of an episode that left a bad taste in Grant's mouth. The first travellers to arrive bought up everything available and complained of exorbitant prices; Marcus Whitman estimated that they spent $2,000 at the fort. The later arrivals found nothing at all to buy and were further enraged to discover that Grant, mindful of the welfare of his own staff in the coming winter, was unwilling to put all the food in his possession on the market. Some overlanders talked of seizing by force all cattle that the Fort Hall traders were unwilling to sell, but in the case of the California-bound pioneers, their anger went beyond threats to violent action. The ringleader was a thirty-year-old native of North Carolina named Julius Martin. University-educated, with a knowledge of Latin and Greek, Martin was nonetheless as much a hardliner as the worst thugs from Kansas. Having first secured a promise of support from some of Frémont's men, who were camped nearby, he and his henchmen sought Grant out and threatened him with dire consequences if he did not sell his secret cache of food.

As a later historian has written, 'the action was little short of robbery'. Martin and his friends obfuscated their actions in a verbal shower of humbuggery: 'unable to resist the clamors of their children for food . . . (they) boldly bearded the lion in his den and succeeded in frightening him into terms.' At least another overlander had the honesty to record that the food was obtained 'by very unpleasant means'. It was a classic case of the ant and the grasshopper. The overlanders of 1843 had failed to take enough supplies, despite the many warnings. Grant had had the foresight to stock Fort Hall adequately. So those who had taken no thought for the morrow simply appropriated the goods of those who had.

The confrontation with Grant was not the only harsh decision made by the overlanders. Another was to dismiss John Gantt from the Oregon-bound party; he immediately joined forces with the California group, for Fort Hall marked the definitive parting of the ways. Joseph Chiles, Bidwell's comrade in 1841, headed a motley group bound for California, including such men as William Baldridge and Julius Martin. They had started from Independence with Frémont but grew tired of his alleged arrogance, left him, and then overtook the main Oregon party. Chiles, a natural 'stirrer', had encouraged some of the splinter groups among the Oregonians to follow him, allegedly because he had several 'very handsome young ladies' in his party. Just west of Fort Laramie, Chiles fell in with the mountain man Joseph Walker and with him planned a route to California. Walker agreed to guide the California party after Fort Hall for a fee of $300. So it was that at Fort Hall Walker led a breakaway group from the main party, bound for California. Among the new recruits were Pierson Reading, John Gantt, John Myers, Samuel Hensley and Milton McGee. John Boardman, originally bound for California, took fright at the lack of provisions at Fort Hall and decided that Oregon, with the plentiful salmon in the Snake River, was a better bet.

Yet the most significant decision taken by the overlanders at Fort Hall was to press on to Oregon in their wagons, even though Grant insisted this was madness. Most suspected that Grant was simply advancing British designs in being so discouraging, as he did not want a sizeable party of settlers at his rear in the disputed Oregon territory. The emigrants therefore accepted with alacrity when Dr Marcus Whitman, for a fee of $80, offered to replace Gantt on the last stage of their journey and guide them safely to the Columbia River. Burnett recorded that the eloquence of Whitman soon overbore the pessimism of Grant. Although a handful of overlanders abandoned wagons at Fort Hall and switched to pack animals, most did not. As Burnett remembered: 'We fully comprehended the situation, but we never faltered in our inflexible determination to accomplish this trip.'

So it was that in the first week of September, the first emigrant wagons ever to penetrate beyond Fort Hall began to inch along the formidable and spectacular Snake River. This was some of the most difficult country they had travelled through so far. The trail ran south-west, west and north-west across modern Idaho, mainly hugging the Snake except where it flowed through sunken canyons. For three hundred miles, the overlanders had to endure desolate country and little game. There were hills and ravines glinting with jagged lava or unyielding obsidian, and there was the dreaded sagebrush or artemisia, which impeded the progress of the animals. Johnson describes the terrain as a 'wild, rocky, barren wilderness, of wrecked and ruined Nature; a vast field of volcanic desolation'.

There were times when the oxen had to tramp over razor-sharp obsidian rocks that cut their feet, leaving the trail soaked with blood. There were other occasions when the men had to march alongside the wagons to prevent them from overturning on the steep mountain defiles; then the wagons would descend to the valley of the Snake only to sink hub-deep in sand until rescued by double-teaming. But worst of all were the clouds of dust which made it impossible for drivers to see the heads of the oxen in front of them. At night the animals suffered agonies from mosquitoes, which settled on them in dark clouds as thick as snowflakes in a heavy snowstorm. Every living thing suffered from these noisome pests, but perhaps worst of all the horses, who whinnied and bayed in agony all night long as the mosquitoes formed a thick black blanket around the pack animals, covering every inch of the body except the eyes.

Breaking a trail through the artemisia was back-breaking toil. Every few miles, five different wagons took it in turn to be at the column's cutting edge, breaking down and crushing the stubble under the wagon wheels and the hooves of the oxen. Since the sagebrush grew to a height of more than four feet, Peter Burnett was not exaggerating when he said that they would have had to hack a passage through it if it had been any stronger. And, paradoxically, watering the stock was no easy matter for, though close to the Snake as the crow flies, they were often three hundred feet above the roaring stream as it cut its way through chasms below. Camping at night high on a basalt cliff, as far as possible from water in hopes of discouraging visits from the ubiquitous mosquitoes, the emigrants then had to lead the animals down to drink in the morning, which meant negotiating a precipitous path a mile long winding down to the water.

Anyone trying to take short cuts to the river soon paid for his ambition. One man tried to ride a mule straight down from the bluff to the water; the mule threw him and he bounced nearly the whole way down to the Snake. Even on the gradual descent, oxen sometimes lost their footing. And, on top of the difficulty of reaching water, there was an increasing shortage of forage. The effort involved in finding grass and water, and the care needed not to lose valuable animals on the cliffs and bluffs or on the descent to the Snake, so wore the travellers out that John Boardman wrote there was no time even to think; he was so exhausted that at night there were no pre-sleep reflections or even any dreams in the course of his heavy slumbers. Even a party not so encumbered with the impedimenta of emigration, like Frémont's, found this three-hundred-mile stretch along the Snake a severe ordeal.

The overlanders of 1843 were particularly unfortunate in that they had to face this wilderness already seriously underprovisioned because of the disappointments at Fort Hall. Their only diet supplement was the salmon they were able to trade from the Shoshone along the Snake, especially at Salmon Falls and other landmarks where the Indians showed off their expertise. Talbot noted: 'The river on this side and all the islands are lined with shanties and black with Indians all occupied in catching or drying salmon.' Fortunately, for the emigrants, the clothing of the whites was a prized item among the Shoshone, and travellers in the wake of the wagon train, like Frémont, could virtually track its progress from the number of Indians they saw dressed in the overcoats, shirts, waistcoats and trousers of the eastern cities.

Thirty miles beyond Salmon Falls the Snake broadened out, wide enough to embrace two small islands. Having followed the southern bank hitherto, the emigrants decided this was on opportune moment to switch to the north shore. At this point the Snake was nine hundred yards wide, but the two shallow islands cut the river crossing into three segments: one hundred yards to the first island, seventy-five yards to the second and a final longer stretch which they aimed to conquer by the time-honoured method of chained-together wagons. The Snake had a reputation for treachery, which it fully lived up to on this occasion. A man named John Stoughton almost drowned when the swift current overcame the wagon he was driving in the rear of the first crossing party – and this was on the supposedly 'easy' stretch to the first island. Only quick thinking by Whitman, who knew the power and ferocity of the Snake, enabled Stoughton to survive.

But the Snake still claimed two victims. The most difficult part of the fording was the final stretch, where the current was so strong that two of the heaviest wagons had to be placed abreast of each other to combat the river as it raged in its deepest channel; at this point the foaming waters were ten inches up the wagon beds. By taking the crossing slowly and steadily, most of the pioneers reached the other side without incident. But a cross-grained curmudgeon of an Englishman, named Miles Eyers, described as 'about sixty', who had already alienated his travelling companions by his stand-offish ways (he liked to camp at least a quarter of a mile away from the rest of the wagon train), decided he needed no help. Plunging into the stream on the final section with a 'fine mule train', he and his animals were almost immediately swept away upstream and drowned; a young man named Cornelius Stringer gallantly (but foolishly) tried to go to his aid and was also drowned. Eyers's wife and family begged their comrades to forgive the arrogance of their paterfamilias and were ferried across without incident; but since Eyers had all his cash strapped to a money belt around his waist, they were left destitute.

The cow column and the main cohorts of the Oregon Emigrating Company got across the Snake before the foul weather struck. But for the stragglers and backmarkers nature had a nasty hand to deal. Steady, teeming rain began to fall continuously, the river rose alarmingly and was soon impassable. Beaten back, Overton Johnson was forced to continue along the south bank, through country he described as the worst between the Missouri and the Pacific. John Boardman breasted the flood between the two islands successfully but, even with pack mules alone, found the final stretch of the three-leg crossing too much for him. Like Johnson, he was forced to continue along the south bank, cursing and complaining about the bad road, the yielding sands, the troublesome sagebrush and the panhandling Indians.

Eight miles beyond the crossing, the main body called a halt and rested for a full day to recover from their exertions. Morale was plummeting, tempers were beginning to fray, and there was a nasty stabbing incident in camp during the night. Food and forage were still scarce but at the stopover oasis they found good grazing, and indeed in the days to come the grass and pasture became more plentiful. As they trekked on towards the Boise River, they passed a number of hot springs to which they designated various titles: the Boiling Spring, Hot Springs Creek, etc. On 18 September, they reached the Boise, detoured down it, and two days later came to the last of the trading posts on the Oregon Trail: Fort Boise, 274 miles on from Fort Hall.

Fort Boise, on the south bank of the river where it emptied into the Snake, was at once a welcoming spot and a foreboding reminder of hazards to come, since the Snake would have to be crossed once more.

Founded in 1834 (the same year as Fort Hall) by the Hudson's Bay Company, it was smaller than the other fur-trading agencies and had fifteen-foot adobe walls surrounding a rectangle no more than one hundred feet square. The commandant in 1843 was the veteran trapper François Payette, who had lived in the Pacific north-west since 1811. The overlanders found him affable and welcoming, polite and courteous in an Old World way. Though, in common with all other fort commanders, he had very few provisions to trade, he pored over maps with the emigrants and marked places where they could find springs of fresh water. But as more and more stragglers trailed in, resentment was rife because the first-comers had swept the place clean of flour, meat, rice and sugar.

Pausing only briefly, the overlanders set out for their second joust with the Snake, this time involving an uninterrupted six-hundred-yard crossing. This turned out to be an anticlimax: the vanguard, splashing across on 20 September, found the river no deeper than four feet six inches, though the cow column, when it plunged into the waters three days later, found the level had risen by an extra ten inches. After the crossing, the wagons headed twelve miles across country to the Malheur River. Twenty-two miles further on they again met the Snake, but at the point where the mighty river swung away sharply to the north through impassable rapids, beetling cliffs and terrifying canyons; ever afterwards this place was called Farewell Bend.

Half a day's journey from the last sight of the Snake at Farewell Bend, the travellers entered the Burnt River Canyon. Here, the River Brûlé slowed to a trickle, so that the valley was more of a ravine and the stream itself more of a creek. The steep sides of the so-called valley made wagonning difficult, especially as the slopes were covered with trees which the overlanders had neither the time nor the energy to cut down so as to clear passage. The diarists had already used up all their superlatives in describing previous terrains as 'the worst yet', but the Burnt River Canyon provoked them to fresh hyperbole – 'the worst road ever', 'the roughest country so far' – and the evidence of frequent double-teaming bears this out. Sometimes it would take eight or nine yoke of oxen to haul a single wagon to the top of a hill, with five men tugging on ropes to keep the wagon steady and stop it tipping over. Sometimes they had to cross and recross the creek eight or nine times in order to find passage. Coming soon after the wagon train, Frémont declared he had never seen a wagon road so bad; it was a pure miracle that the emigrants had got through.

Somehow, painfully, they struggled through the slough of despond, having clocked up no more than twenty-five miles in four gruelling days. From the Pisgah of the last hill in Burnt River Canyon, Peter Burnett saw what looked like the promised land: magnificent forests of pine instead of sand and sage, and a broad valley ten miles wide and thirty long, full of excellent grass and fertile soil. Beyond the forests were snow-capped mountains 'and around their summits the dense masses of black clouds wreathed themselves in fanciful shapes, the sun glancing through the open spaces upon the gleaming mountains'. This was the Powder River valley, with the Lone Pine that Medorem Crawford had described as clearly visible. Burnett saw the tree on the morning of 28 September and used it as a landmark during his descent into the valley.

But already there was a serpent in this paradise. Some mindless emigrants who had preceded Burnett into the valley, knowing nothing of the fame of the solitary tree or heedless of it, chopped it down for fuel but found it was too green to burn anyway. Having seen it an hour before, Burnett thought he was having an optical illusion when he looked again and could no longer see it. As he remarked sadly: 'Had I been there in time I should have begged those woodmen to "spare that tree."' Frémont, following behind the emigrants, had had the merits of *l'arbre seul* dinned into him by Payette at Fort Boise and was eager to see the famous landmark. All he found was a tall pine stretched on the ground, 'which had been felled by some inconsiderate emigrant axe'.

Once into the Powder River valley, the emigrants began to experience what a later traveller would call 'the real Oregon of my imagination'. They ascended the Powder River to the site of present-day Baker City, then north through the first fragmented and snow-capped peaks of the Blue Mountains to emerge at the beautiful valley of La Grande Ronde. The descent on a trail that was 'very sidling and uncomfortably rocky' taxed their endurance, but they were buoyed up by the sight of the greenery in the valley below. Once at the valley bottom, the wagon train rested: animals fed on luxuriant grass, women washed trek-grimed clothes, and bullwhackers lolled in the shade, marvelling at the sound of meadow larks which they had not heard since Kansas. So idyllic were the surroundings that many of the emigrants wanted to end their journey right there; they were prevented from doing so only by lack of provisions and the great distance from the settlements in the Willamette valley.

The caravan trailed ten miles across the valley, which a euphoric Burnett thought was fully one hundred miles in circumference. After losing one of the women (a Mrs Rubey) who died on 1 October – a bad omen, it was thought – they began the stiff climb up the heavily forested Blue Mountains. The ascent proved even more gruelling than the steep descent into La Grande Ronde. Newby spoke of struggling upwards along a rocky canyon over a 'road too bad to describe, crossing the creek ten or fifteen times, passing through tremendous high mountains, double-teaming'. Because of the trees they had to hack their way, using blunt axes that had not been honed since Missouri. Clearing a trail meant cutting a track just wide enough to admit the vehicles, leaving the stumps as evidence of travail. So dense was the forest that a wagoner could not see ten feet in front of him, which meant that keeping track of the cattle was a nightmare.

Their progress was so slow through the Blue Mountains that they often camped at night in sight of the previous night's camp. So strenuous, gruelling and back-breaking was the tree-felling chore that, inevitably, the less appealing side of human nature soon asserted itself. Backsliders and scrimshankers declined to join the daily forty-strong tree-cutting party: some said they had cattle to attend to, which they could not keep track of in this pine-clad wilderness; others simply claimed their 'democratic right' not to obey any order that was personally inconvenient; still others laid quixotic and chimerical plans for a future railway over the mountains, asserting that they would labour in earnest at rail-splitting and the like once the railroad companies commissioned the line.

They were now crossing the main chain of the Blues, a precipitous range, whose western wall seemed almost vertical; additionally, the first flakes of snow fluttered down ominously. Their guide over the Blue Mountains was a Cayuse Indian named Stickus, a Christian convert who spoke no English but communicated effectively in a histrionic form of sign language. In La Grande Ronde, Whitman had received a message telling him he was urgently needed at his mission in Walla Walla. He hurried on ahead, leaving the overlanders in the capable hands of Stickus. Everyone agreed that he was a peerless and totally reliable guide who knew every inch of the terrain and acted as an Ariadne's thread through the forest labyrinth and along what Jim Nesmith swore was 'the roughest wagon route I ever saw'. Stickus's expertise was especially welcome as, in general, the Cayuse were not notably friendly to strangers and travellers; they were known to be accomplished thieves who levied exorbitant prices for everything they sold.

It took four days to cross the Blue Mountains. On the penultimate day they got a warning of the perils awaiting all emigrants still on the trail in late autumn in the shape of a severe but short-lived snowstorm. The one factor that aided them was that once they got above the tree line they no longer had to hack their trail through pine forests. At the western base of the mountains they camped by the Umatilla River close to a Cayuse village. Luck was with them again, for the unpredictable Cayuse were in benign mood and traded vegetables for white men's clothing. Indian corn, peas, pumpkins and potatoes were available in great profusion, and Peter Burnett wrote: 'I have never tasted a greater luxury than the potatoes we ate on this occasion.' The young Jesse Applegate recalled that one of the Cayuse formed an inflated idea of the value of a yellow pumpkin when several emigrants bidded for it. Intoxicated by the putative worth of his pumpkin, he ended by turning down the offer of a suit of clothes worth $25. Ever afterwards, the expression 'like the Indian with his pumpkin' was used for those who drove hard bargains in business.

Reluctantly leaving behind the Indian traders and the quivering aspen groves of the mild Umatilla, the travellers crossed the gently sloping land towards Fort Walla Walla and the Whitman mission. The young Jesse Applegate describes the terrain as 'a kind of sandy desert, with at times rocky ground, sage brush, greasewood and occasionally a few willows'. At this point, the caravan began the process of fragmentation that would reach its apogee at the Cascades: one group headed for Fort Walla Walla, the Hudson's Bay Company post near the confluence with the Columbia River; the other made for the Whitman mission, lured by the rumours of plentiful supplies. The mission itself turned out to be no more than a single adobe house, situated at a spot the Cayuse called Waiilatpu ('the place of the rye grass'). Of the diarists of 1843, Lenox, Newby and Burnett passed by the mission, while Jim Nesmith and the Applegate party made straight for the fort.

At every stopover, the overlanders had complained about the paucity of supplies and the exorbitant prices. The experience at the Whitman mission was no different, but the emigrants obviously expected better than market rates from their erstwhile guide and mentor, and complained bitterly about their treatment. In his diary Newby flatly accused Whitman and his wife of profiteering, Edward Lenox and others spoke of sharp practice and manipulation of the ignorant, while Daniel Waldo laid the even graver charge that Whitman had decoyed them pointlessly to the mission to get possession of their livestock. The rancour in Daniel Waldo's memoir is palpable: 'Whitman lied like hell . . . He wanted my cattle and told me the grass was all burnt between this place and the Dalles. I told him I would try it anyhow. The first night I left for the Dalles I found the finest grass I ever saw, and it was good every night.'

A particular bone of contention was the Whitmans' habit of trading one fresh cow or ox for two of the emigrants' stock. This new version of double-entry bookkeeping enraged the overlanders and was thought of as a double-cross in more ways than one. But the more fair-minded of the travellers admitted that Whitman's cattle were the biblical fat kine and their own poor thin, starvelings. Omitted from the many whingeing memoirs, too, was Whitman's habit of giving free meat to those emigrants who had nothing to trade. Peter Burnett, shrewdest and most perceptive of the diarists of '43, pointed out that Whitman's critics did not compare like with like: they made a straight contrast with Missouri prices, oblivious to freight charges in the Oregon wilderness and the high price Whitman had to pay for the produce in the first place. Burnett was contemptuous of his fellow overlanders: 'The exhausting tedium of such a trip and the attendant vexations have a great effect upon the majority of men, especially those of weak minds. Men, under such circumstances, become childish, petulant and obstinate.'

Those who went directly to the long-established Hudson's Bay Company post at Fort Walla Walla, some twenty-five miles to the west, found less to complain of. The commandant here, Archibald McKinley, really exerted himself for the emigrants even though, in common with all fort commanders, he had little to sell or trade. Newby later contrasted his largesse glowingly with Whitman's alleged meanness, but Nesmith complained that McKinley was such a stickler for Sabbath observance that he would not sell him tobacco on the Lord's Day. Nesmith was anyway in a generally sour mood. The sight of the mighty Columbia did nothing to lift his spirits, and he complained thus: 'Near to the fort are sand banks not possessing fertility enough to sprout a pea, and in fact this is too much the case with all the far-famed Walla Walla valley . . . If this is a fair specimen of Oregon, it falls far below the conceptions which I formed of the country . . . The whole country looks poverty-stricken.'

The Columbia River was where most of the '43 wagon train finally abandoned their wagons. Some loaded their children and effects on horseback, ready to pack the rest of the way to the Willamette valley. But most of the overlanders spent about two weeks at Fort Walla Walla, building rafts for the hazardous run down the Columbia. While they were busy at this chore, Frémont's expedition caught up with them once more, adding a further strain to Walla Walla's slender resources. As the boat-building neared completion, McKinley pushed the boat out in another sense, by inviting Frémont and his captains to a formal dinner with the emigrant leaders. But McKinley was not just a boon to the 'officer class' among the emigrants. He also intervened to prevent a serious clash with the Cayuse. The young Jesse Applegate and other emigrant lads provoked the young boys among the Cayuse to a knock-down, drag-out, no holds-barred fight, which threatened to get seriously out of hand. After stones had been thrown by both sides, paddles wielded by the white boys and arrows shot by the Indian youths, McKinley interposed himself and patched up a shaky peace. But the Cayuse continued sullen, there was an affray around the campfire between adult emigrants and Indians, and in the end McKinley, a proven friend to the Cayuse, had to get the emigrants to sleep within the fort, so acute did he consider the danger of an Indian attack.

Not all the overlanders, however, accepted that this was the point where they would have to abandon wagons. Some continued forty or so miles past the mouth of the Umatilla until the Columbia River started to flow through high bluffs along which no trail could be cut. The itinerary led through several small streams and three broad rivers, starting with the Umatilla itself. Since it was late in the season, the next riverine obstacle, the John Day, was fordable, though the Deschutes proved a tough nut to crack. But finally it became apparent that any wagon train would have to cross the Cascade mountains, and the emigrants baulked at this final hurdle. It was now very late in the season, flurries of snow were falling, and ahead of them loomed the glistening white peaks of the Cascades. They were mortally afraid that they would be trapped in the mountains by winter snows, without adequate supplies, clothing or shelter; above all, it was felt that to attempt the conquest of the Cascades was irresponsible when the first to succumb to cold and hunger were likely to be the women and children.

The emigrants embarking on boats from Walla Walla hoped to reach The Dalles without major incident; this was the place where the Columbia began its scything course through the Cascades. They disposed of their cattle by accepting vouchers from the Hudson's Bay Company, allowing them to exchange their cattle on a one-for-one basis; effectively they would sell their own Kansas kine and buy similar livestock at Fort Vancouver, near the estuary of the Columbia. Much confusion and bitterness was later caused by this trade, for once again the emigrants claimed they had been duped: Missouri cattle, it turned out, were worth twice their Missouri purchase price in Oregon, whereas the inferior Spanish cattle obtainable at Fort Vancouver were a drug on the market. Not the least of the services provided for the 1843 emigrants by Dr John McLoughlin, Hudson's Bay factor at Fort Vancouver, was his cancellation of this inequitable deal; instead, he arranged to have the Missouri cattle brought overland to Fort Vancouver the following spring, having paid the entire bill for pasturage and droving meanwhile.

Now came the ordeal by water. To assist the emigrants McKinley had handpicked the very best Indian guides from the Columbia River tribes: not just the Cayuse but the Walla Walla, Spokane, Wascopum, Klickitat and Chemomichat septs. Every boat leaving in the small armada headed downstream had its own combination of Hiawatha and Palinurus. The Columbia, as viewed from Fort Walla Walla, was calm both up and downstream, but those who ventured on to it expecting an easy hundred-mile passage to The Dalles were soon vexatiously disappointed. Almost as if toying with the puny humans who dared to brave its violent waters, once Walla Walla was dropped astern the river revealed its cruel and forbidding nature, laying out a veritable carpet of obstacles in the shape of shoals, reefs, rocks, whirlpools and rapids. Overton Johnson recalled that he never had an anxiety-free moment on the Columbia.

Peter Burnett thought he had found the answer in a large purpose-built boat purchased from the Hudson's Bay Company. Forty-five feet long, five feet wide and three feet high, piloted both by a veteran of the Ohio rapids and a local Indian guide, the boat was thought to be proof against the perils of the Columbia. The Indian stood at the prow with a long broad paddle while the Ohio pilot, William Beagle, took up station at the stern with a long steering oar which he had often used on the flat bottoms of the Ohio. At first, the boat handled well, skimming from wave to wave, easily mounting their crests and sliding gently down the troughs. But soon Beagle was almost swooning with fear as the boat was swept round and round in the dreadful rapids of the Columbia. Only the Indian pilot kept his head, cool, determined and intrepid in the face of boiling and seething waters far more terrifying than anything seen by eastern boatmen.

The biggest waves on this run down to The Dalles were encountered by the Applegate party. Lindsay Applegate's seven-year-old son Jesse remembered approaching a ferocious stretch of rapids, which required the nicest judgement by the pilot to survive. Their Indian took them on a route through the rapids close to the north bank but, looking back, he saw another, smaller, boat belonging to the Applegates already in severe difficulties. For some reason the pilot of the smaller boat had attempted a route by the even more breaker-tossed south shore. In that boat were seventy-year-old Alexander McClellan, twenty-one-year-old William Parker and his friend William Doke, about the same age, and also three Applegate boys, eleven-year-old Elisha, and Warren and Edward, both nine. Suddenly, the boat capsized beneath a breaking wave and the inhabitants pitched into the churning, sudsy foam. Alexander McLellan and the two nine-year-olds drowned; their bodies were swept away in the flood and never recovered.

We may infer the general ordeal down the river to The Dalles from the fact that two other 1843 diarists had close encounters with death. Peter Burnett's black slave girl was plucked off the bank by a high wave while attempting to fill a water bucket and never seen again. Meanwhile, William Newby and his wife, travelling in a flotilla of three canoes, struck a rock in a narrow defile through a major set of rapids. Their canoe quickly became waterlogged and sank; they managed to cling precariously to a rock, battered by the surge, until a pilot succeded in taking them off, together with the flotsam which now constituted their property. Fortunately for posterity, Newby's diary was part of the baggage salvaged. All in all, four people lost their lives on the passage down the Columbia from Walla Walla to The Dalles and dozens of others suffered close calls.

At The Dalles, where the Columbia boiled, frothed and foamed in frenzy as it forced passage through the Cascade mountains, the overland pioneers who had persevered with the wagons met up with the riverine emigrants for a final reunion. It was now clear that the wagons could not reach the Willamette valley, and it was to be three years before a viable route over the Cascades was laid. The cattle were sent on overland, with the young men acting as drovers, along mountain trails in winter, past Mount Hood, across country where there were no roads, while the wagons were dismantled and the sections placed on rafts for the final hair-raising stretch down the Columbia. The rafts were constructed from pine logs felled in the forest; six or eight logs, each twenty feet long, were lashed together, and then the wagons' running gear and baggage were in turn lashed on top; some used the wagon bed and the canvas covering as a kind of primitive cabin in which the women and children could sleep. To an extent, then, it could be said that the wagons were rebuilt as boats.

Morale among the party was by now at rock bottom. They had come 2,000 miles only to find that the very worst tranche of the entire journey, the sixty miles between The Dalles and the mouth of the Willamette, partly rapids and partly impassable and at that time one of the most dangerous stretches of river in the world, lay before them. And if they had thought Marcus Whitman's mission at Walla Walla mean and inhospitable, in retrospect it seemed a paradise alongside the Methodist mission at The Dalles. Whitman – or rather his agents, for neither he nor his wife Narcissa had been at the mission when the emigrants arrived – had driven a hard bargain, but had at least offered advice and counsel. The missionaries at The Dalles seemed particularly cold and indifferent to the plight of the emigrants, and this impression was reinforced by the experience of later overlanders. The Methodists seemed to feel that seeing to the welfare of newcomers in Oregon was not a matter of Christian charity but a purely administrative matter for the Hudson's Bay

Company – an attitude peculiarly pharisaical in the light of the assistance the missionaries had themselves received from the company.

Casting off from The Dalles, the armada of emigrants made its way downriver painfully and perilously until they reached the dreadful falls of the Cascades. Time and again they tried to force passage only to be pitched out into the boiling waters as giant whirlpools carried them towards the vortex. It was a miracle that there were no further fatalities, though it was often a close-run thing. Men plunged into icy waters to drag helpless women and children to safety on the shore, where they would dry out in front of huge bonfires. The Indian pilots explained that the old fur traders had used lighter, more manoeuvrable craft, expert canoeists and first-class pilots, yet even so had had to portage over the Cascade Falls. At first, the emigrants stubbornly persisted in their futile attempts to get through. Finally, they accepted they would have to portage – a prospect they faced with quailing hearts for, though the distance to be travelled was short, the terrain was forbidding and exhausting.

It is worth pausing to consider how formidable was the barrier posed by the Cascades. Overton Johnson describes it well:

Here the River, compressed into two thirds of its usual width, descends over huge rocks several hundreds of yards, with an inclination of about five degrees; and from the head to the foot of the Rapids, a distance of about four miles, the water descends about fifty feet. From the great agitation of the water, caused by its rushing with such velocity down its rocky channel, the surface of the River, for several hundred yards, is as white as a field of snow. On the South the dark basaltic walls, rising perpendicularly four or five hundred feet, are covered with Pines. There are small islands of rock, both above and below the Falls, many of which are timbered, and huge volcanic fragments cover either shore.

Those emigrants who still had energy left began the difficult process of portage. First, they reconstructed their wagons from the sections lashed on the raft. Then they spent two weeks laboriously building a road around the rapids. Once on the other side of the Cascades, different travellers opted for different solutions. One popular option was to lash canoes together into a raft, then dismantle the wagon beds of a number of wagons so as to make a platform on top of the raft; the running gear would then be taken apart and stowed on top of the platform and the baggage on top of that, all lashed together securely. Finally, using a wagon sheet for a sail, they would erect a mast and hoist sail for Fort Vancouver. But for those without the energy and resources to try the portage, destitution and even starvation loomed. They were still above the falls, existing on boiled rawhide and hemp seeds and, although the Hudson's Bay Company headquarters was just forty miles downstream, because of the barrier of the Cascade Falls, it might just as well have been on the moon.

It was now that the secular saint of 1843 lent a hand. Dr John McLoughlin, the commander of the Hudson's Bay Company post at Fort Vancouver, was a great figure in the history of the West. Despite express orders from his superiors not to aid the 1843 emigrants – on the obvious ground that they would be powerful supporters of the United States in its dispute with Britain over rightful claim to the Oregon territory – McLoughlin put humanity first. The two boatloads of free provisions he sent upriver – and later the free clothing, board and lodging in the fort, drugs and medical attention – were manna from heaven. To enable destitute emigrants to begin a new life, McLoughlin provided tools, seed, wood, cattle and food on generous credit terms (and often free). By the spring of 1844, he had spent $31,000 of company money on four hundred needy settlers, plus large sums from his own pocket. Meanwhile, the ill, exhausted and scurvied had been nursed back to health at Fort Vancouver without being charged a cent.

The 1843 emigration to Oregon had always been shaky in terms of organic solidarity. First, there was the separation into 'express' division and cow column; then the parting of the ways at Fort Hall; next, the bifurcation at Walla Walla; and finally, the disintegration while rafting down the Columbia River. The consequence was that members of the party trickled into Oregon over a period of some two months. For example, Edward Lenox and the Applegates did not finish their journey until the end of November, but Jim Nesmith got in a month earlier. Many of the later arrivals had been at the outer limit of endurance until McLoughlin helped them; the seven-year-old Jesse Applegate remembered eating berries, acorns, yampa, cammas tubers, bulbs and roots but he drew the line at such Indian offerings as caterpillars, wasps' larvae and tainted fish eggs. In general, the early arrivals had escaped the worst hunger pangs, as is evident from Nesmith's eupeptic tone:

Friday, October 27 – Arrived at Oregon City at the falls of the Willamette.
Saturday, October 28 – Went to work.

News of the successful emigration to Oregon in 1843 would cause a sensation in the United States when it was learned. Less attention was made to Chiles's difficult journey to California, possibly because it still did not prove, any more than the Bidwell–Bartleson party had in 1841, that the overland journey to California by wagon was feasible. It will be recalled that Chiles and the mountain man Joe Walker had always intended to break away from the Oregon-bound party at Fort Hall, or Fort Boise at the latest. Somewhere along the trail they introduced a further refinement, arising from a serious lack of food. Chiles would take a fast party of young men on horseback to the Sacramento valley with the intention of bringing back provisions to the others; the main party in mule-drawn wagons, meanwhile, including the women and children, would proceed at a more leisurely pace under Walker's command.

On 17 September, the Chiles party rode ahead. Among the thirteen horsemen were several who would figure in the later history of California: Pierson B. Reading, Samuel J. Hensley, Milton McGee. They reached Fort Boise on 1 October and, two days later, headed west towards the Malheur River. After suffering severe hunger and thirst in the desert wastes, they crossed into the north-eastern corner of present-day California on 20 October. Struggling through early snowstorms, they took their bearings from the icy peak of Mount Shasta to the west and pursued a track south-west through mountain country. On 1 November, they entered the northern end of the Sacramento valley and ten days later, exhausted and at the end of their tether, they limped into Sutter's Fort. Nevertheless, they had achieved their first objective – finding a way round the Sierra Nevada – and had averaged twenty miles a day in supremely difficult country. Yet, they would scarcely have survived but for the skill of their Indian guide.

The second, and principal, task of Chiles's party was to return to the Humboldt Sink with food for the main wagon party. But the mountain passes were snowed in. Sensibly, but perhaps also cynically, neither Chiles nor Hensley, who had boasted of his skill as a frontiersman, so much as attempted the task. Effectively, Walker and the main party were on their own. Sixteen men, four women and five children were left to their own devices in the wilderness. Optimistically, Walker thought he could get to Sutter's Fort in sixty days. He turned the wagons southwards at Calder Creek to the valley of Raft River. So clear were the caravan's tracks and so confident the breaking of the trail that Frémont, following the emigrants to Oregon, turned off to follow Walker, thinking this was the route the emigrants were taking to the Willamette valley. It was some time before an embarrassed 'Pathfinder' realised his mistake and retraced his steps.

Walker continued the steady plod to the Humboldt Sink, following the river (then still called Mary's River), arriving in the last week of October. Hoping to see Chiles and Hensley return with provisions, they settled down to wait and thus wasted eight valuable days. The one benefit of the stopover was that the animals built their strength up on the abundant meadow grass. But when he set off again on 30 October, Walker had already used up forty-five of the sixty days he had allowed for reaching Sutter's Fort and food was getting short. On the plus side, Walker knew the country, for he had passed this way in an easterly direction in 1834, and he recognised landmarks from his 1841 experience with Bidwell and his easterly odyssey of 1842 with Chiles. Walker's intention was to head for the easy pass to the side of the Sierra Nevada later known as Walker's Pass. This was a very long, roundabout route, and if there had been any really experienced mountain men present they would certainly have objected; fortunately for Walker, the only one with the clout to challenge him, John Gantt, had gone with Chiles's fast horseback party.

The route they followed from the Humboldt Sink is not easy to pin down, for none of the travellers kept a diary. The best conjecture is that they must have followed a river to a lake (both of which were later to bear Walker's name), then south across volcanic desert country, dotted with hills of black basalt rock; some think the route was southwards past Mono Lake into Owen's valley. On 20 November, they came to a south-running valley with high mountains to the east and the Sierra Nevada itself to the west. Disregarding the forbidding 14,000-foot snowcaps, Walker led his wagon train along the valley towards the pass that would bear his name. Gradually the towering mountains on their right seemed to diminish in size, until Walker turned west into the defile he had discovered a few years before. On these easy lower gradients before the summit, snow, ice and frost were unknown. But when the sixty-day deadline was reached, and with food stocks running low, Walker ordered the wagons be abandoned near the summit of the pass. The place was near Owen's Lake.

Having cached valuable machinery and saddle-packed the mules, the party made its way wearily to the summit of the pass, trudging through snow six inches deep. They began to descend from the summit on 3 December and slaughtered one of the mules to celebrate. They came down into the San Joaquin valley, narrowly missing a relief party. Chiles had at last bestirred himself and led three men and provisions to Walker Pass, but the mountain man took his party on a northerly sidetrack to what he assured them was a good camping ground. The diversion was ill-considered: it was a drought year, and for three days and nights the wagon train braved the rigours of the desert without food. On these choking alkaline wastes of the arid San Joaquin valley, the early euphoria soon changed to something like despair.

At last, in Peachtree valley, the emigrants reached the promised land. After gorging themselves over the Christmas period on venison and the sweet meat of wild young mustangs, they reached the California settlement on the Salinas River just after New Year's Day 1844. Although Chiles has been hailed in some quarters as the true hero of 1843, greater than Whitman, the truth is that he did not think through the implications of his rash adventure and it was Walker who pulled his chestnuts out of the fire. Those who admire reckless optimism, sanguine energy and making decisions on the wing will always admire Chiles; those who do not will consider him a man who made his mark on the history of the western trails by sheer ubiquitous perseverance. By the end of the decade he had followed the emigrant trails in both directions five times in eight years.

The year 1843 was a decisive one in the history of the emigrant trails. Although a complete California trail had not been established and no wagons had yet travelled all the way from the Midwest to the Pacific, the gap between fantasy and reality was narrowing. Building on the experience of the Bidwell–Bartleson party, Joseph Walker had now properly charted the route from Fort Boise to the Humboldt Sink, leaving only the 250 difficult miles of desert and sierra between the sink and Sutter's Fort to be mapped. The route to Oregon represented an even greater triumph. Horace Greeley had huffed and puffed about the 'suicide mission' on which the emigrants of 1843 were engaged. Yet the 875 souls who arrived in the Willamette valley made him eat his words. True, the emigrants had luck on their side, in the form of McLoughlin's assistance, and in many other ways. In contrast to the volatility of the Cayuse at Walla Walla, the settlers in the Willamette had to contend with the almost extinct Kalapuya Indians, whose numbers had dwindled to five hundred by 1839, having lost 75 per cent of their population in a malaria epidemic in 1831–34; a further epidemic in 1848, this time of measles, finished them off. Yet, for white emigrants, 1844 promised to be the most halcyon of all pioneering years.

SIX

THROUGH FLOOD AND FAMINE

The year 1844 witnessed a quantum jump in emigrant departures to the Pacific paradises of California and Oregon. Whereas in 1841 just thirty-four souls had made it overland to California via the Platte and in 1842 a mere 125 persons reached Oregon after travelling on from Fort Hall to the Willamette valley via Fort Boise, La Grande Ronde, Walla Walla and the Columbia River, 1844 saw no fewer than 1,528 people reaching the west coast on the Oregon and California trails. This total dwarfed even the 'great emigration' to Oregon in 1843, when 875 pioneers reached the Pacific north-west and another thirty-eight under Joseph Chiles got to California. In 1844, additionally, intrepid overlanders blazed a new trail and finally found a viable wagon route all the way to California.

For the first time, too, it began to look as though Independence, Missouri, would no longer enjoy a monopoly as the 'jumping-off' point for the western trails. So far, the story of Independence's growth and prosperity had been an uninterrupted one. Independence, nowadays a suburb of Kansas City, began life in 1827 as the main depot for the flourishing Santa Fe trade; it was thus the starting point for all three westward trails – to California and north-west to the Platte River and thence by the Sweetwater to the Continental Divide at South Pass and points west; and to Santa Fe south-west via the Arkansas River. Set on the west bank, three to four miles south of the bend in the Missouri, where the 'Big Muddy' starts to head north to Nebraska, Independence enjoyed a prospect of rolling hills on the very edge of the Great Plains. By the 1830s it was already a thriving, sprawling town with bare earth streets laid out in a grid pattern, containing half a dozen log huts, two or three clapboard houses, a couple of grog shops masquerading as so-called hotels, a few stores, a bank, printing office and even a church which resembled a large Dutch barn.

Independence went into forced hibernation in the winter months, since the Missouri was frozen over from November through to March and

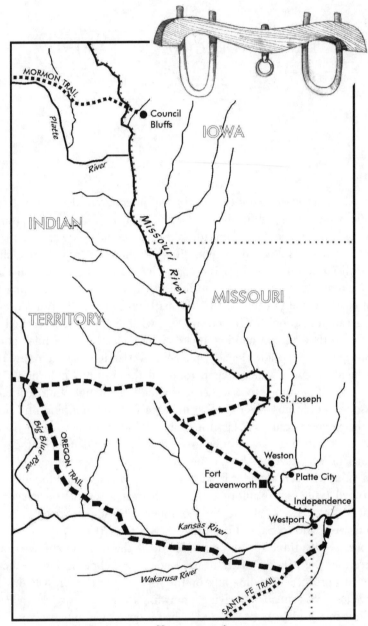

The Jump-Off Points at the Missouri

there were no steamboats until April. But in spring the sleepy town woke from its slumbers to become a cauldron of seething activity. Stevedores singing shanties surged from smoking steamships, straining and heaving under bales and crates of produce, broad-shouldered packers piled wagons high with weighty packages and parcels, droves of drivers cursed and spat oaths as they drilled their dogs ready for the trail. The hubbub and babel of voices created a hustle-bustle that both horrified and bemused travellers. And although there was a paved road six miles long to the Missouri to help trade, there was no paving in the main streets of the town. New arrivals slurped through a morass of red Missouri clay to get to Colonel Noland's tavern or Robert Weston's blacksmith shop. Noland's tavern was billed as the last inn in the USA: it could house four hundred guests provided they slept two in a bed, as was the custom in hotels in the early nineteenth century.

By 1844, Independence had a population of 742; this would rise to between 1,500 and 2,000 in 1849 and to an officially registered 3,164 by 1860. It was a magnet for would-be emigrants from Tennessee, Kentucky, Ohio, Illinois and Missouri, many of whom remained patiently for days on the east bank, waiting to be ferried over but totally ignorant of the dangers both in town and on the trail. By the beginning of May, Independence was buzzing with activity, with people buying and selling at street corners, drawing up constitutions and electing putative officials for the emigrating companies, writing letters, fighting off criminals and conmen, frequenting inns and bars, and wondering if they were doing the right thing. Rookies experimented with yoking oxen, packing mules, cooking over campfires and practising the difficult art of driving a wagon. Outside town, many were the collisions with trees and other tenderfoot teamsters.

Some observers thought that life in Independence had an unreal or fantastic air, like being at a permanent Fourth of July celebration. The young Boston traveller Francis Parkman. who arrived there in the spring of 1846, reported thus:

All conditions of mankind were there in all costumes: Shawnees and Kansa from the Territory and wanderers of other tribes, blanketed, painted . . . Mexicans in bells, slashed pantaloons and primary colors, speaking a strange tongue and smoking shuck-rolled cigarettes; mountain men in buckskins preparing for the summer trade or offering their services to emigrant trains; case-hardened bullwhackers of the Santa Fe trail in boots and bowie knives . . . rivermen and roustabouts, Negro stevedores, soldiers from Fort Leavenworth, a miscellany of transients . . . the lowing of herds pullulated in the town, the smithies and wagon shops rang with iron, whooping riders galloped their ponies, the groggeries were one long aria and out from town the little cluster of tents grew and grew.

The fastidious Boston Brahmin did not care for the polyglot bouillabaisse that was Independence conversation:

He thought the Mexicans' tongue outlandish, and he heard with an intense distaste the high Tennessee whine, the Illinois nasals, the cottonmouth Missouri drawl, the blurred syllables, the bad grammar, the idioms and slang of uncouth dialects.

Yet Independence was not long to retain its pre-eminence as a 'jumping-off' place. Already it was being challenged by St Joseph, two weeks closer to the Platte River by ox team. By 1844, St Joseph, originally a trading post established by Joseph Robidoux and known as Robidoux's landing, and now a town just six months from its birth by charter, had a population of 682, not much less than Independence. St Joseph's real 'take-off' point would come in the 1849 gold rush and soon its newspaper, the *Gazette*, would run a successful propaganda war against Independence, citing cheaper prices, shorter distances and more reliable ferries. Pundits could argue about whether St Joseph retail prices really were 20 per cent cheaper than in Independence, as was assiduously claimed, but certain facts were undeniable: to start from St Joseph sliced at least eight days off the journey and avoided the dangerous crossing of the usually flooded Kansas River. The proof of the pudding was in the eating: St Joseph won the propaganda war and by 1860, with a population of 8,932, was three times the size of Independence.

In the later years of the overland emigration, from 1850 to 1860, St Joseph was in turn challenged by Council Bluffs, originally called Kanesville. Council Bluffs was promoted on two main grounds. First, two hundred miles north-west of Independence, it provided easy access on to the Great Platte River road, and it clearly made more sense for emigrants coming from Illinois, Indiana, Ohio, Iowa and northern Mississippi to start from there rather than St Joseph, let alone Independence even further to the south. Second, it was bruited about after 1847 that the so-called Mormon Trail on the north bank of the Platte was healthier than the traditional route along the southern bank. By 1860, most pioneers started from Council Bluffs, whose population had risen to 2,011; meanwhile, across the Missouri River the rival city of Omaha was developing, with a population of 1,883 by 1860. By this time, in any case, both Independence and St Joseph were starting to lose out to the rising star of Kansas City, which boasted 4,418 inhabitants by 1860. However, in 1844, Independence still held pride of place, but only just. The state of flux in the 'jumping off' points can be seen from one simple fact: six distinct parties started for the Far West that year, but from four different points – Independence, St Joseph, Westport and Council Bluffs. The smallest group was a party of invalid health-seekers and adventurers led by the mountain man Andrew Sublette, which left from Westport, a few miles to the west of Independence (and which is now part of Kansas City). Another exiguous group left from Council Bluffs under the command of John Thorp, bound for Oregon. A third party under Elisha Stephens departed from Council Bluffs along the north bank of the Platte for California. But the two largest parties were those headed by Cornelius Gilliam which crossed the Missouri at various points from Doniphan, nine miles above St Joseph, to Weston (south of St Joseph) and made rendezvous at Fort Leavenworth. A sixth group, under Nathaniel Ford, assembled at Independence; starting behind the Gilliam party, it planned to overhaul them on the trail and then continue west together.

Among those who assembled at Council Bluffs, there was from the very beginning a clear differentiation between those who meant to settle in Oregon and those who intended to branch off to California once they reached Fort Hall. For most of the route to the parting of the ways, the Stephens and Thorp parties travelled close together, with Stephens as nominal supremo but Thorp maintaining a fierce independence as head of the 'Oregoners'. As regards competition with the Oregon-bound Gilliam and Ford caravans, the Thorp wagon train got a head start from Council Bluffs and maintained it all the way to the Pacific. Comprising twenty-seven wagons with forty men plus women and children, the Thorp group had in its ranks James Marshall, a thirty-four-year-old carriage-maker, wheelwright and carpenter from New Jersey, who later became world-famous by discovering gold at Coloma, California, in January 1848. Another pioneer who made his mark was the twenty-four-year-old William Case, six feet tall and wiry, who left a notable memoir of the journey and became prominent in Oregon public life.

The two major Oregon-bound parties of 1844 were altogether more imposing affairs. The Gilliam party rendezvoused at the Great Nemaha Subagency, twenty miles from St Joseph, but already the omens for the journey were less than propitious. Although the vanguard crossed the Wolf River on 11 May, heavy rains and floods washed away the river bridge next day, so that the bulk of the emigrants had to be ferried across the swollen creek on improvised 'canoes'. The rearguard did not arrive at the rendezvous until 17 May but, two days earlier, elections had been held and the caravan organised. Cornelius Gilliam, a veteran of the Black Hawk war and usually referred to as 'Neal' Gilliam, was chosen as general, with Michael T. Simmons as his second-in-command, and he divided his 'brigade' into four companies.

In Gilliam's party were 48 families, 108 men (60 of them classified as 'young'), 48 women and 167 children (323 persons all told), together with 73 wagons, 713 cattle and oxen, 54 horses and 11 mules. The Ford party mustering at Independence was even larger: 358 souls, including 110 married men with wives, 80 single men and 168 children (83 boys and 85 girls), travelling with 64 wagons, 640 cattle, 65 horses and 30 mules. Gilliam wrote to Ford in sanguine, upbeat mood, pointing out that when the two caravans merged it would be by far the largest wagon train ever to cross the Rockies. In all there would be 137 wagons, 119 horses, 41 mules and 1,353 cattle. And for the first time an accurate picture of the social composition of the emigrants emerges. Travelling in the party was a minister of religion, a lawyer, a millwright, a tailor, a ship's carpenter, a cooper, a tailoress, a wheelwright, a weaver, a gunsmith, a wagonmaker and a merchant, plus three millers, two cabinetmakers, three blacksmiths, five carpenters and two shoemakers. Most of the rest were middling farmers.

The final party on the trail that summer was led by Andrew Sublette. Leaving Westport some time after 21 May, this group consisted of a Jesuit priest and twenty other men, presumably trainee Jesuits or postulants of some kind, but mysteriously referred to by Sublette as 'the company of Catholicks'. About half of these itinerant Catholics were invalids, and they had made the unwise decision to travel west on the Oregon Trail for their health. Moses 'Black' Harris, who had been hired as a guide by the Ford caravan, was in close touch with Sublette. One of the most pre-eminent historians of the Oregon Trail has this to say: 'Moses "Black" Harris was hired as guide by Nathaniel Ford's Oregon-bound party, one of the largest of the year; Andrew Sublette was apparently similarly hired by the Cornelius Gilliam party.' This is wrong. What happened was that 'Black' Harris tried to evade the commitment he had entered into with Ford by offering the job to Andrew Sublette; but he declined because he felt an overwhelming sense of responsibility for his invalids.

By 1844, the overland emigrants were already the recipients of a plethora of advice from previous travellers, so had no excuse if they set out under-equipped or under-provisioned. Apart from sturdy wagons, oxen and mules, the pioneers were admonished to bring along knives, axes, hammers, hatchets, whetstones, spades, saws, gimlets, scissors, needles, lasts, awls, nails, tacks, pins, thread, wax, twine, shoe leather, pegs, ropes, cotton cloth, beeswax, tallow, soap, candles, lanterns, spyglasses, drinking cups, washbowls, camp stools, herbs, medicine and linament. Small wonder that the contents of an average covered wagon were said to resemble a hardware store. J.M. Shiveley in his 1846 *Guide* made the point explicit:

> You should take with you an iron pan, the handle so jointed as to fold up; a kind of knife, fork and spoon, that all shut up in one handle – such knives are common in all hardware stores. In addition to this, you will need a fire-proof iron kettle, to make tea, coffee, boil rice, make soup, etc; a tin pan, quart cup and a butcher knife, will about complete your kitchen.

Needless to say, emigrants did not always heed the sensible advice to take only necessities in their wagons, which is one reason that, as the 1840s progressed, the wide prairies came to resemble a thousand-mile-long junk yard. Possessiveness, greed, sentimentality and simple stupidity led them to cling on to their treasured pieces until they wore out the teams, when they were forced to jettison them anyway. Among items abandoned as the going got tough were the following: rocking chairs, mirrors, washstands, iron and steel bars, blacksmiths' anvils and bellows, crowbars, drills, augurs, goldwashers, chisels, trunks, ploughs, grind-stones, baking ovens, cooking stoves, kegs, barrels, harnesses, chains, mattresses, quilts, handsaws, planes, scythes, shoes, hats and other clothing. One emigrant said of his fellow-travellers: 'None of the emigrants know how to fit out for their journey. They are all split upon the same rock.'

The clothes of the emigrants have attracted a lot of attention – the pioneer woman in sunbonnet is virtually an archetype – but they were essentially the normal garb of the Midwestern farmer. One guide recommended a sack coat, a coarse woollen jacket and very large and strong pantaloons of stout sheep's grey cloth together with deerskin hunting shirt and pants. Duck trousers were popular as were blue or striped twilled cotton, hickory or red flannel shirts and cotton socks. Shoes were an important item, stout, large, loose-fitting pegged brogues or brogans with broad soles being the recommended type along with cowhide boots. The mid-nineteenth century was still an era of hats – perhaps reaching its apogee with Abe Lincoln's famous stovepipe – but on the plains the recommended wear was a stout, white felt hat with no glazing, or a palm leaf 'tile'. J.M. Shiveley's guide had this to say:

> Let each man and lad be provided with five or six hickory shirts, one or two pairs of buckskin pantaloons, a buckskin coat or hunting shirt, two very wide brimmed hats wide enough to keep the mouth from the sun. For the want of such hat thousands suffer nearly all the way to Oregon, with their lips ulcerated, caused by sunburn. Take enough coarse shoes or boots to last you through – three or four pairs apiece will be sufficient.

It is a fact of human existence that women's clothes have always attracted more interest than men's, and so it was on the overland trails. Women starting from the jump-off points touchingly wore their best clothes, determined to be 'ladies' even on the high plains, but soon adapted to the harsher environment. Lavinia Porter, one of the shrewdest and most perceptive of travellers to accomplish the California Trail, was endearingly frank about her lowering of sights:

> I started out with two blue cloth travel dresses with an array of white collars and cuffs, scorning advice about homespun and linsey woolsey ... These were soon discarded ... Fortunately I had with me some short wash dresses which I immediately donned, tied my much betrimmed straw hat up in the wagon, put on a big shaker sunbonnet and my heavy buckskin gloves and looked the ideal emigrant woman.

Not short on wry humour, Lavinia added that a huge Indian brave immediately put on the hoop skirt she had discarded and wore it with great pride.

But the most sensational aspect of female fashion on the overland trails was the way the women gradually started wearing trousers or bloomers; in the interests of historical accuracy, it should be pointed out that this was largely a post-1849 gold rush phenomenon. In terms of nineteenth-century bourgeois culture this was a highly rebellious or 'deviant' act, and it took a brave woman to defy male scorn and suspicion on the high plains. Since the Bloomer movement, the brainchild of Amelia Bloomer, was itself an aspect of the brand of nineteenth-century feminism espoused by notable campaigners like Susan Anthony, many men thought that women wearing trousers was an expression of an ideological or political statement. But more sensible males took the point that bloomers were a more practical garb on the overland trail, where dresses quickly collected dirt and mud, where hems were torn to pieces on the trail and where long skirts could even be dangerous if they snagged under a wagon wheel.

Ezra Meeker, whose long life spanned the golden age of the wagon train and the coming of the automobile, spoke his characteristic good sense when he had this to say about the female penchant for trousers:

Of the fortitude of the women one cannot say too much. Embarrassed at the start by the follies of fashion, they soon rose to the occasion and cast false modesty aside. Long dresses were quickly discarded and the bloomer donned. Could we but have had the camera trained on one of these typical camps, what a picture there would be. Elderly matrons dressed almost like little girls of today. The younger women were rather shy in accepting the inevitable but finally fell into the procession, and soon we had a community of women wearing bloomers. Some of them went barefoot, partly from choice and in some cases from necessity.

Where the women were most interested in their clothes, male attention inevitably focused on firearms. The expectation was that these would be used primarily for buffalo-hunting, and the hope was that it would not prove necessary to turn the guns on Indians. Vast amounts of powder and lead were taken on the overland trails, almost always surplus to requirements. The hunting rifle was the favourite weapon, tried and tested. Most of the Midwestern farmers were well accustomed to using rifles, but for the tyro or greenhorn the jump-off towns did a roaring trade in new guns, usually retailing at around $25. Most of these rifles were of the new percussion-cap type, but a few old-timers clung steadfastly to their flintlocks. Shotguns were also in plentiful use, while 'gentleman' travellers liked to deck themselves with a brace of pistols or, in the 1850s, revolvers. Although fear of the red man was a constant among the overlanders, few of them ever drew a bead on an Indian. Fear and paranoia were whipped up by sensationalists like Lansford Hastings who, in his *Guide*, seemed almost to slaver at the mere thought of an encounter with the Plains tribes.

But for every emigrant, male or female, the overriding concern was food. It became almost a cliché (and like all pioneering clichés, was hammered to death in Hastings's *Guide*) that an overlander should have in his wagon two hundred pounds of flour, 150 pounds of bacon, ten pounds of coffee, twenty pounds of sugar and ten pounds of salt. All the evidence suggests that the men and women of 1844 were reasonably assiduous and competent in this regard. The '44 pioneers additionally took large numbers of cows and oxen, which could be slaughtered in an emergency. But the most interesting innovation, on which the diary sources are disappointingly meagre, concerns the first flocks of sheep taken to Oregon, which were a feature of 1844. Sheepmen and shepherds were supposed to be Mexicans, not Anglos, and it was from the vast herds in New Mexico (still Mexican in 1844) territory that the Oregon-bound sheep came. There was no distinct 'cow column' in 1844, like Jesse Applegate's the year before, for such a cattleman would undoubtedly have had the cowboy's traditional loathing of sheep and shepherds and thus exacerbated the already fragile eggshell of 'organic solidarity' among the pioneers of 1844.

Yet well-organised and equipped as the overlanders were, they faced an enemy no previous Pacific-bound emigrants had had to contend with: torrential rains and quasi-biblical flooding, the like of which went beyond living memory. Throughout May and June, rain teemed down almost incessantly, and all the rivers in Kansas became frighteningly engorged. By mid-June the Missouri River was five feet higher than in the disastrous flood of 1826. The steamboat *Mary Tompkins*, carrying a full crew and a boatload of paying customers, was swept out from the river's channel on to the open prairie where, to the screams and ululations of terrified passengers, she smashed down many of the tallest cottonwoods that lay in her path. From Weston to the mouth of the Missouri, the lowlands were flooded, crops destroyed, cattle, sheep, hogs and other stock drowned, and entire homes swept away. By 24 June, the Mississippi at St Louis had risen almost thirty-nine feet above the low-water mark, surpassing by four feet the 'incredible' flood of 1785.

Baptist missionaries in Kansas left a vivid picture of the devastation, all the more cataclysmic in that the 'unprecedented' May floods were followed, after a false dawn in early June when there were a few fine days, by the worst inundations ever experienced. The Kansas River was in spate, at least twenty feet higher than its alleged high-water mark, laying waste the entire bottom land and carrying off everything in its path: houses, farms, cattle, horses, in short, all objects animate and inanimate. Missionary Ira Blanchard of the Delaware mission (at present-day Wynadotte City) wrote:

Thousands of farms along the water courses are without anything to shelter them from the storms and many of them have lost their last morsel of food. The state of things beggars all description. The [mission] station is three-fourths of a mile from the Kansas, and on grounds a little raised from the bottom, so that the water was just to us and did no damage. But the [Delaware] village near us is all destroyed.

There is not even a stalk of corn left in all their fields; and their old stock [of grain] all carried away by the flood.

Blanchard's colleague at the Shawnee Baptist mission (present-day Johnson City) concurred in this apocalyptic vision:

The waters came up over the banks of the creeks and rivers so as to be in many places fifteen feet high where they were never known to come before. Fences were swept away invariably, the newly planted crops destroyed, young orchards etc among the rest, most of the buildings within several miles of the rivers or as far as the river bottoms extended, were swept away, corn cribs and all. Hogs were drownded [*sic*], many horses and cattle also. Many persons barely escaped with their lives, leaving all behind. Many have been drownded in the white settlements. I have not heard of any Indians drownding . . . The roads are almost impassable on account of mud.

Around the site of present-day Kansas City, the swollen river swept away all buildings in the Westport Landing area of Missouri, including the Kansas Town Company warehouse. When the river finally receded at Chouteau's Landing, having left not a trace of human habitation standing, it left its own memorial in the form of a vast expanse of mud five feet deep.

The parties aiming to depart from Independence and Missouri were in a particularly bad case; since they knew nothing as yet of the successful arrival in Oregon of the 1843 emigrants, their perplexity was compounded by the monsoon-like rains and the highest waters ever known in the Midwest. The frustration was all the keener for Cornelius Gilliam's family, as the Gilliam clan had been encamped on the river-bottoms in Doniphan County since 2 March, waiting for other emigrants to arrive, in accordance with the arrangement notified to all prospective overlanders by Gilliam in his public notice of late summer 1843. By the end of April, this 'Kansas camp' held thirty families; technically, the would-be emigrants were squatters on the Sac and Fox reservation, but the Indian subagent had negotiated the necessary permission from the tribal chiefs.

All the emigrant diaries tell the same story: a nightmare journey to the flooded Missouri, attempting a virtual mission impossible in getting cattle across the engorged rivers, followed by a dismal wait at the rendezvous point as the rain pelted down almost continuously. The emigrant John Minto, a twenty-two-year-old ex-coal miner from Pittsburgh, later recorded that during the first two months of his emigrant journey there were only eight days when it did not rain. There were two deaths, one of them a child, before the wagon train even set out. A further delay was caused when marauding bands of Iowa, Sac and Fox Indians stole a large number of cattle. This was a serious matter because without draught and dairy animals there would be no way to clear the land for farms in Oregon, to plough fields, haul logs for cabins, to provide milk and butter or, in emergencies, meat. Gilliam enlisted the help of Indian subagent W.P. Richardson, who went to the respective Indian encampments. The Sac and Fox chiefs took the line that the theft of cattle was a bagatelle, that the emigrants owed them a fee for squatting on their land for more than two months. Richardson composed the dispute, with the result that Gilliam got all his cattle back, except for half a dozen beasts that the Indians had already slaughtered and eaten. As an exemplary punishment, Richardson decreed that six oxen the Indians were supposed to be getting as part of their subsidy would be made over to Gilliam instead, as compensation.

The last two weeks of May were a grim story of constant rains, slow progress and accommodating latecomers, the last of whom trickled in on 19 May. The Revd Edward E. Parrish's diary confirms everything John Minto recorded: rain on the 12th, the 13th, the 15th, the 16th, the 18th, the 19th – the recital becomes monotonous. The only light human relief was provided by the marriage of Martin Gilliam and Elizabeth Asabill on 20 May, in a ceremony performed by the Revd Parrish. Meanwhile, John Minto entered into a peculiar relationship with the Morrison family of emigrants. In exchange for his labour, the Morrisons provided Minto with board and shelter and soon regarded him as one of the family. Minto and the Morrisons were part of the Shaw division in the Gilliam party. William Shaw, commander of Gilliam's rearguard and a loveable forty-nine-year-old, who would live to the age of ninety-two, was married to Gilliam's sister Sarah ('Sally').

Both Shaw and Minto came to be closely connected to one of the most famous families of the overland trail, the Sagers, for the Sager family, evincing the inadequacy that would plague them throughout the journey and bring on tragedy, were one of the two last wagons to join the caravan (on 19 May). Henry Sager, rightly described as 'a restless soul, always dreaming of greener pastures over the western horizon', was one of those infuriating ne'er-do-wells who consistently blame the consequences of their own stupidity on a malign fate. In the autumn of 1843, he sold his farm and blacksmith shop and moved to St Joseph, eager to trek west, despite his wife Naomi's forebodings. The Sagers already had six children – John, thirteen, Francis, eleven, Catherine, nine, Elizabeth Marie, seven, Matilda Jane, five, and Hannah Louise, three – and although he could barely feed this brood, the philoprogenitive Sager had already impregnated his wife yet again; by the time they joined Shaw and the rearguard near the Nemaha River in south-east Nebraska, Naomi was near to full term.

The baby arrived on 30 May and was named Henrietta Naomi. Naomi's labour was long and painful, the birth difficult, the mother lying in a damp Kansas tent while outside the rains teemed down. The Revd Edward Parrish rather oddly recorded that there was 'a frolic in Mr Sager's family today', which presumably means that the irresponsible Henry Sager broke out some liquor to celebrate his daughter's arrival. Naomi Sager certainly did not feel like celebrating. Too weak to travel, the mother was allowed seventy-two hours recovery time; the trek recommenced on 2 June. Parrish's diary rather glumly records the enforced stopover: '31 May. We are encamped to await the arrival of Mr Sager, whose wife is sick. Hope she will be well soon.' '1 June. Camp ordered to remain in its present situation to await the recovery of Mrs Sager. She is reported to be very sick this morning.' The diarist Samuel Crockett concurred: 'Did not travel today on account of Mrs Sagar's [sic] health.'

Once on the trail, they made agonisingly slow progress over flooded terrain and swollen creeks, with heavy rains continuing to fall. On 7 June, after nearly a month on the road, they reached the Black Vermillion, having travelled less than a hundred miles from their starting point. Morale was already very low. John Minto, who had earlier described Neal Gilliam as 'an intrepid and well known soldier of the South', swiftly changed to the opposite viewpoint: he alleged they had had a good chance of getting across the Black Vermillion on the 7th if they had pressed on, but Gilliam insisted on waiting thirty-six hours because his daughter was ill. But from the evening of the 7th the rain teemed down incessantly for ten days. The Black Vermillion rose alarmingly. The travellers had to cut down trees and make 'canoes'. By lashing two of these hollowed-out trunks together, they contrived it so that the centre of each 'canoe' could hold a wagon tightly, with wheels locked in the grooves of the wood. Neal Gilliam's son Washington well expressed the frustration of the party at the 'impassable' and engorged Black Vermillion: 'The rain continued to fall in torrents for days, and the stream to rise correspondingly until it got into the boughs of the trees, and when it commenced falling it was several days before it got into the bank so we could ferry it and swim the stock to safety . . . This little stream that at low water could be stepped over detained us seventeen days in one camp.'

The next obstacle was the Big Blue River, twenty miles distant. The vanguard of Gilliam's party reached the river on 19 June, but the rear did not complete the crossing until the 24th. Whereas they had, with difficulty, managed to swim the cattle over the Black Vermillion, the Blue seemed too high and dangerous. Washington Gilliam, in the van of the party, made light of the difficulties: 'The Big Blue, the next obstacle that detained us, was about twenty miles from the Vermillion; but we found it well in its banks and also had the good fortune to find a couple of large canoes with a platform between them which had been left by a party immediately ahead of us, so all we had to do was to ferry our wagons over and swim the stock, which occupied three days.'

This facile account of the crossing of the Big Blue is belied by Minto's account. He tried riding a four-year-old filly into the river, holding on to its mane. But the horse bucked and reared and threw him into the water. Minto came to the surface to find the panic-stricken filly lashing out in all directions; he just missed being dealt a fatal blow on the head by the horse's hoof. Dragging his drenched body from the rivery deep, Minto joined his comrades in finding a spot three miles further down the river which seemed more fordable, even though the waters were still high and the current strong. Four or five guides went ahead, each with a strong ox which they tried to steer across. Minto was among the first to brave the stream, but found that the eddies produced funnel-shaped whirls which dragged his ox under the water. He was sucked down too and nearly drowned. In his desperation he managed to clutch at an ox that was surfacing. This was sheer luck, as he admitted. He added ruefully: 'I was twice reported drowned that day.'

On the far side of the Big Blue the emigrants were buffeted by a cyclone as they camped in a grove of cottonwoods; their tents were blown down and they were deluged with water. Doggedly they trekked on to the banks of the Little Blue, reached on 2 July. On this day they were able to bag their first big game in the shape of an antelope; previously, the hunters had had to rest content with turkeys and pigeons. For Independence Day on 4 July, Gilliam ordered a day's halt, but it was no day of rest: the women washed clothes while the men hunted. In his eagerness to hunt buffalo, Minto wandered too far from the caravan and had difficulty finding it again. On another occasion, while out hunting on his own, Minto caused a scare when a sentry took him for an Indian. Although the rain had produced an ocean of lush grass on the stretch between the Little Blue and the Platte, the travellers continued to be depressed by the vagaries of the weather. On 6 July, there was another flash flood. Even when the sun came out afterwards, Minto felt downcast by the monotony of the prairie: 'Not a tree or bush was in sight, but a boundless view of grass-covered country.'

Minto continued to gnaw away at the inadequacies of Gilliam's leadership: 'Some signs of dissatisfaction with General Gilliam's leadership are manifest. We travel westward, indeed, but there is not the general eagerness to do and help that there was before we stopped on the east side of the stream [the Black Vermillion] so often for so slight reason.' Gilliam seemed not to care that the young men in the party were undisciplined and that guns were going off accidentally all the time. Minto contrasted Gilliam's shortcomings with the qualities of his beloved Captain 'Billy' Shaw: 'This Captain Shaw, whose wife was a sister of General Gilliam, was by nature much more capable of generalship than her brave, impulsive brother, who from the day we voted him his title had never got his head down to the importance of drill, or even a plan of defense in case of sudden attack.' He took consolation from the growing warmth of his relationship with the Morrison family and the gentle joshing of Mrs Morrison, who regarded him as her own son. After picking some wild flowers, she said to John and his young comrades: 'Here, you young men, is something that will tell whether you are straight or not. If any of you have left girls behind you should have treated better, just touch this weed and it will tell you by wilting.' To his chagrin, Minto's flower wilted.

From the Little Blue to the Platte, the trail ran slightly downhill, the way marked by sandy hummocks or sandhills. In this arid landscape mirages were common, and it was said that a dozen men walking ahead looked like giants fifteen feet tall. As the emigrants passed over the last line of sand dunes and caught sight of the Platte valley below, the mirage effect seemed enhanced, for the Platte appeared like a vast glistening lake or an inland séa. At last, on 7 July, the Gilliam party reached the banks of the Platte. To the Midwesterners, who were used to low-lying rivers, it seemed as though the Platte flowed almost higher than the surrounding landscape and had no true banks. Minto remarked bitterly that it had taken sixty-one days to make two hundred miles: 'Rain and bad generalship were responsible for this.' But immediately the game prospects opened up, as if by magic. Having seen so little wildlife on the trek to the Platte, on the first three days on its shores the emigrants killed thirteen antelope and fourteen buffalo.

The Ford party, meanwhile, was toiling about a week in the rear of the Gilliam caravan. The most notable diarist in this group was fifty-two-year-old ex-fur trapper James Clyman, a veteran of Indian fights in the

Rockies and one-time comrade of Jedediah Smith and Thomas Fitz-patrick. His mid-May diaries mirror almost to the word the state of affairs described by Minto, Parrish and others in the Gilliam party: '14 May. Roads extremely bad owing to the late great rains . . . rained all day.' '15 May. This morning the whole prairie covered in water.' Departing Independence on the 14th and proceeding via Westport, this group was held up at the flooded Wakarusa River from 22 to 25 May, pelted by teeming rains throughout. Riding ahead to the Papins' ferry on the Kansas River, Clyman found that it had been swept away by the floods.

Already the Ford party was becoming strung out along the waterlogged prairie. Clyman estimated that ninety-two men passed muster on 26 May, but there were more coming up behind them all the time. As latecomers tried to crack on the pace from Independence, and impatient frontrun-ners tried to press on ahead, the never very organic solidarity of the Ford caravan was soon in signal disarray. When Clyman's section arrived at the Kansas River on 30 May, the total strength of the Ford emigration was supposed to be at least one hundred wagons and over five hundred souls. Thirty-nine wagons, and about two hundred people, were with Clyman, but between twenty and thirty teams were behind them and an estimated forty-one wagons were already north of the Kansas River. When this splintered party caught up with the Gilliam wagons and later even some of the more advanced caravans, the confusion became almost total, accounting for the notorious difficulty of tracking individual wagons on the 1844 emigration.

On 30 May, Clyman reported the anxiety with which the overlanders faced the crossing of the Kansas River. They were all exhausted after trudging through deep mud, and being assailed by coruscating lightning, deep, growling thunder and the precipitation that went with it. 'We have had almost one continued shower of rain since we left the settlements. We are commencing to cross the Kansas river today, which will occupy all our exertions for the next two or three days. We shall not all get collected in one company in less than eight or ten days.' Next day he continued: 'Our ferrying goes on slowly, it being difficult to get the boat on account of the low grounds being overflown.' On 4 June his diary entry read, 'all hands still engaged getting our stock across the river which is beginning to fall'.

As if the flooded river was not burden enough, they also had trouble with thieving Kansa Indians, who made off with horses and mules. Clyman led a search party to track the thieves but, after forty-eight hours in the saddle, the dispirited posse returned to camp tired and dejected, some facing the prospect of having to walk all the way to Oregon. Clyman complained bitterly that he had lost $200 worth of horses, mules and equipment simply because of the incompetence of the local Indian agent, who never visited the Kansa to give them their treaty goods nor to remonstrate over their braves marauding. But Clyman was no 'Injun-lover', prepared to make excuses for the destitute red man, and pitched into the Kansa as 'too lazy to work and too cowardly to go to the buffalo where they frequently meet with their enemies, get a few killed, and return to dig roots, beg and starve for two months, then make another effort which may or may not be more successful'.

Clyman was determined not to give up and, on 5 June, bearded the Kansa supremo Fool Chief in his camp, complaining bitterly about the theft. Fool Chief, who was killed the following January by a brave who challenged him, appeared to Clyman as 'a tall, lean, wrinkly-faced, filthy-looking man with a forehead indicating deep dissimulation and intrigue, and more like a beggarly scapegallows than a chief, but no doubt these fine qualities are highly prized by the Kaw nation'. Through an interpreter he expressed great indignation about the theft. Fool Chief was conciliatory: he promised that if he saw any of his men with the emigrants' horses, he would restore them. But Fool Chief's reassurances had no effect. Two days later, the emigrants were involved in a brawl with twenty drunken Indians and then, after suffering further heavy rains, they awoke on the morning of 9 June to find two horses and two mules stolen. This time Ford headed the posse that pursued the purloiners; with a dozen men he managed to catch up with the Indians and recover the mounts.

At Cross Creek, heavy rains again beat down on them, and the river rose fifteen feet on 10 June. Eighty hours of steady rain followed, sapping morale among the travellers. Clyman wrote: 'Our tents, beds, blankets, clothing, provisions and everything almost rotting and no prospect of drying them and even our cattle are scarcely able to walk, the muddy weather having given them the fouls [sic].' Even when a day dawned bright and clear, bringing hope to emigrant hearts, the initial good weather soon gave way to hail and rain. By 17 June, they were still being savaged by the elements on a daily basis. Piqued by further petty thefts from the Kansa, Clyman threatened punitive action by a squadron of dragoons at Fort Leavenworth. Although the army was not accompanying the overlanders, as it would in 1845, the cavalry was active on the plains that summer, and the Kansa could not be sure that this was an idle threat.

In continual rain and intermittent thunderstorms with violent lightning, they made their way to the Black Vermillion, which they crossed with ease when compared with the travails of the Gilliam caravan. Now only four days behind their rivals, they were rapidly closing the gap and by 25 June were camped by the Big Blue. But Clyman was in cross-grained, dyspeptic mood. In the privacy of his diary he raged at the incompetence of Moses 'Black' Harris: 'Our pilot, Mr Harris, twenty-two years experience and advice, is perfectly useless.' As he made his way through fog and thunderstorms to the Little Blue River, he amused himself by listing all the males in the party, noting that the country around the Little Blue provided useful timber and fine grass, but most of all by recording his political partisanship for Henry Clay, who was then contesting the 1844 presidential election with James Polk. Despite his fire-eating talk about the Kansa Indians, Clyman admired Clay's gifts for compromise, his attempts to conciliate North and South over slavery, and his dislike of Polk's campaign to admit Texas into the Union.

On 3 July, the Clyman party was overtaken by Andrew Sublette and his cohort of invalids and Catholics. Sublette had caught up with them on 27 June on the fog-shrouded banks of the Black Vermillion, but had then been delayed by the death and burial of one of the invalids, James H. Marshall by name. There was a bitter irony about the Sublette expedition, for his invalids could not have chosen a worse summer to attempt a health-restoring trip on the great plains; in a letter to his brother William, Andrew Sublette confessed that he had never seen rains and floods like this in his entire career. They were scarcely a week out from home base when eleven of the Catholics were seriously ill; Sublette himself had a nasty cough. Shortly after Marshall's death there was a second, featuring a Mr Ketchum of St Louis. Between 3 and 7 July, the Sublette group and the Ford party played overtaking games with each other: first Sublette drew clear, putting Clyman and comrades firmly at the rearguard of all travellers that summer over the western prairie; then Sublette had to pause again to bury a third deceased invalid, this time a man named Browning; by the 13th, the Sublette group were lowering a fourth dead man into the ground.

A pall of gloom hung over the Independence Day celebrations. Clyman wrote: 'The American Jubilee was but little further noted than that the Star Spangled Banner floated from Esquire Roland's wagon throughout the day.' People were complaining of rheumatism and dysentery, and mosquitoes were particularly troublesome. Thunder and lightning were still frequent companions. But a seventeen-mile trek on 10 July brought them to the Platte, which Clyman found more muddy than the Missouri, 'itself the father of mud'. In camp among the cottonwoods of Grand Island, Clyman reflected that this oasis would provide the last significant trees for a long time to come: 'No place in the world looks more lonesome and discouraging than the wide prairies of this region. Neither tree, bush, shrub, rock nor water to cherish him and such a perfect sameness . . . all around you meeting the horizon in all directions.'

Clyman was evidently a man of moods and rapid changes of mind. Although he continued to lament the scarcity of timber, with only the occasional cottonwood or dwarf willow to be seen, on 13 July we encounter the following paean after making twenty miles that day:

> The high level country south of the Ravine (?) are [*sic*] beautiful beyond description, handsomely rolling and thickly set with fine buffalo grass and blue stem almost as soft as a bed and luxuriously covered with wild sunflowers and several other species of wild blossoms which are now in full bloom and scent the air to a considerable distance with a very fine perfume as pleasant as a flower garden.

The Ford party was just three days behind the Gilliam caravan at the Platte but, with stragglers in the latter case and frontrunners in the former, the two wagon trains soon became indistinguishable. On 17 July, Clyman recorded that they passed Gilliam's party last night but had been repassed that morning. Soon the leaders concluded that all this overtaking worked to nobody's advantage. Both sides agreed that they would travel in the near vicinity of each other and would camp no further apart than was necessary for the good of the stock. Clearly the approach to Sioux territory was concentrating the minds. But with a combined caravan of ninety-six teams and wagons, the joint expedition would now be a tough nut for even the largest war party to crack.

It was as well for the Gilliam party that they made common cause with Nathaniel Ford's overlanders, for Gilliam's grandly conceived Company of Oregon Emigrants came close to disintegration during the first week on the Platte. The immediate precipitant was Neal Gilliam's resignation following a vain attempt to impose his authority. Murmurs of opposition to Gilliam's lacklustre leadership became a torrent of open defiance on the Platte, largely because of a fiasco over buffalo-hunting (discussed below). Several strong-minded individuals declared that they had had enough and were forming a breakaway movement. Gilliam then threatened to hang from the nearest tree anyone who left the wagon train. A young man named Daniel Clark called his bluff by jumping on to his horse and calling out: 'If any of you men or boys intend going to Oregon, come on. I'm going.' Gilliam blustered but was powerless and seen to be so. He threatened to shoot Clark and anyone who followed him, but lost credibility by a threat nobody believed in. Even his wife warned him: 'Now, Neal, be careful.' Seeing that he would either have to commit murder or back down and lose face – for it was most unlikely that a general meeting would back sanctions against Clark – Gilliam stormed out. His formal resignation followed on 15 July, followed by that of his close friend B.F. Nicholls and 'Colonel' Michael T. Simmons. The Company of Oregon Emigrants broke up into three independent divisions, one of which was led by Billy Shaw.

Behind the immediate issue of authority and discipline lay a fiasco over buffalo meat, and behind this in turn lay a greedy, wasteful and mindless attitude of the overlanders to the teeming herds of buffalo they encountered along the Platte – 'the best game park in all the world', as John Minto put it. Successive overlanders made the same point. The teeming herds were described as like forests of cedar that turned the prairie black, ten miles wide, containing between one million and two million bison, sometimes moving like a Roman legion, sometimes like a Greek phalanx and often in a V formation. Their stampedes, like rolling thunder, were the most feared experience on the Great Plains. Naturally, emigrant accounts contain a degree of hyperbole, and some critics think it more significant that the overlanders did not often see buffalo once they had left the Platte valley, suggesting that in some sense the teeming herds along the Platte were a freak occurrence. The best scholarly estimate is that the millions attested to by so many witnesses must have been optical illusions, since the Plains may have carried no more than thirty million bison even in the days before the arrival of the horse.

What can be stated with certainty is that, without exception, emigrants on the overland trek behaved with consummate stupidity. Not only did they waste ammunition killing more buffalo than they could eat, but by leaving the rotting carcasses on the plains they alienated the Indians, who in general had been disposed to be friendly to the men and women in wagons. On 12 July, the dissensions in the Gilliam party finally burst forth in an orgy of rancorous recrimination. On one side were the buccaneers, who wanted to slaughter buffalo, cut out the tongues and move on quickly, leaving the corpses to coyotes, carrion crows and other birds of prey. On the other were those who wanted to cook and conserve all the meat against the difficult days to come. The fourteen buffalo killed on the 11th provided almost no meat, as the bison were simply gutted and left unskinned overnight; the hunters had neither the time, the skills nor the inclination for methodical butchery. The result, as Minto trenchantly put it, '40,000 lbs of the best beef spoiled in one night'.

John Minto and others felt that Cornelius Gilliam was directly to blame for this fiasco. Gilliam had headed the faction associated with mindless bison massacre – 'Mr Gilliam had shown himself to be a headlong leader of unreflecting and wasteful slaughter', as Minto put it. When his leadership broke down and he resigned in dudgeon, Gilliam let it be known that henceforth he would accept no man's authority but would devote himself full-time to buffalo-hunting. That there was something self-destructive about Neal Gilliam was perhaps indicated by his untimely end: four years later, when at the age of fifty, he accidentally shot himself dead. In the meantime, Shaw, Minto and others severely criticised the former leader for his gross irresponsibility. Minto's later memoir, painting a glowing picture in primary colours of his honorary parents the Morrisons, also depicts Gilliam in the darkest of hues.

The Ford party were also out buffalo-hunting, also killing wastefully. Their stupidity was of a different kind from Gilliam's. They made the mistake of sweeping in a wide circle looking for bison on 16 July while the wagon train itself pressed on at a fast pace, making eighteen miles. The upshot was that they could take with them only the meat they could carry on a long ride back to the night's encampment, all the time beset by mosquitoes 'with uncommon bloodthirsty appetites . . . and were literally so thick that with all our exertions we could hardly breathe'. As the three-day buffalo hunt by the Ford company continued over 19–22 July, the mosquitoes seemed to realise there were rich pickings among the humans as well as the buffalo. On the 22nd Clyman continued his lamentation: 'The mosquitoes very troublesome. The first time we have been much troubled in camp although they cover a single individual horse and all in a few minutes of evenings and mornings for the last ten days if it happened to be out alone.'

Wasting meat, attracting mosquitoes and alienating Indians were not the only items in the debit ledger of buffalo-hunting overlanders. Shooting bison near the wagon train brought the risk that a buffalo would charge the wagons or the cattle, overturning conveyances or scattering herds for miles which then had to be corralled once more. Valuable horses were worn out by the chase and some gored by angry bulls; others stumbled, broke legs and had to be destroyed, or pitched their riders off, causing broken limbs and even paralysis. Many were the emigrants who arrived in Oregon or California on foot, having worn out their horses on the high plains. Ammunition was wasted, since it took so many of the primitive balls in 1840s guns to kill the great beasts. And the more thoughtful and conservative-minded overlanders deplored the mindless slaughter of herds that could not make up their numbers fast enough to withstand the assaults of the following years' emigrants. Most corrupting of all was the attitude that hunting and killing buffalo was 'good sport'. Even the women, who generally adopted a higher moral tone than the men on the trails, could be corrupted by this insidious argument. Minto said of one hunt along the Platte that 'the scene was so interesting that some of our women actually joined in the chase'.

The combined caravan crossed the fork of the South Platte on 18–19 July. Clyman reported no difficulty, but Minto, who crossed and recrossed six times, found it hazardous. To stop at all was dangerous since 'the bottom of the river was a moving mass of sand, and the wheels of the wagons, hauled by the oxen, sunk in this so quickly that they rattled'. Although it was very hot, with no breeze to keep down the flies and mosquitoes, the travellers were in good spirits as the hunters kept the meat rolling in. Clyman remarked in typically confused or ambiguous mode that by common consent 'this is the finest, richest, sweetest living of any they have ever experienced and all hope that they may last long and broad without stint or diminution'. The emigrants were much taken, as they clocked up twenty-three miles on the trail on 23 July, to see an extensive 'city' of prairie dogs extending over some 4,000 acres, 'thickly settled with an active population living on grass and weeds'. They also noted the peculiarity that the prairie dogs seemed to live in happy symbiosis with rattlesnakes, who might have been thought their natural enemy. Whenever a human approached a prairie-dog hole, an ominous rattling could be heard, almost as though the serpents were protecting their rodent neighbours.

Towards the end of July, there were occasional cool days and on the 21st, when they were about twelve miles west of Ash Hollow, they endured a noonday pelting described by Minto as 'the heaviest hailstorm I ever saw or felt', with hailstones as big as pigeon's eggs. Sublette's small group had also been with them since 13 July and, now that the heavy rains of June had, by and large, ceased and the climate was more equable, the surviving invalids were starting to pick up in health, and even able to participate in buffalo hunts. Accidents and mishaps, such as the overturned and upset wagons that had demoralised the Gilliam party at the beginning of the month, now seemed a thing of the past. The 26th and 27th saw them passing the familiar emigrant landmarks of Court House Rock and Chimney Rock, and on the 29th they camped in the middle of Scotts Bluff. The hills seemed alive with game: full of black-tailed deer, antelope, elk, mountain sheep and even grizzly bears. As they approached Fort Laramie, the prairies seemed on fire, the blaze caused by a party of itinerant Indians ahead of them. Yet, considering the turmoil earlier in the month, it was a reasonably contented combined wagon train that trooped into Fort Laramie on 1 August.

They had arrived almost a month later than the northern party of 1844 emigrants, who had enjoyed much better luck through starting closer to the Platte and to the north of the worst flooded areas, avoiding Kansas. About forty men in twenty-seven wagons had assembled at Council Bluffs, Iowa, in the second week of May and elected Elisha Stephens as their captain for the journey. Stephens was a thirty-eight-year-old former blacksmith and trapper, a strikingly ugly man of slim build, with a long neck and a long and high head, and a tremendous eagle-beak of a nose. Since he had no political skills and was not as good a mountain man as others along on the trip, there is a mystery about why he was elected. One theory was that, for all his drawbacks, he had the mysterious quality of leadership or was, as one scholar of 1844 has expressed it: 'Cautious, polite, hopeful, courageous, prudent, plain, domestic, generous, attached to friends, firm, persevering, successful . . . born to command.'

Yet from the earliest days there were problems with the Stephens leadership. The fundamental issue was that the emigrants were heading for different destinations: Stephens and his coterie were making for California while about one-third of the overlanders had Oregon as their target and looked to John Thorp as their leader. The result was that the Thorp and Stephens parties, though cooperating and often travelling together, had clearly distinct identities. Another salient factor may have been that the Stephens clique contained a strong Irish Catholic contingent, featuring men like Miller, Sullivan and Bray, and families like the Murphys and Martins, whereas the Thorp party was mainly Protestant, albeit of several different denominations. According to Jacob Hammer, a twenty-eight-year-old Quaker bound for Oregon with his twenty-four-year-old wife Hannah, there were four main problems with Stephens. Although elected leader, Stephens refused to be bound by the agreed and democratically voted regulations; he was in a tearing hurry to get across the Missouri at all costs, whereas the Oregonians wanted to take their time, especially as Thorp's wife was ill. Added to which there was the monotony of waiting in teeming rain on the eastern bank of the Missouri River, and simple personality clashes between Stephens and Thorp.

The combined parties set out in the rain on 18 May, crossed the Missouri and headed west to the Platte. They were only a day out when the first trouble occurred. Jacob Hammer explained the situation:

A quarrel arose between A.C.R. Shaw and William Prather which came very near mischief. Myself and William Clemmens were taken aside by William Prather as he supposed we were very civil men and thought we were the men to talk to about the dispute. We told him he had in his manner of speaking given an insult to Shaw. He then acknowledged that it was an insult and further said that if it had been given to him he would have knocked down any man that did it. A.C.R. Shaw was called at this time. I told him I blamed him for flying into such a pashion [*sic*] and threatening to draw his pistols and for swearing so hard. Yet a coolness seems to exist between them.

On 21 May there was further dissension. After clocking up sixteen miles the day before, the emigrants halted for a day to work out the rules and regulations governing them. Hammer and his friends found themselves in a minority against the Stephens faction. To make matters worse, the majority spokesmen then admitted that Hammer's view was the correct and logical one but they intended doing things their way anyhow. There was especial wrangling on the issue of a pilot. Hammer and his adherents argued that to hire a pilot was an unnecessary expense, since the route to Oregon was by now well known; but Stephens and his acolytes insisted that Caleb Greenwood, a veteran mountain man of the upper Missouri country, should be given the position. Since Greenwood was eighty and going blind, Hammer remarked with some asperity that Stephens might at least choose a pilot who could see. If, however, they insisted on hiring Greenwood, they could do so out of their own resources; they would not get a single cent from him.

They now entered the territory of the Potawatomi Indians, suffering very stormy weather and a violent wind which shook the wagons to their foundations. As a sign of friendship, they attended a ceremonial Potawatomi dance and gave the chief a present of two sheep as tribute for passing through his lands. The flooded creeks still gave trouble even at these latitudes, and this occasioned a further division of opinion between the Stephens and Thorp factions. Stephens insisted on driving the cattle into the swollen waters, but the Oregon-bound party refused. Hammer derived much satisfaction from the spectacle of the Californian party finding their cattle mired in mud, from which they extracted them with great difficulty. An 'I told you so' complacency was much in evidence in Hammer's diary.

On 26 May, they entered the territory of the Otoes. Three days later, after incessant rain, the habitual troublemaker A.C.R. Shaw lost his temper with Stephens for blatantly issuing orders that were contrary to the agreed regulations. Shaw made a great show of firing off his gun, reloading it and then telling anyone who cared to listen that he intended killing Stephens. A fresh election was called for to compose the growing differences in the wagon train. Once again Stephens was elected captain, with Thorp receiving the Protestant votes; to his great chagrin, the fire-eating Shaw was not even nominated for office. Doubtless the election simply increased the feelings of paranoia that were so large a part of Stephens's psychological profile and which would, at the end of his life, make him a prickly recluse. On the other hand, it is difficult not to sympathise with the 'captain' when men like the Quaker Jacob Hammer were disobeying orders on the basis of 'revelations' in dreams.

How competent Stephens was in these early days is difficult to determine. One has to discount both the pro-Stephens hagiography and the anti-Stephens demonology of the Thorp faction to get anywhere near the truth. Certainly he seems at an early stage, to have mastered the ticklish craft of getting wagons and cattle across flooded rivers. The traverse of the Missouri was a case in point. At first, the emigrants tried to swim the cattle across, but the beasts panicked in the swirling waters and began swimming in a circle, each trying to climb upon the back of the one in front. The men gave up and led the animals back to the bank, but some were left stuck in mud, 'as tenacious as quicksand'. They had to wait until the water receded before they were able to dig them out with picks and spades. But some of the cattle were so securely fastened by the mud, as if they had manacles on their legs, that it was impossible to rescue them. The luckless beasts were abandoned where they stood, doomed to perish from drowning or starving to death. Stephens finally solved the problem by having two men in a canoe lead across one of the more biddable oxen by tying a rope round its horns and towing it across; the others, seeing the lead oxen get safely across, splashed into the water and swam without fear.

Later, they ferried across the Elkhorn River by making boats out of two wagon beds covered with rawhide and sewn together, and then lashing two of the 'canoes' together. They unloaded all the wagons, ferried everything across, using rawhide ropes stretched across the river and tied to trees on either side. The animals were swum across as at the Missouri. Even though a top-heavy wagon fell off one of the improvised canoes during the crossing of the Elkhorn, and was with difficulty retrieved from the stream, the Stephens party soon learned the knack of using a waterproof nine feet by four wagon box to ferry a ton of goods across a river. This was hard work but it did not involve an impossible number of waterborne trips. Soon they got used to high water and were more concerned about the sand ridges on the bottom land along the river, caused by heavy flooding of the Platte and Elkhorn. After a few bumpy rides, they learned to use the ridges as a good, dry road, avoiding the wet and swampy terrain in the rest of the bottom land.

At the Platte (reached on 3 June), the Murphy family's wagon ran into the river, soaking all their possessions. But this was the last real encounter with hostile water, for henceforth there were no more swollen rivers and all the streams were fordable. The Stephens–Thorp caravan now followed the north bank of the Platte, blazing a trail that would become famous when used by the Mormons in 1847; because Caleb Greenwood had passed this way in the 1830s with a few wagons, pedants object that the men of 1844 cannot be termed pioneers in the true sense. They picked wild cherries and onions, but found the wild peas inedible. Like all other emigrant groups, they succumbed to buffalo mania once they reached the Platte valley. Whether caught in a spontaneous bison stampede or whether they had themselves spooked the animals (it is not clear from the sources), they had a narrow escape when charged by a herd of more than a thousand enraged beasts. William Case, in the Thorp party, described the scene: 'The flying herds of buffaloes passed but a few yards to the rear of the last wagons, and were going at such a rate that to be struck by them would have been like the shock of rolling boulders of a ton's weight.'

On the open plain, dotted with the occasional wild sage or cottonwood, they met several parties of friendly Pawnee, who pointed out to them the ground apples or ground potatoes (which to the emigrants tasted like neither apples nor potatoes). For their own selfish reasons, the overlanders of '44 were glad that the Pawnee had recently been badly mauled by the Sioux, as it was thought the warlike Lakota would not now be hungry for emigrant scalps. They spared no pity for the luckless Pawnee, whose domain was now confined to the grassy plains and sandhills north of the Platte. In this barren land, where the only trees except for an occasional cottonwood were the willow, burr oak and elm on the larger islands in the Platte and the Loup, the Pawnee were hemmed in by a host of enemies. To the west and north-west were the Comanche, Cheyenne, Arapaho and Sioux; to the north-east and south-east were the Omaha and Oto, and to the south were the Osage. Time was when the dominion of the Pawnee was bounded by the Niobrara River to the north, the Arkansas or Canadian rivers to the south, the Missouri to the east and the Fort Laramie area in the west. The key to Pawnee decline was the dreadful smallpox epidemic that swept away 3,000 tribesmen (half their number) in 1832. In 1837–38, another epidemic killed a further 2,000, mostly children who had not gained immunity from the first plague.

The trail blazed by the Stephens–Thorp party on the north shore of the Platte involved leaving the Platte at around the latitude of present-day Columbus, Nebraska, and following the north bank of the Loup River along a roughly parallel course before rejoining the Platte near Grand Island. The reason for this detour along the 'Loup Fork' was that the confluence of the Loup and the Platte made a river crossing too dangerous to attempt at that point. But the Loup itself posed problems, because of the softness of its banks and the quicksands in the river, which meant that the emigrants dared not cross it until much further on. Throughout the days of mid-June, they toiled through heavy rains, sometimes making no more than one and a half miles a day because of the torrents. The devout Jacob Hammer was much exercised about whether the heavy rains were God's judgement on the 'ungodly' party. Finally, on 15 June, they were able to cross the Loup to the south bank – the first time in six days the river was free of quicksand.

Once on the south bank of the Loup they made faster progress, albeit on very sandy and gravelly terrain, averaging sixteen miles on travelling days. There were plenty of wild plums and wild cherries to pick, and the hunters even bagged an antelope. But on the 18th Stephens called another halt. On the one hand John Murphy had the fever, and on the other there had been a further angry altercation which ended with Stephens throwing up his commission in dudgeon. The stopover allowed the travellers to fish and restock the larder with meat from the antelope which were now becoming common and easier to kill. Finally, a few miles above Grand Island, they left the 'Loup Fork' to rejoin the north bank of the Platte. The stream was wide and shallow, once more running through country bare of anything but the occasional cottonwood, but still treacherous and full of quicksands. They again started to average sixteen miles a day, on one occasion taking that long to pass an immense 'city' of prairie dogs, which Hammer thought looked very like squirrels.

On 24 June, there was another dissension-ridden stopover. Since Stephens was still sulking, the emigrants elected a man named Harmon Higgins as his temporary replacement. A more serious problem was illness. Many of the party were far from well and one, a man named Vance, had been dangerously ill for two days but forced by the impatience of his comrades to endure forty jolting miles in the wagon before they would agree to a period of rest and recuperation. But since Vance showed no signs of improvement, Higgins resumed the march. The next four days they made seventy-six miles. Whether this finished off Vance or his position was hopeless anyway, on 28 June he died. Since he was a Baptist, his comrades buried him with the full rites of that denomination.

Pressing on fast, next day they found three splendid water springs – their best supply of fresh water since leaving the Missouri. They were making rapid progress – from the morning of 29 June to the evening of 2 July they clocked up 107 miles, even though the hooves of the cattle were sore and the beasts lowed in pain. On 3 July, they crossed a large tributary and trekked through a landscape full of buffalo chips and strewn with petrified buffalo bones. Game was abundant – white-tailed deer, jackrabbits, timber wolves, grey wolves and coyotes. Less welcome were the clouds of mosquitoes, which particularly made their biting presence felt on Independence Day. But still the cracking pace continued. From 2 to 7 July they marched twenty miles a day, passing Chimney Rock on the 6th and arriving at Scotts Bluff on the 7th.

As they approached Fort Laramie, they were suddenly met by an envoy from the fort commandant Joseph Bissonette. He advised them not to approach the fort at present but to send ahead anyone who spoke the Lakota tongue. Bissonette was concerned by the presence near the fort of a large party of hostile Sioux; at this time of year such a large war party should already be on the borders of the Crow or Blackfoot territory, harrying these traditional enemies unless they intended mischief against the overland wagon trains. The emigrants waited twenty-four hours before getting the 'all-clear' to proceed into Fort Laramie. Bissonette claimed he had asked the Sioux war chiefs for a parley, reminded them that he was a man whose words could be trusted and then warned them that smallpox was cutting a swathe through the wagon trains that year. Surely they did not want to catch this dreaded disease, whose terrible effects were only too well known to the tribes?

Such at least was the story told by William Case, a valuable witness for the exploits of the Thorp party in 1844. Later historians have affected to disbelieve the story, on the grounds that all other emigrants mention the Sioux as being present in large numbers around the fort throughout that summer. George Stewart, the expert on the Stephens party, takes a middle position and says that on the one hand the Sioux were not dangerous since they had squaws and children with them. On the other hand, he writes: 'An estimated 4,000 Sioux were camped nearby, and the emigrants did some trafficking for ponies and mocassins – at the same time feeling a little apprehensive for their own scalps after they should leave the fort.' It seems that Case told a story that was partly true and partly false. Circumstantial evidence from summer 1844 indicates that the Sioux were contemplating an attack on the overland whites – possibly in anger about the wasteful way they were killing the buffalo – and that Bissonette warned them of dire consequences from the US Army. The detail about the smallpox was probably no more than a good yarn told by Bissonette to gullible emigrants to impress them with his cunning.

At Fort Laramie, the Oregon-bound and California-bound parties finally decided to go their separate ways, agreeing informally that they would travel no more than two days' apart in case of serious Indian trouble, with the Stephens caravan in the van. When the Oregon-bound party finally set out from Fort Laramie in mid-July, their progress was so slow (less than ten miles in a week) that new elections were called for. Captain Higgins resigned and John Thorp regained his old position as overall commander, no longer challenged in his authority by Stephens and the contumacious Irish Catholics. Even so, the election of Thorp did not reassure the more impatient overlanders, who hastened ahead to join Stephens, intending to travel with him at least as far as Fort Hall. As proof of his toughness, Thorp cracked on the pace, and in the six days from the morning of 16 July 'ate up' a further hundred miles.

By now indiscipline was the major problem besetting both of the advanced parties of 1844. William Case described the situation among the Oregonians: 'The daily labour of the march was devolved more and more upon the twenty men or so that felt the necessity of pushing on. The majority, however, often spent their evenings playing cards to a late hour, or dancing and fiddling with the young folks around the fire.' The women tried to solve the problem by surreptitiously burning the packs of cards but, as if by magic, new ones appeared. When the scrimshankers continued with their revelry, Case and a few others decided to go on with their wagons, leaving the idlers behind. The Thorp party, having separated from Stephens, was now disintegrating in turn, illustrating the extremes of factionalism on the trail that summer.

Things were no better in the Stephens party. An old man named Derby blatantly disregarded Stephens's orders that no fires were to be lit at night for fear of attracting the Sioux. Derby spat an oath, called Stephens an old granny and swore that he would not put his fire out for him or any man. Stephens called on Dr John Townsend, a semi-qualified physician and horse doctor, to help him out; as a 'professional' man Townsend was thought to have status and gravitas. Townsend extinguished Derby's fire, but the obstinate old man relit it. Townsend returned and ordered him to put it out. Derby made the mistake of trying to browbeat Townsend. 'No, I will not,' he said, 'and I don't think it will be healthy for anyone else to try it.' This was the wrong tone to take with a tough character like Townsend. Again he extinguished the fire and said in a quiet, determined and menacing way: 'It will not be well for you to light that fire again tonight.' Derby sulked all night but did not relight the fire. Next morning, he complained to Stephens who, predictably, found in Townsend's favour. Derby then swore another mighty oath and declared that he would no longer travel with such a crowd. He moved out and camped half a mile behind the caravan but, interestingly, lit no fires. One of Stephens's scouts finally brought the old man to heel by telling him he had seen a large Sioux war party. Derby then returned sheepishly to the camp, apologised and thenceforth obeyed orders.

The Stephens party also did well at procuring fresh meat. The first buffalo hunt after Fort Laramie was notably unsuccessful, and the hunters had to endure the 'humiliation' of bringing back an antelope instead of the shaggy-haired bison. But another hunt near the Sweetwater, led by Moses Schallenberger and Allen Montgomery, was a great success – almost too much so, as the hunters killed seven buffalo while being far from the wagon train. Forced to camp in the wilderness at night, they were surrounded by wolves who bade fair to dispossess them of the carcasses. They were obliged to stay up most of the night, butchering the meat to save it from predators. Early dawn found the wolves massing and nerving themselves up for a raid. Suddenly, the hunters found an unexpected ally. A large bear lumbered into view, sending the wolves scattering. Showing remarkable ingratitude to their ursine saviour, Montgomery and Schallenberger made an unsuccessful attempt to shoot the bear. When their shots scared off the bear, the wolves returned. Seeing that there was now no chance of saving the meat from the pack, the hunters cut up the choice pieces of the buffalo and left the rest for the wolves to devour. It was three in the afternoon before the hunters were ready to mount up and locate the wagons. Having been up all the night before, they were forced to ride through the following night before finally catching up with the wagon train at dawn.

There was a long halt at Independence Rock, partly occasioned by the birth of a daughter to Mr and Mrs James Miller; as they were at Independence Rock they called the child Ellen Independence. They pressed on, past South Pass, where they noticed, as so many had before, that the buffalo ceased to exist, almost as if they had been spirited into the ether. In camp at the Big Sandy, the sixty-four-year-old mountain man Isaac Hitchcock (of whom disappointingly little is known) proposed taking them across country to the Green River by a cutoff. This trek quickly turned into a fiasco. Hitchcock told his comrades that the distance to the Green was a mere twenty-five miles, a single day's march. Accordingly, the party carried no extra water or cut grass for the cattle.

In fact, the distance to the Green was forty-three miles, so that at dusk the travellers found themselves in the middle of desolate country, suffering from thirst and with the cattle faring badly. Although Hitchcock's instinct was right (for the route by which he had led them was the later so-called Sublette's cutoff), he had a lot of explaining to do that night. Fortunately for him and the others, the advance guard, out since dawn in pursuit of straying cattle, found the Green at 11 a.m.

Next morning, after breakfasting at the Green River, Stephens sent out six men to locate all cattle that had strayed on the march from the Big Sandy. Since the six could not agree where the cattle were, they divided and separated: three men scoured the banks of the Green while Murphy and two companions doubled back to the Big Sandy. On the way, Murphy, who was riding ahead, suddenly motioned to the others to turn back. The three men galloped to a canyon and found a hiding place. From there, Murphy pointed out a war party of one hundred painted Sioux warriors, so close that the white men could hear them talking. The Sioux passed within twenty yards of where the trio was lurking in concealment. As one of them commented: 'It was a close call, for had their presence been known, the little band of whites would never have seen the golden plains of California.'

After locating the missing cattle at the Big Sandy, Murphy and his comrades returned to the wagon train, still camped on the Green River. Next morning, there was another shock when two hundred mounted warriors came whooping down on them. Thinking their hour had come, the emigrants grimly seized their weapons. But the Indians made pacific gestures and sent three unarmed braves to parley. They turned out to be friendly Shoshone, on the trail of the very same Sioux war party seen by Murphy the day before. So affable were the Shoshone that they even helped the travellers to swim their cattle over the Green. From there, Hitchcock, now with a smidgin more credibility, persuaded them that the second half of his 'cutoff' would soon bring them to the Bear River, shortening the route by about eighty-five miles and shaving five to six days off their journey. This time there were no mishaps, they reached the Bear, found Peg-Leg Smith's trading post, and there exchanged their tired horses for fresh ponies. They then had an easy passage down through Soda Springs to Fort Hall.

Since Fort Hall marked the point where the California and Oregon parties definitively diverged, the rest of the Stephens story must be told later. Thorp's Oregon party, meanwhile, made good, steady progress, apart from one mistake soon after leaving the North Platte when they lost the way and ended up travelling in a twenty-two-mile circle to achieve just ten miles' progress. Like the Stephens party, they tarried four days at Independence Rock and took a leisurely look at Devil's Gate, and then averaged sixteen miles a day to reach the Sweetwater. At South Pass, Jacob Hammer marvelled at the perpetual snow of the Rockies, but Thorp did not permit many more stopovers. The daily mileages on the Green and Bear river stretches were anywhere from eighteen to twenty-six miles and the journey uneventful, except for some petty thieving by the Shoshone. They reached Soda Springs on 25 August and then left the Bear to proceed along the Portneuf (a tributary of the Snake) to reach Fort Hall on the 29th.

While Thorp and his wagons were at Fort Hall, the bulk of the 1844 overlanders were still at Fort Laramie, 535 miles further east. They took the opportunity to dump Moses 'Black' Harris, who had been unsatisfactory as a guide – many accused him of outright shirking. In his place for the stretch to the new post at Fort Bridger they hired the veteran pathfinder Joseph Walker. The emigrants spent at least forty-eight hours reprovisioning, making repairs and blacksmithing. For Andrew Sublette and his invalids this was the end of the line, but for Clyman and others, who had the long journey to Oregon in prospect, the high prices at Laramie were a particular irritant. Clyman recorded that flour now retailed at $1 a pint (more than twice the 1843 price) and sugar at $1.50 a pint, another increase of at least 100 per cent. Moreover, the traders at the fort were becoming increasingly hard-nosed: no longer would they accept items for exchange or barter but demanded hard cash.

For the Sager family in William Shaw's company, the days at Fort Laramie saw the beginnings of a tragedy that would eventually engulf the whole of this ill-starred sept. Approaching Laramie on 30 July, this accident-prone family tempted fate once too often. The children had grown accustomed to getting out on the tongue of the wagon and then leaping clear without having the oxen even break stride. But while she was playing this dangerous game, the hem of Catherine Sager's dress caught on an axe handle and the wagon wheels ran over her, crushing her leg. Her father ran up and exclaimed in panic: 'My dear child, your leg is broken all to pieces!' Henry Sager then set Catherine's leg in splints, at first adamant that no doctor was needed. Calmer counsels eventually prevailed and a Dutch physician named Theophilos Dagen was sent for. He inspected Henry Sager's handiwork and declared that he could not improve on it.

The psychological profile of the accident-prone child has recently received much attention in clinical studies: suffice it to say that one factor in the Sager tragedy must have been inadequate parenting. Theophilos

Dagen later told Narcissa Whitman that Henry and Naomi's offspring were 'very bad children', badly behaved, inadequately socialised and left to rampage like wild things. Certainly the children's record of accidents during the trek to Oregon is stupefying. Quite apart from Catherine's dreadful accident on 30 July, there had been an earlier incident just after the crossing of the south fork of the Platte, when the family wagon overturned and nearly killed Mrs Sager; Catherine had her dress torn off and Henry Sager's face was badly skinned. Later, the girls went out for a midnight stroll and were nearly killed when a sentry shot at them, mistaking them for Indians. On another occasion, Catherine relates: 'We children narrowly escaped being burned to death by getting the bed-clothes into the fire . . . after this affair Father slept in the tent with us.'

The chapter of accidents went on and on. Elizabeth Sager and her friend Alvira Edes left the wagon train on the most arid, desert-like stretch of the journey, purely for a jaunt. They took no water or compass, got hopelessly lost and were nearly faint with thirst by the time they (by pure luck) stumbled on to the path of the wagon train. Later, in La Grande Ronde area of Oregon, as Catherine relates: 'While encamped there one of my sisters caught fire and would have burned to death had it not been for the timely aid of the doctor.' The three-year-old, meanwhile, got out of the wagon one night and nearly froze to death. And Francis Sager almost blew himself up by sprinkling powder from a powderhorn on the fire: 'his face was blackened and perfectly denuded of eyebrows and eyelashes.'

Fortunately for the state of mind of the emigrants, most of the misfortunes of the Sagers lay in the future when the wagon train quit Fort Laramie, though the lamed Catherine Sager suffered badly with her broken leg from the jolting of the wagon. Once again, the companies that had originally started as Ford and Gilliam's wagon train stuck close together, passing and repassing one another. Despite the alleged success of Bissonette's 'smallpox' ruse and the fact that Minto and others had smoked the peace pipe in Lakota lodges, the presence of so many Sioux at Fort Laramie worried the overlanders; their abiding fear was that the warriors would follow and attack them on the open trail. Perhaps John Minto had an especial worry. While he was in the Lakota encampment, several young Sioux girls took a fancy to him. Through Mrs Morrison they tried to buy him; she then had to explain that John was neither her slave nor her property in any other sense. The Indian girls retreated in confusion, thinking they had misunderstood the situation. Minto worried that on reflection the Sioux elders might construe the 'refusal to trade' as an insult and come after him.

Beyond Fort Laramie, as Minto describes it, 'the country all the way is a rich game park, and swarming with all animals that prey upon game, the large wolf and grizzly bear being most seen'. In another party James Clyman was more impressed by the violent weather – sudden thunderstorms, squalls of wind and frequent flashes of forked lightning – though he did mention the plethora of grizzlies who made their home in heavily timbered boxwood creeks and feasted on their favourite food: chokeberries and red willow berries. They saw plenty of buffalo in the distance, but could not spare the time to turn off the trail and hunt them. By now, everyone saw clearly the implication of the early delays in Kansas – that they might be trapped in Oregon in the snows. As Clyman wrote: 'Our delay on Kaw [Kansas] River was a great detriment to our travelling, bringing us through this dry region in the warmest and driest part of the season.' The travellers were making steady progress – twelve miles on 3 August, eight the next day, seventeen miles on the 8th, twenty miles on the 10th, eighteen miles on the 11th – but Clyman worried about the oxen and cattle: 'Our stock begins to look bad and lose their activity and yet we have not arrived at the worst part of our tiresome journey.'

On 15 August, after marching thirty-six miles in two days, they came to Red Buttes and camped on the Sweetwater. In Shaw's company, John Nichols's daughter, a girl just on the cusp of womanhood, died of fever. Minto, who helped to dig her grave, was much affected: 'From my eight years in the coal mines, I had seen men and boys maimed, crushed or buried by machinery, falling roofs or firedamp, but nothing of that kind affected me like this death scene.' On the 17th, Shaw's company arrived at Independence Rock, a day after Clyman's company, and Clyman joined others in carving his name on the rock. 'I observed the names of two of my old friends, the notable mountaineers Thomas Fitzpatrick and W.L. Sublette, as likewise one of our noblest politicians Henry Clay coupled in division with that of Martin van Buren.'

Despite worrying signs that a large war party of Sioux had recently been in the vicinity, 17 August was given over to hunting. The less adventurous went fishing or tracked down ibex or mountain sheep but, inevitably, the buffalo proved the magnet for the bravehearts in the caravans. Minto managed to wound a yearling, but a great bull interposed itself between him and the wounded calf and while he was pondering whether he had enough ammunition to finish off the bovine paterfamilias, darkness descended rapidly, as it always did on the high plains. Although women could sometimes be caught up in 'bison fever', it was notable that this time they expressed disapproval of the hunt. This was in fact the more normal response to this macho activity, especially when sons and husbands left rotting carcasses behind. In the privacy of their diaries, many of the more spirited and independent female emigrants expressed withering contempt for the 'sport' and the corrupting influence it had on their menfolk. When buffalo were sighted, as one historian has remarked scathingly, 'many men left their responsibilities behind with the women'.

It was almost predictable that the Sager family should have been caught up in the excitement over the buffalo, and with disastrous results. Catherine Sager recorded laconically: 'Father was a perfect Nimrod in his love of the chase.' Elizabeth Sager adds more detail: 'He caused his sickness by chasing some buffalo on a very hot day, for from that day he was taken sick and never got well.' But Sager's hunt merely exacerbated a pre-existing condition. The illness that laid him low was referred to in emigrants' parlance as 'mountain fever' or 'camp fever' but was in reality typhoid fever, contracted somewhere along the North Platte. Typhoid is caused by the ingestion of the enteric bacillus *Salmonella typhi* via contaminated water or food. The normal incubation period is around ten days, followed by two to four weeks' prolonged fever, headache, coughing and abdominal pain; late in the illness the patient suffers delirium and diarrhoea. The mortality rate is about one in eight, death coming from intestinal perforation, intestinal haemorrhage, or both; these result from ulcers caused by the typhoid bacteria as they multiply along the intestines. Obviously, the poor nutrition, scanty rest and hostile environment made a normal 12 per cent mortality rate much higher on the overland trails.

Henry Sager had never been a particularly skilful wagoner – Captain Shaw had had to show him how to manage the animals – but now he lay moaning in the back while Theophilus Degen drove the wagon. The Shaw company proceeded up the north bank of the Sweetwater 'with stupendous rocks on the right of our course and the rounded hills south of the stream flattened into places'. As they approached South Pass, they noted the sudden, almost magical, disappearance of the buffalo. Henry Sager was fading fast, but he was not the first to die. On 23 August, the Gilliam party passed the now halted Ford party, with whom James Clyman was travelling. A man named Joseph Barnett was seriously ill with typhoid and it was resolved to stay put until the crisis passed, one way or the other. While waiting, the fretful Clyman actually admitted to having enjoyed the company of the much-maligned 'Black' Harris, who was now travelling as a private individual. As always, Clyman revealed himself an admirer of women and spoke of their nursing of Barnett: 'Many of the ladies seem emulous to see which should be the most active in giving us advice and assistance for the relief of our apparently dying friend, the Perkins family in particular.'

At 10 p.m. on 26 August, after violent spasms, Barnett died. They buried him on the banks of the Sweetwater 'on which now rests the body of Mr Barnett, the first white man that ever rested his bones on that stream'. They proceeded to South Pass, the Continental Divide, which later prompted this reflection from Elizabeth Sager: 'Mother saw the promised land but did not reach there. I can remember that from the summit of the mountains mother pointed towards the setting sun and said, "Children, look to the westward. That is Oregon. That is where we are going to make our home."' These mountains were familiar to Clyman, though he had last seen them seventeen years earlier. But he was more concerned with the erratic piloting of Joseph Walker. Beyond the Sweetwater, Walker led them towards the Green, vainly trying to locate the cutoff to the Bear River which Hitchcock and Greenwood had successfully (albeit with difficulty) found for Elisha Stephens a month before. Eventually, Walker gave up and took the emigrants down the well-trodden trail to Fort Bridger, but not before Clyman had fully expressed his contempt in his diary.

It was on the Green River that Henry Sager breathed his last. The overlanders arrived there on 28 August, and for many days Sager had been in agony. The emigrant women, so assiduous at nursing, gave him laudanum or some derivative of opium, which lessened the pain, but he was now in the terminal stages of typhoid, suffering the tortures of intestinal perforation and internal haemorrhage. Lapsing in and out of consciousness on 27 August, he found time to pity his lamed daughter Catherine. 'Poor child,' he exclaimed, 'what will become of you?' On the night of 27/28 August, John Minto watched over him: 'the sick man was either wholly or partly unconscious from high fever and did not during the night ask for anything.'

In the morning, when he had a brief lucid moment, Captain Shaw came to see him and found him weeping bitterly. Sager implored him to take his children to the Whitman mission at Waiilatpu and ask the missionaries to care for them. Shaw made a solemn promise to do so. On the morning of 28 August Sager died and was buried immediately on the banks of the Green River. John Minto, fresh from his shattering experience with John Nichols's daughter, was once again a gravedigger and mourner. But there was a macabre sequel. Catherine Sager wrote bitterly: 'Next year's emigration found his bones bleaching upon the plains, having been disinterred by the Indians.' It seems that the

Shoshone did dig up and desecrate the grave, hunting for valuables, and that the coyotes finished off what they had begun.

Duly noting the plentiful antelope, grouse and rabbits south of the Green River, the emigrants trudged on to Fort Bridger, the Gilliam party about two days ahead of Ford's, and made a two-day stopover. There was a starry cast of mountain men at the fort this August, not just Jim Bridger and Louis Vasquez but also Antoine Robidoux and, probably the most famous of all the legendary western pathfinders, Kit Carson. Vasquez and Bridger were able to do a brisk trade with the weary overlanders, but in a sense they were luckier than they knew. The Elisha Stephens party had cut out Fort Bridger by taking the later-titled Sublette Cutoff from the Green to the Bear; had Walker been more skilful, he too would have taken the Ford and Gilliam caravans on a bypass. John Minto was suitably impressed by Bridger ('a powerful built man') and somewhat awed by the miscegenation between trappers and hunters and their Indian 'wives'. It is noticeable that he stuck close to the Morrison family during his time at the fort and complained of his worn-out and threadbare clothes. Mrs Morrison was suitably brisk: 'Yes, John; and if you can trade anything at the fort here, and get some deerskins, I'll fix your pants for you.'

After leaving Fort Bridger on 31 August, with both caravans close together, the overlanders made good progress to Fort Hall, even though the going was far from easy; as Minto related, 'the meander of the valley made the road hugging the foothills longer than the course of the river'. The danger from Indians was now (falsely) thought to be over, so the caravans, already fractured through resignations and personality clashes, splintered still further. Clyman and three other men in the Ford party who were unencumbered by families, pressed ahead with pack horses. The difference was clearly visible in the daily mileages: thirty miles on 4 September, twenty on the 5th, twenty-seven on the 6th and so on. With much complaining about Shoshone thievery, Clyman reached Soda Springs on the 7th, proceeded up the barren Portneuf where there was no game except grouse and where prairie fires had destroyed all forage for horses, and arrived at Fort Hall on the 11th.

John Minto, too, got the itch for solitary travel after Fort Bridger. Even though he was now regarded as the best angler in the party and earned his keep by the number of trout he caught, Minto disregarded the pleas of the Morrisons to stay on with them and displayed the ingratitude of youth by pressing on on horseback with Daniel Clark, the young man who had earlier defied Neal Gilliam. But a few days out he found himself horseless. At night, he heard his horse whinnying but was too tired or lazy to investigate. At dawn, he found that his horse had bolted, having slipped his tether in a panic when wolves tried to eat him; the wolves got no horseflesh but, bizarrely, had devoured thirty feet of rope. As he trudged on morosely, Minto was offered a ride by a Shoshone who had a spare horse. Minto mounted up and galloped to the nearest Indian village. Having been well treated by an Indian male, Minto then got the same reception from a young Shoshone girl, who brought him a gallon pail of luscious blueberries to eat; in exchange he gave her some fishhooks.

On arrival at Fort Hall, Minto tried to trade his ancient gun for a horse but Richard Grant, the Hudson's Bay Company factor at the fort, looked this scarecrow figure up and down and ignored him. Minto and Clark were now ravenously hungry but penniless. In desperation, they went out on to the Portneuf river, two miles away, and shot a duck, which they then feasted on, raw. Back at the fort they managed to cadge some cold bread and side bacon. The dauntless Minto then approached Grant again. The commandant took pity on him and agreed to trade a horse for his gun; when Minto threw in his bullets as a job lot, Grant responded with an Indian saddle. Clearly, Minto was in awe of the bluff, plain-spoken Grant, writing: 'Grant was, I think, a coarser man than Bridger, but carried more outside polish of manner.'

Minto then waited at Fort Hall until the Ford caravan and the Morrison family trooped in. Among those watching the new arrivals was Peg-Leg Smith, who had travelled up from his trading post on the Bear River. Minto described him thus: 'He was now neatly dressed in navy blue, and would have been judged a steamboat captain in St Louis.' Grant, who had shown his Janus face to Minto, again proved controversial. He reiterated his old opinion that it was impossible to get to the Columbia River by wagon but conceded that the 1843 party had somehow managed it: 'You – Yankees will do anything you like,' are the words Minto puts into his mouth. Naturally, this once more fuelled the suspicion that Grant was acting chiefly as an agent of the British government, still locked in a dispute with Washington over the Oregon territory. The feeling was that Grant would do anything to divert the Oregon-bound wagons to California, where aggressive Yankee emigrants would be Mexico's problem.

The emigrants' conflicting opinions about Grant are curious, almost as if they were not talking about the same person. Some stress that he went out of his way to be kind to overlanders, and certainly the tariffs for basic goods consistently show Fort Hall charging less than Laramie or Boise. The historian John Unruh says of the gold rush years: 'Amidst all the turmoil and change of 1849 there was at least one constant – kindly Richard Grant. His hospitality led one overlander to remark that of all posts, only at Fort Hall was there "politeness" and "civility."' But other emigrants had a different story to tell. A particular grievance was the way the Fort traders demanded cash for *their* merchandise but would only offer non-cash barter for any goods the emigrants wanted to dispose of. A later emigrant accused Grant of being 'almost destitute of honesty or human feeling' while the 1847 pioneer Elizabeth Geer ridiculed him as a 'boasting, burlesquing, unfeeling man'. Yet always it was Grant's negativity about Oregon that most rankled. Neal Gilliam's son particularly disliked the way he read out Peter Burnett's advice to Oregon-bound pioneers and then poured 'barrels of cold water' over it; this led Gilliam to regard Grant as a 'badhearted man'.

The stopover at Fort Hall also saw the tragedy of the Sagers almost (but not quite yet) reach its denouement. Naomi Sager had fallen ill soon after her husband's death and, by the time she reached Fort Hall, was in a desperate state of health, apparently suffering from typhoid and scarlet fever at the same time, and thus with no chance of survival. Her situation was exacerbated by understandable anxiety about her children, who now looked certain to end up as orphans. The desolate trail beyond Fort Hall was scarcely designed for convalescence; Clyman described it as 'the most barren, sterile region we have yet passed. Nothing to disturb the monotony of the eternal sage plain'. Over this trail the delirious Naomi Sager travelled on, jolted in the bumpy wagon, and swathed in clouds of dust from the arid trail. In an attempt to screen her from the worst effects of these whorling clouds of dust, a screen was hung over the wagon, but this made it so stuffy that her breathing was impaired. At night, she got momentary relief when she was washed by the heroic pioneer women, who took time off from their own heavy chores to succour a soul in torment.

The end came on 11 September at Pilgrim Springs, halfway between Salmon Falls and the famous Three Island Crossing fork of the Snake River. They were travelling through cruel and unforgiving country – slaked and unslaked lime volcanic rocks and fine and coarse sand, sometimes mixed together, sometimes discrete, in pure form, with, as the sole vegetation, sagebrush, prairie thorn and liquorice plant, shrubby and thickset. Catherine Sager takes up the story: 'The day she died we travelled over a very rough road, and she moaned pitifully all day . . . When the women came in to wash her, they found her pulse almost gone.' But there were enough people around her at the moment of death to confirm that her last words were authentic: 'Oh, Henry, if you only knew how we have suffered!' She was buried immediately. More than ever now William Shaw was determined to make good his promise to Henry Sager. Catherine Sager always remembered that water and food were short in the Snake valley, yet Mr and Mrs Shaw shared their last loaf with the orphans.

By now the emigration of 1844 to Oregon had largely degenerated into a free-for-all, with individual riders heading for the Columbia River as fast as their horses would take them, and a general atmosphere of devil-take-the-hindmost. Everyone knew that there was only a month to go before the first snows could be expected; they might well have to pay dearly for those early floods in Kansas. John Minto tarried at Fort Hall until 16 September then set out with two comrades, intending to show the wagon trains a clean pair of heels. It took him less than forty-eight hours to overhaul the stragglers in the Ford caravan and soon he was overtaking the backmarkers from the Thorp party. He and his comrades experienced no trouble from Indians, except for their annoying habit of starting fires in the sagebrush so that they could harvest roasted crickets, grasshoppers and lizards. After buying fish from Shoshone traders at Salmon Falls, they forded the Snake and even found friendly Bannocks to help them.

James Clyman, meanwhile, was proceeding like a winged mercury. In a single week he clocked up 183 miles, and crossed the Snake at Fort Boise without even bothering to stop at the post. Even the high country beyond the Malheur River did not cause him to slacken his pace very much, except that this daily tally was cut down to seventeen miles on 24 September after riding through 'the worst mountains and over the worst roads we have ever seen'. In just over twenty-four hours, he made another forty-three miles and camped on Powder River. As always, he found the Indians more of an irritation than Minto; this time it was the Bannock habit of setting fire to the grass ahead of any strangers they found in their lands that irked him. Only when he reached La Grande Ronde did he allow himself a day's rest before tackling the Blue Mountains. On 29–30 September, he achieved the Herculean tally of fifty-one miles through mountains and ravines choked with spruce and pine.

Both Minto and Clyman soon swept past the wagoners of the Thorp party, who had had more than a month's lead over them at Fort Laramie. Typical of the problems encountered by the slower wagon trains was this lament from the Quaker Jacob Hammer, who reached Fort Hall on 29 August. After a brief rest and fourteen miles hard slog on the Portneuf River, he wrote: 'One wagon upset in the Portneuf River. We stopped for the man to dry his things. The wagon belonged to a man named Osbourne. A.C.R. Shaw came very near getting drowned in this river while he was hunting property that floated downstream when the wagon upset.' On the Snake River, near American Falls, he and his party had problems of another sort. The Shoshone stole five horses and put into operation their favourite 'scam', whereby they plied for hire to 'find' the stolen horses and then returned, for a reward, the selfsame nags they had just stolen.

Minto, meanwhile, made further good progress, pursuing the meandering trail in Burnt River Canyon and following the bed of the stream to avoid the labour of cutting through the dense thickets on either side. On the steep climb, they continued to overtake emigrants who had left the Midwest months before them. At Lone Pine on the Powder River, Minto noted, as every traveller since the year before had, that the famous 'noble landmark' of the Lone Pine had been cut down. They climbed up the very steep and rough trail to La Grande Ronde, where they found the beautiful valley blanketed in fog. Short of food, they managed to kill a pheasant and a prairie chicken, traded rice, tea and sugar from a party of emigrants they overtook, and bartered food from the Cayuse Indians, using fishhooks as currency. Dreading the stiff climb into the Blue Mountains, they found the going much easier than expected because of the guides provided by the local Cayuse chief and his sons.

By now, Minto and his companions had overtaken all the wagon parties bound for Oregon. After narrowly escaping being robbed by a menacing party of seventeen hostile Cayuse, they debouched on the Columbia River at Umatilla and followed the trail beside the river down to The Dalles, arriving on 15 October. It was a Sunday and they found the Methodist missionaries at prayer, but, as Minto elegantly put it, they 'disregarded' the Sabbath. Minto and his comrades then rode their horses over the Cascades, following the trail that looped round Mount Hood and, after three strenuous days, arrived at journey's end in Oregon City on 18 October.

Even so, Clyman was ahead of them. Travelling with a larger party, Clyman likewise traded with the Cayuse for potatoes, corn, peas and squash but, unlike Minto, he and his men had cows to barter. So close to his goal, the usually tenacious Clyman did not even bother to divert when his mare was stolen by a Cayuse, but responded to the theft by clocking up fifty miles in thirty-six hours. On 3 October, some of his party peeled off to visit the Whitmans at Walla Walla. While complaining about 'the most tiresome travel we had yet found on account of the quantity of sharp fallen rock which filled the path over which we had to travel', Clyman achieved the astonishing tally of 169 miles between 3 and 9 October. Now with the snow-capped Mount Hood clearly in his sights, he did not even bother to disturb the missionaries' Sabbath on 8 October (a week before Minto got there), but swept on through the Cascades to arrive in the Willamette valley on 13 October. Clyman had achieved a great feat of riding, but none of his journey since Fort Hall had been in a wagon train in the true sense.

More authentic was the experience of Jacob Hammer, still toiling along the Snake. To make any significant progress, he and his companions were increasingly forced to travel late into the night. The Snake proved as burdensome to him as to all overlanders and although water and grass were short, at least firewood was not. 'Wormwood is plenty and good for fuel. Many hundreds of miles we have travelled among the wormwood. Some of it grows to the height of six or eight feet and six inches in thickness. If it were not for the wormwood, travellers would be as much put out for firewood as those that travel in the deserts of Arabia.' The company's fortunes changed, however, when, finding that three horses had been stolen by the Cayuse, they formed a posse which seized three Indian ponies as compensation and then demanded the return of the original three. The Snakes prepared for battle, but Thorp sent to nearby Fort Boise for help. Boise fired its cannons to remind the hostiles of the firepower at its disposal while at the same time a party of Nez Percé appeared on the Snake flank. This combined operation had the desired effect.

That incident took place on 24 September, two days after Clyman had passed that way without stopping. Two days earlier, the Revd Edward Parrish, now travelling somewhat to the rear of the wagons, and whose initial reaction to the Snake valley was to marvel at its beauty, recorded a mishap to his daughter that recalled the Catherine Sager accident. 'Today, as little Rebecca was trying to get on or off the wagon, she slipped and fell, the wagon wheel rolling over and breaking her thigh.' As with Catherine Sager, the broken limb was most probably a transverse or oblique fracture of the tibia. And like Catherine Sager, Rebecca Parrish suffered great pain later when the wagon jolted over the rough trails.

The foremost wagons spent late September and early October on the gruelling ascent of the Powder River valley to La Grande Ronde ('beautiful pines . . . very rich mountains and valleys,' Jacob Hammer enthused) and then on the even more daunting climb through the Blue Mountains to its western ridge with the spectacular views to the Columbia River beyond. The lucky overlanders, like Hammer, finished crossing the Blue Mountains to Umatilla before the snows descended and then made their way down the Columbia. At The Dalles, Hammer hired a cedar canoe made by the Chinook Indians and embarked with himself, his wife and children, plus the ubiquitous A.C.R. Shaw and Indian pilots, hiring drovers to take his cattle over the Cascades. They portaged round the Cascade Falls and had an uneventful journey downriver to Fort Vancouver, arriving on 28 October, only a few days after Clyman, who had rested for ten days in the Willamette valley after his exertions.

Yet many emigrants were still struggling with the Blue Mountains when the snows descended, unseasonably early. Frozen with the biting winds and blinding snow, most could make no more than a few miles a day, their plight worsened by semi-starvation, since they were by now out of all provisions except meat. There was no feed available for the cattle, which were simply left to die where they stood trapped in the snowdrifts. Narcissa Whitman, lamenting the fate of both man and beast trapped in the Blue Mountains, estimated late in October that there were still five hundred people out there in the snowy wastes. Relief expeditions were organised, but tired, emaciated and half-starved overlanders continued to trickle in to Oregon through the mountain passes all that year. Statistics telling us that 1,475 reached Oregon in 1844 reveal nothing about the broken health of many of the arrivals.

One party that did get safely over the Blue Mountains was the Shaw company, containing the Sager orphans. At the end of October, William Shaw arrived at the Walla Walla mission with the seven children in tow. Briefly he outlined the history of the family and Henry Sager's dying wish. At first, both Marcus and Narcissa Whitman were appalled at the prospect of playing step-parents to such an unprepossessing brood and suggested to Shaw that they could be temporary guardians only. Shaw then set out for The Dalles and was on the road when an urgent message summoned him back to the mission. This time Narcissa proposed that she take the girls only; she had not liked what she had seen of the unruly Sager boys. But Shaw reminded her of Henry Sager's express wish that his children should not be split up. With great reluctance, Narcissa finally decided to take all seven orphans in. On 6 November, Shaw and the Whitmans signed a document agreeing that henceforth the Whitmans were the children's legal guardians and that they were likewise owners of the pathetic remains of the Sager property, viz. a wagon, three yoke of oxen, a cow and one old steer. Satisfied that he had done his duty, Shaw departed, again, for The Dalles, where he arrived in mid-November.

Narcissa Whitman never forgot the dramatic appearance of the seven waifs on her doorstep that day in late October 1844. The step-parenting proved every bit as arduous as she had feared, as the children were extremely difficult, especially the boys. The impact of the seven orphans, rough-hewn Midwestern brats, on a woman of East Coast patrician breeding was much like that of evacuee children from the East End of London billeted with aristocratic families in rural England during the Second World War. Narcissa found their rough manners as difficult to tame as they found her Brahmin sensibility hard to take; Elizabeth Sager remembered that Narcissa was unpopular with her siblings – too 'stuck-up' – but she liked her. And in Oregon food was plentiful. After the short commons of the overland trek – which at times saw even enterprising woodsmen like James Clyman subsisting on scrawny pheasants and mountain squirrels – Oregon was a cornucopia: one could dine on salmon, oyster, seal, duck, woodcock, snipe and other waterfowl and even on the meat of whales thrown on to the beaches by storms. As a dessert, one could gorge on the plentiful strawberries, blackberries and raspberries.

The year 1844 has claims to be considered the most sensational year overall of the entire calendar of westward emigrations by wagon train, for it had still not finished throwing up new dramas. We left Elisha Stephens and his California-bound party at Fort Hall, where they split from the Oregonians and laid in a certain amount of food for the onward journey. Because of sky-high prices at Fort Hall – one dollar a pound for flour particularly rankled – they decided to trust to luck, arguing that they could always kill some of their cattle for meat. Pausing for a longish (five-day) period of rest at Fort Hall, the small party of twenty-six men, seven women and seventeen children followed the Oregon Trail along the Snake River for a day or two, then swung sharply south at Raft River on or about 17 August.

Elisha Stephens, now clearly confirmed as captain after the Oregonian 'malcontents' had left them, tended to use Dr John Townsend and his brother-in-law Moses Schallenberger as his right-hand men. Also his allies in the long battle against the Oregonians previously were the Murphy clan, comprising Martin Murphy, grandfather and patriarch, Martin Murphy the younger and his siblings, Daniel, Bernard, Ellen and John, and James Murphy. Other Irish Catholics were Patrick Martin and his adult sons Dennis and Patrick, John Sullivan and his younger brothers Michael and Robert, and Edmund Bray, a single man. The older generation was represented by 'Old (Caleb) Greenwood' and Isaac 'Old Man' Hitchcock, and there were a number of single men, acting as cattle herders, ox drivers, drovers and labourers: the French Canadians Francis Deland and Ollivier Magnent, the Americans Vincent Calvin and Matthew Harbin, and John Flomboy, a man of mixed race. Other prominent males were Allen Montgomery, James Miller, and Caleb Greenwood's two half-breed sons John and Britain; both Miller and Patrick Martin had intermarried with the powerful Murphy sept. Women and children made up a significant portion of the party. Hitchcock had a daughter named Isabella Patterson, who was taking six children (two of whom counted as adults) through the wilderness. James Miller's wife was in charge of another four (one son, three daughters), Mrs Allen Montgomery was as yet childless, while both James Murphy and the younger Martin Murphy had their wives with them, plus another five children (four boys, one girl). Dr John Townsend's wife and John Sullivan's wife Mary completed the tally of women. The entire party made up an interesting cross-section of humanity. Three men (Stephens, Hitchcock and Greenwood) had wide experience in the West, Townsend was a physician and Montgomery a gunsmith, and the age range ran the spectrum from ten-week-old Ellen Independence (the child born at Independence Rock) to eighty-year-old Caleb Greenwood. The women were aged between twenty and thirty-six. A much commented-on feature is that twelve of the men were Irish and that the two French Canadians shared their Catholic faith.

From the Raft River, the Stephens party crossed west to Goose Creek, then followed it south-west to the Humboldt River. There was plenty of good grass along the Humboldt and they were not troubled by the alkaline water until they reached the Humboldt Sink, where fresh water was extremely scarce. Like all travellers along the Humboldt, they complained about the panhandling of the 'Digger' Indians, whose language they found incomprehensible, but outright theft was not the problem anticipated – they lost just one pony. Around the beginning of October, they came to the Humboldt Sink, with the humans still in excellent spirits and the oxen in good condition, needing only a little rest. A rest was ordained at the Sink. The cattle were let out to graze, the horses unsaddled, while the women washed clothes. One lot of men repaired wagons and outfits while another formed a hunting party to pick off the abundant antelope, deer, wild duck, geese and sage hens.

While they halted at the Sink, a 'council of war' was held to determine where to go next and how to relate the fragmentary information they had gleaned from Joseph Walker to the features of the landscape around them. Some argued for striking due south, others swore the direct route was due west. This inconclusive conclave came to an end when someone made contact with a Paiute chief named Truckee, leading a hunting party, who communicated with Old Greenwood in sign language and with drawings in the sand. Truckee told them that fifty to sixty miles to the west was a river that flowed in an easterly direction from the mountains, with good grass and trees. Stephens decided to verify Truckee's story. Taking the Indian as a guide, he, Townsend and another man rode out to investigate; after three days they returned to report that the story was true.

Truckee's assistance was a notable example of help given to emigrants by the Indians. As so often, the threat to peace came not from the tribes but from the 'lowlives' among the overlanders. This time the trouble-maker was Caleb Greenwood's son John, a half-breed, who, in a textbook case of self-loathing, hated all Indians with a rare virulence. As was well said of him: 'It seemed as if he was more anxious to kill an Indian than to reach California.' Although despising all red men, he self-contradictorily claimed that his Crow mother gave him 'blood entitlement' to kill Snakes or Paiutes, and was with difficulty restrained from loosing off at the most friendly Indians. Whenever a cow strayed, John Greenwood tried to whip up his comrades by claiming that an Indian had stolen it. Mrs Sarah E. Kealy, an emigrant of 1845 who saw the Greenwoods, father and son, at close quarters, wrote: 'They were mountain men, and dressed the same as Indians . . . I was more afraid of those two men than of the wild Indians.'

But while the wiser heads in the party were watching John Greenwood closely, they failed to reckon with the hot-headed Moses Schallenberger. Ohio-born, the youngest of seven children, Schallenberger was a man of high natural abilities, albeit of limited frontier schooling; reputable authorities reckon him the most intelligent of the California-bound emigrants of 1844. But at the Humboldt Sink, emotion won out over reason in the young man's psyche. Missing a halter, Schallenberger suddenly found a tell-tale trace of it dangling below a short feather blanket worn by one of the Paiute. He laid hands on his purloined property, but the Indian stepped back and fitted an arrow to his bow. Moses retaliated by raising his rifle and drawing a bead on the Paiute. Martin Murphy rushed up and managed to compose things, but for a while it was touch and go, with the Paiutes giving every indication of seeking a pitched battle. They were soon bought off with a generous donation of presents, but not before some heart-stopping moments. Clearly, if Schallenberger had been foolish enough to pull the trigger, the whole Stephens–Murphy party would have perished then and there by the Humboldt Sink.

Dr Townsend rebuked his brother-in-law Schallenberger for his folly and urged him to rehabilitate himself by sterling work on the gruelling march to come. The trek to Truckee River proved every bit as strenuous as feared, even though the travellers had made careful preparations, taking two days' cooked rations and full water vessels. The first stage was a forced march lasting until midnight; they bivouacked at some boiling springs and let the oxen recover. After a two-hour rest they trekked on over a barren desert, knee-deep in alkaline dust, trying to follow the exiguous trail Stephens had blazed on his reconnaissance mission. Around noon, they sighted the promised land in the form of a shimmering dark green line of cottonwoods on the far horizon. As the afternoon wore on, the thirsty oxen and cattle, already without food and water for nearly two days, scented the proximity of water and became maddened. To prevent the teams from stampeding and wrecking the wagons, Stephens ordered the teams unhitched; the crazed animals rushed pell-mell for the water. Hard on their heels came the humans.

That was the evening of 9 October. Without realising it, Stephens's party had crossed eighty miles of desert (later inaccurately named the Forty Mile Desert), which came to be one of the most dreaded landmarks on the route to California. Because there was lush grass and fresh water at the river, the travellers stayed there two whole days, honouring their Paiute guide by naming it Truckee River. They then set out in a westerly direction, following the stream, but it began to wind through narrow canyons, forcing the travellers constantly to cross and recross the water. After some days of very hard going, fortified by the abundance of wood, water and grass and the continuing fine weather, they emerged into the open meadow country in the vicinity of present-day Reno. To the west of the meadows 'the hills began to grow nearer together', and the country was so rough and broken that they had to travel in the bed of the stream. As the river swung back and forth between sheer cliffs, its serpentine course forced them on one occasion to cross it ten times while travelling one mile. This almost constant sloshing through the water softened the hoofs of the oxen, while the rough stones in the river bed wore them down. Eventually, the feet of the cattle became so painful that it was agonising for them to put one hoof in front of another. Meanwhile, the humans were worn out by the stress and strain of wading hip-deep in cold water.

They continued to travel in the bed of the river, partly because the canyon walls were so steep, partly because the cattle were so sore in the feet that, if not taken through water, they refused to proceed at all. To add to their worries, a few light flakes of snow fell, reminding them that it was already mid-October and they were still far from their goal. The optimists in the party insisted this was a false dawn of winter, but had to eat their words when a foot of snow fell, burying the grass on which the animals depended. At night, the oxen lowed and bawled piteously with wretched hunger. An attempt to feed the cattle with pine needles having proved unavailing, the party was close to despair when by chance they found tall rushes protruding through the snow. The cattle devoured these greedily – indeed two of them died from overeating – but the food saved the rest; at last the emigrants knew of a reliable source of forage if only they could locate the rushes.

Around 14 November, they finally came to the confluence of the Truckee and the later-named Donner Creek (near the site of present-day Truckee) and faced a dilemma; whether to follow the main stream which bore away south-west or the tributary that flowed due west towards the snow-capped peaks of the Sierra Nevada. A general council met to resolve the issue. It was decided to hedge bets. The main party would follow the tributary, while a party of six persevered with the main canyon southwards: the six were Mrs Townsend and Ellen Murphy, the two French Canadians and two of the Murphy boys (John and Daniel). After dividing the few provisions, clothes and blankets left, the six in the minor party took the horses (including two spares as pack animals). Some have thought it odd that the horseback party was given all the best equipment, and have speculated that they simply deserted or that Mrs Townsend had had a row with her brother. But this scarcely explains why two of the tightly-knit Murphy clan should have left their kith and kin. Almost certainly the answer had to do with expediency. The idea was that as the half-dozen chosen were the fittest and strongest individuals, they could travel fast and light, get to Sutter's Fort and bring back a relief column to succour the main party.

The principal group with the wagons proceeded a few miles up the tributary (the little Truckee) and came to the limpid waters of Donner Lake (as it was later named). Ahead of them rose the sheer mountain wall; they were not to know that these were the final teeth of the sierra and that beyond lay California. After camping for several days, they decided to split again. Since the oxen were so worn out, six wagons were left behind and three men detailed to guard them, since both the wagons and their contents were valuable. The designated members of the trio were Schallenberger, Joseph Foster and Allen Montgomery. The others set out on the dispiriting one-thousand-foot slog up the forbidding face of the mountains, at first keeping to a course on the north side of the lake. All around them were two-foot snowdrifts. Laboriously, they unloaded the wagons and carried the contents to the summit of the sierra. Then they started up the steep face of the sierra with the unloaded wagons and oxen, using the method of double-teaming.

Halfway up the mountain they came face to face with a vertical rock, about ten feet high. These Midwesterners, with no previous experience of alpinism, at last seemed to have reached the limits of human endurance and will power. It seemed that the only way forward now was to abandon everything except what they could carry on their backs. Suddenly someone – and it may have been Caleb Greenwood, as in the tradition – found a gap or rift in the rock, just wide enough to allow a single ox to pass. Removing the yokes from the oxen, they somehow coaxed them through the chink and thence to the top of the rock. They then reyoked the animals at the top of the ledge, let down chains which were fastened to wagon tongues and hoisted the first wagon to the top. Using the oxen and the first wagon then as a kind of primitive pulley they proceeded to haul up the remainder.

They reached the summit on or about 25 November 1844, and then started a twenty-mile trek west to the headwaters of the Yuba River, going downhill, over very rough country. Their route kept to the ridge on the south of the river, then ran down to Devil's Hill at Hampshire Rocks, but it was tough going all the way, their fears about the imminence of winter storms compounded by anxiety about the pregnant Mrs Martin Murphy, who was coming to full term. Finally, by the waters of the Yuba, Mrs Murphy gave birth to a daughter, Elizabeth Yuba. This was some time in the first week of December. The combination of a new baby, the necessity for a lying-in period and a new fall of snow, piling up drifts three to four feet, occasioned a further crisis. It was agreed that there would be yet another division. The able-bodied started for Sutter's Fort, leaving the women and children under the protection of two men waiting for relief. They built cabins and butchered most of the cattle for meat, hoping that the freezing weather would provide them with nature's own refrigerator.

Those left behind this time included James Miller and old Mr Martin, plus Mrs Martin Murphy and her four boys and new daughter, Miller's wife and four children, Mrs James Murphy and her daughter Mary, and Mrs Patterson and her offspring. About 6 December, seventeen men went on, driving a few cattle, descended beneath the snowline in a few days, and got to Sutter's Fort quite easily. They found the half-dozen members of the horseback party already there. They had ascended the canyon and come to a large and beautiful lake (they were thus the first white people to arrive on the shores of Lake Tahoe), then headed west along the lake and found an easy pass, probably at the head of Mckinney Creek. Next they descended easily along a stream which flowed into the American River. When the expected snowstorms struck, they were at a low enough altitude to escape the full fury. The American River, wide, deep and with strong currents, was more of a challenge and James Murphy narrowly escaped drowning, but they reached the Sacramento valley, finding plenty of game to shoot on the way. They followed the American River all the way to St Clair's ranch, where they were hospitably received, then proceeded to Sutter's Fort.

Unfortunately, they found themselves caught up in the maelstrom of civil war in California, between Manuel Micheltorena, the new Mexican governor, and his enemy José Castro of Monterey. Since Castro wanted to drive the 'Anglos' out of California – or so it was alleged – most Americans, including Sutter, backed Micheltorena. The twenty-one grizzled and hardy pioneering males who suddenly appeared at his fort seemed like manna to Sutter. He cajoled, threatened, forced or blackmailed them to join him and Micheltorena. Micheltorena's fortunes came to a bad end in February 1845 with defeat at Cahuenga Pass north of Los Angeles; he had to sign an agreement to leave California forthwith. At first sight, the spectacle of the Stephens party heading south to fight in a conflict that was no affair of theirs, while their comrades still languished in the snow of the sierras, seems bizarre, but Sutter may have convinced them that rescue was impossible anyway before the spring thaw.

Meanwhile, in mid-December the camp on the Yuba River containing the women and children had surprise visitors in the shape of Foster and Montgomery. Left behind with the wagons, they and Schallenberger had panicked when the worst of the snows started and they calculated that their food might not last through the winter. Fearing starvation, the three of them abandoned the wagons and tried to follow to California in the footsteps of the others. But Schallenberger became exhausted by the sheer physical effort of trudging uphill fifteen miles in improvised snowshoes. Around the campfire at 7,000 feet he told the others he could not go on and would rather return to the cabin and the wagons and take his chances there. Foster and Montgomery, who realised they could end up literally hauling a dead weight, agreed this was the best plan and promised to send a relief party to find him.

With no need for snowshoes on the downhill stretch, Schallenberger virtually skated or slid back to the cabin on icy paths. For two months he survived by trapping coyotes and foxes and shooting the occasional crow. He caught plenty of food and did not go hungry, but his real enemy was fear of the unknown and anxious uncertainty about the food supply; maybe wildlife would simply cease to appear in the vicinity of the cabin. He spent the two months trapping foxes and reading – Byron's poetry and Lord Chesterfield's letters were a particular consolation. In late February, Dennis Martin suddenly appeared. Martin had got tired of the

Micheltorena fiasco and returned to Sutter's Fort, where Mrs Townsend begged him to try to rescue her younger brother, 'Mose'. On 20 February, Martin set out on his solitary quest. On the way to the Yuba River 'women's camp' he was alarmed to discover James Miller and his son on the road to Sutter's Fort, having left the others behind. In the camp on the Yuba River he found to his dismay that all vestiges of altruism and organic solidarity had vanished, leaving a hypertrophied selfishness, where each family competed for food against the others in a 'war of all against all'. He was glad to leave the camp and press on to find Schallenberger.

Martin rescued Schallenberger and coaxed him across the mountain. By mid-March, all the stragglers had been gathered up and were safely at Sutter's Fort. All kinds of dubious claims were later made by assorted individuals trying to cash in on the fame of the Stephens–Murphy party, pretending that they had been prime movers in 'west coast assistance' for the beleaguered overlanders. Quite how much aid Sutter himself gave to the Stephens party is disputed, though he presumably must at least have dispensed some free food and lodgings and maybe even medical assistance. His own claims were certainly magniloquent:

At times my buildings were filled with immigrants. So much so that I could scarcely find a spot to lay my own head to rest. My farm-houses and store-houses were filled every winter during these immigrant times with poor, wet, hungry men, women and children seeking a fortune in a new land . . . Often it was necessary for me to go with my men and cattle to drag them in to safety out of the snow.

The Stephens–Murphy party had achieved great things. They were the first to prove that wagons could be taken all the way to California. One of their number gave birth to the first child born on the trail to California-bound emigrants. Their crossing of the continent was a story with many heroes, among whom the men who endured alone, Dennis Martin and Moses Schallenberger, were pre-eminent. Debate still rages as to what the crucial components of this party really were. Some point to the obsessive personality of Elisha Stephens; others prefer to elevate Dr Townsend as the *éminence grise*; still others think the Murphy clan was the real key to success; a handful put their bets on the unlikely outsider Caleb Greenwood as the true alchemist. It is safest perhaps to conclude that Stephens really was the leader, in fact as well as name, but that his prickly, difficult personality led to a public-relations failure, where his contribution was successively downgraded by historians.

Once in California, he faded into obscurity, and for the last twenty-three years of his life (he died in 1884) lived as a hermit and apiarist near Bakersfield. Schallenberger, who must often have thought he would not survive 1844, let alone 1845, lived another fifty-five years. He worked as a clerk in Monterey in 1845 and later became a prosperous farmer. The other members of the party joined the growing 'Anglo' community in California, increasing by a multiplier the likelihood that the Golden State would go the same way as Texas. Not only had a viable wagon route been found from the United States, but Sutter's Fort itself made a massive hole in the Mexican dyke. As General Manuel Alvarado, a key figure in the anti-gringo faction that defeated Micheltorena, ruefully remarked, the fort had become 'the gateway of communication between the United States and this country which they [the North Americans] covet so much'. It is not far-fetched to draw causal lines between the Stephens overland expedition and California's absorption into the United States. From early 1845, Mexican California was living on borrowed time.

SEVEN

'NEVER TAKE NO CUTOFFS'

Hitherto we have been able to follow closely the fortunes of every single wagon train that left the Midwest for the Pacific. But by 1845, and even more so in the following years, this is no longer sensible even if technically feasible. In 1845, 2,760 emigrants made their way to Oregon and California (2,500 of them to Oregon) in ever more complex organisations and convoluted companies. Even when we can identify which family started at the 'jumping-off' points with which wagon train, this tells us little, since there was immense 'social mobility' between the different caravans as they overtook each other on the plains and different families decided, as it were, to switch horses in mid-stream or, to put it more precisely, to exchange the stern discipline of one captain for the easygoing, *laissez-aller* attitudes of another, or even vice versa. This means that increasingly concentration will be on the unusual, not on the occurrences common to the early wagon trains between 1841 and 1844. The early years of the overland trail are the salient ones, however much historical purists may fulminate about the relative neglect of the later years.

One lesson was already clear from the experience of the first four years on the Oregon and California trails. This was that 'rugged individualism' posed a threat to the viability of wagon trains. Where every man (and the problem was overwhelmingly a male problem) considered himself as good as everyone else, be they never so learned, skilled, erudite, experienced, wise or with years of military experience, the problem of order became paramount, sometimes shading into a problem of crime and punishment. Beyond civilisation's pale, with human beings close to the 'state of nature', there was a clear temptation for the unscrupulous to take an eclectic 'pick 'n' mix' attitude to the provisional civil society of the emigrants: to accept the protection and security afforded by numbers while refusing to accept majority opinion and democracy as an infringement of the rugged individual's 'rights'. Needless to say, mention

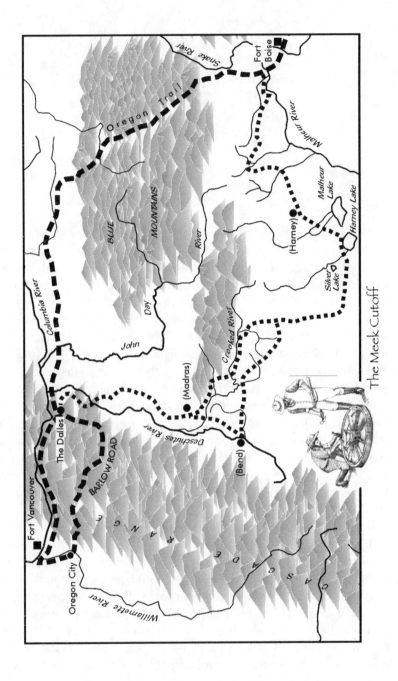

The Meek Cutoff

of corresponding duties was conspicuously absent. Antisocial elements in the wagon trains reserved the 'right' to camp anywhere, to turn off the trail rather than inhale dust from preceding wagons, to refuse to do sentry duty or to stand guard over stock if they themselves had no cattle.

There is ample testimony to the intense reluctance of many emigrants to accept discipline and carry out orders; often they rationalised their anarchy on the grounds that the leaders of the wagon trains were martinets. In 1845 this was to be a constant lament of the most famous wagon-train leader that year, Captain Solomon Tetherow. But 1844 had already thrown up a plethora of incidents. More irritating and comical than serious was the persistent attempt to avoid guard duty. There was one flagrant example of refusal to accept orders in the Shaw company when an ancient harridan screeched at John Minto that her precious son should be exempt from duty. 'It's not John's turn to stand guard tonight,' she yelled. It never was John's turn, whenever he was asked. When Minto reported this to Shaw, he shrugged: 'Well, John, I expect they're afeared. But let's not say anything about it; let's you and me take their places.'

But there were more serious occurrences. In the same caravan, a young man named Clark Edes was staked out as a punishment after he threatened to shoot Minto simply for doing his duty. Shaw ordered the punishment, but Edes was outraged at the mere idea that he should be punished and threatened to kill Minto when he got free; obviously his time in the sun and threats of hanging from Shaw cooled his ardour, for we hear no more of the matter. Part of the problem in the early days of the emigrant trails was that the constitutions of the 'emigrating society' did not seriously consider the problem of sociopaths or those who were prepared to accept their code only selectively. The consequence was that at first banishment from the wagon train was the gravest punishment ordained. To hardened malefactors this was virtually an invitation to a one-man crime wave.

Fortunately, until the 1849 California Gold Rush, there were not many such men on the trails. The greatest causes of violence on the way west were stress, anxiety and enforced togetherness. Families who had lived on isolated farms now came into close contact, in crowded conditions, with people of very different beliefs, values and cultures: Christians mingled with heathens, lowlives with the high-minded, the devout with the blasphemer and – at a slightly later date – the Mormon with the 'Gentile'. There was tension even within families, when the maddening personal tics, scratchings, hummings, whistlings and mutterings which could be accommodated on a spacious farm were now all confined within the narrow circle of a wagon. When strangers outside the tent had dirty, unhygienic, antisocial and slatternly habits to compound these irritations within it, it was not surprising that pent-up rage finally found some external object to fasten on. As one emigrant put it: 'If there is anything in this world that will bring to the surface a man's bad traits, it is a trip across the continent with an ox team.'

The exhaustion and fatigue of the daily treks, the dangers anticipated from Indians and the uncertainty of supply of food, water and forage exacerbated nervous tension. Friction was unavoidable and grumblers and malcontents could always find a focus in other people for their discontents. The emigrant Alonzo Delano had pithy expressions of both cause and effect: on the exhaustion – 'a hyena might have tugged at my toes without awaking me'; and on the myriad frivolous collisions with one's fellows – 'a mean streak will come out on the plains'. The 1845 diarist Jacob Snyder was trenchant: 'A quarrel in camp this morning. Such things are a frequent occurrence and the general resort is to weapons, but measures are always taken to prevent any serious consequences. Here men may display their true character. Not being under the fear of the law, they become careless of consequences.' Women, too, contributed to the general stress. Often, tired out with an exhausting day's washing on the 'rest day', they would return to the wagon at night tired and bad-tempered. A dispute might arise between husband and wife and the aggrieved husband would storm off into the dark to displace the anger he felt towards his wife on to the first person in the wagon train unlucky enough to cross him.

Although more responsible emigrants would intervene, as Snyder says, to prevent homicide or the use of firearms, there was a complaisant attitude on the trail to fist fights, much to the disgust of the women. William Johnston spoke of one such fistic encounter at the Kansas River: 'Fist fight came off this evening between two members of Captain Kirkuff's mess. [The man who] provoked the quarrel . . . was rewarded with rings round his eyes bearing a strong resemblance to ebony goggles.' Southern gentlemen and ex-army officers were particularly sensitive to real or imaginary slights to their 'honour' and made it a point of understanding to display their superior pugilistic skills by thrashing members of the 'lower orders' who were contumacious or impertinent enough to annoy, insult, badger or chivvy them.

Before 1849, serious crime, and therefore serious punishment, was rare on the overland trails. We may discount some of the more fanciful explanations for this, such as the sometimes advanced quasi-Platonist notion that the beauty of the landscape and the scenery of the West had a beneficial effect on the human soul, warding off criminal thoughts. A much more germane consideration is that most of the pre-1849 overlanders were people of the 'middling' sort, Midwestern farmers in the perfect equilibrium situation for emigration. People who could afford the wagon journey west had no reason to commit crime; and for the most part, the dispossessed and wretched of the earth, the social arsenal of criminals, were not present on the plains. Moreover, emigrating companies made sustained efforts to weed out any social 'undesirables' likely to disrupt the routine of the daily march.

Second, the entire ethos of the Midwest in this era militated against crime. To later generations it was a source of amazement that shippers could store crates and hogsheads of merchandise unguarded on river landings for days and weeks without suffering pilferage or 'inventory shrinkage'. Rugged individualism took the form of indiscipline and reluctance to obey orders, but it was a pride-driven ideology, fuelled by notions of 'honour' and the populist conviction that no man should be able to tell another what to do. There was little economically based envy, resentment of the good fortune of others, or hypertrophied egotism of the 'what's in it for me?' variety, and still less, in pioneer society, was there the notion that to lift a finger or get out of bed at all required financial recompense. Many instances of generosity and altruism were recorded on the overland trail which were all the more remarkable for being performed in a context where it was much easier to cheat, lie, steal, be a coward or behave despicably than under the watchful eyes of conventional society. Negatively, in the dislike of being 'given laws', the predominant emigrant ethos can be seen as that of individualism and egotism. Positively, however, collaboration and cooperation predominated over competition and narrow selfishness.

Third, most of the emigrants were God-fearing folk who took seriously the idea that they were answerable to a Supreme Being for their actions. To a modern reader, the agonised discussions among the emigrants as to whether they were compelled to observe the Sabbath on the trail and, if so, what activities (washing, cooking, hunting?) were permissible, sound like the rabbinical jousts with Pharisees recorded in the New Testament or the more esoteric theological ponderings of medieval schoolmen. But to the emigrants these were very serious matters indeed. Over and over again, diarists routinely record the opinion that only faith and religion enabled them to endure when beset by hunger, cold, rain or cholera. Octavius Howe's description of the New England Emigrating Companies in 1849 is justly famous: 'No regiment in Cromwell's Ironsides ever went to battle with more Bibles or more religious instruction than the California companies of 1849.'

After 1849, as the dregs of eastern slums and the get-rich-quick *canaille* joined the lemming-rush to the Californian gold fields, it was not surprising that things changed, that more serious crimes began to be committed and, consequently, that kangaroo courts, lynch mobs, draconian punishment and summary justice became more common. Particularly unpopular were the 'Pikers', poor, usually illiterate and inbred emigrants from the Appalachians. The women attracted contempt and ridicule for their dirty, slovenly, slatternly appearance and habit, while the men, forever cursing, carousing and abusing women and livestock, inspired fear and loathing. Lavinia Porter said of the Pikers that they were 'the roughest, most uncouth, and ignorant people I had ever come in contact with. Perfectly lawless, fighting and quarrelling among themselves, using language terrible to hear.'

Murder became much more common on the overland trail after 1849. Typical were the following, observed by female and male diarists respectively.

A dreadful occurrence took place. A wicked man who had whipped one of his men overheard Ben Farewell say that no man could make him run by whipping. He came into our camp, took an ax and felled him like a beef . . . Will not describe the excitement.

Two men who prepared their outfit in company at Independence, had frequent quarrels in regard to their travelling and camping arrangements. Going into camp near Chimney Rock, the quarrel was renewed . . . In the heat of passion, they drew out their hunting knives and closed in mortal combat. In a few minutes one fell and almost instantly died; the other, fainting from loss of blood, was carried in the shade of a tent where, within an hour, he too expired; and with the grim irony of fate, at sunset they were laid side by side in the same grave.

As more and more women made the journey west, and more and more criminals and sociopaths joined the gold rush, so, inevitably, the first reports of rape on the overland trail began to come in. Yet cases of ravished women were remarkably rare, illustrating the persuasive thesis that it is only in the twentieth century, with the 'legitimating' of violence towards women via pornography and the mass media, that rape has become an epidemic problem. If we further add the factor that the 'demand' from surplus males on the wagon train far outstripped the 'supply' of eligible females, it is clear that cultural factors are of overwhelming importance. Much more common than rape was violence arising from a father's desire to protect his daughter's virginity from over-eager suitors or from a husband's reacting with rage to a wife's infidelity. In one case, the wife's lover shot the husband in self-defence and was then tried by the emigrating company. Having originally ordered a flogging, the company commuted this to simple expulsion, but of the ancient interdiction type, denying fire and water.

As crimes of violence augmented on the trails, the incidence of kangaroo courts, drumhead trials and lynching increased to match. Sometimes malefactors were strung up by angry mobs, sometimes it was a case of 'we'll give him a fair trial and then we'll hang him'. There were even cases where condemned men were given a choice between being hanged or executed by firing squad. The emigrant J.C. Moreland describes what happened to one man condemned by overland rough justice: 'The next morning, just as the sun was breaking over the plains, two wagon tongues were run up in the air and fastened together, and from them he was hanged, and then buried by the side of the road.' Although such hangings were of doubtful legality considered from a US perspective, the plain fact is that there was no law on the plains and, in administering summary justice, wagon trains were usually scrupulous about observing the niceties: in one case where the condemned left a wife and four young children, the emigrating company provided a driver for the family so that they could complete the journey.

Another factor making overlanders determined to mete out their own justice was that handing over malefactors to authorities in California and Oregon usually meant that the criminal escaped punishment through a maze of technicalities and arcane disputes about jurisdiction (California courts had no authority over crimes committed in the wilderness in 'unorganised' territory). If the pioneers made the mistake of delivering murderers to the military at the forts along the trail, the guilty usually escaped because a clever lawyer could claim that the US Army had no jurisdiction in civilian cases. The sober, albeit sombre, conclusion is that, in the absence of government, judiciary, police or jails, wagon trains had no alternative but to administer their own justice. The improvised courts tended to be tough on crime, but less so than other societies 'in a state of nature'. On the California goldfields during 1849, for example, a misdemeanour merited a flogging, a theft head-shaving, branding or ear-clipping, while a more serious robbery could see the miscreant deprived of ears or hands, and three successive thefts brought the gallows.

Clearly, these problems would increase the more people crossed the plains, and 1845 witnessed a genuine population implosion within North America, with nearly 3,000 of the best calibre inhabitants of the Midwest being displaced to the Pacific coast. No less than six major caravans set out from Missouri in May, and there was at least one significant one later in the year. More than five hundred wagons made the journey, with an overall average of 4.3 persons to each wagon. Both Independence and St Joseph reported serious 'Oregon fever'. The St Joseph press recorded the departure of 954 people in 223 wagons, together with 9,425 cattle and 108 horses and mules; males capable of bearing arms numbered 545. Not to be outdone, Independence noted the emigration of at least 278 wagons and more than a thousand people.

The first of the St Joseph companies, consisting of perhaps sixty wagons and between 275 and 300 persons, was led by Indiana-born Captain William G. T'Vault who had been elected on 26 April; also chosen that day were John Waymire as lieutenant and John Clark as pilot. This party was first off the starting block and made steady progress to the Platte, reached on 25 May. The only event worthy of even passing mention was a wedding on 7 May. Close on T'Vault's heels was a party led by Captain Solomon Tetherow, with Hardin D. Martin as lieutenant; they had no need of a pilot as they intended to dog the footsteps of the vanguard party. More detailed statistics – as indeed more information of every kind – is available for this party. There were 293 people in total in this caravan, including 100 armed men (disposing of 170 guns and pistols), 63 women over fourteen, 56 girls under fourteen and 68 boys under sixteen, travelling in 66 wagons, with 624 loose cattle, 398 oxen and 74 mules and horses.

The third caravan to start from St Joseph consisted of something less than 200 persons in about 45 wagons under the command of Captain Samuel Parker. This is an underdocumented wagon train, but slightly more information is available for the last party to leave St Joseph, the so-called 'new London Emigrating Company for Oregon', under the command of Captain Abraham Hackleman. This company consisted of 50 wagons, 214 persons and 666 head of cattle; doubtless the number of the Beast was not considered significant by the plethora of clergymen and Baptist missionaries who travelled with this party. This was late getting under way and by 25 May, when the T'Vault party was already at the Platte, had got no further than the Nemaha Indian Agency, twenty-five miles west of St Joseph. Shortly afterwards, a major division must have occurred, with William Findley of Illinois leading a breakaway movement; by the time the Findley group and the Hackleman party reached Fort Laramie they were in two distinct and completely autonomous groups.

Meanwhile, at Independence, a large party of one hundred wagons made an early start, crossing the Wakarusa on 9 May and the Kansas

River three days later. Other wagon trains, one fifty strong, another with twenty-eight conveyances, were close behind, and there were also freebooting individuals 'island-hopping' between the various companies. The most notable diarist of the emigrants who started from Independence, Joel Palmer, caught up with the main body on 11 May, having 'slipstreamed' various wagon trains in a fast-moving convoy of four wagons. Starting from the Indiana back country and proceeding via Indianapolis, Palmer reached Independence on 6 May, thinking he had plenty of time to outfit, but found most of the emigrants already gone. Although subagent Richardson of the Nemaha Indian Agency commented that the character of the pioneers was much improved on that of 1844, Palmer's initial impressions were not favourable. Before they had encountered any of the rigours of the wilderness, some of his fellow-travellers were rip-roaring drunk. 'From one of the wagons they drew forth a large jug of whiskey, and before bed-time all the men were completely intoxicated.'

Continuing his ski-like progress in a fast wagon, Palmer overtook one caravan of thirty-eight wagons on 8 May and passed another of twenty-eight wagons three days later, even though he had had to divert to round up their horses and mules after a herd of wild Indian ponies 'spooked' them. At nightfall on the 11th, he achieved his immediate objective by overhauling the hundred wagons, but was alarmed to find that the sentries were already so bored with guard duty that they were shooting at the camp dogs to amuse themselves. Next day, he crossed the 750-foot-wide muddy Kansas River in a flat boat: 'so large was our company, and so slowly did the ferryman carry on the necessary operations, that darkness overtook us before half the wagons had crossed the stream.' The emigrants were worried about thefts from the Kansa Indians and so mounted a strong guard, but the real problem came from another direction, in the shape of the most terrific storm, which panicked the cattle and caused a stampede. As Palmer wrote: 'It appeared to me that the very *elements* had broken loose, and that each was engaging madly in a desperate struggle for the mastery.'

To add to the confusion surrounding the caravans proceeding from Independence, there was yet another party on the trail. John Henry Brown was one more mountain man with an eye to the main chance, but there is controversy about whether he really did have the colourful early life he claimed. According to his own story, he had lived among the Cherokee and actually journeyed to California with Cherokee fur traders in an unsung epic of 1843. He returned east in 1844 and was now once again heading for California, directing thirty-eight wagons (many of them bound ultimately for Oregon) and with about 1,000 head of loose cattle. Palmer and the main wagon train from Independence spent much of the summer passing Brown's party and being repassed by it. The wagon trains from Independence were already in a fluid state, with much movement in and out of the various companies; when they merged with the St Joseph parties further along the Platte the confusion would become almost total.

On 13 May, the hundred-strong wagon train was ready to elect its officers. There were two candidates for pilot: T.M. Adams, a promoter of the 1845 emigration, and the well-known mountain man Stephen Meek. Majority opinion was for Meek on general grounds, but the emigrant council baulked at the fee demanded: $250 to be paid at Fort Vancouver on the Pacific and $30 cash on the barrelhead. When Meek saw that he might be passed over, he decided to force the issue. Even as the elders were deliberating, he came running in to say that the Kansa Indians were stealing cattle. The emigrants at once formed a posse and rode to the nearest Kaw village. There, the chief gradually calmed them and convinced them that none of his men was a thief. More perceptive observers like Joel Palmer saw through Meek's transparent ruse at once: the alarm had obviously been raised to disrupt or postpone an election that seemed to be swinging away from the mountain man.

But the plot worked. On 14 May, Meek was chosen as pilot and Dr Presley Welch of Cooper County, Missouri, as captain. Meek celebrated by getting married to a young woman emigrant named Elizabeth Schoonover (said to be an orphan). The wagon train pressed on and made eighteen miles to the Red Vermillion on the 17th, yet this was not a happy caravan; sixteen wagons broke away, but another fifteen joined in, compounding the chaos and confusion that was to mark 1845. Further progress became impossible as a result of massive dissension and factionalism. Disappointed office seekers refused to accept the majority decision that had elected Welch and Meek, so the malcontents forced a compromise. Although Welch and Meek were formally retained in their posts, the wagon train split into three divisions. Each of these was to take turns for a week at travelling in advance of the others, and Welch was to command only this rotating vanguard. Otherwise, each division was to choose its own officers, and it was as a result of this new set-up that Joel Palmer found himself commanding a division of thirty wagons.

And now a fresh problem arose. Under their new leader Hard Chief, the Kansa Indians were proving more of a headache than in the past. Emigrant Jacob Snyder summed up the problem:

Pioneer women: both pipes and sunbonnets

A woman gathers the precious buffalo chips – the peat of the prairie

A pioneer family

Appleton Milo Harmon's journal of the plains across

An Indian chief forbids emigrants to cross his territory

The Sioux Indians in full fig

Buffalo hunting:
a professional business
performed by amateur
emigrants

The mountain man John
Grey's legendary combat
with five grizzly bears

The wagons of the Donner
Party toil up the Donner Pass

James Frazier Reed,
homicidal hero of the
Donner Party

The Donner Party
struggling up the
Sierra Nevada

The rescue of
the Donner
Party

The treasure saved from the
ordeal: Patty Reed's doll

Brigham Young,
American Moses

The Mormons in Winter Quarters

The Mormons on the Platte

A Mormon family on the plains

The Mormon
Pioneers in South
Pass

'Shall We Not
Go On In So
Great A Cause?'

The New
Zion. Salt
Lake City in
1860, the yea
of Sir Richar
Burton's visi

Found the Indians troublesome. They hung about the camp until nine o'clock at night when they left. Came in the morning and demanded pay for passing through their country, which they did not get. The chief's daughter was killed by lightning the day before we arrived. They go in mourning by smearing their faces with mud and clay.

But the Kansa kept nagging away about passage money for the right to cross their territory. Calculating that they might as well give freely what would be stolen anyway, the overlanders agreed a 'tribute'. Snyder was incensed that he had to part with a calf as part of the deal and fulminated about the 'soft' emigrants of earlier years who had given in to the Indians too easily.

Snyder's party was not the only one to be plagued by the Kansa. Samuel Hancock was one of Solomon Tetherow's party out of St Joseph and he found the Kansa in particularly cross-grained mood. When a cow with a bell round its neck warned the pioneers that Indians were stealing cattle, the Kansa shot the cow full of arrows in retaliation. Hancock was then part of a posse which went out to recover the stolen cattle. One of the wagon trains was so vexed by the thieving Kaws that they took a brave hostage as surety for the good behaviour of the others. But the problem was never really solved. Once out of the territory of the Kansa, the overlanders had the thefts of the Pawnee to deal with. The only difference then was that the Pawnee target was the white man's horses rather than his cattle. Hancock found himself riding in posses again; this time they punished the Indians by levying 'compensation' – adding a number of their ponies to the tally of recovered horses.

Trouble with Indians this summer was all the more surprising since, for the first time ever, the emigrants travelled for the first half of their journey virtually under military escort. With 280 well-mounted and equipped dragoons and Thomas 'Broken Hand' Fitzpatrick as guide, Colonel Stephen W. Kearney set out from Fort Leavenworth for a summer on the plains. His orders were to explore possible military roads and make general reconnaissance, to protect the emigrants and, most of all, to overawe the tribes on the Great Plains with a show of force. For a week they followed a course that took them along and across the Wolf, Stranger and Nemaha rivers, then, on 24 May, they reached the Oregon Trail at the Big Blue. Everywhere, as far as the eye could see, were wagons. Kearney at once ordered a forced march to place his dragoons in the van of the emigrants. Palmer noted the soldiers riding past at a great pace on 25 May. The large numbers of Pawnee always visible on the skyline worried the overlanders, and as the dragoons successively overtook the many wagon trains, they were hailed as deliverers. Such were the numbers of emigrants on the plains that summer that it took Kearney twenty days to overtake them all. However, he arrived in Fort Laramie on 14 June, far ahead of even the foremost emigrant caravan.

Among the wagon trains themselves, the story of the trek to Fort Laramie is largely the story of caravans overtaking others and being overtaken, of divisions breaking off from the overall company and joining others, and generally of disorder and indiscipline. A diary entry from Jacob Snyder on 22 May is fairly typical: 'The ten o'clock guard failed to attend to their duty, and the relief guard, having no person to call, slept on and no guard was out this night.' The emigrants saw many traces of previous pioneers, especially the 1843 and 1844 parties. There were many Indian scares and false alarms occasioned by the dreaded cry 'Indians!' but these always turned out to be either friendly tribesmen or returning hunters. Nonetheless, the fear remained, and smaller parties sought the protection of the larger companies. Snyder's diary contains an unwittingly funny story, showing how his small party successively applied for incorporation to the rear, middle and front divisions of a large wagon train before finally being admitted by majority vote to the front division. And Sarah Cummins makes her low estimate of human nature clear by a story illustrating the essential moral and intellectual dishonesty of many overlanders. One family was in the habit of seceding from a caravan at dawn, racing ahead to secure the best pasture, then petitioning for readmission at dusk; the family actually expressed incredulity when it was finally turned down.

The first caravan reached the Platte on 25 May, and for the next week successive waves of wagons debouched on Nebraska's 'sea coast'. The three-week trek along the Platte to Fort Laramie was notable for two things: the violence of the weather and, paradoxically, the appearance of more profuse wildlife than any preceding wagon train had ever witnessed. High winds along the Platte made this one of the testing pioneering years in Nebraska and the climate in mid-June felt more like November. Jacob Snyder reported on 6 June: 'The wind has been very high for several days and today it blew violently, carrying the sand of these bottoms through the air and making it very unpleasant.' Next day, the high winds continued and Snyder noted: 'Four caravans were in motion and the extent of the whole could not be less than twenty miles. So thick was the sand that persons were obliged to place handkerchiefs over their faces to be able to see.'

Big and small game was seen in abundance: elk, buffalo, deer, antelope, bears, rabbits and hares, as well as the inevitable colonies of prairie dogs;

Palmer noted the inevitable symbiosis of the dogs with rattlesnakes. The hunters this year seemed not as talented or successful as those in previous years, and buffalo killings were scarce. One hunter had his horse gored by a bison bull, while another division had to form laager as protection against a buffalo stampede when an inexperienced hunter tried to pick the animals off too close to the wagons. Another shot himself (not fatally) and still another caused an 'Indians!' alert by mistakenly shooting at one of his own men. Most of all this year the emigrants noticed wolves, which hung in clusters on the flanks of the buffalo. This year there seemed to be more wolves than any of the mountain men could ever remember seeing – hundreds of them visible at a time in large packs. A novelty was the large number of prairie owls observed.

The tenor of life is conveyed in Snyder's very full diary. 'The River [sc. the Platte] is covered with small islands making a most romantic and picturesque appearance.' 'Saw numbers of cactus family in bloom, flower pale yellow.' 'Found the water [on the south fork of the Platte] about middle deep and a strong current.' 'The encampment had the appearance of a large military force.' Snyder particularly evinced amused contempt towards the barrack-room lawyers in evidence around the campfires at night: 'Here almost every variety of men are to be met with; questions are introduced and debated and more ridiculous scenes seldom present themselves, even in a city where characters are numerous. The question was love and hunger.'

Palmer's account complements this. We learn that there was a pause for washing days every two weeks. On one of these (2 June) new elections were held, confirming Palmer in his position. It was resolved not to wait for the putative 'parent' wagon train led by Welch but to press on independently; nearby were four other loose and fluid companies, one of thirteen wagons, one of fifty-two and another of forty-three (Palmer's group contained thirty-seven). Palmer prided himself on his men's expertise in jerking meat, and explaining the process gives a marvellous snapshot of wagon life on the plains:

An unoccupied spectator, who could have beheld our camp today, would think it a singular spectacle! The hunters returning with the spoil; some erecting scaffolds [for jerking meat], and others drying meat. Of the women, some were washing, some ironing, some baking. At two of the tents the fiddle was employed in uttering its unaccustomed voice among the solitudes of the Platte; at one tent I heard singing; at others the occupants were engaged in reading, some the Bible, others poring over novels. While all this was going on, that nothing might be wanting to complete the harmony of the scene, a

Campbellite preacher, named Foster, was reading a hymn, preparatory to religious worship. The fiddles were silenced, and those who had been occupied with that amusement betook themselves to cards. Such is but the miniature of the great world we have left behind us, when we crossed the line that separates civilized man from the wilderness.

One by one the overlanders ticked off the familiar landmarks: Ash Hollow, Castle Rock, Chimney Rock, Scotts Bluff. The only noteworthy events on the run to Fort Laramie were a couple of Indian scares. Sol Tetherow's caravan met a large band of Sioux but relations were cordial: Tetherow even invited the Sioux leaders to dinner, at which the chief declared himself delighted. Shortly afterwards, just beyond Chimney Rock, they met a war party of more than two hundred Crow, looking for the Sioux Tetherow had recently entertained. When the Crow asked if there had been any sign of their traditional enemy, the Lakota, Tetherow said he had seen nothing. The Crow were certainly less friendly than the caravan's recent guests. One of them frightened a mule train, which started a stampede of some forty wagons and threw the entire train into disarray. The Crow moved in for a closer look, doubtless hoping to scavenge something under cover of the chaos, but Tetherow sent out a determined guard of twenty well-armed men to warn off the interlopers.

The majority of the 1845 emigrants arrived at Fort Laramie in the two weeks between 14 and 27 June. As always, they found provisions scarce and prices high: flour was $15 a hundredweight and sugar and coffee $1 a pint. But this year most of the attention focused on Kearney's military expedition. On 16 June, he called together the principal Sioux chiefs (including Bull's Tail) and warned them earnestly against ever contemplating harm to the overlanders. Many lofty speeches were made in the council but the anger of the Plains Indians was palpable. They accused the emigrants on the Oregon and California trails of having swept through their country like a plague of locusts, consuming forage over wide tracts of the trail, slaughtering buffalo and starting prairie fires that destroyed both animal feed and precious sources of firewood. Kearney tried to pour oil on troubled waters, then pressed on as far as South Pass. He started back from there on 1 July and was in Fort Laramie again on the 13th. What he had learned in his absence made him concerned enough to call a council with the leading Cheyenne chiefs, again exhorting them to peace and patience.

Joel Palmer did his best to reinforce Kearney's arguments. His party gave a feast for the Sioux at Fort Laramie, dining them on bread, meat, coffee and sugar. The Sioux said they liked trading with the white man but were angry with the incursions the overlanders were making on their traditional hunting grounds and the way they frightened away the buffalo. Palmer then made a spirited speech, stressing that he was the red man's friend. He explained that the emigrants were travelling to the 'great waters of the West', meant no harm, and their pacific intent could be seen because they had women and children with them. The Sioux listened politely, and it was noteworthy that the usual incidence of petty theft was down on the normal for such occasions. The only thing they took this time was a frying pan; Palmer said he did not feel like spoiling the ship for such a ha'porth of tar.

Kearney departed southwards, along the base of the Rockies to the bank of the Arkansas River and the Santa Fe Trail and thence to Fort Leavenworth, having completed a remarkable ninety-nine-day expedition covering 2,200 miles. After an average halt of forty-eight hours in Fort Laramie, the snake-like chain of wagon trains set out for South Pass and Fort Hall. Most of these travellers met Kearney's dragoons along the Sweetwater on the way back from South Pass (many of the troops were sick) and were glad to hear that Kearney had demonstrated the power and efficacy of his howitzer at Independence Rock for the 'instruction' of the Sioux and others. Jacob Snyder, always keen to encounter mountain men (he had met Antoine Robidoux just outside Fort Laramie), visited the army camp and talked to Thomas Fitzpatrick, then recovering after a nasty kick from a horse. Fitzpatrick was confident there would be no trouble from the Indians, but the emigrants continued nervous whenever they saw Sioux in double figures and could never be certain that the wolves they heard howling at night were not painted braves waiting to slaughter them.

The overlanders made slow progress to the north fork of the Platte and had to make frequent stops for repairs to the wagons. Wagon tyres worked loose, and some axle-trees and tongues were broken. Palmer explained their predicament: 'We had neither bellows nor anvil, and of course could not cut and weld tire. But as a substitute, we took off the tire, shaved thin loops and tacked them on the felloes, heated our tire and replaced it.' The pace quickened after Independence Rock (reached by Palmer and Snyder on 12 July) and this year buffalo were found right up to the Continental Divide at South Pass, not to mention thousands of antelope. But, as stated before, the hunters this year were not the most skilful. On one occasion they wounded a bison which ran into camp, where it took twenty men firing point-blank broadsides to finish him off.

On the barren stretches along the Sweetwater, sagebrush was their only fuel (buffalo chips being now as rare as gold dust) and, at 8,000 feet, there were heavy frosts, with ice forming a quarter of an inch thick overnight in water buckets. The only consolation in the extreme, unseasonable (even at this altitude) cold was the sight of the Wind River mountains on their right, about twenty miles distant – a stunning sight as much for the masses of timber swathing the lower slopes of the mountains as for the masses of ice and snow piled peak upon peak. The oversized valley of the Sweetwater provided gentle gradients, but there were the occasional treacherous boggy places, where there was ice under twelve-inch-deep layers of mud, and even quicksands into which buffalo could sink unawares. Parkman, in his 'nature red in tooth and claw' mode, described one such occurrence, which he is unlikely to have witnessed personally. 'Down he sinks; one snort of terror, one convulsive struggle, and the slime calmly flows above his shaggy head, the languid undulations of its sleek and placid surface alone betraying how the powerful monster writhes in his death-throes below.'

A twenty-three-mile march, in an easy climb away from the Sweetwater, brought the travellers to South Pass, from which, next day, it was a downhill twenty-two-mile journey to the Big Sandy River. Ahead yawned the barren forty-mile stretch to the Green River, where the overlanders had to take all their own water and grass – there was nothing to live off on this land. They were rewarded for the two-day ordeal by the sight of the limpid Green, 'a beautiful clear stream, about one hundred yards wide, with a rapid current over the gravelly bottom'. The emigrants appear to have crossed the Green by three distinct methods. Some improvised rafts by laying three canoes alongside each other, bound together and ballasted with logs placed between. Others found that by hoisting up the wagon beds by three inches and laying them on poles they could ferry across without damaging any of their goods. Still others reconnoitred, found a ford half a mile downstream and crossed that way.

Now there was a choice of routes. Some of the emigrants went with Old Greenwood and others on the inaptly named Sublette Cutoff (taken in 1844 by Hitchcock), but many more played it safe and swung south to Fort Bridger. By 25 July Palmer and Snyder were at the fort, where they stayed until the 28th, picking the brains of the famous mountain man Joe Walker, who advised the emigrants that, though none of the ways west was easy, their best bet was to aim for California rather than Oregon. They then proceeded to the watershed of the Green and Bear rivers and descended to camp on the Bear. The first day of August brought euphoria, with Palmer diverting to enjoy a mountaintop panorama of Bear Lake and the Bear valley and Snyder marvelling at the beauty of the landscape: 'This day passed through the most romantic country that I have yet seen on this route.' After the desert between the Big Sandy and the Green, this stretch of river seemed a taste of paradise, with many large mountain trout clearly visible in the pellucid waters, and easy to catch withal.

Next day, 2 August, it was a very different story. The thirty miles made on the 1st now seemed like a dream, as Snyder explained: 'Could not reach the hills without going six miles out of our road. We attempted to cross the river several times on our return and were baffled. The undergrowth was so thick that we could not penetrate it. We finally succeeded and got into the main road again in the bottom from which we came; and in which we camped. The grass was as high as a horse's back and in sufficient quantities to support thousands of cattle and horses.' Hancock, in the Tetherow party, also found the sagebrush tedious but marvelled at the antics of three French Canadians travelling with their Indian wives and extended families. This entire group used the journey along the Bear to lay in a year's food supply, by catching crickets and boiling them into a mush.

Crickets were a new factor in emigrant travel, and a noisome one. Hancock complained that, on top of the sagebrush, he could scarcely put one foot in front of another for crickets, 'the whole surface of the ground being covered with these insects, about an inch and a half long and without wings'. Palmer found the crickets even more detestable:

The ground, for a strip of about four miles, was covered with black crickets of a large size. I saw some that were about three inches in length, and measuring about three-quarters of an inch in diameter; but the common size were [sic] two inches in length and one-half or five-eighths in diameter; their legs were large in proportion to the size of their bodies. Some were singing on stalks of wild sage; others crawling in every direction. Our teams made great havoc among them; so numerous were they that we crushed them at every step. As soon as one was killed, others of them would alight upon it and devour it.

Soda Springs, reached by Palmer and Snyder on 4 August, evoked the usual superlatives. But thereafter, as the Bear turned sharply south to reach its final destination in the Great Salt Lake, the route was again strenuous. Nonetheless, rugged individualism once more reared its head. Knowing that Fort Hall was a couple of days' hard travel away, and hoping to beat others to the scanty supplies likely to be on offer there, more and more individual wagons broke loose from the organised convoys and began a mad stampede to see who could get to Fort Hall first.

But now came a new and totally unexpected problem. Since the beginning of the emigrant trails, the overlanders had basked in the illusion that the real Indian threat to them came from the Plains Indians – the Sioux, Cheyenne and Pawnee – and that, once past South Pass, they were free from danger. Yet in 1845 the Shoshone belied their pacific reputation. Already, at the Green River, there had been a harbinger of possible things to come, when the Snakes (Shoshone) demanded passage money from a company of emigrants. After a twenty-four-hour stand-off, with the overlanders refusing to accede to their demands, the Shoshone gave in and started normal trading. But, on the run from Soda Springs to Fort Hall, they again put in an appearance, this time altogether more menacingly.

William B. Ide, another of the emigrants who chopped and changed along the trail in 1845, was a forty-nine-year-old captain of the 'cattle guard', in charge of rounding up strays. Out on such an errand, Ide had a tense encounter with several Snakes, who had stolen cows. When Ide went to lasso the kine, one of the Indians fitted an arrow to his bow and aimed at him. In response Ide cocked his gun, causing the Indians to flee. It was, as Ide conceded, a near-run thing, but it said something about the temper of the Shoshone this summer. There was worse to come. Hancock's company came under fire when they caught Shoshone riddling their cattle with arrows, and it took a determined charge by the emigrants to flush the Indian snipers out of a thicket. On returning to the caravan, they found arrows as thick as porcupine quills embedded in the wagon beds, but fortunately no casualties. Furthermore, three of the 'independent' wagons that had gone ahead in the race to Fort Hall were attacked by Shoshone. Palmer sent help but one of his scouts in turn was chased by a war party; the Shoshone sheered off only when they saw the size of Palmer's wagon train. The 'independent' wagons crept back fearfully into the safety of the convoy.

At Fort Hall, Palmer tried to learn the reasons for Shoshone hostility. One theory was that they were lashing out at the emigrants in 'compensation' for the mauling they had taken in recent years by Sioux, Crow and Blackfeet – which was why, according to the fort commandant Richard Grant, their numbers had decreased alarmingly in recent years. But soon discussion of the Shoshone took second place to the burning issue of the day: California or Oregon? Once again it was alleged that Grant steered the overlanders in the direction of California, aided on this occasion by the vociferous pro-California propaganda spouted by Caleb Greenwood, who had arrived at the fort with his sons John, Britain and Sam. Impassioned voting took place, which often resulted in a divorce of captain and company, one electing to go to Oregon, the other California. But many listened to Greenwood's mendacious account of the glories of California. He claimed that the route there was far easier than the road to Oregon; that the Indians were more friendly; that Sutter had guaranteed to supply them with potatoes, coffee and dried beef; and that Sutter had a massive Spanish land grant from which he would distribute six sections to each family settling near Sutter's Fort.

Undoubtedly, Old Greenwood was one of several evil geniuses on the trail in 1845. Jarvis Bonney describes him as 'a very picturesque old man. He was dressed in buckskins and had a long heavy beard and used very picturesque language.' The meeting addressed in turn by Barlow and Greenwood descended into a near riot, with the two principals almost coming to blows. Barlow argued that, whereas England was about to give in over Oregon, Mexico would not do the same in California, that the land titles of anyone going with Greenwood would therefore be in jeopardy. When Greenwood seemed to be getting the better of this argument, Barlow lost his temper and said he would 'forbid' anyone to leave the train and go to California; he did not explain how he was going to make his writ run. Greenwood won the debate on points, if not quite by knockout. He got one caravan safely established on the turn-off for California, then returned to Fort Hall for more rabble-rousing public relations on behalf of California. He was remarkably successful; altogether fifty wagons turned off, netting Greenwood the not negligible reward of $125.

Unquestionably, much bad feeling was in evidence at the parting of the ways outside Fort Hall on 13 August. Ide and his family opted for California while the rest of his party carried on for Oregon. Greenwood again showed his mendacious nature by boasting to the California-bound emigrants that he had trapped beaver in these parts twenty-five years ago and could guarantee them the same abundance of trout and salmon they now saw on the Snake River. Bonney has been criticised for hyperbole, but there is every reason to think that the words he put into Barlow's mouth at the California turn-off were authentic in spirit if not in exact vocabulary: 'Goodbye, we will never see you again. Your bones will whiten in the desert or be gnawed by wild animals in the mountains.'

The fifty wagons struck south from Goose Creek and, on 21 August, began following the Humboldt River. They were averaging about fifteen miles a day and were in good spirits. So far Greenwood's boasts about abundant trout had held good, and Snyder was able to experiment in his protein intake by shooting and eating ducks and even a crane: 'the meat of this bird very much resembled that of an antelope both in appearance and flavour.' Although a couple of shots were fired at over-intrusive Snake Indians, by and large the travellers felt such deep contempt that they would often outspan their wagons in lonely spots and spend the night in the bosom of their family, as the Ides did. The Digger Indians they encountered excused their panhandling by telling them that their overlords in the Shoshone tribe treated them as pariahs, leaving them no choice but to grub for a living.

By the beginning of September, they had left the land of milk and honey behind and were in barren terrain where the only vegetation was greasewood and sage. The feet of the oxen were bruised and bleeding and, in their fractious state, they found any hint of nearby buffalo disturbing. The emigrants had to corral the beasts to stop them joining in a buffalo stampede but were only partly successful; on one occasion they were 'spooked' so badly that they rioted inside the enclosure and trampled two of their number to death. To preserve the morale of the plodding animals, the overlanders took turns in the vanguard of the wagon train, serving half a day as trailblazer and then dropping to the rear. The unyielding sagebrush was a trial to the children also, since most of them went barefoot and gashed their feet badly on prickly pear.

Every wagon train had its quota of bad apples, and this time the rotten fruit appeared in the persons of Greenwood's sons and a giant huge-framed Texan named Sam Kinney, six feet four inches tall, weighing upwards of two hundred pounds and sporting the black moustache and beetling eyebrows of a melodrama 'heavy'. Kinney liked to boast that he had killed a number of men in fights, as well as a large number of 'uppity niggers'. A devotee of slavery, Kinney decided that since there were no blacks available to enslave in the wilderness, he would take a Digger Indian as his chattel. He told the others of his plan. They protested that to enslave an Indian would simply turn all his tribesmen out on the warpath. Kinney then swore an obscene oath and said that any man who crossed him would get the treatment he had already meted out to the men he had killed in Texas.

Not surprisingly, therefore, none of the emigrants lifted a finger to stop him when Kinney, spying a Digger in the sagebrush, ran at him, knocked him down with a mighty fist and slapped a pair of handcuffs on him. He then roped him to the back of his vehicle, lashed him with a snakeskin whip and indicated by sign language that there would be more such blows if the Indian did not obey him. After being dragged mercilessly along the ground behind the wagon, the Indian got the savage message. Kinney set out to 'break' the Digger as he would a bronco. By day he dragged him along behind the wagon, lashing at him with the whip; by night he handcuffed him to the wagon wheel. After a week of this, Kinney declared that 'Friday' (as he called the luckless Indian) was tamed and would henceforth work as a drover of oxen. After another week, he decided that he would leave Friday untied at night, since by now he must be so far from his ancestral lands that it would be foolhardy for him to try to escape; besides, Kinney boasted, he had a bloodhound who could track a fugitive slave into the jaws of hell.

One morning, Kinney looked for his slave and found him gone. Also missing were three hams, a blanket, a powder horn and his prized Kentucky rifle, worth a hundred dollars. Kinney raged and rampaged through the camp. In their hearts the others laughed with secret delight but openly they expressed sympathy. Leaving his protesting wife, Kinney took gun and ammunition, set out on his mule with the wonder hound and declared he would bring back Friday's bleeding hulk as a trophy and an awful warning to inferior races who tried to defy the white man. But neither he nor the dog could pick up the Digger's tracks. An expert in woodcraft, he had timed his exit to coincide with a sandstorm that wiped out all traces of his existence. There was no scent for the bloodhound to pick up. Almost apoplectic with rage and vowing infernal vengeance, Kinney rode around the desert like a dervish for half a day, then gave up and rejoined the wagon train.

The next outrage also involved an Indian. John Greenwood could never quite decide whether he hated Diggers and Snakes because he was an honorary white man or whether his self-assigned status as a tribal 'aristocrat' meant that he had to win his spurs and be blooded by killing an Indian. Itching for an excuse, he found it on 6 September. As Greenwood and his comrades were riding along, an Indian suddenly ducked out of cover in the sagebrush, making Greenwood's skittish horse shy and rear. Infuriated by the Indian's 'impudence' as well as by the mocking laughter of his companions, Greenwood seized his rifle. His comrades called on him to desist, and the Indian raised his hand in a sign of peace, but Greenwood fired and shot him through the lung. The caravan's doctor was on the spot within minutes but the Indian was already on the point of death.

Caleb Greenwood had been absent from the wagon train during this incident and it was dusk before he and another son came in from a scouting reconnaissance. Hearing that one of the pioneers had shot and killed an Indian, and knowing that this spelt trouble from the Indian's kin, he announced that he would execute the killer for endangering their lives. In Old Greenwood's mind it was clear that the culprit was Kinney, whom he had been wanting to cut down to size for some time. To his horror, he learned that the killer was his own son. This was a stern test for a mountain man who put kith and kin before all other considerations, but Greenwood rightly saw that his credibility at stake. After making sure there were no extenuating circumstances, that John had not shot in self-defence, he confirmed the execution order, adding that anyone who saw John should shoot him down like a dog. John rode out of camp at full tilt, and was shortly afterwards killed in a quarrel with a Mexican over a card game.

Sure enough, as Old Greenwood had feared, the former wheedling and begging Indians now became confirmed enemies, shooting and killing cattle and oxen, making the travellers jittery and nervous and conjuring fears that every dust cloud presaged war-painted Snakes coming up at a charge. After gorging themselves on the meat of the fallen beasts, the Americans would leave the rest of the carcasses behind. When they saw that the Diggers feasted jackal-like off their leavings, they began deliberately poisoning the meat in retaliation. But even when the overlanders entered the country of the Paiutes they met with hostility; clearly the desert drums must have communicated the message that the white men then passing through were 'bad medicine'. This was not the first time an overlander had gratuitously murdered an Indian (gratuitous, in the sense that none of the normal motives for homicide – revenge, jealousy or financial gain – obtained), but the actions of Kinney and John Greenwood simply added to the drip-drip of depraved actions, ultimately convincing the Native Americans of the West that there could be no trusting the white man.

They continued trekking at an average rate of about fifteen miles a day and arrived at the Humboldt Sink on 13 September. The travelling was becoming increasingly strenuous and gruelling. Successive diary entries by Snyder on 12 and 13 September make the point: 'Our provisions are nearly gone. 15lbs of flour broached yesterday, about 5lbs of bacon and eight of buffalo meat constitute the whole amount, save coffee, of which we have enough to last through.' 'Found the water in the lake as salt as sea water. We have had bad water for several days. The earth is covered with a crust of salt and the water that we use tonight is strongly impregnated with salt, saltpeter and sulphur. It made the horses sick.'

They achieved the arid and barren forty-mile crossing from the Humboldt Sink to the Truckee River without grass or water, both humans and animals suffering grievously in the implacable heat. The vanguard of the wagon train arrived at Truckee River at 11 p.m. on the night of the 14th and the main party at dawn. Since they now beheld wooded country after desert wastes and could replenish their water supplies, Greenwood ordered a two-day stopover. But it was hard going on the 17th, for they found themselves so closely hemmed in by hills that they were obliged to cross the river ten times just to make the day's quota of twelve miles; Ide, indeed, records that the party crossed the Truckee no less than thirty-two times on their descent to Truckee Lake, where they found a log cabin built by the previous year's emigrants.

They pulled the wagons laboriously along the northern shore of the lake. Sarah Ide noted: 'some of the time the water coming almost up to our feet – keeping the women in constant dread of being drowned.' But soon the lapping lake waters seemed a bagatelle, for, at the head of the lake, as they proceeded into a meadow, they were overwhelmed at the sight of the obstacle that loomed ahead: what seemed like a solid wall of granite. A dispute now broke out about the best way to get the wagons over this tidal wave of solid mountain. Greenwood suggested that they dismantle the wagons and carry them over piece by piece. But his star was dipping and his credibility fading, since he could not point out the passes through the Sierra Nevada even though he had been there the winter before. His protestation that he could not remember the way because when he crossed the Sierras with Stephens they were snow-covered, cut no ice, as it were, with the travellers. Ide proposed that they try to construct a bridge or some kind of cog-wheeled railway, but this was dismissed as the merest fantasy.

Nonetheless, the emigrants did construct some primitive roads and causeways, rolling rocks together and 'fixing' them with impacted dirt, building a series of ramps that gradually took them from one level area to the next. They then led the oxen up one at a time, heaving and pulling on ropes to encourage the reluctant creatures. Once the oxen were at a higher level, perched precariously on a small rocky plateau, they could, theoretically, be yoked and then used to pull up the wagons with a long chain. But since a 'pulling team' of oxen comprised twelve beasts, this took up sixty feet of space – usually most of the level area on which they were perched. The travellers therefore had to move the oxen forward inch by inch, block the wagon wheels, shorten the chain, move the wagon a few feet, then repeat the manoeuvre; in this way the wagons were laboriously hitched up the steep slopes. The oxen often slipped, fell on their knees and stained the rocks with their blood. It took four exhausting days to reach the summit.

That was the worst part of the entire journey, but there were more travails to come, for the western edge of the Sierra Nevada was a series of saw-toothed ridges and canyon-striated slopes, which meant they were going uphill and down for a long period as if on a slow-motion switchback. There were muddy streams in the small valleys and the gentle streams concealed jagged boulders and rocks that could capsize a wagon if it struck them. The down slopes of the Sierras were so steep in places that the hard-pressed travellers often had to cut down pine trees and tie them behind the wagons as a brake, to stop the wagons crashing forward over the legs of the oxen. Progress was a nightmare negotiation of ravines, steep ridges, canyons and disappearing trails. Snyder recalled: 'In many places we were obliged to cut the underwood down before we could get our horses along, and in others we would be an hour in passing a few hundred yards, down rough declivities and over rough and broken masses of granite.'

Continuing to travel west, they saw grizzly bears and even killed the occasional deer. At one point they passed the cabin in which Moses Schallenberger had spent the winter of 1844–45; Snyder noticed that the snow must have been very deep, for some of the trees had been cut off eight feet from the ground. They got down beneath the snowline at a canyon later known as Steep Hollow and took consolation from the thought that at least they could no longer be trapped in the Sierras by early winter snows. Shortage of forage for the horses was now the main worry, but morale was bad, and the men grumbled that they had expected to reach the plains long before this. The breakthrough came on 25 September when Snyder was at last able to report good grass and water: 'Stopped early this evening on account of our horses having had but little feed last night. We are evidently approaching the plains. The hills are decreasing in magnitude and everything indicates that we have gotten through the most difficult part of the mountains. This mountain contains a great variety of berries and many species of timber and shrubs.'

At the foot of the Sierras on the Californian side, they camped for three days by a beautiful, ice-cold, crystal-clear mountain stream so that the women could do the washing. Food supplies arrived from Sutter, just as he had promised Greenwood. Jarvis Bonney wandered off by himself along the river and in the waters, on a gravel bar, he saw a shining metal which later enabled him to claim that he was the first man to strike gold in California. Although his friend Dr Gildea advised him that this was not iron pyrites but the real thing, and that he could make a fortune, Bonney failed to follow the matter up (or so he alleged – for the lore of the West is full of tales of people who claimed to have discovered gold before 1848 but to have been too high-minded, disinterested or lacking in energy to take things further). Soon the emigrants were able to press on to Sutter's Fort, where they received the warm welcome Greenwood had promised them.

The immediate sequel was not entirely happy. During the winter of 1845 so many emigrants crowded into Sutter's Fort that they were hit by an outbreak of typhoid; among the victims was Bonney's friend Dr Gildea. But in a wider sense the California party of 1845 had secured an undoubted triumph. Whereas the Stephens–Murphy party of 1844 had scored a 'first' by being the first to take wagons across the Sierra Nevada to California, they just got through by the skin of their teeth; it was open to critics to say that they had been lucky and defied Fate, but that their feat was unrepeatable. The Greenwood caravan – or the Grigsby–Ide party, as it is sometimes unaccountably called – demonstrated beyond question that the California Trail, though strenuous and difficult, was a viable and practicable overland route.

At almost the same time, another overland party arrived at Sutter's Fort. This was a small caravan led by Solomon Sublette, a mountain man with a reputation as a drunken roisterer, but little is known of it or its route west. Frémont the Pathfinder also arrived in California after his exploration of the Great Salt Lake and the eponymous desert in Utah. James Clyman, meanwhile, led a party of discontented Oregonians south to California on one of those bizarre 'internal migrations' in the Pacific area, so characteristic of restless and impatient souls. Altogether, six different sets of overland arrivals have been identified in California in late 1845. But the gung-ho Californian propagandists like Hastings and Greenwood had oversold their bill of goods. Many of those who arrived with Greenwood and Ide, including Truman Bonney, the doctor who attended the Indian shot dead by John Greenwood, not only found California an intense disappointment but emigrated north to Oregon, where they roundly accused Greenwood and Hastings of barefaced lying.

The object of this hatred and ridicule, Lansford Hastings, was meanwhile heading another overland expedition. Having migrated from Oregon to California, Hastings was heavily involved in plots and intrigues to wrest the territory from the Mexicans and force Washington to annex it. In the promotion of such schemes he was in New York in the spring of 1845, from where he travelled to St Louis, lecturing in glowing terms on the advantages of emigration to California, along the lines that would become familiar later in the year when his *Emigrants' Guide* was published. Although it was already very late in the emigrating season, Hastings announced that he would prove the truth of what he was saying by leading an overland party to California. Twenty-two enthusiasts signed up for the expedition, but thirteen of them had second thoughts; it was a nine-man party that Hastings eventually took across the continent. The Hastings party that left Independence on 17 August 1845 was not a wagon train but simply ten young men on horseback with pack mules. They made extraordinarily good time to Fort Laramie, where they were detained for ten days because the Sioux were on the warpath, having vowed to kill any whites or Shoshones they found on the trail (so much for the Kearney mission earlier in the summer). Luckily, they fell in with Jim Bridger, who offered to guide them to his fort by a trail through the Wind River mountains that was impassable to wagons but would avoid the Sioux war parties. The travellers soon concluded that Bridger's mountain trail was the worst in the whole of North America. 'Sometimes climbing precipitous mountains – then down, down to a wild chasm – then assisting their animals with ropes over a precipice they would find themselves in a canyon where sunlight never penetrated – but on – on they went and after 20 days' travel at length reached Fort Bridger.'

After a two-day halt at Fort Bridger, they swung north to Fort Hall but ran short of provisions and staggered into Fort Hall half-starved. A sane man would have wintered here, but not Hastings with his unassailable belief in his own star. He sweet-talked Richard Grant, the commandant, into letting the travellers have provisions against an IOU which he would make good to McLoughlin at Fort Vancouver; since we are talking of Hastings, perhaps it goes without saying that the money was never paid. The travellers turned off for California, made their way down the Humboldt River to the Sink, then negotiated the fearsome desert to the Truckee River. Having been forced to cross and recross this twenty-seven times in eighteen miles, they reached the Truckee meadows, climbed the Sierra Nevada and emerged near present-day Donner Lake. Again perilously short of food, Hastings's fabled luck held when his fever-plagued hunter Napoleon Smith managed to shoot a buck even though his gun-hand was shaking.

After passing a log cabin built by a previous traveller (perhaps the selfsame shack of Moses Schallenberger that the Ide–Greenwood party had seen earlier in the year), they got through the sierra passes before heavy snows blocked them – there would ordinarily have been heavy storms in the mountains at least six weeks earlier. They descended below the snowline and came eventually to Johnson's Ranch on Bear River, California. On Christmas Day, they joined the swelling throng at Sutter's Fort. They had been extraordinarily lucky. As George Stewart comments: 'Hastings's luck had held, though a gambler might have said that he was expending it recklessly.' Dale Morgan is even more forthright: 'Such an attempt at a late crossing of the continent was in fact a foolhardy undertaking, summing up Hastings' extensive ignorance. That the endeavor was nevertheless entirely successful, that he was able to cross the Sierra in mid-December without the slightest difficulty, is one of the many evidences that the Lord sometimes has a forbearing eye for fools and children.'

Although more than 250 emigrants branched off to California with Greenwood and the others, ten times as many overlanders held on for Oregon after the parting of the ways at Fort Hall. Here, again, the golden rule enunciated the following year by Virginia Reed proved its validity: 'Never take no cutoffs.' Some Oregon-bound wagons experimented with a cutoff to the Snake starting at Bear River and suffered grievously from starvation; according to Sarah Cummins, one of the lucky ones who did not take the cutoff, five women and several children died on this trail. Their action was particularly foolish, as no less a personage than General Kearney had strongly advised the emigrants to take the tried and tested route north to La Grande Ronde.

But the great cutoff drama of 1845 would begin only at Fort Boise. Until then, the vast body of emigrants proceeded along the Snake relatively uneventfully. Palmer's journal ticks off the landmarks in the second week of August, as he travelled through stony, dusty and barren lands, the only vegetation sage and wormwood, sometimes shadowed by thousand-foot-high cliffs of black volcanic rock. First, there was the crossing of the Portneuf, next the American Falls and then the final turn-off for California. On 17 August, Palmer's party passed close to the site of one of America's greatest natural wonders (at least before its modern transformation into an electricity generating station), the Shoshone Falls, where the canyon of the Snake is eight hundred feet deep. Palmer appears not to have glimpsed the full cataracts and certainly not the 190-foot drop, equalled as a spectacle only by the falls at Niagara and Yosemite. He may not have seen them properly because of the depth of the canyon or, more likely, because the trail wound back from the river, missing the lower falls.

The principal difficulty during the passage along the Snake was finding adequate forage for the animals; the small amount of grass and green bushes was not enough, so the oxen were always hungry. Water, paradoxically, was also a problem, since the overlanders were often forced to camp on the top of the river bluff and drive the cattle down the bluff one or two miles to water. The problems of rounding up stray cattle then had a multiplier effect, for precious hours were wasted at the beginning of the day, cutting down the daily mileage. Packing water up to the top of thousand-foot steep basalt cliffs for human consumption was another tiresome problem. This was terrain where experience really counted.

Many oxen and cattle collapsed and died along the Snake because of the stupidity of their owners. Not realising that there was little grass along this beautiful river, many companies had been racing each other, trying to overtake and reovertake; they had exhausted their beasts and now found they had little food to give them.

Humans fared better, for at Salmon Falls the Indians did a brisk trade in fresh salmon, which they bartered for fishhooks, powder and ball, knives, calico and clothing. But the crossing at Three Islands took its toll. The river bed here was uneven, with many deep holes, and the water's depth was irregular. Needing at least six yoke of oxen to pull each wagon because of the swiftness of the current, the drivers often found that one yoke was swimming while the others were still paddling through shallow water. The emigrant Sarah Helmick, in the McDonald party, recorded:

Crossing the Snake River was the most difficult part of the journey. The wheels of the wagon were taken off, and they were blocked in such a way as to keep them afloat. Ten yoke of oxen were attached to each wagon. In this way some of the oxen were always on land, and able to keep the rest from being swept downstream. The train enjoyed the distinction of not losing a single wagon or piece of baggage during the crossing.

Most of Palmer's recollections of his journey along the Snake to Fort Boise centred on his fascination with the Shoshone, whom he found experts in theft. 'A young man having a horse which he had taken much pains to get along, when night approached, stalled and hobbled him, that he might not stray off; but at night an Indian stole into the camp, unhobbled the horse, cut the rope, and took him off, leaving the young man undisturbed in his sleep.' A few days later, the Indian sold the horse to another party of emigrants in the rear of the caravan. Horses were the great prize in Indian eyes, and they had many excellent mounts which they were prepared to trade with the overlanders for clothes, but the Shoshone weakness for the white man's fashions allowed the pioneers to have the better of the bargain: a top-class horse could be purchased for a shirt or a coat costing only $10 in the United States.

Palmer was one of the last of that year's emigrants to reach Fort Boise. When he arrived there on 2 September, he was so disgusted by the high price of flour ($20 per hundredweight) that he did not even deign to stay overnight. At Hot Springs, near Fort Boise, he met Elijah White, still intriguing indefatigably in Oregon politics. White was going east to collect his salary as Indian subagent and also to lobby for an appointment as governor of Oregon. It was at Hot Springs that two trails diverged at a cross-stream. Palmer learned that two weeks earlier Stephen Meek had persuaded a large number of wagons that if they followed him on a cutoff, he would take them to the Deschutes River and thence to the Willamette valley. Palmer kept his own counsel on the folly of such a strike into unknown territory.

Palmer's party pressed on up the Burnt River.

[This was] the most difficult road we have encountered since we started. The difficulties arise from the frequent crossings of the creek, which is crooked, narrow and stony. We were often compelled to follow the road, in its windings for some distance, over high, sidelong and stony ridges and frequently through thickets of bush ... sometimes it pursued its course along the bottom of the creek, at other times it wound its way along the sides of the mountains, so sidelong as to require the weight of two or more men on the upper side of the wagons to preserve their equilibrium. The creek and road are so enclosed by the high mountains, as to afford but little room to pass along, rendering it in some places almost impassable.

Surrounded by seemingly perpendicular mountains, they had to hack their way along the trail with axes, for bushes and briars were entangled and intertwined with the trees of cedar, birch, alder and bitter cottonwood. They did all this while attending to broken wagon tongues and strayed cattle. The stress was such that Palmer confessed it was only the knowledge that men before them had conquered the road that gave them the strength to go on.

At last, on 9 September, they reached the pine-clad Powder River, here ten yards wide, its source in the snow-covered mountains away to their left. In the distance they could see the gleaming snowcaps of the Blue Mountains. As they descended the Powder River valley, they fell in with more emigrants who had taken different routes to this junction, some by more northerly routes than Palmer. Although Palmer found the Cayuse friendly and eager to barter horses for cattle, there was a jumpiness in evidence all this summer among the emigrants, and a sneaking feeling that this was the summer when major Indian trouble might be expected. Sarah Helmick reported the panic among her group along the Snake when a scout galloped into camp with the news that 'thousands' of Indians were surrounding them; the 'hostiles' turned out to be friendly Shoshones.

Nevertheless, the emigrants' anxiety in 1845 was not all moonshine and there may have been more to the friendliness of the Cayuse than Palmer at first realised. According to Sarah Cummins, the Cayuse and Walla Walla Indians intended to attack the overlanders in the Oregon mountains. Alerted to their plans, Marcus Whitman sped south with a bodyguard of Nez Percé to warn the pioneers. Accompanied by this escort, the wagons proceeded north and encountered a large Cayuse war party in La Grande Ronde. Surprised to find the white men accompanied by the Nez Percé, their traditional enemy, the Cayuse entered a tense conclave. Their chief declared vociferously that he would oppose passage of the wagons through his lands, to which Whitman replied, with equal vehemence, that if any harm was done to the overlanders, the 'Great Father of the Bostons' would punish the Cayuse severely. Getting nowhere with this line of argument, Whitman lost patience, seized the chief as hostage and warned that he would shoot him down like a dog if he tried to escape or his braves tried to rescue him. The night that followed was a sleepless, tension-filled one, and the issue was resolved only by the arrival next morning of a large party of Nez Percé. No longer liking the odds, the Cayuse agreed to let the wagons proceed.

By the time Palmer reached La Grande Ronde, all was peaceful. He rhapsodised over the spectacular beauty of this immense valley, thirty miles long and twenty miles wide, a paradise for settlers with its fertile soil and vast stocks of elk, deer and salmon, but not yet the ultimate destination for any of the pioneers. Palmer liked the Cayuse and thought them taller, cleaner, more athletic and better looking than any other tribe in the West. He liked their entrepreneurship too and the range of their bartering activities, not just horses for cattle, but wheat, corn, potatoes, peas, pumpkin and fish for clothes, cloth, calico and nankeen. Palmer records with amusement a passage of arms with the Cayuse chief Tiloukaikt, who may have been the Waiilatpu leader involved in the stand-off with Whitman that Sarah Cummins described. The chief pitched his tent about three hundred yards from the emigrants and quizzed Palmer about Christianity. Later, when Palmer was playing cards, Tiloukaikt admonished him for the 'unchristian' practice of playing cards. Palmer wrote: 'You may guess my astonishment at being thus lectured by a "wild and untutored savage" 2500 miles from a civilized land. I inwardly resolved to abandon card playing forever.' Tiloukaikt was an unstable character, both fascinated and repelled by the Christianity of Whitman and the missionaries. Palmer, a straightforward plainsman, probably did not realise that the chief was playing 'mind games' with him.

On 13 September, Palmer started into the Blue Mountains. The first two miles out of La Grande Ronde were very steep and needed six yoke of oxen to each wagon. Then they ran for ten miles along ridges and ravines and, next day, a further nine miles over the main ridge of the Blues, all the time entranced by unsurpassable scenery, with thick groves of yellow pine, spruce, balsam, fir, hemlock and laurel all around, and views clear to the Cascade mountains and Mount Hood to the west. They eased down towards the Umatilla River and the village of Five Crows, the chief of the Columbia Cayuse. The banks of the stream were lined with cottonwood, chokeberries and balm of gilead, and here again a brisk trade was going on between Indians and emigrants. The perceptive Palmer noted that the male Cayuse tended to be drones, with all the work of planting wheat, corn and vegetables done by the women and slaves taken on raids. Entrepreneurship among the Cayuse always coexisted with petty thieving: an attempt to purloin ten cows was thwarted but next morning an ox, a mule and a horse were missing, and the most exhaustive searches could turn up no trace of them.

On 17 September, the advance party that had gone on to the Whitmans' mission returned with the seemingly ubiquitous Marcus, and also with Narcissa. The Whitmans stayed one day, talking mainly about problems at the mission but also commenting on the good weather in 1845, in contrast to the year before, which had enabled most of the Oregon-bound emigrants to arrive a month earlier than expected. Whether Elijah White's violent antipathy for the Whitmans was broached is uncertain, but it is certain that he had been proselytising in an anti-Whitman way that summer, encouraging emigrants to go directly to Umatilla on emerging from the Blue Mountains, bypassing Waiilatpu and Walla Walla. But White was by now deeply unpopular with the Oregon settlements, as much for his hypocrisy as for his small-mindedness. Once Washington realised the true state of affairs in the Far West, White's hopes of becoming Oregon's governor were vain. It was only long after Whitman's death, in the era of Abraham Lincoln, that he returned to Oregon in his old job as Indian agent.

On 18 September, the Whitmans said goodbye to Palmer. He and his group travelled down the Umatilla valley, noting the abundance of prickly pear and intermittently pestered by Walla Walla panhandlers, until they came to the Columbia River three days later, majestic in its three-quarter-mile expanse. The Indians were short of white men's clothes and were offering exorbitant prices in vegetables for items of apparel from the United States. Petty pilfering was rampant. As Palmer wrote: 'We were compelled to keep a sharp look out over our garden furniture as during these visits it was liable to diminish in quantity by forming an attachment to these children of the forest, and following them off.' In the next six days they clocked up seventy-two miles trekking along the shores of the Columbia, sometimes following a road that ran steeply uphill before levelling out on to a long, rolling, grassy plain before descending the bluff again to the bank of the Columbia.

On 28 September, Palmer's party traversed the mouth of the Deschutes River where it emptied into the Columbia. Palmer described the crossing as follows:

> The current of this stream was so rapid and violent, and withal of such depth, as to require us to ferry it. Some of the companies behind us, however, drove over its mouth by crossing on a bar. Preparatory to ferrying, we unloaded our wagons, and taking them apart, put them aboard some Indian canoes which were waiting and crossed in safety; after putting our wagons in order of travel, and preparing to start, we discovered ourselves minus a quantity of powder and shot, two shirts and two pairs of pantaloons, which the Indians had appropriated to their own uses, doubtless to pay the trouble of the ferriage.

Next morning, a quarrel arose among the Indians concerning their canoes. It ended in a vicious scrimmage, a fight unlike any the onlookers had witnessed before. Stones and missiles of every kind rained down on either side. The pioneers wisely kept clear of the affray, and after the battle there was scarcely a Native American left unbloodied, either with red-streaming noses or battered, gore-flecked heads. And so at last, on the 29th, they came to the Methodist mission at The Dalles, the furthest point wagons had ever reached. For Palmer, this was the parting of the ways. Hearing that Samuel Barlow had gone into the Cascades to help build a road that would take wheeled traffic, he at once volunteered and set out for the wilderness on 1 October. Some of the more intrepid souls pressed on, either white-watering on the turbulent Columbia or trying to break trail through the Cascades. One family on the river lost all its possessions when the rapids shook their raft loose from its moorings, sweeping the craft and all the belongings clean away; the destitute family were saved only because some Indians took word of their plight to the nearest settlement. The Cascades group also suffered terribly when they struck into the unknown on 1 October. They were lost for eleven days and staggered into Oregon City more dead than alive.

Yet none of the adventures of the pioneers on the Columbia and its hinterland compared in hardship with the unfortunate plight of those who had turned off on the cutoff just after Fort Boise. For them, the Columbia and the Cascades, for all their perils, would have seemed like the promised land. The villain of this piece was the mountain man

Stephen Meek, who persuaded more than two hundred families to follow him west along the Malheur River, promising to take them on a route to the Willamette valley that would bypass the Columbia River altogether. What followed was disaster, though there is much about this story that is still obscure: parts of the route are hard to identify, there is conflicting testimony about what was in the minds of the overlanders and, above all, there is dispute about the motives and intentions of Stephen Meek.

Let us begin with Meek. The older brother of the better known mountain man Joseph Meek, Stephen was born in Virginia in 1795, was a veteran of the Rocky Mountain fur trade and had worked with William Sublette and Joseph Walker all over the Far West, especially California. In 1840, he had been wagonmaster to the Magoffin brothers in Chihuahua on the Santa Fe Trail and in 1842 guided the Oregon Trail party from Independence to the Columbia. In 1844, he took ship as far south as Valparaíso, Chile, then returned to New York via Panama and revisited his Virginia birthplace. In 1845, armed with letters of introduction from Fitzpatrick and William Sublette, he secured the position as guide to a huge wagon train of Oregon-bound settlers. The day the overlanders set out (11 May), Meek first set eyes on the seventeen-year-old Canadian girl, Elizabeth Schonoover. The smitten Meek paid court and after a week-long romance he married his Elizabeth.

Meek was not a success as a guide. The overlanders were dissatisfied with his performance on the high plains; whenever he was needed to deal with an emergency at the rear of the column he was always miles ahead in the van, and vice versa, leading to the frequently voiced opinion that he was a 'loafer'. Whether Meek was fired just before Fort Hall or left of his own accord is uncertain; what is certain is that he was given only $190 of the $220 owed to him, as some of the families, angry at his lacklustre performance, refused to pay. The consequence was that between Fort Hall and Fort Boise Meek was unemployed. He and his wife rode ahead of the wagon train in company with a young man named Nathan Olney, pondering what to do next.

At Boise, Meek made a major pitch for a 'cutoff' which, he assured the emigrants, would save them time and avoid the manifold problems of the trek north through the Blue Mountains and down the Columbia. In fact, he knew nothing whatever of the country west of the Malheur River, down which he intended to lead his hapless victims. The obvious question then arises: what were his motives and, conversely, what were the motives that induced more than 150 wagons (in some accounts well over 200) to turn off with him? Money was clearly an issue at some level. Samuel Hancock relates that Meek charged the overlanders who went with him $5 a day per wagon for his services, but William Barlow mentions a more plausible figure of $1 a day and board. It is certain that Meek later sued Presley Welch, the leader of the 'turn-off' contingent, for $130 dollars and was initially awarded $66 by a jury (but then received a further $66 on appeal). Money was clearly a running sore between Meek and the emigrants, and he may still have been brooding about the way they 'cheated' him of his full fee for the stretch to Fort Hall. Indeed, some commentators have gone so far as to suggest that Meek deliberately guided the overlanders into a waterless desert out of revenge for their perfidy.

For William Barlow, no despicable action was beyond Meek. 'He proved himself to be a reckless humbug from start to finish. All he had in view was to get the money and a white woman for a wife before he got through. He got the wife and part of the money.' But Barlow's ascription of motive presumably relates to the journey as far as Fort Hall, and his calculation of Meek's fee may also relate to that portion of the trail only. Certainly, if more than two hundred wagons took the 'cutoff' and Meek really did expect to make $5 per wagon, then one can see a clear financial motive. But others considered that machiavellian aspects of Oregon politics formed the background to Meek's scheme. Samuel Hancock thought that the state's cattle ranchers wanted an easier route to the Willamette and had discussed with Meek a cynical way to get others to blaze trail for them.

A great deal of dissatisfaction was expressed in our company towards our guide, Mr Meeks [sic], and it was whispered that two gentlemen having about three hundred cattle between them had contracted privately with our guide to pilot the train into the Upper Willamette country for the extra sum of one hundred dollars each, and the company to be kept ignorant of the arrangement, which it was thought has induced Mr Meeks to depart from the route with which he was acquainted.

Others point the finger at Elijah White and say that, with his fanatical hatred of the missionaries who had earlier dismissed him, he wanted to isolate Walla Walla and the Dalles, leaving the Columbia River as a no-man's-land and to this end had intrigued with Meek. White's defenders allege that he was seeking new roads into Oregon in good faith, that it had nothing to do with his animus towards Whitman and others, but it has to be conceded that White was well capable of the alleged chicanery. At first sight, the problem seems to be that White did indeed meet emigrants on the Oregon Trail in 1845 but they were the later, northward-heading overlanders with Joel Palmer, not Meek and his victims. But this objection that Meek and White did not actually meet on the trail in 1845, since White reached Fort Boise two weeks after Meek had turned off on his 'terrible trail', seems naive, suggesting as it does that it was impossible for the two men to have corresponded or concerted at any previous time.

There is less doubt about what motivated so many pioneers to accompany Meek on the cutoff. The emigrant William Goulder mentions the rumours that the Cayuse and Walla Walla were on the warpath – rumours later confirmed by the wagon train in which Sarah Cummins was travelling. Having had trouble with the Shoshone, Hancock's party was likely to have been swayed by the thought of travelling by a route where no hostiles lay across their path. And, whatever the doubts of those who had found Meek a scrimshanking idler on the way up to Fort Hall, his reputation at least guaranteed that he knew the wilderness. Several overlanders who kept journals mention that careful soundings were taken from the commandant at Fort Boise about Meek's past form and experience; they were told that Meek had passed the fort three times before on his journeys and that there was definitely a pack trail up the Malheur. Besides, the wagon trains did not think they were risking that much. Meek said nothing about cutting across to the Willamette and bypassing the Columbia River entirely. Instead, he spoke of cutting across to the John Day River and then following it north to its confluence with the Columbia – some fifty miles from The Dalles.

Moreover, Meek painted a picture of a land flowing with milk and honey that was particularly welcome to the weary travellers. Even without Indian attacks, the travails of the trail were beginning to tell. Hancock's description of the road between Soda Springs and Fort Hall was typical: 'We found our road extremely dusty, as it had been for some days past, so that it was scarcely endurable; sometimes after travelling a few hours we were unable to distinguish each other, being completely disguised with a coating of black dust which gave us the appearance of Africans, instead of white persons.' And ahead lay the uphill trek to the Powder River, then the ascent of the Blue Mountains, followed by the perilous passage either down the Columbia after The Dalles or across the uncharted Cascades. Meek's route held out a distinct promise of an escape from all that. Nonetheless, most of the emigrants did not branch off without great heart-searching, and many more decided to play safe with the orthodox route.

Meek and his large company of emigrants started up the Malheur on 25 August. James B. Riggs was elected captain of the party, his wagons having merged with those of James McNary and Samuel Parker; large sections of the former T'Vault and McDonald parties also branched off with them. Two hundred families were involved – between 1,000 and 1,500 people – travelling in at least 150 and possibly as many as 300 wagons. They passed modern-day Vale on 'tolerable' roads which swung away about three miles from the river, then, about ten miles east of present-day Harper, were forced back to the Malheur by difficult terrain. On 26 August, they made ten miles, crossing and recrossing the river, finding plenty of grass and water. On the 27th, scouts reported the river ahead impassable, so they swung north-west through high bluffs towards the site of modern-day Westfall through a narrow, stony valley which was a severe test of the resilience of the wagons.

They proceeded up Cottonwood Creek, through the canyon and on towards Buckaroo Springs, aiming for Castle Rock. All around them were the cavernous canyons and high ridges of the Malheur mountains. The trail was full of small, black, hard, razor-sharp nine-pointed stones that made the cattle cringe at every step – Hancock spoke of 'the blood from the feet of our poor animals that suffered almost beyond endurance'. They soon began to lose stock, with three or four oxen a day lying down and refusing to go on. The wagons crossed the Bendire Range at the top of Immigrant Hill, south and east of Castle Rock, and picked their way painfully down the slope to Warm Springs Creek, where the emigrant Jesse Harritt spoke of a 'warm spring bursting from the side of a lofty mountain – a little above blood heat'.

In present-day Agency valley, with plenty of grass and water available, they should have stayed for a few days' rest and retrenchment, but the emigrant diaries clearly show Meek driving them on. The wagons wound round the shoulder of Castle Rock (which Harritt confusingly called 'Frémont's Peak') to the north fork of the Malheur, then followed a difficult, rocky trail along the Malheur for five miles. In this area, on 3 September, the first emigrant death took place, that of Sarah Chambers, a young wife. Already the wagons were stringing out along the difficult trail: some of the companies were by now two days ahead of the former T'Vault wagon train. Soon the wagons had to climb up from the river to the top of a ridge because the creek bed was too rocky; in so doing, they sustained one broken axle-tree and two wagon tongues. Descending on the far side, they reached the head of the Drewsey valley and continued down it to the middle fork of the Malheur near present-day Drewsey.

By now, the itinerary west by south-west was beginning to attract suspicion from the overlanders. On 3 September, one of them wrote in his diary: 'It is now pretty evident that Meek . . . does not intend to fall down to the Columbia via the John Day river at all as he told them on leaving Fort Boise, for we are evidently now through the Blue Mountains and still making a southwest course. It is now said that Meek's intention is to take us over onto the head of the Willamette if he can find a place along the Cascades.' Although the emigrant was mistaken and they were nowhere near the Blue Mountains, even an elementary knowledge of geography indicated that the John Day could not be Meek's target. Yet Meek held them to his compass point. Four miles north-west of Drewsey, the wagon trains swung south-west, gradually ascending the Stinking Water mountains.

Stinking Water Pass is at an elevation of nearly 5,000 feet. The steep ascent meant the wagons had to tack and zigzag up the incline, taking advantage of every slice of flat terrain. Finally, they were through and camped in a 'hollow' among clear springs. There followed another ascent, through rocky, difficult and treeless country, to another summit at the head of Big Rock Creek. Descending into Harney valley, probably by way of East Cow Creek, they travelled along the flat expanses of the valley, rejoicing in the luxuriant grass, plentiful water and abundant wildlife. To the south, they could see the limpid waters of a shimmering lake, with snow-capped peaks away to the south-east reaching what later became known as Silvies River. On 8 September, they came to Harney Lake, but this was to be a crossroads in more senses than one.

Meek's instructions now were to cross the lake and continue in a southerly direction, but the patience of the emigrants with their slippery guide finally snapped. When they reconnoitred the lake and found it marshy, with the bog stretching away in a southerly direction, they rebelled and called Meek to account. Meek always maintained that what happened thereafter was on the overlanders' heads, that if they had persevered and followed his directions, they would have reached the Willamette. But the truth was that he was lost, and the more perceptive leaders among the emigrants were beginning to sense this. The emigrant James Field wrote:

The tale of our going down the John Day River was a mere tale of Meek's in order to get us upon this route and then take us wherever he pleased, but if he now fails to take us across the Cascades his head will not be worth a chew of tobacco to him, if what some of our men say prove true. He is with Owensby's company which is one day's travel ahead of ours, and we make their camps every evening, where we find a note buried at the foot of a stake, stating the distance to the next camp, and the names of the streams.

The volatile mood of the emigrants is understandable, for in the three days at Lake Harney between 7 and 9 September, while the wagons slowly wound round the north and scouts probed the southern limits of the lake, they were assailed from a number of quarters. Having endured a gruelling two-week trek since turning up the Malheur off the main Oregon Trail, they were now beginning to succumb to typhoid fever. In addition to the cattle done in by exhaustion, the local Indians stole ten horses. Then, on 8 September, the entire wagon train was devastated by the first death of a child, from whooping cough. On the 9th, Field wrote:

Last evening a child of E. Packwood, of Illinois, which had been ill a few days died suddenly. At present there are a good many sick about the camp, the majority of them complaining of fever. The child was buried in the dry wormwood barrens, and as we left the camp the wagons filed over the grave, thus leaving no trace of its situation. The reason for our doing this was that the Indians in this part of the country are very fond of clothing, giving almost anything they possess in order to obtain it, and fearing that they might disturb the grave after we left, we took the precaution of leaving a beaten path across it.

The wagons moved on towards the western end of Harney valley and camped on the night of 9 September at Crane Spring, on the shore of the tiny Silver Lake. This was to be the last significant water for almost a week, though the overlanders little realised it at the time. After a late start caused by the child's funeral, they set out at 10 a.m. and trekked all day and past dusk across desert, stopping only at 1 a.m., covering twenty-five miles and desperately seeking water all the time. They made camp near Wagontire Mountain – the place sometimes referred to in emigrant literature as 'Stinking Hollow'. Now, for the first time, Meek openly admitted he was lost. The emigrant William Goulder noted: 'It had been becoming more and more evident to us that Meek had no more knowledge of the country through which we were passing than we had ourselves and that, like us, he was seeing it for the first time.' There were some small springs at Wagontire but not enough water to replenish barrels; unless they found further supplies soon, they were effectively marooned.

The atmosphere at Wagontire was tense, as the pioneers came increasingly close to desperation. Angrily, some of the emigrants asked Meek why he had continued to take them due west, when it was obvious that to reach the John Day they had to turn north. The disingenuous Meek then produced a masterpiece of doubletalk. He claimed that it had always been his intention to find the Deschutes River and follow it on to the Columbia. To the mountain men, the Deschutes was known as the

'John Jay': when he referred to it in such idiomatic terms, clearly the overlanders thought he was referring to the quite different John Day River; so when he said 'John Jay' and they heard it as 'John Day', that was their mistake, not his. Whether anyone was taken in by such transparent flapdoodle is doubtful, but at Wagontire the emigrants had more serious matters to attend to than splitting hairs with the duplicitous Meek.

The next week saw the emigrants engaged in a desperate search for water. Meek was absent for thirty-six hours on 13–14 September but found none. Some wagons went north and were forced back to Wagontire by thirst; another thirty-wagon party decided to brave the desert to the west, but met Meek coming back with grim tales of a wasteland stretching on fifty miles or more. The longer they stayed at Wagontire, the less forage there was for the oxen, and the shortage of grass and water was compounded as the wagons that had been two days behind the leaders began to arrive with thirsty emigrants, oxen and cattle, all adding to the pressure on the exiguous resources of food and water in 'Stinking Hollow'. Sol Tetherow was captain of the previous T'Vault wagon train. A forty-five-year-old patriarch with fifteen children, Tetherow had a thirty-three-year-old partner named Job McNemee. Tetherow and his company arrived at Wagontire two days late, having been delayed rounding up stray cattle and burying McNemee's baby Emmaline. He recorded that twenty of his party had already died of typhoid and that the survivors were in a particularly bad way. As for his cattle, unable to slake their thirst adequately in 'Stinking Hollow', they lay down, refused to get up and slowly ebbed away.

Soon, at least 150 wagons were bivouacked at Wagontire, full of ravenous and thirsty emigrants, angry with Meek and desperate for some solution to their plight. Every day parties scoured the countryside in all directions for the precious water they were sure must be out there somewhere. Tetherow wore out three horses in an increasingly anxious quest. But at the evening of every day it was the same story: no water. Hancock wrote in his diary: 'The number of men on horseback constantly exploring the mountains in quest of water now numbered one hundred, fully impressed with the anxiety with which they were regarded by their fellow travelers; yet these explorations were continued seven days unsuccessfully.' Hardships that could be shrugged off on the trail because movement gave an illusion of progress now had to be faced in all their horror. Starved men and women put salt on grass and ate it, pretending it was meat. Others ate berries and dried grasshoppers (almost literally locusts and wild honey) provided by the Indians. All trace of organic solidarity vanished as morale plummeted and those who had reasonable food stocks hoarded them jealously and refused to help their neighbours.

The radius for the water-searching parties widened to forty, then fifty miles, but still no water. An unprecedented disaster loomed; there was the prospect that more than a thousand people might perish in the wilderness; for the first time, to the accompaniment of violent oaths and piteous tears, people began to realise they might die. They could neither go back nor go forward, and were like sailors hove to in a force-twelve storm that refused to blow itself out. The potential for violence in such an explosive ambience was obvious and, predictably, most of the hatred was directed towards Meek. Hancock wrote: 'The excitement was intense, and famine seemed inevitable. The feelings of our company towards the guide were of that unmistakable character to justify me in telling him his life was in danger; his reply was, "I have known it for several days, but what can I do? I have brought you here and will take you off, if you will go."'

At least two separate attempts were made to lynch Meek on this journey, one here at Wagontire, another on the Deschutes. Many were those who later claimed to be Meek's saviour. Sol Tetherow's account given to his son, describing the reception awaiting Meek when he returned to camp having failed to find water, is typical:

> He found three wagons had been placed facing each other in the form of a triangle, their tongues raised and tied together at the top. The sullen and angry men of the party had put a rope around Meek's neck and were about to hang him. My father, pointing his gun at the men, said, 'The first man that pulls that rope will be a dead man. Steve Meek is the only man who has ever been in this part of the country before. If you hang him, we are all dead men. If you give him a little time, he may be able to recognise some landmark here and find a way out.'

It is a good story, in the Aristotelian tradition of a tale which even if it did not actually happen, might have happened, even should have happened. The problem is that the identical story is told by other men, with themselves in Sol Tetherow's role as saviour; among the others are J.I. Packwood, Daniel D. Bayley and, even more incredibly, Tetherow's partner McNemee. At least three more plausible accounts of what happened are extant. According to Hancock, he and his party decided to separate from the others, to push on and take their chances in the wilderness, reckoning that death at Wagontire was certain anyway. As Hancock still believed in Meek, he offered to hide him in his wagon and tell the other wagonmasters that the guide had left camp in quest of water; once clear of the encampment, he intended to use Meek as his personal guide.

Another version is that no attempt to hang Meek ever took place, that the threats against him were all made behind his back. William Goulder later testified:

> I heard it said in after years that . . . Meek's life was in danger from the indignation and anger of the people upon whom he had imposed. Had this been true, I must certainly have heard about it, but I think I can affirm confidently that there was never a word of truth in the statement. Had it been worthwhile to dispose of Meek by an act of violence, that little piece of work would have been done in the depths of the wilderness, where only coyotes would have been witnesses.

A third version is that threats were made directly to Meek but that he faced down his traducers. According to oral histories collected by Fred Lockley, the story ran as follows:

> One of the men who happened to be just ahead of us said, 'When I get to the top of this hill, if I ever do, I am going to hunt for Steven Meek and if I find him I'll kill him.' Meek was sitting just above us back of a big sagebrush. He stepped out with his gun in his hand and said, awful slow and cool, 'Well, you've found me. Go ahead with the killing.' The man wilted down and didn't have spunk enough to kill a prairie dog. He was like a lot of other bad men – just a bad man with his mouth.

It is likely that Meek did make himself scarce, allowing tempers to cool off and, once he realised the mood in the camp, he might have been justified in putting self-preservation first and disappearing for ever. That he stuck to his task of looking for water is greatly to his credit, and his virtue was rewarded. On 14 September, while being hard-pressed and possibly subjected to the threats detailed above, Meek told the whole company that he had spotted a mountain location about fifteen miles distant which, from its green appearance and the profusion of willow trees there, must contain water. When he left camp on 15 September, it was for that oasis that he was headed. According to Hancock's story, Meek must have been with him, but the emigrant Field clearly states that Meek left camp on the 15th with twenty-one of Tetherow's men, and six of Owensby's company. If Field's account is to be trusted, this provides circumstantial backing for the story that it was the Tetherow and McNemee clan that was Meek's protector. But in such a tangle of conflicting and competing evidence, the truth is irretrievable; the only thing certain is that Meek discovered, intuited or guessed where to find water and then found it.

The joy and relief of the emigrants when scouts returned on the morning of 16 September to say that water had been found can, without exaggeration, be described as ecstatic: if they had been beside themselves with anxiety before, they were now overflowing with happiness and the consciousness that they were not, after all, going to die. Hancock recalled pioneer emotion thus:

> It is impossible to describe the joy with which this news was received; some were so overcome that they could not give utterance to their feelings of joy, while tears of gratitude streamed down their cheeks, others gave vent to their delight in loud exultations; the women and children clapping their hands and giving other demonstrations that they too were enraptured by the announcement of plenty of water. In fact the poor animals seemed to have an appreciation of it too for it is said in scarcity an animal can smell food or water at a great distance; at any rate they travelled along more cheerfully.

Waiting until the heat of the day had abated, the emigrants set out at 4 p.m. and travelled all night, eating up the twenty-five miles that separated them from the precious water. The place they came to was later named Buck Creek Water. Jesse Harritt made a careful inventory of the entire migration and counted 198 wagons, together with 811 oxen and 2,299 loose cattle. The mighty host was finally able to slake its thirst in abundant water. One thing more remained to be decided, however. Now that they had ample supplies of water, should they strike out south, north or west, should they retrace their steps to Fort Boise, or should they send out messengers to beg a relief expedition and meanwhile sit tight where they were? The Cornelius party announced it was going north to the Columbia, whether or not anyone else followed them. They set out in the evening once more, trekked all night, and at 10 a.m. found further plentiful supplies of grass and water. They sent back word to the others, and a mass northward exodus took place.

This next rendezvous point was the south fork of the Crooked River, where giant springs formed pools large enough for animals to bathe in. Ironically, Meek struck water here, for the detachment containing him, Hancock, Tetherow and Owensby contrived to miss Buck Creek by going too far to the west. The sober conclusion would appear to be that there were two finds: one by Meek at the south fork of the Crooked River and another, fortuitous one at Buck Creek by a party following a different route to Crooked River. The main party soon arrived, some having travelled by day and others at night, firing pyres of alkaline-saturated sagebrush to light the way in the dark. Relief should have assuaged the harshest criticisms of Meek, but now men began to clamour that if Meek had led them north-west towards the John Day or even the Deschutes, instead of his madcap scheme to go straight to the Willamette, they would have found abundant water and not suffered the ordeal at Wagontire.

It was probably this animus towards Meek that led the wagon train to split into pro- and anti-Meek factions; the prudential consideration that by taking different routes there would be more chance of finding water and forage for all, may also have played a part. It is certain that at this point the two separate parties headed in two different directions. The main caravan including the McNary, Parker, Hancock and Riggs groups headed due north at first, then north-west, past Cold Springs, Stein's Ridge, Camp Creek and Paulina to the valley of the Crooked River, finding it well named and thus making going difficult, descending to a junction with Ochoco Creek near present-day Prineville (reached on 22 September). From there they proceeded north-west to Madras and the route of the present highway from Bend to The Dalles. North of Madras, Parker, on a sustained scouting probe, found plentiful water at Sagebrush Spring.

The smaller group of wagons under Sol Tetherow headed north-west and west to hit the Deschutes River at present-day Bend. Finding that the going had been much tougher than expected, the leaders began to despair of ever reaching civilisation. Their sufferings had been increasing daily, provisions were running low, the cattle were exhausted and the sick list growing. Meek, travelling with this group, suggested they send riders for help to the Methodist mission at The Dalles, which he estimated was just two days' ride away. Ten men volunteered for the ride, promising to return with food within the week. Those left behind, including Meek, dragged themselves painfully along the trail that ran alongside the Deschutes, passing through modern-day Redmond. They benefited from the luxuriant meadows and clear cold water along the Deschutes, avoided most of the rocky ridges and were able to reach Madras, having bypassed both the Crooked River Canyon and the Gray Buttes. On 26 September, they rejoined the main group at Sagebrush Spring.

The ten men who had volunteered for the ride to The Dalles, thinking it was a two-day stretch, were meanwhile enduring another nightmare. They crossed the Deschutes near modern-day Tumalo, then followed an ancient Indian trading route, passing Box Canyon Creek, Tenino Creek, Dry Creek, Quartz Creek, Nena Creek, Wapinitia, Tygh Valley and Fifteen Mile Creek. It took them ten days to reach The Dalles, during which time they had suffered unimaginably from hunger and thirst. The sole food they had eaten was a solitary rabbit and a salmon bought from an Indian. The men were so done in that when they finally reached The Dalles they could not dismount without assistance. The folly of the Meek cutoff is apparent from one single fact. Palmer had reached Fort Boise two weeks after the wagons that turned off with Meek, yet arrived at The Dalles the day after this mounted party, with the main body still struggling far out in the wilderness.

At Sagebrush Spring, the reunited parties compared notes and swapped yarns. Hancock told of frequent harrying by Indians. On one occasion, they riddled a couple of oxen with arrows and one of the beasts died. On another, they became convinced their luck had turned when a lost band of cows came straggling in, looking like pincushions with a plethora of Indian arrows sticking in them. But most of the talk was of the so-called Blue Bucket gold, a fabulous strike said to have been made somewhere on the trail. Some said this took place on the north fork of the Malheur River, but far the more likely area is somewhere between the south fork of the Crooked River and the Deschutes River, that is, after the caravan had divided. The principals in the find were said to have been the Herren family and they later gave detailed accounts of nuggets which they claimed to have hammered and assayed.

Those prepared to swear they had actually seen the gold – for it was later said to have been lost and no one could remember exactly where it was dug out of the ground – all placed it in that location, and the emigrant Hugh McNary passed on a tradition that the date of 'Blue Bucket' was 17 September. This receives circumstantial confirmation in a curious way. Job McNemee, who claimed to be the prime mover in every single episode on the Meek cutoff, be it the prevention of Meek's lynching or the finding of the gold, claimed that he made the strike and that it was in the Malheur mountains. But he slightly gives the game away with a peevish comment, suggesting he had *not* been present on the day of Blue Bucket: 'The emigrants were more interested in finding the lost trail to the Willamette Valley and securing water for their thirsty children than in discovering gold.'

All this yarning about lost and fabled treasure took place on 27 September when the entire company rested wearily, prior to what they hoped would be the last pull over the mountains. Disease and exhaustion were making an impact by now, as Parker's journal indicates: four deaths on the 23rd, six on the 26th, three on the 29th and five on the 30th. On the 28th, the tired and dispirited emigrants plodded through Hay Creek valley to Trout Creek and camped near the present-day Bolter ranch.

Ahead lay the bulk of Bull Mountain, and the only practicable route was up. The 29th saw them swinging west initially to reach the foot of a long steep ridge, at the top of which were the Shaniko Flats. Jesse Harritt's laconic account as always played down the sheer misery of the day's toil: 'This morning we ascended a huge mountain; were compelled to double our teams. Gained the top at 12 o'clock. We continued our journey over level plain until 8 o'clock when we encamped on the margin of a bluff down which we descended 200 feet and found a small stream of water shaded by a beautiful grove of pine trees.'

The Shaniko Flats were barren scrubland and sagebrush, stony in parts but gentle and rolling. Soon the wagons came to a slope that would take them down to the Deschutes River. They were right above the river, which flowed through a deep, precipitous channel 150 feet below them. The water was tantalisingly close as the crow flies, but the emigrants had to take their time, winding down and down; some of the animals, maddened with thirst, had to be restrained from hurling themselves over the cliff edge into the water. Skirting Bakeoven Canyon, they came to the awesome Deschutes River Canyon two miles south of the entrance to Buck Hollow. There were easier crossings of the Deschutes further north, but in their haste, anxiety and panic the overlanders chose to take their wagons across at the most difficult crossing. The Deschutes was one of the most dangerous rivers in North America, later to have a reputation second only to the Lodore rapids on the Colorado River. Roaring, foaming, seething and eddying, it represented nature at its most terrifying and violent. The mere idea of a ferry was ludicrous, for any conceivable one would simply be swept away in the torrent. Beetling cliffs guarded almost all the entrances to the river, making descent to the banks almost impossible. Great ingenuity was now required if disaster was to be avoided.

The solution found was first of all to dismantle every wagon piece by piece so that individual wheels could be taken across. Next, wagon boxes were caulked and made into improvised boats. Men and oxen then entered Buck Hollow Creek in shallow water to give them confidence, and followed this down to the junction with the Deschutes. The first boats reached the opposite bank, towed by oxen with great difficulty through the foaming water, thirty to forty yards wide and twenty feet deep, battling with a swift current all the way. Once the first party was ashore, ropes and lines could be attached with which ensuing boats, oxen and wagon fragments could be transported to the far bank. It took three or four days to get the first caravan of wagons across, and others were still left on the eastern shore.

Almost before the first emigrants had reached dry land on the far side, a fresh crisis blew up involving Meek. There were men who had not seen him since 15 September when he left Wagontire with Hancock and thought he had deserted, but the pioneers in the vanguard knew better. One of these was an elderly man named Henry Noble, whose two sons, aged eighteen and eleven, had just succumbed to typhoid. In his rage and grief, Noble blamed Meek's incompetence for his sons' deaths and swore he would kill the guide by sundown. Meek decided that this time he should make a final, definitive exit. He and his wife enlisted the help of Indian rivermen, who swam across the river with a rope, secured it to the far bank, then carried Meek and Elizabeth across on a running noose. From there, they secured horses for the ride to The Dalles. They had not been gone more than fifteen minutes when Noble and a henchman rode up on the eastern bank, fully armed, and asked Hancock if he had seen Meek. Told that the guide was gone, old man Noble replied stoically that perhaps it was just as well, as his sons were now buried.

Once the leading wagons were across the Deschutes, they made reasonable progress to The Dalles, travelling via Tygh Ridge, past modern Dufur, into Fifteen Mile Creek and finally Eight Mile Creek; the first wagons reached the mission at The Dalles on 7 October. But there were still wagons stranded on the far side of the Deschutes. These owed their rescue to Meek. To his consternation, the missionaries at The Dalles refused to lift a finger to help. Fortunately, he ran into an old friend from the fur-trapping days, Moses 'Black' Harris. The energetic Harris organised a relief party of tough, experienced mountain men and set off, not a moment too soon. They found the rearguard of the wagon train in dire straits, ill, their food almost gone, and in terminal despair. Harris and his men reinvigorated the 'lost company'. As Palmer explained it: 'A large rope was swung across the stream and attached to the rocks on either side; a light wagon bed was suspended from this rope with pulleys, to which ropes were attached; this bed served to convey the families and loading in safety across; the wagons (sixty-four) were then drawn over the river by ropes.'

It was 14 October when the last of the wagons sadly limped into The Dalles, two full calendar months after they had diverted on to the 'terrible trail' of Meek's cutoff. In terms of loss of life, these biblical wanderings in the wilderness of central Oregon constituted the greatest disaster in the entire history of the overland trails. Twenty-four deaths were documented on the trail, and at least another twenty (mainly children) died during the period of 'convalescence' at The Dalles, either from typhoid or simple privation and exhaustion. But it is quite clear from anecdotal and oral evidence that there were other deaths on the trail that eluded the notice of the diarists. A letter from the emigrant Hiram Smith that was widely published in Midwestern newspapers in 1846 estimated the death tally at fifty, while later scholars have suggested that the true figure may be as high as seventy-five deaths. But for the presence of physicians in the party, the roster of fatalities would have been even higher.

Whatever excuses are made for Stephen Meek, he cannot evade responsibility for this tragedy. He remained adamant that if the emigrants had persevered and followed him to the south of Harney Lake, he would have brought them to the Willamette. What Meek could not argue round was that, by his own admission, he had not known the terrain and was lost. Further danger and privation were added to the lot of the emigrants arriving at The Dalles merely from the time taken on the terrible trail. McNemee, Hancock, Tetherow and the rest now had no option but to complete their journey down the perilous Columbia, for the Cascades were likely to be snowed in at any moment. Once again, the overlanders had to hire drovers to take their stock slowly over the Cascades while they rafted down the rapid-filled Columbia. Hancock got safely to Fort Vancouver; but McNemee remembered with bitterness the labour he expended, after just four days' rest at The Dalles, cutting down trees for a raft, with which he then floated his family down the mighty river.

Meek made a disingenuous attempt to shift the blame on to the Hudson's Bay Company, trying to shelter behind the Anglo-American hostility over the Oregon territory, which had brought the two nations close to war in 1845. He alleged that his information on the cutoff to the Willamette came from the commandants at Fort Hall and Fort Boise, who were obviously trying to sabotage large-scale emigration from the United States to Oregon. But this ploy was negated by the wealth of testimony from the overlanders, who unanimously asserted that the factors at Hall and Boise had strongly advised against the cutoff. So far was the Hudson's Bay Company from sabotaging American immigration that Dr McLoughlin, the company's supremo in the north-west, was accused by the company of dereliction of duty for making the American overlanders so welcome. The British naval lieutenants Henry J. Warre and Mervin Vavasour reported to their superiors that, but for McLoughlin's philanthropy, only thirty American families would be scratching a living in Oregon. McLoughlin's reply was crisp and concise. First, humanitarianism and world opinion demanded the aid he gave. Then, if he had not helped the overlanders, he pointed out, they would have attacked Fort Vancouver in desperation, Indians would have attacked the newcomers and the entire province would have sunk into chaos; besides, his policy was good business, for Americans repaid their loans at 5 per cent interest.

Amazingly, The Dalles was to be the centre for yet another daring emigrant venture in 1845. The Columbia was still the greatest barrier for emigrants wishing to settle in the Willamette valley. It will be remembered that when Joel Palmer arrived there at the end of September, he learned that a scheme was underfoot to build a road through the Cascades. This was urgently needed. So far, emigrants with cattle had either had to swim their stock across the Columbia, skirt the mountains on the far side and ferry back to Fort Vancouver near the mouth of the river, or they had to follow the very tortuous and difficult Indian trails on the south bank winding around Mount Hood. The inspiration behind the idea of building a new road over the Cascades was Samuel K. Barlow, who had already shown that vision and good sense need not necessarily be strangers by resisting the siren voices and refusing to follow Meek on to his cutoff. Barlow was a fifty-one-year-old native of Massachusetts, of Scots descent, who had set out in a wagon train nominally under the command of Dr William Welch. Evidently Welch did not have great leadership qualities, and Barlow soon broke away with a small wagon train of his own.

Barlow was the classic 'can do' American. His credo was: 'God never made a mountain that he had not made a place for some man to go over it or under it. I am going to hunt for that place, but I ask no one who feels in the least the force of the word "can't" to accompany me.' Nineteen men, and women and children, with thirteen wagons, seven horses, sixteen yoke of oxen and a dog, opted to follow him. The party left The Dalles on 24 September and trekked south-west over rolling hills towards Five Mile Creek. But in attempting a conquest of the Cascades with such limited resources, Barlow's party was being absurdly over-optimistic. Folds and folds of sawtoothed ridges had to be crossed before one could descend into the Willamette valley; the ascents were precipitous, the gradients steep and there were no natural passes; there was no way round the peaks and summits, all had to be climbed. Worst of all was the psychological toll of the crests and troughs of the mountains; like oceanic waves in a typhoon, they succeeded one another remorselessly and just when you thought you had come to the dividing ridge, another, higher ridge loomed in front of you. Travellers plunged down into deep, dark, silent, cavernous ravines, from which a steep ascent would then have to be made; at the lowest point of the ravine one's heart sank at the realisation of how high one had been before and how much climbing there would have to be to reach that elevation again.

After a forty-mile trek, Barlow called a halt and made plans to send out a reconnoitring party. When on the Blue Mountains, he had observed a small gap south of Mount Hood and it was through that opening that he hoped to build his road. Barlow decided to lead the reconnaissance himself and took William Rector ahead with him to make surveys. His pitifully small working party of ten men and boys were supposed to cut the road, while the women and children smoothed out the tracks they had made. It was at this base camp in the Tygh valley, among yellow pine timber, that Joel Palmer joined them on 3 October. This was just the sort of adventure the dauntless Palmer enjoyed, and he brought with him another twenty-three wagons and their manpower. A definite start was now made on the road. Despite the lack of good tools, the pioneers at first made rapid progress, since the eastern slopes of the Cascades were not heavily timbered and they had not yet experienced the 'incompatibility of big trees, rusty tools and tender muscles'.

Navvying was not Joel Palmer's style, so next morning he and two comrades set out on their own reconnoitring expedition. For thirty-six hours they rode up ridges, down creeks, through dense forests of spruce and across cedar swamps; only when their food ran out did they return to camp, on the evening of 5 October. Next afternoon, Barlow and Rector returned; on comparing notes with Palmer, they discovered that both parties had followed virtually the identical route to within fifteen miles of Mount Hood. They decided to split the manpower, making some responsible for the wagons while the others continued building the road; the wagons would remain in this base camp and riders would be sent back to The Dalles to purchase and bring up further provisions. By the evening of 10 October, they had completed a twelve-mile road from the valley to the top of the first mountain. Thick laurel bushes had proved the main obstacle so far, but as it was the dry season, they had simply set fire to them and (literally) blazed trail.

But on 11 October they came face to face with a succession of steep ridges. At this point, some of the families gave up and returned to The Dalles. But Barlow and Palmer were determined to find a passable route for wagons. Palmer indulged in another of his thirty-six-hour escapades in the mountains, zigzagging across ravines, trudging through cedar swamps, finding himself in dead ends and box canyons. His two companions became exhausted, but the intrepid Palmer climbed a sheer forty-foot wall of ice and snow in his quest for the elusive pass. Once at the top, he trekked for a mile before realising his sullen comrades were not following him. Euphoric with the sheer joy of mountain adventure, Palmer suddenly realised in the late afternoon of 12 October that he was twenty-five miles from camp with just a biscuit in his pocket. Gingerly, he made a perilous descent and caught up with his comrades. Together, they came to a delicious spring of water and some whortleberry bushes. After a scratch meal of biscuit, berries and spring water, they continued on down the mountains, taking until eleven that night to hit camp. Palmer was tired but happy; his companions were completely exhausted, morose and unhappy.

Back at base camp, Palmer found a miserable state of affairs. The party's provisions were nearly exhausted, many cattle had been lost and Indians had stolen a number of horses. As a consequence, more and more people had to do guard duties around the wagons, leaving even fewer men to work on the road. It was decided that fresh messengers must be sent out, both to The Dalles and Oregon City, to request a relief party. But still Palmer and Barlow would not give up on the quest for the passage through the Cascades. Next morning, Palmer set out again with a single comrade, while Barlow, John Brown and William Berry went ahead to cache the wagons and tools for the next phase of road-building. Originally, the intention had been that the trio would, if necessary, spend the winter in the wilderness at this advance camp but, having found a good place for the cache (the so-called 'Fort Deposit'), Barlow decided that the food would not last three men for a whole winter; Berry was therefore left in solitude as the sole guardian of the wagons until the spring. The decision seems heartless, but, as Barlow's descendant explains, 'wagons were worth from $150 to $200 in the valley, and twenty wagons were indispensable to the pioneers at any price'.

Palmer enjoyed a third joust with the wilderness, battling swamps, scrub and heavy timber. He convinced himself he had found a practicable route but realised it would need huge gangs to work on the labour of tree-felling and clearing the underbrush. His mocassins disintegrated so that he had to walk down mountains barefoot. By now even the intrepid Palmer was getting worried by the clear signs of deterioration in the weather, as indicated by the jittery, scurrying movements of birds, squirrels and other wildlife. His other concern was that in heavy rain the rivers would flood and trap them between two impassable streams, spelling certain starvation. After travelling fifty miles on 14 October, Palmer returned to camp on the 15th with the bad news.

Barlow, meanwhile, returned to base camp to find his party in a state of high anxiety. Not only was food short, but the first snowflakes had fallen and something like panic was sweeping the wagon train at the thought that they might be marooned in the mountains for the winter. Barlow finally took the decision that it was too late in the season for further road-building, and ordered a trek for Oregon City; the women and children would be on horseback with the men leading them. The trek turned into a grim race against time, for without fresh provisions they were unlikely to survive. The daily food quota was now down to a cup of coffee and four small biscuits for each person. They made only three to five miles a day through raging snowstorms, tramping over the most difficult terrain: 'whortleberry swamps confronted us frequently, and many a time all had to wade through them, as the horses mired with the least load upon them.' To make matters worse, some horses died after eating poison ivy. Although the hams were cut out and stored for an emergency, some women were heard to complain that they faced a triple-headed death, from starvation, cold and eating poisoned meat. And it was not just the humans who faced a dilemma. 'With snow over everything but the poison laurel, our horses were forced to eat it and die, or to starve and die.'

Amid the encircling gloom, only Barlow's eldest daughter Mrs Gaines was notably stoical. 'Why,' she said, 'we are in the midst of plenty – plenty of snow, plenty of wood to melt it, plenty of horse meat, plenty of dog meat if the worst comes.' Two things saved the beleaguered travellers. First, the temperature rose so that the snow turned to rain. It rained ceaselessly throughout forty-eight hours from 16 to 18 October, which enabled them to make better progress, even though they sat shivering all night over a fire as the water cascaded down. Then, on the 18th, they met up with the drovers taking cattle over the Cascades, who had left The Dalles eight days before. The drovers informed them that a relief party from Oregon City was camped in the valley below them. Palmer rode the five miles to the camp, only to find that the relief column, despairing of finding survivors, had turned back to Oregon City. Fortunately, they had not gone far and were fetched back.

The plea for help from the settlements had paid a rich dividend. The residents of Oregon City donated 1,100 pounds of flour and 100 pounds of sugar, tea and coffee to the beleaguered pioneers. The rescuers had bought eleven pack horses from the Indians and courageously trekked into the mountains. As Palmer led them back up the mountain, the rain turned to snow, which soon began to drift. For a few hours, Palmer thought he had lost the trail. The night of 19 October was spent in some despondency. But next morning the rescuers set out at 8 a.m. and after seven gruelling hours found the pioneers. Almost starving by now, they were overjoyed at the supplies, now confident that they had enough food to last them through to the settlements. While an advance party was sent to Oregon City to fetch pack horses, the exhausted Barlow party rested for five days before advancing.

On 26 October, the pioneers set out for the downward journey to Oregon City. Starting at 8 a.m., in heavy rain, which soon became snow, they were at first hampered by lack of forage for the horses, all the good grass having been eaten by the herds of cattle already driven over the Cascades by earlier parties of emigrants. They descended Laurel Hill 'like shot off a shovel' and were soon below the snowline. Whatever happened now, their worst troubles were over and they were certain not to starve. They struck the Big Sandy River and followed it for two days, crossing and recrossing. Without stepping stones, this proved difficult, so trees were felled to provide walkways. The vanguard of the pioneers finally left the Big Sandy behind on 29 October and struck across prairie country to Foster's ranch. Here there were ample provisions. Some emigrants immediately pressed on to Oregon City, but others rested and made a leisurely trip of it. The last party did not arrive in Oregon City until Christmas Day 1845, having been on the trail eight months and twenty-four days since leaving Fulton County, Missouri.

Dead reckoning showed that this route from The Dalles south of Mount Hood to Oregon City was 160 miles long, but it was only the middle eighty that needed a road built. Barlow had meanwhile asked the territorial legislature for a charter to build a road across the Cascades. Admiration for Barlow's pioneering heroism as well as continuing anger about the near disaster on Meek's cutoff made the legislators more than willing to listen to plans for avoiding the Columbia. It was agreed that a loan would be made to Barlow, and he would repay it from tolls on wagons using the new road. Armed with the necessary funds and manpower, Barlow waited until the summer of 1846, then returned to the conquest of the Cascades. Beginning at the western end of the Tygh valley, the road ran for eighty miles, the first fifteen following an old Indian trail, but the last sixty-five being hacked from the primeval forests, canyons, creeks and streams of the fearsome Cascades. The Oregon Trail now no longer ended with the ordeal by Columbia, and in 1846 two-thirds of new emigrants entered Oregon via the Barlow Road. By charging $5 a wagon, Barlow repaid the loan by 1847, after which he magnanimously turned his licence to print money over to the territorial government.

Despite the razor-edged experiences of those building the Barlow Road or reduced to despair on the Meek cutoff, in aggregate terms 1845 was a fairly complete triumph for the overland trails. Around 2,500 emigrants made their way to Oregon, the second highest total for the territory in the 1840s. Migration to California also experienced something of a quantum jump, as can be seen by a comparison of the easy travelling of the 1845 overlanders with the travails of the Stephens–Murphy party the year before; Lansford Hastings even got away with an act of consummate folly and hubris. The presence of Kearney's troops and Frémont's soldiers also increased the sense of security on the trails. There is a hint of over-confidence in some of the journals for 1845, which speak of the six-month trek almost as an extended holiday amid beautiful wild flowers and sublime landscapes. Hubris would bring nemesis in 1846 but, as so often, Fate found its victim not in the form of the man who pushed his luck but in gullible innocents whom he had duped.

EIGHT

CALIFORNIA CATCHES UP

Roughly the same number of emigrants ventured forth from Missouri in 1846 as in the previous year, but this time the proportions were very different. Whereas in 1845 only 260 out of a total of 2,760 had gone to California and the rest to Oregon, in 1846 California was the magnet, attracting 1,500 as against Oregon's 1,200, largely as a result of the assiduous propaganda of men like Lansford Hastings and Caleb Greenwood. One consequence of the bifurcation of emigrants was that the complex situation of 1845, with excessive social mobility from party to party and wagon train to wagon train, increased in 1846 by a significant factor. Whereas in 1845 the Greenwood–Ide party had been the only large-scale one travelling from Missouri to California, in 1846 there were three large caravans for California alone. Dale Morgan, the expert on the 1846 journeys, refers to 'the staggering complexity of the overland emigration' in that year.

As in 1845, large trains left from both Independence and St Joseph but, to add to the confusion, there was an increasing tendency to fragmentation on the trail, with smaller and smaller detachments forming breakaway movements from the parent caravans. From St Joseph, three main bodies can be discerned: a company led by William J. Martin, which was the front runner on the way west throughout 1846; a fifty-plus train led by Riley Gregg, which pioneered a new route to the Platte; and a forty-three-strong train under Fabritus Smith, which was the last to leave the St Joseph area. But diarist William Taylor gives an account of the journey with Martin's group that illustrates the extreme fissiparous factionalism of the caravans. An original party of twelve wagons overtook an independent company of eighteen wagons, then merged with Martin's twenty-seven wagons near the Big Blue River. The Martin wagon train in turn merged with a huge caravan (over 130 wagons and 1,000 cattle) which elected Elam Brown as captain, but soon after seceded. Near Soda

Springs, Taylor and eight other men in turn broke away from the Oregon-bound Martin company and struck out for California.

In all, about 274 emigrant wagons left St Joseph in 1846. From the rival 'jumping-off' point, Independence, 267 wagons departed. Four travel permutations were thus possible: St Joseph–California, St Joseph –Oregon, Independence–California, Independence–Oregon. But since so many people switched caravans and destinations en route, no lucid account of the 1846 overland experience can be given. One Oregon-bound party of twenty wagons from Independence chose William Keithly as captain; another of similar size and destination elected John Robinson into the role, but both parties employed the same man, Orus Brown, as pilot. Meanwhile, fifty-five wagons which had mustered at Independence to go to California chose William Henry Russell as their captain. Another twenty-wagon-strong California-bound party opted for Josiah Morin as their leader. The Russell company quickly became the dominant force on the California Trail: by the time this caravan reached the Wakarusa River it totalled seventy-two wagons (containing 130 men, 65 women and 125 children), 700 oxen and 300 mules, as well as numerous cattle and horses.

The emigrants from Independence did not set out in a very happy frame of mind. Jesse Quinn Thornton of Illinois, travelling with his wife, who joined the Russell company on 15 May with nine emigrant wagons (including, surprisingly, Lilburn W. Boggs who had been governor of Missouri in 1836-40), was sniffy about the whole overland experience. Revolted by Independence, which he described as 'a great Babel upon the border of the wilderness', he thought the motives of most of the overlanders in going west singularly confused: 'They agreed in the one general object – that of bettering their condition; but the particular means by which each proposed to attain his end, were as various as can well be imagined.' Thornton's concerns were predominantly military: he wanted the US government to build a chain of permanent military forts along the California and Oregon trails, as well as turnpike roads with bridges and ferries, and to this end weighed up every location and every campsite for its potential as a fort site. Significantly, too, he made a careful inventory of the firepower of the Russell party, which he estimated at 104 pistols, 155 guns, 1,672 pounds of lead and 1,100 pounds of powder.

Both the collective unhappiness of mind and Thornton's martial concerns were prompted by a threefold worry which beset the travellers. The greater aggression evinced by the Kansa Indians under their new chief, as reported by the 1845 emigrants, seemed to portend trouble, and there were those who seriously thought the Kansa in future might be as great a menace as the Pawnee and Sioux. Another Indian-related anxiety derived, oddly, from the unusual number of British army officers and sportsmen on the trail this summer; according to alarmists, these were agents sent from London, where the government, angry with the United States for its recent anti-British moves in Texas, California and (above all) Oregon, had determined to take revenge by raising the Plains Indians against the emigrants. But the most abiding fear was of the Mormons, now starting to move west in search of the promised land. Five thousand 'Saints', all armed with rifles, revolvers and knives, had supposedly vowed to avenge themselves for their persecution by the 'Gentiles' and intended to fall on the overlanders and massacre them once they were outside United States jurisdiction. The presence in the caravans of their arch-enemy Lilburn Boggs, who had persecuted them when governor of Missouri, adds plausibility to the tale.

Maybe this jitteriness manifested itself in a higher level of nervous aggression than usual. In the first three weeks on the trail, three separate serious incidents of violent behaviour were noted. The first involved two drivers, who drew knives; the second involved a quasi-biblical dispute over oxen, with the entire company being drawn in; the third, the gravest yet, escalated from fists to knives to pistols – had the combatants not been parted, one of them would surely have been killed. Edwin Bryant, observing the fistic outbreaks, was detached: 'If a man is predisposed to be quarrelsome, obstinate or selfish from his natural constitution, these repulsive traits are certain to be developed on a journey across the plains. The trip is a sort of a magic mirror, and exposes every man's qualities of heart connected with it, vicious or amiable.'

Yet quarrels not involving violence were also multitudinous this year. On 16–17 May, the first of many dissensions arose in the Russell company when two men who had 140 head of cattle with them were expelled for travelling with stock surplus to their requirements and the good order of the wagon train. On the 17th, while they were camped at the Shunganunga Creek, James G. Dunleavy, a Methodist minister, led a 'disaffected' group which voted to split off from the Russell party; on the 18th, Russell and thirty-five wagons moved forward towards the Kansas River while Dunleavy and another twenty-five wagons stayed put in camp. Bryant missed all the excitement, as he was in an advance party looking for water; while Dunleavy and Russell were at loggerheads, he was making amateur anthropological findings in a camp of Sac Indians.

Not all the disputes involved misfits, sociopaths or 'lowlives'. Jesse Quinn Thornton, a thirty-five-year-old Missouri lawyer, was quite firmly a member of the elite. Virginia-born, educated in London and a friend of Senator Benton, Horace Greeley and Stephen Douglas, Thornton, as his career often shows, had an amazing capacity to rub people up the wrong way. Before starting on the journey west, the cash-strapped Thornton had entered into a partnership with James Goode, whereby he found the means to fit out a wagon and team. Quite what the details were – whether Goode 'grubstaked' Thornton against the lawyer's future earnings in Oregon – does not appear. All we have is the sibylline utterance by an eyewitness that 'Good [sic] had furnished the means and Thornton had furnished the brains, and the means and the brains together did not work very well'. The partners were not many days out on the journey before a dispute arose over true ownership of wagon and team. This was to rumble away through May and finally explode in early June.

On 18 May, Russell and his party crossed the Kansas River by ferry and swam the stock across. The Kansas, though swollen by spring rains, was not quite the obstacle it had been in previous years. Although the Papins' ferry, established in 1843, had been swept away in the great floods of 1844, a Shawnee Indian named Charles Fish now operated a two-boat ferry, which took two wagons a trip on flatboats propelled by long poles, for a charge of one dollar per wagon. Fish and his half-breed partner made $40 from this one transaction alone, and were $400 to the good from ferriage by the end of June. As if to celebrate the trouble-free passage of the Kansas, twin boys were born to a woman named Martha Hall on the opposite bank.

On the 19th, nine wagons from Illinois joined the company, bringing the total in this party back up to forty-six wagons with fifty horses and 320 mules. The nine newcomers belonged to James Frazier Reed and George and Jacob Donner, who would go down in history as the famous (or infamous) Donner party. Reed was a wealthy forty-six-year-old of Polish origin, born in Northern Ireland, with sufficient elite connections to have in his pocket a letter of credential from the governor of Illinois. He had served in the Black Hawk campaign alongside Abraham Lincoln, and had made money as a merchant, railroad contractor and manufacturer. His main motive in travelling west was that his invalid wife needed a more salubrious climate, but he had also sustained some recent business reverses and may have thought it was time to move on to fresh pastures. His lavishly appointed party comprised his thirty-two-year-old wife Margaret and four children, plus Margaret's seventy-year-old mother, three teamsters in their twenties and two young travelling companions, brother and sister, Baylis and Eliza Williams.

The Donners were Reed's friends. The two brothers, George, sixty-two, and Jacob, sixty-five, were classic patriarchs. George had been married three times, and Tamsen, his third wife, was with him, together with her three young daughters and two older girls, the issue of Donner's second marriage. The complicated kinship system of the Donners is shown by the fact that Elizabeth, Jacob Donner's wife, was the sister of George's second wife, and that she in turn had had a previous marriage. Two sons from that marriage accompanied her, besides five children from wedlock with Jacob Donner. With the Donners were four young teamsters in their twenties. Like Reed, the Donners were wealthy. Perhaps the most striking and forceful of them was Tamsen, who had ambitions to open a school for genteel young ladies in California and had brought along paints, books and school supplies for that purpose. A Yankee and one of the first female freelance journalists, Tamsen also had literary ambitions and planned to write a book about the journey west. The *New York Herald* described her thus: 'a perfect specimen of our American women – intelligent, educated, brave and spirited. If the rest of the females of the expedition are like Mrs Donner, there need be no fear of the expedition.'

The march resumed on 20 May. Seventeen more wagons joined the train on 20–21 May, bringing the total back to and beyond the previous level (now sixty-seven); predictably, however, there was further dissension on the 22nd and thirteen wagons under Joseph Gordon and Gallant Dickenson separated and went on ahead. Such was the neurosis of 1846 on the overland trail that they also immediately regretted their action and applied for readmission. At a general meeting of the emigrating company, it was decided not to allow Gordon and Dickenson back immediately but to let them stew for two or three days, giving them time to repent. The tactic did not work. Infuriated that they were being put on probation, Dickenson and Gordon changed their minds again and opted to go it alone.

The next barrier for all travellers was the Big Blue, which proved unfordable this year as a result of terrific storms on 26–27 May; for four nights the emigrants camped on the bank of the flooded river until 30–31 May, when the travellers finally managed to construct an enormous 'canoe' (which they named the Blue River Rover) and took the wagons over. This was a difficult and hazardous operation (because of the swiftness of the river and the weight of the wagons), of which some idea can be gauged from remarks by Bryant: 'The current was so strong, that near the shore, where the water was not more than three or four feet in depth, the strength of a man could with difficulty breast it. One of the canoes was swamped on the western side in drawing the third wagon from it.'

The yo-yo pattern of participation continued on the 28th, when eight more wagons joined the Russell party as it waited fretfully on the banks of the engorged Big Blue. Russell's frustration was all the keener since both parties who had thrown off his yoke (the Dunleavy company and the Gordon–Dickenson dissidents) had managed to get across the Big Blue before it flooded on the 26th. But this was not Russell's only source of frustration. He and Bryant ran up against a brick wall when trying to impose proper discipline. George McKinstry, one of the diarists with this party, wrote: 'The meeting adjourned as soon as possible with a determination not to hold any more meetings as the young men were determined to do their own meeting and their own fighting.'

On the 29th, Mrs Sarah Keyes, who had enjoyed feeble health since joining the wagon train, died and was buried the same day under a tree near the camp. But by this time individual tragedy was subsumed in a general peevishness which finally found expression in a stormy general meeting of the company on 2 June. Having built up its strength since the earlier defections, the wagon train now split in half again, dividing into an Oregon and a California faction. Bryant claimed the decision was made because he and Russell were tired of having to make Solomonic adjudications on matters of no interest or concern to them: what did they care which of the hot-blooded Oregon faction really owned which oxen? But the real reason was tension over the conflicting claims of Jesse Quinn Thornton and his partner John Goode.

A court convened to try to settle this rancorous dispute. At first, it decided to split the assets, with one man having the wagon and the other the oxen. The obvious objection was that the one was useless without the other. The court split into two factions, one favouring Thornton, the other Goode. But Thornton had polish and some political skill; he was clearly a 'gentleman' and that weighed with the majority. On the grounds that Thornton had a wife and Goode was a single man, the majority decided to award the wagon and team to Thornton. Curiously, the pro-Thornton faction consisted of the California-bound emigrants and the pro-Goode of the Oregonians. Thornton, originally bound for Oregon, now declared that he would go with his friends to California.

But that was not the end of the affair. The disgruntled Oregonians refused to accept the majority decision, seized the disputed wagon and announced their own judgement: the assets should be divided and, since Goode had put up the initial money, Thornton should pay it off by driving the team across the plains. Thornton indignantly refused to do physical labour; his status as a gentleman precluded that possibility, in his own mind at least. Once again, he intrigued with the Californians and, with his political skills, convinced them that he had been the victim of injustice. When it became clear that Thornton did not intend to do a hand's turn to pay off his debt, the indignant Oregonians announced a definitive split. By now this solution was accepted with alacrity by both sides, and it was agreed that the Oregon party should press on ahead, putting daylight between them and the Californians. But the decision was not popular among the young women who, in just three weeks, had found beaux and sweethearts; the decision to split the wagon train aborted many a budding romance and engendered emotional and tearful farewells.

As if things were not going badly enough for the caravan, disease now lent a hand. Thornton and his invalid wife, who were supposed to be reinvigorated by the healthful air of the frontier, complained of worsening health; since Thornton was both asthmatic and hypochondriac, it is difficult to be sure how seriously ill he was. He claimed he was 'unwell since coming upon the waters of the Nebraska, owing to mixed salts, glauber salts, alum and magnesia' – a list so precise that suspicions of hypochondria are enhanced. But certainly there was nothing imaginary about some of the other maladies suffered by overlanders on this trip. Pneumonia, tuberculosis, scurvy, typhoid fever, malaria, smallpox, measles, mumps, whooping cough and, above all, dysentery and diarrhoea were all reported. As the historian John Unruh has pointed out, 'the initial portion of the trail to Fort Laramie, otherwise the easiest section of the journey, occasioned the most disease-induced deaths'. The emigrants themselves thought eating fish and the high saline and alkaline content of the water were the main causes of their ailments.

Diarrhoea and dysentery were probably the result of one or more of the following factors: poorly kept food, dirty cooking utensils, bad cooking – 'often a perfect mass of indigestible filth too crude even for the stomach of an ostrich' was one description of a campfire supper – and amoebas in the water. Scurvy was caused by lack of vitamin C: there were no fresh fruit and vegetables and the only source of ascorbic acid was from berries picked by the wayside or vegetables traded with the Indians. The habit of drying and jerking buffalo meat hardly helped, as the vitamin content of the meat was thereby diminished. The two most likely overall causes of emigrant illness, however, were the viruses brought together as if in convention by travellers from many different parts of the United States, which overrode carefully built-up local immunities, and the sheer hardship of life on the trail. Both men and women worked incessantly at back-breaking toil, performed in excessive heat or teeming rain and on bitterly cold and windswept plains or at high altitude (needless to say, the effects of altitude sickness were largely unknown).

The resistance of the human body to bacteria and viruses in such circumstances was unlikely to be great.

Edwin Bryant's background was in journalism – he had been editor of the Louisville *Courier* – but he had picked up a smattering of medical knowledge in his early years. He made the mistake of sounding authoritative when emigrants discussed their ailments with him, and then found that he had the reputation of being a part-qualified doctor. Since very few professional physicians took to the overland trails before the 1849 gold rush, Bryant was soon inundated with requests for help. Typical was an incident on 14 June when the wagon train was moving up the South Platte. A party of outriders from a caravan twenty miles ahead came into camp, looking for a doctor. Bryant was recommended. The riders told him that a ten-year-old boy had fallen from the tongue of a wagon on 5 June, and the wheels had passed over him and crushed one of his legs. His feckless parents laid him in the wagon without even dressing the wound. After a week of agonising pain, the boy said he could feel worms crawling in his leg, and his mother found the flesh swarming with maggots.

After a hard ride to the wagon train, Bryant sized up the situation. The boy had sustained a compound fracture, gangrene had set in, and it was clear that he was dying. Fatalistically, Bryant explained the situation and pointed out that an operation could not save the boy; it would merely be pointless agony. The boy's mother insisted, so Bryant enlisted the help of a French-Canadian drover who had once been a surgeon's assistant. The drover assembled an arsenal of butcher's knives, handsaws and a shoemaker's awl. They gave the boy laudanum but it had no noticeable effect. Then they strapped him to a packing case. The French Canadian first cut through the leg below the knee, releasing an explosion of pus, and had almost severed the limb when he decided he should amputate further up, above the knee. After an hour and three-quarters, he hacked through the bone with a handsaw, but at this point the boy died.

The emigrants accepted the cycle of death and birth with more stoicism than any modern Western society could muster. After dispensing advice to the other sick emigrants, Bryant called on Jesse Quinn Thornton, who had decided, after all, to go to Oregon and had ridden ahead to join the Oregonians (there is an untold story here on which, unfortunately, all the annalists are silent). The Oregon caravan was about a mile away from the macabre sequence with the dying boy and on his arrival the Thorntons invited Bryant to dine with them on roast antelope and buffalo stew. Then, at nine in the evening, after the day's work was done, the travellers assembled at the tent of a Mr Lard, where his daughter Mary was married to Septimus Mootrey. The men had shaved and changed their clothes and the women appeared in their prettiest dresses and had even managed to find candles and make a wedding cake. After a religious service presided over by the Revd Mr Cornwall, the guests formed a procession behind a fiddler and conducted the newly-weds to the honeymoon tent. As if to complete the human life cycle, word came in from a nearby wagon that a woman had just given birth to a son. The moral of 'life goes on' was harped on sententiously and sanctimoniously by the diarists.

The Russell caravan reached the Platte at Grand Island on 8 June without incident. There were the usual broken axle-trees – but this did not detain them as they had brought spares from Independence – and even a minor skirmish with the Pawnee, but for the most part Bryant was able to indulge his passion for botany, and he noted with delight the varied flora of the plains: larkspur, lupin, indigo, pink verbena, wild geranium. The travellers made good progress as far as Ash Hollow, where there was a log cabin that served as an 'emigrant post office'. Known to travellers as 'Ash Hollow Hotel', the cabin, built by trappers in 1845, contained three main kinds of 'mail'. One was genuine post, letters addressed to people in the four corners of the globe, with a request that those finding them should forward them to the nearest US post office. Another was a series of small advertisements of the 'wanted' variety, usually concerned with lost or strayed cattle. Finally, there were open letters, either witty or abusive, dilating on the political situation of the day.

'Ash Hollow Hotel' was merely the finest and most complete of the emigrant 'post offices'. It was the custom of all overland parties to use a 'roadside telegraph' – that is, to leave messages by the side of the trail for others, usually attached to strips of cloth to alert them. The messages were either written on paper, which was then inserted into the notched end of a stick or pinned to trees, bushes or grave markers; or, if paper was not available, would be carved on trees, rocks or on the skulls and bones of cattle, oxen, buffalo, elk, deer or antelope. The messages usually warned of Indian depredations, or poisoned or brackish water, and gave details of accidents and the progress of invalids or convalescents. Given human nature, it was not surprising that occasional idiots tampered with the messages or maliciously left hoax letters or misleading directions to bogus cutoffs.

At Ash Hollow, Russell resigned his post as captain, and all his acolytes, such as Bryant, resigned their minor offices in sympathy. Russell's ostensible reason was the ill-health he had been suffering, but it is clear that the real reason was twofold. He was tired of the indiscipline, the factionalism, the breakaway movements and the seceding wagons; and he wanted to get to California faster – already there were signs that he and Bryant were concerned that they might be trapped in the winter snows of the Sierra Nevada if they did not make faster progress. Now he had the excuse of abandoning the lumbering wagon train to ride ahead to Fort Laramie, whence he would proceed to the Pacific by much faster pack mule. There is some evidence that Russell was widely perceived as a figure of fun. A veteran of the Black Hawk war and one-time secretary to Henry Clay, Russell had the honorary southern title of colonel, given to many Dixieland denizens with the gift for tub-thumping oratory, orotund and prolix rhetoric and good opinions of themselves. He had the nickname of 'Owl' Russell, it was said, because he once heard owls who-whooing in the woods and yelled back into the woods: 'Colonel William H. Russell of Kentucky – a bosom friend of Henry Clay.' He was the classic hail-fellow-well-met, but his Southern courtesy had obviously begun to wear thin on the 1846 emigrants.

But Russell was by no means the only well-connected 'elite' emigrant to discover that social status meant little out in the wilderness, and that men were judged brutally by results alone. Judge Josiah Morin, heading the embryonic version of what later became the Harlan–Young party (at this stage George Harlan was adamant he did not want the post of captain), experienced all of Russell's problems, and more. In the group of wagons he commanded were nine young German-speaking emigrants, three from Alsace-Lorraine, three from Switzerland and three from the fatherland proper; the Swiss Heinrich Lienhard kept a memorable journal of 1846 and was one of the best diarists of the entire overland migration. Another notable in this party was Jacob D. Hoppe, who in the early stages of the journey liked to travel alone (except for his family), separate from the other wagons. The story was that he had killed a black slave in Missouri and crossed into the wilderness to escape punishment. But he feared pursuers or bounty hunters, which was why he was never to be found in his wagon when it was camped or at rest.

A primitive form of class conflict seems to have assailed the Morin caravan. Such at least seems to be the interpretation to put on Lienhard's rather Delphic words: 'Some families who imagined themselves on a higher social level and who displayed a kind of aristocratic attitude brought about the first feelings of discontent among the group.' At any rate, Morin's initial incumbency did not last even as far as the Big Blue. The quasi-democratic rage for frequent elections on the trail played into the hands of Peter Inman, a self-styled preacher but really a horse-thief, who conspired to unseat the judge. Tall, with a squint, Inman got himself elected by the simple expedient of promising to provide free whiskey for his fellow-travellers. But the electors regretted their action as soon as they had done it. One remarked: 'Inman was pretty much of a fool, an uneducated rattle-brained fellow who would like nothing better than to boss other people, and who would be a regular slave driver.'

When Inman failed to make good on his election pledge, there were murmurings which soon became louder until they reached a crescendo: 'Inman is a tyrant'; 'He's a fool'; 'He doesn't know his business.' Camped along the Big Blue, the migrants petitioned for another election. Inman was thrown out and Judge Morin reinstated. The twenty-four-hour captain, who anticipated a famous twentieth-century adage by having just one day of fame, found himself deposed and did not take it well. He yelled at the electors: 'Shoot, go to hell, damn fools you.' But the reinstatement of Morin solved nothing. Next day, thirteen wagons (including the Hoppe family and the two vehicles with the German speakers) deserted him and joined the nearby Dickenson party. The reconstituted parties then became mutually hostile and tried to race each other daily to campsites.

Lienhard was as acute an observer of the trail as Edwin Bryant, and duly noted the buffalo, snakes, prairie dogs, coyotes and wolves, including two huge snowy-white members of the lupine family which had been shot by the emigrants and left on the trail. There was the usual litany of fist fights and even a tense encounter with 150 sullen Pawnee braves. But the besetting sin of the emigrants – factionalism and internecine in-fighting – was never far away. When they reached the Platte, the Germans were on Dickenson's right flank along the north bank, which meant that Dickenson always enjoyed an uninterrupted river view. When the party forded the river and switched to the south bank, the Germans naturally thought it was their turn to occupy the riverside berth. Dickenson, however, insisted on his 'rightful' place next to the river, which caused those on the previous right flank to split off and form a breakaway group under Jacob Hoppe. Thereafter, predictably, the two groups spent the entire passage up the Platte to Fort Laramie passing and repassing each other with the competitive edge of fanatics who no longer really knew what their game was.

As all the wagons approached Fort Laramie, they were strung out across the plains in discrete parties, not so much in ribbon formation but more like a river that disappears underground for a while, then reappears. Since Bryant and Russell and their friends and George McKinstry from the same party rode ahead to Fort Laramie on horseback on 20 June and passed many other wagon trains, we can form a good idea of the location of the various groups, which of course had splintered still further since Independence and St Joseph. They overtook the Dickenson and Gordon group (in which diarist Virgil Pringle was travelling), in fourteen wagons, almost immediately and overhauled the Oregon-bound train (including Thornton) two miles west of Fort Laramie on 23 June. Meanwhile, the party that Bryant had attended with the dying boy (including diarist Nicholas Carriger) and which had been lagging in the rear, overtook what used to be the Russell party on 20 June, leaving that troubled caravan as the backmarker among the significant wagon groups. Most of the wagons on the trail reached Fort Laramie and environs in the last week of June, but were far behind the leaders in this year's race to the Pacific. The wagons led by Charles Taylor, Larkin Stanley and John Craig – that is, the train that started from St Joseph originally as the Martin company – had swept through Laramie as early as 10 June.

Another arrival at Fort Laramie was probably the most famous of all the travellers this year. The man who would be both America's greatest historian and the greatest American historian was, in 1846, a twenty-four-year-old rich Bostonian and recent graduate of Harvard, who harboured a desire to write books about the eighteenth-century Anglo-French wars in North America, and to this end wanted to see something of the wild Indians who would form such a significant part of his narratives. Francis Parkman and his young cousin Quincy A. Shaw met up in St Louis in April and took a Missouri steamer, the *Radnor*, to Kansas Landing (later Kansas City). With Parkman and Shaw now were their guide Henry Chatillon, a buffalo-hunter, and the cart-driver Antoine de Laurier. After visiting Independence and Westport, Parkman made a study of the nearby Shawnee and Wyandot Indians before proceeding to Fort Leavenworth, where he met the men with whom he would travel the Oregon Trail: the British Army captain Bill Chandler, his brother Jack Chandler and an English 'sportsman' named Romaine – the same who had been on the Bidwell expedition in 1841.

After dining with General Kearney at Fort Leavenworth, the Chandler party struck across country and picked up the Oregon Trail on 16 May. A week later they crossed the Big Blue by raft and the same day made their first contact with emigrant wagons – in fact the Keithley party out of St Joseph. Parkman had set out in high hopes of his British travelling companions. He wrote to his mother on 12 May: 'We find them exceedingly intelligent and agreeable and consider ourselves very fortunate in meeting with such a party.' But a month in their company changed all that. His journals and letters increasingly made Romaine and the Chandlers out to be the kind of 'doncherknow' monocle-popping fops and upper-class British morons of a kind beloved of a certain type of Hollywood movie. On 7 June, he wrote in his journal: 'The lagging pace of the emigrants – the folly of Romaine – and the old womanism of the Capt. combine to disgust us. We are resolved to push on alone, as soon as we have crossed the South Fork, which will probably be tomorrow.'

Nonetheless, it was evident that Parkman was sensuously drunk with the austere beauty of the plains – their flora, fauna and even their ascetic landscape. On 8 June, he made notes on yet another emigrant company formed by breakaway movements: this time the Elam Brown company. According to Parkman, the Pawnee had killed one man in this party and so struck them with terror that they had formed laager and not even dared to go out to look for his body; six hundred Sioux had then raided into the camp and carried off all their best horses. The Sioux attack was probably a tall story pitched at Parkman by the pioneers, but the ordeal of the Elam Brown party has a sound enough foundation in fact. Starting from St Joseph, this party was thirty wagons strong by the time it reached the Platte. But there disaster struck. One night, the cattle were spooked by buffalo and started a stampede, which scattered the kine across the plains. The Brown party spent a week trying to round them up, but were still 120 beasts short, including sixty-two oxen. This was a devastating blow, and it was only by buying and borrowing yoke animals from other trains that the party was able to complete the journey to Fort Laramie.

As for lost oxen and cattle, those the Indians did not get would soon fall prey to mountain lions and other predators, especially wolves. Bryant, who later noticed many hard-pressed overlanders abandoning oxen in short-sighted folly, wrote:

Oxen, when footsore, or exhausted by fatigue, are left by the emigrants, and immediately become the victims of the wolves, who give them no rest until they fall. I have sometimes traced an ox, pursued by wolves, along the trail for ten or twenty miles, and noticed the places where he would turn and give battle to his remorseless pursuers. The result in every instance was, that I found the dead carcass or the skeleton of the ox, upon which the wolves and ravens had been feasting. Domesticated animals, unprotected, cannot resist the persevering attacks of the wolves, conducting their warfare with all the skill of instinct, sharpened often by famine. The deer and antelope are compelled frequently to shelter themselves from the attacks of these animals under the strong protection of the buffaloes, and you sometimes see herds of buffaloes and antelopes mingling and grazing together.

Parkman reached Fort Laramie on 15 June, five days after the party containing Taylor, Craig and Stanley. He had a letter of introduction for Bissonette's partner James Bordeaux, who was in temporary command at Fort Laramie, but when introduced to them, Bordeaux at first regarded them with suspicion, as rival traders. Parkman noted with contempt that Bordeaux was illiterate and had to have the letter read to him. Reassured and suddenly recalling his duties as 'mine host', Bordeaux provided Parkman with the best 'apartments' the fort had to offer, which was not saying much. But getting the best meant nothing anyway, as notions of privacy were unknown. Indians walked in unannounced and stretched out on the floor, while curious pioneer women pressed their noses against the window to observe the peculiar scene. Whether because of this, or more likely a natural visceral distaste for the type of person Bordeaux represented, Parkman always loathed the commandant. He took great delight in recounting Bordeaux's fight with a French Canadian named Perrault. Bordeaux got the worse of the encounter and, Parkman says, behaved in a cowardly manner; but he was the commander so he had Perrault kicked out of the fort.

Intermittently for the next fortnight, Parkman watched the emigrants trailing in, acting as a magnet both for the nearby Sioux who hoped to trade and the trappers and mountain men who descended from their fastnesses to fleece the naive newcomers. Parkman's opinion of the emigrants, all of them from middling social sectors, was notoriously low. This is perhaps not surprising from a patrician Boston Brahmin, but one shudders to think what he would have made of the genuine *canaille* who thronged the trails in the gold rush years. In a letter to his mother on 19 June, he is characteristically unsparing:

We have passed on the road eight or ten large companies . . . bound for Oregon or California, and most of them ignorant of the country they are going to and the journey to it . . . Sometimes a thunderstorm will come up and frighten their cattle, or the wolves will make a noise and startle them . . . meanwhile the women will get impatient and cry to go home again, and the men will quarrel and complain till the party splits up into two or three divisions that in future travel separately.

Close encounters with the emigrants did nothing to improve his view of them. He described what used to be Russell's party as a drunken rabble. They had discovered, he wrote, that they had encumbered themselves with too many supplies for the journey to California, so traded their goods for whiskey, which they were quaffing in vast quantities. Almost the worst offender was the Kentucky 'colonel', 'Owl'

Russell himself. Tall, lanky, dressed in dingy broadcloth coat, he harangued the assembled topers in the style of the stump orator. 'With one hand,' wrote Parkman, 'he sawed the air, and with the other clutched firmly a brown whiskey-jug, which he applied every moment to his lips, forgetting that he had drained the contents long ago.' When Parkman was introduced to the colonel, Russell buttonholed him by seizing the leather fringes of his coat and began a long *cri de coeur*. 'His men, he said, had mutinied and deposed him; but still he exercised over them the influence of a superior mind; in all but name he was yet their chief. As the colonel spoke I looked round on the wild assemblage, and could not help thinking that he was but ill-fitted to conduct such men across the deserts to California.'

Parkman spent as little time with the emigrants as he could manage, preferring to conduct anthropological investigations in the Sioux villages in the environs of Laramie – this was, after all, why he had come west. But on 28 June he rode down to the rival collection of log cabins called Fort Bernard and was surprised to meet some educated men; it has been speculated that he might have met Bryant and Thornton, though George Stewart cynically suggests that if the vainglorious Thornton had met a Harvard graduate, he would certainly have mentioned the fact. The inference that Bryant was at hand is strengthened by Russell's presence, on another of his benders: Parkman notes: 'Russel [*sic*] drunk as a pigeon.' On the other hand, Bryant's diary entry for 28 June shows him and Russell already on the trail beyond Fort Laramie. Clearly, one (or both) got their dates mixed up. In any case, that was the end of Parkman's significant observation of the 1846 emigrants. After spending weeks in the Black Hills observing the Sioux, he made his way home by a more southerly route, taking in Pueblo on the upper Arkansas River, Bent's Fort and part of the Santa Fe Trail.

The stopover at Fort Laramie was not just one long drunken carouse, however. The emigrants had serious, life-and-death decisions to take, for the as yet unseen Lansford Hastings was weaving an evil spell that would beguile some overlanders and take others to the jaws of hell. To make sense of it all, we have to remember that 1845 was the year of Hastings's *Emigrants' Guide*, in which he promised those who came to California a miracle route across the desert. Hastings had a wild notion, unwarranted by any geographical or topographical knowledge or surveys, but simply an idea plucked from the top of his head, that the overland route from Missouri to California could be shaved down to 2,100 miles, taking just four months, if wagons left the established trails at Fort Bridger and headed west south-west to the Salt Lake. The giveaway phrase in his guide is 'and thence continuing down to the Bay of St. Francisco', as if it was a pleasant hike through flat green pastureland. As Ray Allen Billington rightly remarks: 'Thus did Lansford Hastings wave away burning deserts and towering mountains, and with a stroke of the pen create the Hastings Cutoff.'

But Hastings had a dazzling aura of infallibility about him, which his rash but successful gamble in travelling from Missouri to California in four months in the winter of 1845 seemed only to enhance. Nothing succeeds like success, and Hastings really did seem like a man on a roll, someone for whom things simply did not go wrong. Encouraged by the triumphant outcome of all his wild gambles hitherto, he was intriguing to get the Mormons, now definitely on the move under Brigham Young, to settle in California and was involved in land speculation with John Sutter. Bidwell, the 1841 pioneer, who knew Hastings well and had helped him to lay the foundations of the new town of Sutterville, testified that there was no end to the man's ambitions; he had brought a party down from Oregon in 1843 with the express intention of wresting California from Mexico and becoming the territory's first governor. The 1843 project had failed, but Hastings's ambitions remained the same.

Attempts have been made to rehabilitate Hastings, but they are unconvincing. His defenders claim that he did not have presidential ambitions, that he did not seek to ape Sam Houston nor did he meet him in Texas in 1844, that many sections of the *Emigrants' Guide* are sound, and that over-the-top pro-California propaganda was also spouted (for their own purposes) by Frémont, Vasquez and Bridger. All this may be true, but it proves nothing to the point. The charge against Hastings was (and is) that he played with other people's lives by exhorting them to take a 'cutoff' of which he had no knowledge. Nobody has managed to shake the substance of the charge against Hastings, which is that he was an irresponsible liar and fantasist. Medorem Crawford, his companion on the 1842 trek to Oregon, scrawled a succession of apoplectic comments in the margin of his copy of the *Emigrants' Guide*: 'absolutely false', 'bosh', 'phenominal [sic] lying'. Bancroft, the great historian of California, called Hastings's work 'a piece of special pleading . . . painted in *couleur de rose*'. Jesse Quinn Thornton, an eyewitness in a position to know, described Hastings as 'the Baron Münchausen of travels', and as a cynic who 'evidently regarded the emigrants as fair game'.

Hastings was in bad odour even before he left California in early 1846. The US consul Thomas O. Larkin was another who thought Hastings's book mendacious trash and reported that even those who welcomed American immigration were angry with him for making California out to be a problem-free paradise. Unaware of or unconcerned with such misgivings, the dauntless Hastings finally got properly under way (after a few reconnaissance forays) on his eastward journey on 27 April. With him went James Clyman, the doyen of the 1844 migrants, James Hudspeth, Old Greenwood and his remaining sons, sixteen other men and a sprinkling of women and children. They reached the summit of the high sierras on 1 May, completed the descent to the Truckee valley a week later, and arrived at the Humboldt Sink soon after. On 16 May, the party split, with Clyman, Hastings, Hudspeth and a handful of men pressing ahead while Greenwood guided the remainder to Fort Hall. The Clyman–Hastings party crossed the Great Salt Lake Desert – a formidable undertaking even for a doughty plainsman like Clyman, as this was an eighty-mile waterless wasteland, home to scorpions, snakes and scaly lizards, and a dustbowl of foul, choking alkaline dust – then swung south of the Great Salt Lake through the Wasatch mountains, the Weber River and Echo Canyon to a resting place on Bear River (near present-day Evanston, Utah). Turning south-east, they reached Fort Bridger on 7 June.

Next day, they parted. Quite why is not explained, but perhaps Clyman had already had enough of Hastings's wild fancies and phantasmagorical cutoffs. Hastings and Hudspeth evidently did some reconnaissance trips and then took up station around South Pass, ready to intercept the emigrants, who all had to pass this way; had he remained at Fort Bridger, they might have eluded him by going on the inaptly named Sublette Cutoff. It was on his eastbound onward journey that Clyman made contact with the leaders of the westbound pack. Swinging south of the Sublette Cutoff, he rafted across the Green River with difficulty and came to South Pass on 18 June. The next significant landmark was Independence Rock and, two days after passing there, on 23 June, he met Taylor, Craig and Stanley, who had originally started from St Joseph with the Martin company. Next day, he passed another three companies, and from then until his arrival in Fort Laramie on the 27th he met a continual stream of emigrants.

Even so, he was not the first eastbound traveller that year to get to Laramie. That honour belonged to the doyen of 1845, Joel Palmer, who was returning from Oregon after his labours on the Barlow Road the previous winter. Starting from Whitman's mission at Walla Walla on 17 April, he made a rapid and uneventful journey – the only excitement being a distant war party of Crows whom Palmer carefully avoided 'as they are generally for a fight' – and arrived at Fort Laramie on 8 June, two days ahead of the first westbound emigrants and a week ahead of

Parkman. He counted the wagon trains as he passed them, and provided an accurate count of 541 vehicles, 212 of them supposedly going to California. On 18 June, he too met the luckless Elam Brown caravan, as well as the Fabritus Smith train, and was able to confirm in detail the death of Edward Trimble at the hands of the Pawnee.

At Fort Laramie, James Clyman met ex-Governor Boggs and James Frazier Reed, old comrades of his from the Black Hawk war. They stayed up late at night, chewing the fat and discussing the route ahead. Boggs introduced him to Judge Morin, who provided Clyman with an excellent cup of coffee, the first proper serving of that beverage he had had since the autumn of 1845. Clyman warned them not to take the Hastings cutoff, which was already being excitedly discussed at Fort Laramie, and was so downbeat about California in general that Morin and Boggs told him next morning they were now determined to go to Oregon (Boggs later changed his mind). But James Reed was unconvinced. Clyman remembered the conversation as follows: 'I told him to take the regular wagon track and never leave it – it is barely possible to get through if you follow it – and it may be impossible if you don't.' Reed then made his famous but fateful reply: 'There is a nigher route, and it is of no use to take so much of a roundabout route.'

In addition to his scepticism about the Hastings cutoff, Clyman poured cold water on the notion of California as a land flowing with milk and honey. From his personal experience, he said, the climate was too dry for successful farming, the soil was arid, and farmers were more likely to starve than make a fortune. Lienhard recalled that a particular impression was made by the women travelling with Clyman, who endorsed his negative views. This had an especially depressing effect on the female emigrants, many of whom began weeping and lamenting and trying emotional blackmail to get their husbands to return to Missouri. A man named William Bryant adroitly called his wife's bluff by offering to pay for her to be escorted back to the Midwest without him. This did the trick, and soon the wailing women concluded there was nothing for it but to press on stoically.

At Fort Bernard, Clyman repeated his unwelcome tenets, but found notable resistance in Edwin Bryant, who confided to his journal that he thought Clyman a liar, a man pursuing some personal hobby-horse or agenda: 'It was easy to perceive . . . that he had a motive for his conduct, more powerful than his regard for the truth.' Why was the opinion about the Hastings cutoff of an experienced mountain man like Clyman so blithely disregarded? It is a question we are entitled to ask. Several answers are possible. Perhaps Clyman muddied the waters by attacking

California *and* the cutoff, so that his more specific warning about Hastings got lost in his general message about California; it is well known that most human beings tend to take in just one piece of information at a time. Perhaps he alienated his audience by describing California as a criminal refuge – 'not a man was to be found in the country, now that he had left it, who was not as thoroughly steeped in villainy as the most hardened graduate of the penitentiary' are the words Bryant puts into Clyman's mouth. Perhaps it was simply snobbery. Jesse Quinn Thornton wrote that Clyman's 'evil report' of California was discounted because of the Clyman party's 'woebegone appearance'. But most likely, Clyman simply collided with a stubborn 'will to believe'; he was telling the emigrants what they did not want to hear, so they ignored him.

Clyman continued his journey down the Platte on 28 June, shortly afterwards meeting Bissonette, on his way back from Missouri with supplies. He met a number of mule-pack teams but no more wagons until 2 July, when, at Ash Hollow, he encountered the so-called 'Mississippi Saints' – the only Mormon wagon train to get this far west, who were dismayed to find that there were no 'Saints' ahead of them. Clyman completed his journey without incident and arrived in Independence on 22 July, having made a careful inventory of all wagons travelling west which almost exactly matches Palmer's similar list. Meanwhile, his *bête noire*, Bryant, was busy preparing a mule train with which he and eight comrades (including Owl Russell) intended to press on at great speed to California, definitively forsaking wagon trains. So strong was Bryant's animus against wagon travel by now that he played the subversive, going round the caravans and trying to persuade other people to join him, especially those he knew well, like Boggs.

The 1846 emigration, the most dramatic of all years in the history of the overland trails, was also notable for lifting a veil on the one subject on which the pioneers were usually silent: sex. Two highly-sexed women made sufficient impression on the diarists and annalists to achieve a tiny footnote in history, and thereby shed light on an area contemporaries liked to shroud in obscurity. Jacob Hoppe, the man with the shady, homicidal past, was travelling with his wife, a pretty young woman in her twenties, and three children, plus a buxom, fair-haired maidservant in her early twenties named Lucinda Jane Saunders. The 'five German boys' (two of them Swiss) who travelled together in one wagon were Heinrich Lienhard, George Zins, Valentine Diel, Heinrich Thomen and Jacob Ripstein. Lucinda earmarked them as possible prey and began by volunteering to do their washing. But Mrs Hoppe spotted the ploy and intervened, saying, 'Lucinda, leave that be. I'll see that you have enough work to do for us, without doing the wash for other people.'

But George Zins was a man with a definite appetite for women and soon made Lucinda his mistress, telling her he would like to marry her but was too poor. The Hoppes threw Lucinda out, so she got a job as servant to the Harlan family. Lucinda then cast her sights on a poor and not very bright eighteen-year-old driver, with whom she actually went through a form of marriage, solemnised by one of the many 'preachers' who frequented the wagon trails. It was a curiosity of the emigrants – or perhaps simply a function of their prudery – that whenever they discovered two young people cohabiting, they would put on their best clothes and appear outside their wagon, saying they had come for the 'wedding', thus trying to pressurise the couple into formal marriage. But after just one night with Lucinda, the groom refused ever to be in the same wagon with her again; the 'marriage' was then considered dissolved.

Further sexual shenanigans arose in the Morin party when the 'husband' of a skinny widow with two children left her wagon saying that he could no longer bear to live with her: 'He wanted to have some rest at night.' The opportunistic Zins, fresh from his fling with Lucinda, moved in and became the woman's lover. Predictably, a crowd of 'wedding guests' appeared outside the woman's wagon in their finery. The widow welcomed the incursion and said that, since Zins had promised her marriage, she was ready to go through with the ceremony. Zins, as always when backed into a corner, pleaded that he could barely keep himself in food and could certainly not afford a wife. The emigrants, baulked of their prey, got their revenge by taunting Zins, who stormed off in a huff.

At Fort Laramie, the widow announced that as no man would agree to be her protector, she would stay at the fort. The five 'German boys' were asked if they would take her in, but quickly made an excuse and left. An emigrant called Wright, who thought it was his Christian duty to succour the poor and homeless, offered to take the woman in his wagon, but Mrs Wright put her foot down very firmly. The incident became something of a *cause célèbre*, as Parkman noted in a letter to his father:

A party that passed yesterday, left at the Fort a woman, who, it seems, had become a scandal to them, and, what had probably much greater weight, caused them trouble to feed and take care of her. She is now lodged among the squaws of the traders – a most pitiable situation; for it is quite impossible that she will be able to get to the settlements before many months at least, and meanwhile she is left alone among the Indian women, and the half-savage retainers of the Company.

In the privacy of his journal, Parkman was more explicit about the case. 'One woman, of more than suspected chastity, is left at the Fort, and Bordeaux is fool enough to receive her.' Nothing is said about the woman's two children and what happened to them. George Stewart is extremely jaundiced about the likely outcome for the widow: 'As for the widow's ultimate fate, we may be permitted after this lapse of time some cynicism. Her career suggests mental deficiency; she had already been acting the wanton and possibly the prostitute. Such a woman was unlikely to starve in the early West, with its surplus of men . . . ' Dale Morgan is more optimistic: 'In all probability, the widow was espoused by a prominent mountain man, but for lack of definite evidence, I forbear naming the husband.'

Parkman, with his contempt for the emigrants, attributed a mercenary motive to the ditching of the widow, who was an abandoned woman in more senses than one. It has often been regretted that America's greatest historian should have been so blinded by his own Brahmin prejudices and his antiquarian predilections that he ignored the great history-making story going on in front of his eyes. Unfortunately, for him the pioneers of the 1840s were comic-cut figures, wheeled on in his narrative for humorous relief. When Parkman's group first caught up with the wagons on the Platte, the Missourians called out to them: 'How are ye, boys? Are ye for Oregon or California?' as if nobody could conceivably be on the Platte for any other reason. On 21 September, on his return journey, Parkman reported another encounter evincing the limited world-view on the plains: 'Whar are ye from? Californy?' 'No.' 'Santy fee?' 'No, the Mountains.' 'What yer been doing thar? Tradin'?' 'No.' 'Huntin'?' 'No.' 'Emigratin'?' 'No.' 'What *have* ye been doing then, God damn ye?'

The emigrants' progress from Fort Laramie turned into a kind of race for the next objective, Fort Bridger (surprisingly, this year hardly any travellers used the Sublette Cutoff). Still well in the lead were the wagons of Taylor, Craig and Stanley, who had started with the Martin company; they were at Independence Rock on 24 June and South Pass on the 30th. Close behind them were thirty Oregon-bound wagons under a Mr John Brown (one of the dozens this year with that surname and not to be confused with the luckless Elam Brown mentioned earlier). On 2 July, Taylor, Craig and Stanley were the first party to have the doubtful privilege of meeting Lansford Hastings, when they reached the Big Sandy and found him and Hudspeth camped there; two days later Hastings would also entice the Brown company with his tall tales of California.

On 7 July, about thirty miles east of Fort Bridger, the Taylor trio met the third of the eastbound parties led by a mountain man celebrity. Solomon Sublette, who had travelled to California in 1845, returned east with Joseph Walker by a southerly route, via Los Angeles, the Cajon Pass and the Old Spanish Trail to Salt Lake and the Bear mountains and thence to Fort Bridger, which they left on 6 July. Appalled by what he heard of Hastings and his irresponsibility, he warned the Taylor trio strongly against the so-called cutoff and repeated the advice next day when he met McBride and John Brown. Sublette tendered the same advice to Bryant and Russell when he met them in the Wind River mountains on 11 July, but in their case to no avail. But between leaving Brown and meeting Bryant, Sublette and his comrades Charles Taplin and Walter Reddick had a narrow escape when they were attacked by a party of about thirty Sioux. Because of the hostility of the Sioux, Sublette and his party decided to pursue a more southerly course after Fort Laramie and ran along the foot of the Rockies to Bent's Fort. Here was another of the ironical double-crosses of 1846. Having bitterly criticised the emigrants for their factionalism, lack of solidarity and disloyalty to each other, Parkman promptly deserted his British comrades on the Platte. He in turn, having made an agreement to travel back east with Sublette, was then deserted by him.

But Sublette's warnings, coupled with those from Joseph Walker at Fort Bridger, had their effect on Brown and McBride in one party, and Taylor, Craig and Stanley in the other: all these wagon trains followed the conventional route to Fort Hall, taking no cutoffs. Once again, we must pause to comment on the obstinacy with which Edwin Bryant and others pursued the will o' the wisp of a shortcut to the Pacific, for Old Greenwood was yet another to add his voice to a growing chorus of anti-Hastings sentiment. Greenwood was apparently at Bear River on 10 June, but proceeded to Fort Bridger shortly afterwards. As his biographer sadly notes, the fame of having successfully guided parties to California both in 1844 and 1845 counted for nothing against the emigration-without-tears formula being ladled out by Hastings and Hudspeth: 'At the fort [sc. Fort Hall] in 1845 he had done a very good job of spellbinding; but the old mountaineer was no match for the silver-tongued Hastings.'

Close behind the Taylor–Craig–Stanley and Brown–McBride parties came Edwin Bryant's mule train. Bryant and his comrades made rapid progress to Independence Rock and Devil's Gate, and on 11 July overtook the Brown company. Bryant found the people in Brown's company much stricken with fevers and bronchial complaints which Bryant, with his primitive knowledge, put down to the effects of bathing in cold water. Once again his rudimentary medical skills were in high demand: he treated a woman who was suffering from pneumonia by recommending that she drink gallons of liquid; no one was more astonished than he when he later heard she had made a complete recovery. In return for Bryant's 'expertise', Brown gave a bravura display of shooting, and killing, a buffalo with a single shot. Bryant soon put daylight between himself and the Brown wagon train and raced on to the Little Sandy (reached on 13 July). Here the problem was mosquitoes which 'manifest an almost invincible courage and ferocity. We were obliged to picket our mules and light fires, made of the wild sage, around and among them, for their protection against the attacks of these insects.'

After being kept awake all night by the mosquitoes, Bryant's party moved across the twelve miles to the Big Sandy on 14 July, in a state of some concern about the racking fever that now assailed Owl Russell. At the Sublette Cutoff they faced a moment of decision, and decided not to strike across country by that route but to go to Fort Bridger instead. Bryant's reasoning was that there was no water in the forty-mile wilderness of the Sublette Cutoff, but the decision took the party closer to the fateful meeting with the siren Hastings, under whose advice they would suffer far more grievous travails than the traverse of a forty-mile wasteland. On the way down to Bridger, they were met by a war party of eighty Shoshone, who asked them with some trepidation about the intention of the Sioux: since it was known they had sworn a war to the knife with Crow and Shoshone this summer, had the white men seen anything of them? Bryant assured them they had last clapped eyes on the Lakota at Fort Laramie.

Bryant's company reached Fort Bridger on 17 July and at once conferred with Hastings and Hudspeth, who had been there for two weeks, waiting to advise overlanders in all good faith or trap them in their spider's web, depending on which interpretation one prefers. Bryant gave Joe Walker's testimony far less weight than that from Hastings and Hudspeth, but it seems he had already made up his mind. One factor may have been the meeting a week earlier, just beyond Devil's Gate, with Wales Bonney, a persuasive pro-Hastings advocate. Bonney is another of those figures whose dark presence resonates right along the Oregon Trail in 1846. Born either in 1799 or 1807 (two different sources announce the different dates with an identical aplomb), Bonney was an Ohio man with a university education, who went to Oregon overland in 1845, but was strongly suspected of having murdered a rich travelling companion in the Cascade mountains and stolen his money. Certainly, it must be significant that Bonney never ventured into the settlements of the Willamette valley, where there were the rudiments of law and order, but spent the winter in a hut in the Cascades and in the spring returned from Oregon alone, saying he found the country disappointing.

Three wholly independent eyewitnesses, moreover, give Bonney the blackest of characters. In Oregon, the Methodist minister, the Revd George Gary, 'fingered' Bonney as a monster of unusual depravity. On the Sweetwater, McBride had his suspicions about him, which were confirmed on arrival in Oregon; although Bonney offered to deliver letters back east for the emigrants and to bring the replies out the following summer, nobody believed he would return to Oregon to face a possible investigation and he never did. Bonney travelled alone for much of his journey back east, but fell in with Solomon Sublette's party for part of the way, and took their roundabout route from Fort Laramie to Independence via Bent's Fort. While on this southern loop, he ran into Parkman, on whom he also made a bad impression, for Parkman noted enigmatically in his journal on 21 August, 'the barefaced rascal Bonny'.

It says something for Bryant's ability to judge character that he should have thought Clyman a liar while being taken in by the likes of Hastings and Bonney. But so it was, and on 18 July his mule train opted to take the Hastings cutoff, with Hudspeth as their guide. Meanwhile, the other, slower wagon trains were still lumbering towards Fort Bridger. All reported seeing large buffalo herds and meeting many Indian parties; this was a restless summer for the tribes. The thirty-six-year-old New Yorker Joseph Aram, travelling with a small caravan captained by Charles Imus, reported encounters with the Cheyenne, who carried the United States flag to indicate their pacific intentions, and with two hundred whooping Bannocks, whose bark proved worse than their bite. Other caravans were collaborating in such a manner that the formation of large trains, such as the Harlan–Young company which came into fully-fledged being after Fort Bridger, was already a distinct possibility.

The 'five German boys' and their small caravan under Jacob Hoppe also made good progress, enjoying excellent water, timbered mountains, fresh trout from the Sweetwater and plentiful game – buffalo, elk, deer, antelope, mountain sheep, beavers, bears, coyotes and the prairie dogs that so fascinated Heinrich Lienhard. The Germans attributed the abundance of game to their being in a no-man's-land between the territories of the Sioux and the Crow; where few hunting parties ventured for fear of encountering a more powerful force of the enemy, the game, safe from indigenous trackers, could thrive unmolested. But the Germans' inexperience in buffalo-hunting came against them. Lienhard stayed out too late on the chase, became dehydrated, was lucky to find a river and finally staggered into camp after dark half-dead.

Another hunting party, having killed a number of bison, nearly died of thirst because of incompetence by Zins and others. The hunters were supposed to stay with the carcasses to ward off wolves until carts arrived to take the meat away and bring a fresh supply of water and food; but Zins forgot to send out the carts, with the result that the hunters sat all day over their kills with parched and aching throats.

After leaving the Platte on 9 July, the Hoppe party passed through Independence Rock and Devil's Gate (where Lienhard inscribed his name in preference to the over-daubed Independence Rock) and were soon in full sight of the peaks in the Wind River mountains. Heinrich Thomen narrowly escaped being bitten by a fat, four-foot-long rattlesnake, but managed to kill the serpent by stunning it with buffalo chips and finishing it off with a sagebrush branch. On 15 July, the Hoppe party overtook the Dickenson caravan, which had split off from Russell's in Kansas. Now the biter was bitten in turn, for Dickenson's erstwhile partner Gordon had already split off from him. The Dickenson and Hoppe wagons started competing with each other but found that, because of the narrowness of the trail, they could not overtake and, willy-nilly, were forced to travel together. The inevitable quarrel then arose. A lout named Dicky in the Dickenson party tried to pick a fight with the twenty-year-old son of a widow, but the Germans parted the combatants.

The next thing was that six of Dickenson's men appeared fully armed and demanded an ox as tribute, claiming that one of their animals had been injured in a collision with the Germans. Lienhard and his comrades sprang to arms, whereat Dickenson's men, seeing the prospect of a shootout, moderated their demands. The Germans made a token payment of a low-denomination coin, which saved face all round. But the incident caused further dissension in the German caravan. A man named Bryant (not to be confused with Edwin Bryant), travelling with his wife, had implored the Germans to give in to Dickenson's armed posse; Lienhard therefore warned him that if he played the coward once more, he would be expelled from their party. There were no other incidents on the trail down to Fort Bridger, and they crossed the Little Sandy, Big Sandy and Green rivers without mishap, except to note that the waters in the 300-foot-wide Green had an unusually strong current and were rising, nearly reaching the wagon beds.

Two days' travel behind the Hoppe party was the Oregon-bound party, in which Jesse Quinn Thornton was now travelling, and the Donner–Reed party, whose destination was California. The first time an inchoate Donner party is clearly identifiable is at Little Sandy on 20 July when the Oregonians parted from them, thus being the first party this year to take the Sublette Cutoff. As yet, however, there was still no distinct Donner party, for Joseph Aram and his wagon train, also bound for California, met the Donners at the Big Sandy and accompanied them down to Fort Bridger. Thornton remembered the Californians being elated and optimistic, except for Tamsen Donner, who was full of forebodings and had grave doubts about the Hastings cutoff. It was presumably now rather than later that Tamsen made the (possibly apocryphal) remark famously attributed to her: 'Oh, who is this Lansford Hastings that he should thus lead us all awry? A wandering lawyer, a briefless boy in his twenties, claiming to be a friend of Sam Houston, he hints darkly at another Lone Star State.'

The Donner party had changed slightly since the early days in Kansas. James Frazier Reed's mother-in-law had died and one of the teamsters had joined Edwin Bryant. But the core of the wagon train remained the two Donner patriarchs' families (George, Tamsen and five children; Jacob, wife Elizabeth and seven children) and Reed's family (James, his wife Margaret and four children). Other important members were Patrick Breen (with wife Peggy, seven children and family friend Patrick Dolan) and John Denton, the Donners' friend, a twenty-eight-year-old English gunsmith. Two teamsters for the Donners (Noah James and Samuel Shoemaker) and five employees of Reed (Baylis Williams, his sister Eliza, Milton Elliott, James Smith and Walter Herron) completed the roster of those who had been with the party from the very beginning.

Despite Parkman's strictures on the 1846 emigrants, most of them were people of well above average wealth. The Donners possessed three wagons, ample trade goods, and credits and bank drafts sufficient to buy a new house in California; additionally, Tamsen had $10,000 in banknotes sewn into a quilt. Reed had equipped his three wagons with bunks and a stove and his own vehicle was stuffed with luxury goods, including fine wines and brandies, barter goods for the Indians and credits for land purchase in California. His thirteen-year-old daughter Virginia had her own pony, which she rode alongside the wagon, and he himself possessed a treasured grey racing mare, which he called Glaucus (though, if he was using Latin, it should presumably have been Glauca). The Irishman Patrick Breen was a successful farmer who also travelled with three wagons, a large herd of horses, milch cows and oxen and a dog called Towser.

These were the original members of the party who had been together since Missouri. Additionally, at the Little Sandy, Tamsen had taken pity on a waif named Luke Halloran, who was dying of consumption. Then there were the families who had joined the Donners after becoming disillusioned with the caravans they started with. One was William Eddy, a carriage-maker from Illinois, travelling with his wife and two children. The most popular man in the party and the best shot and hunter, Eddy had experience as a plainsman and a reputation as a man you crossed at your peril. The fifth and final all-American party was the Murphy clan. Lavinia Murphy was a widow from Tennessee, travelling with four unmarried daughters and two married daughters and their families (Sarah Murphy Foster, her husband William Foster and one child; Harriet Murphy Pike, husband William Pike and two children). The most bizarre rumours circulated about Mrs Lavinia Murphy: some said she was a Mormon refugee who had been in the group of 'Saints' driven out of Nauvoo, Missouri, and was now working her way across the continent as a cook and laundress.

German-speakers were prominent in the 1846 overland journey, and in the Donner party Germany was represented by the Kesebergs and the Wolfingers. Lewis Keseberg, from Westphalia, in his early thirties, was tall, blond and good-looking, an accomplished linguist and certainly the most erudite and well-educated person in the party. Perhaps for this very reason he was as unpopular in the caravan as Eddy was popular. With a reputation as a wife-beater and desecrator of Indian burial grounds – on the Platte he had been temporarily banished from the party for robbing Sioux graves – Keseberg was an enigma, and some claim that he bore an obscure grudge against the world, even though he was no pauper, having four German males in his employ as associates, drivers and assistants: Karl Burger, Joseph Reinhardt, Augustus Spitzer and a man named Hardkoop (for whom, as for Wolfinger, no first name can be discovered). Keseberg certainly bore a grudge against Reed, whom he blamed for his earlier expulsion. Keseberg had a wife and two children, but the other German couple, the Wolfingers, were childless and drew envious glances from the other emigrants because of Mrs Wolfinger's sparkling jewellery and rich clothes.

Finally, there was a miscellaneous group of individuals who had attached themselves to the Donner party at various junctures during the trek over the plains. Charles T. Stanton, thirty-five, short of stature, was a failed businessman from Chicago, with some credentials in botany and geology. There was William McCutcheon, a six-foot-six giant from Missouri with his wife Amanda and one child, who were next to destitute and virtual 'hitchhikers' on the California Trail. Jean-Baptiste Trubode, a teamster hired by George Donner at Fort Bridger and Antoine, a New Mexican herder who had been hired in Independence, completed the roster of the caravan. Altogether, the Donner party comprised twenty-six men aged eighteen or over, twelve women in the same age bracket, six boys and four girls aged between twelve and eighteen, three girls aged between six and twelve, and seventeen infants (eight boys and nine girls) under six.

The Donner party arrived in Fort Bridger on 28 July. No doubt they were as disappointed as Heinrich Lienhard to find that the fort was no more than two blockhouses surrounded by ten-foot-high palisades; as Lienhard, used to European fastnesses, commented; 'it could hardly be defended long against a determined attack'. But Bridger had filled up with emigrants since Clyman found it almost deserted earlier in the year and was now a hubbub of activity. Bryant wrote:

> Circles of white-tented wagons may now be seen in every direction, and the smoke from campfires is circling upwards, morning, noon and evening. An immense number of oxen and horses are scattered over the entire valley, grazing upon the green grass. Parties of Indians, hunters, and emigrants are galloping to and fro, and the scene is one of almost holiday loveliness. It is difficult to realize that we are in a wilderness, a thousand miles from civilization. I noticed the lupin and a brilliant scarlet flower in bloom.

The Donners found that the fragmentation that had beset the 1846 emigrants all the way across the plains was now raised to a new pitch. Travellers had already opted for four different routes. Some, like Thornton, bound for Oregon, turned off at the Sublette Cutoff, avoiding Fort Bridger altogether. But most kept their options open until Bridger and then opted for one of three routes: either they proceeded to Fort Hall and then north to Oregon, as so many had already done before them; or they went to Fort Hall and then followed Greenwood's route south-west to the Humboldt River; or they decided to take the plunge and set off into the unknown along Hastings's cutoff. The Donners had ample warning of what might lie ahead down the cutoff. The Taylor–Craig––Stanley party, in the vanguard, had gone to Fort Hall before making for California, as had another wagon train in which the diarist Nicholas Carriger travelled. Even now it was not too late. Old Greenwood was still at Bridger, offering to guide emigrants to Fort Hall. Joseph Aram, who had been with the Donners at Little Sandy, took up Greenwood's offer and never regretted the decision.

But the Donners seemed mesmerised by Hastings's advice, even though the ambitious lawyer was not at the fort to pitch his ideas at them. What seemed to impress Reed and the Donners was that Edwin Bryant, the Hoppe party and the huge Harlan–Young wagon train had already opted for the cutoff. Had they known what these groups had already suffered they would have been given pause. Bryant and Russell left Fort Bridger on 20 July, crossed the Wasatch and emerged in Great Salt Lake valley. They had endured a six-day nightmare of boulder-filled canyons, impenetrable sage and the ordeal of the Weber River, which was hemmed in between sheer vertical walls on either side. At these altitudes the cold was intense, and ice, the thickness of window glass, congealed in their buckets. On 26 July, they camped in Uinta valley, where the Weber River finally breaks out from the Wasatch Range. Hudspeth decided to reconnoitre to see if wagons could follow them; Bryant spent the time climbing mountains for a view of the Salt Lake.

On 29 July, Hudspeth returned, and the mule train moved south along the lake, passing the site of the future Salt Lake City. Now it was heat rather than cold that assailed them, and ashes from burning oakbrush rained down on them. Still the dauntless Bryant could not be dragged from his reveries about nature or his meticulous sightings of flora and fauna, this time magpies and the sunset colours on the lake. They headed round the southern end of the lake, mentally bracing themselves for the crossing of the Salt Desert. On the morning of 3 August, Hudspeth left them, to return to Hastings at Fort Bridger. The Hastings cutoff had presumably been charted and surveyed by Hastings and his men, so that detailed instructions could now be given? Not a bit of it. Hudspeth simply pointed to the far distant Pilot Peak and said: 'Now, boys, put spurs to your mules and ride like hell.'

The crossing of the Salt Desert nearly finished them, and they had no wagons. In thirty-one hours they slogged across eighty miles of the most barren landscape on the planet, plagued by thirst, tormented by mirages – of horsemen, of cities, cathedrals, lakes, battlements, fountains – choking in dust storms and crunching the powdered salt under foot. At last, the flat terrain gave way to a gently sloping upward incline, and sagebrush began to replace the salt. They made it to Pilot Peak, where there was a spring of abundant clear water. They had survived the greatest test of endurance, reason and moral fibre and, although they still had the Nevada Desert from Pilot Peak to the Humboldt River to negotiate, psychologically they were on the home stretch. But it was always touch and go and nerves were frayed. Bryant describes one consequence, on 7 August, which he had to patch up: 'A disagreeable altercation took place between two members of our party about a trivial matter in dispute but threatening fatal consequences. Under the excitement of angry emotions, rifles were levelled and the clink of locks, preparatory to discharging the death-dealing contents of the barrels, was heard.'

They reached the Humboldt River, followed it to the Sink, where they overtook the year's emigrant leaders – the Craig–Stanley–Taylor party who had gone the orthodox route via Fort Hall – and crossed the desert to the Truckee River. To their amazement, they found that the hard-driving Taylor party, though travelling in wagons, caught up with them here. But there was a price to pay. The race across the desert had taken its toll in the form of madness which descended on one of the wagoners, possibly as a result of drinking contaminated water. The man said he had run his life's course, and was determined to sit by the river and die; Bryant tried to talk him out of it but could make no impression. On 25 August, Bryant and comrades were at Truckee Lake and next day they began the ascent of the Sierras. On 30 August, they saw their first California Indians and next day came to safe haven at the traditional port of call, Johnson's Ranch. Their arrival at Sutter's Fort on 1 September was the first by emigrants that year.

But Bryant, Russell and their companions had had the inestimable advantage of travelling light, without wagons. The next party to try the Hastings cutoff was not a flying column, like Bryant's, but a genuine emigrant wagon train. Many of the smaller caravans, fearful of the unknown yet yearning for a quick route to the promised land, joined together under the leadership of George W. Harlan and Samuel C. Young. The reconstituted Harlan–Young party was about fifty-seven wagons strong, and was to be guided in person by Lansford Hastings, who assured them that his route was four hundred miles shorter than the itinerary via Fort Hall, was less mountainous and was easier on man and beast. The emigrants should have been sceptical from day one, for Hastings's sidekicks led them through the rocky defile of Echo Canyon, skirting the eastern edge of the Wasatch mountains and then west into the Upper Weber Canyon, where they experienced the same problems as Bryant and Russell: through much of its western canyons, the banks rose straight from the river.

The narrow passage through the canyon was blocked with boulders which had to be rolled away or blasted through; three times they had to use a windlass to drag their wagons up the face of cliffs; they made no more than a mile a day for an entire week. They led the wagons down the bed of the stream, sometimes almost falling off the bank, sometimes through willows and cottonwoods. At other stages of the trek, they had to cut a road through trees and along the edge of the canyon, a hundred feet or more above water, levelling boulders, forming a steep path the width of a wagon tread which the exhausted oxen had to climb or descend as best they could. As one chronicler has written: 'Sometimes neither river bed nor bank nor canyon wall was possible and with ropes, windlass, men grabbing at spokes, women tugging at ropes, they had to go over a shoulder of mountain. When a mountain is better travelling than a canyon, you have reached the worst.'

The sole extant diary of the Harlan–Young party is graphic on this via dolorosa:

The sides of the mountains were covered by a dense growth of willows, never penetrated by white men. Three times spurs of the mountains had to be crossed by rigging the windlass on top and lifting the wagons almost bodily. The banks were very steep, and covered with loose stones, so that a mountain sheep would have been troubled to keep its feet, much more an ox team drawing a heavily loaded wagon. On the 1st of August, while hoisting a yoke of oxen and a wagon up Weber mountain, the rope broke near the windlass. As many men as could surround the wagon were helping all they could by lifting up the wheels and sides. The footing was untenable and before the rope could be tied to anything, the men found they must abandon the wagon and oxen to destruction, or be dragged to death themselves. The faithful beasts seemed to comprehend their danger, and held their ground for a few seconds, and were then hurled over a precipice at least 75 feet high, and crushed in a tangled mass with the wagon on the rocks at the bottom of the canyon.

Hastings himself was sometimes with these caravans, sometimes not, busy riding between various parties, almost as if deliberately obfuscating his movements and intentions. Certainly, it was then open for him to claim, and for his apologists since to claim, that the Harlan–Young people had misunderstood him, to which the answer is that there can be no understanding vague turbidity of expression. At any rate, finally the exhausted Harlan–Young party stumbled out on to the arid valley of the Great Salt Lake, thus becoming the first wagon train to reach this spot, a year ahead of Brigham Young and the Mormons. Camped on the Jordan River, music was heard around the campfires for the first time in weeks.

Before Hastings made his final departure, he assured the emigrants that the Salt Desert was only forty miles across and that they would find water after a day. In fact, it was eighty-two miles wide and the overlanders found water only after forty-eight hours of agony. They stuffed their wagons with enough hay and water to last twenty-four hours and set off at nightfall. All night they trekked and all next day, under a burning sun. Heat hazes shimmered in front of them, conjuring up myriad mirages. The dry and brittle atmosphere cracked wagon tongues and the violent jolting stresses sometimes snapped the metal hounds – the sidebars which connected tongue and front of the wagon with the rear. Dry air shrank the wheels, tyres rolled out, spokes came loose and wagons stalled. The hooves of the oxen swelled and festered as they plodded through knee-deep alkaline dust. The whorls of dust tortured the eyes, inflamed the eye sockets and granulated the eyelids. Most emigrants had scorned the alarmist tales of ophthalmia and neglected to buy goggles in Missouri, even though it was known that trachoma was endemic among the desert Indians. A handful of emigrants went blind, but few traversed the Salt Desert without eye trouble of some sort, albeit temporary.

Evening should have brought journey's end, but sunset showed only an everlasting vista of alkaline sand. Cursing Hastings, they continued the trek all night long. Many wagons and teams were abandoned, as outfits merged and survivors formed new units, using the best animals and salvaging the absolutely essential from their vehicles. Daybreak revealed overlanders burned black, brown and dark red by the sun, their lips cracked and chapped. And now, most of all, uncertainty and fear gripped them and the stress of the unknown in this limitless desolation produced a kind of metaphysical *angst* Jack London would later identify as 'the white silence'. As the sun rose higher in the sky on the second morning, something like panic took over. Now the draft animals were dropping in their tracks or were so maddened with thirst that they were uncontrollable. Finally, some time after noon, they found water and came to the end of their worst trial. But the ordeal was not yet over, for water and grass had to be ferried back thirty miles into the desert to rescue the animals and wagons abandoned along the way. Camped on Pilot Peak, the travellers made several forays back into the Salt Desert to round up surviving animals and repair wagons.

The Harlan–Young party would eventually arrive in California in October, about six weeks after Bryant; the rest of the journey after Pilot Peak was relatively uneventful. They were the last overlanders to arrive that year, and were figures of fun for the more fortunate who, ignoring Hastings, had gone the regular route via Fort Hall and merely suffered the average quotient of emigrant woes.

The third party to try the Hastings cutoff was the small nine-wagon Hoppe party, in which Lienhard and the 'German boys' were travelling. Hastings met the Hoppe party on two different occasions on the trail, first on 28 July, and again on 2 August. It is clear from Lienhard's account that wagons were already taking different routes along the cutoff, and the clear impression arises that Hastings was simply making the whole thing up as he went along. Lienhard's account echoes that of the two parties who had preceded him on this trail: the talk of rushes rather than grass, of springs with a disagreeable mineral-salt taste, the sagebrush, the rocky elevations, the 'conglomerate rocks of reddish hue, 300 to 400 feet high'.

Although he was attacked by what he calls a 'badger' (most probably a wolverine), which he killed, Lienhard seems remarkably upbeat at this stage. His account speaks of juneberry trees, eight to twelve feet high, with grapes like blueberries on which he and his comrades gorged, of feasts on red, black and yellow currants. At the second meeting with Hastings, as they were following the Weber River through the Wasatch mountains – with willows and cottonwoods in the valley, firs, cedar, maple, oak and alder on the slopes – he informed them that they were on the wrong route, that they should have turned left on reaching the Weber River. No one thought to ask Hastings why, in that case, he was on the selfsame trail. They followed the Weber River west until it began cascading into boiling rapids, at which point they left it. On 7 August, they came to the shores of the Great Salt Lake.

Many of the emigrants who resisted Hastings's blandishments and proceeded to Fort Hall with the intention of making for Oregon later complained that they too had been gulled by a plausible rogue. In this case the alleged villain was Jesse Applegate (of the 1843 'cow column'), now a prominent citizen in the territory. On 8 August, Applegate arrived in Fort Hall and met Jesse Quinn Thornton and Lilburn Boggs. Applegate related the story of his amazing two-month journey to the fort, which had proved there was a practicable route from the Humboldt River section of the California Trail all the way to the Willamette valley. Since at this time it was not known that the Barlow Road through the Cascades had been completed, the 'Applegate Cutoff' promised a way to avoid the three most dreaded stretches on the Oregon Trail: the Blue Mountains, the Columbia River and the Cascades.

In May 1846, the Oregon settlements sent out a party to locate the southern entrance to the Willamette valley, but lacked the equipment and leadership for success. In June, a more determined group made an attempt. Fifteen of the hardiest and most experienced men in the territory came together for this expedition, including Moses 'Black' Harris, David Goff, Levi and John Scott, and Lindsay and John Applegate. Each man took a pack horse and saddle horse, making thirty animals in all. The Applegates and the Scotts were veterans of the 1843 migration, and Goff of the 1844 trek, while Harris's most recent exploit was the rescue of the unfortunate rearguard of Meek's cutoff party in late

1845. Despite the later fulminations of the embittered Jesse Quinn Thornton, these men were quite literally Oregon's finest.

Starting on 20 June at the foot of the Calapooia mountains, they passed Spencer's Butte and came to the Umpqua River, camping on the night of the 24th opposite Umpqua Canyon. On the 25th, they entered the canyon, at first following the creek but, later, because of fallen trees, winding up a ridge to the top of the mountain. They were nervous about ambushes, for shortly before a party coming from California had been attacked on the summit. Their circumspection was increased by the obvious signs of Indians having recently passed that way. Next day, they divided their forces, leaving one detachment to guard the horses and provisions while the other doubled back to explore the canyon properly. During the night of the 26th, they were aware of the presence of a large party of Indians circling round them and frightening the horses.

Next morning, they moved on cautiously, dismounting with guns primed whenever they had to pass through canyons or other spots where an ambuscade was likely. Applegate wrote: 'Towards evening, we saw a good many Indians posted along the mountain side and then running ahead of us.' As they approached the Rogue River, they saw Indians massed in large numbers, as if to dispute passage of the crossing place on the far side. They decided to camp on the hither bank of the river, and constructed an armed bivouac, with horses picketed in an inner square and sharp stakes driven into the ground in an outer perimeter; if it came to a fight, the crucial thing was to ensure that their horses did not run off. They spent a nervous and largely sleepless night and, after an early breakfast, moved forward tensely for what seemed an imminent battle.

They came on confidently in two divisions, with the pack horses behind. On reaching the river bank, the front division fell behind the horses and drove them over while the rear division covered them; once the horses were safely across, the rear made the crossing under cover of the other men's muzzle-loaders. The Indians baulked at this manoeuvre, as there was no way they could attack without coming under withering defensive fire. The whole operation was a small masterpiece of military precision, especially as the Rogue was deep and for a short distance the horses had to swim. As Applegate rightly remarked: 'Had we rushed pell mell into the stream, as parties sometimes do under such circumstances, our expedition would probably have come to an end there.'

After completing the crossing, they turned up the Rogue. The hidden Indians emerged from thickets in large numbers and tried to provoke them, but the fifteen kept their nerve and rode steadily on. The Indians seemed to lose interest after a while and veered off; later they learned that a large party of French-Canadian mountain men had passed through the canyon about five miles ahead of them but were now pursuing a different route; the Indians had concluded there would be richer pickings from hanging on their flanks. Mightily relieved, on 29 June they ascended a range of hills, giving a splendid view of the Rogue valley from its summit, and that evening camped at the foot of the Siskiyou mountains at Emigrant Creek.

Proceeding to the Siskiyou summit near the present-day Oregon–California border, they spent three days looking for a practicable pass, then followed the Klamath River to Klamath Lake. This was Modoc country, and it was at the lake, less than two months before, that 'Pathfinder' Fremont and Kit Carson had had their notable fight with these most warlike of the Indians in the California–Oregon hinterlands. Frémont had just taken his famous decision to abandon his surveying and return to California to win martial glory against the Mexicans. In his excitement, he neglected to post guards and the usually reliable Carson did not notice the error. The Modocs crept into camp and tomahawked two men; there was a brief, confused fight in the darkness, when the Modoc chief and another of Frémont's men were killed, then both sides blazed away at each other from a distance for the rest of the night. Frémont took his revenge next day by slaughtering every Indian he set eyes on, Modoc, Klamath or other, it mattered not so long as they had a red skin.

Understandably, the Applegate party was nervous.

We could see columns of smoke rising in every direction, for our presence was already known to the Modocs and the signal fire telegraph was in active operation . . . It is likely that the excitement among the Modocs was caused, more than anything else, by the apprehension that ours was a party sent to chastise them for their attack on Frémont. We were but a handful of men surrounded by hundreds of Indians armed with their poisoned arrows, but by dint of great care and vigilance we were able to pass through their country safely.

They continued to edge along the southern shore of lower Klamath Lake, taking all day on 5 July to reach its eastern extremity. Heading for a pass through lava beds thirty miles distant, they came to a large stream later called Lost River which seemed unfordable. By chance they met an Indian and by sign language indicated that they wanted to cross. He led the way half a mile up the river and pointed out a huge rock that straddled the stream. This Stone Bridge on Lost River later became a famous landmark for travellers.

Lost River flowed into Tule Lake, so they rode along the northern rim, then struck due east, coming to Goose Lake on 8 July. They headed through the desolate wilderness of north-western Nevada, checking off landmarks: Surprise Valley, Fandango Pass, High Rock Canyon, Black Rock Mountains, the most notable milestone in the Humboldt Desert, unique with its boiling springs of alkaline water. Here they divided and tried to find the best route to the Humboldt River, one party going east, the other south. The seven men (including Lindsay Applegate) who struck east found a waterhole on the first granite ledge they had seen since the Rogue River. They dug deep and supplied themselves with gallons of water. They were also able to feast on roast rabbit, as the terrain around seemed infested with the creatures. Ever afterwards, the site was known as Rabbit Hole Springs.

They met up with the other party on 17 July, having been apart for three days, and found another waterhole in the desert, full of 'warm, nauseating water', but restorative nonetheless. Next day, they hit the Humboldt River, again providing plenty of water and forage for the horses. Since they were not completely sure of the route they had taken since Rabbit Hole Springs. Levi Scott and Parker doubled back on 22 July, found another spring, then took a bearing to Rabbit Hole Springs, found it again, and returned. With the road now clearly marked, they were confident that they had found a complete route to the Willamette valley, since they knew the Humboldt River would take them to Fort Hall. As the party was now running short of provisions, Jesse Applegate, Moses Harris and three other men went on to Fort Hall to buy fresh supplies. It was agreed that they would rendezvous with the rear party in Hot Spring valley.

While Jesse Applegate's group sped to Fort Hall, the others in the rear party trekked up the Humboldt to the rendezvous at Hot Spring Valley. Somewhere along the river, in the second week of August, their paths crossed those of Bryant's California-bound party. Bryant found that the Oregonians were short of food and were resolved, if the provisions did not return from Fort Hall in a day or two, to start killing their horses for food. Bryant left an interesting account of the meeting:

It would be difficult to decide which of the two parties, when confronted, presented the most jaded, ragged and travel-soiled aspect, but I think the Oregonese had a little the advantage of us in this respect. None of us, within the settlements of the United States, would have been recognized by our nearest kindred as civilized and christianized men ... A singularity of the incident was that, after having travelled across a desert by a new route some three or four hundred miles, we should have met them just at the moment when they were passing the point of our junction with the old trail. Had we been ten minutes later, we should not have seen them.

At Fort Hall, Jesse Applegate propagandised for his new route as vehemently as Hastings had for his 'cutoff': the difference was that Applegate had actually travelled every yard of his. Applegate pointed out that the new route was at least two hundred miles shorter than the tried and tested Oregon Trail; he personally knew the location of every watering hole and pasture and could draw detailed maps. Nearly all the Oregon-bound emigrants at Fort Hall and those who came in subsequently took the new route; altogether five hundred emigrants headed out on the Applegate cutoff. Applegate asked for volunteers to help him clear the road properly, offering $1.50 per day. It was agreed that he and these young men would go ahead and construct the road while John Scott and David Goff would remain behind to guide the overlanders.

Applegate and the emigrants made rendezvous with the rear party at Hot Spring Valley on 10 August and next day set out for Oregon. Applegate and his twenty-one road-makers raced ahead of the wagon train, not before warning the overlanders to travel fast and keep together, for there were hostile Indians on the trail. The warning was timely, for it was only two days out before the road-making party lost their Bannock Indian guide; turning back on foot a few miles to recover a butcher's knife he had left behind at the last halt, leaving his horse with Applegate, he was never seen again, and the obvious conclusion was that he fell victim to the Paiute marauders who hung on the party's flanks. This continuing menace from Indians impeded the work of the pioneering party, for a strong guard had to be set over the horses while the others laboured on the road. Nonetheless, Applegate and the advance party suffered no untoward incidents on their journey back to Oregon.

It was otherwise with the wagon train led by Scott and Goff. They did not set out auspiciously, for the emigrants were already tired, fractious, undisciplined, beset by factionalism and suffering from low morale. Because of the extreme tendency to splinter and fragment in the early stages of the journey, there was no organic unity in the group. Old foes who had split from each other now found that, because they had heeded Applegate's call, they were together again on the trail, with all the old festering enmity unmended. Moreover, some of them were ailing and dying. This was why they took an unconscionable time to drag themselves down the Humboldt River, complaining that this stretch of the journey was much longer than they had expected. When they reached the final turn-off for California on 5 September, Lilburn Boggs and his wagons decided they would risk the Sierras after all and held on for California.

On 6 September, the Oregon-bound emigrants struck into the Black Rock Desert. Virgil Pringle, a notable diarist of '46, grumbled to his journal: 'The new road takes immediately to the desert of fifty-five miles extent with two weak springs on the route.' Twelve miles plodding brought them to Antelope Springs that evening; after a light supper they then travelled all night to the more famous Rabbit Hole Springs, which a disappointed Pringle found weaker than the well at Antelope Springs. Arriving at 4 a.m., they rested until nine then completed the crossing of the desert, arriving in Black Rock at 8.15 p.m. The sterile desert, containing nothing but greasewood and sage, had depressed the travellers, but Black Rock provided a large hot spring and plenty of good grass. After resting for the whole of 8 September, they island-hopped from spring to spring over the next few days before setting out on another desert march.

On 12 September, they were at High Rock Canyon, from which they proceeded via the so-called Little High Rock Canyon and Forty-Nine Canyon to Forty-Nine Hill and then into Surprise valley (reached on the 18th). There was heavy pulling all the way, the oxen were weakening and some of them died. On the 19th, Pringle found one of his oxen with an arrow sticking out of it, and two cows were also reported taken by the Indians. On the 21st, they camped at Goose Lake, where there was another encounter with Indians. A surprise raid succeeded in driving off a number of cattle and oxen, leaving many wagons without an effective team. As Peter Burnett, veteran of the great migration of 1843, explained:

These Indians are amongst the poorest and most degraded of the human race, and are generally thievish and cowardly. They were not disposed to attack the emigrants themselves, but sought every opportunity to destroy their stock, that they might obtain their carcasses, after the emigrants had passed. It became necessary to keep the stock up every night, to save them from the Indian arrow.

They were now in what Pringle referred to as 'the lake country', on the Oregon–California border. Proceeding along the south shore of Goose Lake, the emigrants headed due west on a fairly level gradient to the north shore of Clear Lake (reached on 27 September) and thence north-west to the Modoc mountains, a range of hills between Clear Lake and Tule Lake, making camp on the evening of the 28th near present-day

Malin, barely yards over the modern Oregon boundary line. They were now in the territory of the warlike Modocs (that very day they had passed close to the Lava Beds, later – 1873 – to be the scene of Modoc chief Captain Jack's bloody battles with the US Cavalry) and trouble duly arrived. Even though the emigrant caravan was fifty wagons strong, the Modocs made a daring assault and drove off a large number of cattle; the dauntless overlanders mounted a punitive chase next day and recovered all but ten of them.

Next night, having passed through modern-day Merrill, they camped on Klamath Lake, then skirted the southern shore and followed the Klamath River past present-day Keno towards the Siskiyou mountains. It was on the next uphill stretch that they had particular cause to bless the road-makers ahead of them for any help, since, even with a primitive road cut through the mountains, they had to double- and triple-team to make any progress; Jesse Quinn Thornton indeed claimed that the travellers had to hitch as many as twenty-three yoke of oxen to a single wagon to get it over the summit. Certainly the Siskiyou mountains came close to breaking the spirits of the overlanders: dozens of oxen died and in despair the overlanders began jettisoning precious possessions. Only the beauty and fertility of the landscape, full of clear streams and a wide variety of trees – such a contrast to the sagebrush and greasewood of the Nevada Desert – sustained their morale.

Thornton had to abandon his wagon in the Siskiyous as his oxen had given out. He blamed the Applegates personally for this setback and from then on noted down everything which would redound to the discredit of the road-makers and their cutoff. Thornton asked Goff and his associates to help him transfer his effects and valuables from his abandoned wagons to other wagons and conveyances, but was aghast when they declared this was not part of their normal duties and they would require financial compensation. Thornton took the line that, having enticed emigrants on to his 'short cut', Applegate and his men should thereafter have taken full responsibility for any mishap suffered by travellers on the route, and should have offered their services free when his oxen gave out. An irate Thornton compared Applegate's men to the wreckers off the Florida Keys, deliberately ensnaring voyagers so that they could prey on them and pillage them.

The exhausting passage of the Siskiyous took the best part of two weeks, so that it was not until 11 October that Virgil Pringle's party camped at Bear Creek, north of present-day Ashland, where the California pack trail joined them. It was another three days before they reached the Rogue River and another three before they reached the site of modern-day Grant's Pass. The leisurely progress in the Rogue River valley, though understandable after the exertions in the Siskiyous, was a mistake, for they were assailed by the first of the autumn rains. Thornton thought that Applegate should be held personally responsible for the weather and whipped his fellow emigrants into a rare lather of indignation. Omitted from Thornton's partial record is the salient fact that in the valley of the Rogue, the first of Applegate's relief parties from the settlements arrived with cattle for the hungry overlanders to eat.

The travellers proceeded to the fort of the Umpqua Canyon and began to make their way slowly up the last range of mountains before the Willamette valley. The Umpquas proved to be a range too far and the latter stages of the wagon train's journey to Oregon by the southern route turned into a via dolorosa. The diary entry of the usually laconic Pringle for 21 October shows the stiff upper lip starting to tremble:

The time from this to Monday, 25th, we were occupied in making five miles to the foot of Umpqua Mountain and working the road through the pass, which is nearly impassable. Started through on Monday morning and reached the opposite plain on Friday night after a series of hardships, breakdowns and being constantly wet and laboring hard and very little to eat, the provisions being exhausted in the whole country. We ate our last the evening we got through. The wet season commenced the second day after we got through the mountains and continued until the first of November, which was a partially fair day. The distance through: 16 miles. There is great loss of property and suffering, no bread, live altogether on beef.

Oxen went down by the score, chilled by biting rains, unable to obtain enough forage, exhausted by slurping through flooded creeks. Beasts lay down and died, drowned or simply disappeared, as in one emigrant's mysterious account: 'One yoke of oxen disappeared in the yoke and we never got a trace of them.' The consequence was that most of the migrants had to unload their baggage from the wagons and, in the end, abandon the vehicles as well. There was not a single family that did not take a fearful toll in the canyon. The emigrant Tabitha Brown wrote:

I rode through [the canyon] in three days at the risk of my life, on horseback, having lost my wagon and all that I had but the horse I was on. Our families were the first that started through the canyon, so that we got through the mud and rocks much better than those that followed. Out of hundreds of wagons, only one came through without breaking. The canyon was strewn with dead cattle, broken wagons, beds, clothing and everything but provisions, of which latter we were nearly destitute. Some people were in the canyon two or three weeks before they could get through.

This was not hyperbole. All extant accounts agree that it took weeks for all the wagons on the Applegate cutoff to emerge from the Umpqua mountains. Ill himself and in black humour, Thornton negotiated the worst stretch on 4 November on foot, walking with his invalid wife and fancy greyhound Prince Darco, but more usually wading, since the rains had made the creeks burst their banks, filling the canyon from wall to wall. The canyon was also littered with jettisoned possessions: beds and bedding, household and kitchen furniture, books, carpets, cooking utensils – to say nothing of dead cattle and broken and abandoned wagons. The Thorntons passed people in despair, in a daze, people broken by their ordeal, and others angry and uttering homicidal curses against the Applegates. He rallied one of these catatonic heads of family, whose wife and child looked pathetically on, and helped him get under way again. But still the Calvary went on. They waded one creek forty-eight times in three miles, and all around were people dying, raving, going mad or losing their sight. 'All looked lean, thin, pale and hungry as wolves. The children were crying for food and all appeared distressed and dejected.'

Loss of life on the passage through Umpqua Canyon ran into double figures, mainly affecting the very old and the very young. Typhoid fever played its part, but the main enemies were intense hunger and cold. Thornton and the other diarists, who recorded the earlier deaths of two men named Roby and Burns, fairly hit their stride when the Umpqua Canyon claimed its quota of victims. Here is Thornton: '[James Smith] had been standing at that place a few days before, counseling with some of the party as to the means of escaping their present danger. As he was thus anxiously deliberating, death summoned him away, and he fell dead in a moment, leaving a poor widow with seven helpless and almost starving children ... A Mr Brisbane had also died there, and I was informed that a child had died at this place.' And here is the account of Thornton's friend the Revd J.A. Cornwall: 'Two old men died on the spot ... Many women and children on foot, and some women as well as men with packs on their back.'

Once through the tunnel of death, the emigrants faced the next nightmare: the likelihood of starvation. This spectre had a differential impact on the overlanders, according to their relative skills as hunters and how many trade goods they still retained. The Cornwall party suffered only relative deprivation: while complaining about lack of bread, bacon, flour and coffee, they shot deer, bought cows from other travellers and bartered for edible tubers or camas from the Indians. Pringle's party, while complaining of hunger, bought enough salmon and venison from the Indians to see them through to the Willamette. But undoubtedly many less fortunate emigrants did suffer grievously from dearth and famine. Later, on one of the relief expeditions. Thomas Holt told of entire families who had had nothing to eat for four days but a little tallow boiled in water.

On 14 November, the first substantial rescue expedition under William Kirquendall and Asa Williams returned from the Oregon settlements, bringing relief to all the overlanders in the leading wagon trains. Saved from starvation, Thornton nonetheless complained that he was being charged exorbitant prices for the food, and claimed that the Applegates had brought the overlanders to the brink of starvation so that, in their exhaustion and desperation, they would pay whatever charges the brothers and their associates levied. Thornton also bizarrely suggested that the Applegates were in some way reponsible for a tragedy that occurred the next day. John Newton, one of the men who had originally started with Thornton from Missouri, was travelling a day's journey behind and was inveigled by three apparently friendly Umpqua Indians into making camp next to them and selling them powder and shot. As soon as Newton fell asleep inside his tent, the Indians butchered him with an axe, stole all his belongings and vanished into the night.

After surmounting the final hurdle of the Calapooia mountains, the first of the Applegate cutoff emigrants began straggling into the Willamette valley. Thornton arrived on 18 November, with his wife, a rifle, a knife, his greyhound, a change of clothes and nothing more; abandoned back on the trail were wagon, oxen, household goods, botany notebooks, law books and all the little knick-knacks with which Nancy had hoped to start the new home. But Thornton was one of the lucky ones: within three months he was judge of the Oregon Supreme Court. The weariness of the vanguard can be gauged by Virgil Pringle's progress: in ten days he never travelled more than five miles a day and usually closer to two. He claimed that his was the first wagon that entered the Willamette valley (Thornton was on foot) but he was pleased by what he found: 'The handsomest valley I ever beheld. All charmed with the prospects and think they will be well paid for their sufferings.'

Nevertheless, a major relief effort was needed before the stragglers in the rearguard could be gathered in. Thomas Holt headed a major expedition that left the settlements at the beginning of December and spent until the end of January, often battling through heavy snows, bringing beef and flour to stranded, beleaguered and starving back-markers among the travellers on the southern trail. Holt's diary entries speak for themselves:

Dec. 8th. We met three families packing and one family with a wagon. They tell us they have had nothing to eat today – the children are crying for bread: we let them have fifty pounds of flour.

Dec. 11th. There are three families here that are in a very bad situation; their teams have given out, and they have no provisions. Mr Campbell let them have some flour. I feel for them; it is hard for me to pass them, but when I know there are other helpless families among hostile Indians, I am bound to go on and assist them.

Holt and his comrades backtracked all the way back to the Umpqua mountains, finding stragglers everywhere, battling daily against snow-drifts and being menaced by increasingly hostile and 'very saucy' Umpqua Indians.

It was February 1847 before the last of the emigrants reached a safe haven in the Willamette. In some quarters, the Applegate cutoff became as ill-famed as Lansford Hastings's 'short cut' to California. What was less often pointed out was that without the relief expeditions organised by the Applegates and their friends, hundreds of overlanders would have died in the Umpquas. Thomas Holt displayed particular heroism. As a noted historian of the West has commented: 'He was not the only one who displayed enough energy and interest to ride to the relief of the emigrants; but he must have been one of the few who set out without having relatives or close friends to succor.' Also magnified out of all proportion were the skirmishes with the Modocs and the Umpquas. These were not negligible and at least one death resulted, but they scarcely compared in gravity with the running battle with the Paiutes that Thornton's old comrade Governor Boggs fought, immediately after he had made his decision not to follow the Applegate cutoff but to head for California instead.

Once in Oregon, the vengeful Thornton launched a full-scale verbal onslaught on the Applegates, rehearsing in the newspapers the oft-reiterated charges of culpable negligence, moral responsibility for death and Indian homicide, mendacity and venality. Behind the personality conflict of Thornton and Applegate lay a struggle for mastery of the emigrant routes between the advocates of the northern trail (including Methodist missionaries, Oregon City merchants, the settlers in the lower Willamette valley and the Barlow faction) and the newer Oregon immigrants led by Applegate who championed the southern trail. Faced with Thornton's highly coloured and egocentric version of events, the Applegates hit back with paranoia of their own, charging that the Hudson's Bay Company was the hidden hand manipulating the advocates of the northern trail. Had the company at this late stage been interested in contesting Oregon with the Americans, it would surely have encouraged them to travel by the southern route, away from their sphere of influence.

But in the increasingly charged atmosphere of Oregon politics in 1847, reason did not get much of an audience. David Goff's son-in-law Jim Nesmith, angry that Goff, having done his best in difficult circumstances, was being traduced by a man with a gift for words (whereas Goff was illiterate), decided to stand forth as the champion of the Applegates. This he did in the true tradition of the frontier. First, he came to Oregon City and challenged Thornton to a duel. When Thornton refused to accept the challenge, Nesmith then distributed a handbill, which read:

TO THE WORLD!! J. Quinn Thornton, Having resorted to low, cowardly and dishonorable means, for the purpose of injuring my character and standing, and having refused honorable satisfaction, which I have demanded; I avail myself of this opportunity of publishing him to the world as a reclaimless liar, an infamous scoundrel, a blackhearted villain, an arrant coward, a worthless vagabond, and an imported miscreant; a disgrace to the profession and a dishonor to his country.

Nevertheless, Thornton's propaganda and the lobbying of his faction did their work effectively. Although emigrant travel on the Applegate Trail continued, the cutoff never really caught on. Ironically, given that it was supposed to be an emigrant path to Oregon, it was most used by settlers heading for northern California, like Peter Lassen, who used the first part and then angled south into the hot springs area of California now formed by Lassen Park. It was proposed to construct a proper toll road on the southern route, but nobody wanted to accept the franchise: some thought it immoral to charge immigrants tolls simply for avoiding danger to life and limb on the Columbia, but most were forewarned by the experience of Barlow, who made the mistake of accepting IOUs and notes of hand from travellers on his toll road and then finding it impossible to be paid in cash. Other factors played a part. In the 1850s, the Indian tribes lying across the Applegate Trail turned increasingly hostile. But most of all, the entire idea of cutoffs became anathema when news came from California of the terrible tragedy of the Donner party.

NINE

TRAGEDY IN THE SNOWS

The Donners tarried four days at Fort Bridger, gulled by Hastings's weasel words, which were confirmed by an irresponsible Jim Bridger and his partner Vasquez when they arrived. By one of those Hardyesque ironies on which tragedies turn, a letter from Bryant, warning the Donners of the dangers ahead, was not delivered to them. Even though the stock needed rest and there was blacksmithing to be done, a four-day halt at Bridger was the height of irresponsibility; many wagon trains halted here for just one hour or did not stop at all. There were bad omens already, if the Donners had cared to look for them. Thirteen-year-old Eddie Breen fell from a horse and broke his leg. His mother refused to agree to an amputation and, remarkably, the boy was walking again by the time he reached the Humboldt River.

It was not until 31 July that the Donner party finally quit Fort Bridger, eleven days after Bryant's express mule party and four days after the Hoppe wagon train. On 6 August, they came out of Echo Canyon to the Weber valley, having followed the route of the Harlan–Young party. Already they were slipping behind schedule, for they should have covered the ground in four to five days instead of six to seven. Near the site of modern-day Henefer, Utah, they found a letter from Hastings, advising them to camp at the Weber River and send a man on ahead to find him, since the route ahead was bad and he intended to show them an easier passage. The Donners therefore wasted further time camping by the Weber while Reed, Stanton and McCutcheon went on ahead to find Hastings. On 11 August, Reed returned, without either Hastings or Stanton and McCutcheon – ominously, their horses had broken down. Hastings had by now decided to take the Harlan–Young party across the Salt Desert but had sketched the new route which he and Hudspeth had taken in June. Unfortunately, there was no way for Reed to know exactly where the trail lay: he was in the dark, and so was the Donner party, but

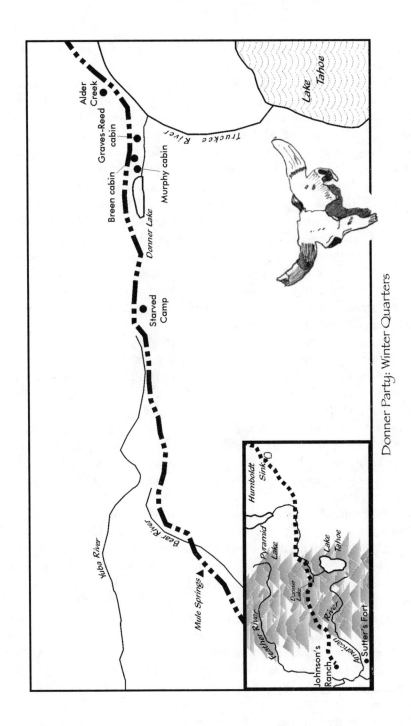

Donner Party: Winter Quarters

Alder Creek

Graves-Reed cabin

Breen cabin

Murphy cabin

Donner Lake

Truckee River

Lake Tahoe

Starved Camp

Yuba River

Bear River

Mule Springs

Humboldt Sink

Pyramid Lake

Donner Lake

Lake Tahoe

Feather River

American River

Johnson's Ranch

Sutter's Fort

by this time they had painted themselves into a corner where they had to take Hastings's fragmentary advice.

On 12 August, not without misgivings, the Donner party proceeded into the Wasatch mountains, where they were confronted by a labyrinth of twisting, circuitous canyons which in a later age had to be dynamited through. Short of able-bodied males, they had to chop through aspen, cottonwood and tangled undergrowth to make a route for the wagons. They felled trees, dug tracks high up on the mountainside, dislodged boulders, built causeways across swamps, coaxed oxen up ridges, round anfractuous paths and past bluffs and spurs. They would often find themselves in a Chinese-box series of canyons, where one simply led to another in a never-ending series, and on ridges that, when scaled, simply revealed another one, and so on ad nauseam. Lienhard's description was a case of Teutonic understatement: 'The narrow valley or canyon often took us almost due south, becoming more and more narrow so that we were forced to cross and recross the creek bed. We finally had to force our way through dense willow thickets.'

After fifteen days, in which they estimated they had come no more than thirty-six miles, the Donners finally reached the last canyon (now known as Parley's Canyon), which once again turned out to be a box canyon in all but name. They had to backtrack to the gulch at which they had entered Parley's Canyon, then struggled up a ridge over the mountain into Emigration Canyon and then out at last into the valley of the Salt Lake. When they emerged into the valley on 27 August, they were eighty-six persons in twenty-three wagons; Stanton and McCutcheon had finally caught up and, additionally, the thirteen-strong Graves family in three wagons joined them. But the increase in personnel was more than matched by a decrease in morale; only with difficulty had the Donners been prevented from dispersing panic-stricken in different directions. During the ordeal in the Wasatch, many emigrants simply had not pulled their weight (either literally or metaphorically) and the real workers in the party deeply resented the scrimshankers. Rage was the predominant emotion: unable to lay hands on Hastings, they sought a scapegoat in James Frazier Reed, who became the butt of envy and transmogrified anger because of his wealth and patrician bearing.

The Donner party was already in serious trouble, as a glance at the calendar shows. Bryant left Fort Bridger on 20 July and was at the Great Salt Lake on 26 July; the Donners left on 31 July and were not at the lake until 27 August. They now headed for the south end of the Great Salt Lake, aware that the Salt Desert was beyond. In the baking sun, one of George Donner's wagons halted long enough for Luke Halloran to die.

The consumptive waif, who cannot have been more than eighteen or nineteen, had become iller and iller through the Wasatch and now died with his head on Nurse Tamsen's lap. The travellers examined Halloran's effects and, to their astonishment, found $1,500 in gold coins and proof of Masonic membership. As George Stewart rightly remarks: 'On the plains in '46 even the waifs seem to have been people of substance.' The other Masons in the party held a lodge meeting, then buried Halloran in a grave of salt mud. Pressing on, in five days they reached Skull valley, the last oasis before the Salt Desert. Here they found fragments of a note from Hastings which, when pieced together by Tamsen, advised them that the crossing of the desert would take two days and nights instead of the twenty-four hours he had previously advised.

The ordeal that lay ahead had just been experienced by Lienhard and the Germans who, after swimming in the lake and experiencing the Dead Sea-like sensation of being buoyed up in the water, had gradually moved away, triple-teaming in the desolate stretch of Skull valley before starting the eighty-mile trek across the desert. Silently, they plodded over loose sand and the harder salt flats with their two-inch thick crusts, the only sounds the scraping of wheels and the clopping of hooves, with nowhere to halt as there was no shade, only the big red, ominous disc of the sun overhead. At midday, they gave the animals some of the grass they had brought and a gallon of water, which the oxen sluiced down and then made clear they would have liked more. Trekking slightly downhill through a 'Sahara-like desert', through high winds that heaped up immense sand dunes, they came, after a solid five-mile stretch of sand in the afternoon, to a desolate plain of grey clay. Everywhere were the bones of dead animals, not just oxen abandoned by the parties ahead, but elk and mountain sheep who had wandered into this waterless death trap.

Night brought some relief, but next morning the sun rose again merciless and unforgiving. They passed more dead and dying animals but this time they found wagons abandoned too; the owners had unhitched the animals. hoping they would run to water; when replenished, they could be brought back to haul the abandoned wagons. Lienhard gave up counting after he had noted twenty-four abandoned wagons, for his attention was in any case distracted by the frequent mirages in the desert. The valley itself looked like a lake in the shimmering heat haze, and emigrants returning from water to pick up their wagons looked like a gigantic snake slithering across the plains. And even when the travellers reached the foot of the mountains, it was still a ten-mile haul to the nearest water.

Lienhard and his comrades spent 18 August and most of the 19th crossing the Salt Desert and congratulated themselves on not losing a single animal or wagon. They stayed all next day for rest and recreation, dancing to fiddle music at night in sheer euphoria, watching the other emigrants toiling back into the desert to fetch their abandoned vehicles, amused at the terrified response of a Shoshone Indian, who fiddled (in a different sense) with a revolver, then nearly died of fright when it went off. The oxen spent two whole hours at the waterhole, slaking their thirst and trying to store, camel-like, further supplies. But there were dangers in such deep draughts and in gorging on the unwonted luxury of grass. A dog belonging to one of the emigrants jumped into the water in sheer joy, lapped the water greedily and took a bath. But when he emerged on to dry land, he suddenly keeled over and died.

In contrast to Lienhard and the Germans, the Donner party took six days to cross this desert. They suffered from the extremes of cold at night and heat in the day; they endured twisting tourbillons of drifting sand, maddening mirages of lakes, rivers and meadows; the multiplying eye whereby each man saw his own projected image increased twentyfold; and the strange wilderness-induced delusion that there were other processions of desert pilgrims with them. The heavily laden wagons of the Reeds and Donners were by now in the rear, and by the third night the water casks had run dry. Reed rode ahead on Glaucus to seek water and, on the evening of the fourth day, found it at Pilot Peak. But by this time all organic solidarity was gone. It was each man for himself, *sauve qui peut*. So it was that when Reed found the water, he also found that William Eddy and the Graves's had got there before him. Reed and Eddy took water back to a stricken ox and remembered seeing a gaunt series of cadaverous spectres eerily blinking at them in the moonlight. All that night, Reed rode past the fragmented Donner party, strung out for miles with no pretence that it was anything but a rabble, until he finally found his family in the rear.

Learning that the teamsters had abandoned them, Reed and his family waited all day for them to return or for the oxen to drift back to them, but in vain; it turned out that all the animals had stampeded through thirst-induced madness and could not be recovered. Finally, Reed and his family took food and water and started walking. As they trudged on, they were charged by a thirst-maddened ox. More dead than alive, they finally staggered in to Pilot Peak on 8 September. No humans had yet died, but Jacob Donner and Keseberg had each lost a wagon while thirty-six oxen (half of them Reed's) were dead or had stampeded into the void. Reed was the real loser from the desert crossing – he had also abandoned two wagons, including the one his daughter Virginia called the 'Pioneer

Palace Car'. Now all he had left was one ox and one cow; he hired two oxen and yoked the two teams thus formed to his remaining wagon. Even when faced with the treachery of his comrades, Reed did not lose his faith in human nature but shared his surplus food with them (a gesture that would not be reciprocated later on).

When comparing the two Napoleons, Marx famously said that history repeats itself, the first time as tragedy, the second as farce. In the Salt Desert in 1846, the tragedy of the Donners came second, the farce first. For Lienhard's gruelling crossing of the desert was thrown into comic relief by the antics of the resident nymphomaniac in the Hoppe party. Just as the travellers were preparing to set out across the desert wastes, there occurred an event best described by Lienhard himself, when someone threw a bundle of clothing out of one or the rearmost wagons.

This bundle belonged to the blonde, stout young lady named Lucinda. The owner of it was probably even less welcome in the wagon than the bundle itself. This bundle was thrown out of Mr Harlan's wagon, in which Miss Lucinda had found refuge twice before, but they got tired of her again and considered throwing out the bundle as the best means of getting rid of the man-crazy Lucinda. If the character of this notorious person hadn't been so well known, this act of Harlan's would have been considered quite heartless. Even now some of the party found it such. Mr Hoppe had taken her with him before we reached the wilderness, but she had left him twice. Hence he was in no mood to take into one of his wagons again this girl, who was walking in the grass with her bundle, apparently in tears. There was much bandying of words, in which one party tried to pass her on to the other, until finally there seemed to be general agreement that one could hardly leave this female alone in the wilderness. So in spite of everything, Hoppe's family *had* to take her in again, which Mr Hoppe did reluctantly.

Lucinda continued to plague the travellers. At the hoedown at Pilot Peak, to celebrate the crossing of the Salt Desert, she was the skeleton at the feast, uninvited and unwelcome, 'like a devil among angels'. She marked the passage of the desert by a one-night stand with a driver named Alfred, but shocked the company by throwing a stick at him, which nearly put his eye out. When the elders asked Alfred if he was prepared to tolerate such behaviour, he shrugged and said anything was better than being her lover; one night was enough, and he had only taken up with her because he was poor and had no friends. The other young girls at the dance tried to freeze Lucinda out, but she was too thick-skinned or stupid to take the hint. After notching up the scalps of Zins,

Alfred and a few others, she bestowed her favours on a driver named Mike, who, predictably, after just one night begged the others to rescue him. Lucinda survived the trail, settled in California and married a man named William Thompson, but he went the way of all flesh, fell ill after the honeymoon and died soon after. She became the mistress of an Irishman named Bray who dumped her, then lived a promiscuous life at Sutter's Fort before departing for San Francisco, where she was said to have had three sailor lovers in six weeks. As Lienhard remarked: 'It's a good thing that I don't know any more stories about Lucinda, because it has been an effort for me to tell this one.'

There were no low comedies with the Donner party, just unrelieved misery. After resting at Pilot Peak, they started towards the Humboldt, without maps, direct trails or guides. The going was dreadful all the way. The multiplier effect of this harsh wilderness raised all the quicksands, razor-edged hills, vertical inclines and narrow ledges to the power of n. Instead of pursuing a straight line, they tacked westwards by north and south tracks, which added a week to the journey. More oxen died and some wagons fell apart. The travellers kept lightening their loads, either caching them in dumps or simply abandoning them in the desert. As oxen failed, more and more goods were transferred into the remaining wagons, thus putting extra strain on the oxen that remained. Suddenly, they realised that their food was getting short and they might have to face starvation as well as snowdrifts. They held a council and, after an acrimonious debate, decided to dispatch envoys to Sutter to get a relief column sent back to them. Stanton and McCutcheon were chosen; they set out on 18 September.

Feeble and dispirited, they resumed their journey, down the south fork of the Humboldt to the point where the cutoff joined the main trail from Fort Hall; on 30 September, they reached the junction with the main trail from Fort Hall, which they should have taken from Fort Bridger two months earlier. They had left Fort Bridger just eleven days after Bryant, but Bryant and his party had by now already been at Sutter's Fort for a month. The absurdity of the Hastings route was plain for everyone to see. Ahead of them, near the site of present-day Elko, Nevada, Lienhard and his Germans cut loose from the Hoppe party and pressed on ahead because they found them dangerously complacent about the potential danger from early snowfalls. Even so, the Germans were themselves overtaken by a party who had left Fort Bridger a fortnight later than they and had taken the orthodox route via Fort Hall.

Along the Humboldt, the ill-starred Donner party experienced more problems with the so-called 'Diggers' than any group of overlanders hitherto. 'Diggers' is a generic term encompassing any of the 'underclass' of Indians from the Shoshone, Bannock, Paiute or Gosiute tribes; it has been speculated that the Diggers were a motley assemblage of outcasts, social inadequates, mentally defectives, sociopaths and other criminals who were beyond the pale of normal tribal society and thus expelled to grub a living from roots and insects or petty pilfering. Certainly at this season of this year the Diggers were unusually aggressive. Although the Donners received them in friendship and allowed them to spend the night with the wagons, they requited this by stealing two oxen and a couple of horses and then began shooting arrows at the overlanders, which wounded some of the oxen.

Why were the Diggers so hostile? Is this simply a case of no good deed going unpunished? Some scholars have speculated that they finally reached snapping point in late 1846 after being the whipping boys for too long for emigrants and mountain men, who had certainly killed a number of them. This idea receives circumstantial support from Lienhard. On 30 August, a party of Diggers asked a 'surly Englishman' for a smoke of the pipe he was puffing. The Englishman was indignant: 'Those dirty Indians are not going to smoke my pipe,' he exclaimed. The Indians did not comprehend his words but they understood the body language only too well. There was a tense moment, with fellow-travellers indignant at the Englishman for alienating the potentially very troublesome Diggers. Then an elderly American woman poured oil on troubled waters by filling her pipe and giving it to the Indian chief to smoke. He passed it round, all smoked contentedly, and all were well pleased. As Lienhard reported: 'While they continued to cast poisonous, revengeful glances at the impolite, raw Englishman, they all without exception smiled graciously at the woman.'

Maybe it was the cold of the long nights and the fading sun of the shorter days, maybe it was the incursions of the Diggers, more likely it was just accumulated stress, but, whatever the reason, on 5 October morale in the Donner party finally reached the nadir. The wagon train was now travelling in two sections, the vanguard under George Donner, the rear under Jacob. The Reeds had by now merged their outfit with the Eddys'. Reed's teamster Milt Elliott hitched Pike's team to a single wagon for an uphill gradient but got into an argument with John Snyder (of the Graves family) over precedence up the hill. Snyder lost his temper, began abusing Reed and finally beat him over the head with a bullwhip. Reed drew his knife and struck home just under the collarbone. Snyder did not appear to feel the blow at first and continued to lash out: he struck Reed twice more and also Mrs Reed, who tried to rush between them. Snyder turned, walked a few paces, staggered and collapsed into the arms of Billy Graves. As Breen came running up, Snyder spoke his last words: 'Uncle Patrick, I am dead.' Within minutes he had expired.

The predictable pandemonium was compounded by the pre-existing neurosis of the Donner party, with everyone displacing his secret fears and anxieties on to everyone else. All rushed to judgement, all were determined to take sides; the Graves family expressly demanded an eye for an eye. Keseberg, who had not forgotten Reed's reprimand on the Platte for despoiling Indian burial grounds, hastened to set up a wagon tongue as a primitive gallows. Reed, backed by Eddy and Elliott, refused to accept rough justice and prepared to fight. Seeing mass bloodshed about to overwhelm the already ill-starred party, the leaders of the rear column finally came to their senses and convened a court. This sentenced Reed to banishment: he was to travel alone and without firearms but meanwhile the wagon train would take care of his wife and children. To travel unarmed and alone in hostile Digger country might have seemed like a death sentence by other means, but Reed somehow acquired firearms (either from his daughter Virginia or from Eddy and Milt Elliott). Since Reed was probably the solidest member of the entire caravan, the Donners were effectively shooting themselves in the foot.

Reed rode ahead on Glaucus, caught up with the forward section and breakfasted with George Donner, who suggested that the best way to let tempers cool would be for Reed to go ahead with another plea for help from Sutter, promising the captain a full refund of all his expenses. Reed therefore rode ahead with a teamster named Walter Herron. But if Donner thought that seeing the back of Reed would help solidarity to form once more, he was soon sadly disillusioned. Still smarting from occasional forays by the Diggers, and disconcerted by a note sent back by Reed that there was more Indian trouble ahead, the Donners uncovered a case of homicide in their own ranks. One night, as they camped on the big bend of the Humboldt River, they noticed that the old Belgian, Hardkoop, was missing. Nearly seventy, the Belgian had been travelling (and presumably eating) in Keseberg's wagon, but Keseberg claimed to know nothing of his whereabouts. But a scout was sent back who found Hardkoop five miles back on the trail; he said that Keseberg had simply thrown him out with a stark order: walk or die.

Hardkoop to Keseberg was like Lucinda to Hoppe and Harlan; forever being reinstated only to be ejected again. Next morning, Eddy, last to leave camp, was approached by a forlorn Hardkoop, who told him that Keseberg had thrown him out again. Eddy said he could not take him in *his* wagon until his oxen had negotiated a difficult stretch ahead, but that if he walked for a bit, Eddy would be able to come back for him later on horseback. This was agreed. The snag was that when Eddy tried to return on horseback, nobody would let him have a horse and Keseberg, though appealed to in the name of humanity, refused to turn his wagon back and pick the old man up. That night they lit fires to guide the old man in, but by morning there was no sign of him. Eddy, Elliott and Pike volunteered to go back on foot to look for him, but the others said that it was on their own heads: they would certainly not wait for them or give them any help, for by now they were worried about their own survival. Whether Hardkoop died of hunger, was scalped by Indians or taken by wolves is uncertain; what is certain is that he perished in the wilderness alone somewhere along the Humboldt River.

The wagon train took most of October to reach Truckee Lake, and the initial passage to the Humboldt Sink and across the forty-mile desert saw no change in its fortunes. They continued to take significant losses from the Diggers all the way down to the Sink. What would they have thought if they could have reflected that Joseph Aram, who had been with them at the rendezvous at the Little Sandy but then taken the regular route via Fort Hall, was already at journey's end in California? Guided by Old Greenwood to the Humboldt Sink, Aram then picked up the best possible guide in the shape of the Paiute chief Truckee, who had steered Greenwood and the Murphy–Stephens party across the Sierras in 1844. So painless (relatively) was his passage that Aram even had time to hunt bears with mastiffs. But Aram's party had unwittingly stored up trouble for the Donners by burning an Indian village near the Truckee River in retaliation for the theft of five oxen.

Digger depredations reached an unheard-of pitch in October 1846. To an extent, the Donners were reaping a whirlwind sown by those who had preceded them. Lienhard and his Germans, who ran ahead, behind and sometimes in tandem with the Harlan–Young party, reported numerous running fights along the Humboldt and the Truckee. Hoppe whipped an Indian in one unsavoury incident, and all continued jumpy at the prospects of retaliatory attacks; the howling of wolves and coyotes at night was invariably ascribed to Indians, whatever its true provenance. Whenever an irresponsible emigrant left his post at night out of laziness or boredom, the waiting Diggers nipped in for further depredations on the stock. And all along the trail the overlanders found notes pinned to trees and twigs warning of battles and skirmishes with Indians ahead. One message spoke of a battle between thirty whites and three hundred Diggers, which the travellers were inclined to file under 'tall tales'. But they revised their opinion when they came upon a dead emigrant – killed in a battle with Indians – who had been dug up out of his grave and mutilated: ears, nose, fingers, genitals and scalp were all cut off.

Lienhard and the others got to safety in California, just in time, before the snows. The Diggers, meanwhile, looked round for the easier target presented by the slow-moving and unwarlike Donners. In a three-night sequence of raids, they virtually cleaned the Donner party out. On the first night, they ran off Graves's horses; on the second, they stole eighteen oxen and a cow and showered the rest of the stock with arrows; on the third night, at the Humboldt Sink, they killed another twenty-one oxen and disabled the rest. Faced with this aggression, the Donner party seemed as helpless as babes; never was the lack of a good, experienced Indian fighter more keenly felt. Since most of the animals (including the horses) were now dead, the emigrants abandoned their wagons and cached their valuables by the wayside, as if they were food deposits, hoping to return some day and reclaim them. The wealth of the Donners was diminishing fast, since most of the oxen killed by the Indians were theirs. Tamsen, who had dreamed of founding her academy for young ladies, sadly buried her crates of books in the desert.

The next stage of the journey was the dreaded forty-mile stretch across the desert to the Truckee River. After the disaster at the Humboldt Sink, there were few oxen to haul wagons, so for most of the party it was a case of proceeding on foot. Nevertheless, the Donners were not the only ones with precious possessions to hide. Wolfinger, realising that he was likely to enter California as a pauper, decided to cache his money and valuables, and foolishly enlisted his German comrades. Reinhardt and Spitzer, to help him find a hiding place. They stayed behind while the others began the trek over the desert. As soon as they were out of sight, the two Germans murdered Wolfinger and made a careful note of where his treasure was stashed. Wolfinger's murder was the third culpable homicide: first Snyder, then the abandoned Hardkoop, and finally the obscure German who has not even handed on a Christian name to posterity. Reinhardt and Spitzer claimed that the Diggers had killed Wolfinger and stolen his effects. It is unlikely that they were believed, but by now nobody cared: all were much too concerned with their own survival.

The crossing of the desert between the Humboldt Sink and Truckee Lake was a nightmare experience for all, but worst of all for Mrs Reed and her children. Eddy and the Donners had been helpful hitherto but now they too were destitute. Eddy was frantic with worry, since no one would take his three-year-old son or the one-year-old Peggy in their wagons. To a point, this was understandable: there were few wagons or oxen left now, and even the incremental weight of a baby might be the straw to break the ox's back. Eddy and his wife therefore trekked across the desert with the boy in his arms, while she held the baby. Eddy's sole remaining possessions were a pack of powder and some bullets and a three-pound bag of sugar; every so often they gave the children sugar to suck, but even so they nearly died of dehydration. Finally, Eddy asked Patrick Breen, who had brimming casks, for some water, but Breen refused. Eddy took it anyway and told Breen he would kill him if he interfered. Refreshed by the water, Eddy borrowed a gun and managed to bag nine geese which he distributed among the families, with no attempt at hoarding. One sympathises with those chroniclers who have discerned a Manichaean struggle going on in the Donner party, with George and Tamsen Donner, Reed and his wife, Stanton, McCutcheon, Eddy and Mary Graves representing the forces of light, while Keseberg, Reinhardt, Spitzer, Breen, Snyder and Franklin Graves represent the forces of darkness.

Compared with the horrors yet to come, the desert crossing might have seemed a bagatelle, but at the time it was perceived as a genuine via crucis. The travellers suffered hallucinations, whereby the sand and rocks seemed like leering demons, and all the browns, reds, yellows and greens of the landscape seemed part of one loathsome all-compassing reptile. The surfaces were sheer torture, as they alternated between light sand so insubstantial that horses sank in it almost to their knees and razor-sharp ridges of obsidian and other volcanic rocks, which cut through mocassins. Eddy, staggering under the load of his child and half mad from thirst, had additionally to endure the stabbing pains as the coral-like rock sliced through his mocassins and turned his feet into a mass of gore. Somehow he and the others endured, and at last they were at the Truckee River. At least now they would always be within reach of water, and death from dehydration no longer beckoned.

At the Truckee they rested for a day, then pressed on up the valley; the going was tough and the few remaining oxen at the end of their tether. They were joined by Reinhardt and Spitzer who came in with their lies about Wolfinger's death; his widow attached herself to the Donners. Plodding on dolefully for three days, on 19 October they experienced a near miracle. Coming towards them was the heroic Stanton, with seven pack mules, two Indian drivers and, incredibly, food, food and more food. Sutter had not failed them, but the true heroism was Stanton's, as he had risked his life to bring back these supplies. He had news of the other outriders too. McCutcheon was ill at Sutter's Fort but Herron and Reed had got through after the most terrible privations. The irony was that Reed, banished to die, had survived, while the party that condemned him was still in mortal peril. Stanton's courage and moral fibre can never be sufficiently praised; to evince further his secular sainthood, Stanton at once took Mrs Reed and her children under his protection.

Finally, they reached the Truckee meadows, and the worst ascent loomed ahead of them. With sound teams they could have got to the summit in three days, but, with exhausted stock, they had to rest the few surviving animals in the meadows. No one was unaware that they were already engaged in a desperate race against time. There had been a few flurries of snow in the days past, and the sky in the Sierras ahead was slate-grey, but even so the party lingered, putting its trust in Stanton, who told them of his recent passage through the mountain defiles and assured them the real snows were not due for another month. But some thought it a bad omen when yet another fatality was recorded. William Pike was cleaning a pistol, when he was distracted by a call for firewood and handed the gun to his brother-in-law with the handle towards him; the gun went off while pointing at Foster, who took a bullet in the back and died almost at once.

After burying him, the party set off for the pass in three detachments. The Breens, Kesebergs and wagonless Eddys went first. But when they pitched camp on 25 October, there was further trouble from the Diggers. A Paiute sharpshooter wounded nineteen oxen, turning them into pincushions with his arrows, but was in turn shot dead by Eddy, finally settling accounts. Stanton, the Reeds, the Graveses and the Murphys formed the second section, while the Donners brought up the rear. But the ill fortune of the Donners continued: one of George Donner's wagons broke an axle, overturned and nearly killed Georgia and Eliza; then, while they were making a new axle, Jacob's chisel slipped and gashed his brother George's hand. While the Donners languished in the rear, the vanguard got as far as a small lake (later named Donner Lake) on the last day of October. They had now taken three months to get this far from Fort Bridger, whereas Bryant had needed only two weeks more to complete the entire journey from Independence, Missouri to Sacramento.

The peaks above them were swathed in snow and the crests were cloud-capped. Apprehension turned to despair when the vanguard got to within three miles of the summit only to be blocked by five-foot snowdrifts which completely obliterated the trail. They turned back to the cabin where Schallenberg had wintered two years before, which was only a mile ahead of last night's camping place. The Breens bagged the cabin, leaving the others to camp in the open, but were soon driven out again when the rain started to pelt (it would continue all next day), penetrating the pine-bough roof with ease. Stanton arrived with the middle section on 2 November, and found the vanguard slumped in inert despair; among other calamities Keseberg had hurt his foot, could not walk and would have to be hoisted on to a horse to make further progress. Stanton exhorted them to try again. On 3 November they did so, but without success. Even though the rain had cleared the snow around the cabin, wagons could be hauled up the steep slope only by all-out effort: men and beasts sweated together, doubling teams, prying with crowbars, blocking wheels with stones and drags, heaving and straining at ropes.

It was all in vain. Foolishly, some of the emigrants had imagined that the rain would wash away the snow from the summit, not realising that, because of altitude, rain at 7,000 feet would mean snow at 8,000 feet. Soon the convoy ground to a halt in thick snow. Stanton and one of the Indians went ahead with the best mule, gained the summit and could have continued on down the western slope to freedom and deliverance. But the samurai-like Stanton once more showed his mettle by coming back to help the others. For all his urging, this time he could not rouse them. They were whipped curs and beaten whelps, defeated, demoralised and apathetic with the indifference of those who had taken one whipping too many; instead of making the supreme effort urged by Stanton, they preferred to huddle round a fire, bickering, quarrelling and apportioning blame. The final nail in their coffin came on the morning of the 4th, when they awoke to a heavy snowfall. They retreated down to the little cabin and huddled there, befuddled, fearful and drained of will power. The party was already little more than a rabble.

The snow caught the rearguard – the Donner family – a few miles further east. They turned into Alder Creek valley, pitched camp and felled trees to make bush huts as there was no time to build cabins; the artless children, unaware of the danger, loved the snow. The danger was acute for, unknown to the Donners, the next relief column had already turned back. The same snow that sank the spirits of those trapped in the Sierras did for Reed and McCutcheon, who were trying to struggle back to them with a pack train of supplies. Setting out from Sutter's Fort, they reached Johnson's ranch with two Indians, thirty-one horses and enough food to tide the trapped travellers over the winter, though they had no conception of the parlous state their comrades were now in. They found a couple named Curtis in Bear valley who were themselves starving, gave them food and pressed on with most of the horses, leaving one of the Indians to bring the others on behind. Next day, they made three miles to Emigrant Gap, but in the night their Indian deserted them, fled back to the Curtises, swept up his comrade and the horses, and disappeared.

Heartbroken, Reed and McCutcheon still persevered for another day, often digging horses out of snowdrifts, then had to admit defeat. They turned back to Bear valley, picked up the Curtises, cached supplies for a later attempt and returned to Sutter's Fort. Sutter warned them that no rescue attempt would be possible until February, which meant that the families out on the sierra faced almost certain starvation.

Breen and Dolan reoccupied the cabin where Schallenberger had spent the winter two years earlier; Keseberg built a lean-to against one of its walls. The Murphy party (including the Fosters and widow Pike and her children) and the Eddys built another log cabin not far away. These were all crude log buildings: the roofs were poles covered with whatever might act as even a partial defence against water. Yet another double cabin was then constructed, of which one half would be shared by the Graveses plus Mrs McCutcheon and child, while the Reeds and the surviving teamsters (Stanton, Denton and two Indians) occupied the other half. Inadequately housed as they were, they were still in far better shape than the Donners, who had likewise put up huts in Alder Creek valley. George Donner built a semicircular cabin of boughs and canvas against a small pine tree, interlacing small branches and throwing over this the quilts and wagon covers. The cabin was divided into two crude rooms and had a hole in the ground for a fireplace. Jacob Donner built a similar but even cruder structure, across the brook from George, but drew the line at taking in the luckless Mrs Wolfinger, who was lodged with his brother. The four teamsters with this party aped the Diggers by building a tepee from brushwood. Altogether, there were sixty people at the lake and twenty-one at Alder Creek.

By now both parties were mainly living on hope alone. The only solid thing in their favour was the cattle Stanton had brought; otherwise food was desperately short. All game had retreated to levels below the snowline, and the emigrants' attempts to catch trout and other fish were lamentably unsuccessful. With his borrowed rifle, Eddy prowled the snowy wastes all the livelong day, but in two weeks his total catch was one grizzly, a coyote, an owl, two ducks and a grey squirrel; most days he bagged nothing. Graves halted the butchery of the mules on the ground that Sutter would want payment for them (clearly he was still optimistic of survival), but they killed the oxen (which were dying anyway), hoping the elements would provide a natural refrigerated larder for the meat. They even began to trade with each other: Pat Breen swapped two of his oxen for Jay Fosdick's gold watch. But as more and more storms deepened the snowdrifts, they found themselves working harder as the calorie intake went down and they grew weaker: Eliza Donner said her daily workload would have worn out the average lumberjack.

On 12 November, thirteen men plus Mary Graves and Sarah Fosdick tried to get over the pass but were beaten back by the ten-foot snows. After resting for a week and a half, the beleaguered emigrants made another attempt on 21 November. Eddy and Stanton, the archangels of the party, were once again the leaders. Twenty-six souls made the effort this time, six of them women, but all were weaker than on the first attempt and worse-provisioned. This time the snow underfoot was like a firm crust, and they got over the divide; Eddy measured the depth of the snow and found it to be twenty-five feet. They spent the night in the snow huddled around the fire, but it was typical of the ill fortune that dogged this caravan that next day the two best men in the party, Eddy and Stanton, fell to quarrelling. The upshot was singularly depressing. Since the two mules used to break trail were terminally exhausted, and Stanton would not go on without them, all had to turn back dismally and return to the lake. Eddy raged that, in his concern for Sutter and the precious rights of private property, Stanton was putting all their lives in danger. But Eddy raged in vain: he and his family returned disconsolately to camp.

To keep their spirits up, the 'mountaineers' of the first two probes vowed to make another attempt on 26 November. But a violent storm broke out and lasted a week, at the end of which all remaining oxen and horses were dead, as well as Sutter's precious mules; by their stupidity, Graves and Stanton ensured that the mules died without providing either meat or an escape route, and perhaps it was significant that both Graves and Stanton were easterners. By the time the storm blew itself out it was December; all their water was frozen, it was unsafe to light fires, and the incessant snowstorms condemned them to virtually perpetual darkness. Graves and Stanton tried to amend their stupidity by teaching their comrades how to make snowshoes out of split oxbows and strips of oxhide. But conditions worsened daily, especially when another blizzard, five days long, prevented them from fetching firewood.

Determined to try again, the besieged travellers at the lake assembled fourteen pairs of snowshoes. But seventeen souls joined the exodus – ten men, five women and two boys – which meant three people would have to do without snowshoes and would inevitably soon be dropped astern in the icy wastes. Just before they set out, they heard the ominous news that at the other camp Baylis Williams, one of Reed's teamsters, had died. It was a motley crew that set out on 16 December. Once again Stanton and Eddy were the leading lights, but Billy Graves, at fifty-seven really too old for this kind of venture, claimed his place by virtue of having made the snowshoes. It truly was survival of the fittest by now: Mrs McCutcheon was so desperate to get across the summit that she left her one-year-old in the uncertain care of invalids. Age and class claimed its privileges: the three condemned to travel without snowshoes were Keseberg's teamster Burger and the two boys.

Ever afterwards, this group that set out on 16 December was known as the 'Forlorn Hope'. Predictably, it was not long into the trek before Burger and one of the boys gave up the unequal struggle; the properly-shod travellers took pity on the other boy and fashioned him a crude pair of snowshoes. On 17 December, they got over the pass, almost done in; they were moving painfully slowly, eating an ounce of food a day and suffering terribly from snow blindness. All had frozen feet and there were many brief, wild, swirling snowstorms, like sudden squalls at sea. There was no sign of any game. Mary Graves started hallucinating and even tough men like Stanton began to fade; snow-blind and faltering, he came into camp at night far behind the rest of them. On 20 December, they camped in Yuba Bottoms, about five miles from where Reed and McCutcheon had cached the food at the head of the Bear valley before turning back. That night, Stanton came into camp very late again, and huddled by the fire, close to death. When the others set out next morning, Stanton sat there glazedly, smoking his pipe. He told the others he would be along shortly. The travellers' last glimpse of him was sitting on a stump, smoking. The baton of unquestioned leadership had passed to Eddy, who got an unexpected fillip that morning when he discovered that his wife had packed half a pound of bear meat as an emergency ration, together with a loving note.

By 24 December, the 'Forlorn Hope' was down to fourteen survivors: eight men, five women and twelve-year-old Lemuel Murphy. After Stanton's death, they lost the trail and began wandering. On Christmas Eve, nine days out from Donner Lake, they finally reached the end of their tether. Having eaten nothing but a mouthful for the last two days, they were at last overwhelmed by months of exhaustion and malnutrition, and their morale snapped: there arose cries that it was hopeless, that they could go no further. Eddy alone, sustained by the bear meat, opposed this and was backed by the women and the two Indians. Twenty-year-old Mary Graves said she was prepared to go as far as she could before dropping. On Christmas Eve, therefore, they finally thought the unthinkable and said the unsayable: survival meant cannibalism. The only other thing to be decided was who should be killed for food: should they draw lots or shoot it out?

They drew lots, but when a man drew the short stick, no one had the heart to kill him. At dusk, they built a fire of little logs on top of the encrusted snow. Nature now took a hand. They were soon engulfed by a blizzard which put the fire out. With men and women screaming hopelessly in the dark, Eddy got them to spread their blankets on the snow, had them sit on them in a circle, then tented the whole over with other blankets. But not before Antoine, the Mexican herder, and Uncle Billy Graves died. All through Christmas Day they stayed almost motionless in the mound in the snow. The storm continued to blow mercilessly and on the morning of the 26th, Patrick Dolan went mad, broke out of the tent and ran into the snow; they brought him back but he died that evening.

There was a brief lull in the snowfall on the afternoon of the 26th. Eddy tried to light a fire from a powder horn inside the tent, but managed only to burn himself, Mrs McCutcheon and Mrs Foster. The snow came on again, but then there was another brief lull, and in this interval they crawled out of the tent, made a fire from a mantua log and roasted Dolan's arms and legs; Eddy and the two Indians refused the meat. That night the delirious Lemuel Murphy became the fourth member of the party to die, expiring in the moonlight in the lap of his sister Mrs Sarah Foster. When the snow finally stopped on the 27th, they butchered the bodies of the four dead, gorged themselves on human steaks and then dried the surplus meat. By now, the Indians were starting to eat the cannibal feast, but still Eddy held aloof. These people were the survivors of the 'Forlorn Hope', and the bivouac in the blizzard was ever afterwards known as the 'Camp of Death'.

On 30 December, slightly stronger after their ravening of the horrible meat, they set off again. The good weather that had appeared on the 27th held and they gradually descended, five to six miles a day, through the snow to where tussocks of earth and grass showed through. When the dried flesh of their dead comrades was eaten, they made a meal from the rawhide of their snowshoes. But this was short commons after the recent anthropophagy, so they began casting predatory eyes on the two Indians; Eddy nipped this murder plot in the bud by telling the Indians what was afoot, and they vanished swiftly and silently. In compensation, Eddy, who was stronger than the rest, offered to forge ahead and try to find meat; Mary Graves, always the doughtiest of the women, volunteered to go with him.

They staggered out into the wilderness, Eddy brandishing the one rifle the 'Forlorn Hope' had with them. Soon they were out of sight of the others and on the trail of a deer, whose proximity Eddy, with his woodcraft, had discerned. Eddy conjectured that the deer had bedded down in a hide for the night, but realised that a single mistake in the hunting of the prey could make the difference between death and survival. He and Mary Graves therefore knelt in prayer, imploring their God to help them. They soon spotted the deer, but Eddy was by now too weak to shoot straight; he had to trust to luck, God and years of experience in the backwoods. He managed to wound the deer, then had just enough strength to crawl forward and cut its throat. A single gunshot alerted the others that he had found meat. Eddy and Mary cooked the deer's guts and slept soundly, expecting the others to find them in the morning.

But it was too late for Jay Fosdick, who died that night. His wife Sarah mounted vigil over the corpse of her twenty-three-year-old husband and lay down beside him, expecting to die. She survived but then had to witness the grisly scene next morning when the others eviscerated her husband and cooked his heart on a stick. Once reunited with Eddy, they spent the day drying both venison and human flesh ready for the onward journey. Only two men were left now and Eddy's rival as bull of the herd, William Foster, was beginning to lose his mind. He demanded further human sacrifice, specifically Mrs McCutcheon whom he accused of being a drag on the chain. When Eddy demurred on the ground that she was a wife and mother, Foster raged that in that case they should take the widow Sarah Fosdick or the unmarried Mary Graves. At this, something in Eddy snapped. He picked up a club, intending to brain Foster, and was only narrowly restrained by the four weak women. Nonetheless, he warned Foster that he would certainly kill him if he made any move against the women.

Next day, they saw bloody footprints in the snow, followed them, and came upon the two Indians, Luis and Salvador, virtually at the point of death. Foster gave them the *coup de grâce* with the gun and began butchering the bodies; that night they again dined on human flesh, but Eddy held aloof and ate grass. The following day they split up: Foster travelled with his wife and Harriet Pike, his sister, while Eddy took the other women (Amanda McCutcheon, Mary Graves and Sarah Fosdick) under his wing. They now often saw deer, but Eddy was took weak to draw a bead on them. Resting every quarter of a mile, they staggered on; Eddy was hard put to it to crawl over the smallest log, while the women frequently broke down into a cascade of tears and lamentation before recovering for one more effort.

On 12 January, they came at dusk to a Digger village. The Indians took pity on these human scarecrows but had nothing to eat themselves except acorns; the women munched a few but Eddy could not manage them. Over the next few days they were handed on from village to village, where they received more acorns and acorn meal. By now Eddy was becoming delirious, but on 17 January a village chief gave him a meal of pine nuts, which miraculously revived him. The others were all in, but Eddy, brought back from the limbo land between life and death by the pine nuts, decided on one last effort. With a pouch of tobacco, he bribed an Indian to act as his guide. He then limped over six miles of rough ground and came at nightfall to a little outhouse on the fringes of Johnson's Ranch, the traditional port of call for all who came over the Sierras towards Sutter's Fort. Eddy collapsed at the feet of a young couple named Ritchie; the wife fed him and got him to bed, while the husband ran out to the other shacks to get help. Soon, a relief party of four well-fed Americans was hastening back to pick up the six survivors of the 'Forlorn Hope'.

Back at Donner Lake, the two teamsters, Milt Elliott (Reed's man) and Noah James (one of Donner's), returned from the Alder Creek camp with further news of that party, especially the deaths of Samuel Shoemaker, James Smith and Joseph Reinhardt, who, before he died, confessed to Jacob Donner that he and Spitzer had murdered Wolfinger. At Alder Creek, there was an unsuccessful attempt to locate the bodies of the dead oxen by poking holes in the snow; foiled in this, the trapped overlanders took to catching and eating the field mice that infested the huts. But the staple diet was boiled strips of oxhide, which they had first singed to remove the hairs, then left simmering for days until it settled into a kind of glue; they also boiled bones until they were soft enough to swallow. Eliza Donner, aged three at the time, later recalled chewing bark and young twigs of pine to assuage the hunger pangs.

Yuletide at the lake was a grim affair. Patrick Breen tried to sustain himself through his devout Catholicism. On the 23rd he had begun reading the Thirty Days' Prayer and the Bible, reading aloud by firelight in the fuliginous cabins. The inspirational literature had its effect: Virginia Reed vowed that if God saved them, she would become a Catholic. On Christmas Day, Breen wrote in his diary: 'Began to snow yesterday, snowed all night and snows yet rapidly; extremely difficult to find wood; offered our prayers to God this Christmas morning; the prospect is appalling but we trust in him.' At least the death toll had stopped at the lake and their huts gave them more protection than those at Alder Creek, as they had hides from which glue could be made, some frozen meat and a few cupfuls of flour.

345

To survive on the diet available – hides boiled to a glue-like paste, powdered bones, and twigs and barks of trees – seemed the height of impossibility. Doubtless the survivors were simply those who had the luckiest endowments in terms of slow metabolic rates. For all that, there was one Christmas dinner at the lakeside. In her half of the cabin shared with the remaining Graveses, Mrs James Frazier Reed assembled the provisions she had carefully squirrelled away. She had concealed ox-tripe in the snow, using it as a refrigerator, and had also saved a cupful of white beans, half a cup of rice, a two-inch square of bacon and a tiny quantity of dried apples; all of these now went into a stew. The children eagerly awaiting this mouth-watering feast were thirteen-year-old Virginia, eight-year-old Patty, Jimmy, five, and Tommy, three. Margaret Reed watched as the children tucked in, and added a warning as poignant as it was ironic: 'Children, eat slowly, there is plenty for all.'

Huddling in their rude huts, the lake party awaited the approach of the new year poised between life and death, in a scene of utter desolation marked by the white silence. As Patrick Breen had remarked earlier: 'No living thing without wings can get about.' Cold, gnawing hunger was the most serious problem but it engendered others: slowly the scarecrows round the lake succumbed to hallucinations, delusion, delirium and incipient madness. Breen's diary, which records the weather and the deaths in a clinical way, is all the more dreadful for its restraint, all the more horrifying for what it leaves unsaid. In lapidary sentences, Breen recorded the death on 30 December of the German Charley Burger and noted (with implied disgust) that Lewis Keseberg immediately appropriated his valuables.

The ordeal was especially acute for Margaret Reed, one of the unsung heroines of the Donner party. Mrs Reed was not a lucky person. She had been married, widowed and married again by twenty-two and now, ten years later, was a confirmed invalid who suffered crippling migraine attacks. On the journey from Missouri, her mother (Mrs Keyes) had died and her husband had been expelled for the killing of Snyder. By this time she was friendless, among strangers and even enemies. Her only ally in her desperate bid to save her children was her teamster Milt Elliott, old beyond his twenty-eight years and described by one historian as 'that type beloved of the novelist – the faithful servitor'. In the new year, Milt agreed with Mrs Reed – whom he habitually called 'Ma' – that the situation was desperate. After Christmas, the Reed family had survived only by killing and eating the family pet dog, Cash, on whose flesh they had eked out another agonising week. Milt concurred with Mrs Reed's bold plan: that the two of them, with Eliza Williams and Virginia Reed, should attempt to cross the Sierras, leaving the three young children behind in the care of others.

On 4 January, the party of four began their trek. As if to make the mission impossible seem even more of a stretch for mind and heart, the three children left behind wept and pleaded piteously with their mother not to abandon them. 'We told them we would bring them back bread,' wrote Virginia, 'and then they were willing to stay.' Tommy was lodged with the Breens, Patty went with the Kesebergs while the Graveses took in Jim. As it happened, they were not orphans long. After only one night in the icy wastes, Eliza turned back; but the others pressed on, missing their way in the blinding snow and nearly expiring at night in the even icier temperatures at the higher altitudes. Finally, with Virginia's feet badly frost-bitten, they reluctantly turned back. Returning to the cabins was touch-and-go: Virginia was so demoralised by turning back that she could scarcely move and Milt was too weak to carry her. Somehow – no one will ever quite know how – they managed to stumble back to the cabins by the lake on the morning of 8 January, more dead than alive.

The following day brought the fifth great snowstorm of the winter which would certainly have done for Margaret, Virginia and Milt if it had caught them in the open. The blizzard raged on until the 13th. By now the Reeds were destitute and without food of any kind so they stayed with the Breens, where they were treated as second-class citizens on sufferance. With fifteen people crammed into the cabin, half stayed in bed all the time. The Reeds had to take the bones which the Breens had already boiled two or three times and boil them for several days more. Virginia, with her frost-bitten feet, was suffering terribly, but Patrick Breen was adamant she could be shown no special favours when they were all in such a desperate case; nevertheless, Peggy Breen, who liked Virginia, would sometimes hand her slivers of meat when her husband was not looking. The Graveses compounded Margaret Reed's problems by confiscating the hides she had bought from them on promissory notes.

Starvation, death and man's inhumanity to man were the principal themes in this dolorous camp from mid-January to mid-February 1847 . Excerpts from Breen's diary convey the flavour.

Sunday 17th. Eliza came here this morning, sent her back again to Graves. Lanthrom crazy last night.

Tuesday 19th. Peggy and Edward sick last night by eating some meat that Dolan threw his tobacco on.

Thursday 21st. Denton came this morning with Eliza she won't eat hides. Mrs Reid [sic] sent her back to live or die on them.

Wednesday 27th. Keysburg [*sic*] sick and Lanthrom lying in bed the whole of his time.

Saturday 30th. The graves seized on Mrs Reid's goods until they would be paid also took the hides that she and family had to live on.

Sunday 31st. Lantron [*sic*] Murphy died last night.

Friday 5th February. Peggy very uneasy for fear we shall all perish with hunger we have but a little meat left and only part of 3 hides has to support Mrs Reid, she has nothing left but one hide and it is on Graves shanty . . . Eddy's child [Margaret] died last night.

Saturday 6th. Murphys folks or Keysburgs say they can't eat hides. I wish we had enough of them.

Sunday 7th. [William McCutcheon's] child [Harriet] died 2nd of this month.

Monday 8th. Spitzer died last night . . . Mrs Eddy died on the night of the 7th.

Wednesday 10th. Milt Elliott died last night . . . J Denton trying to borrow meat for Graves had none to give they have nothing but hides all are entirely out of meat but a little we have our hides are nearly all eat up.

Monday 15th. Mrs Graves refused to give Mrs Reid any hides.

This depressing chronicle shifted a gear on the 19th when Breen recorded laconically: 'Seven men arrived from California yesterday evening with some provisions.' Actually, it is most likely that the relief party arrived on the 19th, but it is hardly surprising that Breen might have got a day wrong in his journal; at the end of his rope, he neither expressed great emotion on the arrival of his deliverers nor thanked the God whom he had so often praised and prayed to. The heroism of Eddy and the Forlorn Hope had paid off. As soon as he staggered into Johnson's ranch on 17 January, Eddy was able to spread the word about his comrades' plight in the mountains. Immediate plans were made to relieve the martyrs in the sierras but there was an obvious problem: California was riven by blood conflict, for the Mexico–US war was also being fought on Californian soil and had drained off most of the able-bodied males. Nevertheless, the word went out, to Sutter's Fort, the Napa valley, Sonoma, to Yerba Buena and San Jose. Captain Edward. M. Kern, USN, commanding officer at Sutter's Fort, offered the generous pay of $3 a day to any man who would volunteer for the relief.

Everyone knew the risk in going with the relief party: that they might well suffer the same starvation and death in the snows from which they were trying to rescue the Donner party. The result was that only three men volunteered at this juncture: Aquila Glover, Septimus Mootrey and Joseph Sels. One of the objections voiced at the public meeting called by

Captain Kern was that Washington might later refuse to pay the wages offered by the captain. When Sutter and another wealthy American rancher John Sinclair promised to be personally responsible for the wages, four more men volunteered: the Mormon brothers John and Daniel Rhoads, Daniel Tucker and Edward Coffeemeyer, men whose names, as George McKinstry rightly said, ought to be recorded in letters of gold. This truly magnificent seven made up the core of the so-called 'first relief'.

Even as the first relief prepared to plunge into the snows of the sierras, James Frazier Reed was preparing the second relief party. Frustrated by the intrusion of the war, Reed finally got to Yerba Buena on 1 February and appealed for help to the navy. Thirteen hundred dollars was raised at a public meeting, and the thirty-one-year-old Passed Midshipman Selim Woodworth volunteered. Caleb Greenwood, meanwhile, arrived from Sonoma, having been promised a bounty of $1,500 if he could organise and lead a relief party into the mountains. Reed and Greenwood then worked together closely to coordinate their efforts with those of Woodworth: it was agreed that the three of them and their men would rendezvous at Hardy's ranch, twenty miles from the 'jumping-off' point at Johnson's Ranch. But Woodworth, proceeding by launch over water, tarried at Sutter's Landing; in disgust, Reed set out without him, once his horses and supplies had been secured.

On 31 January, the seven men of the first relief set out from Sutter's Fort, arriving at Johnson's ranch two days later. Here they collected supplies, ground flour, made snowshoes and recruited six more men, Amazingly, after little more than two weeks' rest and convalescence, the redoubtable William Eddy volunteered to go back with them. They departed on 4 February and made ten miles in very muddy conditions, with horses slipping and sliding on the treacherous surface. Next day torrents of rain cascaded down, washing out the trail and causing flooding so bad that they could not sleep that night but stood huddling round the fire. Throughout the 6th and all the night of 6/7 February the downpour, 'like Noah's flood', never ceased. Although the morning of 7 February was bright and fine, they had to spend the whole of that day drying everything out – not just their clothes, but blankets, flour and jerked beef.

In some ways, they had been lucky. The terrible rains that precipitated on them had fallen as snow at Donner Lake. Setting out at dawn on the 8th, they made good progress until they came to Steep Hollow – usually an insignificant stream but now a raging torrent one hundred feet wide and twenty feet deep. They dealt with this unexpected obstacle by cutting down a pine tree which fell across the torrent and provided a primitive walkway; one man got across and rigged up a series of ropes for them to cling to as they walked the log. They got all their goods across but the horses and mules refused to swim and could not be walked across the long plank. There was nothing for it but to fix ropes on to trees at the other side which could act as pulleys, then attach them to the animals and drag them through the water, forcing them to swim. In a desperate race against time, the passage of the flooded Steep Hollow took up half a day.

On the 9th, they hit the snow on the ridge between the Bear and Steep Hollow. After four miles of floundering through deep snow, they were forced to camp at Mule Springs, where they made their base camp and cached provisions. The snow was already three to four feet deep, there was no forage available for the animals and it was clearly madness to take them further. It was agreed that Eddy, who had not fared well on the trek so far, should go back with them to Johnson's Ranch in company with Joseph Verrot. The main party of ten men, each carrying fifty to seventy-five pounds of dried beef and flour – a crushing load for men having to break trail in the snow – would press on, while George Tucker and Billy Coon were left behind to guard the camp and the caches against the ravages of wild animals.

On the 10th, the ten men pressed on but made only six miles and reached the bottom of Bear River canyon. They travelled in Indian file: each man took it in turns to be at the head of the party, for there was a limit to the time one could spend on this exhausting toil; every step taken plunged the leader knee-deep into the snow and he had to lift his foot correspondingly high for the next step. At night, they had to cut pine saplings, trim them to a length of ten feet, and construct a platform above the snow, where each man sat shivering with blankets around his shoulder, dozing fitfully, unable to lie down. But it was not just lack of sleep that made their progress agonisingly slow; there was little ground covered on the 11th, as their snowshoes proved useless in the soft, wet snows of the lower sierras.

On 12 February, they reached Bear valley, just thirty miles from Donner Lake; by now the snow was ten feet deep. At the upper end of the valley, they dug for the cache left by Reed and McCutcheon in November but found it swept clean by bears. That night, snowfalls alternated with biting, icy rain as the men cowered miserably on their platform of pine logs. Once again, the next day had to be wasted in the drying-out process. Alerted by the depredations of the bears, they began caching some of their provisions in trees, where it would at least be safe from bears, if not from cougars and bobcats. But morale was sinking, especially as the real danger lay ahead. The next leg of the trek lay in the high mountains where they could be caught in a blizzard or get lost; either way, they might never be heard of again. Doubtless it was such considerations that triggered a mutiny. At any rate M.D. Ritchie, Jotham Curtis and Adolph Brueheim now flatly refused to go on. Just when some of the others seemed to be wavering, Daniel Tucker seized the psychological moment and promised $5 a day to anyone who completed the journey.

It is significant that the seven who chose to go on were the exact seven who had first volunteered; more than mere money was at stake here. They began by crossing from the headwaters of the Bear to the Yuba, but then found the Yuba difficult to follow, as it was snow-swathed and indistinguishable from its tributaries, thus making it easy to take a wrong turning. Leaving a trail of charred logs to mark their homeward passage, on 15 February they rounded the bend of the Yuba. They could already see the peaks looming above the pass, but the going was very bad, with snow flurries and squalls; they knew that in a full-scale 'white-out' storm they would be done for. Lack of sleep and exhaustion prevented them making more than five miles on the 16th, but next day the snowfalls ceased and they made eight miles across the open expanse of the Summit valley, ploughing through thirty-foot snowdrifts and caching provisions as they went. By now there was a clear view of the peaks overhead and the gaps between them, through one of which ran the pass to Donner Lake; in summer the walk to the cabins would take no more than two hours, but in these snowdrift conditions the ascent to the pass was a veritable Calvary.

On 18 February, they struggled up the pass and down the other side, beginning the descent at noon. They made their way across the snow that covered the frozen lake and it was nearing dusk when they reached the location Eddy had told them about. They shouted and halloed, and all at once a woman emerged from a hole in the snow 'like some kind of animal'. Daniel Rhoads described the scene: 'As we approached her several others made their appearance in like manner coming out of the snow. They were gaunt with famine and I can never forget the horrible, ghastly sight they presented.' The first woman spoke the memorable words: 'Are you men from California, or do you come from heaven?' Then other voices joined in. 'Relief, thank God, relief!' 'Have you brought anything for me?'

The seven rescuers gave the starving people a little food, taking care not to allow them to gorge on their first meal and, having posted a guard over the packs to prevent pilfering by the famished prisoners of the snow, fell into a deep slumber – their first real sleep for a week. Next morning, three of them proceeded down to Alder Creek. But here was the first shock. Although no more people had died, neither Tamsen Donner nor Jacob's widow Elizabeth would leave with them. Tamsen protested that her husband George was dying and she could not leave him. Noah James and Wolfinger's widow were, however, more than willing to go. So the rescuers took them, along with Tamsen's daughters Elitha and Leanna and Elizabeth's sons George and William Hook; the Donner matrons and their younger children were left in the dubious charge of Jean-Baptiste Trubode, a villain so dark that the historian George Stewart can barely bring himself to mention him without spluttering. Eleven souls were therefore left behind at Alder Creek by the rescuers and six brought out. The trek back to the huts was trying. Elitha and Leanna, richly attired in the fine clothes bought with Donner money, kept collapsing in the snow and crying with pain.

Back at the cabins, the other four rescuers had by now taken full measure of the tragedy in the snows. Since the snow was high above the roofs and there was a slope from the roofs to the crest of the snow-wave, the emigrants had dragged the corpses up the slope with ropes to an icy resting place. The survivors were half mad as well as emaciated and starving. In many respects they were no longer human beings but had descended to a bestial level. Plagued by mirages and hallucinations, the more religious had become fanatical in their pleas to God while others, concluding that the Almighty had forsaken them, were vociferous in their calls for any power, be it Lucifer or Baal, who could deliver them. Religiosity was a precarious thing in the snowy Sierras.

John Rhoads and Tucker, who had been in the trio that went down to Alder Creek, explained to the others the impossibility of persuading Tamsen and Elizabeth Donner to come out. They had ordered the reluctant Trubode to search for the two cattle frozen in the snow and reported Tamsen's ominous parting words, that if the frozen beef was not found, there were other sources of food. But now the question was: who was to return to California with the rescuers and who was to stay? Seventeen from the cabins were chosen to accompany the six refugees from Alder Creek: this included all the Reeds, the failing John Denton and most of the children. On 22 February, the thirty-strong party (seven rescuers, twenty-three refugees) set out from the lake.

It was not long before it became obvious that three-year-old Tommy Reed and his sister Patty could not keep up and were endangering the others. Glover, who had emerged as the real leader of the seven, told Mrs Reed the children must be taken back to the huts. Before agreeing, she made Glover swear on his honour as a Mason that he would return for them from California if their father was unable to do so. Virginia Reed takes up the story: 'That was the hardest thing yet, to come on and leave them there – did not know but what they would starve to death. Martha [Patty] said, "well, Ma, if you never see me again, do the best you can." The men said they could hardly stand it: it made them all cry.' Mootrey and Glover returned with the children to the huts. The Breens gave them an ugly reception and at first point-blank refused to take the children in. As Bernard de Voto puts it: 'Mootrey and Glover had to make detailed promises of reward and at last had to supplement them with threats. Even so they doubted if the children could survive the unwatched charity of the Breens.' When the two rescuers returned to the California-bound party, they wisely kept from Mrs Reed the truth of her children's reception by the Breens.

The escapees had a cold and hard going of it. Denton soon failed, and was left by a campfire, wrapped in a blanket and with several days' food, to await the inevitable. When they reached the first cache, they found it plundered by wolverines or martens. With food again acutely short, they were forced to send the two strongest men, Mootrey and Coffeemeyer, on ahead, lugging the ailing Glover and Dan Rhoads with them, in hopes they would find one of the remaining caches or meet another relief party. Sels, Tucker and John Rhoads were left with the unenviable task of bullying, exhorting and cajoling the starving emigrants and weeping children; they tried to raise morale by building huge fires at night on log platforms. Five days later, after a Herculean journey in the snows under heavy packs, Mootrey and Coffeemeyer returned with the food from the Bear valley depot but also with the alarming news that there seemed to be no relief parties at all in their wake.

In fact, Glover and Dan Rhoads, who were making for the settlements, had already met a relief column, the so-called second relief headed by the dauntless and indefatigable James Reed, who had independently raised $350 for a rescue effort, with which he had hired twelve men at $3 a day. After caching provisions at Mule Springs, Reed's party made fifteen miles into the mountains without snowshoes and encountered Glover and Rhoads. After learning the situation from them, he sent back men to bring up the provisions from Mule Springs and pressed ahead with all speed at daybreak. He was not a minute too soon. Having eaten the beef and bread Mootrey and Coffeemeyer brought back, the disconsolate refugees were trudging on, demoralised by the evidence all around them of children on their last legs. Suddenly, they spotted a caravan winding in single file through the trees. At first, they thought it was Indians but soon, to their joy, they realised it must be a relief column. The cry of 'Bread! Bread!' was heard on the lips of the starving children.

When word was passed that James Reed was the leader of the party, his wife Margaret fainted. Reed called out to the refugees: 'Is Mrs Reed with you?' Virginia Reed, his daughter, struggled forward through the snow in excitement, then collapsed in her father's arms. To his urgently repeated queries about Margaret, Virginia pointed to her lying in the snow. The accounts of Virginia and James Reed are worth quoting in tandem. First, Virginia: 'You do not know how glad we was to see him. For 5–6 months we thought we would never see him again.' And James: 'What were the feelings of Mr Reed when he beheld his wife and two of his children tottering towards him; their forms wasted away, and their countenances pale and haggard from the ravages of famine and cold.' But it was not yet the time for a joyful family reunion, since Patty and Tommy were still at the lake, and Reed had a shrewder idea than his wife what might be their fate at Breen's hands. Having reassured his wife and daughter that the worst ordeal was now over, that there were caches, depots and way stations all the way down the trail to Sutter's Fort (there were not), he pressed on with all speed to the cabins.

In his rush to the lake, Reed missed John Denton's frozen corpse, which was found propped up against a tree a few days later by William Eddy. Since none of his food was eaten, Denton must have died quickly, but before he expired he composed the following affecting verses, remembering his childhood in England:

> O! after many roving years,
> How sweet it is to come
> Back to the dwelling place of youth –
> Our first and dearest home: –
> To turn away our wearied eyes
> From proud ambition's towers,
> And wander in those summer fields,
> The scene of boyhood's hours.

> But I am changed since last I gazed
> Upon that tranquil scene,
> And sat beneath the old witch-elm
> That shades the village green;
> And watched my boat upon the brook –
> It was a regal galley,
> And sighed for not a joy on earth
> Beyond the happy valley.

I wish I could once more recall
That bright and blissful joy,
And summon to my weary heart
The feelings of a boy.
But now on scenes of past delight
I look, and feel no pleasure,
As misers on the bed of death
Gaze coldly on their treasure.

Anxious for his children, Reed sent on an advance party of the youngest and fittest men: Nicholas Clark, C.L. Cady and Charles Stone. The day after the reunion of the Reed family, this trio had got within two miles of the lake. Here they halted, disturbed by signs of Indians. Ten Diggers could be seen on the skyline, and Reed's 'boys' (as he called Clark, Cady and Stone) were both unarmed and fearful that the Indians had massacred the emigrants at the lake. Winnemucca's Paiutes had apparently scouted close enough to the lake to report the presence of white men to their chief; even more alarmingly, the sight of human skeletons on the snowy slopes suggested that the white men were eating each other. Since Paiutes usually wintered on the lower Truckee, their presence at these altitudes was unusual. It has been speculated that the ten Paiutes seen by Reed's advance guard and those seen by Patrick Breen on the same day entered the high sierras out of curiosity about the marooned whites or in hopes of plunder. Certainly there were clear oral traditions among the Paiutes about the Donner party, and Winnemucca is said to have declared that no human lives need have been lost if only the emigrants had appealed to him for help.

On the morning of 1 March, proceeding cautiously, Clark, Cady and Stone edged down to the first hut. They distributed food then moved on to Alder Creek. Meanwhile, Reed's main party arrived at the lake; to his great joy Reed discovered that Patty and Tommy were alive. At first the little boy did not know him, but Patty was soon helping her father by distributing a biscuit each to the survivors. Conditions in the Breen cabin were not as bad as Reed had feared, but in the Murphy cabin was a scene best described as the abomination of desolation. In a noisome foetor of filth and feculence lay a comatose Keseberg; old Mrs Murphy had gone mad and was cackling and weeping by turns; two small children belonging to Eddy and Foster meanwhile lay helplessly in bed crying piteously and incessantly for food. They had not been washed or changed for two weeks and the stench was indescribable, to the point where grizzled mountain man Stone was found by Reed washing the children's clothes. Reed ordered a grand spring-clean: they began by bathing and delousing the two little boys, having first stripped naked themselves to avoid infestation by the vermin that swarmed through the cabin. They soaped, washed and oiled the children, then set to work on the filthy bundle of rags that was Keseberg. Since Keseberg had once tried to hang Reed, here was irony indeed, to the point where the German, momentarily shamed out of his habitual evil, begged that someone other than Reed perform his toilette.

Murphy's cabin was only the taster in a banquet of horror. Outside in the snow, the newcomers found the body of Milt Elliott, erstwhile protector of the Reed family, dismembered and partly eaten. Mrs Murphy, now cackling mad, had made good her threat and gorged herself on Milt's flesh as she had threatened to do and then set to work to construct her own butcher's shop: munched and gnawed limbs were found hidden away in trunks, bones were scattered about, and tufts of human hair, of different colours, were found around the fireplace. At Alder Creek the story was the same. Trubode, sent by Tamsen Donner to beg food from Elizabeth Donner, returned with Jacob's leg and the message that that was the last meat Tamsen would get. When he saw the rescuers, he nonchalantly threw the now unneeded leg back on to Jacob's butchered corpse. Jacob's children were sitting on a log, devouring the roasted liver and heart plucked from their own father, their mouths crimson with blood from the underdone meat. When the newcomers came in, the children appeared not to notice them, nor did they pay them any attention, but continued munching and gnawing on their grisly feast.

There was little to relieve the horror at Alder Creek. George Donner was dying, as was Elizabeth, who had drawn the line at eating the flesh of her own husband. Only Tamsen seemed in reasonably good physical shape, but by now hypertrophied ideas of duty had gripped her. Despite her dying husband's pleas to save herself, she insisted that her place was at his side. Not wishing to separate mother and children, Reed decided the best course was to leave all the younger Donner children (Tamsen's three youngest daughters, Frances, Georgia and Eliza, plus Elizabeth's sons Lewis and Samuel) at Alder Creek. Reed reasoned (erroneously, as it turned out) that the major relief expedition led by Woodworth must be close behind him, and this, supposedly the best equipped of all the rescue parties, could take care of those who remained. Leaving Cady and Clark to care for the people at the creek, he took Elizabeth's three remaining children with him. Back at the lake, he chose to take with him Patrick and Margaret Breen, Mrs Graves and eleven children. That left Keseberg, Mrs Murphy and the three children, Simon Murphy, James Eddy and

George Foster. At the lake the third of his young 'musketeers', Charles Stone, would be in charge.

The fallacy of Reed's thinking was his trust and reliance on Selim Woodworth, a man whose cowardice and incompetence became glaringly clear when Margaret and Virginia Reed reached safety. After Reed and his wife and daughter parted, the former intent on saving Patty and Tommy at the lake, the latter two California-bound, the refugees made good progress. By nightfall all had struggled down to the camp at Bear valley. Here, there were provisions in plenty, and the problem was to stop the starving emigrants overeating. Young William Hook sadly evaded all precautions, gorged himself and died from the after-effects next morning. After burying him, the survivors moved down to Mule Springs, reached two days later. Here, they were effectively below the snowline, green grass grew and there was snow only in small patches. As the pack animals grazed, the female Reeds realised to their horror that their paterfamilias was once more in danger, for here was Woodworth lolling indolently as if at a holiday camp instead of heading the rescue effort.

There were several evil geniuses in the story of the Donner party – Hastings, Keseberg, Jean-Baptiste Trubode, to name but a few – but theirs were sins of commission. In some ways, even more morally culpable was Passed Midshipman Woodworth whose sin was that of massive omission. It almost passes belief that the US Navy should have entrusted the direction of an operation requiring the utmost zeal, energy and commitment to this feckless, fainéant self-advertiser. Parkman, who met him on the trail twice in the summer of 1846, had his measure and described him as 'a great busybody and ambitious of taking command among the emigrants'. John R. McBride, who saw him at close quarters, poured scorn on everything about the man, from his prima donna antics and habit of finding fault with everything to his self-important habit of travelling everywhere with a bodyguard, a half-breed Canadian called Quebec. The thirty-one-year-old Passed Midshipman sported an immense black beard but seemed to McBride 'like a puppy in tall rye . . . in everything but energy he seemed wanting in the qualities of a Western traveller'. Unable to ride or even saddle his horse, he insisted that everything be done navy-style and thought that as he was in command, this made him automatically an expert in everything. He liked to pontificate on the perfectly obvious and to say everything, no matter how banal, twice. The reality of his credentials as a mountain man, as McBride pointed out, was that 'he knew no more how to fasten a pack on a horse than a Bedouin would know how to set the rigging of a ship'. Yet this was the man on whom the fate of the Donner survivors rested.

Virginia and Margaret Reed also quickly took his measure as a cowardly fop, morbidly afraid of frostbite, a man who took to the bottle when there were hard decisions to be made. Disgustedly, Margaret remarked to Virginia: 'We had better take care of him, reverse the order of things.' The Reeds left him behind as they rode on horses with the others down through spring sunshine to the oasis at Sutter's Fort. There, the thirteen-year-old Virginia, a skinny waif, received a marriage offer; such was the shortage of women in California that anyone female, even if not yet nubile, was snapped up. It was no wonder that Virginia wrote to her cousin Mary that any girl wanting to marry should set out at once for California, though she did add her famous advice to would-be emigrants: 'Never take no cutoffs and hurry along as fast as you can.'

At Sutter's Fort, what Margaret Reed learned about Woodworth appalled her even further and raised fears for her husband's safety. The original rescue plan had called for Woodworth to take his schooner with supplies to Hardy's ranch on Feather River, the point where it flowed into the broad Sacramento; this was just twenty miles from the 'jumping-off' point at Johnson's ranch. Reed and his men arrived at the rendezvous at Hardy's Ranch, expecting to find Woodworth and the schooner to ferry them across the Sacramento, but there was no sign of him. So, when Reed set off homewards bearing the rescuees of the second relief, he was sustained by a quite unwarranted belief that Woodworth must be close behind him. In fact, he was unwittingly going in harm's way as definitively as any of the snowbound parties hitherto. The useless Woodworth, paralysed by a morbid fear of the snow, 'liking to command but indisposed to lead', as Dale Morgan puts it, never lifted a finger to help the second relief.

The one advantage Reed enjoyed was the calibre of his men. Apart from the giant McCutcheon, there was Hiram Miller, a tried and trusted comrade, and all the others had experience in the sierras as trappers, hunters and mountain men. The most notable of them was John Turner, a man of thunderous voice, and mighty oaths, a veteran of Jedediah Smith's 1826 overland journey to California and an associate of Greenwood's. Turner was the sort of man who would inspire any leader with confidence. In 1837, he and seven comrades were attacked by Indians. Four of the whites were killed and three others badly wounded, but it was the giant Turner, flailing the Indians with a horsewhip 'like a madman', who put the attackers to flight. Although Reed had left his 'boys' behind, he could also draw on the experience of French-Canadian trappers like Matthew Dofar and Joseph Gendreau.

Reed, the second relief and the refugees left the lake on the journey to

California on 3 March. It was soon apparent that with so many children to carry, the magnificent rescuers were destined to make agonisingly slow progress; the tough mountain men found themselves carrying the weak and emaciated youngsters. Oblivious of possible debacle, Patrick Breen played the violin that Mrs Graves was taking along for her dead son-in-law Jay Fosdick. The mournful tones of the violin around the campfire on the first two nights irritated some, but to the leader they presaged something far worse. Sensing possible disaster, Reed sent Turner, Gendreau and Dofar ahead to bring back food from the nearest cache or urge on Woodworth if they encountered him. The four remaining stalwarts got their fourteen charges over the divide and down to the head of the Yuba. There was no sign of the vanguard: Turner and his comrades had found the nearest cache once again rifled by wolverines and had to press further on.

All day on 5 March the lowering sky had worried Reed and on the 6th the feared tempest broke over them – a storm as fearsome as the one that had assailed the Forlorn Hope. 'I dread the coming night,' Reed confided to his diary. The men were up all night on 6–7 March making fires, but soon snow blindness set in and it was hard to tell where snow ended and fire began. Some of them completely lost their sight, and Reed himself suffered from seriously impaired vision. 'I could not even see the light of the fire when it was blazing against me,' Reed wrote. 'The snow blows so thick that we cannot see twenty feet looking against the wind.' The Hieronymous Bosch nightmare was completed by howling children calling out dolefully, 'Hungry! Hungry!', while their mothers moaned antiphonally, 'Freezing! Freezing!' Reed's last entry on 6 March suggests he thought the end might have come. 'Night closing fast and with it the hurricane increases.'

The storm howled incessantly for two days and three nights. Daylight brought little increase in visibility because of the thickness of the snowfalls. Breen began praying while Reed, Miller and McCutcheon worked heroically, taking ten-minute spells at woodcutting before being compelled by sheer cold and exhaustion to return to the fireside for recuperation. The division of food yielded just a spoonful of flour for each person, and the howling of the wind was counterpointed by the cries of children. Mrs Breen turned on the rescuers and rebuked them with taking three dollars a day just to 'murther' people. McCutcheon silenced her with a volley of oaths. Reed collapsed and seemed near death, while the fourth rescuer, Brit Greenwood, joined Breen in panic-stricken prayer. Only Miller and McCutcheon kept their heads, and it was solely due to them that anyone survived.

Without a fire they were done for, but with the snow drifting up to fifteen feet, it was increasingly difficult to secure the base of the fire. There was an obvious danger that, the higher the level of the snow above terra firma, the more likely it was that the fire pit would simply melt the snow beneath it, collapse into a void and thus extinguish itself. They tried to shore up the fire pit by constructing a substructure of saplings on which the smaller logs would burn, but as the saplings caught fire, the risk was they would become weakened and plunge through the melted snow beneath. This is almost what happened. Only a Herculean effort from McCutcheon on the 6th prevented the fire from collapsing and going out, condemning all to a swift death from exposure. While embers hissed in the pool of snow water at ground level, McCutcheon just managed to save the day. He was so exhausted from his labours that he did not realise he was broiling by the fireside until the heat seared through the four shirts he was wearing and began scorching his skin. Saving the fire brought back hope. The children cried out with pleasure: 'I'm glad we have got some fire. Oh, how good it feels, it's good our fire didn't go out.'

The storm continued to rage and the force of the wind even increased on the second day, but by nightfall, with the fire intact, somehow the feeling quietly crept through the company that they might survive. On the morning of the 8th, they found that five-year-old Isaac Donner had died during the night. Finally, at about noon, the storm ceased. The survivors had been without food and water for twenty-four hours. A decision was taken to split the party. The four rescuers would press on ahead, taking the two Reed children, Solomon Hook (Elizabeth Donner's son) and Mary Donner. The Graveses were too ill to travel and Breen simply refused to go on. Reed raged at Breen and told him that if any of the children died, their blood would be on his head, but Breen was unmoved and muttered pious hopes about Woodworth. Reed answered contemptuously that to rely further on Woodworth 'was leaning upon a broken stick'. The onward party chopped wood for those they left behind and set out. Reed noticed that his daughter Patty seemed to be slipping away and gave her a teaspoonful of crumbs he had saved in his mitten. She revived and her morale rose. 'God has not brought us so far to let us perish now,' she told her father.

Camped beside the Yuba, they hoped soon to see Turner, Gendreau and Dofar. But the men who came into camp were Cady and Stone, who had abandoned their posts and arrived with silver and silk dresses belonging to the Donners. It seems clear that they had agreed to stay behind in the first place only to loot and plunder. At any rate, as soon as

Reed had departed, Stone abandoned his post at the lake and joined Cady at Alder Creek; the third 'musketeer', Clark, was away on a bear hunt. At Alder Creek, Tamsen begged them to take her children to safety; in return she gave them $500 – it is not clear whether she offered the sum or they demanded it. Tamsen then washed and combed Frances, Georgia and Eliza, dressed them in warm, rich clothes and made up a bundle of silk and silver which would defray their expenses in California. After saying farewell to their dying father, the three little girls joined Clark and Cady who set off with them into the wilderness.

Halfway between Alder Creek and Donner Lake, the two men stopped in the snow, drew apart from the children, and held a long animated discussion. It seems they were deciding whether to abandon their charges there and then in the snow. They concluded by taking the children to the cabin occupied by the gruesome Keseberg and dumping them there. They intended to strike out for Mule Springs at once but the same storm that struck at Reed's party drove them back to the huts. Meanwhile, the terrified Donner children crouched in the darkness in Keseberg's cabin while the frenzied German ranted and raved. One of them cried with hunger, and Keseberg yelled: 'Be quiet, you crying children, or I'll shoot you.' Once, Eliza woke to find six-year-old Frances screaming that Keseberg wanted to kill her and imploring him not to pick her up. No account can do justice to the nightmare the children suffered. At Alder Creek there had been starvation, but at least they had their parents; at Donner Lake they were in effect defenceless orphans.

At noon on 8 March, when the storm cleared, Cady and Clark left the three little girls to their fate and, taking money and valuables, made rapid progress down the slopes to join Reed on the Yuba. Reed and his men must have been disgusted by their behaviour, but what could they do? As George Stewart has memorably summed up: 'After all, the expedition was not under military discipline, and if Cady and Clark chose to put their own interests first, no one could well say them nay. Moreover with gentry like them, it was a word and a blow, or perhaps a shot. The sheriff's writ did not run in the mountains of California.' Probably everyone was too taken up with survival for immediate recrimination. Next morning, Cady and Clark set off with the others, all of them frost-bitten and leaving bloody footprints in the snow. That afternoon, they found food hanging from a tree on the end of a rope where Turner, Gendreau and Dofar, having broken into the second cache, had left it for them. They camped that night and made another fire and next day encountered the vanguard of a relief party; later still, the egregious Selim

Woodworth appeared, timidly achieving his highest altitude towards the pass.

Reed and his party were now safe, though in very bad shape; Turner, Gendreau and Dofar had also reached the limits of human endurance during their trek in search of the food depots. But the Breens and Graveses were still back in the snow and behind them, at Donner Lake and Alder Creek, were the last of the starving unfortunates. Immediately, there was talk of the need for a third relief expedition. Here, the prime movers were William Eddy and William Foster of the Forlorn Hope. The two men who had squared up to each other murderously in the snow two months before had become friends through the shared adversity and were determined to rescue their stricken comrades. After recovering their strength at Johnson's, they bearded the useless Woodworth in his lair at Bear valley and browbeat him into accompanying them into the mountains. After earning their contempt for his cowardice and whingeing about having to carry a blanket, Woodworth got off the hook by the fortuitous meeting with Turner, Gendreau and Dofar and later with Reed's second relief itself. Eager to set off without delay, Eddy and Foster could find no one to accompany them except Hiram Miller and an overweight young man named John Starks. Reed persuaded them to return with him to Woodworth's base camp at Bear valley and make more careful preparations.

At Woodworth's camp, Patty Reed finally revealed to her father that she had carried 'treasures' all the way from the lake, never telling the grown-ups lest they demand she lighten the load. Hidden under her dress were a tiny glass salt-cellar, a small wooden doll with black hair and black eyes, and a lock of her grandmother's hair. Safe at last, she was able to tell the doll the story of her terrible adventures. Her father, meanwhile, added his weight to Eddy and Foster's pressure on Woodworth. The harassed Passed Midshipman, in his own fantastic eyes a great captain in both senses, offered pay of $3 a day and a bounty of $50 to any man who would carry down from the sierras a child that was not his. Even so, only two new men took the financial bait. One was Howard Oakley, a Mormon emigrant, and the other was William Thompson. The other members of the third relief were the twenty-year-old giant Starks, who had originally volunteered for no pay, Foster and Eddy, veterans on the Forlorn Hope, and Miller and Stone from the second relief.

It is amazing how often the number seven recurs in narratives of the Donner relief. Once again it was seven men who set out. Eddy and Foster originally intended to bypass Breen, whose character they knew of old, and head straight for the lake and the creek to bring back the survivors.

But Starks, a man of integrity if not also naivety, spoke up. 'No, gentlemen, I will not abandon these people. I am here on a mission of mercy and I will not do half the work. You can all go if you want to, but I shall stay by these people while they and I live.' It was therefore agreed that the relief party would split when they reached the camp in the snow: Foster, Eddy, Miller and Thompson would make for the lake while Starks, Oakley and Stone brought down the Breens and Graveses. There appears to have been method in the division. It seems curious that the mercenary Stone should have volunteered for another ordeal in the mountains, unless he aspired to further Donner riches. Forewarned by Reed, Eddy and Foster most likely deliberately assigned him to the Breen rescue to nip any such intention in the bud.

The seven men set out on the morning of 11 March. It was this group that found Denton's frozen body and his last sentimental verses. Making good progress in bright sunshine, they reached Breen's camp around four o'clock on the afternoon of the 12th. Here, they found themselves on the rim of a crater or great cup, where the fire had melted into the snow and made a pit twenty-five feet deep, with bare ground at the bottom. Patrick and Peggy Breen were sunning themselves, apathetic and insouciant, as indifferent to the horror around them as Kurtz in Conrad's *Heart of Darkness*. Five-year-old Franklin Graves had died since Reed left, but there was no sign of his body or that of Isaac. But more stomach-churning was the sight of Mrs Graves, who lay with the flesh stripped off her arms and legs; her breasts, heart and liver were meanwhile bubbling in a cooking pot by the fire. Her year-old baby sat by the side of its mangled mother, one arm on her body, sobbing bitterly and crying, 'Ma! Ma! Ma!'

Eddy distributed food and comforted the child. Gradually, he pieced together what had happened. It seemed that before dying Mrs Graves had gone mad and tried to kill her own child. The fire had finally burned right down through the snow to the earth, and the survivors had climbed down into the pit to be near it and to shelter from the wind. Breen freely admitted that they had eaten the two children first and then started on Mrs Graves. Even so, there were eleven survivors and Eddy had not expected so many. Seeing his chance, Stone suggested the survivors be left to be picked up by a fourth relief party, but again Starks objected strenuously. It was agreed that the original plan be adhered to. Oakley and Stone took the line of least resistance by taking a child apiece and making a quick descent. It was left to the heroic Starks to bully, coax and cajole the rest of them slowly down the slopes over the next three and a half days, one of the great achievements in the entire Donner story.

Early next morning, Eddy and Foster, racing ahead of Miller and Thompson, reached the cabins at the lake. Mrs Murphy, by now almost blind, told them that their children, George Foster and James Eddy, were dead. The demented Keseberg, now more beast than man, told Foster and Eddy to their faces that he had eaten their sons. Both Mrs Murphy and the three Donner girls, amazingly still alive, confirmed the story. The three girls told how one night Keseberg had taken Georgie Foster to bed and in the morning the child was dead. Mrs Murphy sat down with the dead child, keened over him a long while then burst into violent vituperation against Keseberg, accusing him of strangling the mite. Keseberg said nothing, took the body from her, hung it up on the wall like a piece of meat and later, presumably, treated it like any other piece of meat. Eddy confessed that he wanted to kill Keseberg on the spot, but could not bring himself to club down the pitiful apology for a human being that stood before him.

The only reason that the Donner girls were still alive was that Tamsen Donner had come over from Alder Creek to find them. Just before the third relief arrived at the lake, they met Nicholas Clark and Jean-Baptiste Trubode en route to California. Clark, pinned down at Alder Creek by the great storm of 6–8 March, had then been sent over to the lake by Tamsen Donner to make sure her children had got safely over the divide before the tempest struck. To her horror, Clark returned with news that the children were at Keseberg's cabin in mortal danger; as he put it, 'he believed their lives were in danger of a death more violent than starvation'. Finally, Tamsen had motive enough to leave her dying husband. What opinion we should form of Clark is doubtful. He claimed that he had to leave the lake to save his sanity after the horrors he had witnessed in Keseberg's cabin, but it was noted that instead of taking at least one child to safety he had elected instead to load forty pounds of goods and two guns on his back. Moreover, he did not tell Tamsen Donner of his plans (she thought he and Trubode were now back at Alder Creek) and made no attempt to save Samuel Donner. Also, on the principle that by their company ye shall know them, we have to take account of the fact that he was accompanied by the nefarious Trubode.

Eddy pleaded with Tamsen to come out with the third relief but she was obsessed with the fact that her husband was still not yet dead. Eddy pointed out that his was a hopeless case, so why waste two lives instead of one? But nothing he said influenced Tamsen. She asked him to wait another day while she made a return trip to Alder Creek; if her husband was indeed dead, then she would accompany them. But Eddy pointed out that he could not spare another day: his food supplies were short and he could not risk another storm. So Tamsen once again said goodbye to Frances, Georgia and Eliza, and they finally departed with the third relief. They reached the foot of the pass, caught up with Clark and Trubode and camped for the night. But the Donner girls were always unlucky with strange adults. This time they fell foul of Hiram Miller, who turned nasty on Eliza and was in turn railed at by Frances. Thompson acted as peacemaker. Finding a bundle of silk dresses that had been abandoned by Cady on the trail, Eddy gave it to Thompson who converted the finery into sleeping bags for the three girls. Making good progress, they caught up with John Starks and his unwieldy crocodile of lamed emigrants. On 17 March, there was even more excitement. At last, Woodworth was on the trail, and with him were the veteran rescuers Glover, Coffeemeyer and Mootrey. Like the Reed children, the Donner girls had been among the chosen ones and had at last come through.

Woodworth should now have pressed on and mopped up the Donner relief operation. But meeting the third relief and its refugees gave him just the excuse he needed to turn back and do nothing. It is not surprising that Bernard de Voto delivers this crushing verdict: 'Passed Midshipman Woodworth was just no damned good.' Unfortunately, at Sutter's Fort, McKinstry ordered Woodworth back to his job. He passed the buck to a new relief party, all veterans of the snows: Coffeemeyer, Sels, Tucker, Starks, John Rhoads, William Foster, even William Graves who had had just two weeks of rest and recuperation. This party started on 23 March and got no further than the Bear valley, pleading that they had encountered the wrong kind of snow – too soft for mountain travelling. The truth was that, led by the lacklustre Woodworth, they were more interested in drawing their per diem than rescuing the scarecrows in the mountains. Their reasoning was sound, if cynical. George and Samuel Donner were undoubtedly dead by now, as was Mrs Murphy; Tamsen had been given her chance and made the choice to stay; and as for Keseberg, why, he surely did not deserve to live anyway.

So it was that when the fourth relief expedition got under way, it was primarily designed as a salvage operation, with the goods in the mountains being granted as a sort of 'treasure trove' in legally binding documents to those who dared to go up into the Sierras to appropriate them. By now, all the survivors were safely in the California settlements, and the Reeds and Breens, the only families to have survived intact, were thriving, as were the Donner children. All those who had come through were genetically tough, of wiry farming stock, and it simply needed good food and rest to bring about a remarkable transformation. The one casualty was the Graves baby carried to safety from the snow pit by

Charles Stone. As Thornton sententiously described the death: 'It drooped and withered away like a flower severed from the parent stem. It now blooms in the paradise of God, in a better and happier clime, where the storms and disasters of life will affect it no more.'

The expedition allowed the men to draw a daily wage as well as half of everything they recovered or salvaged. This time the leader was a mountain man named Fallon, a huge Irishman who had trapped in the Rockies, lived in St Louis and New Mexico, and served in the Micheltorena war and in Frémont's California battalion in the Mexico–US war. Once again the magical number seven was in evidence, for Fallon selected just six men to accompany him on his mission. There was only one new face: Sebastian Keyser, a settler who had recently been working at Johnson's Ranch. The others were those well-known veterans of the slopes and sierras: Foster, Tucker, Sels, Coffeemeyer and John Rhoads. They assembled on 10 April, made careful preparations and set out from Johnson's on the 13th.

They proceeded on horseback for two days until they reached the lower end of Bear valley, then sent the horses back and went on with backpacks. Making rapid progress through the impacted and melting snow, they achieved twenty-three miles on their first pedestrian day and camped well up beyond the Yuba bottoms. Next day, they topped the pass and by midday were at the cabins, taking by surprise a party of Paiute Diggers who were already scavenging. They found a scene of desolation, a charnel house of mutilated corpses, which revolted even the case-hardened Fallon. 'We were obliged to witness sights from which we would fain have turned away,' he wrote in his journal,' and which are too dreadful to put on record.' Particularly striking was the corpse of Mrs Eddy, with the limbs severed and a frightful gash in the skull. But there was no one alive. After searching the cabins meticulously for two hours, they started for Alder Creek and soon found footprints in the snow, evidently not an Indian's. They followed them to Jacob Donner's tent only to find that the Friday of the piece had doubled back on the trail. Around the tents was a scene more of plunder than of the desolation at the lake. Books, clothes, firearms, tea and coffee, kitchen utensils and trade goods lay strewn everywhere, much of it sodden by melting snow.

The most sombre find was a large iron kettle, containing human flesh. They found the body of George Donner wrapped in a sheet, evidently the handiwork of his wife. But someone had broken into the burial shroud, mutilated the body, split open the head and removed the brains. The flesh in the kettle was clearly identified as being George Donner's, and it was also clear that he had not been long dead. But there was no trace of Tamsen Donner. Since the day was now well advanced, they camped for the night and began drying out the most valuable items among the flotsam and jetsam. Many questions still remained to be answered. Whose were the tracks in the snow? Where was the Donners' money? It was well known that they had been carrying gold and silver as well as $1,500 in cash. It was decided that in the morning these questions must be answered. To guard against Digger or animal marauders, Fallon, together with Tucker, Coffeemeyer and Keyser would stay at the Creek and cache all the valuable goods they could not carry away; Foster, Rhoads and Sels would meanwhile follow the tracks in the snow.

Next morning, the three men following these footprints found that the trail petered out in the melting snow. They therefore headed straight for the cabins at the lake, where they soon found the answer to their conundrum. In one of the huts, among a mound of human bones, sat a demented Keseberg, and beside him a large pan full of liver and lights recently taken from a human body. Around him were the spoils taken from the dead. As Bernard de Voto puts it: 'like a monomaniac squirrel, Keseberg had filled his noisome burrow with the possessions of the Donners.' To their repeated questions, Keseberg would only answer that everyone else – Mrs Murphy and Tamsen Donner – was dead. When they deduced that the organs in the pan were Mrs Donner's and taxed Keseberg with the murder, he swore up and down that she had simply gone to sleep one night and was dead in the morning. But he admitted to eating her once dead. 'He eat her body and found her flesh the best he had ever tasted!' He further boasted that he had obtained from her body at least four pounds of fat. The three rescuers were left in no doubt that Keseberg had murdered her.

The three interrogators were, however, primarily interested in the Donners' wealth. They asked Keseberg what had happened to the money. He snivelled and whined that he knew nothing of any money and had no one's property. A search soon revealed otherwise. One bundle contained silks and jewellery worth $200 taken from the Donners' camp. Then, on removing a brace of pistols from Keseberg's belt (also stolen from the Donners), they felt a bulge in his waistcoat and uncovered $225 in gold. This, they felt, was just the tip of the iceberg. They asked Keseberg where the rest of the money was hidden and threatened him with Fallon's summary justice; Fallon had a reputation that was known even to a wretch like Keseberg. But Keseberg remained obstinately dumb. Giving him the night to think things over, the trio returned to Alder Creek to report to Fallon.

Next morning, hauling a crushing load of one hundred pounds each, all seven returned to the lake. Fallon immediately quizzed Keseberg on what he had done with the money. When Keseberg again pleaded ignorance, Fallon put a rope around his neck and told him to meet his Maker. He then threw Keseberg to the ground and tightened the rope. Choking and gasping, Keseberg finally promised that he would divulge all if released. Even so, he tried to stall once the rope was off. At last, he realised that Fallon really would asphyxiate him if he did not reveal where he had hidden the money. He took Rhoads and Tucker back to the Donners' camp and pointed out a cache directly underneath the projecting branch of a large tree. Here they found a further $273. They returned with their booty to Fallon and the others, who had meanwhile been moving their packs to the far end of the lake, ready for an early departure.

Keseberg celebrated his return to the cabins by making a greedy meal of the human brains and liver left over from breakfast. At the Donner camp, Fallon's party had found the frozen carcasses of a bullock and a horse, recently released from their icy tomb, with the meat still fresh and good – just one slice had been cut from the bodies. Naturally, then, Fallon asked Keseberg roughly why he had not eaten the bullock and the horse instead of human flesh. 'Oh, it's too dry eating,' he replied, 'the liver and lights were a great deal better, and the brains made good soup.' Realising that they were no longer dealing with a human being in any accepted sense, Fallon's men let it go at that. They suspected that there was further Donner treasure, and certainly money, hidden somewhere, but doubted their ability to gouge the information out of the crazed German. Besides, with more than $60 a head in prize money and trove. they had accomplished the main point of their mission. On 21 April, they started for Bear River valley in snow six to eight feet deep, camped on Yuba River that night, made eighteen miles the next day to the head of the Bear River valley, and reached journey's end on the 25th. Bearing Keseberg as a grisly prize, the fourth relief effectively rang down the curtain on the tragedy of the Donner party.

The Donner disaster was the greatest debacle in the entire history of the wagon trains, even if the death toll on the Meek cutoff in 1845 was probably higher. Forty-two emigrants and two Indian guides died (as well as all animals); however, forty-seven survived, and nearly all went on to live normal lives. This was particularly striking in the case of the Reed and Donner children, all of whom made old bones after coming so close to death on so many occasions. Although none of the survivors later achieved fame or fortune, and James Reed experienced an arc of declining prosperity, albeit without ever descending into indigence, in but a few cases was there evidence of any lasting damage from their privations. Cynics may draw an appropriate moral from the single fact that the most successful figure in later years was Selim Woodworth. Of course, the Donner tragedy was no more a typical outcome for an emigrant journey to the west coast than the *Titanic* disaster was typical of transatlantic travel by liner. But in both cases the enemy was complacency: in such situations eternal vigilance is needed, for, having seemingly conquered nature, mankind often forgets how thin is the margin of victory.

It is not the death toll that most shocks readers of the Donner disaster but the rapid descent of human beings into the heart of darkness. At all moments, it seems, civilisation skates on thin ice. Compounding the routine fact of man's inhumanity to man in the sierras was the spectacle of cannibalism, breaching a human taboo so strong that some writers on the Donner party have simply gone into denial and tried to excise man-eating from the record. In fact, as more and more facts leaked out, the extent of cannibalism came to seem greater, not less. Jean-Baptiste Trubode confided to Lieutenant H.A. Wise of the US Navy that he had eaten both Jacob Donner and a baby. 'Eat baby raw, stewed some of jake, and roasted his head, not good meat, tasted like sheep with the rot,' were his words. But the greatest man-eater was Keseberg. Accused by Coffeemeyer of murdering Tamsen Donner, he sued for defamation, won his case, but was awarded contemptuous damages of one dollar. Ever afterwards he swore he was innocent of the murder and has found believers. For those interested, George Stewart has mounted an effective rebuttal of this naive thesis.

There are critics who allege that historians have exaggerated the significance of the Donners at every level. Some have queried whether the taboo against cannibalism could ever be expected to override the instinct for survival. Others point out that man-eating was a fact of life on the early frontier. Old Bill Williams certainly killed and probably ate one of his comrades; Kit Carson said that, in starvation times, no one sensible ever walked ahead of Williams on the trail. Still others say that the Donners were simply unlucky: they lived out the experiences that many other emigrants would have suffered but for good fortune. It is certainly true that the Bartleson party of 1841 and the Stephens–Murphy outfit of 1844 came close to death by starvation, and Moses Schallenberger even spent the whole winter at Donner Lake. In 1846 itself, the Harlan–Young party nearly perished in the Great Salt Desert. So, allege the sceptics, we have allowed the side issue of cannibalism to blind us, and we have exaggerated the significance of the Donners at all levels. Why, after all, was dying in the snow worse than dying from exhaustion or fever, as some of the men and women of '46 did even before reaching the Truckee, or from pneumonia, as happened to many of the Oregon pioneers that year? These are issues which will doubtless always be debated.

The long-term effects of the Donner tragedy on emigrant travel were slight – one is tempted to say, non-existent. Word of the disaster reached the Midwest too late to deter the emigrants of 1847, and by 1848 news of the gold strike in California swept aside all other considerations. In any case, the press colluded in a conspiracy of silence and suppression of the truth so as not to discourage overland pioneers. By a rich irony, Bryant's book *What I Saw in California* became one of the 'books that won the West'. Even the fearsome Hastings cutoff was used by many travellers in 1850. In retrospect, then, the story of the Donners has a greater moral significance than historical. It is a classic tale of heroes and villains, which seems to have almost every ingredient: cowardice, incompetence, venality, embezzlement, murder, cannibalism and madness (though no suicide, unless we include Denton's 'altruistic' variety) on the one hand; stoicism, will power, endurance, compassion, generosity and humanity on the other. The villains stand out in the dark hues of Webster and Tourneur: Keseberg, Trubode, Reinhardt, Spitzer, Hastings, Wood-worth. The heroes are no less clearly delineated: Reed, Eddy, Stanton, McCutcheon, Starks. There is even a cast of moral ambivalents, including Breen, Clark and Fallon. The Donner tragedy illustrates a perennial truth. There are almost no depths of infamy to which human beings cannot sink, but they are also capable of godlike courage, nobility and self-sacrifice.

TEN

SAINTS AND SINNERS

The year 1847 was one of drama on the overland trail, but the greatest drama was attached to the exodus of the Mormons from Illinois to their new Zion in Utah. The Mormons were the most celebrated, and certainly the most influential, of all the multitudinous Christian sects that proliferated in the United States in the nineteenth century. The core of their belief was (and is) that they were the only true Church upholding the essential teachings of Jesus Christ. Modern children of Israel led by prophets who received direct instruction and continual revelation from God, they regarded themselves as a Chosen People and all non-believers as 'Gentiles'; in the modern era it has been well said that only in Salt Lake City is a Jew a Gentile. Mormons called themselves 'Latter-Day Saints' at once to distinguish themselves from and subtly identify themselves with the 'Former-Day Saints' of the New Testament.

Joseph Smith, the founder of this new religion (always regarded as a fanatical sect by its enemies), was born in Sharon, Vermont, in 1805 and received his first 'revelation' at Manchester, New York, in 1820. Three years later, an angel was said to have told him of a hidden gospel on golden plates, with two stones which would help translate it from the 'Reformed Egyptian'; and on the night of 22 September 1827, the sacred records were delivered into his hands. *The Book of Mormon* (1830) contained a highly fanciful history of America, allegedly written by a prophet named Mormon. America was said to have been colonised during the period of 'confusion of tongues' in the fifth century AD. Despite ridicule, hostility and often overt violence, the new Church of Jesus Christ of Latter-Day Saints rapidly gained converts. Mormon history officially began on 6 August 1830 in Fayette, New York, but a year later Smith set up his headquarters at Kirtland, Ohio. The tradition of nomadism was well entrenched in the early years. Jackson County, Clay County and Caldwell County, Missouri, were successive venues for the travelling church, which ultimately moved to Illinois. Finally, in 1839

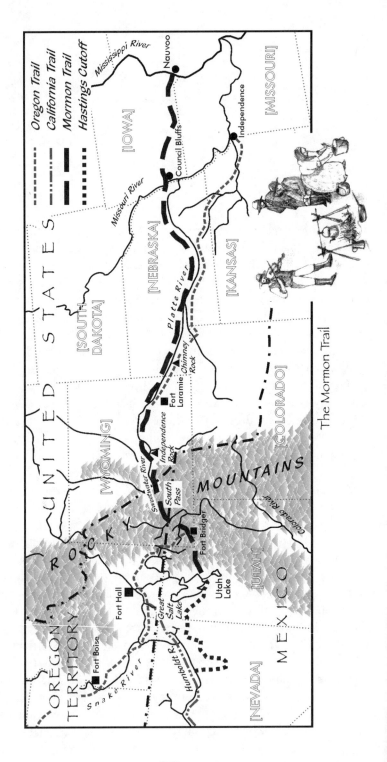

The Mormon Trail

Smith established his last capital at Nauvoo ('beautiful place' in Hebrew) in Illinois.

Smith used his well-honed political skills to play off Whigs against Democrats in the state legislature and so secure a charter for a new city at Nauvoo where he would be king. The 'Saints' set to work to build their Utopia on the Mississippi. Soon 15,000 Mormons lived in 2,000 houses, dominated by a giant stone temple. The houses were brick-built, New England-style, but a contrast and a reproach to the usual jerrybuilt structures of the frontier. Smith quickly gained more and more adherents, usually from the backward agricultural areas of North America or from the industrial slums of England. Making a powerful appeal to the have-nots, the dispossessed and the wretched of the earth, Mormonism's unique selling point was that it promised heaven to come plus an earthly paradise on the frontier; its devotees could be happy both in this life and in the next.

'Gentiles' resented the Saints, but things were peaceful enough until 1844, when Smith made public his latest revelation, which allowed polygamy among the Mormons who could afford it. Some of the Saints became suspicious at this worldly prescription, dubbed Smith a fallen prophet and denounced him to the world. Smith promptly got his associates to expel the 'troublemakers', but they were influential, articulate and, above all, sincere. A newspaper campaign by the expelled William Law in the *Nauvoo Expositor* revealed Smith's plural wives, his secret army of paid assassins, the Danites, his private land speculation and other abuses. Smith in retaliation sent his militiamen to destroy the *Expositor*'s presses. The governor of Illinois issued a warrant for Smith's arrest. Smith had three choices. He could resist by armed force, thus precipitating a civil war in the state which he could not but lose in the long run; he could 'light out for the territory' into Iowa, but this would leave Nauvoo leaderless and at the mercy of his enemies; or he could surrender to the civil authorities. With heavy misgivings he opted for the third path. Jailed in Carthage, Illinois, on 27 June 1844, he and his brother Hyrum were killed by a mob of more than two hundred anti-Mormon militiamen.

In 1835, Smith had appointed twelve 'apostles' as his closest aides, tasked, like the original apostles, with taking the gospel to the heathen. The most prominent of the twelve, Brigham Young, was an obvious choice to succeed Smith, but he had been away from the epicentre of Mormon affairs for significant periods, especially during his mission to England in 1840–41. In his absence, Sidney Rigdon, a skilled orator, had become Smith's right-hand man. On Smith's death, there was a short-lived but ferocious struggle to inherit the prophet's mantle between Rigdon and Young. The forty-three-year-old Young, ex-farm boy, carpenter, house painter and glazier, won the contest. Young was portly, with a tendency to obesity, with fleshy features, sharply pointed nose and thin lips. With long sandy hair, a stooped carriage and homespun clothes, he seemed at first sight an unprepossessing individual. He had no formal education and had a shaky command of grammar and spelling. But he was highly intelligent, with a formidable memory and an indomitable will. He had a powerful gift for invective and possessed the Churchillian knack of being able to enthuse the faithful and convince them that his purposes were their purposes. Most of all, he was an organiser of genius and a born leader.

Such was the man who stood forth as the saviour of the Saints at the moment of their greatest peril. Any lingering chance that Mormons and Gentiles might be able to compose their differences and live together was shattered in September 1845 when the Mormon fanatic Porter Rockwell, one-time bodyguard to Joseph Smith and hired assassin, shot down one of his arch-enemies. Rockwell hid himself among friends in Nauvoo and General Hardin of the Illinois militia vowed he would come into the city and arrest him even if it meant having to raze every last house to the ground. Under such pressure, the 'twelve apostles', under Brigham Young's guidance, issued a proclamation, hoping to buy time: they announced they would quit Nauvoo for good 'as soon as the grass grows and water runs'. By 23 November 1845, 3,285 families were making active preparations for trekking, with 1,508 wagons ready and another 1,892 begun. The apostles had advised each family to acquire a wagon and three yoke of oxen and take 2,700 pounds of goods (1,000 pounds of flour, twenty pounds of sugar, a rifle and ammunition, a tent and tentpoles); additional necessities were two cows, two beef cattle and three sheep.

Where did Brigham Young intend to take his people? Where was the promised land? Various possibilities had been canvassed, ranging from Mexico to Hawaii. The governor of Illinois, under pressure from anti-Mormon zealots to use armed force against the Saints, wrote to Young to suggest a mass exodus to California which he said was 'but sparsely populated by none but the Indian or imbecile Mexican Spaniard', and hinted to him that unless he trekked out soon, the United States government, with its own plans for California, might prevent the Saints from emigrating at all. Oregon and Texas had strong support at times among the counsels of the Saints, as did Vancouver Island. Although it was suggested as early as 1844 that the Mormons approach the infant republic of Texas for a land grant, Young was too shrewd a reader of the runes to be sucked into that particular quagmire. Quite apart from Texas's status as a slave state, it lay between Mexico and the United States and geopolitics suggested strongly that it would soon be a battlefield.

Vancouver Island was, at first sight, more attractive. A master politician, Young knew that an American settlement there would appeal mightily to Washington, locked as it was in conflict with Britain over the disputed Oregon territory; what answer would the Hudson's Bay Company have to 15–20,000 well-armed Mormon settlers? But Young had seen the scale of Gentile emigration to California and Oregon and he knew that these territories, as much as Texas, formed part of the grand design of Manifest Destiny. So, while keeping these options dangling and seeming uncertain where he was heading with the Saints, Young knew as early as 1845 that his objective was the Great Salt Lake desert. If the Saints were to survive, they had to find Zion in a location where ordinary migrating Americans would not be tempted to settle. Young, by his own later admission, was powerfully swayed by Lansford Hastings's account of his notorious 'cutoff' and even more by Frémont's lyrical description of the fertile river-and-creek system of the Great Salt Lake area.

But the anti-Mormons in Illinois wanted the Saints out of the state as soon as possible, and were not prepared to wait while Young debated the location of the promised land with his elders and apostles. There seems to have been a fear that Brigham Young might order one last retaliatory military action in revenge for having to quit Nauvoo. The authorities therefore tightened the screws. At the beginning of 1846, the charters both of the city of Nauvoo and the Nauvoo Legion (the Mormon militia) were withdrawn, thus dismantling the flimsy legal and military protection the Saints enjoyed. At the same time warrants were issued for the arrest of Young and eight apostles on charges of aiding and abetting a river-borne counterfeiting operation; marshals serving the warrant arrested a man named William Miller, who disguised himself as Young, and discovered their error only when they had him back in Carthage. Perhaps most menacingly of all, the Mormons' Gentile friend Thomas L. Kane warned Young that federal troops based at St Louis intended to intercept the migrating Mormons and slaughter them, allegedly to prevent the Saints' military muscle being added to British strength in Oregon. It seems that the authorities, knowing of Kane's links with Young, leaked bogus information to him to exert even more pressure on the Mormons to leave early.

Young brought forward the date of departure from April to February

375

1846. The first group of Saints crossed the Mississippi on makeshift ferries on 4 February. Nine miles inland they found a timbered oasis on the desolate prairie. Here, at Sugar Creek, they pitched camp. Storm-tossed ferries continued to ply across the mighty Mississippi, bringing forlorn parties of men, women and children with their household goods, chattels and animals, but so far the exodus was a mere dribble. Young himself crossed on 15 February with fifteen wagons and fifty members of his family, but boats were sinking on the way across, sickness was rampant at Sugar Creek, and the huddled families sustained themselves as best they could, singing favourite hymns like 'The Spirit of God Like a Fire is Burning', to the raucous accompaniment of brass bands. Seeing the low morale and pitiable state of the faithful, Young wished for a miracle and he got one. On 24 February, the temperature dropped to twelve degrees below, freezing the Mississippi into a lake of ice. Hundreds of wagons streamed across; the American Moses had secured passage for the Chosen People as surely as the original Moses had when he parted the waters of the Red Sea.

The Mormon camp at Sugar Creek in February 1846 has generated contradictory impressions. Some histories claim it as a place of weeping and wailing and gnashing of teeth, where children screamed with hunger, adults moped morosely or chafed in inactivity and all, to a male or female, shivered in intense cold and blinding snowstorms. Others speak of a spartan, stoical spirit, with the Saints simply waiting for the next revelations from the saviour. It was certainly a place of hardship and endurance, if not actual suffering. On 19 February, a blizzard blew down some tents, and every night the temperature was around zero or even below. But it was a true gathering of Zion, in that the great names in early Mormon history were soon here: the scientific Orson Pratt, the martial Hosea Stout, the pious prophetess and hymn-writer Eliza Snow, and Young's right-hand man Heber Kimball.

It is a paradox, noted by Richard Burton among others, that Mormon women, supposedly under the yoke of polygamy, made a more prominent showing in their exodus than Gentile women did in their overland journeys. Apart from Eliza Snow, the midwife Patty Sessions was well to the fore at Sugar Creek and later. Fifty-one years old, Patty was said to have delivered 3,977 babies and to have lost very few of them. As a mother herself, she had been less fortunate, having seen five of the eight children born to her die from infant diseases. Patty was a woman for all seasons: she delivered babies, drove four-ox teams, mended wagon covers, cooked and sewed, and praised God daily with a simple devotion. Her matter-of-fact stoicism comes over clearly in a February 1846 diary item: 'My things are packed ready for the West . . . In the afternoon put Sister Harriet Young to bed with a son. Made me a cap and . . . went to the Hall to see the scenery of the Massacre of Joseph and Hyrum Smith . . . We bade our children and friends goodbye and started for the west. Crossed the river about noon.'

On 1 March, nearly 5,000 Mormons in some five hundred wagons began the trek west through Iowa. The exodus was neither an orderly emigration nor a precipitate flight but somewhere in between. Some of the Saints referred to the experience of the Pilgrim Fathers but, overwhelmingly, the model in their minds was that of the biblical Exodus; nothing whatever seems to have been known about the Boer experience in the Great Trek ten years before. Fifty families formed the basic unit of travel, and each 'fifty' was subdivided into tens, led by a captain responsible for discipline, setting guards, supervising herdsmen and organising the commissary. Young called these moving companies the Camp of Israel and always spoke to them in language modelled on Moses's experience when leading the Israelites out of the land of Egypt. The line of march angled north-west along the Des Moines, passed through Farmington and crossed the Des Moines at Bonaparte, before striking due west to modern-day Centerville. They were not trailblazing and followed territorial roads as far west as possible before using Indian trails. They averaged only three miles a day and took a month to cover one hundred miles.

Why was progress so slow? Many factors were involved. The Mormon Trail was always a two-way affair, unlike either the California or Oregon trails, in that throughout 1846–48 there was a steady eastward traffic for new supplies and converts. Since the Mormons, unlike the Gentile emigrants, had to think of those coming after them, they stopped to build way stations. The first was at Richardson's Point, fifty-five miles from Nauvoo, where successive waves of emigrants would find supplies, wood, tools, blacksmiths and religious counsellors. Disease also assailed the pilgrims during the hegira across Iowa: scurvy, diphtheria, cholera, typhoid, tuberculosis and a range of childhood illnesses. Iowa was a wilderness of bluestem prairie grass and stands of oak and hickory groves, but there were numerous rivers to cross and many dangerous swamps and bogs. The Saints had to lash together tough willow logs and throw them across rolling riverine swells. But what slowed them down most of all was the rain and the mud. It rained almost incessantly throughout March, the wagon wheels sank in deep troughs, mired to the hubs, and, as one cynic wrote, 'it was a middling good road when the mud did not quite reach one's bootstraps while astride a horse'.

On the River Chariton, just above Centerville, the Camp of Israel established a second station and this time planted crops for the use of later waves of Mormon emigrants. Zina Huntington Jacobs gave birth to a son, named Chariton, and another woman, not named in the accounts, gave birth in an improvised shelter – just blankets fastened to poles stuck in the ground, with a bark roof through which the rain was dripping. The sisters held dishes to catch the water, thus preventing the newborn from undergoing a premature baptism. Childbirth was at record levels, for Patty Sessions alone recorded that by 22 April she had delivered four babies and attended three women who miscarried. But still the rain beat down, trying the emigrants' patience. Tired pioneers had to put on sodden shoes in the morning; children had to be whipped whimpering from their beds to milk cows. Sometimes, woodcutting parties were caught out on the prairie by violent storms and had to shiver all night without food or fire. Even those asleep in camp had a cold time of it, for their beds faced the triple peril of inundation – when tents blew down, being soaked by rain that dripped through the wagon covers, or being covered in mud through being spread on wet ground.

Even tough men like Brigham Young's rather dim brother Lorenzo began to complain. After crossing the Chariton on 23 March, he wrote in his diary:

We camped on the hill. It began to rain about noon and rained the rest of the day. About nine o'clock P.M. it began to roar in the west, and the wind began to blow. I stepped to the door of my tent and took hold to it, but in a moment there came a gust of wind and blew the tent flat to the ground. My next care was to hold my carriage, which was under the tent, from blowing away. The rain came down in torrents so fast that it put out the fire. In a few minutes it was all darkness, and it was so cold that it seemed as though I must perish. I stood and held the . . . end of the carriage about one hour. The rain wet me through and through, and I never felt in my life as though I must perish with the cold more than then.

Captain Pitt's brass band, converted en masse in England, was a great consolation to the Saints and a moneymaker when it went among the Gentiles. It received invitations to play at Farmington, Keosaqua and other Iowa towns, where music was an unwonted luxury. It was a great hit in these places and the band would travel anywhere for a fee. Sometimes the fee could be as low as seven dollars or as high as twenty-five plus meals, sometimes the payment would be in bushels of corn or even a pail of honey (that a band member later stole for his own family's use), and on one occasion they played for Indians for the odd fee of ten dollars and ten cents. In camp, the band would perform at the nightly dances, where minuets, cotillions, quadrilles, polkas, Virginia and Scotch reels, square dances and hoedowns were performed (as well as those steps dubbed *varsouvienne, schottische* and money musk), or play hymns at prayer meetings. It was the musicians' proud boast that they put in a full day's work in addition to their entertainment duties and they cited the time they travelled eight miles, split 130 rails before dark, traded them to a farmer for corn and then gave a concert in the evening.

Brigham Young's essential task was to find the equilibrium point between duty and pleasure and between the sacred and the secular. Before the wagons left Sugar Creek, he had explained his system: all must keep strict order and have peaceable relations with everyone they met; young men should hire out as day labourers along the way to buy food and equipment. 'If you do these things,' he told them, 'faith will abide in your hearts; and the angels of God will go with you, even as they went with the children of Israel when Moses led them from the land of Egypt.' The Saints readily complied: men made rails, fences, barns, houses and husked corn, accepting in return not just cash but fodder, hay, corn, vegetables and indeed anything that had a use. But on 22 March, Young and Elder Kimball had to repeat the instructions and, in a major speech, insist on better order; it seemed that the arithmetically smooth system of fifties and tens was not being complied with.

As always, the labours of the Mormon women were much commented on. One sister baked a batch of loaves one day which Eliza Snow declared 'would have done honor to a more convenient bakery than . . . a fire in the wilderness'. When she came to full term, Sister Ann Richards asked a Gentile midwife to help her, but the woman refused unless she was paid a hefty fee in advance. Since Sister Ann had no money, she managed on her own and the child was stillborn. To add to her sorrows, her two-year-old daughter Wealthy died soon afterwards. Her grandmother had gone to one Iowa farm to beg some soup for the ailing Wealthy, but the farmer's wife swore at her. 'I wouldn't sell or give one of you Mormons a potato to save your life,' she exclaimed, and then set her dog on the grandmother. But the amazing thing about Mormon women was how deeply they could be consoled by their religion. At the Missouri River, Ann felt spiritually reborn when Brigham Young said to her: 'It shall be said of you that you have come up through much tribulation.'

From the Chariton, the Camp of Israel headed south-west to Shoal or Locust Creek, where they set up another permanent camp, then turned north-west into present-day Decatur County, recently surveyed but still uninhabited by white men. At Locust Creek, after a brief pause, heavy rains began again and lasted until mid-April. But still the Saints displayed prodigious energy. The men continued to hire out at farms, extending their expertise to the digging of wells, the making of nails and burning of charcoal. When their menfolk were away on such labours or were building bridges or cutting grass at Brigham Young's behest, the women drove the wagons. They were never at rest, either nursing sick children or sewing, knitting, patching, spinning or finding edible roots on the prairie. They even learned to churn butter by using the jolting of the wagon to curdle a pail of cream. Their one moment of pleasure came with the nightly dances, the fiddle music or the stentorian sounds of Captain Pitt's Brass Band, especially when Sister Eliza Snow had devised one of her devotional songs, such as this:

> And it matters not where or whither
> You go, neither whom among,
> Only so that you closely follow
> Your leader Brigham Young.

Knee-deep and axle-high in mud at the beginning of April, the latter-day children of Israel trudged on. On 1 April, Patty Sessions wrote: 'Mud aplenty. The worst time we have had yet . . . Froze our shoes in the tent [and] many could not lie down without lying in the water.' In mid-April, there was finally a dry spell, but someone, whether Indian or white man was uncertain, fired the old grass and caused a prairie fire; on the first dry nights, the Saints were reduced to sleeping on charred ground carpeted with ash and soot. Some of the brethren had complained that the original children of Israel had not had to endure mud, whatever their other travails, but it was almost as though the lament had been heard and punished. The Israelites had suffered a plague of serpents during their wanderings in the desert and now, suddenly, tempted out of their holes by the sunshine, rattlesnakes appeared in hundreds. Lorenzo Young's diary of the trek through Decatur County becomes a daily tally of rattlers slain by the Saints – two on 20 April, another two on the 23rd, one on the 24th, another on the 25th, and William Clayton's journal concurs. But on 23 April, irritation turned to concern as a number of horses were bitten. One, prayed over by an elder, survived, but two more did not. The return of the rains ended the menace for a while but at the next sunny spell the rattlesnakes were again in evidence and killed two more horses on 7 May.

On 24 April, the Saints reached Garden Grove, 155 miles west of

Nauvoo and 130 miles east of Council Bluffs. It was a fertile, beautiful spot, its green, lush valley a contrast to the usual dull, colourless plains of Iowa. Here, Brigham Young ordered a long stopover while a large way station was built. The pioneers acted with the precision of a Roman army. Three hundred and fifty-nine men cleared three hundred acres of land and cut 10,000 rails; some of the lumber was used for coffins to bury those who had succumbed to ten weeks' cold and starvation. One hundred men attacked the bottomland trees with axes while another forty-eight cut them into logs for cabins. Another gang began building a bridge across the Grand River, another made wooden ploughs, while yet another made a foray into Missouri to trade dishes and furniture for food. Road-building and fencing and planting fields completed the task of taming the wilderness, leaving an entire town ready for those who would come after them to the promised land. A large number of people, mainly the sick and dying, were also left behind here; Young was increasingly worried about the dearth of foodstuffs as they plunged deeper into the wilderness: his hunters brought in the occasional wild turkey or sage chicken but nothing more substantial.

The organic solidarity of the Saints was again under threat. Although Brigham Young had explicitly preached a sermon against theft on 12 April, even theft against Gentiles, petty pilfering was reaching epidemic proportions as the hardships of the trail bred selfishness and ruthless instincts of survival. With so many suffering disease and starvation, Christian principles tended to go to the wall. James Hemmic challenged Wilbur Earl to a duel and was excommunicated as a troublemaker; many Saints wanted to give up and return to Nauvoo; members of a counterfeiting gang manufacturing 'boodles of queer' were said to be sheltering among sympathetic Mormons; tempers frayed and minds reached the end of their tether. On 4 May, William Huntington noted that his neighbour William Edwards had gone out of his mind and was considered dangerous. And on 7 May, the very day of the return of the rattlesnakes, Peter Haws's daughter threw a cup of scalding coffee in the face of one of her father's young teamsters, nearly blinding him. The addle-brained Lorenzo Young simply commented: 'The Lord reward her.'

The responsibility for maintaining law and order on the trail lay with Hosea Stout and his hundred-strong force of 'police', answerable directly to Brigham Young. His was not an enviable job. Apart from the routine unpopularity incurred simply because he was a chief of police, he had to enforce the laws on sanitation and the exercise of bodily functions. The Mormons took their cue from Moses, who in Deuteronomy 23:12–15 commanded that each Israelite should bury his or her own excreta far from camp. Stout had to enforce the lavatory rule of 'gentlemen to the right, ladies to the left', at each encampment. He was also the obvious target of the neurotic and the malcontent. Bishop George Miller, one of those hypertrophied individualists who chafed under the command of Brigham Young, refused to give Stout's policemen the password when entering camp on the ground that he was too senior a personage for such commands to apply to him. When Stout insisted, Miller laid a denunciation before Brigham Young, accusing Stout of having tried to kill him with malice aforethought. But Stout was too valuable to Young to be reprimanded. He knew, or soon found out, everything that went on in camp. His investigation of the 7 May coffee-hurling incident itself threw up some interesting facts. It seemed that Peter Haws's daughter had been caught in bed with a young man named Erastus Derby, at which a clique of young men overturned the wagon. Burning with indignation, the shamed girl waited her chance, then hurled the boiling coffee at one of the men she suspected of being involved.

Hosea Stout, indeed, was beset with problems on all sides. Even as he was supposed to maintain discipline and punish malefactors, Stout had a host of problems nearer home. His wife, having suffered severely from pleurisy during her pregnancy, gave birth in a wagon on 21 April, and there were fears for the future of both mother and child. His young son Hyrum died after undergoing agonies from scurvy and whooping cough. With his family sick and his helpers sent back to aid his sister Anna, stranded further back on the trail, Stout had to herd his stock himself. Perennially suffering from migraine, he had to endure the ultimate humiliation of begging food from the twelve on 6 May when his own supplies ran out. He was in particularly wrathful mood when news came in on 27 May that the United States was at war with Mexico. Stout hated the United States, the persecutors of his people as he saw it, and, on the biblical precept of an eye for an eye, openly expressed the hope that Mexico would win the war and the United States be utterly destroyed.

William Clayton, official secretary to the twelve, was in even rawer mood. One of the earliest polygamists, with two wives (Lydia and Margaret) on the trail with him and another back in Illinois, he was a neurotic, troubled by anxiety-filled dreams and neurasthenic ailments, both of which he brooded on for their cosmic significance. On 15 April, Clayton won an immortal niche in Mormon history by composing what is generally agreed to be the finest of all Mormon hymns, 'Come, Come, Ye Saints' (originally entitled 'All is Well'). The occasion is described by Clayton in his journal:

This morning Ellen Kimball came to me and wishes me much joy. She said Dinatha [Clayton's wife back in Nauvoo] has a son . . . Truly I feel to rejoice at this intelligence . . . In the evening the band played and after we dismissed [we] retired to my tent . . . We had a very pleasant time playing and singing until about twelve o'clock and drank health to my son . . . This morning I composed a new song – 'All is Well.'

But Clayton was not usually so euphoric or relaxed. He felt put upon and exploited by an ungrateful rank and file and an arrogant leadership, who took his Herculean labours as their God-given right. Clayton's journals are full of complaints about his fellow Saints. He records the complaints of those worse off than him, who feel that he ought to share all his worldly goods with them, and records his own complaints: that teamsters he has dismissed still expect to be fed by him; that others hauling Church property routinely draw provisions from his private stores; that Mormons left behind at the way stations expect him to support them until their crops grow. Clayton felt that he had a plethora of duties but no rights: the twelve would not share with him, though *he* was expected to share with all those lower on the hierarchical and financial scale. He particularly disliked the way the twelve gave him clerical duties and notes to write up when he could have been chopping trees and making his own living conditions more comfortable; meanwhile, the lazy apostles were out supervising carpentry to make their own wagons dens of luxury. Clayton wrote bitterly: 'It looked as if I had to be a slave and take slave's fare all the journey.'

All this sets in context the Panglossian remarks on the trek that have often been cited. Typical is Thomas Kane's: 'We were happy and contented and the songs of Zion resounded from wagon to wagon, reverberating through the woods while the echo returned from the distant hill.' The truth is that the staged and staggered trek from Nauvoo to Council Bluffs in 1846 was in the main a grim affair. Some emigrants never recovered from the snow and icy rain of February and March, when frost-bitten feet left them with chilblains at best or gangrene at worst. Shoulders and legs stiffened with rheumatism and those who tried to restore circulation by jumping, wrestling and other exercise, like William Clayton, found they simply made matters worse. In the rain and mud, six miles a day was an exceptional tally, and sometimes one mile a day was closer to the mark. With prairie creeks engorged by the rain, caravans had to wait till the floods subsided. If they were caught in a stretch without timber, there would be no fires for two weeks, and hence no cooked food, no dry clothes or bedding. When the sun finally came out, rattlesnakes and mosquitoes came out too. Much attention has focused on the deaths through cholera, scurvy, malaria and typhoid during the trek, but even the survivors and those untouched by major disease suffered from colds, migraines, sinus infections and other minor debilitating conditions. The complaints of men like Stout and Clayton were made in a very severe context indeed.

At last, after a three-week halt, it was time to move on from Garden Grove. Parley Pratt, one of the twelve apostles, was sent ahead to scout out a location for the next permanent settlement and found some round and sloping hills, grassy and covered with groves of timber. To Pratt, the place suggested Mount Pisgah, the famous location from which Moses saw the Promised Land as in the Book of Deuteronomy. He sent back word to Brigham Young that he had found what they were looking for and on 18 May Young's pioneers came to the middle fork of the Grand River and founded another settlement, named Mount Pisgah as Pratt had wished. Once again, cabins arose at astonishing speed and elaborate vegetable gardens were laid; the Saints planted peas, cucumber, beans, corn, buckwheat, potatoes, pumpkin and squash. But there was much sickness and demoralisation. Even stalwarts of the trail like Eliza Snow and Mrs Stephen Markham staggered in ill and collapsed in the crude huts. To his disappointment, William Huntington was appointed president of the Mount Pisgah Council, which meant he could go no further west. Evidently, there was much muttering and complaining at Pisgah, for Heber Kimball felt constrained to deliver another of his fiery sermons, excoriating the travellers for their lack of faith.

Brigham Young and the main party pressed on and reached the Council Bluffs area near the east bank of the Missouri River on 13 June. By common consent, this leg of the journey from Nauvoo, onward from Mount Pisgah, was by far the most pleasant. The sun was high in the sky, the roads had dried out and the grass for the animals was knee-high. Fish, deer and wild turkey were now plentiful and the women and young girls picked gallons of delicious wild strawberries. The pioneers spread out along Indian Creek and Mosquito Creek until, by 22 June, five hundred wagons and nine of the twelve apostles were camped by the banks of the Missouri. A few crossed the river and inspected the old Jesuit mission which the fathers had abandoned in 1841 because of Sioux hostility and alcoholism among the Indians, but most set to and built the first log cabins, which they called Millersville. It had taken them nearly three months to travel 265 miles, but the rest of the Mormons, up to 14,000 of them, were either still back in Nauvoo or were toiling along the trail or in the way stations.

Brigham Young was anxious to get his flock across the river, into the safer territory of Nebraska, but the problem was that these were Indian lands and, according to the laws of the United States, they were forbidden to settlers. He therefore sought the earliest possible meeting with the Potawatomi chief Pied Riche, to whom he proposed an alliance; in return for temporary settlement rights he promised to use the armed might of the Saints to protect the Potawatomi against their traditional enemies the Pawnee. Pied Riche, who knew all about the perfidy of Washington, having been driven west himself by the Indian removal policy, was more than willing to do a deal. When he heard what Young had to say and the story of the persecutions at Nauvoo and elsewhere, he said: 'So we have both suffered. We must help one another and the Great Spirit will help us both. Because one suffers and does not deserve it, that is no reason we shall suffer always. I say we may live to see it right yet. However, if we do not, our children will.'

Having completed a ferry on 29 June, Young took his people to the Nebraska side and swam the cattle across. His original plan was to found a settlement in the Great Basin in late 1846 and that continued to be his policy at least until his arrival at Council Bluffs, as he informed President Polk by letter. But two circumstances changed his mind. The first was the realisation of the size of the task ahead of him. There were too many invalids in the party already and, the twelve apostles warned him, if the leaders themselves forged ahead and formed the vanguard, who would stiffen the backbone of an already backsliding Camp of Israel at Council Bluffs? In any case, the Saints were already far too fragmented as it was, with bodies dotted about all over Iowa and other independent bodies pursuing alternative routes to the West. Pending a final decision, it was best to send available manpower on as wide a sweep as possible, planting and sowing, so that at least the commissariat problems of the onward trek would not be quite so acute. Young faced more vehement opposition than ever before or afterwards over his determination to establish Zion in 1846. But he was always a realist. He backed down; parties of planters were meanwhile sent as far afield as Austin and Florence, twenty miles from modern-day Omaha.

Yet even if Young had been disposed to overrule the twelve, the next development would anyway have made his original plans impossible. On 26 June, Captain James Allen and three dragoons arrived at Mount Pisgah, on their way to see Brigham Young with instructions from President Polk. The US president requested and required that the Mormons furnish a battalion of five hundred men to serve in the Mexican war, specifically to march against Santa Fe and southern California with

General Kearney's Army of the West. This was Polk's way of ensuring the loyalty of the Saints in territory that was still technically Mexican. The astute Young at once saw how the situation could be turned to his advantage. First, he got Allen's 'permission' to settle on the Indian lands, though Allen had no authority to grant it. Then he thought ahead. Faced with the twelve's veto on an advance guard headed by the leadership, and now with the impossibility of a mass advance because of the Mexican war, a Mormon battalion could be just the way he could get a vanguard into the West. While claiming for public consumption that this demand for manpower was yet another example of persecution by Washington, in reality he could get the US government to provide free transport to the West, plus pay and allowances that would provide the surplus for later mass emigration of the Saints.

Young had to be at his brilliant best as a politician to achieve his aims, for opinion among the Saints was overwhelmingly hostile to the idea of giving aid and succour to the hated United States. Hardliners like Hosea Stout (and he was far from being alone) alleged that the recruitment of five hundred men was a transparent ploy: either the Americans planned to leave the families at Council Bluffs defenceless so they could massacre them at will, or they intended to lure the five hundred away into the wilderness and make away with them there; maybe both atrocities were contemplated. More pragmatic objectors in Young's councils pointed out that in his 'cost-benefit' analysis, he had not included the cost of caring for the families of the absent men or for the replacement farmers, hunters, teamsters and even preachers that would be required to fill the gaps of those away on military service. Young countered that the propaganda advantage of a Mormon battalion would be huge; their 'patriotic' service would be the perfect excuse to hold the United States at arm's length once they reached the Great Basin, for Washington could not then claim it had an enemy on the flank of its westward expansion.

Yet most of the Saints had none of Young's subtlety and could at first see only the fact of Mexico's fighting against their old persecutors. More thoughtful critics considered that by overt support for the United States, the Saints might be drawn into unnecessary conflict with Great Britain, a potential ally in the Pacific north-west. Many thought war between Britain and the United States over the Oregon territory only a matter of time. In his journal, Clayton noted the current reports that Britain was pursuing a three-pronged military offensive against Washington: raising and arming the black slaves in the South; whipping up the Indian tribes on the Great Plains; and sending a fleet and an army of 10,000 men round

Cape Horn. Whatever the reason for the objections, Young could at first find no significant numbers of volunteers.

Brigham Young therefore exercised his implicit powers as the heir of Joseph Smith. Declaring that the future of the Saints required this sacrifice he asked of them, he instituted what was virtually a draft. He ordered the Saints to volunteer and told them that, if they refused, he would shame them by forming a battalion of old men and women. Even so, it took him three weeks of threat, bluster, cajolery and unflagging energy to raise five companies. The Mormon battalion eventually comprised 543 males, mainly young but with a few grandfathers, plus large numbers of women and children. To sugar the pill, Young promised the volunteers that none of them would be killed in battle. This astounding 'revelation' was in fact just applied intelligence: Young had already worked out that the chances of his men having to fight were infinitesimal. So it was that on 18 July 1846 an entire Mormon battalion was ready to march from Council Bluffs to Fort Leavenworth for mustering. Reduced in size by the weeding out of cripples, invalids and the old to about a third the official number of effectives, the Mormon battalion nevertheless completed one of the longest military marches on the North American continent to date, from Fort Leavenworth to San Diego. True to Brigham Young's promise, they never came under enemy fire.

Including the computation allowance of $21,000 for the volunteers' clothing, Brigham Young raised more than $71,000 in pay and allowances from the Mormon battalion. To make sure that the men did not remit the money directly to their families, Young sent Orson Pratt after the battalion to make the men hand over their first tranche of pay. Later, he sent his adopted son John D. Lee to Santa Fe to intercept the next payments. Young soothed the ruffled feelings of the battalion members by writing to them that the money was a 'peculiar manifestation of the kind providence of our Heavenly Father at this time'. He then used the cash to buy wagonloads of supplies from St Louis at wholesale prices, though there were murmurings that at least some of the money was appropriated by Young and the apostles for their own comfort.

It was September before Brigham Young hit on a permanent base, the legendary 'Winter Quarters', often referred to as the Mormons' Valley Forge. Before that, he tried and abandoned two sites, the second of which, called Cutler's Park, was later claimed as Nebraska's first city. Still hankering after the idea of somehow getting an advance guard of the Saints to the Salt Lake valley that year, Young sent a party of men to the Elkhorn River, thirty miles west, with instructions to build a ferry or bridge. Young also allowed Bishop George Miller, a cross-grained individual who was always for pushing ahead of his fellow Mormons, to proceed to the Platte valley, then changed his mind and sent a courier telling them to halt where they were on the Loup Fork and establish a branch of Zion there. Miller, who never heeded Young's orders, went north on a nine-day march to the land of the Ponca Indians and ensconced himself there for the winter; while there, he gradually renounced Brigham Young's leadership and ended by leading his men into apostasy.

There was a black day in the Mormon calendar on 17 September 1846. Until then, there had still been about a thousand Mormons left in Nauvoo, mainly the sick and the very poor, together with some high-ranking Saints who had been delegated to complete the sale of real estate and shepherd the rearguard over the Mississippi. As the numbers of Saints decreased over the summer, the boldness and violence of their enemies increased. After a number of killings and outrages in the environs of the city, they finally attacked Nauvoo itself. The hard-pressed Mormons defended themselves for a few days, but were outnumbered and no match for 2,500 vicious, enraged looters. After a long-range exchange of fusillades, a truce was arranged: the Mormons agreed to leave immediately, bag and baggage. Nauvoo was then sacked as thoroughly as Geiseric's Vandals had sacked Rome. Some of the Saints were hurried along to the way stations in Iowa, but many huddled in misery on the Iowa shore of the Mississippi. Soon, disease struck at the aptly named 'Poor Camp' and the Saints began to die like flies.

Brigham Young did what he could to help them, but most of his energies were by now absorbed in the building of Winter Quarters. He had originally intended to winter on Grand Island on the Platte, but his scouts warned him the area was short of grass and water and was a nodal point for the incessant warfare between the Pawnee and Sioux. Accordingly, he set about building a temporary Zion on the western shores of the Missouri. This quickly became a settlement of 631 dwellings housing 3,483 people. Some of the 'homes' were solid cabins constructed of cottonwood logs, but many more were made of 'prairie marble' (sod) or were mere dugouts. All were draughty and cramped, exposed to winds off the Missouri, nearly all windowless and many without doors. When Hosea Stout moved into his new 'home' on 24 November, he reported it to be little more than a bothy, 'neither door nor windows not even but a few of the cracks was yet stopped up and a hard North wind blowing'.

Based in these shacks, the Saints still had to perform back-breaking toil, chopping wood, gathering fuel, hunting and trapping and, above all, herding and droving the 30,000 cattle and innumerable sheep, which the Indians regarded as their own living larder. Young still tried to hire out journeyman labour to the Gentiles and continued with his own moneymaking schemes. One involved women making baskets; another involved the construction of a gristmill. Young himself had an entire church to administer, not just the stricken Saints dotted across Iowa but his missions elsewhere in the United States and overseas. That the seat of Mormon government was what a later observer described as '700 to 800 hovels' is not the least amazing thing about Winter Quarters. It had streets laid out on a grid pattern, a welfare store, shops, woodworking huts, blacksmiths' forges, and much else. Mormon women taught the children, babysat, spun yarn, worked in boarding houses, wove baskets and flour sacks, and made and sold wine from elderberries.

While in their temporary improvised capital, the Saints were stricken by epidemics which some likened to the biblical plagues of Egypt. Although cholera and smallpox were mercifully absent, successive waves of malaria, typhoid fever, dysentery, pneumonia, pellagra and scurvy descended on Winter Quarters and all the Mormon camps throughout Iowa. The outbreaks began as early as August. Among the party building the ferry at the Elkhorn River, more than a third went down at once, so that burial parties could not keep up with the dead. There were mass burials in trenches; women sat in the doorways of tents, keening and mourning for their dead children, whisking the flies from infant corpses that were already decaying. The settlements east of the Missouri suffered even more dreadfully than Winter Quarters, with Garden Grove worst hit of all. In retrospect, the causes were obvious. Mosquitoes proliferated along the Missouri, though the naive Saints, in common with everyone else at the time, did not suspect the insects but thought malaria was caused by 'miasmata'. The lack of vitamin C in the diet was the cause of scurvy, while cold, malnutrition and the sheer exhaustion, physical and mental, of the year's events so far took their toll. Sanitation was primitive or non-existent, the emigrants drank contaminated water, and the sheer close-packed proximity of other human beings spread disease quickly. One six-room house contained six adult women, five adult men and ten children.

The usual figure given for deaths from disease at Winter Quarters between August 1846 and March 1847 is 600. Recent research has established that although the true figure was probably nearer 400, total Mormon deaths in Winter Quarters and all the Iowa way stations were over a thousand. There were no trained physicians among the Saints and their only recourse was to call on their priests to 'cast out' the illness, equated with an evil spirit. A diary entry from William Clayton is typical: 'Twice Heber [Kimball] has rebuked my fever but it has returned.' This underlines the obvious fact that disease did not spare the Mormon elite. Although the idiotic Lorenzo Young could find nothing more significant to record at Winter Quarters than his thirty-ninth birthday, all around him colleagues suffered. At Mount Pisgah, William Huntington died. John D. Lee, thought to be indestructible, hovered near death despite 'rebukes' to the sickness from both Wilford Woodruff and Brigham Young himself. Young and Woodruff were themselves ill for long periods. Worst hit of all was Hosea Stout. Having lost one son (Hyrum) at Garden Grove and his favourite boy William Hosea between Mount Pisgah and Council Bluffs, he sustained a further bitter loss in Winter Quarters when his wife Marinda died in childbirth, along with her child. To cap all, his wife Lucretia ran away; with such a rapid loss of spouses Stout certainly needed polygamy.

Even those who survived were left permanently weakened and unfit for further trekking. Fourteen-year-old Louisa Jeune, niece of Jane Snyder Richards, suffered grievously from scurvy because her family could provide no fresh fruit and vegetables or even any cornbread. She was unable to ingest anything but liquids for six weeks. 'My mouth was so badly eaten with canker, my legs were all drawn up. I could not straighten up any more than if I was sitting down.' She remained that way for a long time afterwards and for years she walked with a cane as one leg was a full two inches shorter than the other. There is more than a suspicion that the suffering could have been lessened if the better-off Saints had been prepared to share their good fortune with their poorer and weaker brethren. The recent convert Ursulia Hascall, for example, had access to a wide variety of food – beans, potatoes, onions, artichokes as well as coffee, sugar and molasses – and came through the winter unscathed.

With death, disease and despair all around them, it is not surprising that many of the weaker brethren began to backslide. Hosea Stout, Brigham Young's strong right arm, had massive unpopularity to add to his woes when he enforced discipline. He in turn started to lose all sense of proportion, initiated a vendetta against William Clayton and swore to kill him once the apostles moved on in the spring. But Stout's most notorious example of draconian discipline involved the serpent that the Mormons of all people ought to have scotched: sexuality. Three young unmarried men, Peletiah Brown, Daniel Barnum and Jack Clothier, were found to have spent fifteen successive nights with young women to whom they had no 'right' according to Mormon law. In the words of the indictment, they had committed the crime of 'adultery or having carnal communication'. As Bernard de Voto remarks: 'In the mores of a polygamous society there is no greater crime.' Stout told them they would be shot, but some of the more retribution-minded of the Saints bruited it about that Brigham Young had ordered exemplary castration.

As it was, the three men received a severe flogging. Daniel Barnum bore up to his eighteen lashes bravely enough. Peletiah Brown, though, broke down towards the end of his ordeal and pleaded with the man wielding the whip. 'O Brother Eldridge, if you will only stop I'll never touch another girl again while hell's afloat.' But the third offender, Jack Clothier, caused the most trouble. His mother refused to accept that her son had done anything wrong and whipped up her extended kin to defend him. There was a tense stand-off between the Clothier clan and Stout's police before they finally extracted the malefactor for his whipping. For his 'contumacity' in trying to evade punishment, Clothier received an extra five lashes, making twenty-three in all. At the end of the punishment he did not come to heel like his two confrères but continued surly and hostile. This punishment for fornication was considered excessive, and there were murmurings among the Mormon rank and file. Ever the pragmatist, Young placated his critics by lifting the usual strict prohibition against strong liquor. Those who could afford it imbibed deeply; some may even unwittingly have saved their lives by the amounts of vitamin C in the wine they drank.

The discontent of the faithful was only one of manifold problems with which Brigham Young contended that winter. Chief Big Elk of the Omaha Indians was not as accommodating as the Potawatomi, and the Omaha and the Oto tribes were accomplished thieves with a particular liking for Mormon sheep. The relationship between Mormons and the Omaha began well enough. When Big Elk met Brigham Young and the Mormon apostles on 28 August he made them welcome with some fine words:

I am probably the oldest man in council and hope you will not take offence if I call you all sons . . . My sons, I like what you say very much and I have it in my heart. I am very weak and because I am weak am imposed upon; If I go to hunt one way I meet enemies and if I turn the other way I meet enemies. I am hunted like the dog on the prairie. We are killed by families without provocation and imposed upon every way and have been for the last ten years. But I have held still because I was advised so to do by the government or I could have done as they have done and killed some too. But I have not done it.

In short, Big Elk endorsed what Pied Riche of the Potawatomi had said. But it was Big Elk, not the white man, who was speaking with forked tongue this time. Big Elk's idea of friendship was for his people to help themselves to the Mormon herds. The response of the Saints was complex. To an extent they were constrained by their own dogma. The Book of Mormon told the story of the struggles of the Nephite and Lamanite peoples, descendants of the prophet Lehi, who led his family from Israel to America at the beginning of the Babylonian captivity. According to Mormon belief, the Lamanites annihilated the Nephites around AD 421 and became the ancestors of the American Indians. Mormons believed that when they joined the Church of the Latter-Day Saints, they were literally transformed into 'the blood of Israel' and therefore felt a special kinship with Indians, whose ancestry made them, like the Saints, children of Abraham. Yet the rapidly increasing tally of cattle thefts by the Omahas made some kind of action imperative.

Young's credo was that it always cheaper to feed Indians than fight them, but he found the Omaha a trial and ordered his guards to fire at Omaha caught stealing cattle, the first time over their heads, then, if they persisted, with deadly aim. He was well aware that the Saints were deeply disillusioned by his standing order that they were not to retaliate on the Omaha for thieving. Some relief came from an unexpected quarter when the Omaha went on the warpath against the Sioux in December and were badly mauled, losing seventy-three dead in a battle. But by this time Young had scant sympathy for them and actually ordered his guard to disperse an Omaha burial party that was making too much noise with its chanting and keening. Eventually, his patience snapped with the constant thievery and he warned Big Elk that any Indian caught stealing would suffer the same penalty for theft as a white man, i.e. a public flogging. It is unclear if Young was influenced in his policy by the advice of Father de Smet, who met the Mormon leaders that winter at Council Bluffs and was impressed with them. De Smet told the Saints the sad story of the mission he had established on this very spot in 1838, only to have to abandon it three years later because of Indian recalcitrance. But de Smet heartened Young and the apostles by giving a glowing account of the Salt Lake valley.

Sometimes it seemed that Brigham Young kept the Mormon movement alive that winter by sheer force of personality and the Saints' love of three-hour harangues. Many factions in Winter Quarters did not like the leader's authoritarianism and what they suspected was a selective communism, whereby the goods of the middling sort were distributed to the Mormon poor but never those of the apostles and the high command itself. Rebukes from Young, Kimball and the rest of the hierarchy came thick and fast. But Young was always a master politician. He tempered strictness with hedonism, and even demonstrated in person the correct way for the Saints to praise God in the dance. Once again the brass band proved to be an effective instrument for achieving organic solidarity. The Saints were diverted with weddings, concerts, choir practices, formal dances, hoedowns, parties and quilting-bees. They were entertained by a curious 'Indian Negro' who could play flute and fife while providing percussion with saucepan and rattle and amused the company by claiming to be a reincarnation of Adam. Children in dugout schools learned spelling from Noah Webster's famous 1783 *Spelling Book*, were taught singing and elocution and took part in mock trials arranged by their teachers. All ages enjoyed the parties when cakes, pies and sweetmeats of hominy and maple syrup were produced. Winter Quarters was a grim experience but it was not all misery.

In the new year of 1847, Brigham Young began to give serious thought to the coming trek to Zion in the Salt Lake valley. On 14 January, he had a convenient 'revelation' telling him how the pioneer wagon train was to be organised: the Saints would use no professional guides or outfitters but place scouts at the front, the rear and on the flanks, shepherding the wagons in a box-like formation, and keeping all Indians, wolves and unsavoury whites at bay. Young would be without John D. Lee, his enforcer, who was acting as his eyes and ears with the Mormon battalion in Santa Fe, but to compensate, the energetic Parley Pratt was about to return from his mission in England, to which he had departed with great speed in September 1846. Heber Kimball would be Young's right-hand man, Orson Pratt would give the pioneers a patina of intellectual respectability, while the ubiquitous Porter Rockwell would do any killing that needed to be done. Noting the bad blood between William Clayton and Hosea Stout, and fearing that Stout might well make good on his threat to 'terminate' Clayton if he, Young, was not around to protect him, Brother Brigham told Stout that he would have to remain at Winter Quarters while Clayton trekked on; Stout's task would be to see to it that enough food was stockpiled to feed the mass emigration of Saints he planned in 1848.

There remained the perennial problem of Bishop George Miller, that reliable thorn in Brigham Young's side. Miller returned from Ponca at the head of the Niobrara River early in 1847 with news that twenty-three Saints had died there of disease; he seemed surprised to find that the figures were far higher at Mount Pisgah, Garden Grove and Poor Camp. It was later estimated that there were 550 deaths at Winter Quarters,

Cutler's Park and Cold Springs, 220 more at Council Bluffs, 115 at Mount Pisgah and 95 at Garden Grove. Miller was a marked man on his return, but was quite capable of giving as good as he got. Hosea Stout alleged that Miller had made gratuitous enemies of the Sioux by his flashy and unnecessary 'alliance' with the Ponca. Brigham Young, in a pointed reference to Miller on 26 January, said there were some men who had to be coaxed by a lump of sugar to keep them from running off to the Gentiles and bringing persecution down on their heads. But the real bone of contention was Brother Brigham's major 'revelation' on 20 January when he first divulged that his target was the Great Basin, to be approached via the north bank of the Platte and Fort Laramie. Miller, who had argued for a route up the Niobrara River so as to avoid the Platte River Road altogether, as that was where 'all the filth and slime' of Missouri and Illinois passed by, declared himself disgusted. When Young dug in, Miller tried to head a breakaway movement to ally the Saints with Mexico and settle between the Nueces River and the Rio Grande. The confrontation ended with Miller's becoming a schismatic. He departed to found his own ill-starred colony in Texas.

Determined to make the earliest possible exodus compatible with the seasons, so that the Saints could plant summer crops when they arrived in Zion, Brigham Young originally set the departure date for 22 March, as soon as the prairie had dried, but there were many false starts. To begin with, Young experienced great difficulty raising the money to outfit and equip a credible caravan. His famous bad temper was often raised to boiling point by the delay in procuring wagons. At a general meeting in early March he warned his followers: 'If you come here again and don't report them fitted out, I'll rub your ears for you – worse than I have done tonight.' On 26 March, he again called his people together and attacked them for their covetousness and meanness in not giving more liberally to the pioneering enterprise. Then Young was forced to delay on 6 April for the annual spring conference of the Saints, marking the founding of the Church seventeen years before. At least he was able to deal decisively with the 'Texas rebels' – Apostle Lyman Wight and High Council member Bishop George Miller – who were not 'sustained' in their positions and headed away in apostasy to found the new colony in Texas. It was at this conference that the fiery advocacy of Heber Kimball finally secured the funds to make sure the exodus occurred with seventy robust and weatherly wagons.

Next, Brigham Young had to decide in detail who was to accompany him. The apostles virtually selected themselves and most of those in the upper ranks of the priesthood had to be placated with an invitation, but thereafter the situation was less clear-cut. Everyone had to wait the 'call' from Young and many, like William Clayton and Thomas Bullock, received it only at the last moment. Young realised that the pioneers could not simply be the top hundred or so individuals in the hierarchy, that frontier skills were at least as important, at any rate until they were settled in Zion. So, among the pioneers in the famous 1847 Mormon trek were carpenters, farmers, blacksmiths, wagon-makers, lumberjacks and mechanics of all kinds. The young men in the party were not particularly devout, and there are many trail journals that record their fondness for card-playing, wrestling, fighting and the telling of lewd stories. Although the advance party was supposed to contain the elite of the Saints, it also contained a number of potential backsliders and one of the most remarkable things about the pioneers is how many of them later quit the Church.

Brigham Young had originally intended that the pioneering party should have the pleasing numerical symmetry of 144 members (twelve times twelve), but his idiot brother Lorenzo ruined his careful plans. Lorenzo was adamant that he had to take along his asthmatic wife Harriet, and no amount of cajolery or bluster from Brigham could move him. Partly to provide Harriet with female company, partly so that he would not appear to disadvantage alongside his brother, Brigham took along one of his wives and allowed Heber Kimball to take one too. Apart from the three women and two children, then, the pioneering party consisted of 144 men, 72 wagons, 93 horses, 52 mules and 66 oxen, to say nothing of 19 cows, 17 dogs and some chickens. Interestingly – for 'Negroes' were not allowed to be full members of the Church – Young took along three black servants: Green Flake, a slave whom Young had baptised as an associate member (second class) of the Latter-Day Saints in 1844, and two slaves from Mississippi named Oscar Crosby and Hank Lay.

The Mormon advance guard of six wagons (under Heber Kimball) assembled at the Elkhorn River, thirty miles to the west of Winter Quarters, on 6 April. Next day, Brigham Young set out, but after one day's journey received word that Parley Pratt had just returned from his mission in England and was at Winter Quarters. He returned to hear Pratt's report and receive the donations from the English faithful. On 9 April, he set out once more, again made a day's travel and then was summoned back a second time. Another apostle, John Taylor, had also returned from England, bringing $500 worth of scientific instruments for Orson Pratt, the Saints' resident scientist, including sextants, telescopes, barometers, thermometers and artificial horizons. Finally, on 15 April, the last of the pioneer wagons rafted the Elkhorn and camped on the bank of the Platte, about three miles below modern-day Fremont, Nebraska.

On 16 April, Young completely reorganised the wagon train, evincing that flair for administration that sometimes toppled over into pedantic fussiness. Although still theoretically assigning to them tens, fifties and hundreds, as on the march through Iowa, Young devised a new quasi-military system, with himself as general and Stephen Markham as colonel. The entire party was divided up into four nightwatches, each to be on duty half the time; there would be regular rotation on the trail, so that no one group of wagons had to break trail all the time; and there would be a series of committees for organising everything from hunting to the pitching of tents. Some have speculated that Young created so many overlapping structures of authority on a 'divide and rule' basis; all disputes about jurisdiction would have to be referred to him, making him the undisputed ruler; so he increased his authority even as he seemed to delegate.

Young intended to follow the north bank of the Platte to avoid coming into contact with Gentiles pursuing the Oregon and California trails along the southern shore. With a marked fondness for Frémont's maps, he was confident, sure that he knew all about the possible dangers of the trail – by this time the fiasco of the Meek cutoff had been widely bruited throughout the West – and was adamant that he would employ no Gentile guides. He insisted on rigid discipline and continued to supplement standing orders with new directives. Each morning at 5 a.m. a bugle would blare out the breakfast call. By 7 a.m. the Saints would be on the march. There would be one-hour stops for 'nooning', and at sunset the wagons would be drawn into a semicircle with the horses secured in the perimeter. The sound of the bugle at 8.30 p.m. meant that each man was to return to his wagon for prayer, and at 9 p.m. 'lights out' was strictly enforced.

The Saints intended to follow the north bank of the Platte all the way to Fort Laramie. They did not in any sense pioneer a 'Mormon Trail' as the north shore had been the preferred route along the river for missionaries and trappers in the 1820s and 1830s. Nor was the route unknown. Bishop Miller's party had travelled a hundred miles as far as the Loup Fork the year before, while Howard Egan, who had been with the Mormon battalion in 1846, had travelled a good part of the Oregon Trail. Besides, they had Frémont's reports, and even Lansford Hastings's *Guide*, one of Brigham Young's favourite books, was reliable enough for the route to Fort Laramie. Nevertheless, the thousand-mile trek to Zion did not begin auspiciously. The Saints were barely on the trail before

Ellis Eames turned back with sickness; he was allegedly spitting blood, but others thought that he was weak in the faith and wanted an excuse to detach himself. To 'compensate', on 19 April Brigham Young decided to take on as assistant to Porter Rockwell a desperado and known murderer named Nathaniel Thomas Brown, mainly, it seems, to thumb his nose at 'Gentile' justice; Brown was on the 'most wanted' list of Missouri sheriff William Bonney.

For four days they made about twenty miles a day, but the early period on the trail was accident-strewn. First, William Clayton found himself unable to fulfil his duties as secretary because of toothache; Luke Johnson diagnosed an ulcerated tooth and yanked it out with pliers. Then James Case, while chopping down cottonwoods for forage, felled a tree on one of his oxen and knocked the animal's eye out of sight into its socket; ten minutes later it reappeared, apparently unharmed. Captain James Brown accidentally shot himself in the leg, while Luke Johnson, the amateur dentist, shot a rattlesnake as it was poised to strike. Worst of all for Brigham Young was that his favourite horse slipped down a ravine and choked to death on its chain. The most pleasant occurrence for the Mormon leaders came on the evening of 24 April, when there was a clear night sky. Orson Pratt set up his new telescope and showed Heber Kimball the planets and stars; together they wondered which was Kolob, according to Mormon belief the closest of all stars to the throne of God.

On 21 April, just before crossing the Loup Fork, the Saints had their first contact with the Pawnee Indians. The Pawnee were distinctive and unmistakable, with painted faces, plucked eyebrows and heads shaved except for a narrow strip of hair from forehead to scalplock, which stood up like a horn. Brigham Young knew their reputation as horse thieves – 'the Ishmaelites of the Prairies – their hands are against every man, and every man's hand is against them', to use Parkman's biblical imagery that would have appealed to the Mormon leader – and he ordered a doubling of the guard. The Pawnee chief Shenifolan rode up to Young and demanded that the intruders on his tribal lands turn back. Young refused. Shenifolan then asked for an amount of tribute that Young found excessive, so again he refused. Somewhat absurdly after such rebuffs, he held out his hand for the chief to shake, but the angry Shenifolan refused him and stormed away in dudgeon. Those who knew the Pawnee thought that was unlikely to be the end of the matter.

Young asked for further volunteers to ward off nocturnal attacks and one hundred answered his call, including all twelve apostles with the exception of Franklin Richards, as Clayton gleefully noted in his diary. They shivered through a night of wind and rain but saw nothing. The

Pawnee were evidently playing a game of cat and mouse, keeping the white man guessing. Meanwhile, the Mormons crossed Looking Glass and Beaver creeks and reached the mission on Plum Creek that had been abandoned the year before. They found a goodly supply of hay here, stacked inside rail fences, which they appropriated. But that this was a war zone became clear when they saw the gutted remains of a government station and a Pawnee village, both victims of Sioux firebrands. The Loup Fork had taken them away from the Platte, so, west of present-day Fullerton, Nebraska, they tried to raft across the Loup to return to the Platte valley. The river was alternately too swift and too shallow for the raft, and the Saints experienced the utmost difficulty in getting across, which they managed with the help of a rubber boat they carried with them in a wagon. They then began angling back to the Platte.

In all the difficulty of getting across the Loup, they had forgotten the Pawnee. But the Pawnee had not forgotten them. In the small hours of 26 April, there was a major alarm in the Mormon camp when Pawnees were seen crawling towards them, trying to steal horses. Some bleary-eyed Saints, answering the tocsin call, wrongly concluded there had been a false alarm. But next day the Indians made their presence felt by getting away with two horses in broad daylight. Potentially the most serious encounter came on 27 April when Brigham Young's hitman Porter Rockwell and three hunters were out looking for a missing mare. It was bad luck for the Pawnee that they chose the most fearsome Mormon to tangle with. Now thirty-four, Rockwell had been jailed in 1843 on suspicion of trying to assassinate Governor Lilburn Boggs of Missouri. Released without trial after eight months, Rockwell was greeted as a deliverer by Joseph Smith who gave him the following Christmas present: 'So long as ye remain loyal and true to my faith, ye need fear no enemy. Cut not thy hair and no bullet or blade can harm thee.'

With his trademark long hair, often worn in braids, Rockwell was a familiar, and much-feared, figure in Mormon circles. While out riding on the 27th with his three comrades, Rockwell suddenly spotted a movement in the long grass. At first, he thought it was a wolf, but in an instant fifteen Pawnee warriors, naked except for breech clouts, seemed to explode out of the grass. Rockwell told his men to hold their fire. The Pawnee advanced; Rockwell waved them back. Ignoring his gesticulations, they started calling 'bacco, bacco' in a wheedling way, but Rockwell noticed that their envious eyes were on his bridle. His second-in-command cocked his pistol and pointed it at the Indian leader, who backed away scowling. The four Saints began to ride away slowly, but when they had gone no more than fifty yards, the Pawnee opened fire. Rockwell turned his horse round to give chase, but in an instant the Pawnee were gone.

In heat and dust (Pratt's thermometer registered 86°F) on 27 April, they came down again into the valley of the Platte and noted a change in landscape, habitat and even ecosystem (though naturally the Saints would not have used such words). As they passed Grand Island on the 29th, they also remarked on the bitter, dry winds that cracked lips and split furniture, as well as the absence of timber, and the change in the grass, which was now short, curly and tufty and would not have concealed any Indians. Clayton noticed, as so many had before him, that prairie dogs, rattlesnakes and owls all coexisted in the same burrows; they began to see antelope and wolves in profusion and finally, on the last day of April, the first of teeming herds of buffalo. There were many other 'firsts': the first buffalo chips they gathered for fuel, the first alkaline flats they had seen, the first time they had to dig for drinking water. The temperature also plummeted alarmingly, down to 30°F by 1 May.

The first week of May witnessed veritable hecatombs of slaughter as Mormon marksmen cut loose among what one writer, using the correct but inelegant collective, calls an obstinacy of bison. 'We were delighted with buffalo hunting. Our eyes had never beheld such a sight – the whole country was covered with them,' one of the brethren wrote. Clayton panned round the plain with one of the new eyeglasses brought from England and counted over a hundred buffalo in as many seconds. Brigham Young tried to restrain the impetuous Saints, some of whom had not tasted fresh meat for months, and ordered that the killing be left to seven designated experienced hunters. Foremost among these was the controversial Porter Rockwell, who demonstrated his prowess by killing a buffalo with a frontal shot in the skull. But Young's advice was at first disregarded, even, it seems, by the apostles, for Heber Kimball, galloping wildly on to the plain, was nearly killed when his horse bolted. Nor did the Saints heed Brigham Young's orders that they should kill only what they could eat, but they did at least respect his order that there should be no killing on the Sabbath.

The mania for buffalo-hunting produced several consequences. In the first place, the buffalo meat, which was described as very sweet and as tender as veal, played havoc with digestive systems unused to fresh meat and produced a mini-epidemic of diarrhoea in the wagon train. Second, the thousands and thousands of buffalo along the Platte (Bullock counted 15,000 within eyesight on 5 May) were soon found to be in competition for forage with the Saints' own cattle and oxen: as Orson Pratt noted:

'Many of our animals are nearly famished for want of food, for every green thing is cut off by buffalo.' Third, the bison became used to the presence of the human predators, with dire results for themselves. Bullock noted the following: 'A calf followed Luke Johnson into camp and at noon halt it was placed in sight of its mother by order of President Young that the mother might get it, but George Brown and another brother very foolishly went in sight, close to the old cow, when she started off and left it. The calf was afterwards seen caught by a wolf and killed.'

Brigham Young's main concern was that the excitement over buffalo-hunting was making the Saints careless; in particular he feared that they might be picked off by the Sioux if they went out hunting in twos and threes. On 4 May, the day after three hundred Indians were reported camped in a hollow only twelve miles away, he issued a formal warning, primed the cannon for action and once again doubled the guard. For a week, this party of Sioux and the Saints were close together, as Erastus Snow noted on 12 May: 'We passed today the carcasses of about one hundred buffaloes lately slaughtered by them. They have taken only hides, tongues, marrow and here and there a choice piece of meat, leaving the balance for wolves, which are by no means scarce or backward in waiting upon themselves.' Indian war parties were never far away. One of their tricks was to fire the prairie in the paths of the Mormons, destroying feed for their teams and horses for many square miles around. There was so much ash swirling around in the air that the Saints looked like chimney sweeps. These prairie fires could produce a tidal wave of flame, twenty feet high, which swept wind-driven across the plains like a devouring Moloch and could overtake a horse or engulf a slow-moving wagon train.

On 6 May, the wagon train passed the hundredth meridian near modern-day Cozad. There was a cold north-westerly wind, and temperatures were at winter levels, with ice forming overnight in water pails. Alongside them flowed the muddy Platte, two miles wide. The tedious tenor of everyday life sometimes surfaces in diary entries like this from Clayton: 'Washed my socks, towel and handkerchief as well as I could in cold water without soap. I then stripped my clothing off and washed from head to foot, which has made me feel much more comfortable.' On 8 May, Clayton estimated that they were 295 miles from Winter Quarters, using the odometer he had suggested to Orson Pratt a month earlier. This was a device using a set of wooden cog wheels attached to the hub of a wagon wheel, which would give a dead reckoning estimate of the mileage travelled. Orson Pratt seemed to have lost interest in the idea and then suddenly, to Clayton's horror and disgust, it turned out he had handed over the idea to another brother, Appleton Harmon, who claimed the odometer as his invention. The whole issue continued to be a running sore with Clayton during the trek.

On 6 May, there also occurred one of Brigham Young's notorious temper tantrums. While he was trying to separate his herd from the buffalo which had intermingled with them, he lost a precious spyglass, one of the consignment of instruments Taylor had brought from England. His volcanic anger was something to see, but not so pleasant for Erastus Snow, whom he castigated publicly for not droving the cows properly. Clayton's diary entry for 7 May, giving an account of the incident, is almost Attic in its brevity: 'The president chastized Elder Snow for not attending to the cows yesterday, causing the president to lose his spyglass, it being Brother Snow's turn to drive the cows according to his own voluntary agreement.' Porter Rockwell agreed to head a search party and to retrace the president's steps over twenty miles. To the great relief of the entire camp, the searchers found it, for until then Brigham Young had been impossible. We are all disposed to blame others if we lose something in the heat of the moment, but perhaps only the leader of a religious movement can get away with it. Nevertheless, Erastus Snow, who was no Bishop Miller, agreed to bow his head and wrote: 'In attempting to exonerate myself from blame, I drew from him a severe chastisement; it is the first I have had since I have been in this Church, which is nearly fifteen years, and I hope it may last me fifteen years to come.'

Brigham Young was far from the only brother whose temper was frayed on the prairie; one might say that the rigours of the plains were enough to try the patience of a Saint. One angry dispute between Thomas Tanner and Aaron Farr drew from Clayton a 'plague on both your houses' judgement. On the one hand it was true that Farr had kept talking after the bugle blew for prayers – a serious offence in Brigham Young's eyes – but on the other Tanner was a stiff-necked humbug who should, Clayton thought, have overlooked this venial sin. However, it was also true that the Mormons were getting bored with the monotony of the trek. On 11 May, several brethren amused themselves after breakfast by digging out four wolf cubs from a hole about a quarter of a mile from camp. They brought the live mammals back to camp and found them to be about six or eight weeks old, about the size of an English hare and very vicious. The Saints knocked them on the head and made fur caps from their skins.

Such pastimes, though cruel, did not endanger morale and good discipline in the wagon train. But Brigham Young thought the widespread penchant for practical jokes and bawdy humour did. To alleviate the boredom, the pioneers arranged mock trials after dinner in which high-ranking Mormons were supposedly haled before a court of their social inferiors to answer 'charges'. Porter Rockwell received one such 'summons' which read:

> You are hereby commanded to bring back, wherever found, the body of Colonel George Mills, before the Right Reverend Bishop Whipple at his quarters, there to answer to the following charge, viz:- That of emitting in meeting on Sunday last, a sound *a posteriori* (from his seat of honor) somewhat resembling the rumble of distant thunder, or heavy discharge of artillery, thereby endangering the steadiness of the olfactory nerves of those present, as well as diverting their minds from the discourse of the speaker.

Another such flysheet announced the 'trial' of James Davenport, caught urinating in the open, 'for blocking the highway and turning the ladies out of their course'. When he got wind of this levity, Brigham Young again exploded with anger and accused the brethren of 'acting the nigger night after night'. He threatened to abort the trek and return to Council Bluffs unless there was instant repentance. 'I understand there are several in this camp who do not belong to the Church,' he thundered. 'I am the man who will stand up for them and protect them in all their rights. And they shall not trample on our rights or on the priesthood. They shall reverence and acknowledge the name of God and his priesthood, and if they set up their heads and seek to introduce iniquity into this camp and to trample on the priesthood, I swear to them, they shall never go back to tell the tale. I will leave them where they will be safe.'

The second and third week of May saw the Saints still trekking through teeming herds of buffalo, but once again disregarding the leader's orders on gratuitous slaughter. On the evening of 18 May Brigham Young called the captains of the tens to his wagon for another of his stern lectures. He brought up the issue of brethren who had left buffalo meat on the prairie and refused to eat it because it was not hindquarter.

> Some would murmur because a hind quarter of meat was allotted to them, which is not right, for God has given us a commandment that we should not waste meat, nor take life unless it is needful, but He can see a disposition in this camp to slaughter everything before them; yea, if

all the buffalo and game that is on our route were brought together to the camp, there are some who would never cease until they had destroyed the whole.

Some historians of the overland trail have remarked, half in jest, that rattlesnakes always seemed to attack Mormons more than Gentiles. Certainly, the pattern of the 1846 trek across Iowa was repeated a year later along the Platte. Even the unobservant Lorenzo Young noticed them, for he wrote on 17 May: 'We found some rattlesnakes, the first we have seen', forgetting or ignorant of the attack on Luke Johnson the month before. But close encounters with the reptiles became a daily occurrence at the beginning of the third week in May. On the 18th, a very large rattlesnake, possibly of the timber variety, nearly bit Brigham Young's horse, then made a lunge at a Saint on foot, who shot it dead with his rifle. On the 20th, at Ash Hollow, another large rattler was shot. On the 23rd, Bullock narrowly missed being struck by a further angry serpent. Finally, on the same day, at Bluff Ruins, one of the ubiquitous reptiles scored a direct hit on the leg of a brother named Nathaniel Fairbanks. The Saints applied tobacco juice, leaves and turpentine to the wound and tied tobacco to his swollen leg, forced him to drink alcohol and water and finally dosed him to make him vomit. Fairbanks was in considerable pain and complained of blurred vision, stomach pains and a dry tongue as well as the swollen leg, but within two days made an almost complete recovery.

The Mormons made good progress on the trek until they came to the first sandhills which ran down to meet the Platte, after which there was heavy pulling. But beyond the sandhills, among the broken lands of the Upper Missouri Basin, they came upon the stretch of the journey that all pioneers found appealing: on the south bank were Courthouse Rock, Chimney Rock and Scott's Bluff, while on the northern shore were Indian Lookout Point and Ancient Bluffs Ruins. Although the wagon train kept on the northern bank, some of the Saints appear to have made individual journeys to the other side to sightsee; Orson Pratt took astronomical observations at Chimney Rock. All the Saints' journals for this period tend to give a curious impression of divergent aims: on the one hand, Orson Pratt making trigonometrical and astronomical observations; on the other, Porter Rockwell blazing away at anything that moved, bagging the occasional wolf or antelope.

The would-be scientific expeditions made some interesting finds, including the fossilised remains of a mammoth, but they were time-consuming. This partly accounts for the slow progress from 20 May (at

Ash Hollow) to arrival at Fort Laramie on 1 June. On 22 May, they were at Ancient Bluffs Ruins, eight miles north-east of present-day Lisco, Nebraska; on the 24th, near Courthouse Rock, where they were visited by a party of curious Sioux; next day, in the vicinity of Chimney Rock; and on the 27th, opposite Scott's Bluff. Apart from the few elite sightseers and tourists, the Saints were again in sour mood, frustrated by persistent panhandling from the Sioux and annoyed by the shortage of game. William Clayton wrote: 'We have seen no game for several days except a few antelopes and hares. The buffalo appear to have left this region and in fact there are little signs of many having been here.'

This discontent lit a trail of spiritual gunpowder that led to Brigham Young's most thunderous explosion to date. Heber Kimball had not featured much on the journey so far, except for the day when he shot two wolves. But, while strolling round the wagons in the Scotts Bluff area on 28 May, he became increasingly disturbed by the levity, gambling and profane language he witnessed. He called the men together and gave a short homily, exhorting them 'to conduct themselves like men of God, or they would be sorry for it'. He made a routine report on the incident to the leader and later that evening was called to Young's tent. Young told him he had had a 'revelation', requiring him to call the camp to repentance and that he intended to preach a major sermon next day against backsliding brethren.

If ever the overworked description 'fire and brimstone' could be used about a sermon, it was surely predictable of the harangue Brigham Young delivered on 29 May. He poured scorn on the lame excuses offered for their misconduct. 'The brethren say they want a little exercise to pass away the time in the evenings, but if you can't tire yourselves bad enough with a day's journey without dancing every night, carry your guns on your shoulders and walk, carry your wood to camp instead of lounging and lying asleep in your wagons.' He deplored the use of foul language, then pitched into card-playing. 'I would rather see in your hands the dirtiest thing you could find on earth than a pack of cards. You never read of gambling, playing cards, checkers, dominoes etc in the scriptures, but you do read of men praising the Lord in the dance, but who ever read of praising the Lord in a game of cards . . . I now tell you, if you don't stop it, you shall be cursed by the Almighty and shall dwindle away and be damned. Such things shall not be suffered in this camp. You shall honour God and confess His name or else you shall suffer the penalty.'

Young then asked for a show of hands, so that those who were prepared to desist from wickedness could be identified; those who were not, should be prepared either to turn round and march back into the wilderness or submit themselves to Mormon justice. Cleverly, he began with the apostles and worked down the hierarchy, leading by example. A forest of hands shot up. Men broke down and confessed their sins in the time-honoured manner of revival meetings. When they pulled out next morning, there was an atmosphere of quiet and calm, with no profane language heard, no quarrelling, no swearing at mules and oxen, not even any laughter. It was a chilling demonstration of social control, evincing Brigham Young as at once efficient autocrat, subtle psychologist and master manipulator. 'It truly seemed,' noted William Clayton, 'as though the cloud had burst and we had emerged into a new element, a new atmosphere and a new society.'

The chastened brethren pulled into the environs of Fort Laramie on 1 June. As Bullock wrote: 'all were anxious to see an habitation once more.' They took comfort in having achieved a trek of more than five hundred miles with no human casualties and the loss of just four horses (two killed in accidents and two stolen by the Pawnee). The Saints had learned a lot from their gruelling experiences in Iowa in 1846 and were now much more experienced, better provisioned and more tightly organised. The main complainants were the three women; Clarissa Decker Young later admitted she had not at all enjoyed the journey with her husband. On 2 June, Brigham Young, Kimball and a few other high-ranking Saints paid a courtesy visit on James Bordeaux, the 'bourgeois' (commander) at the fort in Papin's absence. Bordeaux and the Saints got on surprisingly well. He advised them not to continue along the north bank, which would soon become impassable, but to cross to the south and follow the regular Oregon Trail. He offered to ferry them for twenty-five cents a wagon or to hire out his flatboat. He advised that the Sioux were not to be feared, but the Crow, horse-stealers like the Pawnee, were. He told Brigham Young that the Saints were the best behaved company that had ever arrived at the fort and won their hearts with some scurrilous stories about the bad behaviour of their old enemy Lilburn Boggs, who had passed that way the year before.

On 3 June, the Mormons began ferrying the river, in order to hit the Oregon Trail on the southern bank. They made a contest out of it between the first and second 'hundreds' and averaged eleven minutes for the passage of each wagon. Heavy rain interrupted them, and then came news that 2,000 Gentiles in five hundred wagons were allegedly a few days behind them. Faced with this threat, Brigham Young ordered ferrying operations to restart at 4 a.m. next morning but then unaccountably delayed the march by stopping for another chat with Bordeaux. On the south bank, the Saints were joined by seventeen advance members of the Mississippi Saints, including six women. The Mississippi Saints had intended to join Brigham Young on the Platte in 1846 but, when he stayed in Winter Quarters, they spent the winter of 1846–47 in Pueblo, Colorado, where they were joined by members of the Mormon battalion on sick roster. In the spring of 1847, the advance started north up the Arkansas and arrived at Fort Laramie a few days before Young and his wagon train; most of them, however, plus the sick soldiers from the battalion, were still at Pueblo. Altogether, the Saints now numbered 166 souls and seventy-seven wagons.

Trekking on, they negotiated the steep downhill descent of Mexican Hill and camped on the night of 4 June at one of the emigrant 'post offices' set in a cottonwood oasis and later named Register Cliff. On 5 June, there was a stiff pull up the bluffs near modern-day Guernsey, Wyoming, and there was considerable tension in the wagon train as they started to be passed by Oregon-bound emigrants from Missouri, the home of the Saints' most deadly enemies. Because water and camping sites were scarce, there was enforced fraternisation with this group, but the cohabitation passed off without incident; there were even outbreaks of friendship, with some Missourians coming over to inspect the odometer. The 6th found the Saints marching across rough country on a road full of cobblestones and criss-crossed by a plethora of streams; they had to put road gangs to work to clear the worst rocky obstacles, lamenting betimes that their labour would also benefit the Gentiles. William Clayton, who later produced his own mile-by-mile emigrants' guide, ticked off the landmarks – Horseshoe Creek, La Bonté Creek, Deer Creek – while getting instruction from Orson Pratt in the use of a sextant.

On 8 June, Sister Harriet Crow had a lucky escape after being run over by a wagon. The teams had stopped near the descent from the bluffs and she stepped on the wagon tongue to get a drink. The oxen started up suddenly and threw her under the wheel which passed over her leg below the knee and then continued down over her foot and toes. She screamed and appeared in great agony but was found to have sustained only bruises; miraculously, not a single bone had been broken. The Saints were convinced by this and other things that they were on a lucky streak. For one thing, their diet had improved immensely. Porter Rockwell was bringing deer and antelope into the camp in great profusion, and the pioneers were also discovering a new treat: the salmon and trout that swam in their thousands in Deer Creek. Fishing became a general mania, and the Saints even ate fish for breakfast.

The mood of euphoria was well caught by Erastus Snow who described Deer Creek thus:

This is the most delightful place we have seen since we left the States – a large creek of clear water with a stony bottom, and the way our boys are hauling out the fish is not slow. Excellent feed, timber, plenty of game, beautiful scenery; and added to this, one of the miners had discovered a very excellent bed of bituminous coal up the creek, a sample of which he has brought to the camp; also a quarry of excellent sandstone. I have been agreeably surprised in the country of the Black Hills, over which we have travelled a distance of ninety miles from Fort Laramie. Instead of sand and continual barrenness, without water, as I had expected, we have found hard roads through the hills and at convenient distances beautiful creeks skirted with timber, and bottoms covered with grass, though the country otherwise presents generally a rough and barren appearance.

At La Bonté Creek (near modern-day Douglas, Wyoming), the Saints had met some friends of the trapper Lewis Myers, who told them of a bullboat hanging in the trees near Last Crossing, at the ferrying point of the North Platte. Anxious to establish crossing rights before the Missourians, Brigham Young sent ahead an advance party of forty men with the Mormons' own rubber boat, the so-called 'Revenue Cutter'. The advance party found a ferrying location about four miles from present-day Casper, Wyoming. Some Missourians in the vicinity warned them that this was a favourite spot for dangerous animals, but this was considered typical Gentile scaremongering. The truth of the proposition was soon established: while waiting for the main party to come up, this vanguard of the Saints killed three buffalo, an antelope, plus a grizzly bear and cubs. They could not find the bullboat but they made a fortune out of the Revenue Cutter, which could carry up to 1,800 pounds. They charged the Missourians $1.50 per load and made $34 in one day.

But when the main party of Saints arrived, the Revenue Cutter had to take a back seat, for this boat could not ferry the wagons across, and this was now the urgent business of the day. The river was a hundred yards wide and fifteen feet deep, and was known to be perilous and treacherous. Some of the Saints tried to raft wagons across, but this was dangerous and early attempts were unsuccessful. They therefore tried swinging the wagons across the water on a long rope tied to the opposite bank. But they were overambitious: they tied two wagons together but, once at the other side, these keeled over and sustained extensive damage. They then tried lashing four together; this solved the problem of ballast and balance but the quartet was simply too heavy to manage. They returned to the laborious method of rafting, ferrying one at a time over the boiling waters. It took all day to get twenty-three vehicles across, and the men had to wade into the river, up to their armpits in icy water. Thinking of all the Saints who would come later, Young ordered a proper ferry boat to be made. The Saints built a serviceable ferry boat of cottonwood logs, fashioned from two long dugout canoes which were then planked and caulked. It took three days, until 15 June, to complete the exercise; the sole losses were one horse drowned and one wagon, worth $30, swept away in the flood during the early, impatient phase of the operation.

With his infallible nose for commercial opportunities, Young saw the profit that could be made from a permanent Mormon ferry. There were more than one hundred Gentile wagons piling up on the eastern bank and there were said to be a further thousand between the North Platte and Fort Laramie. Accordingly, Young ordered Thomas Grover and eight other Saints to stay behind, to improve and operate the ferry ready for next year's mass Mormon emigration; in the meantime, they were to charge premium rates ($3 in cash or $1.50 in goods and provisions) for all Gentiles wishing to cross. Later in the year, Grover and his men fought a comic-opera battle with Gentile competitors who established another ferry close by. After failing to cut the Gentile ferry boat loose from its moorings, they simply moved downriver and set up business again, so that overlanders would still come to their installation first.

On 19 June, they finally left the Platte and swung due west towards Independence Rock. Morale was falling again, with individual quarrels on the increase: Thomas Bullock was struck across the face with a whip by George Brown after an altercation, and a few days later had another brush with serpents when he dispatched a large rattlesnake. The terrain was difficult, and by common consent the stretch from the Platte to the Sweetwater was the worst between Nauvoo and Salt Lake, all alkaline flats, swamps and steep hills with bad water, little grass and very few campsites (and those few very bad). Clayton's entry for 20 July catches the atmosphere: 'The first mile was bad travelling, there being several steep pitches in the road making it dangerous for axletrees. A number of the brethren went ahead with picks and spades and improved the road somewhat.' But what sapped the Saints' spirits most of all was an incessant plague of mosquitoes, collected in dense clouds, which seemed to follow the new Moses and his Israelites like some malign form of the pillar of fire. All the pioneer journals speak of the menace from mosquitoes; as with the rattlesnakes, these noisome insects seemed to like the blood of Mormons more than that of the Gentiles.

Just before reaching the Sweetwater there was a bizarre incident. Two scouts, travelling ahead to find campsites for the morrow, were stopped by what appeared to be six Sioux warriors, who indicated by sign language that they were not welcome and motioned to them to go back. When the scouts persisted, the Indians appeared ready to use force to contest passage. Feeling suspicious – since the Sioux had hitherto acted with extraordinary friendliness towards the Saints – the scouts hid behind a ridge then described a large circle to come round behind their adversaries. They found a camp of Missourians and, what was more, observed the six 'Indians' entering the camp, well pleased with their subterfuge. When the scouts reported to him, Brigham Young told them that masquerading as Indians was an old Missouri trick; the best answer to make was a forced march that would take the wagon train ahead of the selfish Gentiles.

The Mormons hit the Sweetwater River on 21 June and pressed on towards Independence Rock, holding their noses to ward off the worst foetors emanating from the small, shallow alkaline lakes around them, gagging on the brackish water when they put it to their parched lips. Because of Brigham Young's careful husbandry, the cattle did not feel so thirsty that they slaked their appetites in the saline water, for it had a reputation for 'busting' any animals that drank it; certainly this area was later a notorious graveyard for exhausted oxen, with hundreds of bleached bones making it an animal Golgotha. Although the water was said to be sickly and even poisonous, the Mormons tried an experiment and gathered bucketfuls of efflorescent white bicarbonate of soda, which they called 'saleratus'. William Clayton describes the sequel: 'After we halted, Sister Harriet Young made some bread using the lake saleratus and when baked was pronounced to raise bread and taste equal to the best she had ever used and it requires less of this than the ordinary saleratus.'

Independence Rock provided the usual opportunities for sightseeing and name-engraving. But the Saints were much more interested in nearby Devil's Gate, which Orson Pratt accurately measured at 1,500 feet long and 370 feet deep. Heber Kimball, intrigued by the diabolical associations of the spot, tried to ride his horse through the water but found the current much too swift; discomfited, he withdrew and remarked wryly that the devil had denied him passage. The Mississippi Mormon children who had joined the wagon train at Fort Laramie caused consternation among the adults by leaning over the side to see the bottom. This was extremely dangerous, as to achieve their aim several children had to form a human chain, holding hands while the last one hung over the precipice at a perilous angle. Needless to say, none of this breached Lorenzo Young's quasi-solipsistic frettings about trivia, and the banality of his diary entries emerges from this, for 23 June: 'Mr Young had a sore thumb; it pained dreadfully, made him sick.'

Lorenzo also found cause to moan about the barren, desolate country they were passing through, as they headed away from Devil's Gate and towards the continental watershed at South Pass. Certainly the Saints had a hard going of it, with severe frosts at night so that they found an icy surface on the water pails in the morning. And on 24 June there was another nasty accident. While bringing up Brigham Young's best horse, a brother named John Holman accidentally shot him dead. Everyone waited for the inevitable explosion from the leader, but he took the loss stoically and spoke not a word of blame. Probably, Young was too much preoccupied with the competition from the Missourians now that water and feed were scarce. Even on the 27th, three years to the day since Joseph and Hyrum Smith had been murdered, when the Saints expected a day of fasting and prayer, the leader kept the wagon train on the move, determined not to be overtaken by the Gentiles.

They arrived at South Pass on 27 June and pressed on some miles to Pacific Springs where they camped. Here, they began to meet a succession of mountain men heading back east. First was Peg-Leg Smith, who had nothing useful to tell them. Next they encountered the famous mountain man Moses 'Black' Harris, who not only knew the country from South Pass to California and Oregon but had even circumnavigated the Great Salt Lake with his still more illustrious confrère Jim Bridger. The Saints found that the rough-hewn Harris took some adjusting to; as one chronicler says of the mountain men: 'their idea of a bath was to place their clothing on an anthill and let the ants eat off the lice and nits.' They discovered in Harris an encyclopedia of information and Western lore, but he was overtly pessimistic about their plans to settle the Great Salt Lake area, citing particularly the lack of timber in the desert. He was more interested in driving hard bargains with the Saints, who were keen to buy new clothes from him; shirts, jackets and trousers made from buckskin were bartered for rifles, ammunition and cash.

The Saints derived more solace from their next encounter with the representatives of the old fur trade, for 28 June brought them face to face with none other than Jim Bridger himself, who was roaring drunk and disconcerted Brigham Young with the whiskey fumes he exhaled as he spoke. Nonetheless, the talks with him were much more fruitful than the previous day's conclave with 'Black' Harris. He was positive that many crops could be grown in the Salt Lake valley and Brother Brigham was so pleased with this intelligence that he gave Bridger a free pass to use at the Mormon ferry on the North Platte. The famous Mormon legend was that Bridger offered to pay $1,000 for the first bushel of corn raised in the Great Basin but, as Clayton noted, it was impossible to tell whether this was a serious offer or even if Bridger knew what he was saying. Clayton spoke archly of 'the imperfect way he gave his descriptions' – a polite euphemism to describe Bridger's inebriation, but it is certain that many Saints did not have Brother Brigham's tolerance for the man's boasting and self-glorification. Their impatience grew when Bridger spoke of petrified birds singing in a petrified forest or the stream that flowed so fast it cooked the trout in it. As a final envoi, Bridger claimed that he had once thrown a rock over the Sweetwater and it just kept growing until it turned into Independence Rock. As Howard Egan remarked mildly: 'from his appearance and conversation I should not take him to be a man of truth.'

The meeting between Brigham Young and Jim Bridger is one of the best documented incidents in the history of the West, but its real significance has divided commentators. There was later very bad blood between Bridger and the Mormons, to the point where, in 1853, Young revoked his licence to trade on Mormon territory and sent a posse to arrest him. Some think that Bridger's optimistic advice to the Saints about the Great Basin was simply a cynical ploy to steer them away from his stamping grounds and that he saw at once that the exodus meant future trouble. These are deep waters. Sober fact must record that, in the light of Bridger's advice, 29 June 1847 saw the Saints clocking up twenty-three wearisome miles, following the Big Sandy to the Green River; the trek was necessary as there was no good drinking water along the trail. On arrival at the Green River, they were sorely disappointed to see that the Missourians (who had again overtaken them), had turned loose their rafts on the river so that the Saints behind them could not use the craft. This meant another halt while fresh rafts were built, for the Green, a major river and the largest tributary of the Colorado, was at this point fifteen feet deep and 180 yards wide.

While the Saints were camped at the Green River on 30 November, they had another visitor, this time one of their own plainsmen. In the winter of 1845–46, Brigham Young had appointed Samuel Brannan to found a Mormon colony in California. He and a party of between two hundred and three hundred had sailed for California via Cape Horn and made a promising beginning by the Pacific. Now he arrived with two comrades to intercept the wagon train, having made an arduous journey from San Francisco over the California Trail via Fort Hall. Brannan made a strenuous pitch for the future Golden State as the right location for the new Zion, and was as committed as the Gentile 'boosters' in the account he gave of the climate and soil there. Young was unconvinced and insisted that the Great Basin was his chosen site. A crestfallen

Brannan accompanied the leader to the Salt Lake, trying all the time to get Young to change his mind. Unsuccessful and therefore increasingly bitter, Brannan broke with Young in August, returned to California, and became yet another in the long list of Mormon apostates.

The halt at Green River also saw the Saints beset by disease. The culprit seems to have been Colorado tick fever – an acute infection starting with splitting headaches and followed by chills, temperatures of 104°F, pains in the muscles, joints and spine, an eruption of a rash of livid spots and sometimes delirium. Clayton and Lorenzo Young were two of the elite to go down with it; at least it was not the more serious Rocky Mountain spotted fever. The Saints were as much at a loss as anyone in this era who had not yet connected the aetiology of illness with insects. The 'scientific' Orson Pratt had this to say about the malady: '[It was] probably occasioned by suffocating clouds of dust which rise from the sandy road and envelop the whole camp when in motion, and also by the sudden changes in temperature.' The legend of 'miasmata' died hard. Ignorant of the illness's cause, the Saints realised its effects only too painfully, for the jolting of wagons compounded the agony for men suffering from headaches and aching joints. Many must have prayed that Brother Brigham would not quickly build the rafts to ferry them across the Green River, but he had two ferry boats built with his usual efficiency and then conveyed all the wagons safely over the river during a four-day period; the animals swam across, as usual.

On 3–4 July, the Saints continued their trek for twenty dusty, choking waterless miles to Black's Fork. Once again they were assailed by an army of mosquitoes. Clayton wrote: 'These insects are more numerous here than I ever saw them anywhere, everything was covered with them.' The fourth of July did not find the Saints in a mood for celebrating, though a few made 'pioneer ice cream' – snow mixed with sugar. The surly tone of the travellers was well caught by Norton Jacob, the artillery officer in charge of the Mormon cannon: 'This is Uncle Sam's day of Independence. Well, we are independent of all the powers of the Gentiles, that is enough for us.' On this day, they were joined by thirteen members of the Mormon battalion who had now been declared fit for duty by the sick bay at Pueblo. Next day, they crossed Ham's Fork and on the 6th again traversed Black's Fork, where it looped back to meet the trail after describing a kind of triangle. The grass began to improve, there were wild flowers and flax, and Wilford Woodruff, one of the apostles, even tried his hand at fly-fishing and caught a dozen salmon trout.

On 7 July, the Saints came to Fort Bridger, which they found a disappointment on many counts. Spoiled by the relative spaciousness of

Fort Laramie, they were taken aback to see 'two double log houses about forty feet long, poles upright in the ground close together, which is all the appearance of a fort in sight'. They set up camp outside the fort and spent two days working on the wagons – checking loose tyres, cracked spokes and broken felloes, repairing weakened axles, loosened bolsters and broken traces, replacing chains, worn hubs and brakes, cracked bows and torn tops. Brother Brigham had warned them against fraternising with the ungodly at the fort, but most of the Saints found the prices too steep to tarry long in the settlement. 'Black' Harris had asked $3 for a pair of buckskin trousers, which the brethren found extortionate, but here the price for the same item was $6. A few shrewd judges of horseflesh may have come out on top in the duel with the Fort Bridger traders. Heber Kimball exchanged two rifles for twenty buckskins and considered he had easily the better of the bargain; an English convert, one of those with the differential bank balance that never ceases to amaze those who investigate the 'brotherhood' of the Saints, bought forty pounds of prime beef for just ten cents a pound.

They were now about to strike off from the Oregon Trail on the Hastings cutoff, which assured them that the Salt Lake was just one hundred miles distant; Clayton estimated that they were now 397 miles from Fort Laramie and 919 from Winter Quarters. Talk of Hastings in the fort turned to the tragic story of the Donner party, which the Saints had not heard till now. Since the Donners were allegedly from Clay County, Missouri, seat of their most bitter enemies, the Mormons considered that divine vengeance had been visited on their foes. Woodruff seemed to remember that he had baptised Mrs Breen into the Latter-Day Saints in Tennessee but that she had apostasised; what better punishment than that she should have been killed and eaten? With little charity in their hearts, the Saints rejoiced to hear the calamities of 'a mob company that threatened to drive out the Mormons who were in California, and started with that spirit in their hearts. But it seemed as though they were ripe for judgement.'

On 9 July, the Saints set off again, initially up a long steep hill, the summit of which lay some eight miles from the fort, then descended on the steepest gradient yet, at times almost a sheer upright of Bridger Butte, and on to the Big Muddy. Those still suffering from 'mountain fever' were unable to manage their wagons without assistance. Thomas Bullock described the descent: 'two steep pitches, almost perpendicular, which on looking back from the bottom looks like jumping off the roof of a house to a middle story, then from the middle story to the ground and thank God there was no accident happened. Presidents Young and

Kimball cautioned all to be very careful and locked the wheels of some wagons themselves.' Next day came a very long, hard and exhausting twenty-mile pull over the Bear River Divide, then down to Sulphur Creek. Orson Pratt's meter recorded an altitude of 7,700 feet, higher than South Pass. But at Sulphur Creek the trail divided, one fork going south, the other west; needless to say there was no mention of this in Hastings's guide or his maps of the eponymous cutoff.

The Saints were saved from their quandary by the fortuitous appearance of yet another mountain man, this time the red-headed Miles Goodyear, whose praises Bordeaux had sung at Fort Laramie; he was able to tell them to take the right-hand fork. Goodyear had founded a trading post in the Salt Lake valley which he called Fort Buenaventura, gambling on traffic coming over the Hastings cutoff; he had enclosed half an acre, built log houses and had corrals for animals and an irrigated garden. Fearing that Buenaventura could become a haven for apostate Saints, Young at once decided to buy him out and, in November, paid him $2,000 for his claim and supplies; this was fortunate for Goodyear, since most emigrants after 1847 avoided the Hastings route and took the Greenwood cutoff instead. At this moment, Goodyear had just covered the Donner route in reverse and had even visited the ill-fated cabins at Donner Lake. Driving a herd of prize Spanish horses from California, he had crossed the Salt Desert and followed the route through the Wasatch mountains. The Saints quizzed Goodyear closely, and he even rode back with Porter Rockwell to point out the route down the Weber Canyon that the Harlan–Young wagon train had followed the year before. Rockwell's experienced eye told him the Mormon wagons could not get through that way. He reported to Brigham Young, who ordered Orson Pratt to take a survey party and find the other route from 1846 – that taken by James Frazier Reed.

The Saints were by now in a ninety-mile-long chain of passes, whose names would become immortalised in the tale of the last days of the pioneer hegira: Coyote Creek Canyon, Cache Cave, Creek Draw, Echo Canyon, Weber River Valley, Main Canyon, East Canyon, Little Emigration Canyon, Emigration Canyon. On 12 July, they crossed the Bear River, whose bed Orson Pratt described as 'completely covered with rounded boulders, some of which were about as large as a human head', shivering as they went in the cold, with the water in the pails solid ice at night. They camped at the head of Echo Canyon but Brigham Young went down with Colorado tick fever and was ill for the next two weeks: he suffered blinding headaches, high fevers and severe aches and pains in the back and joints; worse still, he was 'insensible and raving' and 'almost mad with pain'. as he later put it. Heber Kimball took over and split the wagon train into three: a vanguard of twenty-three wagons and forty-two men under Orson Pratt was to forge ahead; the main body would follow a few days behind; he, Brigham Young and entourage would bring up the rear.

Pratt's advance party basically followed in the tracks of the Donner party, improving the sketchy trail they found, laboriously clearing a road through brush, mountainsides and creeks, hacking, felling, levelling. Pratt's chief lieutenants were Stephen Markham, a member of the Council of Fifty, and John Brown of the Mississippi Saints. Pratt, who did none of the labour himself, was free to enjoy the grandeur of the landscape. As he wrote on 14 July about Echo Canyon:

> Our journey down the Red Fork has been extremely picturesque. We have been shut up in a narrow valley from ten to twenty rods wide, while upon each side the hills rise very abruptly from 800 to 1200 feet; and for most of the distance we have been walled in by vertical and overhanging precipices of red pudding-stones, and also red sandstone, dipping to the north-west in an angle of about 20 degrees (the valley of the Red Fork being about south-west). These rocks were worked into many curious shapes, probably by rains. The country here is very mountainous in every direction.

On 15 July, Brigham Young was well enough to travel in Wilford Woodruff's carriage. But for the advance party the ordeal continued. For them, the last forty-six miles of the journey were even worse than the passage from the Platte to the Sweetwater. They prised huge boulders out of the way with poles and tried to smooth out all the rocks and holes that would break a wheel. The main obstacle was dense stands of willow trees, as thick as porcupine quills; the tree stumps and shivered rocks they left behind had jagged edges as sharp as spears, posing a danger to men and animals, but there was a limit to what Pratt's men could do if they were to achieve any mileage at all. So slow was their progress that, inevitably, the main party began to catch them up. By 19 July, it had passed through Echo Canyon and the Weber River Valley and was crossing the Hog's Back at the summit of Main Canyon (west of modern-day Henefer). Here, they caught their first glimpse of the Wasatch Range of the Rockies – for many a depressing experience as they imagined the worst of the mountains still ahead of them.

After a Sabbath day of rest on 18 July, Orson Pratt and John Brown rode ahead next day and caught their first glimpse of the promised land. From the summit of Big Mountain Pass, at an elevation of 7,400 feet, they descried the Salt Lake valley, an extensive level prairie that they guessed must be close to the lake. But it was two days later that Pratt, this time in company with Erastus Snow, saw the full extent of the Salt Lake valley from the summit of Little Mountain. The Great Salt Lake, fed by rivers denied access to the sea – the Humboldt, Jordan Provo and Weber – which either emptied into the lake or disappeared by evaporation and percolation into sinks, glistened in the sunlight. Pratt wrote:

> We succeeded in getting through . . . and came in full view of the Salt Lake in the distance with its bold hills towering up behind the Silvery Lake . . . After issuing from the mountains among which we had been shut for many days and beholding in a moment such an extensive scenery open before us, we could not refrain from a shout of joy which almost involuntarily escaped from our lips the moment this grand and lovely scenery was within our view.

After following the trail on to the plain, Pratt and Snow returned to report their findings to Brigham Young. But the main party still had some gruelling trekking to do. After overnighting at Broad Hollow beyond the Hog's Back, the caravan entered East Canyon, a meadow-like spot teeming with aspens, birch, poplars and willows, full of wild flowers and trout. But the canyon's beauty was deceptive. The Saints had to negotiate two swamps and cross the same stream thirteen times before they reached the mouth of Little Emigration Canyon. They camped at the junction of East and Little Emigration canyons, at a place they dubbed 'Mormon Flat', then had a hard four-mile pull up the canyon to the crest of Big Mountain. Next they had to lock wheels for the steep descent at the other side of Big Mountain, taking them to Emigration Canyon. Then there was one last camp before Little Mountain, where they breasted the summit and came down to the flat lands of Zion. Thomas Bullock wrote in his diary: 'I could not help shouting, "hurra, hurra, there is my home at last."'

The Saints entered the valley in force on 23 July and immediately began ploughing, planting and irrigating. Brigham Young was determined to make the desert flower by using communal labour systems such as those employed in ancient Mesopotamia or among the Incas and by massive immigration. His great experiment was probably the one example in the Western world of what Marx called 'the Asiatic mode of production' – the authoritarian direction of a population to maximise the yield from supplies of water. But the official entrance into the promised land was 24 July, and has been celebrated as Founders' Day ever since.

All contemporary diary records of the day are prosaic. It was only in 1880, after Brigham Young was dead, that Wilford Woodruff embellished the truth thus: 'President Young was enwrapped in vision for a several minutes. He had seen the Valley before in vision, and upon this occasion he saw the future glory of Zion and of Israel, as they would be, planted in the valleys of these mountains. When the vision had passed, he said: "It is enough. This is the right place, drive on."' It is a striking legend and, as Wallace Stegner says, 'a great statement, one that gathers up in a phrase history and hope and fulfillment'. But it is a legend nevertheless, or rather it is a myth in the fullest archetypal sense, and 'This is the Place' is now celebrated by a sixty-foot monument at the mouth of Emigration Canyon.

The Saints' next task was to found a colony strong enough to survive through the winter of 1847–48 and to prepare the ground for the mass immigration of 1848. They began by renewing their religious covenants by rebaptism. Then they laid out the prospective city, planted crops, assigned building lots, built homes, a stockade, a bowery and opened negotiations with the local Indians. Many exploring parties went out to survey the entire Salt Lake area, and took the opportunity to bathe in the lake, an experience described as being like lounging in a rocking chair. The fort was the pièce de résistance. A square of adjoining log cabins was constructed, opening into an inner court or corral for the cattle, with an adobe wall around three sides of the outer perimeter to ward off marauders. Within three weeks the Saints had completed a wall around the fort and built twenty-nine log houses inside, each one nine feet high, sixteen feet long by fourteen feet wide. The Mormons who remained in Zion built twelve miles of fence and enclosed 5,000 acres during the winter of 1847–48, despite harsh weather.

On 26 August, after just a month at Salt Lake, Brigham Young started the journey back to Winter Quarters, taking 108 men with him. The return journey had been organised as a threefold operation: a vanguard of eleven men left on 11 August, followed by the 'ox party' a few days later. The rearguard, with the leader, would consist of horses and mules only, would travel faster, and thus catch up the ox train; the entire party would then rendezvous on the Platte and return together to Winter Quarters. Various factors conspired against these 'best laid plans'. Part of the reason was that, more familiar with the terrain and with fewer and lighter wagons, the returning Saints travelled much faster, so that it was harder for the backmarkers to catch up; the return from Salt Lake to Fort Laramie occupied just over half the time taken in the reverse direction on the outward journey. Moreover, William Clayton's ox team, having rendezvoused with the vanguard of horsemen at the North Platte ferry on 8 September, did not wait for the main body at Grand Island, as previously agreed, but pressed on at full speed for Winter Quarters; Clayton appears to have done this partly because he was short of provisions and partly to cut short the dissensions in his party, which he lacked Brigham Young's gravitas and authority to deal with.

Brigham Young, meanwhile, travelling with the main (rear) party, had his fair share of adventures. The heartening part of the return journey was the number of Saints they met on the trail already on their way to the Great Basin, which meant that by the onset of winter no fewer than 1,800 Mormons were already settled in the Great Salt Lake valley. But Young, for obscure reasons, seems to have been in a foul mood. When he met Parley Pratt on the banks of the Little Sandy in early September heading one of these caravans, he pitched into him for his lack of organisational skills. Those unsympathetic to Young say that he was jealous of Pratt and saw in him a possible rival for the position of Prophet. Parley Pratt, though, was no Bishop Miller: 'I humbled myself, acknowledged my faults and asked forgiveness.' But a few days later Brother Brigham had real problems to contend with, for on 9 September a Crow raiding party stole up to fifty of their horses, leaving the Saints seriously short of mounts. When, despite punitive forays, the Mormons managed to recover only five of these horses, Brigham Young and Heber Kimball could no longer ride on horseback but had to walk or ride in the wagons.

Nine days later, an incautious Brigham Young narrowly escaped being mauled by a mother bear defending her cubs when the Saints set out on a grizzly bear hunt. Then, on 21 September, the Saints sustained further losses when the Sioux tried to stampede their herd. The Mormons fought back doughtily and repelled the attack, with Porter Rockwell the hero of the hour, but the Indians still managed to uplift eleven of the steeds. When a cross-grained and intemperate Young arrived in Fort Laramie four days later, on 25 September, he was stupefied to find the Sioux comfortably encamped outside the fort, with his horses in full view. The fort's management was, understandably, unwilling to risk an Indian war and possible siege just to get back the Mormons' horses. Young was reduced to patient diplomacy with the Sioux chief, who finally passed the whole affair off as a case of mistaken identity – he thought he was raiding Shoshone ponies, or so he said. After protracted negotiations, which involved having to pay hefty tribute in 'compensation', Young did finally manage to get his mounts back.

There were no further major incidents on the trip, and Young's party spent little more than a month over the trek from Fort Laramie to Winter

Quarters, travelling in mild weather throughout. On 31 October, the wagon train arrived by the banks of the Missouri, having been just nine weeks on the trail from the Great Salt Lake; Young praised his men for their zeal, which meant they had no casualties at all on the journey. Now it was time to organise the mass exodus from Winter Quarters for the spring of 1848. Both 'push' and 'pull' factors were operating by this time, for the United States government was already taking a tough line about the illegal Mormon occupation of Indian lands. The Saints were under orders to evacuate at the earliest possible moment or take the consequences. A wrathful Brigham Young was again in evidence. A young Mormon recorded his impression of the leader in May 1848: 'He was never known to curse so much as on that day. The nation, the land of Missouri . . . and old Colonel Miller an Indian agent for his meanness and abuse to the saints.'

In May 1848, the mass migration began. In three main divisions, 2,408 Mormons trekked west. Brigham Young himself headed the largest wagon train, and Thomas Bullock's minute, pedantic census gives us every last detail. There were 1,229 people in 397 wagons, with 1,275 oxen, 74 horses, 699 cows, 184 loose cattle, 411 sheep, 141 pigs, 605 chickens, 37 cats, 82 dogs, three goats, ten geese, two beehives, eight doves and even a solitary crow. Heber Kimball headed the second division, comprising 662 people, 226 wagons, 1,253 horses, mules and cattle plus an assortment of sheep, pigs, chickens, goats, geese, doves, cats and dogs. Departing on 26 May, Kimball's wagon train was at Chimney Rock on 15 July, Devil's Gate on 12 August, Fort Bridger on 12 September and the Salt Lake on 24 September. Brigham Young's caravan, about four days ahead all the way, reached journey's end on 20 September.

Although it would be tedious to rehearse in detail the daily progress of a trek that was in most regards simply a large-scale replay of the pioneer hegira the year before, a few features are worth noting. First, casualties were higher. On 6 June, the previously peaceful Omaha Indians jumped a detachment of Mormons on the Elkhorn River, killed two (for the loss of four Omaha killed), and wounded three others, including Howard Egan. Four females also died on the trail, including six-year-old Lucretia Cox, who fell off the wagon tongue and was crushed by the front wheel of the wagon. There were also some bad accidents, though the only rattlesnake victim this time was a horse. A young woman named Lucy Groves, who had given birth ten days before, slipped and fell in front of a wagon, which ran over her and broke three ribs and a leg. Brigham Young set the leg, but Lucy's thirteen-year-old daughter accidentally fell on her mother's leg, breaking it again. In severe pain, Lucy begged the others to go on without her, but Brigham Young halted the caravan at once, reset her leg and placed her in a secure hammock.

The establishment of the Mormon nation state after 1848 had some important consequences for the California and Oregon trails, especially the former, as the Saints blazed many new trails and opened up fresh routes. The Salt Lake cutoff meant that the long and arduous trips to Fort Hall or via the Hastings cutoff were no longer necessary; there was also the 'Mormon Corridor', running south-west from Salt Lake City, which was followed by more than a thousand gold-seeking 'Argonauts' in 1849. The Saints not only pioneered and surveyed new routes and cutoffs but made the fruits of their knowledge available in a series of guidebooks, of which William Clayton's was the most famous. But there were others: the vade-mecum produced by B.H. Young and J. Eager sketched the route between Salt Lake and San Francisco, while Joseph Cain and Ariel Brower's book provided an itinerary over the Sierras to California. The Saints also ensured a more peaceful transit for Gentile overlanders by pursuing Brigham Young's policy of appeasement (it's cheaper to feed them than to fight them) of the Indian tribes.

The Mormon oasis at Salt Lake City also helped considerably in the enforcement of law and order on the overland trails. The Mormon judiciary proved extremely useful in resolving disputes that arose on the trail: these could be suits for torts or overcharging, breach of contract cases or felonies involving assault and battery. Although the primary interest of Mormon courts was to deal with emigrants who infringed the Laws of the Church by, for example, letting cattle graze in cultivated fields, Brigham Young's police force reinforced the respectability of the State of Deseret (as the new Zion was called) by acting as impartial and disinterested law enforcers; they once travelled two hundred miles outside Mormon frontiers to apprehend a band of thieves.

By and large the overlanders saw only the negative side of the Mormon achievement. Brigham Young and his followers were highly talented entrepreneurs, and soon the whisper arose that it was entirely appropriate that the Saints should call outsiders Gentiles, since they themselves were the 'Jews' of the West. The accusation of levying extortionate prices does not really stand up, for the cost of staples like coffee and sugar was actually less in Salt Lake City during the gold rush years than at the jumping off points and established forts. Brigham Young himself was not interested in fleecing Gentiles; he would have preferred that they avoid Salt Lake City altogether, especially as they tended to leave their sick behind in the Great Basin for the Saints to look after and let their stock trample over fields full of crops. He wanted a self-sufficient community – economic autarky, to use the jargon – cut off from and independent of the outside world and market forces. He disapproved of trading food to Gentiles that incoming Mormon settlers might need.

But Young was a realist and, seeing that contact with the Gentiles was unavoidable, he advocated charging the highest possible prices. He argued, rightly, that the overlanders had contributed nothing in taxes to the infrastructure – roads, ferries, hospitals, etc. – that made Salt Lake City such an oasis and that such 'tax avoidance' was particularly reprehensible in people like the forty-niners who were interested solely in making individual fortunes. So the attitude of Saints to Gentiles was always characterised by profound ambivalence. On the one hand, the Saints had founded the State of Deseret precisely to escape the contamination of the detested United States; on the other, there were large profits to be made out of trading with the Gentiles and providing them with essential services.

The perfect symbol of this ambivalence was the system of Mormon ferries, which they established on the Greenwood (Sublette) cutoff, on the Green River, the Bear River between Fort Bridger and Salt Lake City, and the Weber River on the other side of Salt Lake. The starting fee was $4 per wagon but in the gold rush years, when there was traffic congestion and cut-throat competition for water, grass, campsites and all the other factors that allowed one to steal a march on a rival, hyperinflation was the norm. The Saints charged whatever the market would bear and, in the case of people craving speed and convenience above all else, the fee for ferrying could go as high as $30 a wagon. The Saints in effect were in a 'no-lose' situation, for either they stood to make thousands of dollars out of the Gentiles or the Gentiles would avoid their domains altogether, which is, at root, what Brigham Young wanted. However, increasingly in the gold rush years, the emigrants beat down the Mormon ferrymen's prices by either threatening to build their own ferries and fords or actually doing so. A very popular ploy was to buy makeshift boats from the outfitting towns in Missouri, to ferry one's own wagon train across, and then to sell them on to the caravan behind, who in turn repeated the manoeuvre, so that everyone ended up with a free crossing.

Apart from complaining about Mormon 'profiteering', Gentiles harboured deep suspicions that they were being used by Brigham Young in devious geopolitical games of his own. Young's initial expansionist dreams included a Pacific seaport and a Mormon domain incorporating most of northern California and Idaho – which would have made the

State of Deseret one-sixth of the size of the United States – and many overlanders felt that the Saints exaggerated and lied about the dangers of the northern routes to California to get them to find new trails through the Sierras which Young would then utilise for his own purposes. One emigrant spoke of his experience at Salt Lake City:

> The Sunday we were there he [Young] stated in his sermon that the Lord had come to him in a vision and told him that no emigrant starting after that time over the northern route to California would arrive there, but would leave their bones to bleach on the plains or in the mountains. Some trains were frightened and went by the southern route, though to their sorrow. We came safely through the northern route but by a tight squeeze.

Yet there was virtually universal agreement that the Mormon 'halfway house' at Salt Lake City greatly eased and attenuated the privations on the Oregon and California trails. At least 10,000 'Argonauts' detoured there in 1849 to get fresh wagons, animals, tools, clothes and food for the rest of the journey. They could also have spectacles and watches repaired, buy unheard-of delicacies and even have their photograph taken. The mere existence of Salt Lake City meant that no one had to outfit for the whole 2,000-mile journey as heretofore. Brigham Young's half-hearted attempts to keep Gentiles at bay by stressing the rigours of an itinerary between Fort Bridger and Salt Lake City had next to no effect. For emigrants, life in Salt Lake City was an unwonted glimpse of luxury. They could board with Mormon families or even rent vacant houses; they could sit down to table and gourmandise on food they had last seen in St Louis or Chicago, all for fifty cents a meal; they could attend Mormon dances and swing pretty Mormon girls on their arm. One forty-niner wrote: 'Our hostess, with despatch, set before us a sumptuous meal of new potatoes, green peas, bread and butter, with rich, sweet milk. It is needless to say that the hungry wayfarers, who for months had not seen these delicacies, did ample justice to this bountiful repast. The memory of the feast will live with me forever.'

The story of the emigrant trail in 1847–48, then, is one of almost complete triumph by the Church of the Latter-Day Saints. Brigham Young's year of decision was clearly 1847. Yet it would be supremely misleading to suggest or imply that the normal 'Gentile' emigration came to a halt in these years. What is true is that migration to California slowed to a comparative trickle – comparative in that although only 450 people, travelling in ninety wagons, reached California in 1847 (less than a third of the 1846 figure), this was still nearly twice the 1845 figure (260). The main cause for the slowdown was the uncertainty engendered by the Mexican war; with little hard information to go on, migrants imagined a scenario where Mexico might have been victorious in California and was conducting a pogrom against 'Anglos'. Another factor was increasing Indian troubles. Chester Ingersoll's wagon train had four oxen, a cow and a horse stolen by the Diggers along the Humboldt River; 'after that,' wrote Ingersoll, 'we shot at every Indian we saw – this soon cleared the way.' Those who received news of the Donner tragedy while on the trail might have also have changed their minds and gone to Oregon instead. At least one party, led by William Wiggins, thought it was possible to reach the Sacramento River via the Applegate cutoff; to Wiggins's credit, once he realised his mistake, he did not attempt to cut back from the present Oregon–California border to Sacramento through unknown mountain ranges, but led his party to Oregon instead.

The beneficiary of the uncertainty over the Mexican war was Oregon, for in 1847 nearly ten times more emigrants (4,000) went there than made the perilous and uncertain trek to California. To the fury of the California 'boosters', the Oregonians decisively won the propaganda war that year, luring a mass migration to the Pacific north-west with cheap provisions, free use of guides and a plethora of trail brochures and other travel information. Two-thirds of these 'jumped off' from St Joseph rather than Independence and most travelled via the Sublette (Greenwood) cutoff, though a few made the longer detour via Fort Bridger. Returning with General Kearney from California on the Sublette cutoff, Captain Henry S. Turner conducted an informative private census at the Sweetwater, which gives an interesting breakdown of that year's emigrants. He listed 1,336 adult males and 789 women, with another 1,384 of both sexes under sixteen – making 3,509 in all. They were travelling in 941 wagons, with 7,946 cattle, 929 horses and mules and 469 sheep. Most of these opted for the Applegate Trail into the Willamette valley, although trouble with the Modocs tended to nudge overlanders back on to the old route north through the Blue Mountains and on to the Columbia River.

Even though the Barlow Road through the Cascades was open, the ordeal by Columbia River still loomed for those who arrived in Oregon too late in the season, when the Cascades were already snowbound. Few Oregon emigrants endured worse miseries than Elizabeth Dixon Smith and her family. It is not entirely clear why they arrived in Oregon so late. It is true that they did not leave St Joseph until 1 June, about a month behind that year's front runners, but they seemed to have made up time quite well en route. However, it was not until 27 October that the Smith family reached The Dalles. With forty-year-old Elizabeth were her husband Cornelius and eight children. The Smith family then joined a queue of people waiting for river passage down the Columbia. Clubbing together with two other families, the Smiths bought a raft, but cold winds and rains prevented its launch until 2 November. For the next eleven days, they endured the worst terrors of white-water rafting, battling monster river waves and treacherous currents, often being forced to put in to the shore, where they huddled, marooned on a rocky outcrop, unable to relaunch because of the seething torrent in the Columbia. Since they had not expected such a tempestuous journey, they soon found that their food supplies dwindled alarmingly; worse, the combination of cruel weather, exposure and poor diet led increasing numbers of the party to fall sick. The temperatures were arctic. On 8 November, still some way from the Cascade Falls, Elizabeth recorded in her diary that her hands were so numb she could scarcely write. The next day, with icicles trickling down from the wagon beds to the boiling river, the first death (Adam Polk, head of one of the other families) was recorded.

They put in to the shore and Cornelius Smith set off to find provisions. Twenty-four hours later he returned, having purchased fifty pounds of beef which he carried on his back for twelve miles. It took them an hour and a half to relaunch on the seething Columbia, and then they endured a beef-only diet for three days until at last, on 13 November, they persuaded the operators of a ferry above the Cascade Falls to transport their effects across the cataract. At the Cascade Falls, they had to reassemble their wagons and portage for five miles in heavy rain to the other side of the rapids before they could restart the voyage on the Columbia, and then they had to compete for space on the river with hundreds of other weary emigrants. By now Cornelius Smith was so ill he could not leave his bed and Elizabeth could no longer wear shoes as her feet were so swollen with cold. Throughout the ordeal on the Columbia, it was always either raining or snowing. At last, on 27 November, Elizabeth managed to secure passage on a flatboat, but the two-day run to Portland was itself no picnic, as the following diary entry indicates: 'Nov. 27. Ran all day though the waves threatened to sink us. Passed Fort Vancouver in the night. Landed below. My husband never has left his bed since he was sick.' On 30 November, thirty-five days after reaching The Dalles, the Smith family crowded into a slum dwelling with the two other families. Just to get food, Elizabeth had to sell all her belongings. Cornelius never recovered from the nightmare on the Columbia and died on 1 February 1848.

Yet, the Smith story apart, most of the mass migration to Oregon in 1847 took place in circumstances of routine, but not noteworthy, endurance and hardship. However, there was one important exception to this general formula, and it portended the serious troubles that would break out in the 1850s and continue for twenty years. For the first time, Indians became a genuine menace on the overland trail. Modocs ambushed a wagon train on the Applegate Trail and massacred all twenty-three people in the caravan. And at the Whitman mission even more shocking events unfolded, as the Walla Walla area was thought to be well inside civilisation's pale. For a long time there had been bad blood between the Cayuse Indians and the Whitmans; Narcissa thought the Cayuse irredeemable as well as 'insolent, proud, domineering, arrogant', while the Cayuse resented the presence of overlanders who diverted to the mission. Then, in 1847, the multitudes of pioneers coming over the Blue Mountains spread the measles among the Cayuse. With no immunity, the Indians died in hundreds. Noting that no whites died, they concluded that the disease was 'bad medicine' deliberately spread by the whites.

On the afternoon of 29 November 1847, three Cayuse, including a man named Tiloukaikt, who had lost three children to the measles, called at the mission and asked to see Marcus Whitman. Once admitted, they hacked him to death. This was the signal for a general massacre. Narcissa Whitman was hit by a musket ball as she stood by the window, then she was dragged outside and killed by enraged warriors, who lashed her face even after she was dead. They then killed eleven other whites, including the two Sager boys who had been adopted by Narcissa together with the rest of the family in 1844. Six-year-old Hannah Sager, ill with measles at the time of the attack, died soon afterwards from lack of medical attention, as did the daughters of mountain men Joe Meek and Jim Bridger who were also at the mission. All the Sager girls and the rest of the survivors were taken away as captives and hostages. The Cayuse eventually ransomed them and they were then hunted down by a pioneer militia. Since fanatical voices in the United States were heard for the extermination of the Cayuse, the five ringleaders in the massacre, including Tiloukaikt, surrendered to save their people from annihilation. They were all hanged.

The Cayuse massacre at the Whitman mission created a sensation and was undoubtedly a factor in the much lower rate of emigration (1,300) to Oregon in 1848. Yet the years 1847–48 saw unrest among the tribes at a level that Washington had not experienced for twenty years. In June 1848 on the Santa Fe Trail, sixty-four US artillerymen with two six-pounders were attacked by two hundred Comanche and used the big guns to devastating effect, though the sound of the salvo stampeded the pack animals, allowing the Indians to get away with twenty-two horses and mules. In the same month, Lieutenant Royall and seventy-one men set out to escort government wagons on the Santa Fe Trail from Missouri. While encamped on the Arkansas River, they were attacked by a huge force of Comanches, maybe five hundred strong, who tried to envelop them in attacks from two directions. The Comanches charged four times and were beaten off with nine warriors killed, but they did manage to uplift a few mules and horses. Royall and thirty-eight mounted men gave chase across the river, only to find themselves surrounded by a huge force of about seven hundred men. The Americans managed to charge through to high ground, dug themselves in and fought off repeated attacks, killing another fourteen braves and wounding scores more. Finally, the Comanche withdrew and Royall was able to get his four wounded men back to camp.

The mass migrations of the wagon trains, to say nothing of the founding of the State of Deseret by Brigham Young, essentially torpedoed Washington's earlier Indian policies. In the 1820s and 1830s, the United States gradually moved back the eastern tribes to new lands west of the Mississippi, Although some tribes, notably the Sacs and Fox of Illinois, fought back stubbornly, especially in the Black Hawk war, by the end of the 1830s Washington seemed in sight of ending Indian warfare for good by separating whites and Indians with a 'Permanent Indian Frontier' that would run north–south from Minnesota to Louisiana. The development of the overland trails destroyed this approach and the acquisition of California, Arizona, New Mexico and Oregon through Manifest Destiny aggression effectively meant that the days of free Indian tribes of the interior were numbered. The backlash by the Indians against the emigrants, noticeable in 1847, could conceivably have had some effect on curtailing overland travel but for the discovery of gold in California in 1848. The California Gold Rush deluged the plains, deserts, mountains and prairies with a human tidal wave beyond the power of Native Americans to resist. It was not just the buffalo that were doomed by Thoreau's famous westward instinct.

EPILOGUE

When James W. Marshall found gold forty miles from Sutter's Fort in January 1848, the overland trails were changed for ever, changed utterly. The story of the trails after 1848 is both quantitively and qualitatively different. The migration triggered by the get-rich-quick urge dwarfed anything that had gone before. California boasted 400 migrants on the California Trail in 1848, but 25,000 in 1849 and a staggering 44,000 in 1850. Yet these figures represented only about half of California's migrants. Additionally, 16,000 people arrived in California via Cape Horn in 1849 and another 12,000 in 1850. Others, finding the California Trail clogged with wagons, opted for the Santa Fe Trail and its extension to California via the Old Spanish Trail, or melded the two routes by travelling to Utah along the traditional California/Oregon Trail and then cutting south-west to the Old Spanish Trail. Another route that burgeoned under the impact of insatiable demand was that via Panama or Nicaragua, across the isthmus from the Gulf of Mexico to the Pacific and thence to San Francisco. Where only 335 people had used this route in 1848, no less than 195,639 were travelling that way in 1860.

It is difficult to convey adequately the mass psychosis that gripped the nation in these years. A San Francisco editor, announcing the closing down of his newspaper because his city had become a ghost town, wrote: 'The whole country from San Francisco to Los Angeles, and from the sea shore to the base of the Sierra Nevadas, resounds with the sordid cry of "gold! *gold*, GOLD!" while the field is left half planted, the house half built, and everything neglected but the manufacture of shovels and pickaxes.' By 1852, the population of California was more than 250,000 or fifteen times that at the beginning of 1848. The Gold Rush phenomenon saw California far outstripping its rivals as a mecca for emigrants. The 1860 census recorded more than 380,000 inhabitants of California as against a mere 40,000 in Utah; Oregon, level-pegging with California in 1848, could manage only 52,000. Gold production, too, was impressive.

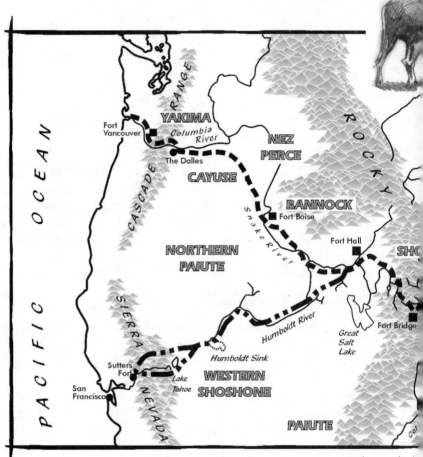

Indian Tribal

Oregon Trail
California Trail

TETON

SANTEE

DAKOTA
(SIOUX)

Missouri River

YANKTON

N

ne River

dependence
k

Chimney Rock

Fort
Laramie

Platte River

PAWNEE

Council Bluffs

MISSOURI

ARAPAHO

KANSA

CHEYENNE

Independence

The peak year was 1852 when over $81 million worth of gold was mined. Even though this fell to $70 million a year by 1853–54, the mines continued to yield fair though no longer spectacular dividends: between 1865 and 1885 the yearly figures oscillated between $15 and $20 million, and the lowest figure in any year until 1900 was $11 million.

On the overland trail, there were some obvious consequences. Emigration was no longer an affair of families seeking to improve their lot by steady toil in the promised land, but of greedy, vicious, venal, ruthless and unscrupulous 'entrepreneurs', many of them no more than gun-toting thugs. The California Trail became a place not of collaboration but of (sometimes literally) cut-throat competition, where bad temper, 'road rage' and quasi-chariot races between contending wagons were the norm. Hysteria, paranoia and fantasy were raised to new heights as people, driven mad by the mere thought of overnight fortunes, demanded the invention of miraculous rapid-transit systems and even aircraft, when the technology and know-how for such inventions still lay far in the future. There was hyperinflation in the prices of food and all basic supplies sold at the forts and trading posts.

Most of all, there were traffic jams on the prairie and severe overcrowding at campsites as the habitat of the Great Plains struggled to accommodate the human tidal wave. A rider on a good horse could easily pass eight hundred wagons in a single day. Alonzo Delano likened the press of people to Napoleon's *Grande Armée* in Russia in 1812 and spoke of the 'greatest crowd of adventurers since the invasion of Rome by the Goths'. Without much exaggeration, one emigrant, Solomon Gorgas, said: 'This certainly is a spectacle the world since its creation has never witnessed.' Mrs Margaret Frink reported that the traffic jam when the roads from St Joseph and Independence met at Marysville, Kansas, was an unbelievable spectacle: 'It seemed to me that I had never seen so many human beings before in all my life.' Naturally, in such a press of people, disease was rampant, and the first obvious consequence of the California Gold Rush was a cholera epidemic that scythed through the travellers all the way from St Louis to Fort Laramie.

The other most noticeable impact of the gold rush years was that it converted the Oregon and California trails into massive rubbish dumps as the emigrants progressively jettisoned animals, teams, goods, valuables and all manner of impedimenta. What happened was that the new race of Argonauts, who had heard every tall story from the Donner tragedy upwards and downwards, overstocked, found they could not make rapid progress and then dumped the stuff, usually within fifty miles from the 'jumping-off' points. Zealous entrepreneurs in St Joseph were able to sortie into the prairie and bring back wagonloads of bacon, flour, ham, bread, beans, stoves, tools, medicine, wagon wheels, axle-trees and clothes, all of which they had sold at premium prices just weeks before. It was estimated that by June 1849 20,000 pounds of bacon alone had been abandoned. Other debris included iron and steel, anvils, bellows, crowbars, drills, augers, baking ovens, cooking stoves, barrels, harnesses, clothes, weapons, ammunition, tobacco, safes, books, bookcases, even a diving bell and breathing apparatus. The word soon spread that you did not even need a 'grub stake' to travel to California's El Dorado, since you could live on what preceding travellers had thrown away.

Next to go were the wagons; over 2,000 of these vehicles were found abandoned in the California desert in 1850. From Fort Laramie to the Truckee, the prairie was littered not so much with trade goods as with the carcasses of dead animals: 190 dead beasts of burden were counted along a 321-mile stretch of the Snake River. But the principal dump-cum-charnel house was in the desert beyond the Humboldt Sink; sometimes the route was so clogged with dead and dying animals that emigrants had to find another route. In the Carson Desert, one traveller found $100,000 worth of dead animals: 2,381 horses and mules and 433 oxen, together with 787 abandoned wagons. A more scientific tabulation of the abandoned wealth left behind in the Gadarene rush to the gold fields finds over $1 million in portable property and several more millions in stock, all jettisoned between Independence, Missouri and Sacramento, and including 4,960 horses, 3,750 oxen and 1,061 mules.

The California Gold Rush is a phenomenon that has launched myriad books in description and explanation; any volume much less than five hundred pages devoted to this peculiar manifestation of 'gold fever' would be woefully inadequate. Its consequences were manifold, on California, on the United States and on the world economy. For our purposes, the most salient consideration is that it was the trigger for trouble with the hitherto mainly peaceful tribes; it also marked a definite caesura between the periods before and after 1848. But, cholera, traffic jams and prairie littering aside, it engendered little that was new in the overland experience. There were no significant technological break-throughs and the obstacles to emigrants remained what they had always been.

Statistics make clear the violent disjuncture between the years before the gold rush and the years after. Until 1848, only 14,247 emigrants had made the trip across the plains to California and Oregon, while a further 4,600 Mormons settled in the new Zion in Utah. But by 1860 almost 300,000 people had emigrated to the three locations – over 200,000 to

California, more than 53,000 to Oregon and nearly 43,000 Saints to the Great Salt Lake valley. In other words, there were fewer than 19,000 emigrants up to 1848 and almost 280,000 in the years 1849–60. Figures for emigrant mortality suggest a rate of about 4 per cent or 10,000 for the entire period 1840–60, and nine-tenths of this was accounted for by disease. As in Africa in the same period, it was the human vulnerability to bacteria and viruses that was the main barrier to conquest of a continent.

Among the known killers on the trail were smallpox, dysentery, scurvy, malaria, pneumonia, diphtheria and tuberculosis, while beyond Fort Laramie the principal scourge was 'mountain fever' – a generic term that embraced typhoid, Rocky Mountain spotted fever and Colorado tick fever. Scurvy particularly hit those on the latter stages of the California Trail, who had little access to fresh fruit and vegetables. At this stage in medical history, even the childhood illnesses – measles, whooping cough, mumps and chickenpox – could have serious consequences. Far and away the most deadly menace was cholera, and it was fortunate for the early emigrants that this was virtually unknown on the trail before 1849. In contrast to mountain fever, most of the cases of cholera occurred on the stretch of the overland trails between Missouri and Fort Laramie. Said to have been carried by rats on ships from Asiatic ports putting in at New Orleans, cholera then pursued a putative course up the Mississippi to St Louis and then on the Missouri to the 'jumping-off' towns. But overlanders were no more vulnerable to it than anyone else; 4,000 people died of the disease in St Louis in 1849.

The problem of disease was compounded by a lack of medical knowledge and a shortage of physicians. Vaccination was not unknown but rarely practised; instead, the overlanders relied on a variety of nostrums, quack remedies and 'panaceas' peddled by snake-oil salesmen. Alcohol, especially brandy and whiskey, featured largely, but some more sophisticated migrants took along a farrago of drugs: opium, laudanum, morphine, calomel, camphor, hartshorn, citric acid and even, in a few cases, a genuine febrifuge in the shape of quinine. Physicians were as rare as gold dust on the trails before 1849, but then quit their practices in huge numbers to join the rush to find the yellow metal. By a freak coincidence, the years 1849–50 were also the peak years for cholera, so they soon found themselves reluctantly drawn back to their old calling. Physicians would place shingles on their wagons and, via the 'prairie telegraph', everyone soon knew where the nearest doctor was. One 1850 practitioner attended seven hundred cholera cases for which, in theory, he received $150. But since many gold rush immigrants had no money, fees usually remained a dead letter, though there are authenticated cases of unscrupulous quacks charging (and receiving) up to $10 a day.

The other main dangers the emigrants faced have already been noted. There were more than three hundred drownings and even more firearms accidents in the years 1840–60, most of them in the post-1849 period when greed, impatience, poverty, meanness and incompetence were at their height among the so-called Argonauts. There were injuries and deaths when emigrants (usually children) fell under wagon wheels, became snarled up in ropes and dragged to death, or were injured by riding animals. Kicking mules fractured bones and lacerated scalps. Men were crushed by rolling horses and there were frequent instances of plunging horses and runaway teams causing concussion or breaking bones. Other injuries were sustained during stampedes, hailstorms or prairie fires. Then there were the freak accidents: six people killed by lightning, four killed by a falling oak tree, one from an overdose of medicine; a child was scalded to death and another died after swallowing a bottle of laudanum.

There were remarkably few deadly encounters with wild animals, all the more surprisingly, considering how many emigrants wandered off on their own or got lost; in such circumstances, a puma or pack of wolves could be dangerous. In general, one could say of the West what could be said of Central Africa in the same period: the chances of being mauled or killed by savage beasts were negligible so long as the traveller did not go looking for trouble. But, as in Africa with the lion- and buffalo-hunters, that is exactly what so many emigrants did. Bison hunts invited stampedes or charges from wounded and maddened bulls, and bear hunts carried their own obvious peril, especially in the case of the fearsome and aggressive grizzlies. There were a few random cases of sleeping emigrants being bitten by wolves, and even one of rabies transmitted in this way, but in general Josiah Gregg's judgement was valid: 'I have never known these animals, rapacious as they are, to extend their attacks to man, though they probably would, if hungry and a favourable opportunity presented itself.'

Rattlesnakes were a persistent menace to the stock, though they rarely bit humans. As Gregg said: 'Rattlesnakes are exceedingly abundant upon these plains: scores of them are sometimes killed in the course of a day's travel; yet they seem remarkably harmless, for I have never witnessed an instance of a man's being bitten, though they have been known to crawl into the beds of travellers. Mules are sometimes bitten by them, yet very rarely, though they must daily walk over considerable numbers.' Yet even

Gregg was not prepared to take chances, as his description of one day on the Santa Fe Trail indicates:

Rattlesnakes are proverbially abundant upon all these prairies, and as there is seldom to be found either stick or stone with which to kill them, one hears almost a constant popping of rifles or pistols among the vanguard, to clear the route of these disagreeable occupants, lest they should bite our animals. As we were toiling up through the sandy hillocks which border the southern banks of the Arkansas, the day being exceedingly warm, we came upon a perfect den of these reptiles. I will not say 'thousands,' though this is perhaps nearer the truth – but hundreds at least were coiled or crawling in every direction. They were no sooner discovered than we were upon them with guns and pistols, determined to let none of them escape.

Yet the worst of all irritants came not from reptiles but from the insect world. Overlander journals are full of complaints about noisome mosquitoes, particularly along the Platte. Emigrants complained that they had been 'eaten up', that their children's faces looked as though they had measles and their own resembled plum puddings. On the Santa Fe Trail in 1846, Susan Shelby Magoffin described what must have been a common occurrence:

I drew my feet up under me, wrapped my shawl over my head till I almost smothered with heat, and listened to the din without. And such a noise as it was, I shall pray ever to be preserved. Millions upon millions were swarming around me, and their knocking against the carriage reminded me of a hard rain. It was equal to any of the plagues of Egypt. I lay almost in a perfect stupor, the heat and the stings made me perfectly sick, till Magoffin came to the carriage and told me to run if I could, with my shawl, bonnet and shoes on (and without opening my mouth . . . for they would choke me) straight to the bed. When I got there they pushed me straight in under the musquito bar, which had been tied up in some kind of a fashion, and oh, dear, what a relief it was to breathe again. There I sat in my cage, like an imprisoned creature frightened half to death.

In the minds of the emigrants at the time, and those of myth-makers since, the greatest obstacle on the overland trail was the threat from Indians. But, statistically, this was a remote danger. In the entire period 1840–60 only 362 overlanders were killed by Indians, while the emigrants accounted for 426 Native Americans. Of the 4 per cent of pioneers who perished on the trail (about 10,000 in total), only 4 per cent of those were the victim of Indian attacks. In the early days of the overland trail, the Indian tribes did not perceive the white travellers as a threat – 'they still looked on the movers as a kind of circus parade, rich with goods but fundamentally comic', in the words of Bernard de Voto. It was only after 1849, when the huge numbers of whites on the plains alerted the tribes to the threat to their buffalo and way of life, that serious trouble broke out. Many of the forty-niners, moreover, were white trash who regarded Indians as subhuman, made gratuitous attacks on peaceful Indians, stole their goods and raped their women and thus invited violent retaliation.

In the 1840s, many Indians helped and cooperated with the pioneers, to the latter's considerable advantage. Overlanders often entrusted wagons, stock and families to Indian boatmen and swimmers at dangerous river crossings, especially on the Platte, Snake and Columbia, paying them in clothing or weapons. Indians helped in other ways, by guiding parties to water or on to unknown trails, gathering wood, carrying provisions, pulling wagons out of mud and ditches, often with their own oxen. They pointed out edible roots, interpreted and even took letters back east. Beyond Fort Boise, there was a considerable trade in fresh and smoked salmon and, besides these, the emigrants could trade for Indian corn, peas, potatoes, pumpkins, onions, wheat and watermelons; in return, the Indians accepted clothes, blankets, buttons, beads, mirrors, needles, thread, guns, ammunition, tobacco, coffee, sugar, beans, flour, bread, soap, fish-hooks, knives and umbrellas.

Before 1849, there were two main sources of friction. The principal grievance on the Indian side was that the emigrants wanted safe passage through their lands but were unwilling to pay tribute. The Indians insisted on it and liked to maintain toll bridges, charging, say twenty-five cents a wagon to cross a river that way. It was exactly the same situation as with the toll or *hongo* demanded by African tribes from European explorers. The aboriginals lived close to subsistence and demanded compensation for the disruption to the buffalo and other animals on their territory and the depletion of grass, timber and water; the whites deemed this blackmail and were tempted to blast passage through the tribal lands. Although the tolls asked were negligible alongside the tariffs levied by mountain men and traders operating ferries along the route, emigrants were infuriated by Indian 'impudence' and their allegedly arrogant ascription of 'rights' to themselves. The obvious way to cut the Gordian knot was for the federal government to guarantee emigrant safety and use treaties and agreements to buy the tribes off with presents – thus preventing direct haggling between Indians and emigrants – which is largely what happened.

The principal grievance of the emigrants was that the Indians were compulsive thieves and rogues. They were particularly expert at stealing horses, with the result that the annual rate of 'inventory shrinkage' from the stock of the pioneers ran to at least a thousand cattle and horses. Even though the tribes were often blamed for theft when animals strayed or stampeded, and for depredations committed by whites, there is no doubting the Indians' larcenous tendencies, which ran the gamut from casual 'shoplifting' of an item in a wagon that took their fancy to robbery with violence against people in ones or twos caught away from the wagon train. The Pawnee had a particularly bad reputation for this; their speciality was to strip their victims of all their clothes so that they had to walk back to the wagons stark naked, and this in an era when a high value was placed on modesty. Indians of all tribes habitually riddled the emigrants' cattle and oxen with arrows; their aim was to cripple them so that the whites left them behind for the Indians to feast on. Emigrants soon became wise to this and turned the tables by butchering the beasts themselves, jerking the meat and travelling on. Yet another speciality was to steal a horse, agree a 'finder's fee' with the emigrants and then return it; this stratagem could be repeated as long as the pioneers stayed in their territory. Even when the overlanders bought horses from Indians, they often found they were purchasing horses that had been stolen from a previous wagon train.

Yet Indians were sometimes unfairly blamed for crimes committed by whites disguised as Native Americans. The most famous example was the 'Mountain Meadows Massacre' carried out by Mormon Danites in 1857. But there were other examples of rape, plunder and murder by whites masquerading as Indians; this was a phenomenon particularly associated with the gold rush years and after, when the *canaille* and lowlives of the eastern slums began to appear on the plains. There were even areas where organised banditry by pseudo-Indians or Comanchero-type criminals collaborating with renegade Indians became almost endemic; this was especially a feature of the area adjacent to the Missouri River settlements, the Utah area beyond Salt Lake City (significantly, this was where the Mountain Meadows atrocity took place), the California end of the trail, and the Humboldt River and Carson River areas. This, of course, was entirely a phenomenon of the 1850s.

Apart from petty thieving, the emigrants never encountered serious trouble until they came to the country of the Pawnee between the Blue River and the Platte. Although rumours sometimes ran round the campfires (as in 1846) that the Kansa and Shawnee were planning treachery, these two tribes were negligible militarily, devoid of martial ability and little more than sneak-thieves; in this respect, they were to the Missouri–Kansas end of the trail what the Diggers were to the California end. The Pawnee were another matter entirely. Intrinsically a formidable tribe, they had taken terrible losses both from smallpox and the Sioux, and displaced some of their impotent anger about this on to the emigrants. Experts in blackmail and cattle-raiding, they were the MacGregors of the plains where their enemies the Sioux were the Clan Campbell; it was said of them that they could almost steal a horse from under its rider. They liked to pick off stray cattle, stampede others, manhandle or even murder stragglers and demand extortionate tolls for the crossing of their territory.

In the 1840s, with a few exceptions where overcomplacent emigrants wandered off from their wagon trains or went out on country promenades unarmed, the Pawnee stopped short of armed violence. But there was a steady escalation of tension, and conflicts over tribute would eventually lead to pitched battles with emigrants in 1852. The overlanders loathed and despised the Pawnee, whereas they gave grudging respect to the Sioux and the Shoshone. The attitude evinced by one emigrant can be taken as typical of the general attitude: 'The Pawnee Indians are the greatest thieves I ever saw – the best way I think to civilize or Christianize Indians is with powder and lead, and this is the way we shall do hereafter.' And in his *Emigrants' Guide*, J.M. Shiveley warned: 'Keep watch all the way, particularly the Pawnee country, from the crossing of the Blue to the crossing of the Platte.' The Pawnee finally resolved their conflicts with whites and the Sioux in the only logically possible way: they became scouts for the US Cavalry in the great decade of Indian warfare, 1866–76.

Once out of Pawnee territory, the emigrants usually encountered the Sioux and their normal allies the Cheyenne, though roving bands of Shoshone, Crow and even Arapaho were sometimes seen. Trouble with the Cheyenne began only in 1856; for twenty years thereafter they were recognised as one of the most formidable challenges faced by the US Cavalry. But in the era of the overlanders they barely rate a mention, and when it occurs, it is honorific. When his entire family died of the cholera epidemic introduced by the 1849 Argonauts, a Cheyenne brave declared a vendetta against the white man and began by killing a young emigrant from St Joseph. His tribe at once dissociated themselves from the killing by executing the brave for murder.

The most formidable of all the tribes of the northern plains, the Sioux, or the Lakota, gave the emigrants very little trouble in the 1840s. Shiveley in his guide pointed out that, unlike the Pawnee, 'the Sioux will not likely molest you in any way'. As true warriors, they despised the stealing of horses and could easily be placated by gifts of food, such as sugar and flour. Even when jittery overlanders fired a few shots in the direction of their war parties, the Sioux, intent on pursuit of their ancient enemies, the Pawnee, the Crow and the Shoshone, understood the reaction for the nervousness it was and paid no attention. The great dynamic on the plains in the 1840s was inter-tribal warfare, though, in subtle ways, this can be seen as a prelude for the eventual white versus Indian conflicts which began in earnest in the 1850s.

Certainly, following the overland trail in the 1850s was a different proposition, for, by then, conflicts between the Sioux and the US military were beginning to grow very serious. Attitudes had hardened on both sides. After their ancestral hunting grounds had been polluted by 70,000 gold seekers in 1849–50, the Lakota reassessed the threat from the white man and realised that it was much more serious than they had realised. The famous story is of an Indian chief suggesting a mass migration east, since surely there could be no whites left there. On the other side, the US Army was taking an unconscionably tough line, demanding draconian penalties for minor offences. Lieutenant John Grattan's arrogant demand for massive compensation for the butchering of a single emigrant cow led to the so-called Grattan massacre of 1854 when the foolish lieutenant and his detail of twenty-eight men were wiped out. The following year, General William S. Harney took revenge in a battle near Ash Hollow where, for the loss of six dead and six wounded, he killed eighty-six Sioux and captured a host of their women and children.

West of South Pass, the emigrants entered Shoshone territory. Once again, the emigrants of the 1840s had little to fear. The Shoshone, or Eastern Snake, though engaged in a deadly struggle with the Sioux, went out of their way to be friendly and helpful to emigrants. Undoubtedly, the key figure here was Chief Washakie, who consistently preached peace and friendship with the white man and held his warriors to the line even under considerable provocation from white ruffians and desperadoes who killed and looted in his territory. One petition, signed by no less than 9,000 emigrants, paid particular tribute to Washakie, who continued his pacific policy even during the difficult years of the 1850s. It should be emphasised that the Shoshone were by no means in the same category as the Kansa or even the Pawnee.

Odysseus's wisdom was said to be proven by his knowledge that the greatest danger in any journey occurs just before the end. In the case of the emigrants, the greatest danger from Indians was at the western end of the Oregon Trail, where 90 per cent of all emigrant fatalities from Indian attack took place. As John Unruh has pointed out, we tend to read back our estimate of the tribes from the very different situation obtaining in the post-Civil War years, when the Sioux, Cheyenne, Comanche and Apache topped the bill as the 'dark other'. In the 1840s, the real threat came from the Bannocks, Cayuse and Modocs, situated in the far western states of Idaho and Oregon. In 1847, as we have seen, there was serious trouble with both the Modocs and the Cayuse and two separate 'massacres' occurred. The far west of the Oregon Trail continued to live up to its bad reputation. In 1854, twenty-five miles east of Fort Boise, eighteen people in a wagon train were killed after a battle precipitated by Indian horse-stealing. What infuriated public opinion about the 'Ward massacre' was that the women in the five wagons had been brutally raped before being murdered.

The area where northern California, southern Oregon and north-western Nevada intersect was the real killing ground in the 1850s. There was serious fighting on the southern Oregon route in 1852. Fourteen emigrants were killed at Lost River that year. Later, a party of volunteers from Yreka, California, reached Tule Lake just in time to rescue a forty to sixty-strong wagon train, which had formed a laager, from the Modocs; between twenty and thirty-five Indians were killed in the counter-attack. Another black year was 1860. The Paiutes went on the warpath and ambushed a large force under Major William Ormsby; the Ormsby party came close to annihilation and lost between forty-six and sixty men but got its revenge when a huge punitive force of eight hundred troops retaliated and killed some forty to fifty Paiutes. In the same year, near the Salmon Falls in Idaho, Snakes and Bannocks besieged a caravan for several days; this was the one and only occasion when the movie stereotype of the wagon train encircled by whooping savages came close to being actualised. Eighteen emigrants died in the fighting and a further four after escaping into the wilderness. More sombrely, scalping, rape and other atrocities were visited on the overlanders, and this was later verified by unimpeachable sources.

The 1849 gold rush marked an invisible watershed in relations between whites and Indians. After that date, not only was there acute pressure from overlanders on Native American resources, principally the buffalo, but the disgorging of the flotsam and jetsam of eastern cities on the Great Plains, with the orgy of murder, rape and atrocity this unleashed, made Indians determine to return tit for tat. It is entirely possible that, had the pioneer parties of 1841–45 faced the determined backlash from the Indians that was seen in the 1850s, the entire overland emigration phenomenon would not have happened. Had the wagon-train movement

439

been postponed until the Federal Government was truly in a position to make its writ run in the West, i.e. until after the Civil War, it might never have happened at all, for by that time the transcontinental railroad was being built. The overlanders were also lucky in that, apart from travellers on the southern route to Oregon after 1846, they missed the most fearsome Indian tribes. Although the Sioux were the most powerful confederacy of tribes in the West, they had to be pushed into confrontation with the whites by blatant provocation and exploitation. Travellers on the Oregon, California and Mormon trails made no contact with the Comanche, Apache or even the Blackfeet, reckoned by experts to be, man for man, the most formidable fighting Indians of all.

The nineteenth century saw the American character at its best, and the best of that best was probably evinced on the wagon trains west. One does not want to go as far as Senator Goldwater, who famously declared that Daniel Boone's greatest merit as frontiersman was that he did not require the cushioning of social security to launch into the wilderness. But it is the intrepidity, self-reliance and mutual cooperation, albeit faltering, that most attracts us to the wagon-train pioneers. It is true that there were no heroes of the calibre of Shackleton on the trail, but Bidwell, Whitman, Clyman and Palmer, to name a handful, bore themselves well and made a quiet contribution to the literature of indomitable endurance. Villains, whether of the active kidney like Keseberg or the passive variety like Passed Midshipman Woodworth, seem thicker on the ground, but maybe this is only because Webster-like dark hues naturally make more impression than quiet, sober, decent individuals. Why, after all, does Macbeth impress more than Mr Pickwick? The overland emigrants have an archetypal significance in American history, representing as they do all the ideals of republican virtue and self-help endeavour. Let us therefore praise obscure men and women and endorse the sentiments of Walt Whitman:

Come, my tan-faced children,
Follow well in order, get your weapons ready;
Have you your pistols? Have you your sharp-edged axes?
Pioneers! O pioneers!

We primeval forests felling,
We the rivers stemming, vexing we, and piercing deep the mines within;
We the surface broad surveying, we the virgin soil upheaving,
Pioneers! O pioneers!

All the pulses of the world,
Falling in, they beat for us, with the western movement beat
Holding single or together, steady moving, to the front, all for us,
Pioneers! O pioneers!

BIBLIOGRAPHY

Abbreviations used:

AHR American Historical Review
M.M. Le Roy R. Hafen, ed. *The Mountain Men and the Fur Trade of the Far West*, 10 vols (Glendale, ca. 1972)
OHSQ Oregon Historical Society Quarterly
OPAT Transactions of the Oregon Pioneers Association, Portland

Unless otherwise stated place of publication is always London.

GENERAL

This contains works which either span the entire chronological period of the study or have been consulted for several different chapters.

Bamforth, Douglas B., 'Historical Documents and Bison Ecology on the Great Plains', *Plains Anthropology*, 32 (1987), pp. 1–16
Bancroft, H.H., *History of Nevada, Colorado and Wyoming, 1540–1888* (SF, 1890)
Bancroft, H.H., *History of Oregon*, 2 vols (SF, 1886)
Bancroft, H.H., *History of California*, 7 vols (SF, 1890)
Bancroft, H.H., *Chronicles of the Builders of the Commonwealth*, 7 vols (SF, 1892)
Barry, Louise, *The Beginning of the West* (Topeka, Kansas, 1972)
Bauer, Erwin A., *Horned and Antlered Game* (NY, 1986)
Beckham, Stephen Dow, *The Indians of Western Oregon: This Land Was Theirs* (Oregon, 1977)
Billington, Ray Allen, *The Far Western Frontier* (1956)
Billington, Ray Allen, and Ridge, Martin, *Westward Expansion: A History of the American Frontier* (NY, 1982)
Brown, David E., *The Grizzly in the Southwest* (Norman, Ok., 1985)

Calloway, Colin G., 'The Inter-tribal Balance of Power on the Great Plains, 1760–1850', *Journal of American Studies*, 16 (1982), pp. 25–47

Cartwright, David, *Natural History of Western Wild Animals and Guide for Hunters, Trappers and Sportsmen*, ed. Mary F. Bailey (Toledo, Ohio, 1875)

Clark, John C., ed., *The Frontier Challenge. Responses to the Trans-Mississippi West* (Lawrence, Kansas, 1971)

Coan, C.F., 'The First Stage of the Federal Indian Policy in the Pacific Northwest, 1849–1852', *OHSQ*, 22 (1921), pp. 46–89

De Lafosse, Peter, ed., *Trailing the Pioneers* (Logan, Utah, 1994)

Denig, Edwin T., *Five Indian Tribes of the Upper Missouri* (Norman, Ok., 1961)

De Voto, Bernard, *Across the Wide Missouri* (1947)

Dodds, Gordon B., *The American Northwest: A History of Oregon and Washington* (Illinois, 1986)

Dodge, Richard Irving, *The Plains of North America and their Inhabitants* (Delaware, 1989)

Dorris, Jonathan Truman, 'Federal Aid to the Oregon Trail prior to 1850', *OHSQ*, 30 (1929) pp. 303–25

Edmunds, R. David, *American Indian Leaders* (Lincoln, Neb., 1980)

Eggenhoffer, Nick, *Wagons, Mules and Men* (NY, 1961)

Eide, Inguard Henry, *Oregon Trail* (Chicago, 1972)

Einarzen, Arthur S., *The Pronghorn Antelope and its Management* (Washington, DC, 1948)

Ewers, John C., 'Intertribal Warfare as a Precursor of Indian–White Warfare on the Northern Plains', *Western Historical Quarterly*, 6 (1975), pp. 397–410

Ewers, John C., *The Blackfeet* (Norman, Ok., 1958)

Faragher, John Mack, *Women and Men on the Overland Trail*, revised edn (Yale, 2000)

Faragher, John Mack, *Sugar Creek. Life on the Illinois Prairie* (New Haven, 1986)

Fanzwa, Gregory M., *The Oregon Trail Revisited* (St Louis, 1972)

Fehrenbach, T.R., *Comanches* (NY, 1979)

Flores, Dan, 'Bison Ecology and Bison Diplomacy: the Southern Plains from 1800 to 1850', *Journal of American History*, 78 (1991), pp. 465–85

Fremont, John Charles, *Memoirs of My Life*, 2 vols (NY, 1887)

Garavaglia, Louis A., and Woman, Charles G., *Firearms of the American West, 1803–1865* (Albuquerque, 1985)

Gibson, James R., *Forming the Frontier: the Agricultural Opening of the Oregon Country, 1786–1846* (Seattle, 1985)

Goetzmann, William H., *Exploration and Empire: the Explorer and the Scientist in the Winning of the American West* (NY, 1966)

Goetzmann, William H., *New Lands, New Men: America and the Second Great Age of Discovery* (NY, 1986)

Graebner, Norman A., *Empire on the Pacific. A Study in American Continental Expansion* (NY, 1955)

Gregg, Josiah, *The Commerce of the Prairies*, ed. Max Moorhead (Norman, Ok., 1954)

Hafen, Le Roy R., ed., *The Mountain Men and the Fur Trade of the Far West; Biographical Sketches*, 10 vols (Glendale, Ca., 1972)

Hafen, Le Roy R., and Ann W., *Relations with the Indians of the Plains, 1857–1861* (Glendale, Ca., 1959)

Hagan, William T., *Quanah Parker: Comanche Chief* (Norman, Ok., 1993)

Haines, Aubrey, *Historic Sites Along the Oregon Trail* (Missouri, 1981)

Harlow, Neil, *California Conquered: War and Peace on the Pacific, 1846–1850* (Berkeley, 1982)

Hasselstrom, Linda M., ed., *Journal of a Mountain Man. James Clyman* (Missoula, Montana, 1984)

Hastings, Lansford W., *The Emigrants' Guide to Oregon and California* (1845)

Hoig, Stan, *Tribal Wars of the Southern Plains* (Norman, Ok., 1993)

Holliday, J.S., *The World Rushed In* (1983)

Hopkins, Sarah Winnemucca, *Life Among the Paiutes* (Boston, 1883)

Hunt, Thomas, *Ghost Trails to California* (Palo Alto, 1974)

Hyde, George E., *Pawnee Indians* (Denver, 1951)

Jackson, W. Turrentine, *Wagon Roads West* (Berkeley, 1962)

Jacobs, Melvin Clay, *Winning Oregon. A Study of an Expansionist Movement* (Caldwell, Idaho, 1938)

Johnson, David Allen, *Founding the Far West* (Berkeley, 1992)

Klauber, Laurence M., *Rattlesnakes. Their Habits, Life Histories and Influence on Mankind*, 2 vols (Berkeley, 1972)

Kurt, Matthew, *Man and Horse in History* (Alexandria, Va., 1983)

Lazarus, Edward, *Black Hills, White Justice. The Sioux Nation versus the United States, 1775 to the Present* (NY, 1991)

Lewis, David Rich, 'Argonauts and the Overland Trail Experience: Method and Theory', *Western Historical Quarterly*, 16 (1985), pp. 285–305

Limerick, Patricia Nelson, *Trails. Towards a New Western History* (Lawrence, Kansas, 1991)

Loveland, Cyprus P., *California Trail Herd*, ed. Richard H. Dillon (Los Gatos, Ca., 1961)

445

Lyman, Walker D., 'Bullwhacking: a Prosaic Profession Peculiar to the Great Plains', *New Mexico Historical Review*, 7 (1932), pp. 297–310

McCann, Lloyd E., 'The Grattan Massacre', *Nebraska History*, 37 (1956), pp. 1–25

McGinnis, Anthony, *Counting Coups and Cutting Horses: Intertribal Warfare on the Northern Plains, 1738–1889* (Evergreen, Colorado, 1990)

MacGregor, Greg, *Overland, the California Emigrant Trail of 1841–1870* (1996)

McLear, Patrick E., 'The St Louis Cholera Epidemic of 1849', *Missouri Historical Review*, 63 (1969), pp. 171–81

Madsen, Brigham D., *The Bannock of Idaho* (Caldwell, Idaho, 1958)

Mails, Thomas E., *The Mystic Warriors of the Plains* (NY, 1991)

Marcy, R.B., *The Prairie Traveller* (1860)

Mattes, Merrill J., *The Great Platte River Road* (Lincoln, Neb., 1969)

Mattes, Merrill J., *Platte River Road Narratives* (Urbana, Ill., 1988)

Mattson, Ray H., ed., 'The Harney Expedition against the Sioux: the Journal of Captain John B.S. Todd', *Nebraska History*, 43 (1962), pp. 89–130

Mayhill, Mildred P., *The Kiowas* (Norman, Ok., 1962)

Meinig, D.W., *The Great Columbia Plain: A Historical Geography, 1805–1910* (Seattle, 1968)

Merk, Frederick, *A History of the Westward Movement* (NY, 1978)

Miller, William C., ed., 'The Pyramid Lake Indian War of 1860', *Nevada Historical Quarterly*, 1 (1957), pp. 37–53, 98–113

Miner, H. Craig, and Huran, William E., *The End of Indian Kansas* (Lawrence, Kansas, 1978)

Mintz, Lannon W., *The Trail: a bibliography of travellers on the Overland Trail to California, Oregon, Salt Lake City and Montana during the years 1841–1864* (Albuquerque, 1987)

Moorhead, Max L., *New Mexico's Royal Road: Trade and Travel on the Chihuahua Trail* (Norman, Ok., 1995)

Morgan, Dale L., *Overland in 1846: Diaries and Letters of the California–Oregon Trail*, 2 vols (Georgetown, Ca., 1963)

Munkres, Robert C., 'The Plains Indians Threat to the Oregon Trail before 1860', *Annals of Wyoming*, 40 (1968), pp. 193–221

Murie, Olaus J., *The Elk of North America* (Harrisburg, Pa., 1951)

Nash, Gerald, *Creating the West: Historical Interpretations 1890–1990* (Albuquerque, 1991)

Nevins, Allan, ed., *Frémont's Narratives of Exploration and Adventure* (1956)

Omwake, John, *The Conestoga Six-Horse Bell Teams of Eastern Pennsylvania* (Cincinatti, 1930)

Peltier, Jerome, 'The Ward Massacre', *Pacific Northwesterner*, 9 (1965), pp. 12–16

Philips, George Harwood, *The Enduring Struggle: Indians in California History* (SF, 1981)

Philips, George Harwood, *Indians and Intruders in Central California. 1769–1849* (Norman, Ok., 1993)

Potter, David, *The Impending Crisis, 1848–1861* (NY, 1976)

Powers, Ramon, and Younger, Gene, 'Cholera on the Overland Trails, 1832–1869', *Kansas Quarterly*, 5 (1973), pp. 32–49

Raymond, Grace, *Washakie* (Cleveland, Ohio, 1930)

Read, Georgia Willis, 'Disease, Drugs and Doctors on the Oregon–California Trail in the Gold-Rush Years', *Missouri Historical Review*, 38 (1944), pp. 260–76

Reynolds, Sidney O., 'The Redskin who saved the White Man's Hide', *American Heritage*, 11 (1960), pp. 50–5, 108–11

Rickard, Madge E., and Bailey, R. Carlyle, *The Midwest Pioneer: His Ills, Cures and Doctors* (NY, 1946)

Rockwell, L.H., *Pioneer Guns and Gunsmiths* (Salt Lake City, 1988)

Rue, Leonard Lee, *The Deer of North America* (NY, 1978)

Russell, Don, 'How many Indians were killed? White Man versus Red Man: The Facts and the Legend', *American West*, 10 (July 1973), pp. 42–7, 61–3

Schwantes, Carlos, *The Pacific Northwest: an Interpretive History* (Lincoln, Neb., 1989)

Shaffer, Leslie, 'The Management of Organised Wagon Trains on the Overland Trail', *Missouri Historical Review*, 55 (1961), pp. 355–65

Shaw, Charles E., and Campbell, Sheldon, *Snakes of the American West* (NY, 1974)

Shumway, George, Durell, Edward, and Frey, Howard C., *Conestoga Wagon 1750–1850* (York, Pa., 1964)

Spaulding, Kenneth A., ed., *Robert Stuart On the Oregon Trail: Robert Stuart's Journey of Discovery* (Norman, Ok., 1954)

Stewart, George R., *The California Trail* (NY, 1962)

Thornton, Russell, *American Indian Holocaust and Survival: A Population History since 1492* (Norman, Ok., 1987)

Tinsley, Jim Bob, *The Puma, Legendary Lion of the Americas* (El Paso, 1987)

Townley, John M., *The Trail West: A Bibliographical Index to Western Trails, 1841–1869* (Reno, 1988)

Trenholm, Virginia Cole, and Carley, Maurine, *The Shoshonis: Sentinels of the Rockies* (Norman, Ok., 1964)

Trigger, Bruce G., and Washburn, Wilcomb E., eds, *The Cambridge History of the Native Peoples of the Americas* (Cambridge, 1996)

Tyler, Ron, *Prints of the West: Prints from the Library of Congress* (Golden, Colorado, 1994)

Unruh, John D., *The Plains Across: The Overland Emigrants and the Trans-Mississippi West, 1840–1860* (Urbana, Ill., 1979)

Van Orman, Richard A., *The Explorers: Nineteenth-Century Expeditions in Africa and the American West* (Albuquerque, 1984)

Van Wormer, Jan, *The World of the Pronghorn* (NY, 1969)

Wagner, Henry R., and Camp, Charles L., *The Plains and the Rockies 1800–1865*, revised and edited by Robert H. Becker (SF, 1982)

Walker, Henry Pickering, *Wagonmasters: High Plains Freighting from the Earliest Days of the Santa Fe Trail to 1880* (Norman, Ok., 1966)

Weisel, George F., *Men and Trade on the Northwest Frontier* (Missoula, Montana, 1955)

White, Richard, 'The Winning of the West: the Expansion of the Western Sioux in the Eighteenth and Nineteenth Centuries', *Journal of American History*, 65 (1978), pp. 319–43

Wilson, R.L., *The Peacemakers: Arms and Adventure in the American West* (NY, 1992)

Wishart, David, *The Fur Trade of the American West, 1807–1840: A Geographic Synthesis* (Lincoln, Neb., 1979)

Worcester, Donald E., *The Apaches: Eagles of the Southwest* (Norman, Ok., 1979)

Word, Samuel, 'Diary of a trip across the Plains', *Contributions to the Historical Society of Montana*, 8 (1917), pp. 37–92

ONE: MANIFEST DESTINY

Barr, Alwyn, *Texans in Revolt. The Battle for San Antonio, 1835* (Austin, 1990)

Bauer, Jack, *The Mexican War 1846–1848* (NY, 1974)

Brack, Gene, *Mexico Views Manifest Destiny, 1821–1846. An Essay on the Origins of the Mexican War* (Albuquerque, 1975)

Chalfont, William Y., *Dangerous Passage: the Santa Fe Trail and the Mexican War* (Norman, Ok., 1994)

Chittenden, Hiram M., *The American Fur Trade of the Far West*, 3 vols (NY, 1902)

Cleland, Robert Glass, *This Reckless Breed of Men. The Trappers and Fur Traders of the Southwest* (NY, 1950)

Connor, Seymour V., *Adventure in Glory. The Saga of Texas 1836–1849* (Austin, 1965)

Drury, Clifford M., *Marcus and Narcissa Whitman and the Opening of Old Oregon*, 2 vols (Glendale, Ca., 1973)

Eisenhower, John D., *So Far from God: the U.S. war with Mexico, 1846–1848* (NY, 1989)

Fehrenbach, T.R., *Lone Star: A History of Texas and the Texans* (NY, 1968)

Galbraith, John S., *The Hudson's Bay Company as an Imperial Factor, 1821–1869* (Berkeley, 1957)

Graebner, Norman, 'The Mexican War: A Study in Causation', *Pacific Historical Review*, 49 (1980), pp. 405–26

Gregg, Josiah, *The Commerce of the Prairies*, ed. Max Moorhead (Norman, Ok., 1954)

Hafen, Le Roy R., and Anne W., *Old Spanish Trail. Santa Fe to Los Angeles* (Glendale, Ca., 1954)

Hague, Harlen, *The Road to California: the Search for a Southern Overland Route, 1540–1848* (Glendale, Ca., 1978)

Hardin, Stephen L., *Texan Iliad: A Military History of the Texas Revolution, 1835–1836* (Austin, 1994)

Hietala, Thomas R., *Manifest design. Anxious Aggrandisement in Late Jacksonian America* (Ithaca, NY, 1985)

Hill, Joseph J., 'The Old Spanish Trail', *Hispanic American Historical Review*, 4 (1921), pp. 444–73

Horsman, Reginald, *Race and Manifest Destiny* (Harvard, 1981)

Jackson, Donald, *Thomas Jefferson to the Stony Mountains: Exploring the West from Monticello* (Urbana, Ill., 1981)

Johannsen, Donald W., *To the Halls of Montezuma: the Mexican War in the American Imagination* (NY, 1985)

Lack, Paul D., *The Texas Revolutionary Experience. A Political and Social History, 1835–1856* (Texas, 1992)

Lavender, David, *The Way to the Western Sea: Lewis and Clark across the Continent* (NY, 1988)

Leckie, Robert, *From Sea to Shining Sea: From the War of 1812 to the Mexican War, the Saga of America's Expansion* (NY, 1993)

McCormac, Eugene I., *James K. Polk. A Political Biography* (NY, 1965)

Milner, Clyde, O'Connor, Carol, and Sandelweiss, Martha, eds, *The Oxford History of the American West* (NY, 1994)

449

Moorhead, Max I., *New Mexico's Royal Road. Trade and Travel on the Chihuahua Trail* (Norman, Ok., 1995)

Pletcher, David, *The Diplomacy of Annexation. Texas, Oregon and the Mexican War* (Columbia, Missouri, 1973)

Price, Glenn W., *Origins of the War with Mexico: the Polk–Stockton Intrigue* (Austin, 1967)

Quaife, Milo M., ed., *The Diary of James K. Polk during his presidency 1845–49*, 4 vols (Chicago, 1910)

Reichstein, Andrew V., *The Rise of the Lone Star: the Making of Texas* (Texas, 1989)

Richardson, James D., ed., *A Compilation of the Messages and Papers of the Presidents, 1789–1902*, 10 vols (Washington, 1903)

Ronda, James P., *Astoria and Empire* (Lincoln, Neb., 1990)

Schroeder, John H., *Mr Polk's War; American Opposition and Dissent, 1846–1848* (Madison, Wisconsin, 1973)

Sellers, Charles G., *James K. Polk, Continentalist, 1843–1846* (Princeton, 1966)

Simmons, Marc, *Murder on the Santa Fe Trail* (El Paso, 1987)

Singletary, Otis, *The Mexican War* (Chicago, 1960)

Stephanson, Anders, *Manifest Destiny* (1995)

Van Leeuwen, Jean, *Bound for Oregon* (1994)

Weber, David J., *The Spanish Frontier in North America* (New Haven, 1992)

Weber, David J., *The Mexican Frontier 1821–1846. The American Southwest under Mexico* (Albuquerque, 1982)

Wishart, David, *The Fur Trade of the American West, 1797–1840: A Geographic Synthesis* (Lincoln, Neb., 1979)

TWO: THE REASONS WHY

Ambler, Charles H., 'The Oregon Country, 1810–1830. A Chapter in Territorial Expansion', *Mississippi Valley Historical Review*, 30 (1943), pp. 3–24

Applegate, Shannon, *Skookum: An Oregon Family's History and Lore* (NY, 1988)

Baur, John E., 'The Health Seeker in the Westward Movement, 1830–1900', *Mississippi Valley Historical Review*, 46 (1959), pp. 91–110

Bell, James Christy, *Opening a Highway to the Pacific, 1838–1846* (NY, 1921)

Benton, Thomas Hart, *Thirty Years' View; or, a History of the Workings of the American Government for Thirty Years from 1820 to 1850*, 2 vols (NY, 1856)

Billington, Ray Allen, *Words that Won the West* (n.p., 1964)

Blue, George Vern, 'The Oregon Question, 1818–1828', *OHSQ*, 34 (1933), pp. 39–59

Bright, Verne, 'The Folklore and History of the "Oregon Fever"', *OHSQ*, 52 (1951)

Dillon, Richard, *Fool's Gold. The Decline and Fall of Captain John Sutter* (NY, 1967)

Douglas, Jesse S., 'Origins of the Population of Oregon in 1850', *Pacific Northwest Quarterly*, 41 (1950)

Egan, Ferol, *Fremont, Explorer for a Restless Nation* (Reno, 1985)

Engelson, Gordon, 'Proposals for the Colonization of California by England in connection with the Mexican Debt to British Bondholders', *California Historical Society Quarterly*, 18 (1939), pp. 136–48

Fender, Stephen, *Plotting the Golden West* (Cambridge, 1981)

Gates, Paul W., *The Farmer's Age. Agriculture, 1815–1860* (NY, 1960)

Goetzmann, William H., *Army Exploration in the American West 1803–1863* (Yale, 1959)

Green, Jonathan S., *Journal of a Tour on the North-West Coast of America in the Year 1829* (NY, 1915)

Gudde, Erwin S., *Sutter's Own Story* (NY, 1936)

Hammond, George P., *The Larkin Papers*, 4 vols (Berkeley, 1953)

Hansen, William A., 'Thomas Hart Benton and the Oregon Question', *Missouri Historical Review*, 63 (1969), pp. 489–97

Hawgood, John A., 'John Augustus Sutter. A Reappraisal', *Arizona and the West*, 4 (1962), pp. 345–56

Hawgood, John A., 'A Projected Prussian Colonization of Upper California', *Southern California Quarterly*, 48 (1966), pp. 353–68

Hawgood, John A., 'The Pattern of Yankee Infiltration in Mexican Alta California 1821–1846', *Pacific Historical Review*, 27 (1958), pp. 27–38

Hollon, W. Eugene, *The Great American Desert, Then and Now* (NY, 1966)

Hudson, John C., 'Migrations to an American Frontier', *Annals of the Association of American Geographers*, 66 (1976), pp. 242–65

Husband, Michael B., 'Senator Lewis F. Lin and the Oregon Question', *Missouri Historical Review*, 66 (1971), pp. 1–19

Jasper, James M., *Restless Nation: Starting Over in America* (NY, 2000)

Johansen, Dorothy O., 'A Working Hypothesis for the Study of Migrations', *Pacific Historical Review*, 36 (1967), pp. 1–12

Limerick, Patricia Nelson, 'John Sutter: Prototype for Failure', in Limerick, *Something in the Soil* (NY, 2000), pp. 16–40

Lyman, George D., *John Marsh, Pioneer: the Life Story of a Trail Blazer on Six Frontiers* (NY, 1930)

Nobles, Gregory H., *American Frontiers* (N.Y. 1997)

Powell, Fred Wilbur, ed., *Hall J. Kelley on Oregon* (Princeton, 1932)

Robins, Roy M., *Our Landed Heritage: the Public Domain, 1776–1936* (Princeton, 1942)

Robinson, W.W., *Land in California* (Berkeley, 1948)

Schafer, Joseph, 'Notes on the Colonisation of Oregon', *OHSQ*, 6 (1905), pp. 379–90

Schroeder, John H., 'Representative John Floyd, 1817–1829: Harbinger of Oregon Territory', *OHSQ*, 70 (1969), pp. 333–46

Simpson, George, *Narrative of a Journey Round the World*, 2 vols (1847)

Sutter, John A., *The Diary of John Augustus Sutter* (SF, 1932)

Wardell, M.L., 'Oregon Immigration prior to 1846', *OHSQ*, 27 (1926), pp. 41–64

Weber, David J., *The Mexican Frontier, 1821–1846. The American Southwest under Mexico* (Albuquerque, 1982)

White, Richard, *'It's Your Misfortune and None of My Own'* (Norman, Ok., 1991)

Zollinger, James P., *Sutter: the Man and His Empire* (NY, 1939)

Zollinger, James P., 'John Augustus Sutter's European Background', *California Historical Society Quarterly*, 14 (1935), pp. 28–46

THREE: TO BOLDLY GO

Beard, Charles A., and Mary, *The Rise of American Civilization*, 2 vols (NY, 1929)

Berrien, Joseph W., 'Overland from St Louis', *Indiana Magazine of History*, 56 (1960), pp. 273–352

Berthong, Donald J., *The Southern Cheyenne* (Norman, Ok., 1963)

Bidwell, John, *Echoes* (Chicago, 1928)

Bidwell, John, *A Journey to California* (SF, 1937)

Burns, Robert Ignatius, *The Jesuits and the Indian Wars of the North-West* (Yale, 1966)

Caughey, John W., *California* (1959)

Child, Andrew, *The Overland Route to California* (LA, 1946)

Chittenden, Hiram Martin and Richardson, Alfred Talbot, eds, *Life,*

Letters and Travels of Father Pierre-Jean de Smet, S.J. 1801–1873, 4 vols (NY, 1905)

Cleland, Robert G., *From Wilderness to Empire* (NY, 1944)

Dawson, Nicholas, *California in '41* (Austin, Texas, 1894)

Donnelly, Joseph P., trans. and ed., *Wilderness Kingdom. Indian Life in the Rocky Mountains. The Journals and Paintings of Nicholas Point, S.J.* (1967)

Ellison, Eobert S., *Independence Rock: the Great Record of the Desert* (Casper, Wyoming, 1930)

Ewer, John C., ed., *Adventures of Zenas Leonard, Fur Trapper* (Norman, Ok., 1959)

Farnham, Thomas J., *Travels in the Great Western Prairies* (NY, 1841)

Garraghan, Gilbert G., *Chapters in Frontier History* (Milwaukee, 1934)

Garraghan, Gilbert G., *The Jesuits of the Middle United States*, 3 vols (NY, 1938)

Ghent, W.J. *The Early Far West* (NY, 1931)

Giffen, Helen S., *Trail-Blazing Pioneer. Joseph Bellinger Chiles* (SF, 1969)

Grinnell, George, *The Cheyenne Indians*, 2 vols (1923)

Hafen, Le Roy R., *Broken Hand: The Life of Thomas Fitzpatrick: Mountain Man, Guide and Indian Agent* (Denver, 1973)

Hafen, Le Roy R., 'Fraeb's Last Fight and how Battle Creek got its name', *Colorado Magazine*, 7 (1930), pp. 97–101

Hafen, Le Roy R., and Anne W., *To the Rockies and Oregon, 1839–1842* (Glendale, Ca., 1957)

Hafen, Le Roy R., and Young, Francis Marion, *Fort Laramie and the Pageant of the West, 1834–1890* (Glendale, Ca., 1938)

Heath, Minnie B., 'Nancy Kelsey – the first pioneer woman to cross the Plains', *The Grizzly Bear Magazine*, 40 (1937), pp. 3–7

Hill, Joseph J., 'Antoine Robidoux, Kingpin in the Colorado Fur Trade, 1824–1844', *Colorado Magazine*, 7 (1930), pp. 125–32

Hines, George H., ed., 'The Diary of James St John (sc. James John)', *St John (Oregon) Review* (March–April 1906)

Hunt, Rockwell D., *John D. Bidwell, A Prince of Californian Pioneers* (Caldwell, Idaho)

Hussey, John A., 'New Light on Talbot Green', *California Historical Society Quarterly*, 18 (1939), pp. 32–63

Ingalls, Eleazer, *Journal of a Trip to California by the Overland Route across the Plains* (Wankegan, Ill., 1852)

Lathrop, Gloria Ricci, trans. and ed., *Mengarini's Recollections of the Flathead Mission* (Glendale, Ca., 1977)

Laveille, E., *The Life of Father de Smet, S.J.* (NY, 1915)

McDermott, John Francis, 'De Smet's Illustrator: Father Nicholas Point', *Nebraska History*, 33 (1952), pp. 35–40

McDermott, John Francis, ed., *The Frontier Reexamined* (Urbana, Ill., 1967)

Mattes, Merrill J., 'Robidoux's Trading Post at Scott's Bluffs', *Nebraska History*, 30 (1949), pp. 95–138

Mattes, Merrill J., 'Fort Laramie, Guardian of the Oregon Trail', *Annals of Wyoming* (1945), pp, 3–20

Mattes, Merrill J., 'Chimney Rock on the Oregon Trail', *Nebraska History*, 36 (1955), pp. 1–26

Menefree, C.A., *A Historical and Descriptive Sketch Book of Napa, Sonoma, Lake and Mendocino* (Napa City, Ca., 1873)

Miller, David E., 'The First Wagon Train to cross Utah, 1841', *Utah Historical Quarterly*, 30 (1962), pp. 41–51

Morgan, Dale L., *The West of William H. Ashley, 1822–1838* (Denver, 1964)

Morgan, Dale L., *Jedediah Smith and the Opening of the West* (Indianapolis, 1953)

Munkres, Robert L., 'Soda Springs: Curiosity of the Trail', *Annals of Wyoming*, 43 (1971), pp. 215–35

Munkres, Robert L., 'Independence Rock and Devil's Gate', *Annals of Wyoming*, 42 (1970), pp. 5–43

Munney, Nolie, *The Life of Jim Baker 1818–1898* (Denver, 1931)

Nunis, Doyce B., ed., *Josiah Belden. California Overland Pioneer, His Memoirs and Early Letters* (Georgetown, Ca., 1962)

Partoll, Albert J., ed., 'Mengarini's Narrative to the Rockies', *Frontier and Midland History*, 18 (1938), pp. 193–202, 258–66

Phillips, Charles, *Missouri: Mother of the American West* (Northridge, Ca., 1988)

Platt, Philip L., and Slater, Nelson, *Travellers' Guide across the Plains upon the overland route to California* (SF, 1963)

Royce, Charles R., *John Bidwell, Pioneer, Statesman, Philanthropist* (Chicago, 1906)

Schoenberg, Wilfred P., *Paths to the North West. A Jesuit History of the Oregon Province* (Chicago, 1982)

Spaulding, Kenneth A., ed., *On the Oregon Trail: Robert Stuart's Journey of Discovery* (Norman, Ok., 1954)

Stewart, George R., 'The Prairie Schooner Got Them There', *American Heritage*, 13 (1962), pp. 4–17, 98–102

Terrell, John Upton, *Black Robe. The Life of Pierre-Jean de Smet* (NY, 1964)

Tobie, H.E., 'From the Missouri to the Colummbia, 1841', *OHSQ*, 38 (1937), pp. 137–59

Unrau, William E., *The Kansa Indians: A History of the Wind People, 1673–1873* (Norman, Ok., 1971)

Wallace, William S., *Antoine Robidoux* (LA, 1953)

Webb, W.L., 'Independence, Missouri, A Century Old', *Missouri Historical Review*, 22 (1927), pp. 30–50

Williams, Joseph, *Narrative of a Tour from the State of Indiana to the Oregon territory in the years 1841–42* (Cincinatti, 1843)

Zenor, B.J., 'By Covered Wagon to the Promised Land', *American West*, 11 (July, 1964), pp. 30–41

FOUR: THE WOMAN IN THE SUNBONNET

Adair, Owens, *Some of her Life Experiences* (Portland, Ore., 1921), pp. 234–6

Adams, Cecilia Emily McMillan, 'Crossing the Plains in 1852', *OPAT* (1904), pp. 288–329

Adams, Inez Eugenia, 'Early Recollections of Oregon Pioneer Life', *OPAT* (1928), pp. 17–36

Allen, A.J., *Ten Years in Oregon. Thrilling Adventures, Travels and Explorations of Dr Elijah White* (NY, 1859)

Allen, Eleanor, *Canvas Caravan* (Portland, Ore., 1946)

Allyn, Henry, 'Journal of 1853', *OPAT* (1928) pp. 372–435

Armitage, Susan, 'Women and Men in Western History: A Stereoptical Vision', *Western Historical Quarterly*, 19 (1988), pp. 381–95

Armitage, Susan, and Jameson, Elizabeth, eds, *The Women's West* (Norman, Ok., 1987)

Bailey, Washington, *A Trip to California* (n.p., 1915)

Belshaw, Maria Parsons, 'Diary', ed. J.W. Ellison, *OHSQ*, 33 (1932), pp. 318–33

Bourne, Edward Gaylord, 'The Legend of Marcus Whitman', *AHR*, 6 (1901), pp. 276–300

Collins, Elizabeth Gilliam Martha, 'Reminiscences', *OHSQ*, 17 (1916), pp. 358–72

Coone, Elizabeth, 'Reminiscences of a Pioneer Woman', *Washington Historical Quarterly*, 8 (1917), pp. 14–21

Crawford, Medorem, 'Occasional Address', *OPAT* (1881), pp. 9–19

Cummins, Sarah J., *Autobiography and Reminiscences* (Oregon, 1920)

Delano, Alonzo, *Across the Plains and among the Diggings* (NY, 1936)

Dorris, Jonathan T., 'The Oregon Trail', *Journal of the Illinois State Historical Society*, 10 (1918), pp. 473–547

Drury, Clifford M., *Marcus and Narcissa Whitman and the Opening of Old Oregon*, 2 vols (Glendale, Ca., 1973)

Drury, Clifford M., *First White Women over the Rockies*, 3 vols (Glendale, Ca., 1966)

Duniway, Abigail Scott, *Captain Gray's Company* (Portland, Ore., 1859)

Ellmaker, Enos, 'Autobiography', in *The Ellmaker Narrative* (Eugene, Ore., 1962)

Faragher, John, 'History from the Inside Out: Writing the History of Women in Rural America', *American Quarterly*, 33 (1981), pp. 537–57

Faragher, John, and Stansell, Christine, 'Women and their families on the Overland Trail, 1842–67', *Feminist Studies*, 2–3 (1975), pp. 150–66

Fischer, Christine, ed., *Let Them Speak for Themselves: Women in the American West, 1849–1900* (Connecticut, 1990)

Fremont, John Charles, *Report of the Exploring Expedition of 1842* (Washington, 1845)

Fowler, William H., *Women on the American Frontier* (NY, 1970)

Frizzell, Louisa, *Across the Plains to California in 1852* (NY, 1915)

Frost, John, *Pioneer Mothers of the West* (Boston, 1875)

Geer, Elizabeth D. Smith, 'Diary', *OPAT* (1907) pp. 153–85

Guerin, E.J., *Mountain Charley or the Adventures of Mr E.J. Guerin* (Norman, Ok., 1968)

Hafen, Anne W., 'Lancaster P. Lupton', *M.M.* ii. pp. 207–16

Hafen, Le Roy R., *Broken Hand* (Denver, Colorado, 1973)

Haines, Francis, 'Goldilocks on the Oregon Trail', *Idaho Yesterdays*, 9 (1966), pp. 26–30

Hastings, Loren B., 'Diary of Loren Hastings', *OPAT* (1923), pp. 12–26

Hewitt, Randall, *Across the Plains and Over the Divide* (NY, 1964)

Hines, Celinda E., 'Diary of Celinda E. Hines', *OPAT* (1918), pp. 69–125

Hixon, Adrietta Applegate, *On to Oregon! A True Story of a Young Girl's Journey into the West* (Idaho, 1947)

Hough, Emerson, *The Passing of the Frontier* (Yale, 1921)

Husband, Marcus B., 'William I. Marshall and the legend of Marcus Whitman', *Pacific Northwest Quarterly*, 64 (1973), pp. 57–69

Ivins, Virginia Wilcox, *Pen Pictures of Early Western Days* (NY, 1905)

Jacobs, Wilbur R., ed., *The Letters of Francis Parkman*, 2 vols (Norman, Ok., 1960)

Jeffrey, Julie Roy, *Frontier Women: the Trans-Mississippi West 1840–1880* (NY, 1979)

Jones, Brian, 'Those Wild Reshaw Boys', in Francis B. Taunton, ed., *Sidelights of the Sioux Wars* (1967) pp. 5–46

Longmire, James, 'Narrative of a Pioneer', *Washington Historical Quarterly*, 23 (1932), pp. 47–60

Lovejoy, Asa L., 'Lovejoy's Pioneer Narrative, 1842–48', ed. Henry E. Reed, *OHSQ*, 31 (1930) pp. 237–60

Lyman, H.S., ed., 'Reminiscences of F.X. Matthieu', *OHSQ*, 1 (1900) pp. 73–104

McClure, Andrew S., *The Diary* (Eugene, Ore., 1959)

McDermott, John Dishon, 'James Bordeaux', *M.M.* v. pp. 65–80

McDermott, John Dishon, 'Joseph Bissonette', *M.M.* iv. pp. 49–60

McGaw, William Cochran, *Savage Scene: the Life and Times of James Kirker, Frontier King* (NY, 1972)

McIntosh, Walter H., *Allen and Rachel, An Overland Honeymoon in 1853* (Caldwell, Idaho, 1938)

Malone, Michael P., ed., *Historians and the American West* (Lincoln, Neb., 1983)

Mattes, Merrill J., and Kirk, Elsey J., eds, 'From Ohio to California in 1849', *Indiana Magazine of History*, 46 (1950), pp. 297–318

Meek, Stephen Hall, *Autobiography of a Mountain Man, 1805–1889* (Pasadena, Ca., 1948)

Merk, Frederick, 'The Oregon Pioneers and the Boundary', *AHR*, 29 (1924), pp. 681–99

Miles, Edwin A., 'Fifty-Four or Fight: An American Political Legend', *Mississippi Valley Historical Review*, 44 (1958), pp. 291–300

Munkres, Robert L., 'Wives, Mothers, Daughters: Women's Life on the Road West', *Annals of Wyoming*, 42 (1970), pp. 191–224

Myres, Sandra L., *Westering Women and the Frontier Experience 1800–1915* (Albuquerque, 1982)

Myres, Sandra L., *Ho for California* (Albuquerque, 1980)

Nixon, Oliver, *How Marcus Whitman Saved Oregon* (Chicago, 1895)

Pengra, Charlotte, *Diary of Mrs Bynon T. Pengra* (Eugene, Ore., n.d.)

Perriam, Eve, ed., *Growing Up Female in America. Ten Lives* (NY, 1971)

Philips, Paul C., ed., '"Dick's Works," an overland journey to California in 1856. The Journal of Richard Owen Hickman', *Frontier*, 9 (1929), pp. 242–60

Pletcher, David, *Diplomacy of Annexation: Texas, Oregon and the Mexican War* (Columbia, Mo., 1973)

Porter, Lavinia, *By Oxteam to California* (Oakland, Ca., 1910)

Rawling, Gerald, 'The Oregon Trail', *History Today*, 11 (1961), pp. 743–52

Richmond, Robert W., 'Developments along the Oregon Trail', *Nebraska History*, 33 (1952), pp. 154–79, 237–47

Riley, Glenda, *Frontierswoman: the Iowa Experience* (Ames, Iowa, 1981)

Riley, Glenda, *Women and Indians on the Frontier 1825–1915* (Albuquerque, 1984)

Riley, Glenda, *The Female Frontier: A Comparative View of Women on the Prairie and the Plains* (Lawrence, Kansas, 1988)

Riley, Glenda, 'The Specter of a Savage: Rumors and Alarmism on the Overland Trail', *Western Historical Quarterly*, 15 (1984), pp. 427–44

Riley, Glenda, 'Women on the Great Plains: Recent Developments in Research', *Great Plains Quarterly*, 52 (1985), pp. 81–92

Ross, Nancy Wilson, *Westward Women* (Berkeley, 1985)

Ruiz, Vicki L., and Monk, Janice, eds, *Western Women: Their Lands, Their Lives* (Albuquerque, 1988)

Schlissel, Lillian, ed., *Women's Diaries of the Westward Journey* (NY, 1982)

Schlissel, Lillian, Gibbens, Byrd, and Hampsten, Elizabeth, eds, *Far from Home. Families of the Westward Journey* (NY, 1989)

Schlissel, Lillian, Ruiz, Vicki L., and Monks, Janice, eds, *Western Women: Their Lands, Their Lives* (Albuquerque, 1988)

Schmitt, Martin, '"Meat's Meat." An account of the flesh-eating habits of Western Americans', *Western Folklore*, 11 (1952), pp. 185–203

Smith, Elizabeth C., *Mexican War Service* (Bloomington, Ill., 1848)

Smith, Helena H., 'Pioneers in Petticoats', *American Heritage*, 10 (1959), pp. 101–3

Smith, Page, *Daughters of the Promised Land. Women in American History* (Boston, 1970)

Smith, Ralph A., 'The Scalphunter in the Borderlands 1835–1850', *Arizona and the West*, 6 (1964), pp. 5–22

Staats, Stephen, 'Occasional Address', *OPAT* (1878), pp. 46–59

Stauffer, Helen Winter, and Roswski, Susan J., eds, *Women and Western American Literature* (Troy, NY, 1982)

Stewart, Helen Maurice, *The Diary of Helen Maurice Stewart* (Eugene, Ore., 1961)

Thissell, G.W., *Crossing the Plains in '49* (Oakland, Ca., 1903)

Tobie, Harvey E., 'Stephen Hall Meek', *M.M.* ii. pp. 225–40

Troxel, Kathryn, 'Food of the Overland Emigrants', *OHSQ*, 56 (1955), pp. 12–26

Weisel, George F., *Men and Trade on the Northwest Frontier* (Missoula, Montana, 1955)

FIVE: THE GREAT MIGRATION

Adair, Sarah D., 'Pioneer of 1843', *OPAT* (1900), pp. 65–82

Alter, J. Cecil, *Jim Bridger* (Norman, Ok., 1962)

Applegate, Jesse, *Recollections of My Boyhood* (Oregon, 1914)

Applegate, Jesse, *A Day with the Cow Column* (Chicago, 1934)

Arthur, John, 'A Brief Account of the experience of a Pioneer of 1843', *OPAT* (1887), pp. 96–104

Barry, Louise, 'Overland to the Gold Fields by John Hawkins Clark', *Kansas Historical Quarterly*, 11 (1942), pp. 227–96

Beidelman, Richard D., 'Nathaniel Wyeth's Fort Hall', *OHSQ*, 58 (1957), pp. 197–250

Boardman, John, 'Journal of John Boardman', *Utah Historical Quarterly*, 2 (1929), pp. 99–121

Bourre, Edward Gaylord, 'The Legend of Marcus Whitman', *AHR*, 6 (1901), pp. 276–300

Burnett, Peter, 'The Letters of Peter H. Burnett', *OHSQ*, 2 (1902), pp. 405–19

Burnett, Peter, 'Recollections and Opinions of an Old Pioneer', *OHSQ*, 5 (1904), pp. 64–99

Cannon, Miles, 'Fort Hall on the Saptin River', *Washington Historical Society Quarterly*, 7 (1916), pp. 217–32

Carter, Harvey L., 'John Gantt', *M.M.* v. pp. 101–15

Coffman, Lloyd W., *Blazing a Wagon Trail to Oregon* (Springfield, Ore., 1993)

Dale, Harrison C., 'The Organisation of the Oregon Emigrating Companies', *OHSQ*, 16 (1915), pp. 205–27

Edwards, Frank S., *A Campaign in New Mexico with Colonel Doniphan* (Philadelphia, 1847)

Field, Matthew C., *Prairie and Mountain Sketches*, ed. K.L. Gregg (Norman, Ok., 1957)

Foreman, Carolyn Thomas, 'Colonel Jesse Henry Leavenworth', *Chronicles of Oklahoma*, 13 (1935), pp. 14–29

Fowler, Loretta, 'The Great Plains from the Arrival of the Horse to 1885', in Bruce G. Trigger and Wilcombe E. Washburn, eds, *The Cambridge History of the Native Peoples of America* (Cambridge, 1996), Vol. 1 Part 2, pp. 18–25

Fremont, John C., *Report of the Exploring Expedition to the Rocky Mountains in the Year 1842 and to Oregon and California in the Years 1843–44* (Washington, 1845)

459

Geer, Elizabeth, 'The Diary of Elizabeth D. Smith Geer', *OPAT* (1907) pp. 153–85

Hobbs, James, *Wild Life in the Far West* (1875)

Howard, M., and Edith M., eds, 'John Shiveley's Memoir', *OHSQ*, 81 (1980)

Humphreys, Alfred Glen, 'Thomas L. (Peg-Leg) Smith', *M.M.* iv. pp. 311–30

Husband, Michael B., 'To Oregon in 1843: the "great Migration"', *Kansas Quarterly*, 5 (1973), pp. 7–16

Husband, Michael B., 'William I. Marshall and the legend of Marcus Whitman', *Pacific Northwest Quarterly*, 64 (1973), pp. 57–69

Jeffrey, Julie Roy, *Converting the West. Narcissa Whitman* (Norman, Ok., 1991)

Johnson, Overton, and Winter, William H., *Route Across the Rocky Mountains* (Princeton, 1932)

Lenox, Edward Lewis, *Overland to California*, ed., Robert Whitaker (Oakland, Ca., 1904)

Looney, Jesse, 'From the Far West', *Journal of the Illinois State Historical Society*, 22 (1929), pp. 354–6

McCarner, 'McCarner Diary', *OHSQ*, 4 (1903)

Murray, Keith A., 'The Role of the Hudson's Bay Company in Pacific Northwest History', *Pacific Northwest Quarterly*, 52 (1961), pp. 24–31

Nesmith, James W., 'Diary of the Emigration of 1843', *OHSQ*, 7 (1906), pp. 329–59

Nesmith, James W., 'The Occasional Address', *OPAT* (1876), pp. 42–62

Nevins, Allan, ed., *Narratives of Exploration and Adventure by John Charles Fremont* (NY, 1956)

Newby, William T., 'Diary of the Emigration of 1843', ed. Harry N.M. Winton, *OHSQ*, 40 (1939), pp. 219–42

Nixon, Oliver W., *How Marcus Whitman Saved Oregon* (Chicago, 1895)

Oliphant, J. Orin, ed., 'Passing of an Immigrant in 1843', *Washington Historical Society Quarterly*, 15 (1924), pp. 205–10

Penrose, S.B.L., 'The Wagon Train of 1843 – its Dual Significance', *OHSQ*, 44 (1943), pp. 361–9

Penter, Samuel, 'Recollections of an Oregon Pioneer', *OHSQ*, 7 (1906), pp. 56–61

Porter, Mae Reed, and Davenport, Odessa, *Scotsman in Buckskin* (NY, 1963)

Preuss, Charles, *Exploring with Fremont* (Norman, Ok., 1958)

Reading, P.B., 'Journal of Pierson Barton Reading', ed. Philip B. Bekeart, *Journal of the Society of California Pioneers*, 6 (1930), pp. 148–98

Rich, E.E., ed., *The Letters of John McLoughlin from Fort Vancouver to the Governor and Committee 1839–44* (Toronto, 1943)
Rolle, Andrew, *Fremont. Character as Destiny* (Norman, Ok, 1991)
Sage, Rufus B., *Rocky Mountain Life* (Boston, 1857)
Schafer, Joseph, 'Notes on the Colonisation of Oregon', *OHSQ*, 6 (1905), pp. 379–90
Schoenberg, Wilfred P., *A History of the Catholic Church in the Pacific Northwest, 1743–1983* (Washington, 1987)
Scott, Leslie M., 'Influence of American Settlement upon the Oregon Boundary Treaty of 1846', *OHSQ*, 29 (1928), pp. 1–19
Sprague, Marshall, *A Gallery of Dudes* (Lincoln, Neb., 1979)
Staples, David Jackson, 'Journal', *Journal of the California Historical Society*, 22 (1943), pp. 119–50
Stewart, J.M., 'Overland Trip to California', *Publications of the Historical Society of Southern California*, 5 (1901), pp. 176–85
Talbot, Theodore, *Journals 1843*, ed. Charles H. Carey (Portland, Ore., 1931)
Templeton, Sardis, *The Life and Adventures of Pegleg Smith* (LA, 1965)
Tracy, Albert, 'Journal of Captain Albert Tracy', *Utah Historical Quarterly*, 13 (1945), pp. 1–117
Walker, Ardis M., 'Joseph R. Walker', *M.M.* v. pp. 372–3
Watson, Douglas S., *West Wind. The Story of Joseph Reddeford Walker* (LA, 1934)
Watt, Joseph, 'Recollections of Dr John McLoughlin', *OPAT* (1886), pp. 24–7
Whitman, Narcissa, *Letters 1836–1847* (Fairfield, Ore., 1987)

SIX: THROUGH FLOOD AND FAMINE

Abbott, Carlisle S., *Recollections of a California Pioneer* (NY, 1917)
Alter, J. Cecil, *James Bridger. A Historical Narrative* (Norman, Ok., 1962)
Bailey, Washington, *A Trip to California* (n.p., 1915)
Bancroft, H.H., *Chronicles of the Builders of the Commonwealth*, 7 vols (SF, 1890)
Been, Henry Putney, 'The Army and the Oregon Trail to 1846', *Pacific Northwest Quarterly*, 28 (1937), pp. 339–62
Brooks, Elisha, *Pioneer Mother of California* (SF, 1922)
Camp, Charles L., ed., *James Clyman, Frontiersman* (Portland, Ore., 1960)
Cannon, Miles, *Waiilatpu. Its Rise and Fall, 1836–1847* (Boise, 1915)

Cannon, Miles, 'The Snake River in History', *OHSQ*, 20 (1919), pp. 1–23

Carleton, James Henry, *The Prairie Logbooks*, ed. Louis Pelzer (Chicago, 1943) pp. 87–9

Clark, C.M., *A Trip to Pike's Peak* (San Jose, 1958)

Cole, Cornelius, *Memoirs of Cornelius Cole* (NY, 1908)

Collins, Martha Elizabeth Gilliam, 'Reminiscences', *OHSQ*, 17 (1916), pp. 358–72

Cooke, Lucy R., *Crossing the Plains* (Modesto, Ca., 1923)

Crockett, Samuel B., 'Diary of Samuel Black Crockett', ed. Vernon Carstensen, in Charles Miles and Otis B. Sperlin, eds, *Building a State. Washington 1889–1939* (Tacoma, 1940), pp. 594–607

Davis, Henry T., *Solitary Places Made Glad* (Cincinnati, 1890)

Davis, W.N., 'The Sutler at Fort Bridger', *Western Historical Quarterly*, 2 (1971), pp. 37–54

Eels, Myron, *Marcus Whitman, Pathfinder and Patriot* (Seattle, 1909)

Ellison, Robert S., *Fort Bridger: A Brief History* (Cheyenne, Wyo., 1981)

Fenton, W.D., 'The Winning of the Oregon Country', *OHSQ*, 6 (1905), pp. 343–78

Fisher, Ezra, 'Letters', *OHSQ*, 16 (1915), pp. 379–411

Flora, S.D., 'The great flood of 1844 along the Kansas and de Cygnes rivers', *Kansas Historical Quarterly*, 20 (1952), pp. 73–81

Foote, H.S., ed., *Pen Pictures from the Garden of the World* (Chicago, 1888)

Frantz, Joe B., and Choate, Julian E., *The American Cowboy. The Myth and the Reality* (Norman, Ok., 1955)

Gilbert, Bil, *Westering Man: the Life of Joseph Walker* (NY, 1983)

Gilliam, Washington Smith, 'Reminiscences', *OPAT* (1904), pp. 202–20

Gowans, Fred R., *Fort Bridger. Island in the Wilderness* (Provo, Utah, 1975)

Gowans, Fred R., 'Fort Bridger and the Mormons', *Utah Historical Quarterly*, 42 (1974), pp. 49–67

Guinn, J.M., *History of the State of California and biographical details of the Coast Counties, California* (Chicago, 1904)

Hafen, Le Roy R., and Young, F.M., *Fort Laramie* (Glendale, Ca., 1938)

Hayden, Mary Jane, *Pioneer Days* (San Jose, 1915)

Hopkins, Sarah Winnemucca, *Life among the Paiutes. Their Wrongs and Claims*, ed. Mrs Horace Mann (Boston, 1883)

Hughes, Willis B., 'The First Dragoons on the Western Frontier, 1834–1846', *Arizona and the West*, 12 (1970), pp. 115–58

Humphreys, Alfred Glenn, 'Pegleg Smith', *Idaho Yesterdays*, 10 (1966), pp. 28–32

Hyde, George E., *Pawnee Indians* (Denver, 1951)

Ide, Simon, *A Biographical Sketch of William B. Ide* (Glorieta, NM, 1880)

Ingersoll, Chester, *Overland to California in 1847* (Chicago, 1937)

Kelly, Charles, *Old Greenwood* (SLC, 1936)

Kilgore, William T., *The Kilgore Journal* (NY, 1949)

Langworthy, Franklin, *Scenery of the Plains* (Princeton, 1932)

Latrobe, Charles J., *The Rambler in North America*, 2 vols (1836)

Lockley, Fred, *Oregon Trail Blazers* (NY, 1929)

Lomax, Alfred L., 'History of Pioneer Sheep Husbandry in Oregon', *OHSQ*, 29 (1928), pp. 99–143

Lyman, H.S. 'Reminiscences of William M. Case', *OHSQ*, 1 (1900), pp. 269–95

McDermott, John D., 'Joseph Bissonette', *M.M.* iv. pp. 49–60

McDermott, John Francis, ed., *The Frontier Reexamined* (Urbana, Ill., 1967)

Mattes, Merrill J., 'The Council Bluffs Road', *Overland Journal*, 3 (1985), pp. 30–42

Meeker, Ezra, and Driggs, Howard, *Covered Wagon Centennial and Ox Team Days* (NY, 1932)

Miller, Thelma B., *History of Kern County, California*, 2 vols (Chicago, 1929)

Minto, John, 'Reminiscences', *OHSQ*, 2 (1901), pp. 119–67

Minto, John, 'Sheep Husbandry in Oregon', *OHSQ*, 3 (1902), pp. 219–47

Minto, John, 'Mrs Nancy Morrison', *OPAT* (1892), pp. 61–74

Minto, John, 'Robert Wilson Morrison', *OPAT* (1895), pp. 53–62

Mullins, W.H., *The History of Kansas City* (Kansas City, Mo., 1881)

Nesmith, James W., 'Appointment of Dr Marcus Whitman as guardian of the Sager children', *OHSQ*, 11 (1910), pp. 312–13

Nunis, Doyce, *Andrew Sublette. Rocky Mountain Prince* (LA, 1960)

Nunis, Doyce, 'Andrew Sublette', *M.M.* viii. pp. 349–63

Parrish, Edward Evan, 'Crossing the Plains in 1844', *OPAT* (1889), pp. 82–122

Pleasants, William J., *Twice Across the Plains* (SF, 1906)

Potter, Theodore Edgar, *Autobiography, 1832–1910* (Concord, NH, 1913)

Quigley, Hugh, *The Irish Race in California* (SF, 1878)

Ramsdell, T.M., 'Reminiscences', *OPAT* (1896), pp. 108–12

Rees, Willard H. 'Oregon Immigrants of 1844', *Washington Historical Quarterly*, 18 (1927), pp. 93–102

Rumer, Thomas A., ed., *This Emigrating Company. The 1844 Oregon Trail Journal of Jacob Hammer* (Spokane, Washington, 1990)
Sager, Catherine, Elizabeth and Matilda, *The Whitman Massacre of 1847* (Washington, 1981)
Schama, H.B., *Overland Journey to California* (n.p., 1918)
Shaw, T.C., 'Captain William Shaw', *OPAT* (1887), pp. 49–51
Smith, C.W., *Journal of a Trip to California* (n.p., 1918)
Staples, David Jackson, 'Journal', *California Historical Society Quarterly*, 22 (1943), pp. 119–50
Stewart, Agnes, 'The Journey to Oregon', *OHSQ*, 29 (1928), pp. 77–98
Stewart, George R., *The Opening of the California Trail* (Berkeley, 1953)
Sunder, John E., *Bill Sublette* (Norman, Ok., 1959)
Swasey, W.F., *The Early Days and Men of California* (Oakland, Ca., 1891)
Thissell, G.W., *Crossing the Plains in '49* (Oakland, Ca., 1903)
Thompson, Erwin, *Shallow Grave at Waiilatpu* (Portland, Ore., 1985)
Trotter, F.I., Loutzenhiser, F. H. and Loutzenhiser, J.R., eds, *Told By Pioneers*, 3 vols (Olympia, 1938)
Ward, Harriet, *Prairie Schooner Lady. The Journal of Harriet Sherrill Ward* (LA, 1859)
Webb, W.L., 'Independence, Missouri, A Century Old', *Missouri Historical Review*, 22 (1927), pp. 30–50
Wells, Eugene T., 'The Growth of Independence, Missouri, 1827–1850', *Bulletin of the Missouri Historical Society*, 16 (1959), pp. 33–46
Wells, Merle, 'Richard Grant', *M.M.* ix. pp. 165–86
White, Richard, '"The Winning of the West": The Expansion of the Western Sioux in the Eighteenth and Nineteenth Centuries', *Journal of American History*, 65 (1978), pp. 319–43
Whitman, Narcissa, 'Letters', *OPAT* (1894), pp. 53–219
Wyman, Walter, 'Council Bluffs and the Westward Movement', *Iowa Journal of History*, 47 (1949), pp. 99–118
Wyman, Walter, 'Omaha: Frontier Depot and Prodigy of Council Bluffs', *Nebraska History Magazine*, 17 (1936), pp. 143–55
Wyman, Walter, 'The Outfitting Posts', *Pacific Historical Review*, 18 (1949), pp. 14–23

SEVEN: 'NEVER TAKE NO CUTOFFS'

Bailey, Walter, 'The Barlow Road', *OHSQ*, 13 (1912), pp. 287–96
Bancroft, H.H., *History of Oregon* (SF, 1886)

Barlow, Mary S., 'History of the Barlow Road', *OHSQ*, 3 (1902), pp. 71–81

Barlow, Samuel K., 'Reminiscences of Seventy Years', *OHSQ*, 13 (1912)

Belshaw, Maria Parsons, 'Diary', ed. J.W. Ellison, *OHSQ*, 33 (1932), pp. 318–33

Bonney, Benjamin F., 'Recollections', *OHSQ*, 24 (1923), pp. 36–55

Brooks, Noah, 'The Plains Across', *Century Magazine*, 63 (1902), pp. 803–20

Carleton, J. Henry, *The Prairie Logbooks*, ed. Louis Pelzer (Chicago, 1943)

Carter, Harvey L., 'Caleb Greenwood', *M.M.* ix. pp. 187–92

Clark, Keith, and Tiller, Lowell, *Terrible Trail. The Meek Cutoff 1845* (Bend, Ore., 1966)

Clarke, Dwight L., *Stephen Watts Kearny. Soldier of the West* (Norman, Ok., 1961)

Cleland, Robert Glass, *History of California* (NY, 1922)

Conyers, Enoch W., 'Diary', *OPAT* (1905), pp. 423–512

Cooke, Lucy R., *Crossing the Plains* (Modesto, 1923)

Cummins, Sarah J., *Autobiography and Reminiscences* (Oregon, 1914)

Delano, Alonzo, *Across the Plains and among the Diggings* (NY, 1936)

Evans, Elwood, *History of the Pacific Northwest* (Portland, Ore., 1889)

Findley, William, '1845 Overland Journal', *Pacific Northwest Quarterly*, 37 (1946), pp. 19–30

Fisher, Ezra, 'Letters', *OHSQ*, 16 (1915), pp. 379–411

Galbraith, John S., *The Hudson's Bay Company as an Imperial Factor, 1821–1869* (Berkeley, 1957)

Goulder, W.A., *Reminiscences of a Pioneer* (Boise, Idaho, 1909)

Hancock, Samuel, *Narrative of Samuel Hancock* (NY, 1927)

Harrison, Dale C., 'Organisation of the Oregon Emigrating Companies', *OHSQ*, 16 (1915), pp. 205–27

Harritt, Jesse, 'Diary', *OPAT* (1911), pp. 506–26

Hewitt, Randall H., *Across the Plains and Over the Divide* (NY, 1964)

Howe, Octavius T., *Argonauts of '49* (Boston, 1923)

Howell, John Ewing, 'Diary of an Emigrant of 1845', *Washington Historical Quarterly*, 1 (1907), pp. 138–58

Hughes, Willis B., 'The First Dragoons on the Western Frontier, 1834–1846', *Arizona and the West*, 12 (1970), pp. 115–38

Ide, Simon, *A Biographical Sketch of the Life of William B. Ide and the conquest of California by the Bear Flag Party* (Glorieta, NM, 1880)

Johnston, William G., *Experiences of a 49er* (Pittsburgh, 1892)

Kelly, Charles, *Old Greenwood* (SLC, 1936)

Langum, David J., 'Pioneer Justice and the Oregon Trails', *Wyoming Historical Quarterly*, 5 (1974), pp. 421–39

Lassell, O.O., *The Doctor in Oregon* (Portland, Ore., 1947)

Leader, Herman A., 'McLoughlin's Answer to the Warre Report', *OHSQ*, 33 (1932), pp. 214–29

Lockley, Fred, 'The McNemees and Tetherows with the Migration of 1845', *OHSQ*, 25 (1924), pp. 353–77

Lockley, Fred, *Captain Sol Tetherow, Wagon Train Master* (Portland, Ore., 1960)

Lyman, Albert, *Journal of a Voyage to California and Life in the Gold Diggings* (Hartford, Connecticut, 1852)

McCoy, John, *Pioneering on the Plains* (n.p., 1924)

McNary, Lawrence A., 'Route of the Meek Cutoff, 1845', *OHSQ*, 35 (1934), pp. 1–9

Martin, John, *Portrait and Biographical Record of Willamette Valley* (Chicago, 1903)

Mattes, Merrill J., 'Joseph Rhodes and the California Gold Rush', *Annals of Wyoming*, 23 (1951), pp. 52–71

Maxwell, William A., *Crossing the Plains. Days of '57* (SF, 1915)

Meek, Stephen H.L., *The Autobiography of a Mountain Man* (Pasadena, 1949)

Meeker, Ezra, *Covered Wagon Centennial and Ox Team Days* ((NY, 1932)

Minto, John, 'Reminiscences', *OHSQ*, 2 (1901), pp. 119–67

Moreland, J.C., 'Annual Address', *OPAT* (1900), pp. 26–34

Murray, Keith A., 'The Role of the Hudson's Bay Company in Pacific Northwest History', *Pacific Northwest Quarterly*, 52 (1961), pp. 24–31

Nesbit, Virginia, 'Sarah Helmick and Helmick Park', *OHSQ*, 26 (1925), pp. 444–7

Norton, L.A., *Life and Adventures* (Oakland, Ca., 1887)

Nunis, Doyce B., 'The Enigma of the Sublette Overland Party', *Pacific Historical Review*, 28 (1959) pp. 331–49

Palmer, Joel, *Journal*, vol. xxx of R.G. Thwaites, *Early Western Travels*, 32 vols (Cleveland, 1907)

Partoll, A.J., ed., *Frontier Omnibus* (Helena, 1962)

Peltier, Jerome, 'Moses "Black" Harris', *M.M.* iv. pp. 103–117

Perriam, Eve, ed., *Growing up Female in America: Ten Lives* (NY, 1971)

Prucha, Francis Paul, *The Sword of the Republic* (NY, 1969)

Rich, E.E., ed., *The Letters of John McLoughlin* (Toronto, 1944)

Rogers, Fred B., *William Brown. Ide Bear Flagger* (SF, 1962)

Shaffer, Leslie L.D., 'Management of the Organised Wagon Trains on the Overland Trail', *Mississippi Historical Review*, 55 (1961), pp. 355–65

Shaw, D.A., *Eldorado, or California as seen by a Pioneer* (LA. 1900)
Snyder, Jacob R., 'Diary', *Quarterly of the Society of California Pioneers*, 8 (1930), pp. 224–60
Staples, David Jackson, 'Journal', *California Historical Quarterly*, 22 (1943), pp. 119–50
Steele, John, *Across the Plains* (Chicago, 1930)
Stewart, Agnes, 'The Journey to Oregon', *OHSQ*, 29 (1928), pp. 77–98
Stewart, Helen Marnie, *The Diary of Helen Marnie Stewart* (Eugene, 1961)
Taylor, Bernard, *El Dorado: or Adventures in the Path of Empire* (NY, 1949)
Tetherow, Samuel, *Captain Sol Tetherow. Wagon Master* (Portland, Ore., 1923)
Tobie, Harvey E., 'Stephen Hall Meek', *M.M.* ii. pp. 225–40
Trenholme, Virginia Cole, and Carley, Maurine, *The Shoshonis: Sentinels of the Rockies* (Norman, Ok., 1964)
Ward, Harriet, *Prairie Schooner Lady. The Journal of Harriet Sherrill Ward* (LA, 1959)
Whipple-Haslam, Lee, *Early Days in California* (California, 1923)
Wilkins, Mary B., 'Samuel Kimbrough Barlow: A Pioneer Builder of Oregon', *OHSQ*, 26 (1925), pp. 209–24
Wojcik, Donna M., *The Brazen Overlanders of 1845* (Portland, Ore., 1976)
Wood, John, *Journal. Cincinnati to the Gold Diggings* (Columbus, 1871)

EIGHT: CALIFORNIA CATCHES UP & NINE: TRAGEDY IN THE SNOWS

Allen, William L., and Avery, R.B., *California Gold Book. First Nuggets. Its Discovery and Discoverers* (SF, 1893)
Aram, Joseph, 'Reminiscences', *Journal of American History*, 1 (1907), pp. 617–32
Andrews, Thomas F., 'The Controversial Hastings Overland Guide: A Reassessment', *Pacific Historical Review*, 37 (1968), pp. 21–34
Andrews, Thomas F., 'The Ambitions of Lansford W. Hastings: A Study in Western Myth-Making', *Pacific Historical Review*, 39 (1970), pp. 473–91
Applegate, Lindsay, 'The South Road Expedition', *OHSQ*, 22 (1921), pp. 12–45
Bagley, Will, 'Lansford Warren Hastings: Scoundrel or Visionary?' *Overland Journal*, 12 (1994), pp. 12–26

Bagley, Will, and Schindler, Harold, ed. and rev., *West from Fort Bridger: The Pioneering of Emigrant Trails Across Utah, 1846–1850* (Logan, Utah, 1994)

Bieber, Ralph P., *Wah-to-Yah and the Taos Trail* (Cincinnati, 1850)

'The Breen Journal', in Morgan, *Overland* i. pp. 306–22

Brown, John, *Autobiography* (SLC, 1941)

Bryant, Edwin, *What I Saw in California* (1849)

Burcham, Mildred Baker, 'Scott and Applegate's Old South Road', *OHSQ*, 41 (1940), pp. 405–23

Carey, Charles, ed., *The Emigrants' Guide* (Princeton, 1932)

Carey, Charles, ed., 'Diary of Reverend George Gary', *OHSQ*, 24 (1923), pp. 302–11

'The Carriger Diary', in Morgan, *Overland* i. pp. 143–58

Carter, Tolbert, 'Recollections', *OPAT* (1906), pp. 67–72

Cleland, Robert G., *A History of California. The American Period* (NY, 1922)

Cleland, Robert G., *From Wilderness to Empire. A History of California 1542–1900* (NY, 1944)

Daniels, Roger, ed., *Essays in Western History in Honor of Professor T.A. Larson* (Laramie, 1971)

DeLafosse, Peter H., *Trailing the Pioneers: A Guide to Utah's Emigrant Trails 1812–1869* (Logan, Utah, 1994)

De Voto, Bernard, *1846. The Year of Decision* (1957)

Diamond, Jared, 'Living through the Donner Party', *Discover* (March, 1992) pp. 100–7

Evans, Elwood, ed., *History of the Pacific Northwest*, 2 vols (Portland, Ore., 1889)

'The Fallon Diary', in Morgan, *Overland* i. pp. 360–6

Favour, Alpheus M., *Old Bill Williams. Mountain Man* (Norman, Ok., 1962)

Garrison, A.E., *Life and Labours of A.E. Garrison* (Oregon, 1943)

Grayson, Donald K., 'Donner Party Deaths: A Demographic Assessment', *Journal of Anthropological Research*, 46 (1990), pp. 223–42

Hall, Carroll D., ed., *Donner Miscellany* (California, 1947)

Harlan, Jacob W., *California '46 to '48* (SF, 1888)

Harlow, Neal, *California Conquered: War and Peace on the Pacific, 1846–1850* (Berkeley, 1982)

Hawkins, Bruce, and Madsen, David, *Excavation of the Donner–Reed Wagons: Historic Archaeology Along the Hastings Cutoff* (SLC, 1990)

Helfrick, Devere, 'The Applegate Trail', *Klamath Echoes*, 9 (1971), pp. 1–106

Holmes, Kenneth L., ed., *Covered Wagon Women* (Lincoln, Neb., 1995)
'The Holt Diary', in Morgan, *Overland*, i. pp. 189–204
Hopkins, Sarah W., *Life among the Paiutes* (Boston, 1883)
Houghton, Eliza P. Donner, *The Expedition of the Donner Party and Its Tragic Fate* (Chicago, 1911)
Jacobs, Wilbur R., *The Letters of Francis Parkman*, 2 vols (Norman, Ok., 1960)
Johnson, Kristin, ed., *'Unfortunate Emigrants.' Narratives of the Donner Party* (Logan, Utah, 1996)
Kelly, Charles, *Salt Desert Trails* (SLC, 1930)
King, Joseph A., *Winter of Entrapment. A New Look at the Donner Party* (Toronto, 1992)
Korns, J. Roderick, ed., 'West from Fort Bridger', *Utah Historical Quarterly*, 19 (1951)
Lienhard, Heinrich, *From St Louis to Sutter's Fort*, trans. and ed. E.G. and E.K. Gudde (Norman, Ok., 1961)
Lotchin, Robert W., *San Francisco 1846–1856: From Hamlet to City* (Lincoln, Neb., 1979)
McCurdy, Stephen A., 'Epidemiology of Disaster; The Donner Party (1846–1847), *Western Journal of Medicine*, 160 (1994), pp. 338–42
McGlashan, C.F., *History of the Donner Party* (Truckee, Ca., 1879)
'The McKinstry Diary', in Morgan, *Overland* i. pp. 203–18
Miller, David E., 'The Parting of the Ways on the Oregon Trail – the East Terminal of the Sublette Cutoff ', *Annals of Wyoming* 45 (1973), pp. 47–52
'The Miller–Reed Diary', in Morgan, *Overland* i. pp. 245–68
North, Arthur W., 'The Cutoff ', *Sunset*, 35 (1915), pp. 1095–1104
Paden, Irene D., *Prairie Schooner Detours* (NY, 1949)
Parkman, Francis, *The Oregon Trail* (1969)
Peltier, Jerome, 'Moses "Black" Harris', *M.M.* iv. pp. 103–17
'The Pringle Diary', in Morgan, *Overland* i. pp. 163–72
Read, Georgia Willis, 'Disease, Drugs and Doctors on the Oregon–California Trail in the Gold-Rush Years', *Missouri Historical Review*, 38 (1944), pp. 260–76
'The Virginia Reed Account', in Morgan, *Overland* i. pp. 278–88
'Daniel Rhoads' Account', in Morgan, *Overland* i. pp. 323–60
Riddle, Jeff C., *The Indian History of the Modoc War* (Medford, Ore., 1973)
'M.D. Ritchie's Diary', in Morgan, *Overland* i. pp. 331–2
Rucker, Maude Applegate, *The Oregon Trail and Some of its Blazers* (NY, 1930)

Steed, Jack, *The Donner Party Rescue Site, Johnson's Ranch on Bear River* (Fresno, Ca., 1988)

Steed, Jack and Richard, 'The Rediscovery of Johnson's Ranch', *Overland Journal*, 4 (1986), pp. 18–32

Stewart, George, *Ordeal by Hunger* (Boston, 1960)

Sunder, John E., 'Solomon Perry Sublette. Mountain Man of the Forties', *New Mexico Historical Review*, 36 (1961), pp. 49–61

'Diary of William E. Taylor', in Dale Morgan, *Overland in 1846*, 2 vols (California, 1963) i. pp. 118–42

Thornton, Jesse Quinn, *Oregon and California in 1848*, 2 vols (NY, 1849)

Thornton, Jesse Quinn, 'Occasional Address', *OPAT* (1878), pp. 29–71

'The Tucker Diary', in Morgan, *Overland* i. pp. 331–6

Wade, Mason, ed., *The Journals of Francis Parkman*, 2 vols (NY, 1952)

Winter, Oscar Isburn, 'The Development of Transportation in Oregon, 1843–49', *OHSQ*, 40 (1939), pp. 315–26

Wise, Henry Augustus, *Los Gringos* (NY, 1849)

TEN: SAINTS AND SINNERS

Alexander, Thomas G., *Things in Heaven and Earth: the Life and Times of Wilford Woodruff* (SLC, 1991)

Alexander, Thomas G., and Allen, James B., *Mormons and Gentiles: A History of Salt Lake City* (Boulder, 1984)

Allen, James B., *The Trials of Discipleship* (Urbana, Ill., 1987)

Allen, James M., Leonard, Glen M., *The Story of the Latter Day Saints* (SLC, 1976)

Anderson, Maybelle Harmon, ed., *Appleton Milo Harom Goes West* (Berkeley, 1916)

Arrington, Leonard J., *Charles C. Rich: Mormon General and Western Frontiersman* (Provo, Utah, 1974)

Arrington, Leonard J., *Brigham Young, American Moses* (NY, 1985)

Arrington, Leonard J., *Great Basin Kingdom. An Economic History of the Latter Day Saints* (Cambridge, Mass., 1958)

Arrington, Leonard J., 'Persons for All Seasons', *Brigham Young University Studies*, 20 (1979), pp. 39–58

Arrington, Leonard J., 'The Economic Role of Pioneer Mormon Women', *Western Humanities Review*, 9 (1955), pp. 145–65

Arrington, Leonard J., and Bitton, Davis, *The Mormon Experience* (NY, 1979)

Bagley, Will, ed., *The Pioneer Camp of the Saints. The 1846 and 1847 Mormon Trail Journals of Thomas Bulloch* (Spokane, Washington, 1997)

Beecher, Maureen Ursenbach, 'Women's Work on the Mormon Frontier', *Utah Historical Quarterly*, 49 (1981), pp. 276–90

Bennett, Richard, *The Mormons at Missouri, 1846–1852* (Norman, Ok., 1987)

Bennett, Richard, 'Finalizing Plans for the Trek West. Deliberations at Winter Quarters, 1846–1847', *Brigham Young University Studies*, 24 (1984), pp. 312–18

Bitton, Davis, 'Mormons in Texas: the ill-fated Wight Colony, 1844–1858', *Arizona and the West*, 2 (1969), pp. 5–26

Bringhurst, Newell G., *Brigham Young and the Expanding American Frontier* (Boston, 1986)

Britton, Rollin J., 'Early Days on Grand River and the Mormon War', *Missouri Historical Review*, 13 (1919), pp. 112–34;14 (1920), pp. 459–73

Brodie, Fawn M. *No Man Knows My History: the life of Joseph M. Smith the Mormon Prophet* (NY, 1945)

Brooks, Juanita, 'Indian Relations on the Mormon Frontier', *Utah Historical Quarterly*, 12 (1944), pp. 1–48

Brooks, Juanita, ed., *On the Mormon Frontier: the Diary of Hosea Stout* (SLC, 1964)

Brooks, Juanita, and Cleland, Robert G., *A Mormon Chronicle: The Diaries of John D. Lee 1848–1876*, 2 vols (San Marino, Ca., 1955)

Brown, John L., ed., *Autobiography of Pioneer John Brown* (SLC, 1941)

Bryson, Conrey, *Winter Quarters* (SLC, 1986)

Burton, Richard F., *The City of the Saints* (1861)

Bushman, Richard L., *Joseph Smith and the Beginnings of Mormonism* (Chicago, 1984)

Camp, Charles L., ed., 'William Alexander Trubody and the Overland Pioneers of 1847', *California Historical Society Quarterly*, 16 (1937), pp. 122–43

Campbell, Eugene E., 'Brigham Young's Outer Cordon – a Reappraisal', *Utah Historical Quarterly*, 41 (1973), pp. 220–53

Campbell, Eugene E., *Establishing Zion: the Mormon Church in the American West, 1847–1869* (SLC, 1988)

Campbell, Eugene E., ed., *The Essential Brigham Young* (SLC 1992)

Cannon, M. Hamlin, 'Migration of English Mormons to America', *AHR*, 52 (1947)

Clayton, William, *William Clayton's Journal* (SLC, 1921)

Clayton, William, *The Latter Day Saints' Emigrants Guide* (St Louis, 1848)

Cosgrove, Hugh, 'Reminiscences', *OHSQ*, 1 (1900), pp. 255–69

Creer, Leland H., *The Founding of an Empire, The Exploration and Colonisation of Utah, 1776–1856* (SLC, 1947)

Crosby, Jesse W., 'History and Journal', *Annals of Wyoming*, 11 (1939), pp. 145–219

Egan, Howard, *Pioneering the West, 1846 to 1878* (Richmond, Utah, 1917)

Faulring, Scott H., ed., *An American Prophet's Record: the Diaries and Journals of Joseph Smith* (SLC, 1988)

Findley, Jane L., 'Sketch of Pioneer Days', *OPAT* (1926), pp. 23–5

Fleming, L.A., and Standing, A.R., 'The Road to Fortune: The Salt Lake Cutoff', *Utah Historical Quarterly*, 33 (1965), pp. 248–71

Foy, Mary E., 'By Ox Team from Salt Lake City to Los Angeles, 1850', *Historical Society of Southern California, Annual Publications*, 14 (1930), pp. 271–337

Geer, Elizabeth Dixon Smith, 'Diary', *OPAT* (1907), pp. 153–79

Gentry, Leland H., 'The Mormon Way Stations. Garden Grove and Mount Pisgah', *Brigham Young University Studies*, 21 (1981), pp. 445–61

Greeley, Horace, *An Overland Journey from New York to San Francisco* (NY, 1860)

Gunnison, John W., *The Mormons or Latter-Day Saints in the Valley of the Great Salt Lake* (Philadelphia, 1856)

Harrell, James E.A., 'Reminiscences', *OHSQ*, 24 (1923), pp. 186–92

Hastings, Loren B., 'Diary of a Pioneer', *OPAT* (1923), pp. 12–26

Hill, Donna, *Joseph Smith, the First Mormon* (NY, 1977)

Holmes, Kenneth L., ed., *Covered Wagon Women* (Nebraska, 1995)

Holzapfel, Neitzel, and Holzapfel, Jeni Broberg, *Women of Nauvoo* (SLC, 1992)

Hunter, Milton R., 'Brigham Young Coloniser', *Pacific Historical Review*, 6 (1937), pp. 341–60

Hunter, Milton R., 'The Mormon Corridor', *Pacific Historical Review*, 8 (1939), pp. 179–200

Huntres, Keith, ed., *Murder of an American Prophet* (SF, 1960)

Ingersoll, Chester, *Overland to California in 1847* (Chicago, 1937)

Jackson, Richard H., 'Utah's Harsh Lands, Hearth of Greatness', *Utah Historical Quarterly*, 49 (1981), pp. 4–25

Jackson, Richard H., *The Mormon Role in the Settlement of the West* (Provo, Utah, 1978)

Jenson, Andrew, *Latter Day Saints Biographical Encyclopedia*, 4 vols (SLC, 1901)

Jenson, Andrew, *Day by Day with the Utah Pioneers*, new edn (SLC, 2000)

Johnston, William G., *Overland to California* (Oakland, Ca., 1948)

Jory, James, 'Reminiscences', *OHSQ*, 2 (1902), pp. 271–86

Kane, Thomas L., *The Mormons. A Discourse Delivered before the Historical Society of Pennsylvania* (Philadelphia, 1850)

Kelly, Charles, 'Gold Seekers on the Hastings Cutoff', *Utah Historical Quarterly*, 20 (1952), pp. 3–30

Kelly, Charles, 'The Salt Desert Trail', *Utah Historical Quarterly*, 3 (1930), pp. 35–52

Kelly, Charles, ed., *Journals of John D. Lee* (SLC, 1938)

Kelly, William, *An Excursion to California*, 2 vols (1851)

Kennedy, Scott G., ed., *Wilford Woodruff's Journal* (Midvale, Utah, 1979)

Kilgore, William T., *The Kilgore Journal* (NY, 1949)

Kimball, Stanley B., *Heber C. Kimball: Mormon Patriarch and Pioneer* (Urbana, Ill., 1981)

Kimball, Stanley B., 'The Iowa Trek of 1846', *Ensign*, 2 (1972), pp. 36–45

Kimball, Stanley, *Discovering the Mormon Trails, New York to California, 1831–1868* (SLC, 1979)

Kimball, Stanley, 'The Mormon Trail Network in Iowa, 1838–1863: A New Look', *Brigham Young University Studies*, 21 (1981), pp. 417–30

Kimball, Stanley, and Knight, Hal, *111 Days to Zion* (SLC, 1978)

Larson, Andrew Karl, *Erastus Snow: The Life of a Missionary and Pioneer for the Early Mormon Church* (SLC, 1971)

'Letters of a Proselyte: The Hascall–Pomeroy Correspondence', *Utah Historical Quarterly*, 25 (1957)

Little, James A., 'Biography of Lorenzo Dow Young', *Utah Historical Quarterly*, 14 (1946)

Lockley, Fred, *To Oregon by Oxteam in '47* (Portland, Ore., n.d.)

Ludlow, Daniel M., *Encyclopedia of Mormonism*, 5 vols (NY, 1992)

McCall, Ansel James, *The Great California Trail in 1849* (NY, 1882)

Morgan, Dale L., 'The Mormon Ferry on the North Platte: the Journal of William A. Empey', *Annals of Wyoming*, 21 (1949), pp. 111–67

Morgan, Dale L., 'Miles Goodyear and the Founding of Ogden', *Utah Historical Quarterly*, 21 (1953), pp. 195–218, 307–29

Morgan, Dale L., 'Letters by Forty-Niners, Written from Great Salt Lake City in 1849', *Western Humanities Review*, 3 (1949), pp. 98–116

Morgan, Dale L., *The State of Deseret* (Logan, Utah, 1987)

Morgan, Martha, *A Trip Across the Plains* (SF, 1864)

473

Neff, Andrew L., *History of Utah 1847 to 1869* (SLC, 1940)

Nibley, Preston, *Exodus to Greatness. The Story of the Mormon Migration* (SLC, 1947)

Noall, Claire, 'Mormon Midwives', *Utah Historical Quarterly*, 10 (1942), pp. 84–144

Oaks, Dallin H., and Hill, Marvin S., *Carthage Conspiracy: the Trail of the Accused Assassins of Joseph Smith* (Urbana, Ill., 1975)

Petersen, William J., 'The Mormon Trail of 1846', *Palimpsest*, 47 (1966), pp. 353–67

Poll, Richard D., ed., *Utah's History* (Provo, Utah, 1978)

Pratt, Orson, 'Diary', *Latter Day Saints Millenial Star*, 12 (1850), pp. 1–180

Pratt, Parley, *Autobiography* (NY, 1874)

Pratt, Stephen P., 'Parley P. Pratt in Winter Quarters on the Trail West', *Brigham Young University Studies*, 24 (1984), pp. 383–6

Read, George Willis, and Gaines, Ruth, eds, *Gold Rush*, 2 vols (NY, 1944)

Remy, Jules, and Brenchley, Julius, *A Journey to Great Salt Lake City*, 2 vols (1861)

Richards, Mary Parker, *Winter Quarters. The 1846–1848 Life Writings of Mary Haskin Parker Richards* (Logan, Utah, 1996)

Ricketts, Nora Baldwin, *The Mormon Battalion in the US Army of the West 1846–1848* (Logan, Utah, 1996)

Roberts, B.H., ed., *History of the Church of Latter Day Saints. Period II. Apostolic Interregnum* (SLC, 1932)

Root, Riley, *Journal of Travels from St Joseph to Oregon* (Galesburg, Ill., 1850)

Rugh, Susan Sessions, 'Patty Sessions', in Vicky Burgess-Olson, ed., *Sister Saints* (Provo, Utah, 1978)

Schindler, Harold, *Orrin Porter Rockwell: Man of God, Son of Thunder* (SLC, 1983)

Ships, Jan, *Mormonism: the Story of a New Religious Tradition* (Urbana, Ill., 1985)

Smith, George D., ed., *An Intimate Chronicle* (SLC, 1991)

Smith, Herman C., 'Mormon Troubles in Missouri', *Missouri Historical Review*, 4 (1910), pp. 238–51

Snow, Erastus, 'Journal', *Utah Humanities Review*, 2 (1948), pp. 107–28, 264–84

Sortore, Abraham, *Biography and Early Life Sketch* (Alexandria, Mo., 1909)

Spencer, Lucinda, 'Pioneer of 1847', *OPAT* (1887), pp. 74–8

Staker, Susan, ed., *Waiting for World's End: the Diaries of Wilford Woodruff* (SLC, 1993)
Stanley, Reva, *Archer of Paradise. A Biography of Parley P. Pratt* (Caldwell, Idaho, 1937)
Steele, John, *Across the Plains* (Chicago, 1930)
Stegner, Wallace, *The Gathering of Zion* (NY, 1964)
Tullidge, Edward W., *Women of Mormondom* (SLC, 1877)
Udell, John, *Incidents of Travel to California across the Great Plains* (Jefferson, Ohio, 1856)
Van der Zee, Jacob, 'The Mormon Trails in Iowa', *Iowa Journal of History and Politics*, 12 (1914), pp. 3–16
Van Wagoner, Richard, *Sidney Rigdon: A Portrait of Religious Excess* (SLC, 1994)
Ward, Maurice Carr, *Winter Quarters* (Logan, Utah, 1996)
Whitney, Orson F., *History of Utah* (SLC, 1904)
Winther, Oscar O., ed., *The Private Papers and Diary of Thomas Leiper Kane, a Friend of the Mormons* (SF, 1937)
Young, Clara Decker, 'A Woman's Experience with the Pioneer Band', *Utah Historical Quarterly*, 14 (1946), pp. 173–6
Young, John R., *Memoirs of John R. Young, Utah Pioneer of 1847* (SLC, 1920)
Young, Lorenzo Dow, 'Diary', *Utah Historical Quarterly*, 14 (1946), pp. 133–70

NOTES

ONE: MANIFEST DESTINY

Page 8 'vivacious, attractive, gregarious, idealistic and sentimentally religious' quoted in Dan L. Thrap, *Encyclopedia of Frontier Biography* (Lincoln, Neb., 1988), iii, p. 1560; original in Clifford M. Drury, *Marcus and Narcissa Whitman and the Opening of Old Oregon*, 2 vols (Glendale, Ca., 1973)

p. 8 'I fear' Melvin Jacobs, *Winning Oregon* (Caldwell, Idaho, 1938), p. 26

p. 9 'to overspread' quoted in Paul S. Boyer, *The Oxford Companion to United States History* (Oxford, 2001), p. 470 from original in Frederick Merk, *Manifest Destiny in History* (1963)

p. 10 'They seem to look upon' Walter Colton, *Three Years in California* (NY, 1850), p. 118

p. 10 'There is in fact' Albert K. Weinstein, *Manifest Destiny* (Baltimore, 1935), pp. 140–1

p. 15 'No covered wagons followed' John A. Hawgood, *The American West* (1967), p. 143

p. 16 'No one has ever exaggerated' Bernard de Voto, *The Year of Decision* (1943), p. 250

p. 17 'War parties have' Josiah Gregg, *The Commerce of the Prairies*, ed. Max Moorhead (Norman, Ok., 1954), pp. 432–9

TWO: THE REASONS WHY

p. 19 'It is palpable homicide' Unruh, *The Plains Across*, pp. 38–9

p. 19–20 'For, what, then' ibid.

p. 20 'Oregon is mountainous and rugged' ibid.

p. 20 'It is impossible, of course' David J. Weber, *The Mexican Southwest under Mexico* (Albuquerque, 1982), p. 196

p. 21 'The present is emphatically' William H. Goetzmann, *Army Exploration in the American West 1803–1863* (Yale, 1959), p. vi

p. 21 'eastward I go' Henry David Thoreau, 'Walking', in *Works of H.D. Thoreau* (1913), v. pp. 168–9

p. 21 'the westward urge' David Lavender, *Westward Vision: the Story of the Oregon Trail* (NY, 1963), p. 26

p. 21 'was as natural' George R. Stewart, 'The Prairie Schooner Got Them There', *American Heritage*, 13 (February 1962), pp. 4–17 (at p. 8)

p. 22 'An American will build' Alexis de Tocqueville, *Democracy in America*, ed. J.P. Mayer and Max Lerner (N.Y. 1966), p. 508

p. 22 'What do you think' Sarah J. Cummins, *Autobiography and Reminiscences* (1914), p. 19

p. 23 'the United States entered upon' James Christy Bell, *Opening a Highway to the Pacific, 1838–1846* (NY, 1921), pp. 119–25

p. 24 'The Senator from South Carolina' Thomas Hart Benton, *Thirty Years View*, 2 vols (NY, 1856), i. pp. 470–2

p. 25 'Take what may be necessary' Peter Burnett, 'Recollections and Opinions of an Old Pioneer', *OHSQ*, 5 (1904), pp. 64–99 (at p. 65)

p. 25 'If I live' John Minto, 'Reminiscences', *OHSQ*, 2 (1901), pp. 119–67 (at p. 122)

p. 25 'The motive that induced' Phoebe Goodell Judson, *A Pioneer's Search for an Ideal Home* (Washington, 1925), p. 9

p. 25–26 'The impulse towards removal' Clarence H. Danhof, *Change in Agriculture: the Northern United States, 1820–1870* (Harvard, 1969), p. 150

p. 26 'The bad climate' Parkman, *Journals*, ii, p. 442

p. 26 'Mr Ames is travelling' Dale Morgan, *Overland*, i, p. 205

p. 26 'The motives which thus brought' Jesse Quinn Thornton, *Oregon and California in 1848*, 2 vols (NY, 1849), i. p. 26

p. 26 'I remember his answer distinctly' John Bidwell, *Echoes* (Chicago, 1928), p. 14

p. 27 'In the hands of an enterprising people' Richard Henry Dana, *Two Years Before the Mast* (NY, 1936), p. 193

p. 27 'the deep, rich, alluvial soil' Hastings, *Emigrants' Guide*, p. 81

p. 28 'I was everything' Erwin G. Gudde, *Sutter's Own Story* (NY, 1936), pp. 66–7

p. 28 'All of them' John A. Sutter, *The Diary of John Augustus Sutter* (SF, 1932), p. 19

p. 32 'the gateway of communication' Weber, *The Mexican Southwest*, pp. 204–5

p. 32 'It is too late now' James P. Zollinger, *Sutter: the Man and his Empire* (NY, 1939), pp. 134, 145–6, 177

p. 33 'It is the security' Bancroft, *California*, iv, pp. 612–16

p. 33 'hear the Gospel before' Jonathan S. Green, *Journal of a Tour on the Northwest coast of America in the Year 1829* (NY, 1915), p. 18; Billington, *Far Western Frontier*, p. 79

p. 33 'such fascinations as almost' Edwin Bryant, *What I Saw in California* (1849), p. 16

p. 34 'A young woman' George D. Lyman, *John Marsh. Pioneer: The Life Story of a Trail Blazer on Six Frontiers* (NY, 1930), p. 249

p. 35 'to the wilderness' Billington, *Far Western Frontier*, pp. 86–7

p. 35 'pigs are running about' Edward Lenox, *Overland to Oregon in the Tracks of Lewis and Clark. History of the First Migration to Oregon in 1843* (Oakland, 1904), p. 13

p. 36 'I cannot but contrast' Revd H.H. Spalding to Joel Palmer, 7 April 1846, *Palmer's Journal*, in Thwaites, ed., *Early Western Travels 1748–1846* (Cleveland, 1906), xxx, pp. 283–98 (at pp. 287–9, 291–2)

p. 36 'with nothing intervening' ibid., pp. 292–4

p. 36 'he was ready to aver' Unruh, *Plains Across*, p. 36

p. 36 'Why, man alive' Minto, 'Reminiscences', loc. cit. p. 142

p. 37 'Out in Oregon' Verne Bright, 'The Folklore and History of the "Oregon Fever"', *OHSQ*, 52 (1951), p. 252

p. 37 'In Oregon there are no' Unruh, *Plains Across*, p. 123

p. 39–40 'Analyzed in detail' Goetzmann, *Army Exploration*, p. 103

p. 40 'thanks to Frémont's enthusiastic' Unruh, *Plains Across*, p. 233

p. 41 'the nation failed' Mary S. Barlow, 'History of the Barlow Road', *OHSQ*, 3 (1902), pp. 71–81 (at p. 71)

p. 41 'Father was a great fisherman' Benjamin Bonney, 'Recollections', *OHSQ*, 24 (1923), pp. 36–55 (at p. 36)

p. 41 'My father used to' H.S. Lyman, 'Reminiscences of William M. Case', *OHSQ*, 1 (1900), pp. 269–95

p. 43 'a land of genuine Republicanism' Hastings, *Emigrants' Guide*, pp. 133, 152

p. 44 'the benefactors of their race' P.L. Edwards, *Sketch of the Oregon Territory: or, Emigrants' Guide* (Liberty, Missouri, 1842), p. 20

p. 44 'Father had come to' Elizabeth Gilliam Collins, 'Reminiscences', *OHSQ*, 17 (1916), pp. 358–72 (at p. 365)

p. 45 'Who wants to go' Morgan, *Overland in 1846*, ii, p. 491

p. 46 'The Oregon emigrants' Hastings, *Emigrants' Guide*, p. 58

p. 47 'the reckless and unprincipled' Dorothy O. Johansen, 'A Working

Hypothesis for the Study of Migrations', *Pacific Historical Review*, 36 (1967), pp. 1–12 (at pp. 9–10)

p. 47 'The health of pine' 'Autobiography of William Henry Rector', *OHSQ*, 29 (1928), pp. 323–36

p. 47–8 'It is hard for me' Thoreau, 'Walking', loc. cit.

THREE: TO BOLDLY GO

p. 49 'Compared to the trials' Charles and Mary Beard, *The Rise of American Civilization*, i, p. 600

p. 51 'his description' Bidwell, *Echoes*, pp. 13–14

p. 52 'being rather fond' Nunis, *Belden*, p. 35

p. 52 'Our ignorance of the route' Bidwell, *Echoes*, pp. 15–16

p. 52 'Where my husband goes' Stevens, *California Trail*, pp. 19–20

p. 53 'a young man of evident culture' Dawson, *California in '41*, p. 13

p. 56 'it was well we did' Bidwell, *Journey to California*, p. 23

p. 58 'already somewhat advanced' Donnelly, *Wilderness Kingdom*, p. 26

p. 59 'Plains on all sides!' Schoenberg, *Paths*, p. 19

p. 59 'I hope that the journey' Laveille, *The Life of Father de Smet*, p. 121

p. 61 'he was not the best man' Bidwell, *Echoes*, pp. 21–2

p. 61 'The terrain between Westport' Donnelly, *Wilderness Kingdom*, p. 30

p. 62 'There were some as wicked' 'The Joseph Williams Tour', in Hafen and Hafen, *To The Rockies*, p. 221

p. 62 'Our leader, Fitzpatrick' ibid.

p. 63 'King Lear,' Alonzo Delano, *Across the Plains* pp 51–2

p. 64 'without law or license' 'Joseph Williams Tour', p. 222

p. 64 'That night dreadful oaths' ibid., p. 223

p. 65 'Dark clouds' Bidwell, *Journey to California*, p. 5

p. 65 'For league after league' Parkman, *The Oregon Trail*, p. 65

p. 66 'I am still weary' 'Joseph Williams Tour', p. 223

p. 66 'A young man' Bidwell, *Journey to California*, p. 7

p. 67 'the name is not' Richard F. Burton, *The City of the Saints*, p. 92

p. 68 'The Chimney was seen' Bidwell, *Journey to California*, p. 7

p. 69 'He wished some religion' Chittenden and Richardson, *Life, Travels and Letters of de Smet*, i, pp. 296–7

p. 72 'In my opinion' ibid., p. 298

p. 72 'This night we have the sound' 'Joseph Williams Tour', p. 228

p. 72 'Today Col. Bartleson' ibid., p. 229

p. 75 'only by having fastened' Dawson, *California in '41*, p. 14

p. 75 'deists and swearers' 'Joseph Williams Tour', pp. 230–2

p. 77 'He was genial' Bidwell, *Journey to California*, p. 16

p. 77 'They started purely' *Life, Travels and Letters of de Smet*, i, p. 295

p. 77 'Not only did he' Bidwell, *Echoes*, pp. 38–9

p. 78 'Though this was' Schoenberg, *Paths*, pp. 20–1

p. 78 'If the road to' ibid., p. 21

p. 80 'We have been up' Rockwell D. Hunt, *John Bidwell, Prince of California Pioneers*, pp. 58–9

p. 83 'Bidwell and Kelsey' Dawson, *California in '41*, p. 23

p. 85 'Now we have been' ibid., p. 31; Hunt, *John Bidwell*, pp. 64–5

p. 85 'nothing but horse broth' Nunis, *Belden*, p. 42

p. 86 'He seemed to be heartily sick' Hunt, *Bidwell*, p. 66

p. 86 'mountains whose summits' Bidwell, *Journey to California*, pp. 24–5; Dawson, *California in '41*, p. 23

p. 88 'We had expected' Dawson, *California in '41*, pp. 29–30

p. 88 'they were not generally' Bidwell, *Journey to California*

p. 91 'a man whose wit' quoted in Dan L. Thrapp, *Encyclopedia of Frontier Biography*, i, p. 312, from original in Bancroft, *History of California*

FOUR: THE WOMAN IN THE SUNBONNET

p. 94 'fussy . . . self important' David Lavender, *Westward Vision*, pp. 250, 263, 307, 344

p. 95 'of that obliging and flattering' Dan L. Thrapp, *Encyclopedia of Frontier Biography*, iii, pp. 1549–50

p. 97 'Fort Vancouver' A.J. Allen, *Ten Years in Oregon*, pp. 145–6

p. 97–98 'A noble sight' ibid., p. 147

p. 97 'Now all was high glee' Lansford Hastings, *Emigrants' Guide*, p. 6

p. 98 'The American character' ibid., p. 6

p. 99 'While the destruction' Allen, *Ten Years in Oregon*, p. 149

p. 99 'May 18' Medorem Crawford, 'Occasional Address', pp. 9–10

p. 100 'symptomatick fever' ibid., p. 10

p. 101 'Take plenty of bread' T.H. Jefferson, 'Guide', in Dale Morgan, ed., *Overland in 1846*, i, pp. 237–44

p. 102–3 'For breakfast' Charles M. Tuttle, 'California Diary', *Wisconsin Magazine of History*, 15 (1931), pp. 69–85

p. 104 'I am now in Indian country' Allen, *Ten Years in Oregon*, p. 153

p. 104 'cattle's feet' Medorem Crawford, 'Occasional Address', p. 10

p. 104 'Oh, my Philly' Allen, *Ten Years in Oregon*, p. 159

p. 104 'It affected all' ibid.

p. 105 'The emigrants commonly' Rawling, 'The Oregon Trail', loc. cit., p. 751

p. 106 'in view of the fact' Hastings, *Emigrants' Guide*, p. 9

p. 106 'They disposed of' Frémont, *Report of the Exploring Expedition*, p. 35

p. 106 'They were plundered' Francis Parkman to his mother, in Wilbur R. Jacobs, *Letters of Francis Parkman*, 2 vols, i, p. 44

p. 107 'a sleek looking gentleman' H.S. Lyman, ed., 'Reminiscences of F.X. Matthieu', *OHSQ*, 1 (1900), pp. 73–104 (at p. 79)

p. 107 'They could not but' ibid., pp. 79–80

p. 108 'Perfect unanimity' Hastings, *Emigrants' Guide*, p. 9

p. 108 'He [Bailey]' Allen, *Ten Years in Oregon*, pp. 154–5

p. 109 'July 14. Buried Baily' Medorem Crawford, 'Occasional Address', pp. 12–13

p. 111 'His [Fitzpatrick's] repeated' Allen, *Ten Years in Oregon*, pp. 156–7

p. 112 'A great band of Sioux' 'Reminiscences of F.X. Matthieu', loc.cit., pp. 81–2

p. 113 'assured him that his path' Hafen, *Broken Hand*, p. 137

p. 113 'I have no doubt' Fremont, *Report of the Exploring Expedition*, p. 41

p. 113 'About five or six thousand' 'Reminiscences of F.X. Matthieu', p. 82

p. 117 'His implorings' Allen, *Ten Years in Oregon*, p. 165

p. 117 'extremely hilly' Hastings, *Emigrants' Guide*, pp. 37, 137

p. 118 'Left camp at 11 o'clock' Medorem Crawford, 'Occasional Address', pp. 15–17

p. 118 'The tree is a large' ibid., p. 18

p. 118 'struck us with' ibid., pp. 18–19

p. 119 'Sept 14. We arrived' ibid., p. 19

p. 119 'heads bent' 'Reminiscences of F.X. Matthieu', loc.cit., p. 86

p. 119 'horrid road' ibid.

p. 123 'The chief figure' Emerson Hough, *The Passing of the Frontier* (Yale, 1921), p. 93

p. 123 'However much help' 'The Shiveley Guide', in Morgan, *Overland in 1846*, pp. 734–42 (at p. 736)

p. 123 '20 May. Two fine looking young ladies' Camp, *Clyman*, pp. 69, 89

p. 124 'I thought I never' ibid., pp. 69

p. 124 'Here let me say' ibid., p. 71

p. 125 'I have been in bed' Mattes, *Great Platte River Road*, p. 65

p. 125 'Disquiet, anxiety, melancholy' John Mack Faragher, *Women and Men on the Overland Trail*, pp. 14–15, 176–7

p. 127 'our washing' James Longmire, 'Narrative of a Pioneer', *Washington Historical Quarterly*, 23 (1932), pp. 47–60 (at p. 51)

p. 127 'Did they rig up' Stewart, *California Trail*, p. 125

p. 128 'I have always' Elizabeth Gilliam Collins, 'Reminiscences', *OHSQ*, 17 (1916), pp. 358–72 (at p. 367)

p. 129 'We may suspect' Stewart, *California Trail*, p. 10

FIVE: THE GREAT MIGRATION

p. 131 'There are many' *Letters of Narcissa Whitman*, p. 211

p. 131 'The immigration of 1843' H.H. Bancroft, *History of Oregon 1848–1888* (SF, 1888), p. 425

p. 131 'This day was' James W. Nesmith, 'Diary', loc. cit., p. 330

p. 131 'We have now bid farewell' P.B. Reading, Journal of Pierson Barton Reading', loc. cit., p. 149

p. 131 'I have learned' Peter Burnett, 'Letters', loc. cit., pp. 405–6

p. 132 'No scene appeared' Peter Burnett, 'Recollections and Opinions', loc. cit., p. 65

p. 135 'These men were running' Field, *Prairie and Mountain Sketches*, pp. 26–7

p. 135 'It was really very funny' Letter in *New Orleans Picayune*, reproduced in *OHSQ*, 1 (1900), p. 400

p. 137 'The man with a black eye' Burnett, 'Recollections and Opinions', loc. cit., p. 66

p. 138 'The whole atmosphere' 'Journal of Pierson Barton Reading', loc. cit., p. 155

p. 138 'Tuesday 6th' 'Journal of John Boardman', loc. cit., p. 100

p. 139 'I adopted rules' Burnett, 'Recollections', loc. cit., p. 68; 'Letters', loc. cit., p. 418

p. 139 'They were probably' Applegate, *A Day with the Cow Column*, pp. 27–9

p. 140 'the most miserable' Burnett, 'Letters', loc. cit., p. 410

p. 141 'generally fertile' ibid., p. 412

p. 142 'a treacherous, cowardly banditti' Parkman, *Oregon Trail*, p. 63

p. 142 'the most notorious rascals' Overton Johnson, *Route across the Rocky Mountains*, p. 11

p. 142 'a proud and honourable' 'Journal of Pierson Barton Reading', loc. cit., p. 158

p. 143 'a drowsiness has fallen' Applegate, *A Day with the Cow Column*, p. 38

p. 144 'It is necessary to dig' Burnett, 'Letters', loc. cit., p. 414

p. 145 'poured down upon us' Overton Johnson, *Route across*, p. 9

p. 145 'It is to me rather hard' 'Journal of Pierson Barton reading', loc. cit., p. 159

p. 147–8 'possessed a great and good' James Nesmith, 'Diary', loc. cit., pp. 337–8

p. 147 'From the time he joined us' Applegate, *A Day with the Cow Column*, pp. 40–1

p. 148 'a range of' Overton Johnson, *Route across*, p. 76

p. 150 'the boys at Fort Platte' James Nesmith, 'Diary', loc. cit., p. 340

p. 150 'some of the company got gay' Boardman, 'Journal of John Boardman', loc. cit., p. 103

p. 150 'We had a beautiful' John Minto, 'Reminiscences', *OHSQ*, 2 (1901), pp. 119–67

p. 150 'The night of our arrival' Rufus B. Sage, *Rocky Mountain Life* (Boston, 1857), p. 68

p. 153 'a beautiful spring' Overton Johnson, *Route Across*, p. 15

p. 154 'large enough for a beaver' 'Journal of Pierson Barton Reading', p. 170

p. 156 'I have established' Alter, *Jim Bridger*, pp. 209–10

p. 158 'a picture of home beauty' Nevins, *Narratives of Exploration and Adventure*, pp. 217–18

p. 160 'the action was little short of robbery' Stewart, *California Trail*, p. 45

p. 160 'unable to resist . . . by very unpleasant means' 'Journal of John Boardman', loc. cit., pp. 111, 113

p. 160–1 'We fully comprehended' Burnett, 'Recollections', p. 77

p. 161 'wild, rocky barren' Overton Johnson, *Route Across*, p. 27

p. 162 'The river on this side' Talbot, *1843 Journals*, p. 54

p. 165–6 'Had I been there' Burnett, 'Recollections', p. 82

p. 165 'which had been felled' Nevins, *Narratives*, p. 282

p. 165 'road too bad' William T. Newby, 'Diary', loc. cit., pp. 235–6

p. 166 'the roughest wagon route' Nesmith, 'Diary', loc. cit., p. 354

p. 167 'I have never tasted' Burnett, 'Recollections', p. 82

p. 167 'like the Indian' Applegate, *A Day with the Cow Column*, p. 99

p. 167 'a kind of sandy' ibid., pp. 100–1

p. 167 'Whitman lied like hell' quoted in Coffman, *Blazing a Wagon Trail*, p. 149

p. 168 'The exhausting tedium' Burnett, 'Recollections', loc. cit., pp. 82–3

p. 168 'Near to the fort' Nesmith, 'Diary', loc. cit., p. 355

p. 172 'Here the River' Overton Johnson, *Route Across* pp. 38–39

p. 173 'Friday, October 27' Nesmith, 'Diary', p. 559

SIX: THROUGH FLOOD AND FAMINE

p. 179 'All conditions' De Voto, *The Year of Decision*, p. 141

p. 180 'He thought' ibid, p. 142

p. 182 'Moses "Black" Harris' Unruh, *The Plains Across*, p. 110

p. 183 'You should take with you' 'The Shiveley Guide', in Morgan, ed., *Overland in 1846*, ii, p. 735

p. 183 'None of the emigrants' Russell E. Bidlack, *Letters Home: the Story of Ann Arbor's Forty-Niners* (Ann Arbor, Michigan, 1960)

p. 184 'Let each man' 'The Shiveley Guide', loc. cit., p. 736

p. 184 'I started out' Lavinia Porter, *By Oxteam to California*, op.cit.

p. 185 'Of the fortitude of the women' Ezra Meeker and Howard Driggs, *Covered Wagon Centennial*, op.cit.

p. 186–7 'Thousands of farms' *Baptist Missionary Magazine*, 5 (1944), pp. 282–4; cf. *Kansas Historical Quarterly*, 8 (1940), pp. 472–4

p. 188 'a restless soul' Drury, *Marcus and Narcissa Whitman*, op. cit., ii, pp. 116–17

p. 189 '31 May. We are encamped' Parrish, 'Crossing the Plains', loc. cit., p. 87

p. 189 'Did not travel today' Crockett, 'Crockett Diary' in Miles and Sperlin, *Building a State*, op.cit. p. 601

p. 189 'The rain continued' Gilliam, 'Reminiscences', loc. cit., p. 203

p. 190 'The Big Blue' ibid., p. 203

p. 190 'I was twice' Minto, 'Reminiscences', loc. cit., pp. 138–9

p. 191 'Not a tree' ibid., pp. 137, 140, 141, 142

p. 191 'Some signs of dissatisfaction' ibid., p. 140

p. 191 'This Captain Shaw' ibid. pp. 140–1

p. 191 'Here, you young men' ibid., p. 143

p. 191 'Rain and bad generalship' ibid., p. 145

p. 192 '14 May. Roads extremely bad' James L. Camp, ed., *James Clyman*, pp. 67–71

p. 192 'We have had' ibid., pp. 71–2

p. 192 'Our ferrying' ibid.

p. 192 'all hands' ibid.

p. 193 'too lazy to work' ibid., pp. 72–3

p. 193 'a tall, lean, wrinkly-faced' ibid., p. 74

p. 193 'Our tents, beds' ibid., p. 75

p. 194 'Our pilot, Mr Harris' ibid., pp. 76–80

p. 194 'The American Jubilee' ibid., p. 82

p. 195 'No place in the world' ibid., p. 84

p. 195 'The high level country' ibid.

p. 195 'If any of you men' Minto, 'Reminiscences', loc. cit., pp. 150–2

p. 196 'the best game park' ibid., p. 154

p. 196 '40,000 lbs of the best' ibid., pp. 146–7

p. 197 'Mr Gilliam had shown himself' ibid., pp. 147–50

p. 197 'with uncommon bloodthirsty' Camp, *Clyman*, p. 85

p. 197 'The mosquitoes very troublesome' ibid., p. 86

p. 198 'the scene was so interesting' Minto, 'Reminiscences', p. 153

p. 198 'the bottom of the river' ibid.

p. 198 'this is the finest' Camp, *Clyman*, pp. 85–7

p. 198 'thickly settled' Edward Parrish, 'Crossing the Plains', loc. cit., p. 96

p. 198 'the heaviest hailstorm' Minto, 'Reminiscences', pp. 154–6

p. 199 'Cautious, polite, hopeful' Stewart, *The Opening of the California Trail*, pp. 39–41

p. 199–200 'A quarrel arose' Rumer, ed., *This Emigrating Company. The Journal of Jacob Hammer* (hereinafter *Hammer Journal*), p. 47

p. 201 'as tenacious as quicksand' Stewart, *Opening*, p. 51

p. 202 'The flying herds' H.S. Lyman, ed., 'Reminiscences of William M. Case', loc. cit., pp. 272–3

p. 204 'An estimated 4,000 Sioux' Stewart, *Opening*, p. 54

p. 205 'The daily labour' Lyman, ed., 'Reminiscences of William M. Case', loc. cit., pp. 275–6

p. 205 'No, I will not' Stewart, *Opening*, p. 55

p. 207 'It was a close call' ibid., p. 61

p. 208 'My dear child' Sagers, *Whitman Massacre*, pp. 14, 101, 107; Thompson, *Shallow Grave*, pp. 19, 21, 152, 158, 169

p. 209 'We children narrowly escaped' Sagers, *Whitman Massacre*, pp. 12–13

p. 209 'While encamped there' ibid., pp. 17–18

p. 209 'his face was blackened' ibid., p. 182-3

p. 209 'the country all the way' Minto, 'Reminiscences', p. 158

p. 210 'Our delay on Kaw' Camp, *Clyman*, p. 90

p. 210 'our stock begins' ibid., p. 93

p. 210 'From my eight years' Minto, 'Reminiscences', p. 159

p. 210 'I observed the names' Camp, *Clyman*, pp. 94-5

p. 211 'many men left' Faragher, *Women and Men on the Overland Trail*, p. 85

p. 211 'Father was a perfect' Sagers, *Whitman Massacre*, pp. 13, 101, 184, 188

p. 211 'with stupendous rocks' Minto, 'Reminiscences', pp. 161-2

p. 211 'Many of the ladies' Camp, *Clyman*, pp. 97-8

p. 212 'on which now rests' ibid., p. 98

p. 212 'Mother saw the promised land' Sagers, *Whitman Massacre*, p. 183

p. 212 'Poor child' Parrish, 'Crossing the Plains', loc. cit., p. 103

p. 212 'the sick man' Minto, 'Reminiscences', p. 163

p. 212 'Next year's emigration' Thompson, *Shallow Grave*, pp. 158-9

p. 213 'Yes, John' Minto, 'Reminiscences', pp. 164-6

p. 214 'Grant was, I think' ibid., p. 216

p. 214 'He was now' ibid., pp. 217-18

p. 215 'almost destitute' Washington Smith Gilliam, 'Reminiscences', pp. 205-6

p. 215 'boasting, burlesque, unfeeling' Elizabeth Dixon Smith Geer, 'Diary', loc. cit., p. 163

p. 215 'barrels of cold water' Washington Gilliam Smith, 'Reminiscences', pp. 205-6

p. 215 'the most barren' Camp, *Clyman*, pp. 103-4

p. 215 'The day she died' Thompson, *Shallow Grave*, pp. 30, 159; Sagers, *Whitman Massacre*, pp. 16-17, 188-91

p. 216 'the worst mountains' Camp, *Clyman*, pp. 106-9

p. 216 'One wagon upset' *Hammer Journal*, pp. 125, 159

p. 217 'the most tiresome travel' Camp, *Clyman*, pp. 110-16

p. 218 'Wormwood is plenty' *Hammer Journal*, p. 162

p. 218 'Today, as little Rebecca' Parrish, 'Crossing the Plains', loc. cit., pp. 108, 109-10, 112

p. 218 'beautiful pines' *Hammer Journal*, pp. 162-7

p. 222 'It seemed as if' Simon Ide, *Biographical Sketch of William B. Ide*, pp. 34-5

p. 222 'They were mountain men' ibid.

p. 223 'the hills began to grow' Stewart, *Opening*, p. 67

p. 227 'At times my buildings' James Peter Zollinger, *Sutter: the Man and his Empire* (1939), pp. 112–13

p. 228 'the gateway of communication' David J. Weber, *The Mexican Frontier 1821–1846. The American Southwest under Mexico* (Albuquerque, 1982), p. 205

SEVEN: 'NEVER TAKE NO CUTOFFS'

p. 231 'It's not John's turn' Minto, 'Reminiscences', loc. cit., p. 156

p. 232 'If there is anything' Edwin Bryant, *What I Saw in California* (NY, 1849), p. 49

p. 232 'a hyena might have' Alonzo Delano, *Across the Plains and among the Diggings* (NY, 1936), pp. 50, 100–101

p. 232 'a mean streak' ibid. p. 124

p. 232 'A quarrel in camp' Jacob R. Snyder, 'Diary', loc. cit., p. 235

p. 232 'Fist fight came off' William G. Johnston, *Experiences of a 49er*

p. 233 'No regiment in Cromwell's' Octavius T. Howe, *Argonauts of '49*, p. 14

p. 234 'the roughest, most uncouth' Lavinia Porter, *By Ox Team* p. 78

p. 234 'A dreadful occurrence' Sandra Myres, *Westering Women*, p. 137

p. 234 'Two men who' John Steele, *Across the Plains*, p. 2

p. 235 'The next morning' J.C. Moreland, 'Annual Address', loc. cit. pp. 26–34

p. 237 'From one of the wagons' Joel Palmer, *Journal*, p. 34

p. 237 'so large was our company' ibid., p. 35

p. 237 'It appeared to me' ibid., p. 38

p. 239 'Found the Indians' Snyder, 'Diary', loc. cit., pp. 225–6

p. 240 'The ten o'clock guard' ibid., pp. 227–30

p. 240 'The wind has been' ibid., p. 231

p. 240 'Four caravans' ibid.

p. 241 'The River is covered' ibid., p. 229

p. 241 'Here almost every variety' ibid., p. 233

p. 241 'An unoccupied spectator' Palmer, *Journal*, pp. 53–4

p. 243 'We had neither' ibid., pp. 66–9

p. 244–5 'Down he sinks' Parkman, *Oregon Trail*, p. 278

p. 244 'This day passed through' Snyder, 'Diary', pp. 243–4

p. 245 'Could not reach' ibid., p. 245

p. 245 'the whole surface' Hancock, *Narrative*, p. 22

p. 245 'The ground, for a strip' Palmer, *Journal*, p. 79

p. 247 'a very picturesque' Bonney, 'Recollections', loc. cit., pp. 38–9

p. 247 'Goodbye, we will never see you' ibid., p. 40

p. 247 'the meat of this bird' Snyder, 'Diary', pp. 247–51

p. 250 'Our provisions' ibid., p. 253

p. 251 'some of the time' Stewart, *California Trail*, pp. 100–1

p. 252 'In many places' Snyder, 'Diary', p. 256

p. 252 'Stopped early this evening' ibid., p. 257

p. 254 'Sometimes climbing precipitous mountains' Morgan, *Overland in 1846*, i, pp. 30–1

p. 254 'Hastings's luck had held' Stewart, *California Trail*, p. 105

p. 254 'Such an attempt' Morgan, *Overland*, p. 30

p. 256 'Crossing the Snake River' Virginia Nesbit, 'Sarah Helmick', loc. cit., p. 445

p. 256 'A young man' Palmer, *Journal*, pp. 96–8

p. 257 'the most difficult road' ibid., pp. 101–3

p. 258 'You may guess my astonishment' ibid., pp. 105–8

p. 259 'We were compelled' ibid., pp. 114–18

p. 260 'The current of this stream' ibid., p. 119

p. 262 'He proved himself' Barlow, 'Reminiscences of Seventy Years', loc. cit., p. 254

p. 262 'A great deal of dissatisfaction' ibid.

p. 263–5 'We found our road' Hancock, *Narrative*, p. 25

p. 264 'It is now pretty evident' Clark and Tiller, *Terrible Trail*, pp. 33–4

p. 265 'The tale of our going down' ibid., pp. 38–41

p. 266 'Last evening a child' ibid., pp. 41–2

p. 266 'It had been becoming' Goulder, *Reminiscences*, p. 126

p. 267 'The number of men on horseback' Hancock, *Narrative*, p. 29

p. 268 'The excitement was intense' ibid., p. 30

p. 268 'He found three wagons' Fred Lockley, *Captain Sol Tetherow*, p. 6

p. 269 'I heard it said' Goulder, *Reminiscences*, p. 126

p. 269 'One of the men' Clark and Tiller, *Terrible Trail*, pp. 140–1

p. 270 'It is impossible to describe' Hancock, *Narrative*, p. 32

p. 272 'The emigrants were more interested' Fred Lockley, 'The McNemees and Tetherows', loc. cit., p. 355

p. 273 'This morning we ascended' Jesse Harritt, 'Diary', loc. cit., p. 525

p. 274 'A large rope was swung' Palmer, *Journal*, p. 123

p. 276 'God never made' Mary S. Barlow, 'History of the Barlow Road', loc. cit., p. 72

p. 279 'whortleberry swamps' ibid., p. 76

p. 279 'With snow over everything' ibid., p. 77

p. 279 '"Why," she said' ibid.

EIGHT: CALIFORNIA CATCHES UP

p. 282 'the staggering complexity' Morgan, *Overland*, i, p. 115

p. 283 'They agreed in the one' Jesse Quinn Thornton, *Oregon and California*, i, pp. 14, 26, 67–8; Thornton, 'Occasional Address', loc. cit., p. 34

p. 284 'If a man is predisposed' Edwin Bryant, *What I Saw*, pp. 50–5

p. 285 'Good had furnished' Morgan, *Overland*, i, p. 406

p. 286 'a perfect specimen,' *New York Herald*, 3 August 1846

p. 286 'The current was so strong' Bryant, *What I Saw*, pp. 49–50

p. 287 'The meeting adjourned' 'McKinstry Diary', loc. cit., p. 208

p. 288 'unwell since coming' quoted in Merrill Mattes, *Great Platte River Road*, p. 82

p. 288 'the initial portion' Unruh, *The Plains Across*, p. 408

p. 291 'Some families who imagined' Lienhard, *From St Louis to Sutter's Fort*, p. 21

p. 292 'Inman was pretty much' ibid., p. 26

p. 292 'Inman is a tyrant' Jacob W. Harlan, *California '46 to '48*, pp. 33–5

p. 292 'Shoot, go to hell' Lienhard, *From St Louis*, pp. 24–31

p. 293 'We find them exceedingly intelligent' Parkman to his mother, 12 May 1846, in Wilbur R. Jacobs, *The Letters of Francis Parkman*, i, pp. 38–9

p. 294 'The lagging pace' Parkman, *Journals*, ii, p. 435

p. 294 'Oxen, when footsore' Bryant, *What I Saw*, pp. 110–11

p. 295 'We have passed' Parkman to his mother, 19 June 1846, *The Letters of Francis Parkman*, i, pp. 42–4

p. 296 'With one hand' Parkman, *Oregon Trail*, p. 135

p. 296 'His men, he said' ibid., p. 136

p. 296 'Russel drunk as a pigeon' Parkman, *Journals*, ii, p. 447

p. 297 'and thence continuing down' Hastings, *Emigrants' Guide*, pp. 137–8

p. 297 'Thus did Lansford Hastings' Ray Allen Billington, *The Far Western Frontier 1830–1860* (1956), p. 108

p. 297 'a piece of special pleading' Bancroft, *History of California*, iv, p. 397

p. 297 'the Baron Munchausen' Thornton, *Oregon and California*, i, pp. 83, 242

p. 298 'as they are generally' Palmer, *Journal*, pp. 241–54

p. 299 'I told him' Camp, *Clyman* p. 225

p. 299 'There is a nigher route' ibid.

p. 299 'It was easy to' Bryant, *What I Saw*, p. 94

p. 300 'not a man was to' ibid.

p. 300 'evil report ... woebegone countenance' Thornton, *Oregon and California*, pp. 110–11

p. 301 'Lucinda, leave that be' Lienhard, *From St Louis*, pp. 13–14

p. 301 'He wanted to have sonme rest' ibid., pp. 54–6

p. 301 'A party that passed' Parkman to his father, 28 June 1846, *Letters*, i, pp. 45–7

p. 302 'One woman, of more than suspected' Parkman, *Journals*, ii, p. 47

p. 302 'As for the widow's' Stewart, *California Trail*, p. 160

p. 302 'In all probability' Morgan, *Overland*, i, p. 110

p. 302 'How are ye, boys?' Parkman, *Oregon Trail*, p. 57

p. 303 'At the fort' Kelly, *Old Greenwood*, pp. 96–8

p. 304 'manifest an almost invincible' Bryant, *What I Saw*, p. 113

p. 305 'the barefaced rascal Bonny' Parkman, *Journals*, ii, p. 474

p. 307 'Oh, who is this' Joseph Aram, 'Reminiscences', loc. cit., pp. 624, 627

p. 309 'it could hardly be defended' Lienhard, *From St Louis*, p. 95

p. 309 'Circles of white-tented' Bryant, *What I Saw*, p. 122

p. 310 'Now, boys, put spurs' ibid., pp. 135–48

p. 310–12 'A disagreeable altercation' ibid., pp. 149–65

p. 311 'Sometimes neither river bed' De Voto, *Year of Decision*, p. 314

p. 312 'The sides of the mountains' William L. Allen and R.B. Avery, *California Gold Book*, pp. 64–5

p. 314 'conglomerate rocks' Lienhard, *From St Louis*, pp. 96–9

p. 315 'Towards evening' Lindsay Applegate, 'The South Road Expedition', loc. cit., pp. 17–18

p. 315 'Had we rushed pell-mell' ibid., p. 18

p. 316 'We could see columns' ibid., pp. 20–4

p. 317 'It would be difficult' Bryant, *What I Saw*, pp. 171–2

p. 317 'The new road takes' 'Pringle Diary', loc. cit., i, p. 181

p. 319 'These Indians are amongst' Elwood Evans, ed., *History of the Pacific Northwest*, ii, pp. 190–1

p. 321 'The time from this' 'Pringle Diary', loc. cit., i, p. 185

p. 321 'One yoke of oxen' Morgan, *Overland*, i, pp. 395–6; ii, p. 785

p. 321–22 'I rode through the canyon,' 'A Brimfield Heroine – Mrs Tabitha Brown', *OHSQ*, 5 (1904), pp. 199–205 (at p. 204)

p. 322 'All looked lean' Morgan, *Overland*, ii, pp. 782–3

p. 322 '[James Smith] had been standing' Thornton, 'Occasional Address', loc. cit., pp. 54–5

p. 322 'Two old men' Morgan, *Overland*, ii, pp. 778, 782, 786

p. 323 'The handsomest valley I ever' 'Pringle Diary', loc. cit., p. 186

p. 324 'Dec 8th. We met' 'Holt Diary', loc. cit., i, pp. 191–7

p. 325 'TO THE WORLD' Morgan, *Overland*, ii, pp. 670–2, 688–9

NINE: TRAGEDY IN THE SNOWS

p. 328 'The narrow valley' Lienhard, *From St Louis*, p. 99

p. 329 'On the plains in '46' Stewart, *Ordeal*, pp. 41–2

p. 331 'This bundle belonged' Lienhard, *From St Louis*, p. 109

p. 332 'It's a good thing' ibid., pp. 120–2

p. 333 'Those dirty Indians' Morgan, *Overland*, i, p. 272

p. 333 'While they continued' Lienhard, *From St Louis*, pp. 127–8

p. 334 'Uncle Patrick' McGlashan, *History of the Donner Party*, p. 47

p. 345 'Began to snow yesterday' 'Breen Diary', loc. cit. i, p. 313

p. 346 'Children, eat slowly' McGlashan, *History of the Donner Party*, p. 98

p. 346 'that type beloved' Stewart, *Ordeal*, pp. 168–9

p. 347 'We told them' 'Virginia Reed Account', loc. cit., i, p. 284

p. 347 'Sunday 17th. Eliza' 'Breen Diary', loc. cit., i, pp. 316–20

p. 348 'Seven men arrived' ibid., i, p. 320

p. 351 'As we approached her' 'Daniel Rhoads' Diary', loc. cit., i. p. 328

p. 353 'That was the hardest thing' 'Virginia Reed Diary', loc. cit., i, p. 286

p. 353 'Mootrey and Glover had to make' De Voto, *Year of Decision*, p. 431

p. 354 'Is Mrs Reed' 'Reed Diary', loc. cit., pp. 297, 339

p. 354 'You do not know' 'Virginia Reed Account', i, p. 286

p. 354 'O! after many roving years' De Voto, *The Year of Decision*, p. 434

p. 357 'a great busybody' Parkman, *Journals*, ii, pp. 411, 434

p. 357 'like a puppy' Morgan, *Overland*, i, pp. 98–9

p. 358 'Never take no cutoffs' Virginia Reed to Mary Keyes, 16 May 1847, Morgan, *Overland* i, pp. 287–8

p. 358 'liking to command' ibid., i, p. 352

p. 359 'I dread the coming night' McGlashan, *History of the Donner Party*, p. 174

p. 360 'I'm glad we have got' ibid., p. 175

p. 360 'God has not brought us' Stewart, *Ordeal*, pp. 227–30

p. 361 'Be quiet, you' ibid., pp. 231–6

p. 361 'After all, the expedition' ibid., p. 235

p. 362 'No, gentlemen, I will not' Morgan, *Overland*, i, p. 356

p. 364 'he believed their lives' McGlashan, *History of the Donner Party*, pp. 163–9, 199–201

p. 365 'Passed Midshipman Woodworth' De Voto, *Year of Decision*, p. 442

p. 365 'It drooped and withered' Thornton, *Oregon and California*, ii, p. 221

p. 366 'We were obliged to witness' Eliza P. Donner Houghton, *The Expedition of the Donner Party and Its Tragic Fate*, pp. 365–70

p. 367 'like a monomaniac squirrel' De Voto, *Year of Decision*, p. 443

p. 367 'He eat her body' Harlan, *California '46 to '48*, pp. 61–5

p. 368 'Oh, it's too dry' 'Fallon Diary', loc. cit., i, pp. 364–6

p. 369 'Eat baby raw' Henry Augustus Wise, *Los Gringos*, p. 75

TEN: SAINTS AND SINNERS

p. 377 'My things are packed' Susan Sessions Rugh, 'Patty Sessions', loc. cit.

p. 377 'it was a middling good' Stanley B. Kimball, *Heber C. Kimball*, p. 132

p. 378 'We camped on the hill' 'Diary of Lorenzo Dow Young', loc. cit., p. 134

p. 379 'If you do' John R. Young, *Memoirs of John R. Young* p. 16

p. 379 'would have done honor' Arrington, 'Persons for all seasons', loc. cit.

p. 379 'I wouldn't sell' Edward Tullidge, *Women of Mormondom*, p. 309

p. 379 'It shall be said' De Voto, *Year of Decision*, p. 95

p. 380 'Mud aplenty' Kimball, *Heber Kimball*, pp. 133–5

p. 381 'The Lord reward her' 'Diary of Lorenzo Dow Young', p. 138

p. 383 'This morning Ellen Kimball' *William Clayton Journal*, p. 19

p. 383 'It looked as if' ibid., pp. 31–2

p. 383 'We were happy' *Diary of Hosea Stout*, pp. 141, 143, 146

p. 385 'So we have both' O.O. Winther, *A Friend of the Mormons. The Private Papers and Diary of Thomas Leiper Kane*, pp. 25–9

p. 387 'peculiar manifestation' Norma Baldwin Ricketts, *The Mormon Battalion*, pp. 36–7, 258–9

p. 390 'Twice Heber has rebuked' *William Clayton Journal*, p. 61

p. 390 'My mouth was so badly' Conrey Bryson, *Winter Quarters*, p. 73

p. 391 'In the mores' De Voto, *Year of Decision*, pp. 449–50

p. 391 'O brother Eldridge' *Diary of Hosea Stout*, pp. 190–1

p. 391 'I am probably' ibid., pp. 188–9

p. 393 'If you come here again' Arrington, *American Moses*, p. 130

p. 398 'So long as ye remain' quoted in Thrapp, *Encyclopedia*, iii, p. 1232

p. 399 'We were delighted' *William Clayton Journal*, pp. 118–20; *Bullock Journals*, pp. 142–4; 'Erastus Snow Diary', loc. cit., pp. 115–16

p. 399 'Many of our animals' 'Diary of Orson Pratt', 8 May 1847, loc. cit.

p. 400 'A calf' *Bullock Journal*, p. 147

p. 400 'We passed today' 'Erastus Snow Diary', p. 119

p. 400 'Washed my socks' *William Clayton Journal*, pp. 125–6, 137–8, 149, 152–3

p. 401 'The president chastized' ibid., pp. 134–5

p. 401 'In attempting to exonerate' 'Erastus Snow Journal', p. 117

p. 402 'You are hereby commanded' Schindler, *Orrin Porter Rockwell*, p. 157

p. 402 'for blocking the highway' Egan, *Pioneering the West*, pp. 52–7

p. 402 'I understand there are several' *William Clayton Journal*, pp. 189–97

p. 402 'Some would murmur because' 'Lorenzo Dow Young Journal', loc. cit., p. 158; *Bullock Journal*, pp. 158–9, 'Diary of Orson Pratt', loc. cit., p. 66; 'Erastus Snow Diary', p. 120

p. 403 'We found some rattlesnakes' 'Lorenzo Dow Young Journal', p. 159

p. 404 'We have seen no game' *William Clayton Journal*, p. 183

p. 404 'to conduct themselves' Kimball, *Heber Kimball*, pp. 159–61

p. 404 'The brethren say' James B. Miller, *The Trials of Discipleship*, pp. 230–1

p. 404 'I would rather see' Roberts, *Comprehensive History*, iii, pp. 184–5

p. 405 'It truly seemed' *William Clayton Journal*, pp. 197–205

p. 405 'all were anxious to see' *Bullock Journal* pp. 175–8

p. 407 'This is the most delightful' 'Erastus Snow Journal', 10 June 1847, quoted in Roberts, *Comprehensive History*, iii, p. 196

p. 409 'After we halted' *William Clayton Journal*, pp. 251–2

p. 409 'Mr Young had a sore thumb' 'Diary of Lorenzo Dow Young', p. 162

p. 410 'their idea of a bath' Kimball, *Heber Kimball*, p. 165

p. 411 'the imperfect way' *William Clayton Journal*, pp. 273–8

p. 411 'from his appearance' Egan, *Pioneering the West*, pp. 87–9

p. 412 '[It was] probably occasioned by' 'Diary of Orson Pratt', p. 163

p. 412 'These insects are more numerous' *William Clayton Journal*, p. 282

p. 412 'This is Uncle Sam's day' Stegner, *The Gathering of Zion*, pp. 159–60

p. 413 'two double log houses' *William Clayton Journal*, pp. 285–6

p. 413 'a mob company' George Smith, *An Intimate Chronicle*, p. 349; De Voto, *Year of Decision*, p. 464

p. 415 'Our journey down the Red Fork' 'Diary of Orson Pratt', p. 165

p. 416 'We succeeded in getting through' ibid., pp. 178–9

p. 416 'I could not help' *Bullock Journal*, p. 232

p. 417 'President Young was enwrapped' Kimball, *Heber Kimball*, p. 170

p. 417 'a great statement' Stegner, *The Gathering of Zion*, p. 168

p. 418 'I humbled myself' Stephen P. Pratt, 'Parley P. Pratt', loc. cit.

p. 419 'He was never known' Roberts, *Comprehensive History*, iii, p. 293

p. 422 'Our hostess, with despatch' Ansel James McCall, *The Great California Trail in 1849*, pp. 55–7

p. 423 'after that we shot at' Charles Ingersoll, *Overland to California*, pp. 38–9

p. 424 'Nov 27. Ran all day' 'Diary of Elizabeth Dixon Smith', in Kenneth L. Holmes, ed., *Covered Wagon Women*, pp. 141–4

EPILOGUE

p. 430 'This certainly is' Mattes, *Great Platte River Road*, p. 31

p. 430 'It seemed to me' ibid.

p. 433 'I have never known these animals' Gregg, *Commerce of the Prairies*, p. 375

p. 433 'Rattlesnakes are exceedingly' ibid., p. 382

p. 434 'Rattlesnakes are proverbially abundant' ibid., p. 46

p. 434 'I drew my feet up under me' Susan Magoffin, *The Diary of Susan Shelby Magoffin, 1846–1847* (Lincoln, Neb., 1982), p. 33–34

p. 435 'they still looked on the movers' De Voto, *The Year of Decision*, op. cit

p. 437 'The Pawnee Indians' Alonzo Delano, *Across the Plains*, p. 20

p. 437 'Keep watch all the way' 'The Shiveley Guide', in Morgan, *Overland*, ii, p. 735

p. 437 'the Sioux will not likely,' ibid., p. 735

INDEX

accidents on the overland trail,
208–09
  drownings, 2, 19, 117, 134,
  150, 152, 157, 162–63,
  170–71, 190, 216, 225, 251,
  433
  firearms discharged, 2, 66–67,
  72, 76, 108, 109, 112, 117,
  146, 197, 209, 338, 433
  crushing by wagons, 151, 208,
  209, 218, 289, 338, 406, 419,
  433
antelope, 62–63, 71, 74, 81, 83,
  102, 141–42, 190, 191, 198,
  203, 206, 212, 221, 240, 243,
  294, 305, 399, 406, 407
Apache Indians, 16, 92, 97, 439,
  440
Applegate Jesse, 23, 320, 321,
  322, 323, 324–45, 423, 425
  and 1843 'Cow Column', 39,
  47, 135–36, 139–40, 142,
  143, 144, 146, 147–48, 149,
  153–54, 163, 167, 168–69,
  170, 173, 186
  and the Applegate Cutoff,
  314–18, 323, 324, 325, 423,
  425
Arapaho, 11, 16, 202, 437
Arizona, 5–6, 10, 30, 41, 97, 426

Baker, Jim, 74–75
Bannock Indians, 216, 305, 318,
  333, 439
Barlow, Samuel, 41, 247, 260,
  276–81
  and Barlow Road, 276–81, 314,
  325, 423
Bartleson, John, 52, 58, 61, 62,
  70, 72, 77, 81, 82, 84, 85,
  86, 87, 88, 89, 90, 91, 92,
  129, 130, 131, 148, 174, 176,
  369
bear (black, brown and grizzly),
  71, 72, 74, 79, 115, 123,
  157, 198, 206, 210, 240, 252,
  305, 335, 340, 350–51, 360,
  407, 418
Bear River, 2, 3, 39, 74, 75, 79,
  80, 115, 157, 158, 159, 207,
  208, 212, 213, 244, 245, 255,
  303, 414, 421
Belden, Josiah, 52, 76, 84, 87, 89
Bidwell John, 26, 29, 34, 92,
  129, 130, 131, 148, 160, 174,
  176, 293, 294, 440
  and 1841 journey to California,
  49–91
bighorn sheep, 68, 74, 102, 198,
  210, 305
Big Blue River, 100, 189, 190,

murdered, 425–26
Whitman, Walt, 440–41
wild animals (see under
 individual species), 19, 51,
 55, 62, 87, 100, 125, 141,
 198, 203, 204, 209–10, 212,
 240, 272, 294, 305, 314, 340,
 350, 351, 359, 407, 433
Willamette Valley, 7, 9, 34, 35,
 76, 78, 120, 122, 128, 165,
 171, 173, 174, 176, 177, 218,
 219, 257, 261, 262, 263, 265,
 271, 275, 276, 304, 314, 323,
 324, 423
Williams, Joseph, 62, 64, 66, 67,
 69, 72, 75, 76, 78, 141
Williams, Old Bill, 369
Wolfinger family, 308, 336, 337,
 340, 345, 352
wolves, 62, 63, 72, 87, 98, 196,
 204, 206, 210, 212, 213, 226,
 241, 292, 294, 295, 305, 306,
 335, 340, 399, 401, 404, 433
women on the overland trail (see
 also individual women): 1, 8,
 19, 22, 42, 45–46, 51, 52,
 96, 100–101, 102, 103, 104,
 111, 113–14, 120, 133, 138,
 143, 144, 153, 154, 155, 165,
 169, 171, 172, 174, 176, 181,
 183–85, 188, 190, 198, 205,
 210–11, 220–21, 222, 224,
 225, 226–27, 232, 234–35,
 236, 238, 240, 241–42, 255,

256, 257, 262, 264, 279, 285,
 286, 287, 288, 290, 295, 299,
 304, 312, 333, 336–37, 341,
 344, 358, 376–77, 379–80,
 382, 384, 389, 405, 406, 409,
 419, 422, 423–24
 general overview of, 123–29
Woodruff, Wilford, 390, 412,
 413, 415, 417
Woodworth, Selim, 349, 356–57,
 358, 359, 360, 361, 362, 365,
 368, 370, 440
Workman, William, 13–14

Young, Brigham, 40, 78, 297,
 312, 373–76, 378, 379, 380,
 381–82, 384, 385–88, 390,
 391, 392, 393, 394, 395–421,
 426
 personality of, 374
 political talent of, 385–87
 plans for exodus to West,
 374–76
 and trek to Council Bluffs,
 376–84
 in Winter Quarters, 385–95
 and trek to Utah, 395–415
 rebukes the Saints, 404–5
 founds Salt Lake City, 416–17
 in 1848, 417–20

Young, Lorenzo, 378, 380, 381,
 390, 395, 403, 409–10